U.S. GOVERNMENT

Principles You Need to Know

A Customized Version of
American Government: Political Culture in an Online World,
Sixth Edition, by Chapman Rackaway.
Designed Specifically for
Gwinnett Technical College

Kendall Hunt
publishing company

Cover image © Shutterstock.com

www.kendallhunt.com
Send all inquiries to:
4050 Westmark Drive
Dubuque, IA 52004-1840

TEXT ISBN: 978-1-5249-7336-0
PAK ISBN: 978-1-5249-7275-2

Published in the United States of America

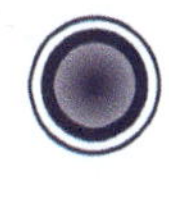

Contents

UNIT 1—FOUNDATIONS OF GOVERNMENT 1

CHAPTER 1—**The Political Culture of American Democracy** 3

CHAPTER 2—**The Development of American Constitutional Democracy** 37

CHAPTER 3—**Federalism: A Nation of States** 75

CHAPTER 4—**Civil Liberties and Individual Freedom** 111

CHAPTER 5—**Civil Rights and the Struggle for Equality** 149

UNIT 2—POLITICAL CULTURE AND PARTICIPATION 197

CHAPTER 6—**The Mass Media** 199

CHAPTER 7—**Public Opinion in American Politics** 237

CHAPTER 8—**Popular Participation in Politics** 273

UNIT 3—THE POLITICAL PROCESS 307

CHAPTER 9—**Campaigns and Elections** 309

CHAPTER 10—**Political Parties** 363

CHAPTER 11—**Interest Groups** 403

UNIT 4—INSTITUTIONS OF GOVERNMENT 443

CHAPTER 12—**Congress** 445

CHAPTER 13—**The Presidency** 489

CHAPTER 14—**The Supreme Court and the Federal Judiciary** 541

CHAPTER 15—**The Federal Bureaucracy** 575

The Constitution of the United States 613

Index 635

Unit 1

Foundations of Government

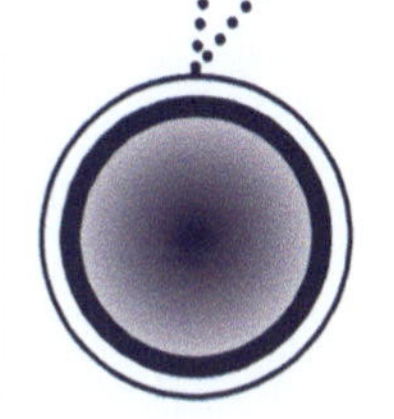

Chapter 1

The Political Culture of American Democracy

OUTLINE

Key Terms 3

Expected Learning Outcomes 4

1-1 Politics, Government, and Political Culture 4

- **1-1a** Government 6
- **1-1b** The Importance of Political Culture 8

1-2 The Meaning of Democracy 13

- **1-2a** The Intellectual Foundations of Modern Democracy 14
- **1-2b** Democratic Regimes 16
- **1-2c** Democracy and Capitalism 18
- **1-2d** Political Culture and Democracy 20

1-3 The Contours of American Political Culture 21

- **1-3a** Regional Variations in American Political Culture 22
- **1-3b** The American Political Consensus 23
- **1-3c** Institutions and American Political Culture 28
- **1-3d** The Evolving American Political Culture 31
- **1-3e** Ideology 31

1-4 Conclusion: Politics and the American Future 33

Questions for Thought and Discussion 34

Endnotes 35

KEY TERMS

anarchy
aristocracy
authoritarian regime
authority
capitalist economy
citizen
civic engagement
communitarians
conservatives
constitutional democracy
coup d'état
cultural conservative
democracy
dictatorship
economic conservative
elites
equality
freedom
free, fair, and open elections
government
governmental institutions
ideology
individualism
institution
intermediary institutions
laissez-faire
legitimacy

liberals
libertarians
limited government
majority/individual problem
majority/minority problem
majority rule
masses
moderates
multiculturalism
natural law
natural rights
participatory democracy
political culture
political socialization
politics
popular culture
populists
private enterprise
private property
progressive
public benefits
public interest
regionalism
regulatory state
representative institutions
rule of law
social contract
socialism
social capital
socialist economy
societal culture
societal institutions
sovereignty
state of nature
universal suffrage
welfare state

EXPECTED LEARNING OUTCOMES

After reading this chapter and completing the supplemental online materials, students will:

- Define government, politics, and other fundamental terms to understanding government
- Compare democracies with other forms of government
- Describe the roles and responsibilities of citizens in modern, technology-centered democracies
- Identify ideological categories of the American political system
- Analyze the relationship between economies and types of governmental systems
- Contrast regional political cultures within the United States

1-1 POLITICS, GOVERNMENT, AND POLITICAL CULTURE

What is a typical day like for you? Go to class, perhaps you have a job on- or off-campus, spend time with friends, eat, sleep. In that span, you also probably consume a lot of online content. Planning things with friends on Facebook, using Twitter or Reddit to keep current on what's going on in the world, gaming with friends half a world away on Xbox Live, texting your family to keep them in touch. Today's world is a constant stream of wireless exchange. Cellular, online, and social communications media have changed the way we interact, work, and even think. Those tools have certainly changed the way we look at politics, what we expect from our government, and our general orientation towards others. In this book we will pay particular attention to how changes in our society have changed our politics, and us.

Nobody who was present during the early colonial days of the American republic could have envisioned a world where you could communicate with someone on the other side of the country instantaneously or travel to the other side of the world in a day. Our country was founded during a time of great isolation, where people rarely went outside of their own communities and a place as close as two states away might as well be another planet.

These changes are important because there are two important things intertwined here: politics and culture. Politics, as we will see, is a reflection and extension of a nation's existing culture. So as culture changes, politics will (usually slowly) follow suit and change as well. When society changes quickly, our politics often struggles to keep up. During the Civil Rights movement of the mid-twentieth century, society's views on equal rights for African Americans changed quickly, but it took the government more than a decade to catch up to the new reality of American society.[1]

Our politics tells us a lot about our culture, and vice versa. The preferences people have for candidates, parties, and issues reflect their core beliefs, giving us an insight into the culture they inhabit. Issues change, new candidates enter the fray regularly, and people's attitudes towards government morph with the times. Citizen political activity is a good way to examine shifts in our culture.

For instance, picture yourself in Chicago's Grant Park on the night of November 4, 2008. Thousands of people have gathered in the cold of an impending Lake Michigan winter to hear the remarks of the newly elected president of the United States of America. In some ways, the scene was nothing new: thousands of the faithful gather to hear the words of the president-elect every four years. But one obvious fact about the newly chosen chief executive made 2008 different: Barack Obama became the first African American president. Obama's election was a sign of one constant in American politics: change. Obama's campaign made a mantra out of the word "change," and in electing him the United States acknowledged a significant change for us as a people. Politics is a reflection of a people. A nation's values, sense of right and wrong, aspirations, and sense of its own identity are all wrapped up in its politics and government.

ONLINE 1.1

Watch video of President Obama's 2008 election victory speech: **http://www.youtube.com/watch?v=3K8GWCI7P7U**

Barack Obama's election is a sign of a society whose vision of race and identity is undergoing a significant shift. The first black president is simply a sign of changes that have been building in the United States for decades now.

The faithful who gathered in Grant Park to hear Obama's acceptance speech were mostly political activists. But the crowd looked different than the typical political hangers-on. There were more non-white faces in the crowd, and the crowd was younger. Thousands of people under the age of 25 became involved in politics for the first time in 2008, inspired by Obama or his Republican opponent, John McCain. As a college student, you are likely in that age group yourself. The 2008 election demonstrates that there is political power in all people, even those without much political experience. America's democratic political culture dictates that any person can express his or her ideas, vote, or even run for and become president. Politics provides people an opportunity to participate and take leadership in government on every level, for the purpose of making change. As the diverse demographics of the Obama victory rally show, technology isn't the only aspect of American culture experiencing drastic change. The American political culture even holds up the participation of the masses as a valuable thing, regardless of the change occurring around us. We believe in citizen-led democracy, even if the element most people think of is running for office.

When asked about politics, most Americans immediately think of the process of running for public office. The word *politics* brings to mind an image of a candidate making a speech, meeting with supporters, or staging a media event. But politics involves much more than the activities associated with elections and campaigns. **Politics** is the process by which societies govern themselves. In every society, conflicts arise that must be resolved. Politics is the process through which people resolve their conflicts peacefully. In its most successful form, politics lifts society out of chaos and violence.[2] Thus, politics is fundamentally about getting along.

1-1a GOVERNMENT

Because people need rules to live by, every society needs a government. When a society establishes a government, a few important questions must be asked: What type of government will a society have? What role will government play? What functions will it perform? What values will it promote? Which groups will it favor? How much power will leaders have, and how will they use their power? The answers to these questions cannot be ascertained in a cultural vacuum. The role and scope of government reflect a people's view of human nature and of individual capability and responsibility. Few societies are in complete agreement on these questions. Over time, however, societies develop answers to these questions. As a consensus emerges, these answers form a nation's political culture. Politics is about creating rules and enforcing cooperation with them.

The term **government** refers to the institutions that have the authority to make rules that are binding on society. Government is necessary to avoid what the English political philosopher Thomas Hobbes (1588–1679) called "the war of every man against every man." Without government, wrote Hobbes, there is "continual fear and danger of violent death and the life of man [is] solitary, poor, nasty, brutish, and short."[3] Anarchy, or total freedom, would lead to a life not much removed from that of animals. The world has witnessed many examples of what happens when governments disappear—in Lebanon, Bosnia, Somalia, and many other places. People are brutalized. They lose their jobs, their homes, and their possessions. Cities are plundered and devastated. Entire peoples are even subjected to genocide.

© Steven Frame, 2013. Used under license from Shutterstock, Inc.

Another way of defining government is to say that it consists of those institutions that hold a monopoly on the legitimate use of force in society. Government is legitimate when it is generally perceived as having the right to rule its population. Even if a government is universally regarded among its people as legitimate, it must, on occasion, use force to back up its rules and policies. Even if force is rarely used, the threat of it is always there. By using force, a government can exist without being perceived as legitimate. In such a situation, citizens may not recognize the government's laws and policies. However, no government wishes, or can afford for long, to rule where it is not accorded **legitimacy** by the people it governs. If the public does not have faith in their government, the laws passed build resentment among the public and eventually democracy can break down.

ONLINE 1.2

Look at an interactive map of governments around the world: **http://www-958.ibm.com/software/data/cognos/manyeyes/visualizations/regime-types**

Although the fundamental purpose of government is to maintain order, peace, and security, governments do much more than that. Governments play a role in managing their economies, providing for the public welfare, fostering the growth of knowledge,

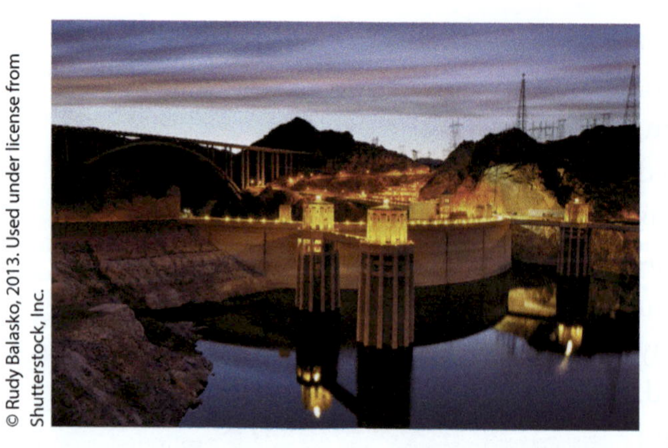

and maintaining a healthy environment. They also provide **public benefits**, such as projects and programs that benefit society as a whole—roads, dams, water and sewer systems, schools, and parks, for example. Ideally, governments provide public benefits in which all citizens have an equal interest, but in reality governments often redistribute burdens and benefits among different groups in society. Even when governments do not redistribute burdens and benefits, they set the rules by which these elements are distributed. The importance of the distributive aspect of government decision making has led some political scientists to define politics as "who gets what, when, [and] how."[4]

1-1b The Importance of Political Culture

In this text, politics and government are presented as they reflect the political culture of the United States. **Political culture** consists of the values that most members of a society hold about what politics ought to address and how these matters should be addressed. Political culture gives people a sense of what government ought to deal with, what is appropriate, and what is not appropriate for public consideration. This basic understanding affects the way people look at government—what they expect government to do and how they expect it to be done. Political culture also embraces people's emotional reactions to the "symbols, institutions, and rules that constitute the fundamental political order."[5] Political culture is thus a broad term referring to shared values, expectations, and feelings having to do with politics and government.

ONLINE 1.3

Why is culture important for any civilization and government? **http://www.youtube.com/watch?v=gbddciQiYdg**

The importance of political culture was made abundantly clear when world attention focused on Afghanistan following the terrorist attack on the World Trade Center and the Pentagon on September 11, 2001. The ruling Taliban wielded its political power based on an extreme interpretation of the Koran—the sacred scriptures of Islam. For some time the Taliban had supported and received support from the al Qaeda terrorist network, headed by Osama bin Laden. By harboring bin Laden and al Qaeda, the terrorist organization he heads, the Taliban converted Afghanistan into a base for training terrorists who would strike at the United States and its allies. The Taliban ruled Afghanistan with an iron hand, ruthlessly suppressing dissent and enforcing its harsh version of Islam. Women were not permitted to hold jobs or leave their homes without covering themselves from head to toe. Girls were not permitted to attend school. The Taliban shocked the world when it destroyed ancient Buddhist monuments and required Hindus to wear identifying labels. Although religious tolerance and the separation of church and state are fundamental components of American political culture, the Taliban rejected these values.

ONLINE 1.4 *9/11 in Real Time*
You can watch video of the 9/11 attacks as they happened.

Although the Taliban's fusion of religion and government is unthinkable in a Western-style democracy, to many Afghans and others in the Islamic world, that mixture seemed perfectly natural. Human beings in Afghanistan and the United States did not come to hold these different beliefs by accident. From childhood onward, people in every society are bombarded with a variety of messages and images that set the boundaries for what they come to regard as possible and desirable. Of course, at the same time, each person develops a sense of what is impossible or undesirable. Many of the limits of and possibilities for politics are determined by the limits and possibilities that the broader societal culture sets for all behavior.

It is important to recognize that political cultures evolve. Usually, cultural change comes about slowly, but sometimes it can be rapid and dramatic. Consider the Arab Spring of 2011 in countries like Egypt, Libya, Syria, and Bahrain. Fueled by text- and Twitter-organized protests, dissidents in all of those countries built their disagreement with the ruling regimes into changes in leadership. Egyptian president Hosni Mubarak stepped down, and Gadhaffi was killed by rebels after retreating from the capitol.[6] Like in the aftermath of Operation Iraqi Freedom's hostilities eight years before, immediately many held out hope that democracy would flourish in the formerly authoritarian cultures. Toppling the regimes was relatively easy. But one does not simply graft democracy

onto a society and have it work. Like planting seeds, democracy takes time to grow, developing roots into a culture. Societies accustomed to authoritarian systems do not automatically shift effortlessly into a republic without significant work. So as Iraq maintains a fragile attempt to democratize, a hard-line Islamic sect in the Muslim Brotherhood has taken control of Egypt. Removing one authoritarian regime does not guarantee its replacement with a democratic one.

Political Culture and the Larger Societal Culture

Political culture is embedded within the larger **societal culture**, which includes all socially transmitted patterns of behavior as well as all the beliefs, customs, and institutions within the society. Culture embraces the arts, music, literature, science, philosophy, and religion and includes the ways that we entertain ourselves—sports, movies, magazines, and television. Culture includes the ways we communicate with one another, the words and images we use, and the media that transmit those words and images. In short, culture embraces all the products of work, thought, and experience that are characteristic of a particular people.

Just as political culture sets the stage for what government considers as viable options, the broader societal culture provides individuals with options for personal activities. Cultures simplify the lives of individuals by limiting choices. Cultures determine values, such as who can marry whom and what types of entertainment are acceptable. As cultures change, they often give individuals more freedom, but at a cost. In nineteenth-century America, for instance, churches, schools, and families communicated a clear set of standards regarding appropriate sexual behavior. An individual could "choose" to be promiscuous, but few felt that they could really opt for that choice. Society, through the church and other powerful institutions, clearly disapproved. After the sexual revolution of the 1960s and 1970s and again during today's debates over sexual orientation, individuals found themselves receiving complex and contradictory cultural messages about sexuality. Behavior that was clearly frowned upon in the past was becoming acceptable. The wide array of options presented to Americans fostered confusion and frustration among people of both sexes. The culture changed, but with this cultural change came conflict. Today, four decades after the onset of the sexual revolution, American culture is considerably more tolerant of choices once considered immoral or deviant, while the debate continues on more recently developed societal changes. California passed a gay marriage ban, Proposition 8, in 2008.

ONLINE 1.5

You can watch a debate about California's Proposition 8: **http://www.youtube.com/watch?v=Af0mndnF6mY**

Today's American society is very mobile. The amount of information and personally relevant materials we can store on our phones and share at will is staggering. Our ability to connect with people vast distances away makes the prospect of moving to another town, state, or even country a regular occurrence today, but such distance from family was unthinkable to most even fifty years ago. Likewise, we come to expect immediate response and action because we are able to connect with others at any time. We no longer have to wait three to five days for a letter to get to someone—we can talk to, text, e-mail, or instant message them and get a response back just as quickly. Governments, which are made to move slowly and deliberately, have a difficult time providing their citizens with the rapid response that today's communication technology allows us.

Culture and Authority

As another example of the interaction of culture and politics, consider the matter of authority. Essentially, **authority** is the right to tell others what to do. Some cultures are more supportive of authority than others. Many people have wondered how the Germans could have gone along with the atrocities committed by the Nazis during World War II. Noting that German culture stresses obedience to authority, an obedience that is ingrained from childhood, some have speculated that the Germans' cultural definition of authority spilled over into their political culture; that is, patterns of behavior from the culture at large became patterns of behavior in politics. What happened in Nazi Germany probably could not happen in the United States, although no one can be certain of it. Clearly, though, the political culture of modern America is significantly different from that of Nazi Germany.[7] Americans are distrustful of authority and are not accustomed to blind obedience.

Popular Culture: A Reflection of the American Experience

The American experience is chronicled and analyzed by historians, sociologists, political scientists, and even novelists. It is also depicted in **popular culture** (or "pop" culture), a term often used to denote the elements of culture that masses of people find enjoyable or entertaining. In this book, we use the term *popular culture* to include movies, books, plays, and, of course, television programs. Sometimes popular culture deals explicitly with political themes. An obvious example is the highly successful television series *The West Wing*, which depicted life inside the White House in a very compelling way, drawing heavily on real political events and issues and offering a heavy dose of political commentary.

Hollywood has a long history of making feature films of this genre, from the 1939 classic *Mr. Smith Goes to Washington* to the 2012 Will Ferrell comedy *The Campaign*. While films, plays, and television series dealing with political themes reflect many different perspectives on politics, they all help to shape (or sometimes reinforce) political attitudes and opinions. *Mr. Smith Goes to Washington* inspired moviegoers with its depiction of a courageous young senator battling forces of corruption on Capitol Hill. By presenting a narrative in which an embattled president employs a media specialist to boost his approval rating by creating an illusion of war, *Wag the Dog* appealed to (and probably reinforced) popular cynicism about politics and mass media.

Films like *V for Vendetta*, television series such as *Political Animals*, and entertainment programs like *The Colbert Report* are not standard fare. The great mass of American pop culture is nonpolitical, offering entertainment with heavy doses of comedy, sexual innuendo, and violence. Yet even mainstream entertainment can be quite revealing of the attitudes and beliefs that underlie American politics. Consider the standard Hollywood "cop" movie in which the hero is usually something of a rebel or a renegade. Excellent examples include the Matt Damon/Jeremy Renner *Bourne* series of films. In these films the hero is a government agent who goes rogue against a system he believes to be immoral and corrupting. He is constantly struggling, not only against the villains but also against "the system." The authorities are often portrayed as stupid or selfish bureaucrats and politicians. Agents of the government either unwillingly play into the aims of the villains or are the villains themselves. Of course, in the end, the rebellious hero saves the day and vanquishes the villains. These movies resonate with Americans precisely because they reflect the distrust of authority, disdain for bureaucracy, and hostility toward politicians that are deeply embedded in the American personality.

In the online world it is equally impossible to escape the intersection of politics and culture. Political candidates have ubiquitous Facebook presences, Twitter feeds, YouTube channels, and Pinterest boards. Wherever we spend our free time, political figures will try to have a presence. Sometimes the merger of popular and political culture is even clearer. Videos themselves become the object of political controversy. That was certainly the case in the case of the YouTube video "The Innocence of Muslims," which was reported as a driver behind anti-American violence in the Middle East throughout September of 2012.[8] Pop culture is often the vehicle through which conflicting cultural values are explored. Twitter has become the modern-day equivalent of the public town hall or square, a zone where all ideas can be shared and the president has the same 144-character limit that a high school student has.

ONLINE 1.6 *"The Innocence of Muslims"*

Social media provides an opportunity for us to interact with political figures like at no other time in our history. During a high school trip to her state capitol, Kansas teen Emma Sullivan tweeted critically about her state's governor, Sam Brownback, using the hashtag #heblowsalot. The immediacy and lack of a filter on social media allows people to speak their minds about politics and elected officials, even in ways that would normally be considered inappropriate. Brownback's staff demanded an apology, but later withdrew the demand and apologized to Sullivan. Without the public and immediate nature of social media, Sullivan and Brownback would never have made news, but today they can. Our interactions can be positive, critical, and even inappropriate, as the Sullivan example shows.[9]

1-2 THE MEANING OF DEMOCRACY

Belief in democracy is one of the fundamental elements of American political culture. Many Americans mistakenly consider their political system to be thoroughly democratic. *Democracy* is a broad term encompassing a variety of related ideas and practices—and some facets of the American political system would be considered undemocratic by many people around the world. Nevertheless, the study of American politics logically begins with an examination of the idea of democracy.

The term **democracy** is derived from the Greek word *demos*, meaning "the people," and *kratia*, meaning "rule" or "authority." Literally, then, democracy means "rule by the people." The Greek philosopher Aristotle (384–322 BC) defined democracy as the rule of the many, as opposed to **aristocracy**, which means the rule of the few.[10] More familiar to Americans is Abraham Lincoln's definition of democracy as "government of the people, by the people, and for the people."[11]

In the real world, even under the most favorable conditions, democracy only approximates the ideal of "government by the people." In every human association, power inevitably is wielded by the few over the many.[12] Every society can be divided into two basic groups: those who lead and those who follow. Political scientists refer to leaders—whether of government, business, science, education, the mass media, or the arts—as **elites**. Although every society has its elites, societies vary greatly in the way their elites are structured, the way power is distributed among them, and the relationship the elites have to the **masses**.

In an **authoritarian regime**, power is concentrated in one elite or a few elites, who are not accountable to the masses except in the rare instances of revolutions. In the most extreme case, a **dictatorship**, power is concentrated in the hands of one individual. Adolf Hitler's Germany and Joseph Stalin's Soviet Union are good historical examples of dictatorships. In both cases, no one dared challenge or even question the dictator. Iraq under Saddam Hussein provides a familiar recent example of a dictatorship. Usually, though, power in an authoritarian regime is wielded by one ruling family, a dominant political party, or a group of religious leaders.

In a democracy, on the other hand, power is distributed among multiple elites in society. Moreover, elites in government are accountable to the masses through free and fair competitive elections. In a democracy, governmental power changes hands from time to time, if not at regular intervals, between rival political parties. This change comes about peaceably, through the electoral process. In an authoritarian system, changes in political leadership require some extraordinary event, such as the death of the dictator, a **coup d'état**, or a revolution. After revolutions, though, what does a newly democratic nation do? Libya and Egypt are currently in the process of determining whether they will return to authoritarian systems or emerge as democracies.

ONLINE 1.7 *Zahra Langhi TED Talk*
https://www.youtube.com/watch?v=qtcWebAYmKY

The closest approximation to the ideal of pure democracy was the *polis*, or city-state, of Athens from approximately the mid-fifth to the mid-fourth century BC. All citizens were members of the assembly, which held monthly meetings to enact laws, dispense justice, set foreign policy, and manage the city-state's finances. After free and open debate, decisions were made by majority vote. As with modern government, the policies established by the assembly had to be carried out by administrators. These officials were selected in two ways: The assembly elected administrators for posts that required special knowledge or skills, and positions that required only ordinary ability were filled by administrators selected annually by lottery from among the citizenry. This procedure ensured that Athenian government was truly conducted by its citizens. Citizenship was not universal in the Athenian *polis*, as women, children, slaves, and newcomers to Athens were excluded, so participation in Athenian democracy was confined to a small minority of the population who owned property. Although contemporary Americans might question whether such a system was truly a democracy, the culture of ancient Greece found slavery acceptable and did not think that women should participate in the political process.

1-2a The Intellectual Foundations of Modern Democracy

After the decline of ancient Athens, the idea of democracy lay dormant until it was resurrected in Europe during the late seventeenth century, when intellectuals began to question the legitimacy of monarchs and aristocrats, whose authority was based solely on heredity. The most influential political thinker in the late seventeenth and early eighteenth centuries was England's John Locke, whose principal work, *Two Treatises of Government*, laid the foundation for modern democratic theory. Locke, along with other writers, provided the intellectual roots for the American version of democracy. Although most Americans are probably not familiar with John Locke or his writings, they tend to view his ideas as "self-evident truths," to use the language of the Declaration of Independence.

One of Locke's principal motivations in writing the *Two Treatises* was to justify the Glorious Revolution of 1688, where the English Parliament asserted its power over the monarchy. Locke started with the premise that humans are rational beings who are capable of acting in their own self-interest and discovering the **natural law** ordained by the Creator for the conduct of human affairs. Locke postulated a **state of nature**, a condition of society in which no government exists. Although Locke's hypothetical state of nature is characterized by perfect freedom and total equality, it is also fraught with danger. Because this state has no authority, people are insecure. Nothing can stop the strong and cunning from exploiting the weak and vulnerable. In Locke's view, government exists by virtue of a **social contract** among rational individuals who prefer to be ruled by others than to live in the chaos and insecurity of the state of nature. **Sovereignty**, or the right to rule, is thus vested ultimately in the people, not in the rulers. When the government does not protect peoples' basic freedoms, called **natural rights**, they have the right to remove that government and replace it with a better one.

Locke's ideas were built on those of another English philosopher, Thomas Hobbes. Hobbes, who also wrote in the seventeenth century, envisioned a state of nature that was much worse than Locke's. Writing in *Leviathan* (1651), Hobbes thought that people were so anxious for security that they would give up all their freedom by surrendering all power to a king. This king would have absolute power because government's only obligation to the people is to keep them safe. In Hobbes's view, no middle ground exists between **anarchy**, the total absence of government, and an all-powerful king. People are not capable of governing themselves.

Locke had a more optimistic view of human nature. In Locke's view, people are capable of surrendering authority to government on a limited basis, retaining certain rights while allowing the government adequate powers. This idea, **limited government**, is the basis of the U.S. Constitution. The idea is a powerful one, but one that demands a great deal from human beings. It requires them to make informed decisions about what is in their best interests and what is the appropriate role for government. The concept of limited government requires that people pay attention to what their government is doing and speak out when they believe that government has acted improperly. At the same time, it requires that people obey the government when it acts within its legitimate sphere of authority. In short, limited government requires that the individual become a **citizen**.

Rousseau and the French Revolution

After Locke, the preeminent democratic thinker of the Enlightenment was the Frenchman Jean-Jacques Rousseau (1712–1778). Rousseau began with similar assumptions, postulating a state of nature and a social contract. But Rousseau advocated a more direct, **participatory democracy** than Locke believed to be possible or desirable. Rousseau believed that representative institutions could only distort the general will of the people, which he regarded as infallible. In France, Rousseau's extreme version of popular sovereignty came up against ideas of absolute monarchy—with explosive consequences. But the French Revolution of 1789, largely based on Rousseau's ideas, failed to establish a successful democracy. Rather, it brought about a "reign of terror" in which no one was safe from the guillotine. The French Revolution eventually degenerated into a militaristic dictatorship that wreaked havoc on Europe. Given the awful experience of the French Revolution, the appeal of Rousseauian ideas of democracy has diminished considerably, at least insofar as they might be applied to mass societies.

Lockean, rather than Rousseauian, thinking became part of the intellectual tradition of the United States. Perhaps the reason is that, unlike France, whose revolution shook the foundations of French society with incredible violence, the United States of America came into being without a tremendous upheaval in society. Although the British colonial rulers were defeated and expelled, the basic structures of society were not shaken.

1-2b Democratic Regimes

In the nineteenth and twentieth centuries, as the essential democratic idea caught on, theories of democracy proliferated. Today, one can find a variety of theories of democracy. As democratic theories vary, so do their practical applications. Societies differ in wealth, geography, history, language, and the number of religious and racial groups. Consequently, no two democratic regimes look exactly alike, and some seem to work much better than others. Despite these differences, one can distill the essential features that make a political system democratic.

First, a democracy must have one or more **representative institutions** empowered to make decisions for the society. Authoritarian regimes, seeking to gain legitimacy by posing as democracies, sometimes have "representative" assemblies that have no real policy-making power or influence over the government. Second, in a democracy, members of the representative assemblies must be elected in **free, fair, and open elections**. Here, too, authoritarian systems trying to display the trappings of democracy often hold elections that are neither free nor fair nor open. One good indicator that a political system is truly democratic is that power changes hands from time to time. Whatever its superficial appearance, any system in which power is exercised by the same party or group over a long period is unlikely to qualify as a democracy.

Universal Suffrage

Although the participation of all citizens in the day-to-day governance of their country is a practical impossibility, all citizens—at least all adults—ought to have the right to participate in elections. Indeed, voting is generally considered to be the elemental act of political participation in a representative democracy.

Universal suffrage means that all adult citizens have the right to vote. In many democratic countries, protracted and sometimes bloody struggles were necessary to achieve universal suffrage. The thought simply did not occur to John Locke and the classical liberals of the Enlightenment that women ought to have the right to vote; indeed, the franchise was not extended to all women in the United States until 1920. At the time of the American Revolution, the overwhelming majority of people of African descent living in this country were slaves. A bloody civil war, several constitutional amendments, a series of important acts of Congress, and numerous judicial decisions would be required over a period of more than a century before African Americans could enjoy the right to vote. Does the lack of universal suffrage in the United States over most of its history mean that America was not a democracy? In Chapter 2, "The Development of American Constitutional Democracy," we see the Founders of the American republic were not entirely enthusiastic about democracy. Yet two centuries of social, economic, political, and legal change have brought about the democratization of the United States.

ONLINE 1.8

View the Freedom House's "World Freedom Map 2013": **http://www.freedomhouse.org/sites/default/files/Map%20of%20Freedom%202013%2C%20final.pdf**

Democracy and Human Rights

Whether one considers Lockean liberalism or other formulations of democratic theory, the two core values of democracy are clearly **freedom** and **equality**: All citizens are entitled to certain basic rights, and all citizens must be treated equally by the state. Given their philosophical underpinnings, democracies tend to be much more supportive of human rights than do authoritarian regimes. Yet nothing in the structure of representative democracy per se requires the system to respect or foster human rights.

Representative democracy, which is based on the principle of **majority rule**, is subject to two basic problems: the **majority/individual problem** and the **majority/minority problem**. In a system based squarely on majority rule, no guarantee exists that the majority will not run roughshod over the rights of the individual. Nor does any assurance exist that the majority will respect and tolerate an ethnic, racial, or religious minority group.

One approach to dealing with the majority/individual and majority/minority problems is to specify in law the rights of individuals and minorities and to establish legal constraints on the power of the majority to infringe upon those rights. But how is this process to be accomplished if the majority can change the law? What can ensure that democracy will not degenerate into tyranny of the majority? The answer of the Founders of the American Republic was to enact a constitution, a fundamental law superior to the will of transient majorities and changeable only through extraordinary means requiring a firm national consensus. Thus, in describing the American form of government, the term **constitutional democracy** is as appropriate as the term *representative democracy*. Of course, the United States is not the only democratic country to have adopted a written constitution to protect the rights of citizens and limit the power of popular majorities. Yet in no country is the written constitution taken as seriously in the day-to-day operations of government as it is in the United States. It is one of the features that makes the American system of government unique and interesting.

1-2c Democracy and Capitalism

Politics and economics are not totally separate spheres of activity. What happens in the political system can have enormous consequences for the economy and vice versa. Both politics and economics deal with the distribution of power in society. To a great extent, economic power translates into political power. The United States has, for the most part, a **capitalist economy**—it is based on the principles of **private property** and **private enterprise** (see Table 1-1). Political theorists have debated at length about the relationship between democracy and capitalism. Some argue that private property and free enterprise are desirable, if not strictly necessary, conditions for democracy, in that

TABLE 1-1 Socialist Economies Versus Capitalist Economies

SOCIALIST	CAPITALIST
Government-controlled industry	Private enterprise
Collective property	Private property
Less-stratified economic classes	Stratification of economic classes
Free or low-cost access to education, health care, transportation; extensive government-run social services	Competitive for-profit educational, health care, and transportation companies
State-provided minimum housing	Open market housing
Government intervention in economy	Self-regulating market economy

they help to limit the power of the state. Others believe that the economic inequalities inherent in capitalism are inconsistent with the egalitarian ideals of democracy. Some democratic theorists believe that people must be more or less equal economically if they are to be equal politically. These theorists prefer a **socialist economy**, where government controls major industries and works to eradicate differences in wealth. In many democracies, **socialism** is an accepted alternative to be considered within the democratic institutions of that country. These countries, such as France, Italy, and Sweden, have viable socialist parties, some of which have captured the government at various times.

For most of its history, the United States was a fiercely capitalistic country, favoring minimal government involvement in the economy. However, as time progresses, cultures change. For eighty years the federal government has gradually expanded its role in the economy generally. Over time, people became more accepting of governmental involvement in the economy. Today, most Americans accept economic policies that once were considered radical. As the people change in their attitudes, so society and politics will follow suit. It is also true that policy changes will often produce changes in attitudes.

The world's most successful democracies do seem to be found among the advanced, industrialized nations, most of which are essentially capitalist. Included in this category are Great Britain, of course, as well as Canada, France, Germany, Italy, Japan, and a number of others. As one scholar notes, capitalism and democracy "are historically tied together because in the forms in which they have arisen…both are manifestations of constitutional liberalism."[13] The fledgling democracies of Eastern Europe have by and large adopted capitalist economies; it remains to be seen how well they will succeed.

The case of China has been unique. In the 1980s, China began a significant movement toward capitalism, which led to demands for political reform. Following the massacre of student protesters at Tiananmen Square in Beijing in June 1989, the government crushed the attempt to develop democratic political institutions. During the 1990s, China continued its movement toward capitalism, but did so under authoritarian means. During the 2000s, China has developed into a world power and has opened up a number of opportunities for capitalist-style economy within its borders. The question remains whether a growing middle class will pressure for democratic reform following the Chinese economy as it becomes more fully capitalist and the standard of living continues to rise.

China's example suggests that democracies function best when a large middle class exists. A society in which a small minority of the population is very rich and the rest of the people are very poor is not a good candidate for a successful democracy. A tremendous disparity in wealth intensifies social conflict and makes consensus and compromise virtually impossible. This concept helps to explain why achieving democracy has been so difficult among the world's least-developed nations.

1-2d Political Culture and Democracy

A democratic form of government cannot simply be created out of thin air nor imposed on a country by a dominant foreign power (although it has been tried from time to time). Not only must economic conditions be favorable, but the country must also have an integrated political culture that is welcoming to democratic values and institutions. A nation accustomed to authoritarianism would have difficulty adjusting to the cultural requirements of democracy.

Democracy requires, at a minimum, a tolerance of different groups and ideologies, an abiding faith that conflicts can be resolved through reasoned discussion and compromise, and the willingness to abide by decisions that one does not like and to support one's government even when it is dominated by the political opposition. Most fundamentally, democracy requires a degree of trust between its leaders and its masses.

This element of democratic political culture is, of course, challenged when a nation fears for its safety. Following the September 11, 2001 terrorist attacks, there were reports of hate crimes against Muslims and Arabs, although at levels far below what some had predicted. President George W. Bush called for tolerance of persons of the Islamic faith, and leaders throughout the country echoed this call. The overwhelming majority of Americans were able to make a distinction between Islam and terrorism. Most Americans did not define the "war on terrorism" that followed the terrorist attacks on the United States as a war against Islam, although Osama bin Laden and his followers sought to characterize the conflict in such terms. The public response to President Bush's actions and messages after the terrorist attack indicated a high level of public trust in the president. Unfortunately for President Bush, public trust in his leadership waned considerably after the controversial decision in early 2003 to invade Iraq and topple Saddam Hussein.

1-3 THE CONTOURS OF AMERICAN POLITICAL CULTURE

American political culture is not only fundamentally democratic and antiauthoritarian, but also varied and complex. It varies across regions of the country and among groups in society. Moreover, American political culture is constantly evolving, reflecting the demographic, economic, and technological changes in society. Despite the tremendous diversity that now characterizes this country, the broad outlines of American political culture remain clearly discernible.

To a great extent, contemporary American political culture still reflects the values of the European people who settled this country hundreds of years ago. Settlers did not come with a blank cultural slate; they brought with them elements of the cultures of their native lands. Educated people brought with them the knowledge of political philosophy. Many regarded America as a grand experiment in political science—a place where the best ideas from the history of political thought could be put into practice. Most people who came to this country in its early days were not, of course, highly educated. Yet they brought with them something as important as knowledge of political theory: a thirst for freedom and a desire for a better way of life.

American political culture is also a product of the land itself. Geographically, America was very different from Europe. The challenge of confronting the wilderness and the frontier made different demands on the political system than had been the case in relatively civilized Europe. Much of what is special about American culture is related to its frontier history. When people would become tired of the lack of opportunity or being in the minority in a given area, they would collect their families and possessions and head west to start a new life. On the frontier, settlers did not have the luxury of a social support system, but had to face challenges themselves. Thus, the individual came to be, and still remains, at the core of American values. Thus, the dominant characteristic of American political culture is **individualism**.[14] One of the main writers advocating individualism in American democracy was Ayn Rand. Many of the leading lights in the modern libertarian movement point to her works, like *Atlas Shrugged*, as the philosophical underpinnings of their beliefs.

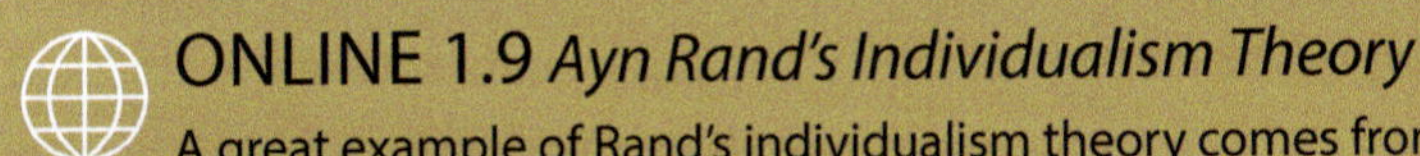
ONLINE 1.9 *Ayn Rand's Individualism Theory*
A great example of Rand's individualism theory comes from this classic movie monologue.

To many people, individualism means self-reliance, or what has been called "rugged individualism." To a great extent, rugged individualism is a thing of the past, a vestige of the frontier. All of us are dependent now on each other and on government to an extent that many of us do not realize. But Americans still value individualism.

We admire the entrepreneur, the inventor, and the artist. For the most part, Americans understand that individualism also means the right to express an alternative point of view or pursue an unconventional lifestyle, even one that most people find offensive. To a great extent, the rugged individualism of the American frontier has been replaced by the "expressive individualism" of an increasingly diverse, rapidly changing society. A person's choice of music, dying their hair a bright color, tattoos and piercings, and style of dress are all ways people can express their individualism and separate themselves from others while still living within the larger societal culture.

1-3a Regional Variations in American Political Culture

Individualism is inextricably intertwined with Americans' faith in democracy. But individualism does not have a monopoly on the political culture. Individualism exists in constant tension with Americans' attachments to traditional values and their desire to foster a good society. One can find various mixtures of these competing cultural values in different regions of the country, reflecting the predispositions to government and politics of the groups that settled there.

In the 1960s, the political scientist Daniel Elazar helped to popularize the concept of political culture as a way of understanding American politics. According to Elazar, the European settlers brought with them two competing perspectives on what politics in America should be about. The first perspective views government's role as that of protecting a marketplace of individuals and groups as they pursue their economic self-interest. The second perspective is that government should protect and nurture that which individuals and groups have in common.[15] In this view, the role of government is to nurture society in general rather than nurture the potential for individuals to achieve success.

Elazar sought to explain the variation in political cultures among the American states as blends of these two competing cultural currents. He described the fabric of American political culture as a tapestry of three subcultures, each of which found a different way to combine protecting the individual with fostering the needs of society.[16] In the *individualistic political culture*, government exists mainly to keep order in the marketplace. The role of government is quite limited; it need not concern itself with fostering the "good society," and responsibility for one's own actions is stressed. This culture would leave people alone to own and use their property and lives as they see fit. The government in a *moralistic political culture* stresses the public good over the rights of the individual and enters people's lives in a variety of ways to ensure that the "general welfare" is advanced and the "good society" achieved. One might expect states in which this culture is dominant to tax and spend more and to provide more social services. In a *traditionalistic political culture*, government becomes somewhat involved in defining the "good society." Rather than expect government to ensure a certain level of public welfare, however, this culture would support government involvement to protect traditional values.

Elazar's work was relevant in the 1960s, but since then things have changed significantly. Elazar's model saw the different cultures identified by state, partly because people saw themselves as citizens of their state first and the United States second. As power and focus shifted towards the federal government, state-level differences morphed into multistate differences. American political culture has developed a strong strain of **regionalism**.

Colin Woodard describes modern America as a collection of regional political cultures in his work *American Nations*.[17] Woodard traces the settlement, history, and culture of each region. For instance, American commercial history and success can be traced all the way back to Dutch mercantile entrepreneurs. Hence, Woodard terms the New York City metro area "New Amsterdam," while the egalitarian, middle-class settled and dominated midsection of the country is "The Midlands," stretching from Pennsylvania all the way to New Mexico. The "Deep South" covers much of the Old Confederacy and traces its roots to Barbadan slavelords. Woodard claims the end product is an authoritarian and unequal political culture. The Far West, a gigantic region spanning the interior of the West Coast to just east of the Rocky Mountains, tends to be pro-business, stemming from the need for corporate industry to settle its challenging terrain.

1-3b The American Political Consensus

Although individualism and support for democratic institutions are the fundamental characteristics of American political culture, a number of other important values also comprise what is called "the American national character," "the American political consensus," or "the American way of life." Chief among these values are commitments to individual freedom, equality of opportunity, and the rule of law. These commitments are far from complete, not universally shared, and are sometimes overtaken by competing values and sentiments.

The Commitment to Individual Freedom

In the abstract, *liberty* is the right of the individual to be free from undue interference or restraint by government. Liberty presupposes that individuals are capable of rationally determining what is in their best interests. Americans are lovers of freedom. The word resonates through our culture. American literature, music, cinema, theater, and poetry all celebrate the idea of human freedom. But what do Americans mean by "freedom"?

Certainly, most Americans support the idea of free expression that is enshrined in the First Amendment to the Constitution. Americans believe in the right to speak one's mind, especially to offer criticism of the government. But in the mid-twentieth century, the American people supported a variety of restrictions on those who embraced communism and other radical political ideas. The public seemed unwilling to support freedom of expression when it involved "un-American" ideas. The question of free expression now has more to do with the issues of pornography and violence than with radical political ideas. Some people feel that pornography is degrading to women and actually perpetuates sex discrimination. Many believe that graphic depictions of violence in television shows, movies, and video games contribute to the epidemic of violence in society. Although no one claims to support pornography and violence, the public seems to have strong appetites for both. Those who produce and profit from such fare claim the protection of the First Amendment. But history suggests that when the American public feels seriously threatened, the constitutional guarantee of freedom of expression will give way.

Faith and Freedom

One of the principal reasons that people left Europe to come to the New World was to escape religious persecution. Recognizing the centrality of religion in the life of the American people, the framers of the Bill of Rights included in the First Amendment a guarantee of the free exercise of religion and a prohibition against government establishing one religion as the official creed of the United States. Religion remains important in the lives of Americans. Americans are more likely to express a belief in God and to attend church than are citizens of the democracies of Western Europe. Polls reveal that a strong majority of people in this country think that believing in God is an important part of what it means to be a "true American." As Yale law professor Stephen Carter notes, "deep religiosity has always been a facet of the American character."[18]

This country was settled primarily by Protestants, although Roman Catholics and Jews have always had a significant presence in the United States. The proportions of Jews and Catholics in the population increased significantly as a result of the great waves of immigration from Southern and Eastern Europe in the late nineteenth and early twentieth centuries. These new immigrants were not always greeted with hospitality. The Ku Klux Klan and other nativist groups fanned the flames of intolerance. Jews, in particular, have often been the victims of discrimination and even persecution. The Constitution guarantees people the right to exercise their religion freely, although it does not (and cannot) guarantee social acceptance. Now, however, anti-Semitism and anti-Romanism have largely subsided in this country. The contemporary conflict over religion has a very different character.

The conflict over religion now has more to do with whether, and to what extent, government acknowledges, accommodates, and supports religious beliefs and practices. No one doubts that the framers of the Bill of Rights meant to prohibit the establishment of a national religion. But does the Constitution also require a strict separation of religion and government? Is government required to be neutral and detached on matters of religious belief?

The Pledge of Allegiance calls America "one nation under God." The Declaration of Independence invokes the "firm protection of divine Providence." Our currency bears the slogan "In God We Trust." Congress begins its sessions with a prayer. Even the Supreme Court begins its public sessions with the statement "God save the United States and this honorable Court." Christmas is a national holiday. Our most popular patriotic song is "God Bless America." Only the strongest advocates of the separation of church and state would object to public affirmations of America's religious heritage. But what about organized prayer and Bible reading in public schools? Or religious invocations at public school graduation exercises? Though supported by large majorities in the communities where they took place, these practices have been challenged and declared unconstitutional by the courts. In one controversial decision in the mid-2000s, a federal appeals court ordered the words "under God" to be struck from the Pledge of Allegiance.

Freedom, Autonomy, and Privacy

America has a strong tradition of personal and familial privacy. Americans have always reacted negatively to attempts by government to interfere in people's private lives, whether through eavesdropping or legislation. The courts have recognized that people have a right of privacy under the Constitution.[19] The growing consensus now is that government should not interfere in people's sexual relationships. The old laws forbidding adultery, fornication, and contraception have largely been done away with through judicial decisions, legislative action, or simple nonenforcement. The Supreme Court has even said that the constitutional right of privacy is broad enough to include the right of a woman to have an abortion.[20] And although many people are troubled by the number of abortions performed in this country, and a vocal minority intensely opposes legalized abortion, public opinion is generally supportive of a woman's "right to choose."

Today, one of the most heated public issues is that of gay rights. Historically, gay men and lesbians generally remained "in the closet." But in the 1960s and 1970s, many began to "come out" and admit their sexual orientation. Many did so at the risk of alienating friends and losing their jobs. In the 1980s, gays organized and began to push for social acceptance, political power, and legal protection against discrimination. Today, people are rarely prosecuted for engaging in private homosexual conduct, at least outside the military services. Again, most people do not believe that government should intervene in people's private lives. Expressing this cultural theme, the Supreme Court in 2003 struck down a Texas law that criminalized private, consensual homosexual conduct. Voters in many states now face ballot measures that either provide homosexual couples marriage rights or deny them. No federal effort has been successful, but the many state attempts mean the issue is advancing and will continue to be at the forefront of the government's agenda for some time to come.

Economic Liberty: Support for the Free Enterprise System

The area of American social life in which our individualism has manifested itself most clearly is the economy. America has a capitalist economy built on deep-seated cultural commitments to the values of private property and free enterprise. The overwhelming majority of Americans credit the free enterprise system for making the United States a great country. Until the late nineteenth century, American government followed the doctrine of ***laissez-faire***, or minimal interference with the free enterprise system. As the Industrial Revolution progressed, however, public support for government intervention began to grow. Increasingly, people began to look to government to regulate the excesses of the market economy and ensure a minimal standard of living. Changing attitudes led to the establishment of the modern **regulatory state** and the **welfare state**, terms that highlight the modern relationship of government to the economy. Although American political culture has come to accept, and even demand, a role for government in managing the economy, there is clearly a limit to which the public will support government efforts to redistribute wealth to the less fortunate.

Equality in American Political Culture

Another core value of democracy is equality. Americans believe in equality. After all, the Declaration of Independence declares that "all men are created equal." But what type of equality do Americans believe in? The Constitution guarantees "equal protection of the laws," that is, equality before the law. Historically, however, African Americans, women, and various minority groups have been denied legal equality. To a great extent, these legal inequalities have been eradicated, although social and economic inequalities clearly remain.

When polled, the overwhelming majority of Americans agree that people should be treated equally without regard to their race, sex, or religion. Of course, not everyone lives up to this ideal. People in this country, as elsewhere in the world, still harbor prejudices that affect their attitudes and behavior toward people who are "different." Prejudice in the form of racism, sexism, and religious bigotry is one cause of economic inequality, although it is certainly not the only cause.

The Rule of Law and the Problem of Violence

Americans are committed to the **rule of law** as a core democratic value. This commitment is most clearly expressed in the U.S. Constitution and the judicial institutions that interpret and enforce its principles. The American legal system is highly developed and tremendously complex. If citizens feel that they have been wronged by others, they have opportunities to seek justice through the courts, which operate according to rational and clear procedures. Likewise, criminal behavior is clearly defined by government, with specific rules limiting government officials as they arrest and prosecute those suspected of having committed a crime. In many ways, this society's commitment to the rule of law is reflected in its very large number of attorneys. The United States has more attorneys per capita than any other nation on earth.

The murder rate in American cities remains far higher than in any other advanced nation. Moreover, major incidents of students murdering their classmates in Colorado, Kentucky, Oregon, Mississippi, Arkansas, and Michigan have become imprinted on the nation's conscience.

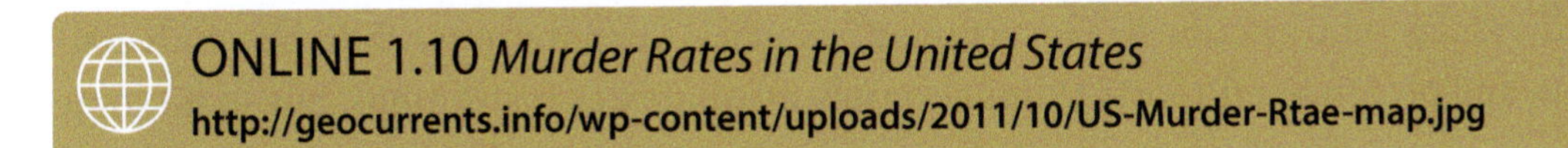

ONLINE 1.10 Murder Rates in the United States
http://geocurrents.info/wp-content/uploads/2011/10/US-Murder-Rtae-map.jpg

How could this lawlessness persist in a nation committed to the rule of law? Or, to put it another way, how can a nation remain committed to the rule of law when so many operate outside the law? Is this violence an indelible part of our national character? Does it suggest a breakdown of social norms and institutions? Is it a function of the easy availability of guns? Is it being encouraged by our mass media and popular culture? Obviously, the answers to these questions are not mutually exclusive.

Some have attributed America's seeming obsession with violence to the influence of the frontier culture on the American character.[21] Since the frontier days, Americans have widely believed that firearms should be easily available. But as crime and violence reached epidemic proportions in the 1980s, many people began to question the wisdom of allowing guns to be produced, sold, possessed, and used without significant restrictions. In the 1990s, a sharp, and often angry, debate developed between the advocates of gun control and the proponents of the "right to keep and bear arms." This debate continued into the first decade of the twenty-first century and will likely go on for years to come.

Many believe that the violence on television and in recorded music stimulates violent behavior, especially among young people. In the 1990s, a loud outcry occurred over the movie *The Matrix* because the two students behind the Columbine High School massacre in Denver were inspired by violent scenes in the film to commit the terrible acts upon their classmates.

The debate remained: Were the media merely reflecting the national mood, or were they in fact contributing to it? Although this question was not easily answered, politicians were feeling the heat. Some members of Congress threatened to consider regulating the content of network television. A large segment of American society wanted government to rein in some elements of the popular culture. The rule of law seemed preferable to the law of the jungle. Nevertheless, characterizing Americans as being of one mind on these issues would be a mistake. Although some people thought that government ought to assume responsibility for community safety, others remained skeptical of enforcing community values that would limit the rights of individuals. Of course, this disagreement was not new. Americans have always disagreed about the appropriate role of government. As you have seen, much of this disagreement is traceable to the differing cultural backgrounds of the people who came to this country and their experiences in settling it.

1-3c INSTITUTIONS AND AMERICAN POLITICAL CULTURE

An **institution** is an established pattern of behavior that transcends and outlives the individuals who occupy it. Government agencies, corporations, churches, universities, and professional sports teams certainly all qualify as institutions, but so do some social arrangements that may not be so obvious. You can divide American institutions into three broad categories: **governmental institutions**, the existence of which may be traced to the federal and state constitutions; **intermediary institutions**, which are quasipublic institutions, such as political parties, that mediate between government and the people; and **societal institutions**, which exist primarily by custom and are not primarily political in character. The family is a good example of a societal institution.

GOVERNMENTAL INSTITUTIONS

Much of this book is devoted to describing the workings of governmental institutions in the United States: the Congress, the presidency, the Supreme Court and other courts of law, and the many bureaucratic agencies that exist at all levels of government. At the beginning of the twenty-first century, serious concern exists over whether governmental institutions that were designed in the eighteenth century can manage the complex problems of the postindustrial age and meet the demands of an increasingly diverse society. The American people appear to be losing faith in their institutions. Long-term trends in public opinion show that Americans now have less confidence in their institutions and less faith in their leaders than they did thirty years ago. Since the early 1970s, due in part to the failure in Vietnam and the Watergate scandal, popular trust and confidence in government have been in decline. Given this declining public trust and the increasingly difficult problems to be managed, one must ask whether American institutions can continue to govern without serious modification. The question is far from academic—and the answer has implications for the quality of life of future generations of Americans.

Intermediary Institutions

Governmental bodies are not the only institutions of importance in the United States or in any democracy. Political scientists consider political parties, interest groups, and the mass media to be nearly as important as government in the political system. Because these entities provide linkages between the governing elites and the masses, they are sometimes referred to as *intermediary* institutions. These institutions help connect people to the political process by providing channels for political participation or at least a means of following what government is doing. Few people are elected or appointed to high public office, but millions of people can join interest groups or get involved in political parties. And nearly everyone in society has access to television, radio, and newspapers.

Societal Institutions

Basic societal institutions—such as the family, school, and church—although not primarily political entities, play an important role in **political socialization**, the transmission of political values and beliefs. Accordingly, as primary agents of political culture, these institutions may provide considerable support for a particular political system. Over the past several decades, some commentators have expressed concern about the apparent erosion of these institutions: the breakdown of the family, the decline of organized religion, and the crisis in the public schools. This concern is partially motivated by the important role these institutions have played historically in holding the nation together, maintaining social order and stability, and transmitting values that foster political and economic progress.

Some commentators believe that the tremendous social and economic change that America has experienced over the past century has undermined the societal institutions that have nurtured our democratic political culture. These commentators, who may be referred to as **communitarians**, believe that unbridled individualism is corrosive to a democratic political system. They fear that American citizens are losing their sense of community and their commitment to the **public interest**. Communitarians worry that Americans are increasingly unwilling to make the kinds of sacrifices that are sometimes necessary to ensure the long-term survival of the political system. In his widely read book *Habits of the Heart*, sociologist Robert Bellah argues that Americans "have committed what to the republican founders of our nation was the cardinal sin: We have put our own good, as individuals, as groups, as a nation, ahead of the common good."[22]

One element that our democratic political culture holds up is the idea of the citizen-leader. **Civic engagement** is "working to make a difference in the civic life of our communities and developing the combination of knowledge, skills, values and motivation to make that difference. It means promoting the quality of life in a community, through both political and non-political processes."[23] For democracy to work, people must participate in politics, be knowledgeable, and understand how the political system operates. In 2000, Harvard political scientist Robert Putnam published the book *Bowling Alone*, where he showed that Americans have become less civically engaged over time.[24] The reduction in people who join civic organizations like the Rotary or Kiwanis clubs, the decline in church membership, and the decline in collective activities like participating in bowling leagues pointed to an absence of what Putnam calls **social capital**. Social capital is similar to legitimacy, including elements like faith in the decisions and qualities of elected officials. Since the publication of *Bowling Alone*, a new trend has emerged with programs like the American Democracy Project, which seeks to build civic engagement skills among American college students.[25]

While we do not view this textbook as a manual to good citizenship, we do see this book as an opportunity for students to build their own bank of social capital by becoming more informed about the workings of government and how the citizen plays a vital, and often forgotten, role in democratic politics. As you will see, young people do not participate in politics to the same extent that other age groups do. A truly integrated political culture sees all age groups with a similar desire and ability to govern through a democratic process.

Unfortunately, two powerful forces work against the maintenance of an integrated political culture in this country. One is our highly successful capitalist economy, which is "a relentless engine of change, a revolutionary inflamer of appetites."[26] The other is the ever-increasing ethnic, racial, and religious diversity of our society. And the goal of maintaining an integrated political culture seems hard to reconcile with the current drive toward **multiculturalism**, the belief that different cultures can and should coexist in the same society. The nation's old motto "E pluribus unum," meaning "Out of many, one," has fallen into disfavor in some quarters. The traditional idea that America should be a melting pot for people of different cultures is increasingly being rejected in favor of the belief that immigrants should strive to maintain their distinct cultural identity. Yet, when polled, most Americans still come down on the side of the melting pot. Native Americans are the only exception to this trend. By a margin of 2-1, Native Americans believe in maintaining their own distinctive culture. Asian Americans are the most likely to favor the concept of the melting pot, which may help to explain their rapid economic advancement in this society.

ONLINE 1.11 *Diversity in the United States*
http://radiomankc.blogspot.com/2010/08/census-data-diversity-by-county-5-pct.html

The historian Arthur M. Schlesinger puts the issue succinctly: "The question America confronts as a pluralistic society is how to vindicate cherished cultures and traditions without breaking the bonds of cohesion—common ideals, common political institutions, common language, common culture, common fate—that hold the republic together."[27]

1-3d The Evolving American Political Culture

American political culture is constantly changing. Of course, by their very nature, cultures change slowly. Values persist, and culture persists. Yet American political culture has been evolving in a number of ways. First, although regionalism is still an important force in American politics, American political culture has become somewhat nationalized. The South, the part of the country with the most distinctive political culture, has become much more like the rest of the country. Two major reasons underlie the nationalization of American political culture. First, the media in the United States are national. No matter where people live, they likely watch the same television programs, read the same news magazines, and watch the same news. Second, the national government has clearly become dominant over the states, and the federal courts have long since ruled that states may not restrict the rights of minorities in order to maintain the region's traditions.

Other changes in American political culture reflect shifts in the larger societal culture. American society has become much more open than it once was. Fewer constraints are placed on personal expression. One can see this readily in the popular culture—movies, music, television, novels, plays, and the like. For example, the difference between television programs in the early part of the twenty-first century and those from the late 1950s and early 1960s is tremendous, especially in the portrayal of sexuality and family life. "Ozzie and Harriet" has given way to "Here Comes Honey Boo-Boo."

In addition to wider boundaries for personal expression, Americans are now much more tolerant of a variety of lifestyles. Some states and cities now have laws prohibiting discrimination on the basis of sexual orientation. Many American political jurisdictions now allow live-in partners to receive health benefits formerly reserved for spouses. In some cities, such as New York, gay and lesbian couples can be considered partners for purposes of receiving benefits. In Vermont and five other states, gay and lesbian couples can enter into civil unions that legally resemble marriages or marry with the exact same rights as heterosexual couples. Such policies would have been inconceivable as recently as a decade ago.

1-3e Ideology

When people talk of political conflict in the United States, they typically frame the conflict in terms of two opposing ideologies—liberalism and conservatism. The concept of **ideology** is related to political culture, but is conceptually distinct. Ideology refers to a coherent system of beliefs and values that lead people to form opinions on social, economic, and political questions. In the United States, the ideological system is more complex than can be captured in a single liberal-conservative continuum because of differences in attitudes toward regulations of different types of behaviors. A person may believe that one's personal choices, such as whom to marry and whether or not to take narcotic drugs, is an important area to regulate while believing in a relatively regulation-free *laissez-faire* economy. The opposite may be true as well, so we must separate American ideologies according to a two-axis system creating four general areas to fit our ideologies into (see Figure 1-1). People who believe in more regulation across the board are **populists**, while those who favor less regulation consistently are known as **libertarians**. In the corners are **conservatives**, who believe in free-market economics while favoring more regulation of individual behaviors, and their opposite are known as **liberals**, favoring fewer behavioral restrictions but more aggressive oversight of economic matters. For a growing number of Americans, the typology does not fit them at all. Calling themselves **moderates**, they are in the middle of the ideological spectrum without a defined ideology or party to anchor them. As their numbers have increased to roughly a third of the electorate today, they are a highly sought-after voting bloc in elections, but are less predictable and harder to understand and reach than their more ideologically driven counterparts.

ONLINE 1.12 *Where Do You Stand?*

To see where you might stand, link to an online quiz that lets you determine your ideological placement: **http://www.people-press.org/typology/quiz/**

Liberals *Favor*: Greater economic regulation and social welfare spending *Oppose*: Greater personal choice/lifestyle regulations	**Populists** *Favor:* Greater economic regulation and social welfare spending *Favor:* Greater personal choice/lifestyle regulations
Libertarians *Oppose*: Greater personal choice/lifestyle regulations *Oppose*: Greater economic regulation and social welfare spending	**Conservatives** *Favor*: Greater regulation of personal choice/ lifestyle issues *Oppose*: Greater economic regulation and social welfare spending

Figure 1-1 *The Liberal-Conservative Typology*

The meaning of the ideologies "conservative" and "liberal" have changed over the last twenty years. Conservatives can now be thought of in two different categories: one is the **economic conservative**, who favors a fiercely capitalist ideology that favors free-market solutions to problems and minimal government intervention in the economy. The other type of conservative, the **cultural conservative**, believes in maintaining traditional values and institutions, opposing abortions, gay marriages, and other policies they feel to be morally improper for government to allow. Liberals on the other hand favor government as a mechanism of reform and progress. Cultural conservatives are generally pessimistic about the desirability and possibility of social progress. They prefer order and stability to progressive experimentation. For liberals, who have taken to calling their movement **progressive**, progress is defined in terms of equality. Thus, liberals have sought to use the power of government to promote economic equality and social justice. Conservatives have argued against government interference in the free enterprise system but have looked to government as a means of preserving the social order.

1-4 Conclusion: Politics and the American Future

Because of the inherent dynamism of capitalism, the ever-increasing diversity of American society, and the constantly accelerating pace of life in the information age, politics in America is complex and dynamic. The student of American government may at times feel overwhelmed by the myriad perspectives, theories, and ideologies of American politics, let alone the tremendous volume of factual information being generated on the subject. No one, from presidents to pundits, can legitimately claim to understand all there is to comprehend about American politics and government. Nevertheless, in a democratic society such as ours, citizens must make the effort.

The dynamics of American politics take place in an evolving political culture that sets the limits for political discourse and action. This culture, with its roots in the American frontier and its commitment to free-market capitalism, has changed greatly as the broader societal culture has been transformed. At the beginning of the twenty-first century, the American political system faces a number of serious challenges. Perhaps the most fundamental of these is the governance of a society that is becoming increasingly diverse. How can such a society maintain the integrated political culture necessary to sustain democratic institutions? Can American democracy survive an attack by outsiders who characterize their grievances in terms of a religious war without a lessening of religious tolerance in this country? In the decades to come, American democracy must find a way to ensure that diversity is a source of strength rather than a threat to the viability of the system.

Questions for Thought and Discussion

1. Why do Americans tend to hold negative views of politics and politicians?

2. Is it possible to conceive of a political system in a modern mass society in which all citizens who desire could participate equally in the making of public decisions?

3. How rapidly do political cultures change? What are the factors that cause them to change?

4. Why is individualism the dominant characteristic of American political culture? How is the nature of American individualism changing?

5. How have the liberal and conservative ideologies changed since the United States was founded? Do any underlying continuities exist in these opposing ideologies?

Endnotes

1 Jeff Goodwin and James Jasper, *Rethinking Social Movements: Structure, Meaning and Emotion* (Lanham, MD: Rowman and Littlefield, 2004).

2 See, generally, Bernard Crick, *In Defense of Politics*, 4th ed. (Chicago: University of Chicago Press, 1993).

3 Thomas Hobbes, *Leviathan* (New York: Macmillan, 1947), p. 82.

4 Harold D. Lasswell, *Politics: Who Gets What, When, How* (New York: McGraw-Hill, 1936).

5 Walter A. Rosenbaum, *Political Culture* (New York: Praeger, 1975), p. 4.

6 "Libya: Gadhaffi's Last Stand in Sirte," October 27, 2011, http://allafrica.com/stories/201110271091.html

7 Gabriel Almond and Sidney Verba, *The Civic Culture* (Princeton, NJ: Princeton University Press, 1963), p. X.

8 "Making the Innocence of Muslims." *Vanity Fair*, December 27, 2012, http://www.vanityfair.com/culture/2012/12/making-of-innocence-of-muslims

9 "Clamor Erupts over Teen's Tweet about KS Governor Sam Brownback," November 24, 2011, http://www2.ljworld.com/news/2011/nov/24/kansas-city-teens-tweet-draws-ire-brownback-admini/

10 *The Politics of Aristotle*, ed. and trans. by Ernest Barker (New York: Oxford University Press, 1958); see, generally, "Oligarchy and Democracy," pp. 110–37.

11 Abraham Lincoln, *Gettysburg Address*, November 19, 1863.

12 The classic formulation of the so-called iron law of oligarchy can be found in Roberto Michels' *Political Parties: A Study of the Oligarchical Tendencies of Modern Democracies* (New York: Free Press, 1962).

13 Charles Lindblom, *Politics and Markets* (New York: Basic Books, 1977), p. 162.

14 See J. Harry Wray, *Sense and Non-Sense: American Culture and Politics* (Upper Saddle River, NJ: Prentice-Hall, 2001), in particular Chapter 3, "Making It Alone."

15 Daniel J. Elazar, *American Federalism: A View from the States* (New York: Thomas Crowell, 1966), pp. 85–86.

16 Ibid., pp. 90–95.

17 Colin Woodard, *American Nations: A History of the Eleven Regional Cultures of North America* (New York: Penguin Books, 2012).

18 Stephen L. Carter, *The Culture of Disbelief: How American Law and Politics Trivialize Religious Devotion* (New York: Basic Books, 1993), p. 4.

19 See, for example, *Griswold v. Connecticut*, 381 U.S. 479 (1965).

20 *Roe v. Wade*, 410 U.S. 113 (1973).

21 Joe B. Frantz, "The Frontier Tradition: An Invitation to Violence." In *The History of Violence in America: A Report to the National Commission on the Causes and Prevention of Violence* (New York: Bantam Books, 1969), pp. 157–64.

22 Robert Bellah, et al., *Habits of the Heart* (Berkeley: University of California Press, 1985), p. 285.

23 Thomas Ehrilch, *Civic Responsibility and Higher Education* (Oryx Press, 2000), preface.

24 Google Books, http://books.google.com/books?id=rd2ibodep7UC&dq=putnam+bowling+alone&printsec=frontcover&source=bn&hl=en&ei=At5MSq24DoaeMaa-mfkD&sa=X&oi=book_result&ct=result&resnum=4

25 American Association of State Colleges and Universities, "About ADP," www.aascu.org/programs/adp/

26 George Will, *The Pursuit of Virtue and Other Tory Notions* (New York: Simon & Schuster, 1982), p. 36.

27 Arthur M. Schlesinger, Jr., *The Disuniting of America*, rev. ed. (New York: Norton, 1998), p. 138.

Chapter 2

The Development of American Constitutional Democracy

OUTLINE

Key Terms 38
Expected Learning Outcomes 38
2-1 The Constitution and American Political Culture 38
2-2 Establishment of the American Colonies 40
  2-2a Government in the Colonies 41
2-3 The American Revolution 42
  2-3a Causes of the Revolution 42
  2-3b Contrasting Political Cultures 43
  2-3c American Independence 44
2-4 The "Disunited" States of America 45
  2-4a Government under the Articles of Confederation 46
2-5 The Constitutional Convention 48
  2-5a The Delegates 48
  2-5b Consensus on Basic Principles 50
  2-5c Conflict and Compromise in Philadelphia 53
  2-5d The Signing of the Constitution 54
2-6 The Framers' Constitution 55
  2-6a The Institutions of the New National Government 55
  2-6b The System of Checks and Balances 56
  2-6c Restrictions on the States 56
  2-6d Individual Rights 57
  2-6e An Undemocratic Document? 57
2-7 The Battle over Ratification 58
  2-7a Federalists versus Anti-Federalists 58
  2-7b The Ratifying Conventions 59
2-8 Amending the Constitution 60
  2-8a Constitutional Change through Judicial Interpretation 64
  2-8b Democratization of the Constitutional System 67

2-9 Conclusion: Assessing the Constitutional System 71
Questions for Thought and Discussion 73
Endnotes 74

KEY TERMS

advice and consent
Articles of Confederation
bicameral legislatures
bill of attainder
Bill of Rights
Boston Tea Party
checks and balances
commander-in-chief
common law
Constitutional Convention
Court-packing plan
Declaration of Independence
democratization
direct democracy
distributive articles
divided-party government
due process of law
electoral college
English Bill of Rights
equal protection of the laws
ex post facto law
federalism
First Continental Congress
habeas corpus
Magna Carta
malapportionment
Mayflower Compact
Necessary and Proper Clause
New Deal
New Jersey Plan
one person, one vote
original jurisdiction
police power
poll tax
Prohibition
protective tariffs
reapportionment
representative government
republic
Second Continental Congress
Shays' Rebellion
sovereign immunity
Stamp Act
states' rights
tyranny of the majority
unicameral legislature
unitary system
veto
Virginia Plan
writ of mandamus

EXPECTED LEARNING OUTCOMES

After reading this chapter and completing the supplemental online materials, students will:

- Describe how the early attempts at American self-governance influenced Constitutional political development
- Identify philosophical influences on the U.S. Constitution
- Compare proposal for Constitutional design presented at the Constitutional Convention
- Describe the powers, structure, and amendment process of the U.S. Constitution
- Analyze the ratification process for the Constitution

2-1 THE CONSTITUTION AND AMERICAN POLITICAL CULTURE

As Chapter 1, "The Political Culture of American Democracy," points out, the American political consensus embraces a commitment to individual freedom, democratic institutions, equality of opportunity, and the rule of law. All these values are enshrined in the U.S. Constitution—some in its original concept and others added as it has evolved over two hundred years. Through twenty-seven formal amendments and many more changes in interpretation, the U.S. Constitution is this country's evolving political covenant. It sets forth the general parameters of government and defines the citizens' relationship to that government. The Constitution represents the most basic expression of our shared political culture.

The U.S. Constitution is extremely resilient. It has withstood the Civil War, two world wars, the Cold War, the Great Depression, massive social upheavals, and the technological changes that have recently remade our society. The Constitution is now being tested by an altered economy. The "Great Recession" that began in 2008 presaged a significant shift in government's interaction with the economy. Yet with all the discussion of bailouts and handouts, no one has suggested that the existing constitutional order was fundamentally inadequate to meet the challenge of a changing economy. Americans are convinced of the viability and adaptability of their constitutional system.

The American people believe in their Constitution, even though relatively few have even read it. They believe that the Constitution has worked well over the years, although they acknowledge that the political system has changed dramatically since the time the Constitution was adopted. Indeed, support for the Constitution itself, and for the system of government it created, is an essential element of American political culture. A 2010 survey by the Associated Press and the National Constitution Center found that nearly three in four Americans believe the Constitution has endured because of its continuing relevance, while less than a quarter think the document has outlasted its usefulness.[1]

Probably no idea is more basic to what it means to be an American than the view that government is limited and that individuals have rights that the government may not transgress. The Bill of Rights (Amendments I through X of the Constitution) reflects the ideals of early America more than its reality. However, these ideals have gained such force that they have done much to guide the evolution of our culture. And with the changing culture has come a changed sense of what the Constitution means. This idea of change within the framework of guiding principles is probably the most fundamental aspect of American constitutional democracy. Many constitutional disputes are framed in terms of whether the Constitution should be understood according to the Founders' original intentions or whether the meaning of the document should be adapted to the needs of the present day.

Nearly all Americans understand the need for the Constitution to be amended from time to time, and most believe that the meaning of the Constitution should evolve to reflect changing social and economic conditions. But Americans are understandably opposed to any attempt to change the Constitution wholesale. Indeed, they are even

wary of holding a new constitutional convention to try to improve on the document. But they are comfortable with some gradual change in what the Constitution means. As long as the meaning of the Constitution changes to reflect an evolving societal consensus, its legitimacy is not seriously threatened.

The Constitution begins with the phrase "We the people…" This phrase is somewhat ironic in that the Constitution itself was written by aristocrats. But over the years, the Constitution has come to be accepted by the American people and, in many ways, to embody their values and aspirations. Frequently, the most oppressed and least powerful people in our society have turned to the Constitution as their weapon for change. Somewhat ironically, the document that is the legal foundation of American government is also the basis for protecting individuals from their government. Such is the legacy of the "living Constitution."

2-2 Establishment of the American Colonies

To comprehend the contemporary constitutional system, you must understand how it has evolved over time. Although the origin of the American constitutional system might reasonably be seen as the Declaration of Independence in 1776 or the adoption of the Constitution in 1787, those documents emerged from the political culture that had developed in the American colonies. Accordingly, our examination must begin with the colonial background of the nation.

Colonies were established in the New World primarily for economic reasons. Governments in Europe saw the colonies as sources of raw materials for industry and as consumer markets for finished products. Ambitious Europeans, frustrated by rigid class structures and guild systems, viewed the colonies as places of economic opportunity. Yet economics and the desire for a better standard of living were not the only motives that led Europeans to make the long, hazardous journey across the Atlantic Ocean. Just as important was the desire for religious and political freedom.

The Protestant Reformation of the fifteenth and sixteenth centuries gave rise to a new religious diversity in Europe, but also led to a plague of religious warfare and persecution. Groups like the Puritans established their colony at Plymouth to create a religious safe haven for their strict variety of Calvinist Protestantism. In *Democracy in America*, written some two hundred years later, Alexis de Tocqueville credited the Puritans with providing the moral foundation of American democracy. Certainly, the Puritan values of hard work, self-reliance, and personal responsibility were instrumental in creating a society in which self-government could succeed. For many years, these values remained at the core of American political culture. Whether they still do is open to question.

By the 1770s, 2.5 million inhabitants were spread over thirteen American colonies from New Hampshire in the north to Georgia in the south. Although 60 percent of the colonists were of English origin, many other ethnic groups were present, including the Dutch, Welsh, Scots, and Germans. In the southern colonies, 28 percent of the population were slaves forcibly brought to America from Africa. Thus, diversity, which is still a source of both pride and conflict, is rooted in the early settlement of the country.

Although most colonists were dissatisfied with the established order in Europe, they were certainly not anarchists. From the beginning, they understood the need for government. Before the Puritans' ship arrived at Plymouth, forty-one of the male passengers signed the **Mayflower Compact**, the first written agreement for self-government in America. Since the compact authorized the adoption of laws for the common good and committed all members of the colony to obey those laws, it foreshadowed the adoption of the U.S. Constitution 167 years later. Samuel Eliot Morison has written that the Mayflower Compact "is justly regarded as a key document in American history. It proves the determination of a small group of English emigrants to live under a rule of law, based on consent of the people, and to set up their own civil government."[2]

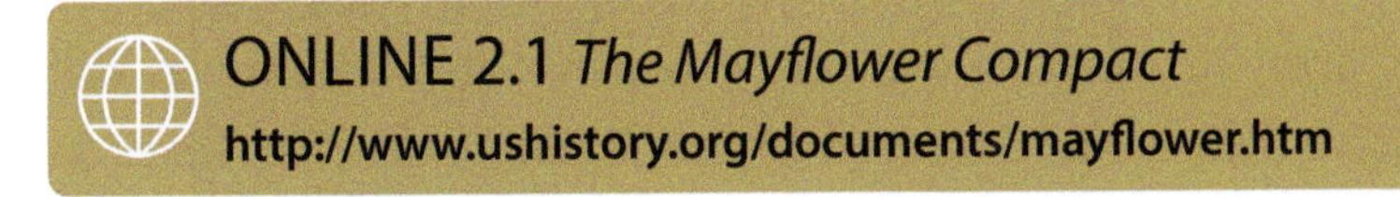

ONLINE 2.1 *The Mayflower Compact*
http://www.ushistory.org/documents/mayflower.htm

2-2a Government in the Colonies

The powers exercised by the colonial governments were generally limited by written charters, predecessors to the state constitutions that would be written after the American Revolution. The idea that government must be based on a written charter is thus deeply rooted in American political culture. Except for Pennsylvania, the colonies had **bicameral legislatures** (two-house legislatures). In most colonies, the upper house of the legislature was appointed by the governor and consisted largely of aristocrats. The lower house was elected by "the people," that is, by white male adult property owners. All colonial governors had broad powers, including the absolute right to **veto**, or reject, legislation and the authority to appoint all judges. The colonial courts followed the **common law**, which was the traditional law of England. Because the courts were bound by an elaborate body of law that had developed over the centuries, and were not making new law, they were by far the least important institutions of government during the colonial era.

2-3 THE AMERICAN REVOLUTION

One can argue that the American Revolution was made virtually inevitable by the British defeat of France and Spain in the Seven Years War (also known as the French and Indian War), which lasted from 1756 to 1763. The British victory removed the threats to the American colonies from France in the north and Spain in Florida and the west. As the historian Paul Kennedy has observed: "Freed from foreign threats which hitherto had induced loyalty to [England's government], American colonists could now insist upon a merely nominal link with Britain, and, if denied that by an imperial government with different ideas, engage in rebellion."[3] Thus, the seeds of independence were sown. As the colonies were no longer defenseless outposts subject to the constant threat of attack, the colonies began to exist independently from British rule.

The British, as a result of their victory, acquired the extensive lands of the Ohio and Mississippi river valleys. To the restless American colonists, these lands beckoned for settlement. The British, however, worried about the difficulties and costs they would incur in trying to protect settlers from conflicts with the Native Americans who occupied the lands over the mountains. Consequently, Parliament prohibited the colonists from purchasing land west of the Appalachians. To enforce this policy, the British sent an army of ten thousand troops to the colonies. Many colonists were outraged by what they considered to be a wholly inappropriate use of military power during peacetime.

2-3a CAUSES OF THE REVOLUTION

Maintaining a large standing army in America was very expensive, and Britain was still struggling to repay the massive debt it had incurred in the Seven Years War. Taxes in Britain were considerably higher than in the colonies—indeed, more than twenty-five times higher for the average taxpayer. Not surprisingly, the British looked for a way to make the colonies pay more of the cost of their own defense. This idea seemed only fair to the British, who were still resentful that the colonies, which had been the principal beneficiaries of the British victory in the Seven Years War, had contributed little to the war effort.

In March 1765, Parliament passed the **Stamp Act**, which required the colonists to purchase stamps to be placed on envelopes, newspapers, wills, playing cards, college degrees, marriage licenses, and land titles, among other things. Violators were subject to trial without jury. Colonial reaction to the Stamp Act came fast and furious. Americans have never been fond of taxes, but the colonists were particularly angry that Parliament would impose a tax on British subjects who were not represented in the House of Commons. In Boston, the self-styled Sons of Liberty hung in effigy the agents and supporters of the king. They also looted the home of Andrew Oliver, the king's agent for stamp distribution in Massachusetts. Oliver resigned from office and was never replaced. In October 1765, delegates from all thirteen colonies met in New York. This "Stamp Act Congress" demanded repeal of the despised legislation and called for a boycott of British goods. Faced with declining exports to the colonies, Parliament gave in to the colonists' demands.

In 1766, Parliament enacted the Townshend duties, another revenue-raising measure that imposed taxes on a variety of imports to the colonies. The colonists protested, and the duties were repealed except for the tax on tea. In 1773, Parliament passed the Tea Act, which granted the East India Company the exclusive right to sell tea to American distributors. This monopoly, which eliminated American importers from the tea trade, prompted the **Boston Tea Party**, in which some 150 colonists disguised as Native Americans dumped tea from British ships into Boston Harbor. Parliament responded quickly to this act of lawlessness by passing the Coercive Acts, which were dubbed the "Intolerable Acts" by the Massachusetts colonists. These acts closed the port of Boston until reparations were made to the East India Company, restricted public assemblies, increased the powers of the governor, and, most onerous of all, required colonists to quarter British soldiers in their homes.

The Intolerable Acts helped to galvanize public opinion against Great Britain throughout the colonies. Responding to this new climate, disgruntled delegates from twelve colonies convened in Philadelphia in September 1774. Calling itself the **First Continental Congress**, the assembly called for a boycott of English goods. Some of the more radical delegates urged revolution, although more moderate sentiments prevailed. Yet forces were in motion that would propel the colonies into a violent uprising against the British.

2-3b Contrasting Political Cultures

One underlying cause of the antagonism between the colonies and Great Britain was their contrasting political cultures. By the eighteenth century, Britain was moving slowly but steadily in the direction of political democracy. The age of absolute monarchy had passed with the Glorious Revolution of 1688. Yet, because of property qualifications for voting, less than 20 percent of the adult male population of Britain was entitled to vote in parliamentary elections. Parliament therefore still retained much of an upper-class bias.

In contrast, the American colonies were considerably more democratic. Voting in elections for colonial assemblies was limited to white men of property, of course, but property qualifications were much less stringent than in Britain. Consequently, more than half the adult male population was entitled to vote. The colonial assemblies reflected this enfranchisement. Among the members of the lower houses of the colonial legislatures were the owners of small farms, shopkeepers, and artisans as well as lawyers, physicians, and planters. Consequently, the assemblies came to reflect the more democratic sensibilities of the colonies. This more democratic political culture certainly reflected the more egalitarian nature of American society, a society in which traditional European ideas about social class and hierarchy were being rapidly discarded.[4]

In 1775, the voyage from Bristol, England, to Boston took at least a month. Because of their remoteness, the American colonists lost their sense of attachment to

Great Britain and developed an independent sense of political identity. And because the colonies were spread out along the Atlantic seaboard, the colonists developed a strong sense of localism. Most Americans in the 1770s believed that their affairs were better governed by their local and state assemblies than by Parliament in faraway London. Colonists, especially those who had been born in the New World, began to think of themselves as Georgians, Marylanders, and New Yorkers rather than as English subjects.

2-3c American Independence

With so many of the colonists no longer identifying with Britain, a violent break became almost inevitable. The Revolutionary War began in April 1775 when a band of sixty Minutemen armed with muskets confronted six companies of the British army in the village of Lexington, Massachusetts. The British were on their way to Concord, Massachusetts, to seize a cache of weapons that the rebellious colonists had been stockpiling. No one knows which side fired "the shot heard round the world." When the badly outnumbered colonists retreated, eight of their compatriots lay dead on the village green. Although the fighting began in Lexington, John Adams was quite correct in observing that "[t]he Revolution was affected before the war commenced. The Revolution was in the minds and hearts of the people."[5]

If the colonies were to act as a nation, they needed a way to govern themselves, even if initially only for the purposes of waging war. A transitional government was needed before a fighting force could be organized and funded. Convening in May 1775, the **Second Continental Congress** decided to raise an army to oppose the British. It also opened channels of communication to European powers in an effort to obtain military support. Despite a rising tide of revolutionary sentiment in the colonies, the Continental Congress declined to declare independence from Britain. Over the next year, a great debate took place between radicals who wanted full independence and moderates who believed that reconciliation with Britain was still possible.

One of the most influential and colorful radicals was Thomas Paine, a recent arrival from England. His pamphlet *Common Sense*, published in January 1776, helped to stir the revolutionary cauldron. In the first three months after it was published, *Common Sense* sold more than one hundred twenty thousand copies, making it by far the best-selling book of 1776. Paine's pamphlet portrayed the struggle of the American colonies against George III as part of a larger democratic struggle against corrupt and decadent monarchies. But the colonists were most impressed by Paine's eminently practical argument that it was silly to think that "a continent could be perpetually governed by an island."

By the spring of 1776, it was apparent to most Americans that independence from Britain was both necessary and desirable. On July 2, the Second Continental

Congress adopted a resolution of independence. Two days later, it approved the **Declaration of Independence**. Authored by Thomas Jefferson, the Declaration outlined the colonies' grievances against King George and asserted the right of revolution. The ideas expressed in the Declaration were by no means original to Jefferson or to the American colonies. They were articulated a century earlier in John Locke's *Two Treatises of Government*. When the Declaration of Independence refers to "life, liberty and the pursuit of happiness" as being the "inalienable rights" of individuals, it echoes Locke's formulation of the natural rights of "life, liberty and property." Although the Declaration asserted American independence, it did so by drawing on ideas that had already taken hold in Britain. Thus, in a sense, the Declaration of Independence was an affirmation of the links between the British and American political cultures. Despite the considerable cultural differences that led to the Revolution, the essential ideas of the Declaration of Independence came from Britain.

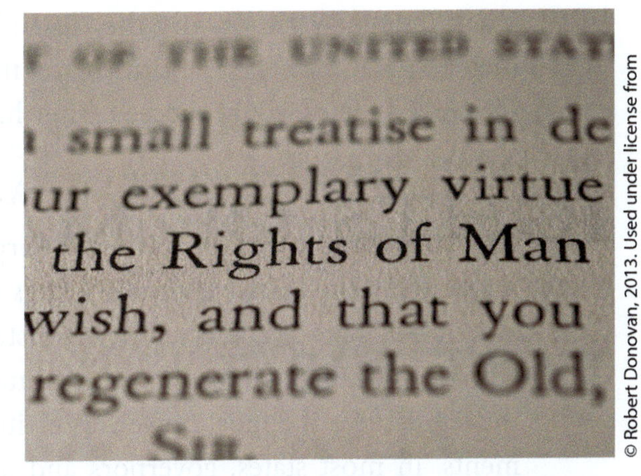

ONLINE 2.2 *The Declaration of Independence*
http://www.history.com/topics/american-revolution/videos#declaration-of-independence

2-4 THE "DISUNITED" STATES OF AMERICA

Several weeks before the Declaration of Independence was adopted, Richard Henry Lee, of Virginia, proposed to the Continental Congress that a "plan of confederation" be prepared for the colonies. The plan was drafted by a committee and adopted by the Continental Congress in November 1777. By its own terms, the **Articles of Confederation** had to be ratified by all thirteen states. Persuading all thirteen states to go along took six years, but on March 1, 1781, the Maryland legislature finally ratified the document. Thus, on March 2, 1781, the old Continental Congress became the "United States of America in Congress Assembled."

ONLINE 2.3 *The Articles of Confederation*
http://www.loc.gov/rr/program/bib/ourdocs/articles.html

When Lord Cornwallis, the British commanding general, surrendered to General George Washington at Yorktown in October 1781, Americans were generally optimistic about their new nation and the "league of friendship" they had established among their respective states. The British and many Europeans, however, were doubtful that the United States would succeed. They had ample reason for their skepticism.

2-4a Government under the Articles of Confederation

The "Articles of Confederation and Perpetual Union" were written with the idea of maintaining the thirteen separate states as sovereign entities. During the Revolution, all thirteen states established new constitutions and political institutions. In keeping with the prevailing philosophical sentiments of the Revolution, the constitutions made the legislatures the most powerful institutions of the newly constituted state governments. In most states, governors and judges were appointed by the legislature. By the mid-1770s, all thirteen states had well-established political systems, which they intended to protect against encroachments by the national government.

The national government created by the Articles of Confederation was intentionally minimalist in character. Congress, the sole institution of the national government, was provided with little meaningful power. Congress was a **unicameral** (one-house) **legislature**, where each state had one vote. A supermajority of nine states was required to adopt any significant measure, making it impossible for Congress to act decisively.

Using the name "government" for the institutions established under the Articles is overstating things. The entire national government was so weak it collapsed under its own light weight. Every institution was designed to be weak, which was a particular problem in addressing the common interests of the states and massive debt accumulated during the War for Independence. Congress' greatest deficiency under the Articles, for instance, was that it lacked the power to tax. It could only request funds from the states, which were less than magnanimous. During the first two years under the Articles, Congress received less than $1.5 million of the more than $10 million it requested from the states. This arrangement became especially problematic as Congress tried to fund the Continental Army, which remained at war with the British until the Peace of Paris was signed in 1783. After the peace, Congress struggled to repay the massive war debt it had incurred; the states, for the most part, treated the national debt as somebody else's problem.

The Articles of Confederation did not give Congress any power to regulate foreign and interstate commerce. Commercial regulations varied widely among the states, which sought to protect their interests by instituting **protective tariffs** and fees. A tariff is a charge imposed on a product being brought into a country or, in this case, a state. In addition to raising money, the purpose of a tariff is to protect domestic producers by increasing the price of imported goods. Of course, when one state instituted a tariff, other states retaliated with tariffs of their own. These impositions frustrated the emergence of a national economy and depressed economic growth. Although Congress could coin money, states were not prohibited from issuing their own currency, which further inhibited interstate economic activity.

Under the Articles, there was no president to provide leadership and speak for the new nation with a unified voice. This omission was deliberate, of course, because many Americans feared a restoration of the monarchy. But as a consequence, states began to develop their own foreign policies; some even entered into negotiations with other countries.

Nor did the Articles of Confederation provide for a national court system to settle disputes between states or parties residing in different states. The lack of predictable enforcement of contracts between parties in different states also inhibited interstate economic activity. The fact that no one could look to any overarching authority to settle disputes or provide leadership contributed to the sense of disunity. Finally, by their own terms, the Articles could not be amended except by unanimous consent of the states. Any state could veto a proposed change in the confederation. As a result, under the Articles of Confederation, the national government was ineffectual. Meanwhile, much to the delight of the European colonial powers, the "Perpetual Union" was disintegrating. It soon became clear that the Articles could loosely guide a collection of states, but were incapable of providing government for a nation.

The Annapolis Convention

Among those who were extremely dissatisfied with the Articles of Confederation were James Madison of Virginia and Alexander Hamilton of New York. Together they engineered a conference, which was held in Annapolis, Maryland, in 1786. Officially called for the purpose of discussing issues of commerce, the Annapolis convention was actually a forum for expressing dissatisfaction with the Articles of Confederation. Although only five states sent delegations to Annapolis, the convention adopted a resolution calling for a convention to revise the Articles. Shortly after the close of the Annapolis Convention, the idea of a new constitution gained considerable support from an event in Massachusetts: **Shays' Rebellion**.

Shays' Rebellion

In the wake of the American Revolution, most owners of small farms were saddled with high debts. By the mid-1780s, a rash of foreclosures occurred. In some states, legislatures provided relief by passing laws prohibiting foreclosures. In other states, judges permitted debtors to reschedule their debts. In Massachusetts, however, no such relief was provided. Debtors were routinely thrown into jail, and farms were seized for debt. In the fall of 1786, an angry mob of some fifteen hundred farmers, armed with muskets and pitchforks, marched on a courthouse in western Massachusetts. The rebellion was led by Daniel Shays, a veteran of the Revolutionary War. Shays' Rebellion, as it came to be called, was finally put down in early 1787 by the state militia. Congress provided no assistance. Shays and his cohorts were eventually pardoned by the governor of Massachusetts.

Shays' Rebellion galvanized dissatisfaction with the Articles of Confederation. A consensus developed, at least among the nation's elites, that the national government needed to be strengthened. In particular, bankers and other creditors believed that the national government needed the power to protect contracts and other property rights, both from popular uprisings and from state legislative and judicial action. Responding to these concerns, Congress finally adopted a resolution calling for a convention to be held at Philadelphia for the express purpose of "revising" the Articles of Confederation.

ONLINE 2.4 *Shays' Rebellion*
http://www.youtube.com/watch?v=3ImIEcsTEVo

2-5 The Constitutional Convention

Fifty-five men from twelve states assembled in Philadelphia during the hot summer of 1787 to see whether they could make the national government work. The Rhode Island legislature refused to send a delegation, fearing that the convention would greatly strengthen the national government and thereby threaten the sovereignty of the states. While ostensibly gathering to update the Articles, the convention soon validated those concerns by moving far beyond a mere revision of this discredited document.

2-5a The Delegates

When the state legislatures named their delegates to the **Constitutional Convention**, Thomas Jefferson was serving as the American minister to France. After reading the names of the delegates in a Paris newspaper, Jefferson remarked that the convention would be "an assembly of demi-gods."[6] To be sure, the fifty-five delegates were an impressive lot. Twenty-one of them had fought in the Revolution; eight had signed the Declaration of Independence; seven had served as state governors. Among the delegates were six planters, three physicians, eight businessmen, and thirty-three lawyers. They were highly educated, wealthy, and quite influential in their respective states. The delegates were, quite simply, a representative sample of the young nation's elite. In James Madison's words, they were "the best contribution of talents the states could make for the occasion."[7]

The Motives of the Delegates

In 1913, historian Charles A. Beard argued that the primary motive of the delegates to the Constitutional Convention was a desire to protect their own upper-class economic interests. According to Beard, the Constitution was "an economic document drawn with superb skill by men whose property interests were immediately at stake."[8] Beard pointed out that most of the signers of the Constitution were merchants, lenders, wealthy landowners, or speculators. In other words, they were people who stood to benefit from a strong national government that would protect contracts and foster economic growth. Several scholars have since challenged, if not refuted, Beard's thesis. Forrest McDonald, for example, after studying the delegates, asserts that only a minority were motivated primarily by personal economic concerns or the interests of the upper class.[9] Historian John Garraty has written that "to call men like Washington, Franklin and Madison self-seeking would be utterly absurd."[10] The author of another book that is sympathetic to the Beard interpretation acknowledges that "most general discussions of the issue today argue that the Constitution came about because of a consensus to improve the general well-being of the country, not as a result of a conflict over economic interests."[11]

Philosophical Influences on the Delegates

The discussions leading to the creation of the Constitution were based much more on philosophy than on the crass economic interests of the delegates and the social class from which they were drawn. The eighteenth century was, after all, the Enlightenment and the Age of Reason, and the delegates prided themselves on being enlightened and reasonable men. As an educated lot, the delegates were generally familiar with the writings of Baron de Montesquieu, Adam Smith, Jean-Jacques Rousseau, and other philosophers. Without question, the greatest influence on the delegates was exerted by the English philosopher John Locke, whose major work, *Two Treatises of Government* (1690), was published almost a century before the Constitutional Convention.

Although Locke's ideas provided the philosophical underpinnings of the Constitution, as well as of the Declaration of Independence a decade earlier, the ideas of a Frenchman, Baron de Montesquieu, had the greatest impact on the delegates' thinking about the structure of the national government. Montesquieu's Spirit of the Laws, published in 1748, argued that the essential functions of government—legislative, executive, and judicial—must be separated into different branches of government. A failure to do so would, in Montesquieu's view, lead inevitably to tyranny. The success of parliamentary systems in such modern European democracies as France, Germany, Sweden, and Italy raises serious doubts about Montesquieu's insights. Yet to the Framers of the Constitution, Montesquieu's idea of separation of powers was gospel.

Another Source of Influence: The English Constitutional Tradition

You must understand that the delegates to the Constitutional Convention were not beginning with a clean slate. Although they intended to scrap the Articles of Confederation, they were not out to do something original. Rather, they meant to perfect, or at least significantly improve, the idea of constitutionalism that had its roots in the Old Testament covenant between God and the Israelites. This idea of a covenant found historical expression in the **Magna Carta** of 1215, in which England's King John consented to limitations on the power of the monarchy. This idea was extended by the **English Bill of Rights** (1689), which guaranteed the supremacy of Parliament over the monarchy. In America, the idea of constitutionalism appeared first in the Mayflower Compact of 1620 and later in the state constitutions adopted after the American Revolution.

POLITICAL CONSIDERATIONS FACING THE DELEGATES

In addition to being men of wealth and learning, the Framers of the Constitution were, above all, practical politicians who understood the need for compromise. They were distinctly aware that they represented well-established states with varying interests and that the product of their labors would ultimately have to be approved by conventions in their states. Their political sensitivity, skill, and sophistication have been praised by numerous commentators, including political scientist John P. Roche, who has written that "the Philadelphia Convention was not a College of Cardinals or a council of Platonic Guardians...it was a *nationalist* reform caucus which had to operate with great delicacy and skill in a political cosmos full of enemies to achieve the one definitive goal—popular approbation."[12] As Roche suggests, uppermost in the minds of the delegates was the need for the popular acceptance of the new constitution. That is why the Constitution of 1787, unlike the Articles of Confederation, begins with the majestic phrase "We the People of the United States..."

2-5b CONSENSUS ON BASIC PRINCIPLES

When the convention began in May 1787, the delegates made a number of significant procedural decisions. First, they selected George Washington to preside over the convention. Washington, easily the best known and most admired American of his day, lent prestige and credibility to the proceedings, and his association with the convention probably assisted subsequent ratification efforts.

After selecting Washington to preside, the delegates decided to conduct their business in secret. The doors and windows were kept closed despite the heat and humidity of the worst summer to afflict Philadelphia in many years. By modern procedural standards, the delegates' decision to hold secret sessions seems rather undemocratic. Certainly, a secret constitutional convention today would arouse a firestorm of controversy. Ironically, the delegates thought secrecy was necessary to encourage free and open debate on the difficult issues before the convention. Secrecy probably contributed to the convention's success by enabling delegates to compromise, something that can be difficult for people who have taken a position publicly and feel compelled to maintain it. Fortunately, James Madison, who was an assiduous note taker, recorded the proceedings of the convention for posterity. The notes were made public only after Madison's death in 1836.

The delegates argued over many ideas at the convention, but were in agreement on basic principles. They believed in popular sovereignty—the Lockean idea expressed in the Declaration of Independence that power is vested ultimately in the people, not in the government. Accordingly, the delegates believed in **representative government**, or the idea that most policy decisions ought to emanate from legislatures that represent the people, even if indirectly (see Figure 2-1).

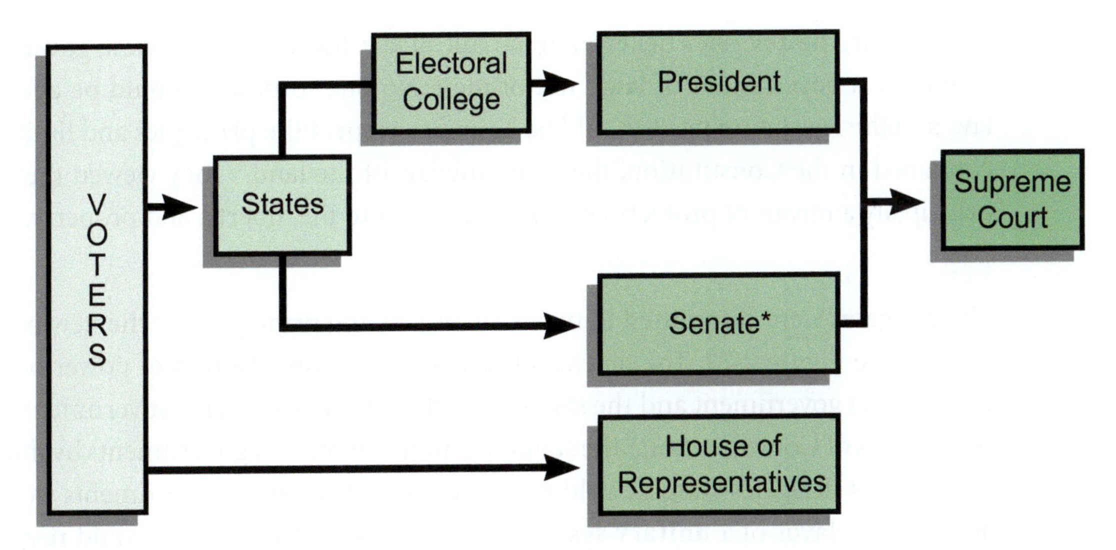

Figure 2-1 *The Use of Indirect Elections in the Constitution*
The delegates rejected the concept of direct democracy, in which the masses would be involved in government on a regular basis, choosing instead a method of indirect elections except for the House of Representatives.
*The Seventeenth Amendment, which provided for direct election of senators by the people, eliminated the state legislatures' role in choosing senators in 1913.

Yet the delegates rejected the concept of **direct democracy**, in which the masses would be involved in government on a regular basis. In fact, many delegates equated the term *democracy* with mob rule. They sought to build a **republic**, not a democracy. When they looked to ancient models, their inspiration was the Roman republic, not the Athenian democracy.

The delegates also believed in limited government. Government exists to ensure the social contract and to accomplish what people cannot do by acting alone. The new national government would be designed to accomplish what the several states could not do on their own—namely, provide for the national defense, settle disputes between states, and create a legal climate in which interstate commerce could flourish. The new national government was not to be a leviathan—a mammoth government that dominates its people and values order above all. This type of government is not limited at all and has no implied contractual arrangement with the governed other than to protect them. This form of government had been advocated by Thomas Hobbes, whose book *Leviathan* was a blueprint for government in the turbulent environment of seventeenth-century Europe.[13]

Finally, the delegates believed in the rule of law. Ideally, in their view, government should be a government of laws, not of men. No one in power should be above the law, and the legislature itself should be bound to respect the principles and limitations contained in the Constitution, the "supreme law of the land." They viewed the law as principally a means of protecting individual rights to life, liberty, and property.

FEDERALISM

The delegates were committed to two basic organizing principles for the new political system (see Figure 2-2). The first was **federalism**, the distribution of power between the national government and the states. As noted in section 2-4a, "Government under the Articles of Confederation," the states had well-established governments by the mid-1770s. Most delegates simply could not conceive that the state governments would be abolished in favor of a **unitary system**, in which all political power would rest in the central government.

The decision to retain the states as units of government was much more than a concession to political necessity. The delegates, who represented their respective states at the convention, believed in federalism as a means of dispersing power. After a revolutionary war fought against distant colonial rulers, the Founders believed that government should be closer to the governed. Moreover, given the dramatically different political cultures of the states, a distant national government could never hope to command the loyalty and support of a diverse people. Finally, the delegates recognized the practical problems of trying to administer a country spread out along a thousand-mile seaboard. The states were much better equipped for this task.

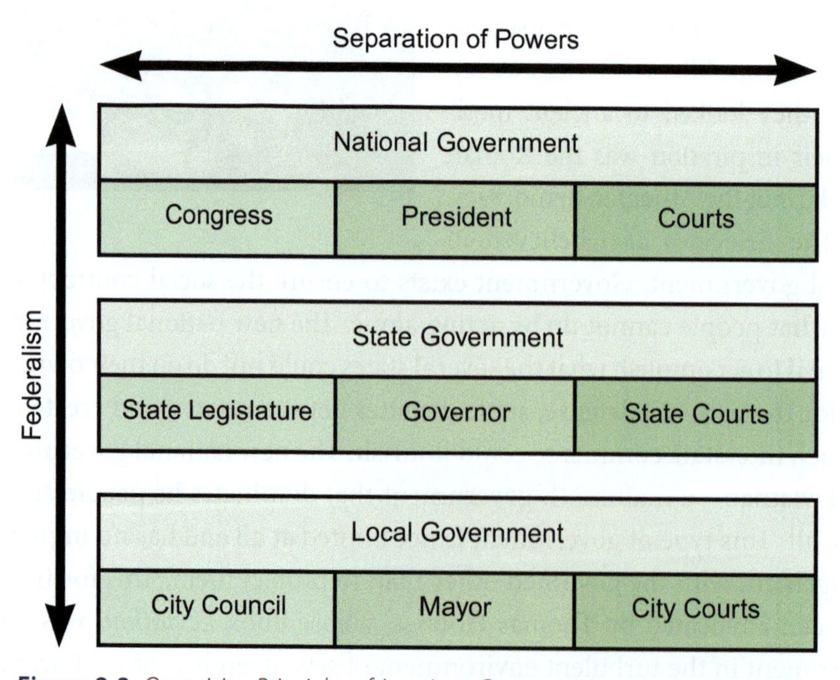

Figure 2-2 *Organizing Principles of American Government*

Separation of Powers

The second basic organizing principle for the new government was the separation of powers. The delegates had no interest in creating a parliamentary system. They believed that parliaments could be manipulated by monarchs or captured by impassioned but short-lived majorities. Accordingly, parliaments provided insufficient security for liberty and property. The delegates believed that only by allocating the three basic functions of government (legislative, executive, and judicial) into three separate branches could power be appropriately dispersed. In James Madison's words, "The accumulation of all powers, legislative, executive, and judiciary, in the same hands...may justly be pronounced the very definition of tyranny."[14]

As you have read, the separation of powers was not an original idea. Not only were Madison and the other delegates well aware of Montesquieu's arguments for separation of powers, but the new state constitutions adopted during or after the Revolutionary War were based on that principle. Yet the Framers were also aware that in most states the legislatures dominated the executive and judicial branches. At Madison's urging, the delegates agreed that a system of **checks and balances** would be necessary if separate branches of government were to be maintained. As Madison would later argue in *The Federalist* No. 51, "Ambition must be made to counteract ambition."

ONLINE 2.5 *Checks and Balances Interactive*
http://www.cyberlearning-world.com/lessons/civics/checksandbalances/interactive_checks_and_balances_flow_chart.htm

2-5c Conflict and Compromise in Philadelphia

Although the delegates agreed on basic assumptions, goals, and organizing principles, they differed sharply over many other matters. By far the greatest sources of disagreement were the conflict between the small and large states over representation in Congress and the cleavage between northern and southern states over slavery. But a number of other issues were also divisive. Should we have one president or a multiple executive? How should the president be chosen? Should we have a national system of courts or merely a national supreme court to review decisions of the existing state tribunals? What powers should the national government have over interstate and foreign commerce? Some of these disagreements were so serious that several delegates packed their bags and left Philadelphia, and for a time it appeared that the convention might fail altogether.

Representation in Congress

As noted in section 2-4a, "Government under the Articles of Confederation," under the Articles of Confederation all states were equally represented in a unicameral Congress. Representatives of the larger states preferred that representation be proportional to state population. The **Virginia Plan**, conceived by James Madison and presented to the convention by Governor Edmund Randolph of Virginia, called for a bicameral Congress in which representation in both houses would be based on state population. Delegates from the smaller states, fearing that their states would be dominated by the large states under such an arrangement, countered with the **New Jersey Plan**, which called for preserving Congress as it was under the Articles. Supporters of the New Jersey Plan, including William Paterson and David Brearley, of New Jersey; John Dickinson and Gunning Bedford, of Delaware; Luther Martin, of Maryland; and Elbridge Gerry, of Massachusetts, argued that a constitution based on the Virginia Plan would never be ratified. After a few days of intense debate described by Alexander Hamilton as a "struggle for power, not for liberty," Roger Sherman, of Connecticut, proposed a compromise. Congress would be composed of two houses: a House of Representatives, in which representation would be based on a state's population, and a Senate, in which all states would be equally represented.

SLAVERY

Although not fully apparent in 1787, the most fundamental conflict underlying the convention was the division between North and South over the slavery question. The conflict involved more than human rights; it was also a clash of different economies and political cultures. The South had a thriving plantation economy based on slave labor, which generated considerable wealth for the plantation owners. The political culture of the South tended toward the aristocratic and traditional. By contrast, the North was on the verge of an industrial revolution. Northern agriculture was based on family farms. The political culture was more democratic and, from the southern point of view, considerably more moralistic. Southern delegates at the Constitutional Convention feared that the new national government would try to end the slave trade and possibly try to abolish slavery. At the same time, southern delegations wanted slaves in their states to be counted as persons for the purpose of determining representation in the new House of Representatives. Northern delegates, realizing that southern support was crucial to the success of the new nation, finally agreed to two compromises over slavery: First, Congress would not have the power to prohibit the importation of slaves into the United States until 1808. Second, for purposes of representation in Congress (and the apportionment of direct taxes), each slave would count as three-fifths of a person.

2-5d THE SIGNING OF THE CONSTITUTION

After three months of debate, Governor Morris presented the final draft of the Constitution to the convention. On September 17, 1787, thirty-nine delegates representing twelve states placed their signatures on what they hoped would become the nation's new fundamental law. They then adjourned to the City Tavern to celebrate their achievement and discuss a final challenge: Before the Constitution could become the supreme law of the land, it would have to be ratified by the states.

ONLINE 2.6 *Text of the U.S. Constitution*
http://www.archives.gov/exhibits/charters/constitution.html

2-6 THE FRAMERS' CONSTITUTION

The Framers' Constitution was a brief document, only about four thousand words. It was not designed to spell out every detail of the new government, but rather to provide a structure; basic institutions; and a set of powers, principles, and prohibitions. The document reflected, naturally, those principles essential to the Framers' philosophy of government: consent of the governed, limited government, separation of powers, checks and balances, and federalism.

2-6a THE INSTITUTIONS OF THE NEW NATIONAL GOVERNMENT

The first three articles of the Constitution, known as the **distributive articles**, defined the legislative, executive, and judicial branches, respectively, of the new government. The distributive articles divided the powers of government across three independent, coequal branches in keeping with the Framers' commitment to the principle of the separation of powers.

Article I vested "all legislative Powers herein granted" in a "Congress of the United States." This was the lawmaking body, but the grant of power to make laws was intentionally limited. In addition to these specific powers, Article I, Section 8 contained a clause allowing Congress to "make all Laws which shall be necessary and proper for carrying into Execution the foregoing powers, and all other Powers vested by this Constitution in the Government of the United States, or in any Department or Officer thereof." The **Necessary and Proper Clause** would later emerge as perhaps the most significant language of Article I. (See the discussion of *McCulloch v. Maryland*, 1819, in Chapter 3, "Federalism: A Nation of States.") Congress gained through this clause much of the lawmaking power it now exercises.

Article II vested "the Executive Power" in the president of the United States. Article II, Section 2 spelled out the president's powers, the most significant of which are the powers to serve as **commander-in-chief** of the armed forces; make treaties with foreign nations, with the **advice and consent** of the Senate; and appoint ambassadors, federal judges, and other high officials, again with the advice and consent of the Senate. Today, "advice and consent" refers to the two-thirds majority of the Senate that must approve treaties and presidential appointments. In no way did the language of Article II anticipate the power and prestige of the modern presidency. Although some Framers—most notably Alexander Hamilton—took a broad view of what constituted "executive power," most of them conceived of the president's role primarily as one of faithfully executing the laws passed by Congress.

Article III gave "the judicial Power of the United States" to "one supreme Court" and "such inferior courts as Congress may from time to time ordain and establish." Section 2 extended the judicial power to "all Cases…arising under this Constitution, the Laws of the United States, and Treaties made…under their Authority." Article III made no mention of what was to become the cornerstone of judicial power: the right to invalidate legislation found to be contrary to the Constitution. This power, known as judicial review, was assumed by the Supreme Court in a landmark decision in 1803 (see the discussion of *Marbury v. Madison* in section 2-8a, "Constitutional Change through Judicial Interpretation"). The Framers of the Constitution were aware of judicial review, but could not agree on whether the federal courts should be given this power. Some, including Alexander Hamilton, wanted the courts to be able to nullify acts of Congress that violated the Constitution. Others thought it dangerous to place the power to nullify legislation in the hands of appointed judges with life tenure. Ultimately, the Framers left the question of judicial review to be worked out in practice.

2-6b The System of Checks and Balances

Under the proposed Constitution, the president was authorized to veto bills passed by Congress, but Congress could override the president's veto by a two-thirds majority in both houses. The president was given the power to appoint judges, ambassadors, and other high government officials, but the Senate could reject presidential nominees to these positions. The president was made commander-in-chief, but Congress was given the authority to declare war, raise and support an army and a navy, and make rules governing the armed forces. The president was empowered to call Congress into special session, but was duty-bound to appear "from time to time" to inform Congress about the "state of the Union." These provisions were designed to create a perpetual competition between Congress and the executive branch for control of the government, with the expectation that neither institution would permanently dominate the other.

The Framers were concerned with not only the possibility that one institution might dominate the government but also that a popular majority might gain control of both Congress and the presidency and thereby institute a **tyranny of the majority**. An important feature of the system of checks and balances was the different terms for the president, members of the House, and U.S. senators. Representatives would be elected every two years; senators would serve for six-year terms. Presidents, of course, would hold office for four years. The staggered terms of the presidency and the Senate, in particular, were designed to make it difficult (although certainly not impossible) for a transitory popular majority to get and keep control of the government.

2-6c Restrictions on the States

Article I, Section 10 imposed a series of restrictions on the state governments. States were prohibited from entering into treaties, alliances, or confederations among themselves or with foreign powers. They were also prohibited from coining their own money, imposing their own tariffs on imports and exports, and, most importantly, impairing the obligations of contracts. These restrictions on the economic powers of the states were a direct response to the conditions that existed under the Articles of Confederation.

2-6d Individual Rights

The Framers did not believe that a bill of rights was a necessary component of the Constitution, for three reasons:

1. Because rights were founded in natural law, their existence did not depend on their enumeration in the Constitution.
2. An enumeration of specific rights might imply that citizens lacked other rights not specified.
3. The new national government was to be limited in power and thus would pose little threat to life, liberty, and property.

Yet, conversely, without creating a bill of rights, the Framers did recognize several rights in the text of the Constitution. Article I, Section 9 recognized the ancient common-law right to petition the courts for a writ of ***habeas corpus***, a means by which an individual could challenge and, if successful, escape unlawful confinement. Section 9 forbade Congress from suspending the writ "unless when in Cases of Rebellion or Invasion the public Safety may require it."

Article I, Section 9 also prohibited Congress from passing bills of attainder and *ex post facto* laws. Article I, Section 10 imposed these same prohibitions on the state legislatures. A **bill of attainder** is a legislative act imposing punishment on a party without the benefit of trial in a court of law. An ***ex post facto* law** retroactively criminalizes some action that was not a crime when it was committed. The British Parliament had on occasion used both bills of attainder and *ex post facto* laws to punish opponents of the Crown. The Framers were well aware of these abuses of legislative power and wanted to make sure that neither Congress nor the state legislatures would succumb to them.

2-6e An Undemocratic Document?

The Framers' Constitution contained a number of elitist elements that strike modern sensibilities as being downright undemocratic. In particular, many important choices were left to the elites of society rather than to the common people. First, Article I, Section 3 provided that members of the Senate would be chosen by the state legislatures rather than by the people directly. Second, the president was to be chosen not by direct popular election, but rather by the **electoral college** composed of delegates from the states. Third, federal judges were to be appointed, not elected, and would hold office for life. These elitist elements of the Constitution were controversial even in 1787. The more democratically minded Founders, such as Patrick Henry of Virginia, thought that the new Constitution should be rejected.

2-7 The Battle over Ratification

Today, U.S. citizens look to the Constitution as a statement of their national consensus—an expression of their shared political culture. But in 1787 the Constitution was a divisive political issue, and ratification was by no means a foregone conclusion. Interestingly, although the smaller states had been the obstacle at the Philadelphia Convention, opposition to ratification was most intense in the largest states: Massachusetts, New York, and Virginia. But division existed in every state.

Unlike the Articles of Confederation, the Constitution of 1787 did not require the unanimous consent of the states to be ratified. Instead, it would take effect after ratification by nine of the thirteen states. Rather than allow the state legislatures to consider ratification, the Constitution called for a popular convention to be held in every state. By rejecting a motion to hold another constitutional convention, the Framers presented the states with an all-or-nothing situation. These features, in addition to provisions for amending the Constitution later, were intended, in the words of Forrest McDonald, to "stack the deck" in favor of ratification.[15]

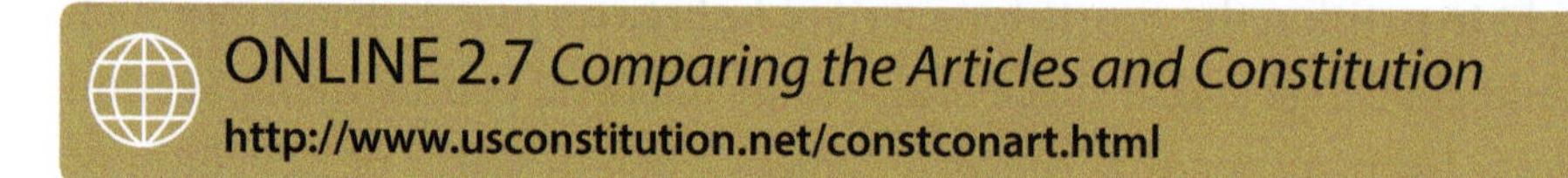

ONLINE 2.7 *Comparing the Articles and Constitution*
http://www.usconstitution.net/constconart.html

2-7a Federalists versus Anti-Federalists

Supporters of the Constitution called themselves Federalists; opponents were dubbed Anti-Federalists. Federalists were found mainly in the cities, among the artisans, shopkeepers, merchants, and, not insignificantly, newspaper publishers. Anti-Federalist sentiment was strongest in rural areas, especially among small farmers. The Anti-Federalists were poorly organized and, consequently, less effective than their Federalist opponents. Moreover, they were constantly on the defensive. Because they were opposing a major reform effort, they were perceived as defending a status quo that was unacceptable to most Americans. Still, the Anti-Federalists had considerable support and succeeded in making ratification a close question in some states.

The most eloquent statement of the Anti-Federalist position was Richard Henry Lee's *Letters of the Federal Farmer*, published in the fall of 1787. Lee, a principal architect of the Articles of Confederation, thought that the proposed national government would threaten both the rights of the states and the liberties of the individual. Perhaps Lee's most effective criticism of the new Constitution was that it lacked a bill of rights. Lee pointed out that state constitutions, without exception, enumerated the rights of citizens vis-à-vis their state governments. The only conclusion Lee could draw was that the Philadelphia Convention and its handiwork, the Constitution, did not place a premium on liberty. However wrongheaded this criticism, it touched a nerve among the American people. Ultimately, the Federalists would only secure ratification of the Constitution by promising to support a series of amendments that would create a bill of rights.

Despite their popular appeal, *Letters of the Federal Farmer* and the other Anti-Federalist tracts were no match for the brilliant essays written by James Madison, Alexander Hamilton, and John Jay in defense of the Constitution. *The Federalist Papers* were published serially in New York newspapers during the winter of 1788 under the pen name Publius. Without question, *The Federalist Papers* helped to secure the ratification of the Constitution in the crucial state of New York. Yet *The Federalist*, as the collected papers are generally known, was much more than a set of time-bound political tracts. As historians Charles and Mary Beard recognized, it was "the most profound single treatise on the Constitution ever written." Accordingly, it ranks "among the few masterly works on political science produced in all the centuries of history."[16]

ONLINE 2.8 *The Federalist and Anti-Federalist Papers*
http://www.constitution.org/fed/federa00.htm
http://www.constitution.org/afp/afp.htm

2-7b The Ratifying Conventions

Approximately three months after the close of the Philadelphia Convention, Delaware became the first state to ratify the Constitution. Within nine months after the convention, the necessary ninth state had signed on. But the two largest and most important states, Virginia and New York, became battlegrounds over ratification. Although the Constitution became the "supreme law of the land" when the ninth state, New Hampshire, approved it in June 1788, it was vital to the success of the new nation that Virginia and New York come on board.

At the Virginia ratifying convention, Patrick Henry, a leader of the Anti-Federalist cause, claimed that four-fifths of Virginians were opposed to ratification. But the oratory of Edmund Randolph, combined with the prestige of George Washington, finally carried the day. The Federalists won Virginia by a vote of 89–79. The news that Virginia had approved the new Constitution gave the Federalists considerable momentum. In July, New York followed Virginia's lead and approved the Constitution by three votes. The two holdouts, North Carolina and Rhode Island, not wanting to be excluded from the Union, followed suit in November 1789 and May 1790, respectively. The new Constitution was in effect and fully legitimized by "the consent of the governed."

After its ratification, the Constitution became an object of popular reverence—a sort of secular Bible. Yet, despite the widespread Constitution worship, the Constitution, like the Articles of Confederation that preceded it, had certain deficiencies.

Of course, the Framers anticipated this problem and provided mechanisms for changing the Constitution. At the same time, these mechanisms were intentionally designed to make it difficult to change the Constitution. Because the Constitution represents the supreme and fundamental law of the land, amending the Constitution should be considerably harder than passing a statute. Otherwise, whenever a majority in Congress wanted to pass a law prohibited by the Constitution (for example, a law abridging the freedom of speech), they could easily change the Constitution to allow that law. Because the Constitution exists in large part to protect minority interests from abuse by the majority, mere majority approval is not enough.

2-8 Amending the Constitution

The two methods by which the Constitution can be amended are outlined in Article V. Both methods assign a formal role to the states. Most commonly, two-thirds of the members of each house of Congress propose an amendment, which must then be approved by three-fourths of the state legislatures. Thus, with this method, state legislatures around the nation must consider the proposed amendment, and a quarter of the states can block a change. In the 1970s, for example, opponents of the Equal Rights Amendment were able to concentrate on selected state legislatures and eventually succeeded in stopping the proposed amendment. The votes of certain state legislators in Illinois became pivotal as consideration of the amendment continued.

The second method of proposing an amendment to the Constitution has never been used. It allows two-thirds of the states to initiate the process by petitioning for a national constitutional convention. The logic of this second method is that it allows the states to overcome a stubborn Congress that might be unwilling to make widely supported changes in the Constitution. In either case, the Constitution cannot be altered without the participation of the state legislatures.

This difficulty of amending the Constitution prevents a "bandwagon effect" driven by short-term emotions. For example, politicians might react to popular outrage at constitutional interpretation by the courts and immediately suggest changing the Constitution. The amendment process gives opponents time to marshal their resources and make their arguments. It also allows them to target their opposition toward a small number of states. Merely having to face a drawn-out ratification process is enough to keep all but the most thoroughly considered constitutional changes from being formally proposed. For instance, in 1989, the Supreme Court held that flag burning was a legitimate form of political speech and declared unconstitutional a state law making flag burning a crime.[17] An immediate firestorm of reaction against the decision occurred. Not surprisingly, several members of Congress suggested an amendment that would specifically exempt flag burning from the protection of the Bill of Rights. As the debate continued, however, it became clear that there was much sentiment against tampering with the Bill of Rights in this way. The push for an amendment soon subsided, although the issue seems to resurface prior to every presidential election.

On the other hand, a workable constitution should not present insurmountable obstacles to change. When a clear consensus for changing the Constitution exists and no opposition group can argue effectively against it, amendments can, and do, pass. For example, the Twenty-Sixth Amendment, which established a national eighteen-year-old voting age, represented a near-consensus in American society and passed with little trouble in 1971. In all, the amendment process seems to strike an almost perfect balance. Efforts at change are infrequent and generally reflect shifts in very broad principles. With the exception of the Eighteenth Amendment, which outlawed the sale of alcohol, constitutional amendments have been accepted as part of the political fabric. Evidently, the American people approve of the process by which the Constitution is amended. When polled in 1987, 60 percent of a national sample said the process was "about right."[18]

The most glaring imperfection of the Constitution of 1787 was the absence of a bill of rights, a deficiency that almost derailed the ratification of the Constitution in Virginia and New York. When the First Congress adopted the **Bill of Rights** in 1789, it was making good on an agreement that had been instrumental in securing ratification. Although Congress was under no legal compulsion to act, most members believed that adding the Bill of Rights to the Constitution was desirable, either as an end in itself or as a means of engendering popular support for the new Constitution and government. James Madison, the prime mover behind the Bill of Rights in the House of Representatives, appealed to both the idealistic and pragmatic sentiments of his fellow members. In a speech on the House floor in June 1789, Madison said:

> *It cannot be a secret to the gentlemen of this House that, not withstanding the ratification of this system of government...yet there is a great number of our constituents who are dissatisfied with it, among whom are many respectable for their talents and patriotism and respectable for the jealousy they have for their liberty.... We ought not to disregard their inclination but, on principles of amity and moderation, conform to their wishes and expressly declare the great rights of mankind secured under this Constitution.*[19]

After considerable debate, Congress adopted twelve amendments in the fall of 1789 and submitted them to the states for ratification. Ten of these amendments were promptly ratified and officially became part of the Constitution in 1791. Interestingly, one of the two "failed" amendments prohibited Congress from giving its members a pay increase that would go into effect before the next congressional election. The amendment was resurrected and finally ratified in 1992 amidst widespread public anger at Congress.

Guaranteeing States' Rights: The Tenth and Eleventh Amendments

Although the term *Bill of Rights* refers collectively to the first ten amendments to the Constitution, only the first nine deal with individual rights. The Tenth Amendment was designed to reassure the state governments that powers not delegated to the new national government would be reserved to them. Similarly, the Eleventh Amendment was designed to limit the power of the federal courts to invade the **sovereign immunity** of the state governments—that is, their traditional protection against being sued in the courts without their consent. Thus, both the Tenth and Eleventh Amendments deal with **states' rights** and, accordingly, are examined in depth in Chapter 3, "Federalism: A Nation of States."

Correcting a Constitutional Malfunction: The Twelfth Amendment

The Framers of the Constitution did not anticipate, nor did they desire, the emergence of political parties. By the late 1790s, however, a two-party system was becoming established (the Federalists versus the Jeffersonians). Under the Constitution, the president and vice president were to be elected by the electoral college, which was made up of delegates from the states, rather than by the American people directly. The Constitution provided that the presidential candidate receiving a majority of votes in the electoral college would be elected president; the runner-up would become vice president. This procedure resulted in John Adams having a "hostile" vice president in Thomas Jefferson (1797–1801). The Adams-Jefferson administration was anything but harmonious.

The electoral college malfunctioned badly in the next presidential election. In 1800, Thomas Jefferson and Aaron Burr, both of whom were Democratic Republicans, received the same number of electoral votes (73), even though it was well known that Burr was seeking the vice presidency. Under the procedures outlined in Article II, Section 1, the election was thrown into the House of Representatives, which, much to Jefferson's chagrin, was controlled by the rival Federalist party. To make matters worse, the ambitious Burr, no longer content to become vice president, tried to capture the presidency. After a battle in the House, Jefferson finally prevailed, but only after thirty-six ballots and securing the support of his old political enemy, Alexander Hamilton. The unpleasant episode prompted Congress to adopt, and the states to ratify, the Twelfth Amendment. Essentially, the Twelfth Amendment requires members of the electoral college to vote separately for the president and vice president. This method permits two individuals to run as a party ticket. The Twelfth Amendment became part of the Constitution on September 25, 1804, just in time for the next presidential election.

The Civil War Amendments

The impact of the Civil War (1861–1865) on American political culture, the institutions of government, and indeed the entire political system can hardly be overstated.

The Civil War changed the Constitution in several ways, most obviously through the addition of three new amendments: the Thirteenth (1865), Fourteenth (1868), and Fifteenth (1870). The Thirteenth Amendment abolished slavery, thus reaffirming and extending President Abraham Lincoln's Emancipation Proclamation of 1863. The Fourteenth Amendment, among other things, prohibited states from denying persons within their jurisdictions due process of law and the equal protection of the laws. **Due process of law** refers to the legal procedures that must be observed before the government can deprive an individual of life, liberty, or property. **Equal protection of the laws** means that all citizens have an equal right to the various protections the law affords.

The primary motivation for the Fourteenth Amendment was to provide constitutional protection for the civil rights of the newly freed former slaves. Section 5 of the Fourteenth Amendment gave Congress the authority to enact "appropriate legislation" to enforce the broad guarantees of due process and equal protection. Finally, the Fifteenth Amendment guaranteed citizens of all races the right to vote in state and federal elections and, like the Fourteenth Amendment, authorized Congress to enforce the guarantee by appropriate legislation. The effect of the Civil War amendments was not immediate, but over the long run their influence has been profound. These amendments have served to protect not only the civil rights of African Americans and other minorities but also the civil rights and liberties of all Americans. In addition, by empowering Congress and the federal courts to protect civil rights against incursions by the state governments, these amendments had a tremendous impact on federalism.

Other Important Amendments

Twelve amendments have been added to the Constitution since 1870; the latest is the Twenty-Seventh Amendment, adopted by Congress in 1789 but not ratified until 1992. Although none of these amendments ranks in magnitude with the Bill of Rights or the Civil War amendments, several had a significant impact on the constitutional system. Three amendments—specifically, the Nineteenth (1920), the Twenty-Fourth (1964), and the Twenty-Sixth (1971)—expanded the right to vote to include groups that had previously been locked out of the political process. Accordingly, these amendments are discussed in section 2-8b, "Democratization of the Constitutional System."

The Sixteenth Amendment (1913) authorized Congress to "lay and collect taxes on incomes." This amendment was a direct response to an 1895 Supreme Court decision which held that Congress lacked the constitutional authority to impose an income tax.[20] By dramatically increasing the revenues of the national government, the Sixteenth Amendment facilitated the increasing responsibility (and power) that the national government assumed during the twentieth century. Accordingly, it must be considered an important modification of the constitutional system—a further departure from the limited role that the Founders envisioned for the national government.

The Eighteenth Amendment (1919) prohibited the manufacture, sale, or transportation of alcoholic beverages in the United States. Congress implemented this amendment through the Volstead Act, which went into effect in 1920. This statute in essence attached criminal penalties to the prohibitions of the Eighteenth Amendment. **Prohibition** was brought about in large part by pressure groups, such as the Anti-Saloon Leagues, that believed alcohol abuse was a serious social problem that the national government should address. Prohibition was never popular or effective. Organized crime vaulted into the national consciousness as gangsters like Al Capone took over the business of importing and distributing liquor. In all, Prohibition was judged a tragic failure, and the Eighteenth Amendment was repealed by the Twenty-First Amendment in 1933 during the darkest days of the Great Depression. Prohibition was significant, however, in that it greatly increased the role of the federal government in law enforcement and crime control, a function previously left to the states. In a sense, Prohibition was the predecessor of the "war on drugs" being waged by the national government today.

The Twenty-Second Amendment, ratified in 1951, limited a president to no more than two consecutive terms. Before the election of Franklin Delano Roosevelt, who won four presidential elections (1932, 1936, 1940, and 1944), no president had sought a third term. In 1949, the Republican Congress reacted to Roosevelt's feat (as well as to the centralization of power in Washington that attended his presidency) by adopting the Twenty-Second Amendment. Ironically, in the mid-1980s, Republicans lamented that Ronald Reagan, a popular Republican president, was barred from seeking a third term. Some Republicans went so far as to call for the repeal of the Twenty-Second Amendment. When Reagan expressed no interest in a third term, the movement to amend the Constitution subsided.

2-8a Constitutional Change through Judicial Interpretation

In this chapter, you have read about constitutional changes that came about through the formal amendment process. Turn now to significant modifications in the constitutional system that came about through changes in the way the Constitution is interpreted. Constitutional interpretation has become the principal, but not exclusive, domain of the courts as a result of a key Supreme Court decision in 1803.

In *Marbury v. Madison* (1803), the Supreme Court asserted the power to review acts of Congress and declare them null and void if found to be contrary to the Constitution (see Case in Point 2-1).[21] Seven years later, the Court extended this power to encompass the validity of state laws under the federal Constitution.[22] The power of the federal courts to rule on the constitutionality of legislation is nowhere explicitly mentioned in the Constitution, although many commentators have tried to justify it in terms of the Supremacy Clause of Article VI. The Framers of the Constitution were not unanimous in their support for judicial review, but most likely expected the courts to exercise this power. In any event, the Supreme Court assumed this authority and, in so doing, greatly enhanced its role in the system of checks and balances. Moreover, the Court took on primary responsibility for interpreting the Constitution. In *McCulloch v. Maryland* (1819), Chief Justice John Marshall observed, "We must never forget, that it is a constitution we are expounding."[23] Marshall went on to observe that the Constitution "was intended to endure for ages to come, and consequently, to be adapted to the various crises of human affairs."[24] Clearly, Marshall had in mind that the courts would be principally responsible for making such adaptations.

Case in Point 2-1

The Establishment of the Power of Judicial Review

Marbury v. Madison (1803)

After the national election of 1800, in which the Federalists lost the presidency and both chambers of Congress to the Jeffersonian Republicans, the Federalists tried to preserve their influence within the national government by expanding their control over the federal courts. The "lame duck" Congress, in which the Federalists held a majority, quickly passed the Judiciary Act of 1801, which was signed into law by President John Adams. The act created a number of new federal judgeships, which Adams would be able to fill with loyal Federalists. Congress also adopted legislation creating several minor judgeships for the newly established District of Columbia.

William Marbury was one of many Federalist politicians appointed to judicial office in the waning days of the Adams administration. Marbury's commission as justice of the peace for the District of Columbia had been signed by the president following Senate confirmation on March 3, 1801, Adams' last day in office. The responsibility for delivering the commission fell to Secretary of State John Marshall. For some reason, yet to be fully explained, the commission was never delivered.

Thomas Jefferson was sworn in as the nation's third president on March 4, 1801. The new secretary of state, James Madison, refused to deliver the commission to Marbury. Marbury filed suit against Madison in the Supreme Court, invoking the Court's original jurisdiction—that is, its power to hear cases that have not been previously decided by lower courts. In his suit, Marbury asked the Court to issue a **writ of mandamus**, an order directing Madison to deliver the disputed judicial commission.

The Supreme Court's presumed authority to issue the writ of mandamus was based on Section 13 of the Judiciary Act of 1789. Section 13 granted the Court the authority to "issue...writs of mandamus, in cases warranted by the principles and usages of law." According to Chief Justice John Marshall's opinion in *Marbury*, the Court could not issue the writ because the relevant provision of Section 13 was unconstitutional. Under Article III of the Constitution, Congress may regulate the appellate jurisdiction of the Court, but not its **original jurisdiction**. According to Marshall, Section 13 was invalid because it expanded the Court's original jurisdiction. Thus, the power of judicial review was first asserted in a case involving a technical legal question. Since 1803, the power has been used to address much more important questions of public policy, such as abortion, racial segregation, and school prayer.

The Constitution, *Laissez-Faire*, and the New Deal

A colossal struggle over the government's role in regulating the economy provides an excellent illustration of how a change in the way the Constitution is interpreted can affect government institutions and public policy making. The Framers of the Constitution believed in limited government, but they did endow the national government with the power to regulate interstate commerce. Under their **police power**, however, states had the authority to enact laws regulating economic activity for the purpose of promoting public health, safety, and welfare. At the same time, it is fair to say that the Framers did not expect either the federal or the state governments to attempt to manage the economy in any comprehensive way. Though not hardcore advocates of *laissez-faire* capitalism, in which the free market operates with no government intervention, the Founders did believe in the primacy of private enterprise.

After the Civil War, as the United States experienced rapid growth and change as a result of the Industrial Revolution, both the national and state governments began to enact measures designed to regulate the economy. By modern standards, these regulatory measures were relatively modest. Yet, beginning in the 1890s, a conservative Supreme Court limited the power of Congress to tax and regulate interstate commerce.[25] Moreover, the Court interpreted the Due Process Clauses of the Fifth and Fourteenth Amendments to create a barrier to federal and state legislation designed to regulate the industrial workplace. In case after case, the Court held that government efforts to regulate wages, working hours, and working conditions were violations of the liberty of both employers and employees. In *Lochner v. New York* (1905), the leading case of the era, Justice Rufus Peckham asserted that "the freedom of master and employee to contract with each other in relation to their employment, and in defining the same, cannot be prohibited or interfered with, without violating the Federal Constitution."[26]

In 1929, the nation plunged headlong into the Great Depression. In 1932, Franklin D. Roosevelt was elected to the presidency on a promise to provide a **New Deal**. Roosevelt's New Deal consisted of unprecedented efforts by the federal government to regulate and manage the economy. The New Deal was enacted through a series of important statutes passed by Congress beginning in 1933. In a series of decisions between 1933 and 1937, the Supreme Court declared these statutes invalid. Although the particular reasons varied, the Court's essential objection was that these laws expanded the powers of the national government beyond the permissible scope delineated in the Constitution. Not surprisingly, Roosevelt, most members of Congress, and a substantial segment of the attentive public viewed the Court's decisions as unnecessarily obstructionist—even reactionary. Roosevelt began to refer to the Court as the "nine old men" whose "horse and buggy" views of the American economy were preventing the government from orchestrating a recovery.

In early 1937, Roosevelt proposed his infamous **Court-packing plan**, under which the president would be authorized to appoint one new justice to the Supreme Court for each current justice over the age of seventy. Although the Court-packing plan failed in Congress, the Supreme Court evidently got the message and in an abrupt turnaround in the spring of 1937 upheld the National Labor Relations Act, a key piece of New Deal legislation.[27] In the years to follow, the Court repudiated altogether the doctrines by which it had earlier blocked government efforts to regulate the economy. In rejecting these doctrines, the Court helped to bring about a veritable constitutional revolution.

As a result of the New Deal, President Lyndon Johnson's Great Society legislation of the 1960s, and various programs enacted under Republican as well as Democratic presidents, the national government has taken more and more responsibility for managing the economy and ensuring the economic well-being of the nation. This tremendous change in public policy, and in the power of government agencies, came about not through a formal amendment to the Constitution, but rather through changes in the way the Constitution was understood.

2-8b Democratization of the Constitutional System

The growth of government at all levels to meet demands engendered by economic and social change is perhaps the most obvious change in the constitutional system since its founding more than two centuries ago. Yet equally important is the **democratization** of the constitutional system, which simply means that the system has become more democratic than it was designed to be. Like other major changes in the constitutional system, this change has come about through both formal amendments and changes in constitutional interpretation. Even more fundamentally, though, the democratization of the constitutional system represents a profound change in American political culture.

Expanding Constitutional Protection of Liberty and Equality

By protecting the rights of all citizens against the power of the national government, the Bill of Rights took a major stride in the march toward constitutional democracy. Certainly, the First Amendment, which protects the right of all citizens to speak freely and assemble and organize for the purpose of petitioning the government for a redress of grievances, has proved to be essential to American democracy. Without question, the Fourteenth Amendment, which provided broad protection for the civil rights of all Americans, must be regarded as a giant step forward in the evolution of American democracy. The Fourteenth Amendment guarantees, among other things, equal protection of the laws. This provision rests on the premise that individuals should be equal before the state, which is *the* fundamental principle of democracy.

Enfranchising African Americans

In *Scott v. Sandford* (1857)—better known as the Dred Scott case—the Supreme Court ruled that persons of African descent were not, and could not become, citizens of the United States.[28] Indeed, they had no constitutional rights. This decision, which is now considered morally outrageous, was overturned by the ratification of the Fourteenth Amendment in 1868. The Fourteenth Amendment conferred citizenship on "all persons born or naturalized in the United States." It did not, however, specifically guarantee African Americans the right to vote. Congress corrected this oversight by adopting the Fifteenth Amendment (1870), which provides that "the right of citizens of the United States to vote shall not be denied or abridged by the United States or by any State on account of race, color, or previous condition of servitude."

The Constitution is not a self-executing document. Nearly a century passed before the promise of the Fifteenth Amendment was fulfilled. A number of states resisted the extension of the franchise to African Americans, and some adopted measures that frustrated black citizens' efforts to register and vote. Eventually, however, these impediments were swept away by Supreme Court decisions and acts of Congress, such as the landmark Voting Rights Act of 1965. These decisions and enactments involved both assertions of power by the national government vis-à-vis the states, and changes in constitutional interpretation (for further discussion, see Chapter 5, "Civil Rights and the Struggle for Equality"). As a result of the enforcement of the Fifteenth Amendment, African Americans can register and vote without encountering legal and structural obstacles.

Direct Popular Election of the Senate

As noted in section 2-6e, "An Undemocratic Document?" the Constitution initially provided that members of the U.S. Senate would be elected by the state legislatures. The Seventeenth Amendment, ratified in 1913, required that the Senate be chosen directly by the people. The House of Representatives had proposed the amendment on several occasions, but the Senate had resisted. Finally, in 1912, after public opinion became aroused, the Senate relented. It took only one year for the states to ratify the measure, which had attracted widespread popular support. In reality, though, the Seventeenth Amendment merely formalized what had been occurring informally in half the states, where the legislatures routinely followed the will of the people expressed at the ballot box.

Women's Suffrage

The Nineteenth Amendment (1920), which guaranteed women the right to vote, was the culmination of a movement that began in the 1840s. But the Nineteenth Amendment applied only to voting. It said nothing about the numerous state and federal laws that discriminated against females in matters of property, marriage and divorce, employment, and the professions. In 1923, an amendment was introduced in Congress to provide wider constitutional protection for women's rights. Not until 1972, however, did Congress submit the Equal Rights Amendment to the states. After a protracted and, in some states, bitter struggle, the amendment failed to win ratification. But its failure did not leave women's rights without protection under the federal Constitution. The Equal Protection Clause of the Fourteenth Amendment has been interpreted to provide a substantial degree of protection against official, government-sponsored sex discrimination (see Chapter 5, "Civil Rights and the Struggle for Equality"). Moreover, Congress has used its enforcement powers under the Fourteenth Amendment to enact statutes that further protect women against discrimination.

Lowering the Voting Age

The Twenty-Sixth Amendment (1971) effectively lowered the voting age to eighteen in both state and federal elections. Congress had already decided in 1970 to lower the voting age in federal elections; the amendment came in response to a Supreme Court decision which held that a constitutional amendment was necessary to force the states to lower their voting ages.[29] Considerable impetus for lowering the voting age came from young men aged eighteen to twenty-one, who were eligible to be drafted into military service and sent to die in the jungles of Vietnam, but who were unable to vote for or against the politicians who formulated policies like the draft and the conduct of the Vietnam War. The amendment was ratified quickly and with little opposition. Even state legislatures that supported maintaining the voting age at twenty-one were reluctant to deal with the costly administrative problems that would follow if the federal and state voting ages were different.

Eliminating Economic Restrictions on Voting

When the Constitution was framed, the states were given almost total discretion in determining eligibility to vote. They were limited only in that those who were deemed to be eligible to vote for members of the state house—technically, "the most numerous branch of the state legislature" —would be eligible to vote in elections to the U.S. House of Representatives. In all states, voting was restricted to white men of property, although specific property requirements varied somewhat. By the time Andrew Jackson was elected president in 1832, all states except New Jersey and North Carolina had abolished property requirements for voting.

One of the ways in which states limited the vote was through the **poll tax**. Throughout the nineteenth century, many states, especially in the South, charged a tax for the privilege of voting. Of course, the idea was to limit the participation of the poor, both black and white. In 1964, the Twenty-Fourth Amendment was added to eliminate the poll tax, which had already fallen into some disfavor. The amendment applied only to federal elections, however, and some states continued the practice. Two years later, though, the Supreme Court ruled that these state poll taxes violated the Fourteenth Amendment's Equal Protection Clause, and this device was effectively eliminated from the American political landscape.[30] The removal of the poll tax through formal constitutional change (the Twenty-Fourth Amendment) and the extension of this limitation to the states through constitutional interpretation signified a change in the American notion of political participation: voting is for all citizens, not just the wealthy.

Reapportionment: One Person, One Vote

The right to vote is devalued if one person's vote counts for less than the votes of other citizens. Unfortunately, this was the case before the 1960s. Congressional districts, state legislative districts, even local electoral districts (school boards, county commissions, and the like) were often grossly unequal in terms of population, a condition known as **malapportionment**. When districts are unequal, the influence of each voter in the more populous districts is diminished, and the influence of voters in the less-populated districts is enhanced.

Historically, malapportionment of the state legislatures and U.S. House of Representatives favored the less-populated rural districts over the more-populated urban ones. Constituents from urban areas attempted to get the legislatures to reapportion themselves, but with little success. Finally, after it became clear that the legislatures were not going to act, the federal courts entered the "political thicket" of legislative apportionment. First, in the landmark case of *Baker v. Carr* (1962), the Supreme Court overturned a precedent that had prevented the lower courts from intervening in matters of apportionment.[31] Then, in *Reynolds v. Sims* (1964), the High Court held that state legislative districts had to be reapportioned according to the principle of **one person, one vote**.[32] Districts then had to be redrawn to be made equal in population. Other Supreme Court decisions extended this requirement to U.S. House districts and to districts for local governing bodies.

Considered fairly revolutionary in the 1960s, **reapportionment** is now an accepted part of American political life. Every ten years, after the federal government completes its census, state legislatures reapportion themselves and the congressional districts in their respective states. Failure to do so inevitably means that they will be sued and ordered to undertake reapportionment by a federal court. Indeed, even when the legislature does reapportion itself, certain parties are bound to be displeased. Thus, lawsuits challenging reapportionment plans have become fairly routine in the federal courts. Although reapportionment can be tricky, both legally and politically, unquestionably the reapportionment revolution has rendered the political system more democratic. In a democracy—which rests, of course, on the premise that all citizens are equal before the state—no justification exists for one person's vote to count for more than another's. Political equality has thus become a fundamental aspect of American political culture.

2-9 Conclusion: Assessing the Constitutional System

The American Constitution is the oldest written constitution still in effect in the world. Its longevity can be attributed to a number of factors. One is its basic design, incorporating the separation of powers and federalism. This arrangement creates an inherent bias toward deliberation and consensus building and against quick government responses to social and economic problems. Given the gridlock that often occurs in Washington, especially during periods of **divided-party government** (when one party controls Congress and the other the presidency), some people have questioned the intelligence of that design. Yet no appreciable public demand exists to substitute a parliamentary system for the Framers' basic constitutional design.

At first glance, the Constitution has changed little over the nation's first two hundred years. The number of formal amendments is really quite small. Since the first ten amendments were ratified, which were a de facto part of the original document, fewer than twenty changes have been made. For the most part, these formal changes have dealt with structural corrections, the end of slavery, and the expansion of the franchise. A deeper examination, however, reveals that the constitutional system has undergone tremendous, even fundamental, changes. Notwithstanding the Founders' commitment to the ideal of limited government, government at all levels has expanded to address political demands engendered by social, economic, and technological change. A civil war, two world wars, a great depression, social unrest, and a four-decade-long cold war have had profound consequences for the constitutional system.

Three "meta-trends" in American constitutional development can be identified:

1. *The changing nature of federalism.* Over two hundred years, the relationship between the national government and the states has changed profoundly. Not only has the national government emerged as clearly dominant over the states, but the relationship between the national government and the states has become much more complex (see Chapter 3, "Federalism: A Nation of States").
2. *The growth of government.* This phenomenon involves all levels of government, moving from the eighteenth-century model of limited government to the contemporary model in which government assumes ultimate responsibility for the social and economic well-being of the nation. We alluded to this megatrend in our discussion of the New Deal and the constitutional revolution of 1937 (see section 2-8a, "Constitutional Change through Judicial Interpretation"). We also discuss it in Chapter 3 and at various points in this book, especially Chapter 15, "The Federal Bureaucracy."

3. *The democratization of the constitutional system.* The constitutional republic established by the Founders has become, through formal and informal changes, a constitutional democracy. This has occurred most notably through the achievement of universal suffrage, but also has involved structural changes to allow for greater citizen participation in government and to make government more responsive to the popular will. These changes are highlighted throughout the book, but especially in Chapters 3, 5, and 6.

The political system has changed, the institutions of government have changed, and the political culture has changed. Yet the basic design of American government, conceived more than two hundred years ago, remains intact. It works reasonably well, even though America now faces challenges that were unimaginable decades—let alone centuries—ago. Even in an age of mass communications, electronic media, and computer technology, the Constitution is capable of protecting individual rights and channeling the resolution of conflicts in a way that most citizens find acceptable. Through wars, depressions, and cultural revolutions, the Constitution has shown remarkable flexibility and adaptability. Even in the midst of the contemporary war on terrorism, its viability does not appear to be in jeopardy. Simply put, Americans continue to believe in their Constitution.

Questions for Thought and Discussion

1. Why were the leaders of the American Revolution not content to remain loyal British subjects?

2. What were the main reasons for the failure of the Articles of Confederation?

3. Why did the Framers of the U.S. Constitution reject the idea of a parliamentary system? What would the Framers say about the failure of legislation to pass because of the "gridlock" that sometimes develops when Congress is of one party and the president is of another?

4. How has the Constitution been adapted to cope with fundamental social and economic change?

5. In interpreting provisions of the Constitution that do not have obvious meanings, should contemporary Americans try to find out what the Framers of the Constitution intended and follow those intentions as closely as possible? Why or why not?

ENDNOTES

1 Anonymous, "The AP-National Constitution Center Poll," The Associated Press, August 20, 2010. Available at http://surveys.ap.org/data/GfK/AP-GfK%20Poll%20August%20NCC%20topline.pdf

2 Samuel Eliot Morison, "The Mayflower Compact." In *An American Primer*, ed. Daniel J. Boorstin (Chicago: University of Chicago Press, 1966), p. 1.

3 Paul Kennedy, *The Rise and Fall of the Great Powers* (New York: Random House, 1987), p. 93.

4 See Gordon S. Wood, *The Radicalism of the American Revolution* (New York: Vintage Books, 1993).

5 Charles Francis Adams, ed., *The Works of John Adams*, vol. 10 (Boston: Little, Brown, 1856), p. 282.

6 Quoted in Catherine Drinker Bowen, *Miracle at Philadelphia* (Boston: Little, Brown, 1966), p. 4.

7 Quoted in Clinton Rossiter, *The Grand Convention* (New York: Macmillan, 1966), p. 159.

8 Charles A. Beard, *An Economic Interpretation of the Constitution of the United States* (New York: Macmillan, 1960), p. 188.

9 Forrest McDonald, *We the People: The Economic Origins of the Constitution* (Chicago: University of Chicago Press, 1958).

10 John A. Garraty, *The American Nation*, 4th ed. (New York: Harper and Row, 1979), p. 123.

11 Robert A. McGuire, *To Form a More Perfect Union: A New Economic Interpretation of the United States Constitution* (Oxford: Oxford University Press, 2003), p. 30.

12 John P. Roche, "The Founding Fathers: A Reform Caucus in Action," *American Political Science Review*, vol. 55, 1961, pp. 799–816.

13 Thomas Hobbes, *Leviathan* (New York: Macmillan, 1947).

14 *The Federalist*, No. 47.

15 Forrest McDonald, *We the People* (Chicago: University of Chicago Press, 1958), p. 113.

16 Charles A. Beard and Mary R. Beard, *A Basic History of the United States* (New Home Library, 1944), p. 136.

17 *Texas v. Johnson*, 491 U.S. 397 (1989).

18 CBS/*New York Times* poll, May 1987. Respondents were asked, "Do you think it is too easy or too hard to amend the Constitution, or is the process about right?" Eleven percent responded "too easy," 20 percent responded "too hard," 60 percent responded "about right," and 9 percent were not sure.

19 Quoted in Charles S. Hyneman and George W. Carey, *A Second Federalist: Congress Creates a Government* (New York: Appleton-Century-Crofts, 1967), pp. 260–61.

20 *Pollock v. Farmer's Loan and Trust Co.*, 158 U.S. 601 (1895).

21 *Marbury v. Madison*, 5 U.S. (1 Cranch) 137 (1803).

22 *Fletcher v. Peck*, 10 U.S. (6 Cranch) 87 (1810).

23 *McCulloch v. Maryland*, 17 U.S. (4 Wheat.) 316, 407 (1819).

24 17 U.S. (4 Wheat.) at 415.

25 In *Pollock v. Farmer's Loan and Trust Co.*, 158 U.S. 601 (1895), the Court invalidated an income tax measure passed by Congress. In *U.S. v. E. C. Knight Co.*, 156 U.S. 1 (1895), the Court substantially limited the scope of the Sherman Anti-Trust Act of 1890.

26 *Lochner v. New York*, 198 U.S. 45, 64 (1905).

27 *National Labor Relations Board v. Jones & Laughlin Steel Corp.*, 301 U.S. 1 (1937).

28 *Scott v. Sandford*, 60 U.S. (19 How.) 393 (1857).

29 *Oregon v. Mitchell*, 400 U.S. 112 (1970).

30 *Harper v. Virginia State Board of Elections*, 383 U.S. 663 (1966).

31 *Baker v. Carr*, 369 U.S. 186 (1962).

32 *Reynolds v. Sims*, 377 U.S. 533 (1964).

Chapter 3

FEDERALISM: A NATION OF STATES

OUTLINE

Key Terms 75

Expected Learning Outcomes 76

3-1 The Idea of Federalism 76

- **3-1a** Inventing American Government 79
- **3-1b** Alternative Modes of Allocating Power 79

3-2 Federalism in the Constitution 81

- **3-2a** Defining the Federal Relationship 82
- **3-2b** The Supremacy of Federal Law 82

3-3 The Development of Federalism: The Founding to the Civil War 83

- **3-3a** Implied Powers and National Supremacy 83
- **3-3b** The Civil War: A Battle between Two Ideas of Federalism 85

3-4 Evolving Federalism in the Modern Era 86

- **3-4a** Civil Rights: A Case Study in Federalism 87
- **3-4b** "Electoral Federalism" and the Right to Vote 89
- **3-4c** Civil Liberties, State Action, and the Bill of Rights 91
- **3-4d** Economic Regulation: A Historic Conflict in Federalism 93
- **3-4e** States, Cities, and the Federal Government: The Evolving Federal Relationship 94

3-5 The Complex Character of Contemporary Federalism 99

- **3-5a** Areas of Federal–State Cooperation 99
- **3-5b** Fiscal Federalism 103

3-6 Assessing American Federalism 104

- **3-6a** The Advantages of the Federal System 104
- **3-6b** The Disadvantages of Federalism 106

3-7 Conclusion: Federalism and Political Culture 106

Questions for Thought and Discussion 108

Endnotes 109

KEY TERMS

Black Codes

block grants

categorical grant

confederation

cooperative federalism

devolution

dual federalism
enumerated powers
federal system
fiscal federalism
general revenue sharing
grants-in-aid
implied powers, doctrine of
initiative and referendum
legislative proposal
marble cake federalism
Missouri Plan
nation-centered federalism
nullification, doctrine of
secession, doctrine of
state-centered federalism
Supremacy Clause
unfunded mandates

EXPECTED LEARNING OUTCOMES

After reading this chapter and completing the supplemental online materials, students will:

- Compare different models of national/state power distribution
- Describe the types of power allocated to different levels of government
- Understand the role of American federalism in the concept of government power
- Identify levels of government by their assigned power
- Trace the history of the balance of power between the federal and state governments

3-1 THE IDEA OF FEDERALISM

Think about the state you grew up in. For some of you, think about the states you grew up in. When you think about yourself as a citizen, do you think about yourself as a citizen of that state, or those states, or do you first think of yourself as an American? The question isn't trivial—it helps us to understand the dual nature of being an American. For the first time in history, citizens belonged to a state and to a nation under the American federal system.

Even under a system with a strong national government, for most of American history citizens identified first and foremost as being from their home state first and Americans second. Considering the federal government was a severely limited entity and most people rarely traveled outside the borders of their home states, the identification with a state over the nation isn't surprising. As the world, American society, and our governmental priorities changed, so did the typical American's perception of their identity. Travel, relocation, communication, and America's role in the world drew identification from one's state to the nation in general. Today, most of us consider ourselves American citizens—and those that don't probably consider themselves citizens of the world. The borders in which we associate our citizenship have definitely expanded, and with them our views of government. But states and localities still exist and have important roles in the governmental system, even if we do not recognize them or pay as much attention to them as we do the federal government.

New Orleans, Louisiana is one of the unique American cities. Andrew Jackson believed, during the War of 1812, that no city (not even Washington D.C.) should be defended as fiercely as New Orleans. America's international shipping has long relied heavily on New Orleans. With the Mississippi River and Gulf of Mexico as part of the city's landscape and culture, New Orleans was also in a precarious spot. When Hurricane Katrina made landfall on August 28, 2005, the city was devastated. Floods swept through the city as inadequately prepared levees failed. Those levees were built by the federal government's Army Corps of Engineers.

© justasc, 2013. Used under license from Shutterstock, Inc.

Police officers from the city fled the flood waters, leaving no local response. Louisiana's state emergency management agency and governor had failed to request the coast of their state be included in federal emergency declarations, and the federal government did not respond quickly. The result was thousands of people crammed into the New Orleans Superdome as a shelter, and thousands more dead in homes throughout the area. The United States is one nation, but is subdivided into states. Those states have governments, and while we would expect the local, state, and federal governments to work in concert to solve problems, they often do not. Conflict, complex rules, and geographic distance all make potential problems when disaster strikes. Not all disaster responses are failure, though.

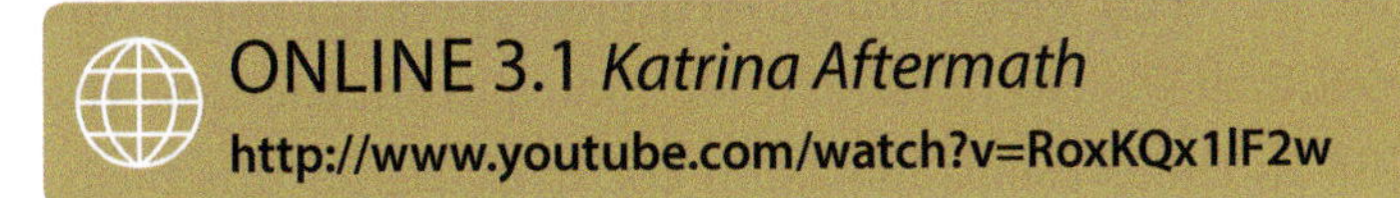
ONLINE 3.1 *Katrina Aftermath*
http://www.youtube.com/watch?v=RoxKQx1lF2w

When the United States was attacked by terrorists in September 2001, the first government personnel to respond to the tragedy were the frontline troops of local government: firefighters and police officers. New York's mayor, Rudy Giuliani, was widely praised for his efforts in coordinating and leading the city's response to the tragedy. However, because the terrorist attack was an attack on the entire country, Americans looked to their national government in Washington, D.C., for a *national* response to the attack. In times of national crisis, Americans typically look to Washington for action. First responders to 9/11 share their stories in the video linked at the online supplement.

ONLINE 3.2 *9/11 First Responders*
http://www.youtube.com/watch?v=otd2s9cjfgg

Although local police and firefighters were the first to respond to the attacks, state and national agencies were not far behind. Indeed, within hours of the attacks, the Federal Emergency Management Agency (FEMA) was present on the scene of the attacks and helped to coordinate the national, state, and local responses. In the weeks that followed the attack of September 11, Americans saw government at all levels swing into action.

At the national level, Congress responded to the crisis with new legislation strengthening the powers of federal agencies to deal with suspected terrorists. President Bush promptly mobilized the military in an effort to destroy terrorist bases in Afghanistan. America's diplomatic corps, under the leadership of Secretary of State Colin Powell, worked tirelessly to assemble and maintain an international coalition in support of America's war on terrorism. National security and intelligence agencies worked behind the scenes around the globe to gather intelligence and forge alliances aimed at rooting out terrorist networks.

Various agencies of the national government, including the Federal Bureau of Investigation (FBI), the Immigration and Naturalization Service (INS), and the Federal Aviation Administration (FAA), were called on to dramatically upgrade domestic security. Even a new federal bureaucracy, the Department of Homeland Security (DHS), was created to coordinate the national government's efforts in this area and bring multiple agencies of government under one roof.

What happened in the aftermath of September 11 can be viewed as a case study in American federalism. Essentially, *federalism* refers to a political system in which constitutional authority is divided between a national government and a set of provincial or state governments. The political system of the United States, from the time the Constitution was ratified in 1788 to the present, has been constructed on this basis. In the United States, the nation and the fifty states exist simultaneously as sovereign political entities. Although this arrangement has always been the case, the character of the federal system, and in particular the relationship between the national government and the states, has changed profoundly. As this chapter will make clear, our country has moved from a state-centered model of federalism to a nation-centered model. This chapter examines the development of American federalism from the founding of the American republic to the complex character of the contemporary system. The chapter also examines the structures and functions of state and local governments, which remain essential components of the federal system.

3-1a Inventing American Government

The United States of America officially became a nation when the Declaration of Independence was enforced by a successful war for independence from Great Britain. Having successfully asserted its independence, a formidable task of nation building lay ahead. It would be some time before Rhode Islanders, Virginians, Pennsylvanians, Georgians, and New Yorkers would regard themselves as Americans sharing a common identity with other former colonies. Fortunately, they did have the essential materials from which to build a nation. Americans of all thirteen states shared a common language. Moreover, despite significant economic and social differences between North and South, Americans of the Revolutionary era shared the rudiments of a common political culture in their individualist philosophy.

No real doubt ever existed that the thirteen former British colonies were to be the basic building blocks of the new nation. No one seriously argued that the former colonies should be left to fend for themselves as individual republics, nor did any support exist for merging the colonies under one central government. The Articles of Confederation represented a temporary first attempt to find a middle ground between these undesirable extremes. As observed in Chapter 2, "The Development of American Constitutional Democracy," the Articles failed essentially because they had not allowed the central government enough power.

Of course, the fear of a centralized government had been, to a great degree, a major motivating force behind the Articles. The residents of what would become the United States had become accustomed to the colonies, many of which had unique histories. The idea of a larger unit was more than a little frightening. Nevertheless, the Framers of the Constitution were faced with the task of inventing an organizational scheme that combined a central government with the existing state governments that had evolved from the colonies. Their task was to divide power between these two levels in a way that was acceptable to enough residents of the states to ensure ratification. The **federal system** they created represented a uniquely American solution to the universal problem of governing.[1] In a federal system, authority and responsibility are divided between a central government and a set of regional governments. In the United States, federalism refers to the distribution of governmental power between the national government in Washington, D.C., and the fifty state governments.

3-1b Alternative Modes of Allocating Power

When the Constitution was written, two basic models existed by which power could be apportioned between the national government and the states: a *unitary system* and a **confederation**. The Framers rejected both of these alternatives, opting instead for a federal system. When the American federal system was created in 1787, it was altogether new. It is now recognized as a model that other countries forging new constitutions may choose to emulate.

Unitary Systems

In a unitary system, *sovereignty*, the right to rule, is vested in one central government. A government is sovereign if it is the seat of final authority. No other unit of government can eliminate or restructure it. In a unitary system, the central government cannot be altered by any agreement among the nation's smaller political units, such as cities, counties, states, or provinces. However, these smaller entities can be altered or eliminated by the central government—they do not have the protection that sovereignty brings. France and Japan are good examples of strong democracies that utilize unitary systems of allocating power.

In essence, had the Framers of the Constitution opted for a unitary government, they would have rendered the states no more than administrative units that were closer to the people and better able to deliver some services, but a unitary system was never seriously considered. The experience with British rule had soured the Founders on the idea of one government with centralized and ultimate power. The new Americans did not care if tyranny came from a central government in America rather than from across the Atlantic—they wanted to make the potential for tyranny as remote as possible. Moreover, in 1787, the states were sovereign entities, having been loosely held together since the Revolution by the Articles of Confederation. Because they were originally established as separate colonies, each with its own administrative machinery, the states became viable political entities after independence was declared. During the Revolution, each state adopted a constitution establishing a legislature, executive branch, and court system. The states had no intention of entirely surrendering their sovereignty to a new national government, and any constitution that required them to do so surely would not have been ratified.

Confederations

The existing alternative to the unitary system was one that had already been tried: a confederation. In a confederation, the states are sovereign and the central government is not. The central government exists only at the will of the states, which can eliminate or restructure it at will. This was essentially the situation under the Articles of Confederation.

If the experience with Britain made a unitary system unthinkable, the years under the Articles likewise eliminated a confederation from serious consideration. Without some independent authority, a central government would be too weak to function, and the chaos experienced under the Articles could be expected to continue. Clearly, creating another confederation would have doomed the new country to be a weak, fragmented collection of states. The realities of the world at that time mandated nationhood, which was not possible under a confederation.

The Federal Alternative

The Framers of the Constitution were both innovators and compromisers. Had they been otherwise, the Constitution they produced could not have been ratified. The federal system they adopted was a compromise between the advocates of a strong central government, such as Alexander Hamilton, and those, like George Mason, who favored strong states and a weak national government. Federalism was an innovation, based not on experiments that had been tried elsewhere, but rather on ideas that had been suggested by political philosophers of the Enlightenment.

In a federal system, both the states and the central government are sovereign within the sphere of powers the Constitution grants them. Neither can do away with the other nor alter the other's structure. Each has its own compact with the governed and its own role in performing the governing task. Both the national government and the states can act directly to affect the lives of individuals, although in different ways. Of course, this shared sovereignty greatly complicates the process of governing. Any federal system involves overlapping functions and inevitable tensions between the national and state governments. Much of the history of the American political system reflects the tensions of competing national and state interests.

3-2 Federalism in the Constitution

At the time the Constitution was being written and discussed, the failed Articles of Confederation provided the only national structure. State governments still functioned independently, however. Because the Constitution was creating a new national (federal) government, it was reasonable to presume that this new government could do only what the Constitution specifically allowed. This presumption was very important, for some conflict over the respective roles of the new national government and the states seemed inevitable. When the state conventions ratified the Constitution, they agreed to let this new government take away some of their powers and responsibilities. Naturally, the states were apprehensive, and some were quite hesitant to ratify the Constitution. Advocates of states' rights insisted that the Constitution would have to be amended to make explicit the fact that the states were relinquishing only those powers delegated to the national government. This, of course, was the purpose behind the Tenth Amendment, which, along with the rest of the Bill of Rights, was adopted by the First Congress in 1789 and ratified by the states in 1791.

The fact that the proposed Constitution had to be ratified by nine states, voting individually as states, underlined the logic of the federal system. A bare majority in the five smallest states could have blocked the new government had they found it unsatisfactory. This routing of national decisions through states, as states, rather than through a "national" mechanism, is a hallmark of the American system. In fact, the

American people have no mechanism for making a purely national decision. In the Senate, states are equally represented. Even our presidential elections are conducted by the states. This system ensures a continuing role for the states as political units. As long as the states remain actors, they cannot be completely overshadowed, no matter how strongly the national government exerts its power.

3-2a Defining the Federal Relationship

The Constitution was ratified with the full knowledge that the new national government would have substantial but limited powers. The Tenth Amendment "reserved" all powers not delegated to the national government for the states. However, the Necessary and Proper Clause in Article I of the Constitution provided a gray area for the federal government to expand its powers where no clear grant of authority to either level of government exists. Therefore, the list of such delegated powers was of crucial importance. The Framers defined the powers of the new government by carefully specifying the types of laws that Congress could enact. These **enumerated powers** are contained in Article I, Section 8 of the Constitution. They include such tasks as collecting taxes, declaring war, providing for the national defense, coining money, regulating interstate commerce, establishing policies on immigration and naturalization, establishing a postal service, setting up a system of federal courts, and various other jobs associated with the administration of the new government. Most significantly, Article I, Section 8 permitted Congress to "make all Laws which shall be necessary and proper for carrying into execution the foregoing powers, and all other powers vested by this Constitution." This passage would turn out to be one of the most important in the Constitution.

As originally conceived, the national government was quite limited in scope. The states were clearly responsible for passing laws that defined criminal behavior; funded local roads, education, and sanitation; and regulated business. In a nutshell, the states were to have the *police power*, the power to make and enforce laws to protect the public health, safety, morality, and welfare. Of course, the Constitution establishes only a broad framework for governing. It does not provide a detailed blueprint. Indeed, as one scholar has observed, the Constitution "virtually ensured continuing controversy about the respective roles of the national and state governments by creating sufficient ambiguity to leave many of the important questions unresolved."[2]

3-2b The Supremacy of Federal Law

Any federal system has to address the possible friction between the national and regional governments. The second paragraph of Article VI, known as the **Supremacy Clause**, makes it clear that federal laws and the U.S. Constitution take precedence over state laws and state constitutions when they are in conflict. The meaning of this clause seems straightforward. The laws of Congress are ultimately superior to the laws of the states, and the Supreme

Court is likewise superior to the state supreme courts in determining the meaning of the U.S. Constitution. Although both the states and the national government are sovereign, the national government is superior when the two sovereigns conflict (assuming the national government is acting within the scope of its constitutional authority).

3-3 The Development of Federalism: The Founding to the Civil War

Whatever understandings may have existed when the Constitution was ratified, it did not take long for disagreements over the appropriate roles of the federal and state governments to arise. These types of disputes were almost inevitable, given the general, and sometimes rather vague, nature of the Constitution. The political culture supported two different views of what the new republic should be. Thomas Jefferson envisioned a rural society with the national government playing a minimal role. Alexander Hamilton held a strikingly different vision, one of a country of shopkeepers and merchants involved in trade. This latter perspective supported a more active national government, playing a greater role in fostering interstate trade and protecting domestic markets from foreign competition. Jefferson's perspective soon evolved into a states' rights view of the Constitution, and Hamilton's became associated with a stronger central government. Together, they represented the two endpoints on a scale that defined the political discussion of the day. The politics of the era revolved around this debate, in much the same way as the politics of the mid-nineteenth century revolved around the issue of slavery and the politics of the 1960s revolved around civil rights and the Vietnam War.

3-3a Implied Powers and National Supremacy

The first major constitutional issue involving federalism concerned the economy. Alexander Hamilton, the first secretary of the treasury, believed that Congress needed to establish a national bank to promote economic development and strengthen the nation's economy. In 1791, Congress, acting largely at Hamilton's behest, created the First Bank of the United States. The bank acted as a clearinghouse of sorts for federal funds. The federal government was the bank's largest depositor and principal director.

From the outset, Thomas Jefferson objected to the bank as unnecessary and improper. Moreover, he believed that the bank was unconstitutional, going beyond what Congress could enact under Article I, Section 8. Jeffersonians charged that the bank was corrupt and was merely a tool enabling the Federalists to use the power of the national government for their own political and economic ends. In this regard, Jefferson was expressing the concerns of many rural residents who were suspicious of urban banking and trading interests. When the bank's charter expired in 1811, Congress, which was controlled by the Jeffersonians, opted not to renew it.

Within a few years, however, sentiment in Congress turned in favor of reestablishing the bank. Congress chartered the Second Bank of the United States in 1816. This new national bank was quite active, and many states became concerned that they would lose their state-chartered banks. In response, state legislatures moved to fight the national bank. The Maryland legislature enacted a law that imposed a heavy tax on the Baltimore branch of the Bank of the United States. But when presented with the state's tax bill, McCulloch, the cashier of the national bank at Baltimore, refused to pay. The state of Maryland filed suit and prevailed in the state courts, which upheld the payment order. McCulloch then appealed to the U.S. Supreme Court, which overturned the Maryland courts' decision.[3]

The Court based its decision in *McCulloch v. Maryland* on a broad interpretation of the Necessary and Proper Clause of Article I, Section 8. Although the power to charter a bank was not specifically mentioned in the enumeration of national powers, Chief Justice John Marshall believed that a bank was implied from the listing of powers involving taxation, credit, money, and the regulation of commerce. Thus, from Marshall's opinion in *McCulloch v. Maryland* emerged the **doctrine of implied powers**, one of the fundamental doctrines of American constitutional law.

Having justified the action of Congress in establishing the bank, Chief Justice Marshall turned his attention to the Maryland tax. Because the national government was, under the Supremacy Clause of Article VI, "supreme within its sphere of action," the states had no power to impede the legitimate actions of the national government. Because the power to tax involved "the power to destroy," the state of Maryland was impeding, and quite possibly destroying, a legitimate enterprise of the national government. Having decided that creating a bank was a legitimate activity of the federal government, the Supreme Court had no trouble in forbidding Maryland, or any other state, from taxing it. *McCulloch v. Maryland* dealt a major blow to the forces of states' rights and substantially enlarged the powers of the national government.

The Supreme Court cemented its commitment to national supremacy with its 1824 decision in *Gibbons v. Ogden*, which affirmed the dominant role of the national government in the regulation of commerce.[4]4 In *Gibbons*, the Court struck down a New York law that granted a monopoly to operate steamboats in state waters. The law prevented a competitor from operating a ferry service between New York and New Jersey under a "coasting" license issued by the federal government. Writing for the Supreme Court, Chief Justice Marshall upheld the validity of the federal license and struck down the state monopoly. In an opinion reminiscent of *McCulloch v. Maryland*, Marshall expounded on the broad character of the federal power to regulate interstate commerce and the invalidity of state laws that collided with the federal power.

Both *McCulloch v. Maryland* and *Gibbons v. Ogden* were based on an interpretation of the Constitution that favored a stronger central government. These decisions allowed considerable discretion for Congress to respond to a changing society without worrying about whether its laws fit precisely within the list of enumerated powers in Article I, Section 8. This situation opened the door to broad federal legislation, especially in the twentieth century. Many laws Congress has passed in recent decades would not have been possible without the Supreme Court's broad interpretation of the Constitution in *McCulloch v. Maryland* and *Gibbons v. Ogden*.

3-3b The Civil War: A Battle between Two Ideas of Federalism

Without question, the fundamental social and political issue of the mid-nineteenth century was slavery. As noted in Chapter 2, "The Development of American Constitutional Democracy," the question of slavery was not effectively resolved at the Constitutional Convention of 1787. The issue was left to fester and eventually erupted into civil war when it became clear that the southern states were not going to relinquish what they thought was their "right" under the Constitution.

In the infamous Dred Scott decision in 1857, the Supreme Court gave support to the southern states' hard-line position.[5] In a complicated decision, the Court ordered, among other things, that people of African origin or descent were not citizens of the United States at the time the Constitution was adopted; nor could they become citizens. Moreover, slaves were property, not persons with rights of their own. In the Court's view, when Congress outlawed slavery in certain territories under the Missouri Compromise of 1820, it deprived slaveholders in "free" territories of their "property" without due process of law. The decision was reviled in the North and celebrated in the South, showing how deep-seated the regional cleavage was, even with respect to what the Constitution meant. Far from resolving the question of slavery, the Dred Scott decision revealed a basic division between the political cultures of the North and South.

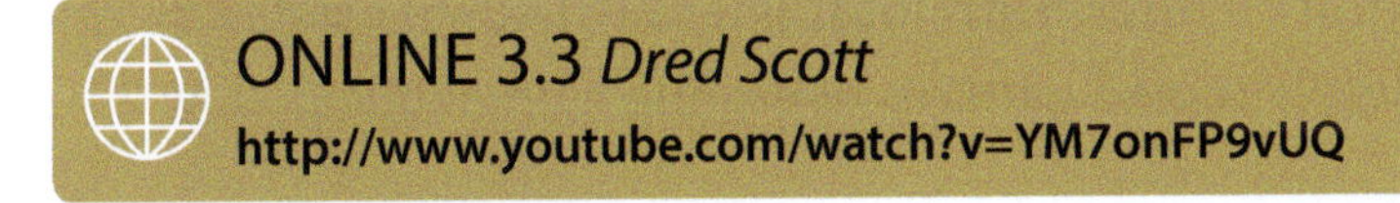
ONLINE 3.3 *Dred Scott*
http://www.youtube.com/watch?v=YM7onFP9vUQ

The Doctrines of Nullification and Secession

As the increasingly democratic political culture of the United States became less and less hospitable to slavery, many in the South looked for a justification for continuing their way of life. Slavery had become very much identified with that way of life. Clearly, many leaders in the South felt loyalty not to the still-youthful nation, but to their respective states and to the local political cultures those states were protecting.

Out of the growing division between the southern states and the national government emerged the **doctrine of nullification**, which held that a state could decide for itself whether it would recognize, and ultimately abide by, a law passed by the national government. The logical extension of this position was the **doctrine of secession**—the idea that a state could secede, or withdraw, from the Union. In seceding from the Union, the southern states were making the ultimate claim under a states' rights interpretation of the Constitution—the right to withdraw their ratification of the Constitution. Of course, in conducting the Civil War, President Abraham Lincoln used the power of the national government to implement his position that the states could not choose to leave the United States. Lincoln's position, which would prevail, was that after states had agreed to join the Union, their decision was irrevocable. In *Texas v. White*, issued four years after General Lee's surrender at Appomattox Courthouse, the Supreme Court pronounced, once and for all, that "the Constitution, in all its provisions, looks to an indestructible Union, composed of indestructible States."[6]

The Victory of Nation-Centered Federalism

In addition to being a conflict over the morality of slavery, the Civil War was a contest between two visions of American federalism. The Union victory vindicated a **nation-centered federalism** and spelled the end of the **state-centered federalism** espoused by the South. By the end of the Civil War, the basic fabric of federalism had taken shape. Although the states were certainly major players, the federal government had become the first among equals. Its supremacy was well established, and the supreme role of the federal courts in resolving questions of federal and state power was ensured.

3-4 Evolving Federalism in the Modern Era

In the wake of the Civil War, as the country changed from a mostly agrarian economy of farms and small towns to an urban, industrial society, the character of federalism continued to evolve in the direction of national dominance. Increasingly, the national government saw fit to move into areas of policy traditionally reserved to the states. In each instance, there was resistance, and sometimes sharp conflict. Each situation brought about a clash of political cultures, with local interests taking a states' rights position, usually to preserve deeply rooted patterns of dealing with public policy.

3-4a CIVIL RIGHTS: A CASE STUDY IN FEDERALISM

The Civil War ended in 1865. That same year, slavery was formally abolished throughout the United States by the ratification of the Thirteenth Amendment to the Constitution. Nevertheless, many states passed laws to perpetuate the secondary social and economic status of African Americans within their borders. The **Black Codes**, as they were called, limited the economic freedom and property rights of blacks and even denied them access to the courts of law. Congress responded by passing the Civil Rights Act of 1866, the first in a long line of federal civil rights laws. The Civil Rights Act of 1866 was designed to nullify the Black Codes, but many questioned whether Congress possessed the constitutional authority to act in this field. To alleviate these doubts, Congress proposed the Fourteenth Amendment, which was ratified in 1868.

THE IMPORTANCE OF THE FOURTEENTH AMENDMENT

The Fourteenth Amendment prohibited the states from denying "any person" (a veiled reference to African-Americans) within their jurisdiction the equal protection of the laws, which is precisely what the Black Codes had done. Moreover, Section 5 of the Fourteenth Amendment gave Congress the power to enforce the Equal Protection Clause, as well as the other substantive provisions of the amendment, by "appropriate legislation." This language provided a firm constitutional foundation for congressional action in the civil rights field.

Although the Fourteenth Amendment and the Civil Rights Act of 1866 effectively dismantled the Black Codes, the southern states devised new means of legally subordinating blacks. These enactments, known as *Jim Crow laws*, took a multitude of forms. Whether mandating separate schools for black and white children or establishing segregated public facilities, these laws had the effect of keeping the races apart and restricting African Americans to menial positions. In addition, because the Constitution gave to the states the responsibility for conducting elections, the southern states were able to devise ways to keep blacks from voting. These measures were consistent with the dominant, traditional culture of the Deep South, which viewed persons of African descent as being inferior to whites. Look at Table 3-1 and imagine that you are a newly freed slave in the post–Civil War South. The column on the right describes how the Black Codes and Jim Crow laws affect your life. In the web supplement for the text, you can view a video with testimony from African Americans about the experience of living under Jim Crow laws.

3.4 *Jim Crow*
http://www.youtube.com/watch?v=VnlbKKxJvbU

TABLE 3-1 Life under the Black Codes

SITUATION	EFFECT OF BLACK CODES
You want to farm your own land but are too poor to purchase any, so you try to rent some.	In Mississippi, you can't rent or lease land outside a city or town. Do you try to find work inside a town?
You live outside a town and need to pick up supplies at a store, or perhaps you're looking for work in a city.	In Opelousas, Louisiana, you are barred entry into cities and towns unless you have a note from your employer, stating your reason for being there and how long you are allowed to stay. If you are found in a city after 10 p.m., you will be locked up in the local jail.
You live in Mississippi and have fallen in love with a white northerner. You want to marry.	The Black Codes of 1865 in Mississippi outlaw interracial marriage, and you and your husband or wife can be imprisoned for life if you are caught.
You and several friends, all over the age of eighteen, gather together for a political meeting.	You can be arrested for unlawful congregation and vagrancy, fined fifty dollars, and spend ten days in jail. White people associating with you and arrested at the same time pay two hundred dollars and can serve up to six months in jail. Why do you think there is such a difference?
You live in Texas and witness a fight between two white men that leaves one severely injured. Surely it's your duty to testify at the trial, isn't it?	As a freeman in Texas, you cannot vote, hold office, sit on a jury, or testify in court except in cases involving other blacks.
Compiled from: http://www.nilevalley.net/history/jim_crow_laws.html http://www.pbs.org/wnet/jimcrow/ http://www.tsha.utexas.edu/handbook/online/articles/view/BB/jsb1.html	

The Jim Crow laws were passed in accordance with the rules of the states; that is, majorities of elected representatives voted to enact these laws, and state courts held that they were consistent with the state constitutions. In fact, many state constitutions explicitly required separation of the races. Despite the passage of the Thirteenth, Fourteenth, and Fifteenth Amendments, the U.S. Supreme Court did not have the will, or the means, to confront these state actions.[7] The prevailing political culture allowed the southern states to use state action to maintain their "way of life." This view prevailed until 1954, when, in the landmark decision in *Brown v. Board of Education*, the Supreme Court ruled that black citizens' rights to equal treatment under the law outweighed states' rights to maintain segregated school systems.[8]

ONLINE 3.4 *Brown v. Board*
http://www.oyez.org/cases/1950-1959/1952/1952_1

The Development of a National Consensus on Civil Rights

Initially, the Supreme Court's desegregation rulings were met with howls of disapproval. Governors of some southern states refused to abide by the Court's mandates. Many southerners resented what they felt was an unconstitutional intrusion into state affairs. In some places, such as Little Rock, Arkansas, the reaction to desegregation was so violent that federal troops had to be mobilized to restore order. By the 1960s, the idea (if not the implementation) of desegregation had begun to gain acceptance, even in the Deep South. But in the 1970s, as federal courts began to mandate the busing of students to dismantle segregated public schools, white resistance flared up again. Interestingly, the most intense reactions to forced busing came not in Dixie, but rather in the big cities of the North and West.

The Supreme Court's pioneering decisions invalidating segregation in public schools were eventually followed and reinforced by congressional and presidential action. The most important of these efforts was the enactment of the Civil Rights Act of 1964, which, among other things, barred the transfer of federal funds to educational institutions (public or private) that practiced racial discrimination. By the 1980s, the political culture of the United States no longer supported the idea of racial segregation. Americans had come to accept the laws and court decisions that had been fostered by the national government to promote civil rights. No longer did any widespread sentiment exist for the old style of states' rights, under which state governments were free to discriminate against groups of their citizens. Americans had come to a consensus that equality under the law was a basic right.

3-4b "Electoral Federalism" and the Right to Vote

The Supreme Court's ruling in *Brown v. Board of Education* made clear that the federal courts would be willing to take an active part in overturning state systems that violated their citizens' constitutional rights. By the mid-1960s, Congress was also willing to cast a critical eye on the ways in which states had been conducting their elections. Historically, African Americans in some states had been denied an equal opportunity to register and vote. The passage of the Voting Rights Act of 1965 was the first major foray of the national government into the conduct of state and local elections, which had been always considered a state responsibility under federalism. The initial intent of this legislation was concerned with registering minority voters and eliminating devices that had been used to limit minority participation. In upholding the Voting Rights Act against a challenge brought by the state of South Carolina (one of the main targets of the legislation), the Supreme Court expressed hope that "millions of non-white Americans will be able to participate for the first time on an equal basis in the government under which they live."[9]

In 1980, the Supreme Court ruled that urban electoral systems could be invalidated under the Fourteenth Amendment (and the Voting Rights Act) *only* if it could be proved that they had been created with the intent to discriminate against minority voters.[10] This decision came down just before congressional hearings on the extension of the Voting Rights Act. When the extension was granted in 1982, Section 2 was amended to outlaw electoral systems that could be shown to lead to "minority vote dilution," regardless of any original intent to discriminate. This reworking of the Voting Rights Act led to a great surge in federal court involvement in the structures of local governments. As a result of litigation in this area, state and local governments are being held responsible for creating systems in which candidates preferred by African Americans can be elected. In many cases, cities have been ordered by federal courts to change their form of government. Systems of electing city councils at-large, rather than by district, had been a major component of the early twentieth-century movement to reform American cities. These systems came under challenge in the 1980s under the Voting Rights Act on the ground that they were diluting the voting strength of minorities. At-large systems have proven to be difficult to defend legally, despite the fact that their original intent had not been to limit African American participation.

In addition, the federal courts have become embroiled in the drawing of district lines for Congress and state legislatures. For instance, to ensure the election of a black representative to Congress in North Carolina, a district was created that connects a number of predominantly black areas by including a two-hundred-mile length of interstate highway. The district that was created meandered across the entire state but was invalidated by the Supreme Court in 1995's *Shaw v. Reno*. In the Court's view, vote dilution suffered by African American voting in congressional elections throughout North Carolina is "not remedied by creating a safe majority-black district somewhere else in the State."[11] Under prevailing constitutional interpretation, states cannot make race the dominant factor in drawing district lines, but it can be considered along with other factors.[12]

3-4c Civil Liberties, State Action, and the Bill of Rights

As noted in section 3-2, "Federalism in the Constitution," the Bill of Rights was intended as a set of limitations not on the states, but rather on the national government. States were expected to protect their citizens through their own constitutions. For protection of their rights from infringement by the state governments, citizens had to look to their respective state constitutions, as interpreted by the state courts. However, the adoption of the Fourteenth Amendment in 1868 created the legal basis for changing the relationship of the Bill of Rights to the states. In addition to requiring states to extend "equal protection of the laws," Section 1 of the Fourteenth Amendment prohibited states from depriving anyone of life, liberty, or property "without due process of law" or abridging the "privileges and immunities of citizens of the United States." In other words, a state could not deny Bill of Rights protections to its own citizens. Although legal scholars have debated the intentions of the Framers of the Fourteenth Amendment, the Supreme Court eventually came to accept the idea that the Fourteenth Amendment "incorporated" most, if not all, of the protections of the Bill of Rights, making them enforceable against the state governments.

The Incorporation of the Bill of Rights

The first instance in which the Supreme Court accepted the doctrine of incorporation was in 1896, when it decided that the Fourteenth Amendment required state and local governments to provide "just compensation" to persons whose property had been taken for public use.[13] In essence, the Court decided that the Just Compensation Clause of the Fifth Amendment constituted an essential element of due process, and thus was binding on the states under the Fourteenth Amendment.

In 1925, the Supreme Court held that the First Amendment freedoms of speech and press were "among the fundamental personal rights and 'liberties' protected by the Due Process Clause of the Fourteenth Amendment from impairment by the states."[14] In 1940, the Court extended the doctrine of incorporation to include freedom of religion.[15] The First Amendment prohibition against "establishment of religion" was applied to the states in 1947.[16] By the late 1960s, virtually all the provisions of the Bill of Rights had been incorporated into the Fourteenth Amendment and thereby made applicable to the states.

The application of the Bill of Rights to the states was far more than a matter of legal abstraction. It permitted individuals who believed that their basic rights had been violated by a state government to challenge that government in a federal court.[17] This ability greatly expanded the supervisory power of the federal courts over the state governments. Although this dramatic expansion of federal judicial power met initial resistance, most Americans eventually came to accept the need for federal judicial supervision of state actions that impinged on individual liberties. Liberty, like equality, came to be seen as a fundamental value that was not to be sacrificed on the altar of federalism.

The Rights of the Accused: A Case Study in Federalism

As a result of the nationalization of the Bill of Rights, the states gradually lost their ability to establish their own criminal justice policies. As late as the 1930s, some states routinely held trials in which the accused did not have legal counsel, even if the possible punishment after conviction included the death penalty.[18] Some states did not provide protection in their constitutions against double jeopardy, that is, being tried or punished twice for the same offense.[19] In many states, police could conduct searches and seizures that would have been considered to have violated the accused's Fourth Amendment rights had the searches been conducted by the national government.[20] By the 1960s, however, the Supreme Court had decided that most of the Bill of Rights applied to the states via the Fourteenth Amendment, including nearly all the provisions of the Fourth, Fifth, Sixth, and Eighth Amendments, which address the rights of the accused.

As a result of the Supreme Court's incorporation of the Bill of Rights into the Fourteenth Amendment, much more of a national set of policies is now in place in the criminal justice field. Most Americans are generally familiar with the exclusionary rule, which prohibits the use of illegally obtained evidence in a criminal trial,[21] and the *Miranda* warnings that police are required to provide criminal suspects before interrogating them.[22] Many Americans dislike the constraints that the courts have placed on the police under the Bill of Rights, but, at the same time, most of us take comfort in the fact that we do not live in a police state. When pressed, most Americans express support, at least in the abstract, for the idea of subjecting state criminal justice policies to the scrutiny of the federal courts.

Judicial Federalism

You should not assume the relationship between the federal courts and the states consists entirely of the federal courts trying to make the states live up to their obligations to protect civil rights and liberties.[23] In recent years, as the federal courts have become more conservative as a result of judicial appointments by Republican presidents, a number of state courts have gone beyond federal judicial requirements in protecting the civil rights and liberties of their citizens. This statement is especially true with respect to the rights of persons accused of crimes. For example, what constitutes a reasonable search and seizure under the federal constitution may not qualify as reasonable under the relevant provisions of the New Jersey Constitution. You must not forget that states may provide more, but not less, protection to their citizens than is required by the U.S. Constitution.

3-4d Economic Regulation: A Historic Conflict in Federalism

In the late nineteenth century, the federal government began to assert its power to regulate interstate commerce, focusing first on railroads and manufacturing. The government's major concern was the emergence of large corporations that often combined to form monopolies, thus stifling competition and driving up rates and prices. Although some states had attempted to regulate railroad rates, state governments were generally incapable of dealing with large corporations with activities in many states. In 1886, the Supreme Court further hampered state regulatory efforts by ruling that an Illinois railroad regulation intruded on the commerce power of the national government.[24] While conservatives argued for a *laissez-faire* approach to the economy in general, increasing political pressure was brought to bear on the national government to act to stem the power of the large corporations.

In 1887, Congress adopted the Interstate Commerce Act, which created the Interstate Commerce Commission (ICC), the first permanent federal regulatory agency.[25] Though initially limited in its powers, the ICC marked the beginning of a trend toward the creation of national bureaucratic agencies to regulate facets of the economy. It also signaled the beginning of a new era of federal involvement in economic policy making, including areas traditionally regarded as state functions.

The Supreme Court and Federal Regulation of the Economy

As noted in Chapter 2, "The Development of American Constitutional Democracy," the Supreme Court of the late nineteenth and early twentieth centuries resisted the trend toward federal involvement in economic policy. In one leading case, the Court struck down a federal law which prohibited the interstate shipment of goods manufactured by companies that used child labor beyond federal guidelines.[26] According to the Court, the federal law had invaded an area of policy reserved to the states under the Tenth Amendment. The Court was exercising one of its major roles: umpire of the federal system.

The Supreme Court continued to resist federal efforts to regulate the economy until the late 1930s. From the 1940s until the 1970s, the Court was dominated by liberal judges appointed by Democratic presidents. These judges brushed aside the Tenth Amendment and gave the federal government broad power to regulate commerce. Writing for the Court in 1941, Justice Harlan Fiske Stone observed that the Tenth Amendment "states but a truism that all is retained [by the states] which has not been surrendered [to the federal government]."[27] In recent years, however, a more conservative Supreme Court has moved to devolve some power to the states,[28] although the broad regulatory power of the federal government in the economic realm remains well established.

3-4e States, Cities, and the Federal Government: The Evolving Federal Relationship

The Constitution was written in an age when America was a country of farms and small towns whose inhabitants viewed cities with some suspicion, if not hostility. City residents were certainly in the minority. The first census showed that only one in twenty Americans lived in urban areas of more than twenty-five hundred persons. The rest were little concerned with the services that city residents might want—fire and police protection, sanitary sewers, well-lighted streets, and public parks, for example.

By the early nineteenth century, urbanization had begun in earnest, with New York, Philadelphia, and Boston gradually becoming major urban centers. By 1820, nine cities had populations of more than one hundred thousand. The main growth in American cities took place in the late nineteenth and early twentieth centuries, however, when millions of immigrants flocked to American cities to work in factories. These people brought with them tremendous needs for governmental services, and they looked to the cities for help. Later, the urban migration included millions of blacks fleeing the rural South in search of decent jobs and an opportunity to live without the shackles of segregation. Naturally, they also looked to the cities for help.

Washington and the Cities

The Constitution does not mention cities. It did not have to, for cities were, and are, creatures of the states. States determine the means by which cities are created, their structure, the taxes they can collect, and the ways in which their boundaries can be enlarged. For most of our history, cities' fates were determined solely by the state legislatures. Before the 1930s, the relationship between the national government and the cities was limited to occasional, scattered public works projects. During the 1930s, the tremendous social and economic problems of the Great Depression overwhelmed the cities, and the states were not in a position to provide much help. As part of President Franklin D. Roosevelt's New Deal, the federal government established a number of programs to help urban residents because no other level of government was willing or able to meet their needs. Characterized by Roosevelt as "enlightened centralism," the New Deal programs provided work for urban residents, such as constructing public buildings, parks, and other facilities. These programs required the cooperation of the city governments, because much of the federal funding was distributed through the local political structures.

Whereas the political culture of the nineteenth century would not have supported the idea of massive, direct federal aid to, and involvement in, the nation's cities, by the mid-twentieth century the political culture had changed markedly. People had become accustomed to the idea of looking first to Uncle Sam for solutions to social and economic problems. The political culture had become hospitable to the new federal role in distributing aid directly to the cities.[29] That support has evolved into an expectation and, consequently, federal aid to the cities is now institutionalized.

THE FEDERALISM OF THE 1960S

The programs of the New Deal were responses to the crisis of the Great Depression. By the early 1960s, the United States faced another set of urban problems. Affluent and middle-class city residents were moving in great numbers to the suburbs. This migration, which was greatly aided by federal mortgage and tax policies, left the cities with tremendous social and economic problems that they seemed unable to solve. As before, many looked beyond the states to the federal government for assistance. To complicate the situation, race became a major factor. As whites fled to the suburbs, many larger cities were increasingly inhabited by African Americans and other minorities. Issues thus became framed in racial as well as economic terms.

The political culture of the 1960s was quite different from that of the 1930s. The new generation was impatient with government officials, who seemed unable or unwilling to respond to increasing urban decay. Many believed poverty could be fought only by empowering the poor—that is, letting them play a major role in deciding how to spend federal antipoverty dollars. This feeling was somewhat understandable, considering the outcome of certain federal programs of the era. For instance, beginning with the Housing Act of 1949, Washington had spent a great deal of money on urban renewal projects that seemed to do little more than reduce available housing for the poor while benefiting developers and others in the local business community.

Federal dollars had been traditionally provided as **grants-in-aid**, in which federal money is allocated to a particular local project, usually after an application and review process. Before the 1960s, state and local governments could obtain federal grants without any meaningful involvement by those whom the grants were designed to benefit. The new grant-in-aid programs of the 1960s mandated the involvement of the poor in the application process as well as in deciding how the money would be spent after a grant was obtained. Web supplement 3-6 invites you to look at comparative state highway spending to see how dependent on federal money most state roadways are.

ONLINE 3.5 *Highway Spending by State*
http://www.commonwealthfoundation.org/doclib/20100623_highwayspendingbystate2008.pdf

This new approach was embodied in a series of ambitious programs founded under the general umbrella of the "war on poverty," which President Lyndon Johnson was able to push through Congress in 1964 and 1965. The most controversial program was known as Model Cities.[30] Under this program, poor residents could elect representatives to decide how federal poverty funds could be spent. In many cases, this procedure bypassed city officials and gave them no say in how the money was spent. Not surprisingly, when it was discovered that the funds were sometimes spent in a questionable manner, such as a Chicago street gang that used money obtained through the program, Model Cities came under political fire.

The Nixon Retreat

One of President Nixon's top priorities was to dismantle many of the social programs of the Johnson years. The Nixon administration sought to strengthen the state role along with that of elected officials by replacing many grants-in-aid with a new program, **general revenue sharing**, that went into effect in 1972. Revenue sharing provided states and cities with money that could be spent as elected officials saw fit.

This trend continued with the enactment of the Housing and Community Development Act of 1974, which replaced many **categorical grant** programs with **block grants**. Block grants are provided to state and local governments to be spent in specified general areas, such as housing or law enforcement; these grants do not carry the restrictions and requirements of categorical grants. The Nixon administration did not invent block grants, which had been in use for many years, but it did revitalize the concept, which was consistent with the administration's philosophy of shifting decision making from the national bureaucracy to state and local governments.

Under the Nixon administration, the relationship between the national government and the cities changed dramatically. Attempts at actively organizing the poor to act as spokespersons on their own behalf disappeared as federal money was channeled through existing power structures. Local elected officials were given more discretion than ever in deciding where the money would be spent. Of course, this policy also gave less discretion to bureaucrats in Washington. Nixon's policies marked an important change in the federal system. They shifted power away from both the urban poor and the decision makers at the national level and toward state and local elected officials. The Nixon years reflected a growing suspicion in American political culture about the national government's role in dealing with the cities. Although Jimmy Carter was a Democrat, his "outsider" presidency did nothing to change this antipathy toward Washington.

Coercive and Regulatory Federalism

Ironically, during Nixon's administration the federal government began to much more aggressively use its regulatory power to force the states into line. As the federal government had expanded its authority using spending power and legislation in the 1960s, Washington now supervised many duties of the states. The federal government is under no obligation to provide grant money to all states, so Congress began attaching preconditions to the eligibility of federal grants. For instance, when the national government wanted to establish a countrywide drinking age of 21, the only justification possible was using grants-in-aid for highways. Since states had control of their own highway policies, the federal government could not step into that area. However, more than 80 percent of all money spent on roads in the states was provided by the federal government at that time. So the National Minimum Drinking Age Law of 1984 simply made having a 21-year-old drinking age as a precondition for eligibility to that large pool of highway money. The aggressive regulations, followed fifteen years later by requirements for .08 blood alcohol levels as a national standard for drunk driving prosecutions as a precondition for highway fund eligibility, sparked a revolt against the federal government's fiscal powers and reach by conservatives.

The Reagan–Bush Years and Beyond: From New Federalism to Devolution

The election of Ronald Reagan in 1980 had major consequences for the federal arrangement. Over the years, the cities had become quite dependent on federal aid. In fact, some communities relied on the federal government for the major part of their budget. In an early televised address to the nation, President Reagan stressed his commitment to reducing the federal government's size while recognizing and increasing the role of the states. However, Reagan's main contribution to the federal arrangement was the **cutback**. Whereas Nixon had given the states more discretion in how they spent the money they received from the national government, Reagan sought to reduce this funding altogether.

The idea behind the Reagan approach was simple: If the states and cities want programs, they should pay for them. The federal government would do its part by eliminating costly rules and regulations—cutting the authority of federal bureaucrats. Some states moved to aid their cities in new and creative ways, but the ability of state governments to undertake major initiatives is limited. Three factors undercut their ability to provide much aid to the cities:

1. *Politics.* Despite legislative reapportionment, the states have not been particularly hospitable to the interests of the cities. Quite often, urban delegations in the state legislatures find themselves outvoted by coalitions of rural and suburban representatives.
2. *Money.* The states raise money through a variety of means, but, unfortunately, none can really compete with the federal income tax. The revenue from many types of taxes and fees does not increase as fast as the states' costs for basic programs. Moreover, the states must balance their

budgets, leaving little room for new programs, especially in an age of fiscal austerity. Finally, state revenues are dependent on the national economy. In bad times, states find themselves in deep trouble.

3. *Additional responsibilities.* During the 1970s, the federal courts began to hold the states responsible for the constitutional rights of prisoners in state facilities. In some cases, the courts even took over a state's correctional system until the state prison facilities met minimum standards. This situation put tremendous pressure on state budgets. In addition, the federal government imposed greater funding burdens on the states for health care. The states have the primary responsibility for funding Medicaid, which provides medical care to low-income residents. With medical costs escalating rapidly throughout the 1980s, states' Medicaid obligations doubled and sometimes tripled in just a few years.

Clearly, the Reagan revolution removed some of the regulatory burden from state and local governments. This freedom from federal oversight brought new responsibilities, however. States often found themselves in the front lines of defense against an onslaught of new social and economic problems without the ability to confront them effectively. To some degree, that was exactly what the Reagan revolution was about—reducing reliance on government, especially the federal government, to solve problems that many thought could be better handled through private action.

In the early 1990s, states and cities became increasingly vocal in objecting to a new phenomenon: unfunded mandates. **Unfunded mandates** are programs or policies that the federal government requires but does not fund. For instance, the federal Clean Water Act increased the water quality standards for rivers and streams in urban areas. The costs of meeting the increased standards were quite high, and virtually all had to be borne by city governments. Congress found this approach quite appealing, however, because it could appear to be responsive to national policy concerns by passing legislation while passing the cost on to other levels of government. For example, unfunded federal mandates cost Tennessee cities more than $164 million in 1993 alone.[31] A study of 134 cities conducted by the U.S. Conference of Mayors in 1993 found that federal mandates consumed, on average, nearly 12 percent of local budgets.[32] Los Angeles County, California led the nation in federally mandated spending, laying out roughly $1 billion in 1993.[33]

Responding to widespread concern about unfunded mandates, Congress passed the Unfunded Mandates Reform Act (UMRA) in 1995. This legislation was designed to make it difficult for the federal government to make state and local governments pay for programs that they did not enact or even necessarily approve. Under the act, the Congressional Budget Office (CBO) is required to estimate the costs for any bill that would have an impact of $50 million on state and local governments. Any bill must provide funding to cover the cost of any new mandated spending in states and cities. However, the act did not apply to mandates existing at the time of its passage, and many conservatives complained that the act "lacked teeth." Web supplement section 3-7 reviews unfunded mandates by the Congressional Budget Office.

ONLINE 3.6 *Unfunded Mandates*

The elimination of unfunded mandates was part of the Contract with America that helped the Republicans to gain control of Congress in 1994. One political buzzword of this period was **devolution**, the idea that federal power should be devolved to the state and local governments. The idea took hold not only in Congress, but within the Supreme Court's conservative majority in the mid-1990s. The transfer of power and responsibility from the federal government to the states took place to some extent in the 1990s, but no one really expected a fundamental change in the character of modern federalism. And if some people did, they were disappointed. Despite some shifting of power and responsibility, the national government retains its dominant position in the political system, and it is difficult to imagine that it could ever be otherwise.

3-5 THE COMPLEX CHARACTER OF CONTEMPORARY FEDERALISM

The direct federal–city linkage is indicative of the complex nature of contemporary American federalism and the difficulty of dividing powers and responsibilities cleanly. The classical approach, called **dual federalism**, has never really characterized the American system. A more accurate description might be called **cooperative federalism**, with state and federal governments working together to deal with the problems of a growing and increasingly urban society. But some commentators point out that the cooperation has sometimes been less than abundant.

3-5a AREAS OF FEDERAL–STATE COOPERATION

Political scientist Morton Grodzins coined the term **marble cake federalism** to describe the mix of federal and state activities throughout the policy-making process.[34] This metaphor does fit much of the way the federal system works. In virtually any area of American public life, from roads to health care to education to law enforcement, the federal and state governments work side by side, if not always in perfect harmony. Of course, it is important to recognize that in most instances, the national government is the dominant partner, and when conflicts arise, the national government usually prevails.

Protecting the Environment

Environmental protection is an area of public policy that nicely demonstrates the cooperative federal–state approach. Consider, for example, the Clean Air Act and the Clean Water Act. These federal statutes, enacted in the 1970s, represent the main thrust of the national effort to control air and water pollution. These acts are enforced primarily by the Environmental Protection Agency (EPA), a major federal regulatory agency, but states are given enforcement powers under these acts as well. The EPA works, in turn, with state agencies to develop implementation and enforcement plans. In 1995, responding to criticisms that their relationship was not always harmonious or productive, the EPA and state officials agreed to establish the National Environmental Performance Partnership System (NEPPS). Consistent with prevailing attitudes about federalism in the mid-1990s, the new system sought to give states greater flexibility in the implementation of national environmental policies. It also sought to allow each state to focus its energies on the environmental problems that most affected it. Under the new system, the EPA and each state enter into an agreement that sets forth priorities, goals, strategies, and responsibilities. At least on paper, NEPPS is an excellent example of cooperative federalism.

Law Enforcement

Usually, Washington plays a significant role in two areas: funding and coordination. Law enforcement provides a good example of both. For instance, because bank robbery violates both state and federal law, both the local police and the FBI become immediately involved. For all serious crimes, the federal authorities enter investigations when the suspect flees from one state to another to avoid prosecution.

In addition, Congress has established programs that provide funding (usually grants-in-aid) to state and local police departments. The funds often go toward the purchase of new computer systems or equipment. Under President Clinton's crime bill, which became law in September 1994, the federal government transferred money to cities to allow them to hire additional law enforcement personnel. State and local police work very closely with the federal databases to identify and track suspects. State and federal authorities often cooperate in conducting investigations and making arrests, especially where interstate criminal activity is involved.

The "war on drugs" provides many examples of cooperation among federal, state, and local agencies. Consider, for example, the marijuana-eradication programs that are underway in many states. These efforts are funded by the National Office of Drug Policy but are organized on a state-by-state basis. In each state, a task force under the leadership of the governor organizes an effort involving state and local law enforcement agencies, the federal Drug Enforcement Administration (DEA), and even the state's national guard. National Guard helicopters and other military equipment are used to locate marijuana patches and even indoor "grows." Searches, seizures, and arrests are then made by the law enforcement agencies involved. Depending on various factors, the persons arrested are prosecuted for drug offenses in federal or state courts.

Because federal and state laws overlap in regard to many crimes (the distribution of illicit drugs, for example), an accused criminal may be subject to prosecution in either state or federal court. In some instances, defendants are subject to prosecution in both state and federal courts. This was the case in 1992, when four Los Angeles police officers accused of using excessive force in the arrest of motorist Rodney King were prosecuted by both the state of California and the federal government. The police officers were acquitted in the state case, but two of them were convicted in a subsequent federal trial.

In the 2000 presidential election campaign, one issue of disagreement was whether the federal government should enact legislation against "hate crimes." A prominent example of a hate crime is the horrible incident that took place in Jasper, Texas, in 1999, when a black man, James Byrd, Jr., was dragged to his death behind a pickup truck. In fact, this incident was the topic of discussion in the campaign and the subject of a controversial television campaign ad. Candidate Al Gore cited the Byrd incident as an example of why federal legislation is needed. George W. Bush pointed out that the men responsible for the crime had been convicted of murder and punished severely under Texas law. In Bush's view, federal hate crimes legislation was unnecessary. But proponents of federal law claimed that state and local authorities were not always willing to enforce existing state hate crimes laws.

The general trend in recent decades has been for Congress to create new federal offenses to supplement the state criminal codes. An excellent example is the area of drug offenses, in which there are now parallel prohibitions at the national and state levels. Although some critics object to the nationalization of the criminal law, state and local officials often appreciate the opportunity to enlist the support of federal law enforcement officials. And state and local prosecutors often turn drug cases over to federal prosecutors, because "the feds" often have greater resources and offenders are likely to be sentenced to longer prison terms under the very punitive federal drug laws.

EDUCATION

Traditionally, education was a matter of state and local concern. Beginning in the 1960s, however, the federal government became more involved in this area. Congress provided federal grants to states and local communities, but used this support to leverage control over various aspects of school administration. In the 2000 presidential election, education became a major topic of discussion, with both candidates pledging to improve a troubled educational system, albeit by very different means. Among other things, candidate George W. Bush promised to return control of schools to the local level, a theme that has played well in recent decades, especially among conservatives.

However, the No Child Left Behind Act of 2001,[35] which President Bush trumpeted as one of his major domestic policy successes, brought greater federal involvement in the field of education, much to the chagrin of conservatives.[36] It must be noted, though, that the new federal law made provisions for local control and flexible implementation, unlike many of the federal education policies of previous decades.

Welfare

Historically, the federal government had little to do with matters of social welfare. That changed in the wake of the Great Depression, as President Franklin Roosevelt promised the American people a "New Deal." Part of the New Deal was the federal government assumption of responsibility for ensuring social welfare. This assumption grew dramatically in the 1960s as part of President Lyndon Johnson's Great Society program. The idea was to use the forces of government, primarily the federal government, to overcome poverty. Aid to Families with Dependent Children (AFDC) and other federal programs were funded primarily by the federal government, but the states were given primary administrative responsibility. Of course, with federal funding came federal control, which by the 1990s had become quite unpopular.

In 1996, the Republican-controlled Congress adopted, and President Clinton signed into law, the Personal Responsibility and Work Opportunity Reconciliation Act. The act dramatically changed the nation's welfare system. The old AFDC was replaced by a new program, Temporary Assistance for Needy Families (TANF). As the name of the program suggests, welfare assistance was made temporary, rather than a lifelong entitlement. The new program also emphasized job training to help move recipients off the welfare rolls and into gainful employment. Finally, welfare reform eliminated many of the federal controls and let states determine criteria for eligibility for welfare.

Disaster Response and Relief

When Hurricane Andrew struck Florida and Louisiana in August 1992, state and local governments shouldered the principal burden of responding to the disaster. However, state and local officials made clear that they expected that Washington would pay for most of the clean-up expenses. On September 17, 1992, their expectations were fulfilled as Congress appropriated, at President George H.W. Bush's request, more than $10 billion to pay for the damage wrought by the hurricanes and help people restore their homes and businesses. The same thing happened in 2004 as Florida was plagued by a series of devastating hurricanes. People expected federal aid to flow to state and local governments to assist in the massive clean-up and restoration efforts and to buttress social services overextended by the social effects of the storms. Because 2004 was a presidential election year, and because Florida was expected to be a "battleground state," President George W. Bush wasted no time in coming to Florida to assure residents and civic leaders that federal assistance would be forthcoming.

Hurricane Katrina, which flooded New Orleans and devastated much of the Gulf Cost in 2005, overwhelmed the capacities of state and local governments. Given the magnitude of the disaster, officials and ordinary citizens looked to the federal government to respond. Unfortunately, the federal government's response was slow, uncoordinated, and ineffective. Of course, there were failures at the local and state levels as well, but media and public attention focused on the federal response, particularly that of President Bush and the Federal Emergency Management Agency (FEMA). The Katrina debacle negatively affected not only President Bush's approval rating, but the public's perception of the federal government.

3-5b Fiscal Federalism

The preceding discussion of areas of federal–state cooperation highlights not only the cooperative relationship between the federal government and the states in certain programmatic areas but also the fiscal dependence of the states on Washington. As we have pointed out, states and cities have become dependent on federal dollars in a wide variety of areas, a dependency only partially reduced by the Reagan revolution of the 1980s and the devolution of the 1990s. But with funding comes control. Congress routinely attaches conditions to this aid. The national minimum drinking age law and .08 legal limit for intoxication mandates are perfect examples of the aggressive fiscal federalism practiced by Washington.

This nationalization of policy making reflects the increasing sense that our problems are of national scope and hence need national attention. Congress and the president often find themselves under some pressure to act, regardless of federal theory. The Los Angeles riots of 1992, for example, were regarded not just as reactions to local concerns, but as symptoms of national urban problems. Often, the quickest way to act is to require the states to take action, especially if additional laws are considered necessary. States and cities receive so much federal aid in so many areas that requiring state action as a condition of receiving federal funds is certainly an appealing strategy.

The dominance of federal dollars has become so complete that it has led to the use of the term **fiscal federalism** to describe the federal relationship based on money. In many ways, this term reflects the evolution of the American federal system. The emphasis on money is possible because the country's collective attention has been diverted from program differences rooted in state and regional variations. To a great degree, the United States has succeeded in developing a national political culture.

Because the actions of the federal government changed the segregationist culture of the Deep South, regional and state differences in public policy have faded. Although some variation among the states persists, states in the future are unlikely to take actions designed to preserve themselves as distinct cultural entities.

3-6 ASSESSING AMERICAN FEDERALISM

Clearly, the character of American federalism has changed dramatically since the Constitution was written in 1787. Yet the basic structure and fundamental principle of dual sovereignty remain reasonably intact. The national government cannot abolish the states, although the federal courts can redraw state legislative districts and even impose significant changes on local government structures. In most areas, the national government cannot dictate policy to the states, but it can, and does, coerce them to participate in national programs or abide by national policies. Still, the states remain more or less autonomous political entities that have enormous influence over the day-to-day lives of their citizens. Indeed, in some areas, such as education, health care, and the environment, some states have assumed leadership roles, adopting innovations that have served as models for other states (and even the federal government).

3-6a THE ADVANTAGES OF THE FEDERAL SYSTEM

Despite enormous changes over the past two centuries, American federalism retains the basic advantages and disadvantages that are inherent in the federal arrangement. On the positive side, federalism allows government to be closer to the people. Despite the concentration of power in Washington over the past century, the federal system continues to provide a degree of decentralization. Imagine how much more concentrated power would be if the federal structure were abolished in favor of a unitary system! For someone living on Maui, in the Hawaiian Islands, traveling to Honolulu to petition the state government for a "redress of grievances" is more convenient (and considerably less expensive) than to make the several-thousand-mile journey to Washington, D.C. Federalism is well suited to a country that spans a continent (and beyond).

Federalism also allows policies to be tailored somewhat to local and regional differences. For example, the state of Nevada, reflecting the traditional libertarian culture of the frontier, is much more permissive than most states with respect to the "vices" of prostitution and gambling. Similarly, Wyoming, which retains much of the political culture of the Old West, is much more permissive about the possession and use of firearms than is New York, for example. Not only does federalism allow policies to reflect the different tastes and values that are found among the states, but it also allows the states to innovate and experiment with new policies and programs. In this sense, states can be viewed as "policy laboratories" where new ideas can be tested without committing the entire nation to a policy that may turn out to be ineffectual or counterproductive.

In the wake of the terrorist attacks of September 11, 2001, many people realized that federalism has another advantage. Suppose that Washington, D.C. were to be destroyed or contaminated by a nuclear or biological attack. It is somewhat comforting to realize that even if the national government were paralyzed, state and local governments would still be able maintain order and provide essential services.

What Americans Think about
Federal, State, and Local Government

The following data, taken from a Gallup survey conducted in September 2007, suggest that Americans have greater confidence in their state and local governments than they do in the federal government.

	GREAT DEAL	FAIR AMOUNT	NOT VERY MUCH	NONE AT ALL	NO OPINION
How much trust and confidence do you have in our federal government in Washington when it comes to handling international problems—a great deal, a fair amount, not very much, or none at all?	8%	43%	34%	13%	1%
How much trust and confidence do you have in our federal government in Washington when it comes to handling domestic problems—a great deal, a fair amount, not very much, or none at all?	6%	41%	38%	14%	1%
How much trust and confidence do you have in the government of the state where you live when it comes to handling state problems—a great deal, a fair amount, not very much, or none at all?	18%	49%	23%	9%	1%
And how much trust and confidence do you have in the local governments in the area where you live when it comes to handling local problems—a great deal, a fair amount, not very much, or none at all?	22%	47%	19%	10%	2%

Source: Adapted from Jeffrey M. Jones, "Low Trust in Federal Government Rivals Watergate-Era Levels," The Gallup Organization, September 26, 2007. Online at http://www.gallup.com/poll/28795/Low-Trust-Federal-Government-Rivals-Watergate-Era-Levels.aspx

3-6b The Disadvantages of Federalism

On the debit side of the ledger, federalism necessarily entails inefficiency in the implementation of national policies and the solution of national problems. States may be slow to act, and when they do, they may act in a fashion that contradicts what other states or the national government is doing.

Decentralization entails the diffusion of power, which is generally regarded as a good thing, but it also increases the opportunity for corruption. Contrary to commonly held stereotypes, the national government tends to be the least corrupt level of government because it conducts its business under the watchful eye of the mass media. State and local governments typically are subject to less intense media scrutiny. To be fair, though, state and local governments are probably now less corrupt than they were in the days of the powerful political machines and bosses. Because states and local communities have primary governmental responsibility for the public welfare, the federal system permits what is sometimes an alarming variation in the degree of state and local support for education and social services. Traditionally, this variation extended also to civil rights and liberties, but this is less true now because of federal judicial oversight.

The inconsistencies of laws among the states and between the states and the federal government have made the legal system extremely complex. The complexity is apparent not only in the criminal law but also in rules of court procedure and jurisdiction, business law, family law, wills, estates, trusts, insurance, real property, licensure, environmental regulations, and zoning—the list goes on and on. Unquestionably, federalism has been a boon to lawyers. (Those planning to go to law school may see this as an advantage rather than a disadvantage of federalism!)

Finally, but not least significantly, federalism renders the American political system considerably less intelligible to the average citizen. In a democracy, which puts a premium on citizens paying attention to and participating in their government, federalism adds much complexity. The average citizen may have difficulty figuring out what agency at which level of government is responsible for acting or failing to act in a certain fashion. On balance, though, one must conclude that American federalism has worked reasonably well. There now appears to be no compelling justification for its abolition, or, for that matter, no real prospect for its demise.

3-7 Conclusion: Federalism and Political Culture

Like all societies, the United States has troubling divisions among its people: racial, ethnic, social, and economic. These divisions do not correspond now to states or regions. America has become a unified nation. Fostering this unity took a civil war, a monumental depression, two world wars, and a decades-long cold war, but it was finally achieved. Not only have crises brought the nation together, but advances in communications and transportation systems have also helped to foster identification with the national community. Today, a person may be born in one state, grow up in another, go to college in a third, move to a fourth to start a career, and finally move to a fifth state to enjoy retirement. This high degree of mobility erodes loyalties to states. In their place, one develops a loyalty to the nation. Whereas people living in the United States in 1787 thought of themselves primarily as Virginians or Marylanders or North Carolinians, people living in this country today think of themselves first and foremost as Americans. The development of the national identity has helped hold the system together during times of crisis; it also explains the emergence of the nation-centered model of federalism.

Since the Constitution was adopted, power in the American federal system has certainly tilted toward the national government. Nevertheless, the states have retained their political vitality and still play a significant role in the day-to-day lives of their citizens. Despite the nationalization of the American political culture, the states still approach their problems in a variety of ways. However, the variation is not of such magnitude or of such emotional import as to threaten the existence of the United States as a unified nation. The states still have vital roles in virtually every area of American public life. It remains as true today as when the Constitution was adopted: To understand the American political system, from the functioning of the criminal justice system to the conduct of elections to the construction and maintenance of highways, you must understand the unique nature of American federalism.

QUESTIONS FOR THOUGHT AND DISCUSSION

1. Why did the Framers of the Constitution opt for a federal system rather than a unitary one?

2. How has the evolution of the federal system affected the civil rights and liberties of American citizens?

3. How does the federal government get the states to adopt policies they might otherwise not adopt?

4. Do Americans generally believe that the federal government has too much power, not enough power, or about the right amount of power?

5. In today's world, do the advantages of federalism outweigh the disadvantages?

ENDNOTES

1 Samuel H. Beer, "Federalism, Nationalism, and Democracy in America," *American Political Science Review*, vol. 72, 1978, p. 11.

2 Lawrence J, O'Toole, "American Intergovernmental Relations: An Overview." In Lawrence J. O'Toole, ed., *American Intergovernmental Relations*, 3rd ed. (Washington, D.C.: CQ Press, 2000), p. 5.

3 *McCulloch v. Maryland*, 17 U.S. 316 (1819).

4 *Gibbons v. Ogden*, 22 U.S. (9 Wheat.) 1 (1824).

5 *Scott v. Sandford*, 60 U.S. (19 Howard) 393 (1857).

6 *Texas v. White*, 74 U.S. (7 Wall.) 700 (1869).

7 See, for example, the Civil Rights Cases, 109 U.S. 3 (1883) and *Plessy v. Ferguson*, 163 U.S. 537 (1896).

8 The seminal case in this regard was *Brown v. Board of Education*, 437 U.S. 483 (1954), which is discussed at length in Chapter 5, "Civil Rights and the Struggle for Equality."

9 *South Carolina v. Katzenbach*, 383 U.S. 301 (1965).

10 *City of Mobile v. Bolden*, 446 U.S. 55 (1980).

11 *Shaw v. Reno*, 517 U.S. 899 (1995).

12 *Hunt v. Cromartie*, 532 U.S. 204 (2001).

13 *Chicago, Burlington and Quincy R.R. Co. v. City of Chicago*, 166 U.S. 226 (1897).

14 *Gitlow v. New York*, 268 U.S. 652 (1925).

15 *Cantwell v. Connecticut*, 310 U.S. 296 (1940).

16 *Everson v. Board of Education*, 330 U.S. 1 (1947).

17 The Eleventh Amendment, which would seem to prevent such challenges, was effectively circumvented by permitting individuals to sue state officials, rather than the states as sovereign entities.

18 See, for example, *Powell v. Alabama*, 287 U.S. 45 (1932).

19 See, for example, *Palko v. Connecticut*, 302 U.S. 319 (1937).

20 See *Wolf v. Colorado*, 338 U.S. 25 (1949).

21 See *Mapp v. Ohio*, 367 U.S. 643 (1961).

22 See *Miranda v. Arizona*, 384 U.S. 436 (1967).

23 William J. Brennan, "Guardians of Our Liberties—State Courts No Less Than Federal." In *Views from the Bench: The Judiciary and Constitutional Politics*, eds. David M. O'Brien and Mark Cannon (Chatham, NJ: Chatham House, 1985).

24 *Wabash, St. Louis, and Pacific Railway Co. v. Illinois*, 118 U.S. 557 (1886).

25 Actually, the agency was abolished in 1995 after its regulatory functions were curtailed or transferred to other agencies.

26 *Hammer v. Dagenhart*, 247 U.S. 251 (1981).

27 *United States v. Darby*, 312 U.S. 100, 124 (1941).

28 See, for example, *United States v. Lopez*, 514 U.S. 549 (1995); *Seminole Tribe v. Florida*, 517 U.S. 44 (1996); *Printz v. United States*, 521 U.S. 898 (1997).

29 Christopher Hamilton and Donald Wells, *Federalism, Power, and Political Economy* (Englewood Cliffs, NJ: Prentice-Hall, 1990), p. 172.

30 The official name of the law was the Community and Demonstration Cities Act.

31 Pam Park, "Sasser to File Bill Easing Effect of Mandates," *Knoxville News-Sentinel*, October 27, 1993, p. A-5.

32 Marty Bauman, “Federal Mandates,” *USA Today*, November 16, 1993, p. 15A.

33 Ibid.

34 Morton Grodzins, “The Federal System.” In *The American Assembly: Goals for Americans* (Englewood Cliffs, NJ: Prentice-Hall, 1960), p. 250. Grodzins's “marble cake” metaphor is meant to contrast with the “layer cake” nature of classical federalism.

35 For official information on the law and the program it established, go to http://www.ed.gov/nclb/landing.jhtml.

36 See, for example, George F. Will, “Reelect Bush, Faults and All,” *Washington Post*, October 31, 2004, p. B07.

Chapter 4

Civil Liberties and Individual Freedom

OUTLINE

Key Terms 112

Expected Learning Outcomes 112

4-1 Individual Rights in a Democratic Society 112

- **4-1a** Where Do Rights Come From? 113
- **4-1b** Substantive and Procedural Rights 115

4-2 Rights Protected by the Original Constitution 116

- **4-2a** Habeas Corpus 116
- **4-2b** Bills of Attainder and Ex Post Facto Laws 117

4-3 The Bill of Rights 118

- **4-3a** Nationalization of the Bill of Rights 119

4-4 Protection of Private Property 121

4-5 First Amendment Freedoms of Expression, Assembly, and Association 121

- **4-5a** The Scope of Protected Expression 122
- **4-5b** The Prohibition against Censorship 124
- **4-5c** The Clear and Present Danger Doctrine 125
- **4-5d** Fighting Words and Profanity 125
- **4-5e** Obscenity and Pornography 126
- **4-5f** Defamation 127
- **4-5g** The First Amendment and Electronic Media 128
- **4-5h** Freedom of Assembly 129
- **4-5i** Freedom of Association 129

4-6 Freedom of Religion 130

- **4-6a** Separation of Church and State 130
- **4-6b** Religion, Government, and Ideology 131
- **4-6c** The Free Exercise of Religion 132

4-7 The Right to Keep and Bear Arms 133

4-8 Rights of Persons Accused of Crimes 134

- **4-8a** Freedom from Unreasonable Searches and Seizures 135
- **4-8b** Protections of the Fifth Amendment 136
- **4-8c** Sixth Amendment Rights 136
- **4-8d** Freedom from Cruel and Unusual Punishments 137

4-9 The Right of Privacy 138
  4-9a Reproductive Freedom 139
  4-9b Privacy and Gay Rights 140
  4-9c The Right to Die 142
4-10 Conclusion: Civil Liberties—A Question of Balance 143
  Questions for Thought and Discussion 145
  Endnotes 146

KEY TERMS

actual malice
bifurcated trial
civil liberties
civil rights
clear and present danger doctrine
compulsory self-incrimination
cruel and unusual punishments
double jeopardy
exclusionary rule
expressive conduct
fighting words
freedom of association
grand jury
gun control
imminent lawless action
indictment
Miller test
probable cause
public defender
reasonable time, place, and manner regulations
right of privacy
right to keep and bear arms
search warrant
selective incorporation
subpoena
symbolic speech

EXPECTED LEARNING OUTCOMES

After reading this chapter and completing the supplemental online materials, students will:

- Compare natural and civil rights
- Identify sources of civil liberties in the U.S. Constitution
- Analyze the power of governments to restrict protected liberties in the U.S. today
- Contrast restrictions on political rights and criminal trial rights
- Apply Supreme Court decision-making processes to civil liberties controversies

4-1 INDIVIDUAL RIGHTS IN A DEMOCRATIC SOCIETY

How private is your private life? Where does the government's right to involve itself in your daily life start, and where does it end? Can the government read your private e-mails? Text messages? The things we share publicly on social media are fair game, of course. But what about the things we only say to each other privately? What freedom do you have to keep your words, actions, and thoughts private in an interconnected and constantly online world? Today the amount of information we share that can be recorded and possibly used against us is significant. The government has access to massive databases, larger than anything imaginable when the Bill of Rights was written. Communication technology may have undermined the right to privacy we hold dear in this country.

ONLINE 4.1

Privacy Rights Online at the Electronic Frontier Foundation **https://www.eff.org/**

In every democratic government, individuals possess certain basic rights. Although the catalog of individual rights under American democracy is extensive, it can be summarized along two underlying dimensions: the right to be free from both unreasonable interference in one's beliefs, associations, and activities and the right to equal treatment by the government and society. The former defines the realm of civil liberties, the subject of this chapter. The latter, which encapsulates the subject of civil rights, is dealt with in Chapter 5, "Civil Rights and the Struggle for Equality." In a nutshell, then, **civil liberties** deal with freedom from government; **civil rights** involve equality where government actively protects them. These basic values—freedom and equality—are fundamental in not only American politics but also all democratic societies. Of course, considerable disagreement exists over the specific definition and application of these values. Moreover, because of their nature, civil liberties and civil rights issues put a great strain on the political system.

Nothing strains the majority's support for civil liberties more than does a feeling of vulnerability, especially from enemies living within the society. In the wake of the terrorist attacks on America on September 11, 2001, government at all levels took stronger measures to protect domestic security. However, law enforcement agencies found themselves bound by legal limitations designed to protect the freedom and privacy of Americans. One such limitation was the federal law that limited wiretap requests to a specific telephone rather than to an individual who might be using a number of phones. Technology often allows people to exploit antiquated legislation to bypass the literal extension of rights, as in this case. At the urging of the Bush administration, Congress quickly and by a wide margin voted to ease this restriction. Although most Americans seemed to support the legislation, many cautioned against sacrificing civil liberties in the war on terrorism. Civil libertarians expressed concern that the civil liberties of all Americans might be sacrificed on the altar of domestic security. On the other hand, what good are civil liberties if no domestic security exists? The challenge to government, and especially to courts, is to strike a reasonable balance between these values, taking into account the changing circumstances of our national life.

4-1a Where Do Rights Come From?

The ideas of liberty and equality are embedded in democratic political culture. Clearly, not all societies recognize liberty and equality as

© Kheng Guan Toh, 2013. Used under license from Shutterstock, Inc.

rights. In these societies, democratic institutions function poorly, if at all. Without a consensus in a society, rights do not exist or have no real meaning, regardless of any claims to the contrary. Often, the consensus is built on claims that a particular right comes from God or *natural law*.

Natural Rights

In the view of the American Founders, as expressed in the Declaration of Independence, individuals "are endowed by their Creator with certain unalienable Rights," among which are "Life, Liberty and the pursuit of Happiness." In the Founders' view, these unalienable rights are born to all human beings. They are given by natural law and discoverable by human reason. *Natural rights* are not granted by governments, but do depend on government for their security. Recalling John Locke's theory of the *social contract*, the Declaration of Independence further declares: "To secure these Rights, Governments are instituted among Men, deriving their just powers from the consent of the governed." Governments that cannot protect those natural rights, according to Locke, must be changed or removed. Thus, one of the basic tests for a functioning government is the protection of rights for the citizenry.

In the minds of the Founders, individual rights preceded, and were superior to, the powers of government. Therefore, government should be a vehicle to protect these rights and should have no authority to abridge them. At the same time, the Founders were well aware of the tendency of governments to infringe on, rather than protect, individual rights. This tendency could be found in all types of governments. In an authoritarian form, the infringement stemmed from tyrants as they sought to keep and expand their power. In a democracy, the threat was from the passions of citizens who sought to use the power of government to do their bidding at the expense of others.

An Evolving Social Contract

The more modern view of rights is that they are the legitimate claims that members of a civilized society may make to limit the actions of their government and each other. In this view, rights evolve along with the political culture of the society. What was not a fundamental right in the eighteenth century, such as the right to be free from involuntary servitude, is universally regarded as fundamental in the early twenty-first century. The practice of witchcraft was grounds for execution in seventeenth-century New England. Although most people find witchcraft (now generally referred to as Wiccanism) bizarre or even repugnant, it is now generally accepted that one has the right to practice witchcraft as long as it does not threaten the rights of others. The issue of abortion poses a more difficult question. On one side, abortion is condoned as an expression of a woman's right to control her own body. On the other side, it is condemned as the murder of innocent human beings. Abortion is an issue on which no societal consensus exists; hence, some people refuse to characterize it as a right, even though the courts have defined it that way.

4-1b Substantive and Procedural Rights

In the United States, the federal and state constitutions, backed by the power of judicial review, are the primary ways the rights of individuals and minority groups are protected. Constitutional challenges to majority rule generally fall into two categories: challenges to the substance of a policy that the government has adopted and challenges to the procedures by which the government implements a policy. Through a number of provisions, the U.S. Constitution limits both what government may do and how it may do it. Government may not take actions that threaten the substantive rights of individuals, such as the right to free exercise of religion, nor may it take actions that threaten the life, liberty, or property of the individual without following due process of law. For example, a person accused of the crime of distributing obscene material might make a substantive constitutional challenge, based on the First Amendment, to the government's right to outlaw obscenity. The accused might also challenge the procedures used by the police in gathering evidence of the crime, claiming that they violated the Fourth Amendment prohibition against unreasonable searches and seizures.

Rights of the Accused

The overwhelming majority of constitutional challenges to government action are brought by individuals accused of crimes. Most of these cases involve procedural challenges. For the most part, their claims are made under the Fourth, Fifth, and Eighth Amendments, which prohibit unreasonable searches and seizures, compulsory self-incrimination and double jeopardy, and cruel and unusual punishments, respectively, or under the Sixth Amendment, which guarantees a speedy, public trial by an impartial jury, the right to confront witnesses, and the assistance of counsel. The Founders knew the potential for the criminal law to be used as an instrument of oppression. That is why they imposed limits on how police and prosecutors could do their job of ferreting out crime. Of course, every measure that protects the rights of the accused increases the probability that a guilty person will go free. In a society beset by crime, tremendous pressure exists to ignore or at least relax the rights of the accused, who by the very fact of being accused of a crime are accorded little sympathy by society.

4-2 Rights Protected by the Original Constitution

As noted in Chapter 2, "The Development of American Constitutional Democracy," the thirteen states comprising the newly formed Union experienced a difficult period of political and economic instability after the Revolutionary War. Many citizens, especially farmers, defaulted on their loans. To alleviate the plight of debtors, some state legislatures resorted to various measures, including making cheap paper money into legal tender, adopting bankruptcy laws, restricting creditors' access to the courts, and prohibiting imprisonment for debt. These now-common statutes were objectionable to the Framers of the Constitution, who regarded contracts, including debts, as sacred. The Framers believed that serious steps had to be taken to prevent the states from forgiving debts and interfering with contracts.

Thus one of the motivations behind the Constitutional Convention of 1787 was the desire to secure overriding legal protection for contracts. Article I, Section 10 prohibits states from passing laws "impairing the obligation of contracts." The Contract Clause must be included among the provisions of the original Constitution that protect individual rights—in this case, the right of individuals to be free from governmental interference with their contractual relationships. By protecting contracts, Article I, Section 10 performed an important function in the early years of American economic development.

4-2a Habeas Corpus

Article I, Section 9 states that "the privilege of the Writ of Habeas Corpus shall not be suspended, unless when in Cases of Invasion or Rebellion the public Safety may require it." Grounded in English common law, the writ of *habeas corpus* ensures the individual will not unlawfully be held in custody. Specifically, *habeas corpus* enables a court to order the release of an individual found to have been illegally incarcerated. Although the right has many applications, it is used most commonly in criminal cases, when an individual is arrested and held in custody but denied due process of law.

In adopting the *habeas corpus* provision of Article I, Section 9, the Framers wanted not only to recognize the right but also to limit its suspension to emergency situations. The Constitution is somewhat ambiguous about which branch of government has the authority to suspend the writ of *habeas corpus* during emergencies. For example, President Lincoln unilaterally suspended the writ early in the Civil War, and Congress soon confirmed this decision by statute. During World War II, the writ of *habeas corpus* was suspended in the territory of Hawaii, allowing the military to take "necessary" measures to deal with persons of Japanese extraction without interference by the civilian courts. The post-9/11 Patriot Act allowed the suspension of *habeas corpus* for suspected enemy combatants, though that key provision of the law was later invalidated by the courts. (See Case in Point 4-1.)

These types of "emergencies" present real difficulties not only for *habeas corpus* but also for all devices that guarantee the liberties of individuals relative to the government. In wartime or during a riot, governments are under tremendous pressure to maintain security and order. Any society makes some provision, either explicitly or implicitly, for dealing with such situations. As reasonable and necessary as such provisions might seem, they are certainly subject to possible abuse. Those siding with potential enemies are not easily tolerated. Those appearing to side with countries with whom we are at war are often despised.

Federal *Habeas Corpus* Review of State Criminal Cases

The writ of *habeas corpus* is an important element in modern criminal procedure. As a result of legislation passed by Congress in 1867 and subsequent judicial interpretation of that legislation, a person convicted of a crime in a state court and sentenced to state prison may petition a federal district court for *habeas corpus* relief. The federal court is then permitted to review the constitutional correctness of the arrest, trial, sentencing, and punishment of the state prisoner. Here, as elsewhere, a state's criminal justice system must pass federal review to ensure that a prisoner's rights as a citizen of the United States are not violated by the state.

Under Chief Justice Earl Warren (1953–1969), the Supreme Court broadened the scope of federal *habeas corpus* review of state criminal convictions by permitting prisoners to raise issues in federal court that they did not raise in their state appeals.[1] The more conservative Court under Chief Justice Warren E. Burger (1969–1986) switched direction and restricted state prisoners' access to federal *habeas corpus* relief.[2] Nevertheless, the frequency of federal *habeas corpus* cases challenging state criminal convictions prompted a movement in Congress to further restrict the availability of the writ. In 1996, Congress enacted the Antiterrorism and Effective Death Penalty Act, which, among other things, created a gatekeeping mechanism to reduce successive federal *habeas corpus* petitions. These new restrictions were upheld by the Supreme Court under Chief Justice William H. Rehnquist (1986–2005).[3] Federal *habeas corpus* review of state criminal cases still occurs, but is now less common. On the other hand, state courts have in recent years become more hospitable to the rights of the accused, so the need for federal oversight of state court convictions is no longer as compelling.

4-2b Bills of Attainder and Ex Post Facto Laws

The Constitution prohibits (in Article I, Sections 9 and 10) Congress and the states, respectively, from adopting bills of attainder. A *bill of attainder* is a legislative act that imposes punishment on a person without benefit of a trial in a court of law. For example, when Congress passed a law that prohibited members of the Communist party from serving as officers in trade unions, the Supreme Court declared the law unconstitutional, saying that Congress had inflicted punishment on easily ascertainable members of a group without providing them with a trial by jury.[4]

Article I, Section 9 also prohibits Congress from passing *ex post facto* laws. Article I, Section 10 imposes the same prohibition on state legislatures. *Ex post facto* laws are laws passed after the occurrence of an act that alter its legal status or consequences (see Case in Point 4-1). In 1798, the Supreme Court held that the *ex post facto* clauses applied to criminal but not to civil laws.[5] Thus, the *ex post facto* clauses do not prohibit retroactive laws dealing with civil matters. For an act to be invalidated as an *ex post facto* law, two key elements must exist. First, the act must be retroactive—it must apply to events that occurred before its passage. Second, it must seriously disadvantage the accused. The changes must be more than procedural; they must render conviction more likely or punishment more severe.

Case in Point 4-1

Civil Liberties in a Post-9/11 World

Rumsfeld v. Padilla (2004)

On May 8, 2002, Jose Padilla, a U.S. citizen, flew from Pakistan to Chicago's O'Hare International Airport. As he stepped off the plane, Padilla was arrested by federal agents executing a material witness warrant in connection with its investigation into the 9/11 attacks. Padilla was suspected of participating in the plot to detonate a "dirty bomb" on U.S. soil. Since Padilla was considered a "material witness," no charges were filed. Padilla was denied the right to counsel as allowed under the Patriot Act. Later, the federal government began calling him an "enemy combatant," which meant that he could be imprisoned indefinitely.

After a lower court upheld the government's right to detain Padilla, his lawyer appealed the case the United States Court of Appeals, where Padilla's case was overturned. The Appeals Court stated that the president did not have authority to order military detentions when the suspects were American citizens.

The federal government appealed to the U.S. Supreme Court, which threw the case out on a technicality. Padilla's case went to trial in 2006, and in 2007 he was found guilty of conspiracy and sentenced to seventeen years in prison for his involvement in the plot. Prior to his conviction, however, Padilla was an example of the government's power to strip citizens of their civil liberties under the post-9/11 Patriot Act.

4-3 The Bill of Rights

As discussed in Chapter 2, "The Development of American Constitutional Democracy," the failure of the Framers of the Constitution to include a more complete list of protected rights was a potential stumbling block to the ratification of the document.

However, the Federalists and the Jeffersonians reached an agreement that led to the adoption of the Bill of Rights by the First Congress in 1789. Though not an exhaustive catalog of individual liberties, the Bill of Rights enumerates those freedoms that most concerned the Founders: the right to speak and write freely without governmental censorship, the right to assemble peaceably, the right to exercise one's religion without coercion or penalty, the right to be free from unwarranted arrest and prosecution, and the right to be secure in one's property, among others.

4-3a Nationalization of the Bill of Rights

When the Bill of Rights was ratified, it was widely perceived as limiting only the powers and actions of the national government. Through judicial interpretation of the Fourteenth Amendment, however, the Bill of Rights has been *nationalized*, or extended to the states. Section 1 of the Fourteenth Amendment imposed broad restrictions on state power, requiring the states to provide equal protection of the law to all persons, respect the "privileges and immunities" of citizens of the United States, and, most importantly, protect the "life, liberty, and property" of all persons. Specifically, the Fourteenth Amendment prohibited states from depriving persons of these basic rights "without due process of law." (For an extensive discussion of the civil rights implications of the Equal Protection Clause, see Chapter 5, "Civil Rights and the Struggle for Equality.")

The ratification of this amendment in 1868 provided an opportunity for the Supreme Court to reconsider the relationship between the Bill of Rights and state and local governments. Although no conclusive evidence exists that the Framers of the Fourteenth Amendment intended for it to "incorporate" the Bill of Rights and thus make the latter applicable to actions of state and local governments, the Supreme Court has endorsed a doctrine of selective incorporation by which most of the provisions of the Bill of Rights have been extended to limit actions of state and local governments.

The principal thrust of the process of **selective incorporation** is that, with few exceptions, policies of state and local governments are now subject to judicial scrutiny under the same standards that the Bill of Rights imposes on the federal government (see Table 4-1). The prohibition of the First Amendment against the establishment of religion, for example, applies with equal force to a school board in rural Oklahoma and to the U.S. Congress. Likewise, the Eighth Amendment injunction against cruel and unusual punishments applies equally to high-profile federal prosecutions for treason and to sentences imposed by local courts for violations of city or county ordinances. Note, however, that in a few instances, such as those governed by the Sixth

Amendment right to trial by jury, the Supreme Court has been willing to give the states slightly greater latitude than the federal government in complying with Bill of Rights requirements.

TABLE 4-1 Supreme Court Decisions Incorporating Provisions of the Bill of Rights into the Fourteenth Amendment

SUPREME COURT CASE AND YEAR					
Amendment Right					
First Amendment	Fiske v. Kansas (speech) 1927	Near v. Minnesota (press) 1931	Employment Division (Oregon) v. Smith. (free exercise of religion) 1990	DeJonge v. Oregon (assembly) 1937	*Lemon v. Kurtzman* (establishment of religion) 1971
Second Amendment	DC v. Heller 2008	McDonald v. Chicago 2010			
Fourth Amendment	*Wolf v. Colorado* (unreasonable searches and seizures) 1949	*Mapp v. Ohio* (exclusionary rule) 1961		*Rumsfeld v. Padilla* (detention of prisoners) 2004	
Fifth Amendment				*Malloy v. Hogan* (self-incrimination) 1964	*Benton v. Maryland* (double jeopardy) 1969
Sixth Amendment		*In re Oliver* (right to public trial) 1948	Gideon v. Wainwright (right to counsel) 1963	Klopfer v. North Carolina (right to speedy trial) 1967	*Duncan v. Louisiana* (right to jury trial) 1968
Eighth Amendment			*Robinson v. California* (cruel and unusual punishment) 1962		

Note: The Third and Seventh Amendments have not been incorporated. Also, the right to indictment by a grand jury (Fifth Amendment) and the prohibitions against excessive fines and bail (Eighth Amendment) have not been incorporated.

4-4 Protection of Private Property

As we have seen, protection of private property was a fundamental concern of the Framers of the Constitution. The authors of the Bill of Rights also expressed concern for private property rights. Specifically, the Fifth Amendment prohibits the federal government from taking private property for public use without just compensation. This prohibition has been extended to the state and local governments via the Fourteenth Amendment.[6] A state may use its power of eminent domain, for example, to create a lane of access across private property to the seashore to enhance recreational opportunities for the public. But if it does so, it must provide reasonable compensation to the property owners.[7]

The Due Process Clauses of the Fifth and Fourteenth Amendments prohibit the federal and state governments, respectively, from taking private property without due process of law. For example, a person whose property is being taken by the state is entitled to challenge the reasonableness of the state's action in court. The guarantee of due process also protects people against the arbitrary termination of government benefits.[8]

In 2005, the Supreme Court decided to endorse the power of local governments to use their right of eminent domain. The city of New London, Connecticut wanted to sell a neighborhood to a developer, who in turn wanted to build a hotel, health club, and commerical office space. The city was attracted to the higher amount of taxes that the commercial properties would bring compared to the low revenues generated by private property taxes. The city and homeowner Susette Kelo could not come to an agreement on a price to pay for her house in the area in question. Rather than relocating the project, the city of New London condemned Kelo's home and evicted her without compensation. Eminent domain is usually used for public goods projects such as roads, but never before had private property been claimed to turn over to another private owner. Kelo sued all the way to the U.S. Supreme Court, who denied Kelo's appeal. As a result, eminent domain powers for local governments are stronger now than ever.

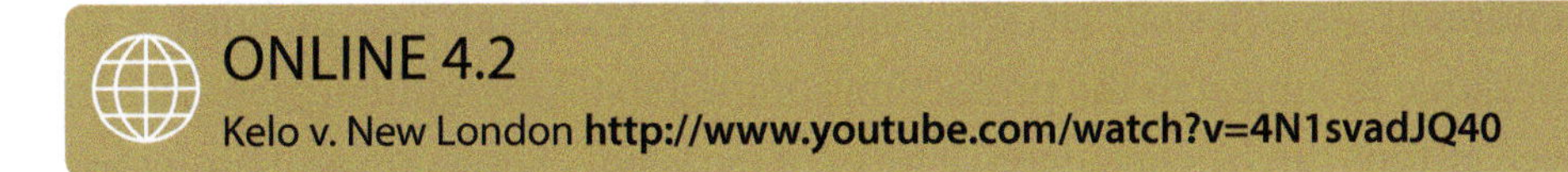
ONLINE 4.2

Kelo v. New London **http://www.youtube.com/watch?v=4N1svadJQ40**

4-5 First Amendment Freedoms of Expression, Assembly, and Association

The First Amendment protects, among other things, freedom of speech and freedom of the press. Both of these freedoms are generally subsumed under the broader heading "freedom of expression." Freedom of speech has been rightly called "the matrix, the indispensable condition, of nearly every other form of freedom."[9]

Justice Hugo L. Black, a champion of First Amendment rights on the Supreme Court, once wrote: "Freedom to speak and write about public questions is as important to the life of our government as is the heart to the human body."[10]

The Framers of the Bill of Rights understood that every utterance could be the mechanism through which an unpopular idea could become popular. Through the power of persuasion and the value of their ideas, minorities could eventually become majorities. But what if such ideas are considered dangerous? What if the expression of these ideas tends to undermine the very system that protects the freedom to hold unconventional ideas? During much of the first half of the twentieth century, many people believed that communism was a grave danger to American society. The courts often held that the federal and state governments acted appropriately in enacting laws restricting the activities of avowed Communists. Since the decline of communism around the world and the demise of the Soviet Union, the issues of free speech are now very different.

4-5a THE SCOPE OF PROTECTED EXPRESSION

The Supreme Court has recognized that the underlying purpose of the First Amendment is to protect human communication from government interference. Thus, under current interpretation, the First Amendment protects not only speech and writing in their purest, most literal forms, but also a range of **symbolic speech** and **expressive conduct**. Wearing a political button, holding a sign, placing a bumper sticker on one's car—all are examples of symbolic speech or expressive conduct protected by the First Amendment. As you shall see, even burning the American flag qualifies as an act of expression that is subject to the protections of the First Amendment (see Case in Point 4-2). Even tattoos can be considered a form of personal expression and protected by the Constitution.

ONLINE 4.3

Tattoos as Expression **http://www.firstamendmentcenter.org/ariz-high-court-rules-tattoos-are-form-of-protected-expression**

Case in Point 4-2

Is Burning the American Flag an Exercise of Free Speech?

Texas v. Johnson (1989)

The most dramatic and controversial instance of expressive conduct to be afforded First Amendment protection is the public burning of the American flag as an act of protest. After burning the American flag on the street outside the 1984 Republican National Convention in Dallas, Gregory Johnson was prosecuted under a Texas law prohibiting flag desecration. Johnson was convicted at his trial, but his conviction was reversed by the Texas Court of Criminal Appeals, which held that Johnson's conduct was protected by the First Amendment. The U.S. Supreme Court agreed, splitting 5–4. Writing for the Court, Justice William Brennan observed that "the expressive, overtly political nature of [Johnson's] conduct was both intentional and overwhelmingly apparent." Brennan rejected the argument that "the State's interests in preserving the flag as a symbol of nationhood and national unity justify [Johnson's] criminal conviction." Dissenting, Chief Justice Rehnquist challenged the idea that flag burning is a form of political speech, saying that "flag burning is the equivalent of an inarticulate grunt or roar that . . . is most likely to be indulged in not to express any particular idea, but to antagonize others." Rehnquist stressed the "unique position" of the flag "as the symbol of our Nation, a uniqueness that justifies a governmental prohibition against flag burning."

The Supreme Court's decision in *Texas v. Johnson* (1989) was met with a firestorm of criticism. Conservatives were outraged by the ruling and shocked that two Reagan appointees to the Supreme Court, Justices Anthony Kennedy and Antonin Scalia, had concurred in the decision. Congress began debate on a proposed constitutional amendment that would remove flag burning from the protection of the First Amendment. The amendment failed, but Congress did adopt a new statute making it a federal offense to desecrate the American flag. However, like the state law struck down in *Texas v. Johnson*, the new federal statute was invalidated by the Supreme Court in *United States v. Eichman* (1990). Did the Court adopt the right interpretation of the First Amendment? Should freedom of speech include the right to burn the American flag?

It is important to realize that just because a particular form of conduct is expressive in nature does not mean that it is immune to government regulation or even criminal prosecution. The courts have recognized that certain types of expression are beyond the pale of the First Amendment. Even when the First Amendment does apply, courts often weigh the individual's interest in expression against countervailing societal interests. When expression is purely commercial or entertainment-oriented, the courts tend to tolerate greater restrictions. For example, in 2000, the Court rejected a constitutional challenge to a local ordinance that restricted nude dancing in bars. The city of Erie, Pennsylvania, adopted an ordinance making it an offense for anyone to "knowingly or intentionally appear in public in a state of nudity." To comply with the ordinance, erotic dancers were required to wear pasties and G-strings. The owners of Kandyland, a club that featured all-nude erotic dancers, filed suit in a state court to challenge the constitutionality of the new ordinance. The Supreme Court upheld the ordinance, finding that the requirement that dancers wear pasties and G-strings was "a minimal restriction" that left dancers "ample capacity" to convey their erotic messages.[11]

4-5b The Prohibition against Censorship

The Founders wanted individuals to be able to speak their minds and publish their opinions without fear of government censorship. Thanks to the adoption of the First Amendment and the development of a political culture that supports the value of free expression, this country has been freer of censorship than most other countries, including many of the world's other democracies. From time to time, however, our government has sought to prohibit the publication of information or ideas deemed detrimental to the public interest. Quite often, these instances have involved considerations of national security. In a landmark case in 1971, the federal government attempted to prevent *The New York Times* and *The Washington Post* from publishing excerpts from a classified study titled "History of U.S. Decision-Making Process on Vietnam Policy" (the Pentagon Papers). The Supreme Court held that the government's effort to block publication of this material amounted to unconstitutional censorship.[12] The Court was simply not convinced that such publication—several years after the events and decisions discussed in the Pentagon Papers—constituted a significant threat to national security.

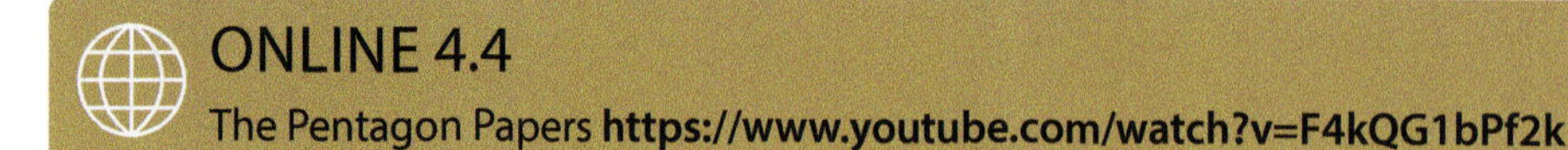

ONLINE 4.4

The Pentagon Papers **https://www.youtube.com/watch?v=F4kQG1bPf2k**

Today's online world has given us a new version of the Pentagon Papers issue: Wikileaks. Founder Julian Assange and his allies believed that governments should be transparent in their dealings. Secrecy led, in Assange's mind, to the worst violations of civil rights and liberties in the modern world. Armed with a group of coders and hackers, Assange began compiling and posting classified documents from governments across the world online. The U.S. government was one of Wikileaks' targets, and in 2010 hundreds of classified communiques were available for download online, provided by a young U.S. attache named Bradley Manning. The U.S. government had plans to intervene because a traditional media partner, the *Guardian* newspaper from Britain, was involved. However, before things could progress, Assange was arrested on sexual assault charges in Europe. Assange could be extradited to the U.S. for trial stemming from the Wikileaks release of the classified documents.[13]

4-5c The Clear and Present Danger Doctrine

Societies strive to keep order in many ways. To many, it is appropriate for legislatures to pass laws to protect the community's moral climate. Others think that it is necessary to control "dangerous ideas" in times of crisis. To the degree to which these ends seem justified, the bounds of expression are not limitless. It is well established that the First Amendment does not provide absolute protection for freedom of expression. In a widely quoted Supreme Court opinion, Justice Oliver Wendell Holmes, Jr., once observed that "the most stringent protection of free speech would not protect a man in falsely shouting fire in a theater, and causing a panic." Holmes concluded that "the question in every case is whether the words used are used in such circumstances and are of such a nature as to create a clear and present danger that they will bring about the substantive evils that Congress has a right to prevent."[14] From the 1920s through the 1960s, this classic statement of the **clear and present danger doctrine** was the guiding principle behind most Supreme Court decisions having to do with the rights of political dissenters. The Warren Court modified the doctrine somewhat to allow greater leeway to free expression. In 1969, the Court held that "the constitutional guarantees of free speech and free press do not permit a State to forbid or proscribe advocacy of the use of force or of law violation except where such advocacy is directed to inciting or producing **imminent lawless action** and is likely to incite or produce such action."[15] Thus, the possibility that violence may erupt when an extremist addresses a hostile crowd is not enough to justify restrictions on free expression. The situation must be so dangerous that violence is inevitable unless the authorities intervene.

ONLINE 4.5

Timeline of Free Speech **http://www.firstamendmentcenter.org/first-amendment-timeline**

4-5d Fighting Words and Profanity

The courts have also recognized that **fighting words**, direct personal insults that are inherently likely to provoke a violent reaction from the person or persons at whom they are directed, are not protected by the First Amendment. In one historic case, the Supreme Court used the fighting words doctrine to uphold the breach-of-the-peace conviction of a speaker who called a law enforcement officer "a damned fascist" and "a God-damned racketeer."[16] On the other hand, in another celebrated case, the Court refused to regard as fighting words an individual's public display of the slogan "F___ the draft."[17] After entering the Los Angeles County Courthouse wearing a jacket bearing that slogan, Paul Cohen was arrested for breach of the peace. In reversing his conviction, the Supreme Court noted that "no individual actually or likely to be present could reasonably have regarded the words on the appellant's jacket as a direct personal insult."

PROFANITY

Despite the Supreme Court's decision in *Cohen v. California*, a number of jurisdictions outlaw profanity. Most of these laws were enacted long ago when prevailing attitudes in this area were much more conservative. Today profanity laws are seldom enforced, but when they are, defendants almost always raise a First Amendment defense. Consider the widely publicized case of the "cussing canoeist." When Timothy Boomer fell out of his canoe and into Michigan's Rifle River in 1999, he unleashed a torrent of profanity in a very loud voice. Boomer was arrested and convicted of violating an 1897 Michigan law that provided "any person who shall use any indecent, immoral, obscene, vulgar or insulting language in the presence or hearing of any woman or child shall be guilty of a misdemeanor." However, on appeal his conviction was overturned and the law was declared unconstititional.[18]

4-5e OBSCENITY AND PORNOGRAPHY

One of the more difficult First Amendment problems over the years has been the issue of pornography and obscenity. *Pornography* is the portrayal of sexual conduct, either in words, pictures, or performances, in a manner that many people find offensive. Obscenity is pornography that the law prohibits. Needless to say, pornographers are not a class of people accorded much respect. Many people are frustrated by any move to protect the right to produce, distribute, or possess material they deem to be morally reprehensible. Not surprisingly, severe tension develops when the many seek to use the instruments of government to promote a healthy moral climate, only to be challenged by the few, who want to pursue their own interests without regard for a moral climate they may not respect.

State and federal laws have long prohibited the production, sale, and even possession of obscene materials. The Supreme Court has held that such prohibitions are constitutional because obscenity is beyond the pale of the First Amendment. What, however, constitutes an obscene book, movie, or play? For years, the courts have struggled with the practical problems of defining obscenity. In the leading case on the subject, the Supreme Court has held that to be obscene, a particular work must meet a three-part test. Because the test is set forth in the Court's decision in *Miller v. California* (1973), it is called the **Miller test.**[19] To be obscene under this test, a particular work must be patently, or obviously, offensive. Second, it must appeal to a prurient, or unnatural, interest in sex. Finally, it must lack serious redeeming artistic, scientific, political, or literary value. Still, law enforcement agencies, prosecutors, judges, and juries struggle with the definition of obscenity. In many jurisdictions, the laws prohibiting obscenity go unenforced, except in the most extreme situations, because of the difficulty of proving the crime. Adult bookstores now abound, at least in big cities, and hardcore pornography is readily available online. Clearly, societal attitudes, which ultimately drive the law, have changed dramatically in this area. With the exception of child pornography, which both the law and society condemn, sexually oriented expression has by and large achieved social and legal tolerance in this country.

Pornography Online

In 1996, Congress adopted the Communications Decency Act (CDA), which made it a crime to display "indecent" material on the Internet in a manner that might make it available to minors. The American Civil Liberties Union brought suit to challenge the statute on First Amendment grounds. In *Reno v. American Civil Liberties Union*,[20] the Supreme Court invalidated the challenged provisions of the CDA. Writing for the Court, Justice John Paul Stevens concluded that, with respect to cyberspace, "the interest in encouraging freedom of expression in a democratic society outweighs any theoretical but unproven benefit of censorship." Some hailed the Court's decision as a virtual Declaration of Independence for the Internet. Others lamented that Congress was prohibited from trying to protect children from the dangers of cyberspace. Now, largely as a result of the *Reno* decision, pornography is widely available on the World Wide Web. Theoretically, Internet pornography that rises (or sinks) to the level of obscenity can be prohibited, but little effort has been made to ferret out the obscene from the merely pornographic material on the Web. However, federal authorities (principally the FBI) have been aggressive in their efforts to combat child pornography in cyberspace. Those efforts received something of a setback in 2002 when the Supreme Court ruled that the child pornography laws could not be enforced against those who produce or distribute "virtual child pornography," that is, child pornography consisting of computer-generated images as distinct from real human subjects.[21]

4-5f Defamation

The laws of every state protect people against defamation of character. *Defamation* consists of making injurious, false public statements about someone. If the statements are made verbally, the offense is called *slander*; if they are made in writing, the offense is termed *libel*. An individual who is slandered or libeled may sue to recover actual and punitive damages for the injury to his or her reputation. The Supreme Court, however, has held that the First Amendment "prohibits a public official from recovering damages for a defamatory falsehood relating to his official conduct unless he proves that the statement was made with **actual malice**—that is, with knowledge that it was false or with reckless disregard of whether it was false or not."[22] Indeed, the Court has extended this prohibition to apply to all "public figures," not just to public officials.[23] This category includes all persons who have sufficient access to the media that they can effectively defend themselves against false charges. It is difficult, but not impossible, for a public person to prevail in a libel suit. This type of plaintiff has to show that the person being sued made the injurious statement with actual malice or reckless disregard of the truth. The rationale for making it hard for public persons to win defamation suits is that if it were easy to sue people for making false statements about others, public debate and criticism, especially in political matters, would be inhibited. On the other hand, many people now feel that certain elements of the media, in particular the supermarket tabloids, abuse their freedom under the First Amendment. Without the threat of libel suits, irresponsible publications may write whatever they want about celebrities.

4-5g The First Amendment and Electronic Media

Freedom of the press now involves much more than publication of newspapers, books, and magazines. With the advent of electronic media, the First Amendment guarantee of free expression has taken on new significance. Mass media now play an extremely important role in our daily lives, and certainly in the political life of the nation. Without question, the protection of the First Amendment applies to expression via electronic media, although in a somewhat diluted form.

From the inception of television and radio, the federal government has extensively regulated the broadcasting industry. Television and radio stations must obtain licenses from the Federal Communications Commission. Among other things, the FCC requires that television stations provide a "family hour" of evening programming and prohibits the broadcast of obscene programming at any time. Stations that violate these and other regulations are subject to having their licenses suspended, revoked, or not renewed. For the most part, the courts have upheld the policies and procedures of the FCC against a variety of challenges, some of which were based on the First Amendment.

The FCC rules against indecent programming do not apply to channels transmitted only by cable. Because cable stations do not, strictly speaking, engage in broadcasting, they are not subject to the regulations that affect the public airwaves. Consequently, cable companies may transmit programs to subscribers that would not be permitted on broadcast television. HBO, The Movie Channel, Showtime, and other premium channels routinely show R-rated movies that could not be shown on broadcast television without substantial editing. Most cable companies now offer their subscribers X-rated programming on a pay-per-view basis. May a city enact an ordinance prohibiting a cable company from transmitting X-rated films to subscribers? Would the programming have to meet the legal test of obscenity before a court would permit a community to prohibit it? This question remains an open one, but the law is clearly evolving in the direction of granting protection to the suppliers of adult-oriented television programming, as long as it is made available only to those consumers who specifically choose to have access to such material.

Social media create a new wrinkle in the free speech fabric. People are free to say what they want within the traditional limits established by the courts. But people can create entirely false identities (or use those of others) online, and use them to manipulate others. The phenomenon, known as "catfishing," led to a movie and TV series where people who had become involved in fake relationships online had the opportunity to meet the real people masquerading. No person has been sued or arrested for impersonating another person online, though the case of former Notre Dame linebacker Manti Te'o being catfished by Ronaiah Tuiassosopo may develop into a court case. Likewise, cyberbulling has become a signficant problem in many areas.[24]

4-5h Freedom of Assembly

Public assemblies have been and continue to be important mechanisms of political participation. From the assemblies on village greens before and during the American Revolution to the antiwar and civil rights demonstrations of the 1960s, public assemblies have played a key role in galvanizing public opinion. The political importance of free assembly is obvious, yet so too are the dangers that go along with assemblies by unpopular groups. Concern over public safety often prompts local authorities to take measures to restrict public assemblies. In 1977, when the American Nazi party announced plans to march through the predominantly Jewish town of Skokie, Illinois, the town council passed an ordinance prohibiting the march. The Nazis went to court and won a decision declaring the ordinance unconstitutional under the First Amendment.[25] On the other hand, the courts have consistently held that authorities may impose **reasonable time, place, and manner regulations** on public assemblies. The Supreme Court relied on this doctrine in 1983 in upholding a Washington, D.C., ordinance that prohibited assemblies within five hundred feet of foreign embassies.[26]

4-5i Freedom of Association

Although the Constitution makes no explicit reference to **freedom of association**, the courts have long recognized the right to associate with persons of one's choosing as an implicit First Amendment freedom. This freedom is very important in politics because it is the legal basis for the formation of political parties and interest groups. In a democracy, people must have the freedom to join (and leave) political groups of their own accord.

What about extremist groups? Does the First Amendment give a person the right to join the Ku Klux Klan or the Nazi party? Generally speaking, freedom of association applies to all groups, regardless of the content of their ideology or the nature of their political objectives. The only exception to this principle comes when groups are committed to the destruction of lawful governmental authority by force or violence. In these types of cases, the clear and present danger doctrine may permit government to infringe freedom of association. For example, Section 2 of the Internal Security Act of 1940, better known as the Smith Act, made it a crime merely to belong to the Communist party. In a 1961 decision, the Supreme Court upheld Section 2, but made clear that the prohibition applied only to active members of the Communist party who had a specific intent to bring about the violent overthrow of the U.S. government.[27] Under current constitutional doctrine, the government would have to show that lawless action by the group in question is imminent before the courts would permit restrictions on the group's freedom of association.

In recent years, state and local governments have utilized civil rights laws in an attempt to force social and civic groups to accept members of minority groups. By and large, these efforts have been successful. However, in the spring of 2000, the Supreme Court made national headlines when it invoked the doctrine of freedom of association in upholding the Boy Scouts' policy of refusing to allow openly homosexual men to serve as Scout leaders. The Court noted that "homosexuality has gained greater societal acceptance," but concluded that "this is scarcely an argument for denying First Amendment protection to those who refuse to accept these views." Although the Court's decision was strongly criticized by gay rights and other civil rights organizations, it was applauded not only by the Boy Scouts but also by many private groups who fear governmental interference with their activities.[28] By early 2013 the Scouts were considering an end to the ban, though gay boys can participate in Scouts, but gay adults are still banned. Decision was made in July 2013.

4-6 Freedom of Religion

The desire for religious freedom was one of the principal motivations for people coming to the New World. It is no accident that the Framers of the Bill of Rights placed freedom of religion first in the First Amendment: "Congress shall make no law respecting an establishment of religion or prohibiting the free exercise thereof." Freedom of religion as a constitutional principle has two distinct components: the prohibition against official establishment and the guarantee of free exercise.

4-6a Separation of Church and State

Some people believe that the Framers of the Bill of Rights intended, as Thomas Jefferson said, to erect a "wall of separation" between church and state. Others think that the

Framers intended merely to prevent the national government from setting up one denomination as an official religion that the American people would be required to support. Although the intentions of the Framers of the Bill of Rights are debatable, the Supreme Court has generally opted for the stricter interpretation, requiring a greater separation between church and state. And, although the First Amendment's Establishment Clause applies only to Congress, the Court has incorporated the principle under the Fourteenth Amendment. More specifically, the Court has held that to survive a challenge under the Establishment Clause, a government policy must have a secular, or nonreligious, purpose; must neither inhibit nor advance religion to any significant degree; and must avoid excessive entanglement between government and religious institutions.[29]

Without question, the most controversial issues involving separation of church and state have arisen in the context of public schools. In a series of well-known decisions, the Supreme Court of the 1960s prohibited public schools from sponsoring religious exercises, including prayer and Bible reading.[30] In 1985, the Court reinforced and extended its school prayer decisions in striking down an Alabama law that required public school students to observe a moment of silence for the purpose of "meditation or voluntary prayer." And, in 1987, the Court invalidated a Louisiana law that forbade the teaching of the theory of evolution unless accompanied by instruction in creation science. The Court concluded that the principal purpose of the law was "to endorse a particular religious doctrine."[31] Although the contemporary Supreme Court is more conservative than the Court of the 1960s, it has maintained a commitment to the idea of strict separation of church and state in the public school setting. For example, in the spring of 2000, the Court struck down the practice of student-led invocations before high school football games.[32]

4-6b Religion, Government, and Ideology

The question of school prayer—indeed, the larger issue of the relationship between religion and government—is one that divides liberal and conservative ideologies. Liberals typically believe in strict separation of church and state, fearing that any government entanglement with, or endorsement of, religion constitutes a serious threat to liberty. Thus, liberals often attack practices such as using taxpayers' money to pay chaplains for state legislatures, placing nativity scenes and other religious symbols on public property, and even allowing churches to be exempt from paying property taxes.

Most conservatives, on the other hand, bemoan the increasing secularization of government and society. Many conservatives believe that inasmuch as both religion and government should foster public morality, the two are joined in a common cause. In the conservative view, government should find ways to enhance and encourage religious values and institutions. At the very least, government should be permitted to acknowledge the importance of religion in the social and political life of the nation. Thus, conservatives typically do not object to attempts to require public schools to teach the biblical account of creation alongside the theory of evolution or to the many policies and practices that mingle religion and public life. As noted at the beginning of this chapter, the dispute over the relationship of religion and government goes beyond clashing ideologies. It represents something of a cultural war in the United States between traditional and modern thinking and between rural and urban societies.

4-6c The Free Exercise of Religion

The reason the Framers of the Bill of Rights prohibited an official establishment of religion was not that they were opposed to religion. On the contrary, most Framers of the Bill of Rights—indeed, the overwhelming majority of those who founded this country—were deeply religious. Their principal motivation in separating church and state was to protect the free exercise of religion. The Founders were painfully aware of the bloody religious warfare that had plagued Europe for centuries. Compared to most European countries of the late eighteenth century, America already had tremendous religious diversity. Catholics, Jews, and Protestants of many denominations had come to this country seeking freedom from persecution and a chance to practice their beliefs in peace, without interference or coercion. Two hundred years later, the Free Exercise Clause of the First Amendment retains the importance it had to the founding generation. Indeed, given the increased religious pluralism of our society resulting from immigration from all over the world, the clause may be more important now than it was two hundred years ago.

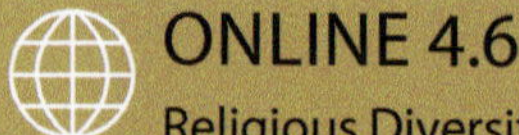

ONLINE 4.6
Religious Diversity in America **http://religions.pewforum.org/reports**

What the Free Exercise Clause Does and Does Not Protect

The Free Exercise Clause absolutely protects religious belief, and it grants extensive protection to solicitation and proselytizing by religious groups.[33] The most difficult problem of interpreting the Free Exercise Clause is determining the extent to which it protects unconventional religious practices. In 1879, the Supreme Court decided that the Free Exercise Clause did not protect a Mormon who practiced polygamy from prosecution for the crime of bigamy.[34] Although this decision has never been overturned, the modern Court tends to give wider berth to unconventional religious practices. For example, in 1972, the Court prohibited the state of Wisconsin from prosecuting a group of Old Order Amish who refused to send their teenage children to high school.[35] Yet the courts generally refuse to grant First Amendment protection to religious activities that offend the public morality or threaten people's health or safety. For example, courts have upheld laws prohibiting the use of poisonous snakes in religious exercises (a practice that still continues in remote parts of Appalachia). On the other hand, laws that outlaw socially undesirable practices only insofar as they are a part of religious ceremonies are subject to being declared unconstitutional. For example, in 1990 the Supreme Court ruled that the Native American Church, which considers the narcotic drug peyote part of its rituals, could not exempt its use from illegal drug testing in the workplace.[36] Furthermore, in 1993 the Supreme Court struck down a Hialeah, Florida, ordinance prohibiting animal sacrifice in religious exercises. The law was aimed at the practice of Santeria, a mixture of ancient East African religions and Roman Catholicism that involves the sacrifice of live animals. The Supreme Court said that, in enacting the law, city officials "did not understand, failed to perceive, or chose to ignore the fact that their official actions violated the Nation's essential commitment to religious freedom."[37]

4-7 The Right to Keep and Bear Arms

Most Americans believe that the Constitution protects their **right to keep and bear arms**. Yet the Second Amendment refers not only to the keeping and bearing of arms but also to the need for a "well regulated Militia." The Second Amendment provides: "A well regulated Militia, being necessary to the security of a free state, the right of the people to keep and bear arms shall not be infringed." The courts have generally interpreted the Second Amendment to allow broad governmental regulation of the sale, possession, and use of firearms. In one case, *United States v. Miller* (1939), the Supreme Court upheld a federal law banning the interstate transportation of certain firearms.[38] The defendant, who had been arrested for transporting a double-barreled sawed-off shotgun from Oklahoma to Arkansas, sought the protection of the Second Amendment. The Court rejected Miller's argument, asserting that "we cannot say that the Second Amendment guarantees the right to keep and bear such an instrument." In upholding a federal gun control act in a 1980 decision, the Court said:

> *These legislative restrictions on the use of firearms are neither based on constitutionally suspect criteria, nor do they trench upon any constitutionally protected liberties. . . . The Second Amendment guarantees no right to keep and bear a firearm that does not have "some reasonable relationship to the preservation or efficiency of a well regulated militia."*[39]

As it's now interpreted, the Second Amendment does not pose a significant constitutional barrier to the enactment or enforcement of **gun control** laws, whether passed by Congress, state legislatures, or local governments. However, in May 2002, Attorney General John Ashcroft sent a letter to the National Rifle Association in which he argued that the Second Amendment conferred an individual right rather than a collective right to bear arms. This letter, along with the criticism accompanying it, demonstrated the divisions in American culture over the issues of gun ownership and the regulation of firearms.

When John Hinckley tried to assassinate President Ronald Reagan in 1981, Jim Brady, Reagan's press secretary, was seriously wounded. In the mid-1980s, Brady and his wife, Sarah, became the best-known advocates of national gun control measures. The Brady bill, as it came to be known, called for the imposition of a five-day waiting period for the purchase of a handgun; during that time, a background check would be conducted to see whether the purchaser was a convicted felon or had a history of mental illness. Hinckley, who had a history of mental problems, used a handgun he had purchased just a few days earlier with no background check in his attempt to assassinate the president of the United States. Even though President Reagan was a victim of this attack, he opposed the Brady bill for many years. So did his successor, George Bush. But early in 1993, President Bill Clinton made clear that he supported the bill, and after much partisan wrangling, the Brady bill finally became law. Advocates of gun control hailed the victory, but called it a first battle in the war against easily available handguns. Opponents of gun control, such as the powerful National Rifle Association, lamented the passage of the Brady bill as a step on a slippery slope that would lead ultimately to the banning of privately owned firearms. The idea that gun ownership is a personal right is so deeply imbedded in American political culture that it is difficult to imagine the government's going too far in the gun control area.

Between 2008 and 2010, two cases would solidify the power of the Second Amendment. The Supreme Court invalidated a 1975 Washington D.C. law banning the ownership of firearms, and then followed it in 2010 with a full incorporation of the Second Amendment to states and localites with the McDonald decision, which nullified Chicago's strict firearms ban.[40]

4-8 Rights of Persons Accused of Crimes

Protecting citizens against crime is one of the fundamental obligations of government. In the United States, however, government must perform this function while respecting the constitutional rights of individuals. Courts of law are continually trying to balance the interest of society in crime control with the rights of individuals accused or convicted of crimes. Although violent crime has declined in recent years, the public remains quite fearful of crime. To some extent, this fear may be a function of continual frightening portrayals of crime in the media and popular culture. In any event, tremendous political pressure exists to "get tough" on criminals; courts of law are often blamed for coddling them.

4-8a Freedom from Unreasonable Searches and Seizures

The Fourth Amendment protects people from unreasonable searches and seizures conducted by police and other government agents. It requires that police have **probable cause** and obtain a **search warrant** from a judge before subjecting a person to a search for weapons, contraband, or other evidence of crime. Reflecting a serious concern of the Founders, the Fourth Amendment remains extremely important now, especially in light of the pervasiveness of crime and the national "war on drugs." In the twentieth century, the Fourth Amendment has been the source of numerous important judicial decisions and has generated a tremendous and complex body of legal doctrine. For example, the Supreme Court under Chief Justice Warren expanded the scope of Fourth Amendment protection to include wiretapping, an important tool of modern law enforcement.[41] In its landmark decision in *Mapp v. Ohio* (1961), the Warren Court also extended to the state courts the **exclusionary rule**, which prohibits the use of illegally obtained evidence at trial.[42] Since the 1970s, the Court has been more conservative in the Fourth Amendment area in an attempt to facilitate police efforts to ferret out crime. In several significant decisions rendered in the 1980s, the Court relaxed the probable cause and search warrant requirements and created a number of exceptions to the exclusionary rule. For example, in *United States v. Leon* (1984), the Court held that the exclusionary rule does not apply where police officers acting in good faith seize evidence on the basis of a warrant that is later held to be invalid.[43] Conservatives applauded the Court's newfound emphasis on law and order; liberals were outraged at the erosion of individual rights.

ONLINE 4.7
Your Rights

Technology and the Fourth Amendment

The Fourth Amendment is one of the areas of law in which the impact of changing technology is most profound. Police are quick to employ new technological means of detecting illicit activities that are obscured from public view. One increasingly common device used in the "war on drugs" is the infrared thermal imaging device, which detects heat waves emanating from inside homes, greenhouses, and other structures. This type of device can provide a strong indication of whether marijuana is being grown inside the closed structure. Is the use of this type of device a "search," even if the officers using it are not physically positioned on a suspect's property? If so, officers must normally have probable cause and, if possible, must obtain a search warrant before employing the heat detector. The Supreme Court has held that any means of invading a person's "reasonable expectation of privacy" is considered a "search" for Fourth Amendment purposes.[44] The question is whether the use of thermal imagers by police violates a reasonable expectation of privacy. In 2001, the Supreme Court answered this question in the affirmative. In *Kyllo v. United States*, the Court held that the use of a "thermal imager" by law enforcement agents is a "search" within the meaning of the Fourth Amendment.[45] In this case, police had used the device without first obtaining a warrant to scan a home they suspected to be housing an indoor marijuana growing operation. Therefore, their search was invalid, and the case against Kyllo could not go forward. The *Kyllo* case is important because it shows how changing technology creates new and difficult Fourth Amendment problems. As technology in this area advances, courts will continue to confront these types of problems.

4-8b Protections of the Fifth Amendment

The Fifth Amendment contains a number of important provisions protecting the rights of persons accused of crime. It requires the federal government to obtain an **indictment** from a **grand jury** before trying someone for a major crime. It also prohibits **double jeopardy**, or being tried a second time for the same offense after having been found not guilty. Additionally, the Fifth Amendment protects persons against **compulsory self-incrimination**, which is what is commonly meant by the phrase "taking the Fifth."

In its well-known *Miranda v. Arizona* decision of 1966, the Warren Court interpreted the Fifth Amendment Self-Incrimination Clause to require police officers to advise criminal suspects of their constitutional right to remain silent.[46] Under *Miranda*, failure to provide the warning means that any admission made by the suspect cannot be used in court. This controversial decision has been somewhat limited by the Court in recent years, however. The Court has identified certain situations in which confessions that would have been suppressed under a strict reading of *Miranda* may nevertheless be used in evidence. As in the case of the Fourth Amendment, conservatives cheered and liberals bemoaned the departures from the precedents set by the Warren Court. In the spring of 2000, the Supreme Court reconsidered and reaffirmed its landmark *Miranda* ruling, suggesting strongly that the once-controversial decision is now firmly established as part of the legal landscape.[47]

4-8c Sixth Amendment Rights

The Sixth Amendment is concerned exclusively with the rights of the accused. It requires, among other things, that people accused of crimes be provided a "speedy and public trial, by an impartial jury." The right of trial by jury is one of the most cherished rights in the Anglo American tradition, predating the Magna Carta of 1215. The Sixth Amendment also grants defendants the right to confront, or cross-examine, witnesses for the prosecution and the right to have "compulsory process" (the power of **subpoena**) to require favorable witnesses to appear in court. Significantly, considering the incredible complexity of the criminal law, the Sixth Amendment guarantees that accused persons have the "Assistance of Counsel" for their defense. The Warren Court regarded this right as crucial to a fair trial, holding that defendants who are unable to afford private counsel must be provided with counsel at public expense.[48] The Burger and Rehnquist courts have not significantly retreated from this holding, and most criminal defendants now rely on a **public defender** or other appointed counsel to represent them. One must realize, however, that in many areas of the country, public defender offices are underfunded and overburdened with cases. Even in jurisdictions where public defenders are well funded, the resources available to them seldom match those available to the prosecutor.

4-8d Freedom from Cruel and Unusual Punishments

In prohibiting **cruel and unusual punishments**, the Framers of the Eighth Amendment were concerned with prohibiting the tortures that were common in Europe as late as the eighteenth century. The authors of the Bill of Rights probably had no expectation that the Cruel and Unusual Punishments Clause would be used to challenge the legality of the death penalty. After all, the Bill of Rights seems to assume the existence of capital punishment in its references to "capital" crimes and defendants being placed in "jeopardy of life or limb." Yet the Supreme Court has said that the Cruel and Unusual Punishments Clause "must draw its meaning from the evolving standards of decency that mark the progress of a maturing society."[49] As the death penalty became controversial in the 1960s, courts invoked the Eighth Amendment to scrutinize capital punishment.

In a landmark 1972 decision, *Furman v. Georgia*, the Supreme Court struck down Georgia's death penalty.[50] Of the five justices who voted to invalidate the death penalty, only two held that capital punishment was inherently unconstitutional. For the other three justices in the majority, the problem was the manner in which the law permitted the death penalty to be imposed. Trial juries were given virtually unlimited discretion to decide when to impose capital punishment. The result, according to Justice Potter Stewart's opinion in *Furman*, was that the death penalty was "wantonly and . . . freakishly imposed."

In the wake of the *Furman* decision, the Georgia legislature rewrote the state's death penalty law. The new law, which became a model for many other states, provided a special procedural structure for judges and juries to follow in deciding who should get the death penalty. The revised Georgia law requires a **bifurcated trial** for capital crimes: In the first stage, guilt is determined in the usual manner; the second stage deals with the appropriate sentence. To impose the death penalty, the jury must find at least one of several aggravating factors. The law also provides for automatic appeal to the state supreme court. The appellate review must consider not only the procedural regularity of the trial but also whether the evidence supports the finding of the aggravating factor and whether the death sentence is disproportionate to the penalty imposed in similar cases. The new law was upheld by the Supreme Court in 1976 in *Gregg v. Georgia*.[51] Subsequently, thirty-seven other states and the federal government adopted new death penalty statutes modelled after the law upheld in *Gregg*.

As crime rates rose during the 1960s and 1970s, public opinion became increasingly supportive of the death penalty. It was thus no surprise that the more conservative Supreme Court of the 1980s was willing to support capital punishment in the great majority of cases. Indeed, in the early 1990s, the Court took steps to prevent lower federal courts from interfering with the carrying out of death sentences imposed by state courts. For example, in January 1993, the Court refused to allow a lower federal court to stop an execution, even though several witnesses had come forward ten years after the fact to assert the innocence of the condemned man. In the Supreme Court's view, the question of guilt or innocence was a matter for the state courts that tried the individual and adjudicated his appeals.[52]

In Eighth Amendment cases, as in cases dealing with criminal justice generally, the Supreme Court under Chief Justice William Rehnquist has been much more oriented toward the goal of crime control than the goal of due process. Of course, as politics and public opinion ebb and flow, so do the tides of opinion on the nation's highest court. It is not inconceivable that, a decade from now, a more liberal Court might repudiate some of the conservative decisions now emanating from the federal bench.

4-9 The Right of Privacy

We come finally to one of the most controversial of all constitutional rights: the **right of privacy**. It is controversial for two reasons. First, the term *privacy* is nowhere mentioned in the Constitution. The right of privacy has been recognized by the courts as an implicit freedom. To some extent, this recognition is buttressed by the Ninth Amendment, which asserts the existence of rights not enumerated in the Bill of Rights.

Yet critics charge that the right of privacy is nothing more than a judicial invention, unwarranted by the text or history of the Constitution. The second reason for the controversial nature of the right of privacy is its application to tough social issues, such as abortion, gay rights, and euthanasia.

4-9a Reproductive Freedom

Although foreshadowed in earlier decisions, the right of privacy was first recognized by the Supreme Court in *Griswold v. Connecticut* (1965).[53] Estelle Griswold, the director of Planned Parenthood in Connecticut, was convicted and fined $100 for aiding and abetting persons in using contraceptive devices, an offense under Connecticut law. The Connecticut courts upheld her conviction, rejecting the contention that the state law was unconstitutional. The Supreme Court struck down the Connecticut birth control law by a vote of 7–2, holding that it violated a constitutional guarantee of marital privacy. Seven years later, the Court ruled that the right of privacy was not limited to marital couples, but rather is a right enjoyed by all adults.[54]

The Supreme Court's 1973 ruling in *Roe v. Wade* is, without question, the modern Court's best-known and most controversial decision.[55] Norma McCorvey, also known as Jane Roe, was a twenty-five-year-old unmarried Texas woman who was faced with an unwanted pregnancy. Because abortion was illegal in Texas, Roe brought suit in federal court to challenge the constitutionality of the antiabortion statute. The district court declared the Texas law unconstitutional, but refused to issue an injunction against its enforcement. Roe appealed directly to the Supreme Court.

On appeal, the Supreme Court handed down a 7–2 decision striking down the Texas law. Justice Harry Blackmun wrote the Court's majority opinion, concluding that the right of privacy is broad enough to encompass a woman's decision to terminate her pregnancy. However, Blackmun noted, "the right [to abortion] is not unqualified and must be considered against important state interests." Although a fetus was not, in the Court's view, a "person" within the meaning of the Constitution, states would be permitted (except in cases in which the mother's life would be endangered by carrying the fetus to term) to ban abortion after "viability" (the point in gestation at which the fetus is capable of surviving outside the mother's womb). Dissenting, Justice Rehnquist wrote that "the fact that a majority of the States . . . have had restrictions on abortion for at least a century is a strong indication . . . that the right to an abortion is not 'so rooted in the traditions and conscience of our people to be ranked as fundamental.'"

Roe v. Wade touched off a firestorm of legal and political controversy that has not yet abated. As the Supreme Court became more conservative in the 1980s, support for *Roe v. Wade* among the justices began to erode. Pro-life groups were disappointed, however, that justices appointed by Presidents Reagan and Bush—namely, Sandra Day O'Connor, Anthony Kennedy, and David Souter—refused to go along with a reversal of *Roe v. Wade*. At the same time, pro-choice forces were alarmed at the degree to which the more conservative Court of the late 1980s and early 1990s permitted states to regulate abortion.[56] However, President Clinton's appointment of Ruth Ginsburg, an advocate of women's rights, to the Supreme Court in 1993 made it unlikely that the Court would move further in a conservative direction on the abortion issue. Indeed, this belief was borne out in the spring of 2000, when the Court struck down Nebraska's ban on partial-birth abortion. The Nebraska law in question defined partial-birth abortion as a "procedure in which the person performing the abortion partially delivers vaginally a living unborn child before killing the unborn child and completing the delivery." The Supreme Court, dividing 5–4, invalidated the law because it lacked an exception for the preservation of the health of the mother and imposed an undue burden on a woman's right to choose abortion.[57] Although many people are offended by the partial-birth abortion procedure, the Court pointed out that the real issue is the woman's right to choose, not the method by which abortion is performed.

Public opinion on abortion has remained fairly stable over the years. Survey research has shown that nearly 90 percent of the American people believe that abortion should be legal in cases in which the life of the mother is in jeopardy. About 80 percent believe that it should be available in cases of rape. A similar percentage supports legal abortion in instances of birth defects. Only about 40 percent support the idea that abortion should be available as a means of birth control.[58] Even though the opposition to abortion is intense, the idea of legalized abortion has taken hold in the American culture. The law is unlikely to ever return to the pre–*Roe v. Wade* state. Even if the Supreme Court were to overturn *Roe*, it would still be up to the state legislatures to decide whether to reinstate prohibitions against abortion that are now considered unconstitutional. And even then, state courts could declare these laws unconstitutional under their respective state constitutions. No doubt, if *Roe v. Wade* were overturned, some states would attempt to restrict abortion rights, but by no means would there be a nationwide prohibition on abortion.

4-9b Privacy and Gay Rights

If the right of privacy implies the right of an individual to make his or her own choices in matters of sex and reproduction, how can laws that prohibit homosexual activity be justified? That was the difficult question addressed by the Supreme Court in 1986.[59] Michael Hardwick, a gay man living in Atlanta, was charged with committing sodomy with a consenting male adult in the privacy of his home. Although the state prosecutor decided not to take the case to the grand jury, Hardwick brought suit in federal court, seeking a declaration that the statute was unconstitutional.

The Supreme Court, dividing 5–4, upheld the Georgia law, refusing to recognize "a fundamental right to engage in homosexual sodomy." Writing for the Court, Justice

Byron White stressed the traditional legal and moral prohibitions against sodomy. Responding to the argument that the state has no right to legislate solely on the basis of morality, White wrote that law "is constantly based on notions of morality, and if all laws representing essentially moral choices are to be invalidated . . . the Courts will be very busy indeed." Dissenting, Justice Harry Blackmun disputed the Court's characterization of the issue. For Blackmun and three of his colleagues, the case was not about a "fundamental right to engage in homosexual sodomy," but the more general right of an adult, homosexual or heterosexual, to engage in consensual sexual acts with another adult.

In the wake of the *Hardwick* decision, a number of state courts, relying on their state constitutions, struck down state laws prohibiting homosexual conduct. Indeed, the Georgia Supreme Court invalidated the very law that the U.S. Supreme Court upheld in the *Hardwick* case.[60] Of course, the Georgia court based its decision on the Georgia state constitution as distinct from the U.S. Constitution. Such decisions make an important point about civil liberties in the American federal system. The responsibility for protecting civil liberties rests not only with the Supreme Court and other federal courts; the state courts have an important role to play under their respective state constitutions.

The fact that a number of state courts invalidated their respective states' sodomy laws, combined with the liberalization of American attitudes on the subject of homosexuality in the 1990s, made it almost inevitable that the U.S. Supreme Court would reconsider and overturn *Bowers v. Hardwick*. That is exactly what happened in 2003 when the Court, dividing 6–3, struck down a Texas law criminalizing "deviate sexual intercourse." Writing for the Court, Justice Anthony Kennedy summed up the Court's reasoning as follows:

> *The case. . . involve[s] two adults who, with full and mutual consent from each other, engaged in sexual practices common to a homosexual lifestyle. The petitioners are entitled to respect for their private lives. The State cannot demean their existence or control their destiny by making their private sexual conduct a crime. Their right to liberty under the Due Process Clause gives them the full right to engage in their conduct without intervention of the government. . . . The Texas statute furthers no legitimate state interest which can justify its intrusion into the personal and private life of the individual.*[61]

In his dissenting opinion, Justice Antonin Scalia accused the Court of signing on to an "agenda promoted by some homosexual activists directed at eliminating the moral opprobrium that has traditionally attached to homosexual conduct." Scalia also predicted that the Court's decision would give greater impetus to the legalization of gay marriage, a prediction that was validated in 2004 (see Chapter 5, "Civil Rights and the Struggle for Equality").

Given the contemporary societal debate over the rights of gay men and lesbians, the legal battle over gay rights undoubtedly will continue, both in the courts and in the legislative branch of government. Ultimately, the issue will be resolved by the American people, en masse, who must decide whether to maintain traditional attitudes of disapproval toward homosexuality or adopt a greater level of tolerance.

4-9c THE RIGHT TO DIE

For many years, going back to the famous Karen Quinlan case of the mid-1970s, state courts have recognized that the constitutional right of privacy grants a "right to die" in situations in which an adult is faced with an irreversible, terminal medical condition.[62] Thus far, the right to die has meant the right to force doctors to discontinue treatments that maintain life. Some courts have gone so far as to permit termination of feeding in order to induce death.[63] But where does one draw the line? Can we make a principled distinction between withholding medical care or food and water and active intervention to produce death? Are we moving inexorably down a slippery slope to the legalization of euthanasia? Some countries—most notably, the Netherlands—already have legalized euthanasia centers where people go to die. Would such a policy make sense for this country to emulate? If the right of privacy is the right to control one's own body, why shouldn't any competent adult have the right to commit suicide for any reason? Why should Dr. Jack Kevorkian, the so-called suicide doctor who is now serving a prison sentence for murder, be prosecuted for assisting terminally ill patients in taking their own lives? Courts and legislatures, indeed the American people, are still grappling with these difficult questions.

A real-life drama involving the right to die played out in the national spotlight in 2005. At the center of the drama was Terry Schiavo, a young woman who was in a "persistent vegetative state" due to brain damage she experienced fifteen years earlier. Terry's husband obtained a court order to remove the nasogastric tube that was providing Terry with water and nutrition. But Terry's parents, backed by pro-life organizations, objected to the removal of the tube and fought a protracted but ultimately unsuccessful legal battle to keep their daughter alive. Had Terry made a "living will," a binding declaration of her wishes, before she suffered the brain damage that rendered her unable to communicate, the long legal battle would have been avoided. Nearly all states now have laws allowing competent adults to make living wills. In the absence of such documentation, courts have to make hard decisions about what patients would prefer if they were unable to communicate, or they have to rely on the wishes of surrogates like husbands, parents, and siblings. When family members agree on what should be done, there is no problem. But when they are at odds, as was the case with Terry Schiavo's family, courts have to decide which family member's wishes are controlling. In Florida, the law stated that a spouse's wishes should be determinative, which is why the Florida courts sided with Terry's husband and against her parents. But, again, the struggle over the right to die is much more than a legal or political battle. It is ultimately a cultural struggle between traditional and modern, or postmodern, notions of individual rights and responsibilities.

Controversy

Civil Liberties, the Patriot Act, and the War on Terrorism

Most Americans understand that in time of war or national emergency, civil liberties claims must give way to considerations of national security. Certainly, that has happened many times historically, most notably during the Civil War and World War II. The terrorist attacks of 9/11 and the subsequent "war on terrorism" raised this issue again, but in a very different context. The war on terrorism is an unusual war. The enemy is not a nation-state, and the enemy combatants are not conventional soliders. The war on terrorism may go on for decades. Does the war on terrorism provide a justification for the curtailment of civil liberties?

Shortly after 9/11, Congress enacted the Patriot Act of 2001. The law signficantly enhanced the powers of law enforcement and intelligence agencies to investigate suspected terrorists and other national security threats. For example, the law authorized law enforcement agencies to conduct a "sneak and peek" search of a residence—a search in which the occupants are not immediately informed, as long as the Attorney General has determined that the search is necessary to protect national security. The act also made it easier for federal officials to obtain wiretap orders and engage in other forms of electronic surveillance. It allowed government agents access to student records, library records, and even medical records. The law also provided for indefinite incarceration of non-U.S. citizens without any sort of trial, again as long as the Attorney General has determined such persons to be a threat to national security. The Patriot Act also removed legal barriers against the sharing of information by law enforcement and intelligence agencies.

During the 2004 presidential campaign, President Bush repeatedly extolled the virtues of the Patriot Act, which the White House said was "needed to stop terrorists before they strike, fulfilling America's duty to win the War on Terror." Civil libertarians took a very different view of the issue. The American Civil Liberties Union and numerous other organizations have been waging their own sort of war against the Patriot Act. They have tried to sway public opinion against the act. They have lobbied Congress not to renew the legislation, which was due to expire at the end of 2005. They have even gone to court to challenge the constitutionality of certain parts of the legislation. The future of the Patriot Act rests with federal judges and members of Congress, but these officials will likely be swayed both by public opinion and by events.

4-10 CONCLUSION: CIVIL LIBERTIES—A QUESTION OF BALANCE

Individual rights are widely seen as an indispensable feature of democracy. That is certainly true in the case of American democracy, in which individual rights are guaranteed by the U.S. Constitution. Yet individual rights exist in constant tension with majority rule, another essential feature of democracy. Individual rights must be balanced against legitimate societal interests in morality, order, public health and safety, and even national security. When policies reflecting these interests conflict with constitutional rights, the principal responsibility for striking a balance belongs to the courts. Yet the courts are influenced by the events of the day, by the other institutions of government, by public opinion, and, ultimately, by the political culture of the nation. At the same time, one must recognize that landmark court decisions—indeed, all political events—have an impact on the underlying political culture. Sometimes the political culture will evolve to accept, even embrace, court decisions that were once regarded as extremely controversial. To many people, especially those of a conservative persuasion, American society has come to value individual rights to such a degree that the very fabric of society is now threatened. One can point to numerous examples—including gay rights, pornography, and legalized abortion—that many regard as undermining traditional values.

The American people are now alarmed by the persistent threat of terrorism. Naturally, people look to government to protect them against this and other threats to their security. In dealing with these types of threats, the danger exists that government will go too far in curtailing the rights and liberties of American citizens. Of course, it is the role of courts, applying the principles of the Bill of Rights, to see that this situation does not happen or at least to minimize the curtailment of freedom. It will be interesting to see whether, in the face of the terrorist threat, American political culture will come to value domestic security over individual liberty. More likely, society will continue to struggle to balance these competing values, and the law of civil liberties will ebb and flow accordingly.

Questions for Thought and Discussion

1. Could the Framers of the Bill of Rights have conceived of pornography as "speech" that would be protected by the First Amendment? What is the rationale for granting this type of expression a degree of constitutional protection?

2. What is meant by the term *hate speech*? Does it fall within the protections of the First Amendment? Does the First Amendment give a person the right to use racial and ethnic slurs in public?

3. To what extent does the First Amendment apply to the Internet? Does the First Amendment protect someone's right to put up a website devoted to propagating hatred against minorities? What if the site advocates violence against specific types of people and suggests means whereby such violence might be carried out?

4. Would the Second Amendment, which speaks of "the right to keep and bear arms," prohibit Congress from enacting a law generally prohibiting the sale and possession of all handguns?

5. Do the federal courts now favor the rights of the accused over the rights of crime victims?

6. Was the Supreme Court correct in finding a "right of privacy" in the Constitution?

7. Is Congress' recognition of Christmas as a national holiday a violation of the principle of separation of church and state? Why or why not?

8. Would a federal statute banning partial-birth abortion be likely to withstand constitutional scrutiny?

9. What arguments can be made for and against the constitutionality of the death penalty?

10. Are civil liberties seriously threatened by the government's efforts to prevent domestic terrorism?

Endnotes

1 See, for example, *Fay v. Noia*, 372 U.S. 391 (1963).

2 See, for example, *Stone v. Powell*, 428 U.S. 465 (1976).

3 *Felker v. Turpin*, 518 U.S. 1051 (1996).

4 *United States v. Brown*, 381 U.S. 437 (1965).

5 *Calder v. Bull*, 3 U.S. (3 Dall.) 386 (1798).

6 *Chicago, Burlington and Quincy Railroad v. City of Chicago*, 166 U.S. 226 (1897).

7 *Nollan v. California Coastal Commission*, 483 U.S. 825 (1987).

8 *Goldberg v. Kelly*, 397 U.S. 254 (1970).

9 Justice Benjamin Nathan Cardozo, writing for the Supreme Court in *Palko v. Connecticut*, 302 U.S. 319 (1937).

10 *Milk Wagon Drivers Union v. Meadowmoor Dairies*, 312 U.S. 287 (1941).

11 *City of Erie et al. v. Pap's A.M.*, 529 U.S. 277, 120 S.Ct. 1382, 146 L. Ed. 2d 265 (2000).

12 *New York Times Co. v. United States*, 403 U.S. 713 (1971).

13 "Prosecutors say Manning collaborated with Wikileaks' Assange in stealing secret documents," *The Washington Post*, December 22, 2011. http://articles.washingtonpost.com/2011-12-22/national/35287366_1_david-e-coombs-wikileaks-assange-julian-assange

14 *Schenck v. United States*, 249 U.S. 47 (1919).

15 *Brandenburg v. Ohio*, 395 U.S. 444 (1969).

16 *Chaplinsky v. New Hampshire*, 315 U.S. 568 (1942).

17 *Cohen v. California*, 403 U.S. 15 (1971).

18 *People v. Boomer*, 655 N.W.2d 255 (Mich. App. 2002).

19 *Miller v. California*, 413 U.S. 15 (1973).

20 *Reno v. ACLU*, 521 U.S. 844 (1997).

21 *Ashcroft v. Free Speech Coalition*, 535 U.S. 234 (2002).

22 *New York Times Co. v. Sullivan*, 376 U.S. 254 (1964).

23 *Curtis Publishing Co. v. Butts*, 388 U.S. 130 (1967).

24 "Manti Te'o Girlfriend Hoax," *USA Today Online*. http://www.usatoday.com/topic/d460b578-e191-4e1f-bb7c-957e01c4e031/manti-te'o-hoax/

25 *National Socialist Party v. Village of Skokie*, 432 U.S. 43 (1977).

26 *Boos v. Barry*, 485 U.S. 312 (1983).

27 *Scales v. United States*, 367 U.S. 203 (1961).

28 *Boy Scouts of America v. Dale*, 530 U.S. 640 (2000).

29 *Lemon v. Kutzman*, 403 U.S. 602 (1971).

30 See, for example, *Engel v. Vitale*, 370 U.S. 421 (1962); *Abington School District v. Schempp*, 374 U.S. 203 (1963).

31 *Edwards v. Aguillard*, 482 U.S. 578 (1987).

32 *Santa Fe Independent School District v. Doe*, 530 U.S. 290 (2000).

33 See, for example, *Cantwell v. Connecticut*, 310 U.S. 296 (1940).

34 *Reynolds v. United States*, 98 U.S. 145 (1879).

35 *Wisconsin v. Yoder*, 406 U.S. 205 (1972).

36 *Employment Division, Department of Human Resources of Oregon v. Smith*, 494 U.S. 872 (1990).

37 *Church of the Lukumi Babalu Aye, Inc. v. City of Hialeah*, 113 S.Ct. 2217 (1993).

38 *United States v. Miller*, 307 U.S. 174 (1939).

39 *Lewis v. United States*, 445 U.S. 55 (1980).

40 *District of Columbia v. Heller*, 128 S. Ct. 2783 (2008); *McDonald v. Chicago*, 561 U.S. 3025 (2010).

41 *Katz v. United States*, 389 U.S. 347 (1967).

42 *Mapp v. Ohio*, 367 U.S. 643 (1961).

43 *United States v. Leon*, 468 U.S. 897 (1984).

44 *Katz v. United States*, 389 U.S. 347 (1967).

45 *Kyllo v. United States*, 121 S.Ct. 2038 (2001).

46 *Miranda v. Arizona*, 384 U.S. 436 (1966).

47 *United States v. Dickerson*, 530 U.S. 428 (2000).

48 *Gideon v. Wainwright*, 372 U.S. 335 (1963).

49 *Trop v. Dulles*, 356 U.S. 86 (1958).

50 *Furman v. Georgia*, 408 U.S. 256 (1972).

51 *Gregg v. Georgia*, 428 U.S. 153 (1976).

52 *Herrera v. Collins*, 113 S.Ct. 853 (1993).

53 *Griswold v. Connecticut*, 381 U.S. 479 (1965).

54 *Eisenstadt v. Baird*, 405 U.S. 438 (1972).

55 *Roe v. Wade*, 410 U.S. 113 (1973).

56 *Webster v. Reproductive Health Services*, 492 U.S. 490 (1989); *Planned Parenthood v. Casey*, 112 S.Ct. 2791 (1992).

57 *Stenberg v. Carhart*, 430 U.S. 914 (2000).

58 For a nice summary of public opinion on abortion from 1965 to 2002, see Harold W. Stanley and Richard G. Niemi, *Vital Statistics on American Politics, 2003–2004* (Washington, D.C.: Congressional Quarterly Press, 2003), p. 160.

59 *Bowers v. Hardwick*, 478 U.S. 186 (1986).

60 *Powell v. State*, 510 S.E.3d 18, 26 (Ga. 1998).

61 *Lawrence v. Texas*, 539 U.S. 558, 578 (2003).

62 *In re Quinlan*, 355 A.2d. 647 (N.J. 1976).

63 See, for example, *Bouvia v. Superior Court*, 179 Cal. App. 3d 1127 (1986).

Chapter 5

CIVIL RIGHTS AND THE STRUGGLE FOR EQUALITY

OUTLINE

Key Terms 150

Expected Learning Outcomes 150

5-1 Equality and American Democracy 150
- **5-1a** Equality and the Founding of the Republic 151
- **5-1b** Two Faces of Discrimination 152

5-2 The Struggle for Racial Equality 153
- **5-2a** Civil Rights Measures Enacted after the Civil War 154
- **5-2b** The Cementing of Second-Class Citizenship 155
- **5-2c** The Decline of "Separate but Equal" 159
- **5-2d** The Civil Rights Movement 162
- **5-2e** The Civil Rights Act of 1964 164
- **5-2f** Dismantling Segregation: An Active Role for Government 166
- **5-2g** Affirmative Action 168
- **5-2h** Racial Discrimination in Voting Rights 170
- **5-2i** Civil Rights for Other Racial and Ethnic Groups 173

5-3 Sex Discrimination 176
- **5-3a** Women's Struggle for Political Equality 177
- **5-3b** Women in Military Service 178
- **5-3c** Sex Discrimination by Educational Institutions 179
- **5-3d** Women in the Workforce 180
- **5-3e** Affirmative Action on Behalf of Women 180
- **5-3f** Sexual Harassment 181

5-4 Other Civil Rights Issues 182
- **5-4a** Age Discrimination 183
- **5-4b** Discrimination against the Poor 183
- **5-4c** Discrimination against Persons with Disabilities 184
- **5-4d** The Controversy over Gay Rights 185

5-5 Conclusion: Evolving Notions of Equality 191

Questions for Thought and Discussion 193

Endnotes 195

KEY TERMS

affirmative action
apartheid
at-large voting
busing
civil rights movement
cracking
de facto segregation
de jure segregation
discrimination
equality of opportunity
equality of result
gerrymandering
grandfather clause
Jim Crow laws
judicial federalism
literacy test
majority minority districts
packing
proportional representation
racial profiling
separate but equal
sexual harassment
vote dilution
white primary

EXPECTED LEARNING OUTCOMES

After reading this chapter and completing the supplemental online materials, students will:

- Compare civil liberties and rights
- Identify sources of civil rights in the U.S. Constitution
- Evaluate the protection of civil rights throughout U.S. history for group victims of discrimination
- Contrast civil rights controversies among different groups over time
- Evaluate the expansion of civil rights protections over time

5-1 EQUALITY AND AMERICAN DEMOCRACY

For the last fifty years, the civil rights portion of American government textbooks and courses focused primarily on the 1960s-era civil rights movement and the relations between the African American minority and the white majority in American society. The election of Barack Obama as President signaled enormous changes that American society has experienced regarding race relations. Black-white relations are not perfect by any means, and important civil rights questions involving race remain on the public agenda. But in recent years these issues have been joined by a variety of other civil rights controversies involving the rights of women, the poor, and immigrants who are in this country illegally. Without question, the most salient civil rights issue of the last decade has been the rights of lesbians, gays, bisexuals, and transsexuals (LGBT). Discrimination on the basis of sexual orientation has been attacked on many fronts, and policies and attitudes have changed markedly in recent years. But in most states same-sex marriage is still prohibited, which means that gay men and lesbians are denied the legal and economic benefits associated with marriage. As of 2011, gay and lesbian Americans are now permitted to serve openly in the military. And while some states and communities have adopted laws prohibiting discrimination on the basis of sexual orientation, the federal government has yet to adopt such laws. Thus, civil rights remains very much a contested and dynamic area of public policy. By 2013 multiple cases went before the Supreme Court seeking to clarify the murky legal status of gay marriage in America.

ONLINE 5.1
Gay Marriage Rights in the States
http://graphics.latimes.com/usmap-gay-marriage-chronology/

Civil rights can be thought of as the intersection of majority rule and minority rights. One potential deficiency of democracy is the way majorities deal with minorities. An unfortunate but undeniable element of the human condition is the tendency of many people to distrust and dislike those who are unlike them. Because the political system is the device by which a democratic society allocates its values, majorities tend to use political institutions to their benefit and to the detriment of minority groups. Left unchecked, this tendency can lead to the dehumanization of those who are different. "Difference" can be based on any number of criteria, including race, religion, gender, age, sexual orientation, physical disability, or political affiliation. The Founders, well aware of this "majority/minority problem," placed institutional limits on the power of majorities.

At any time, any identifiable group faces the potential of discrimination. Although African Americans have been the most obvious victims of discrimination in America, other groups have been singled out for adverse treatment, often in times of war or threats of war. For instance, during World War II, Japanese Americans on the West Coast were "relocated" to detention camps as fears grew that they might engage in sabotage or espionage. In the wake of the terrorist attacks of September 11, 2001, many people feared that persons of Middle Eastern descent might be subjected to hate crimes or singled out for investigation by law enforcement authorities. In contemporary America, this type of treatment is characterized as a civil rights issue.

A *civil right* is a legal assurance of equal treatment by the society. Of course, a right is not self-executing—it has no meaning unless it is supported by a reasonable degree of societal consensus. For example, a right to equal treatment based on race did not exist in revolutionary America. It would take two centuries of social, economic, and political change, including a bloody civil war, before African Americans would acquire the right to equal treatment before the law. Even now, some people doubt whether African Americans have fully received equal treatment.

5-1a Equality and the Founding of the Republic

The term *democracy* did not elicit particularly positive reactions from elites in colonial America. The term brought to mind images of a mob, possibly driven by emotion, certainly motivated by self-interest, taking control of the machinery of government. Despite the physical separation of the colonies from Europe, there can be no denying the impact of European politics on American thinking and values. In France, the monarchy had been toppled in a revolution that shook the foundations of French society. Liberty and equality had been the watchwords of the French Revolution. In their name, virtually all institutions were shaken to the core. Blood truly flowed in the streets of Paris. Americans probably felt comfortable with the overthrow of the monarchy and the French aristocracy, but the chaos that followed was frightening. Thus, the prevailing political culture of late-eighteenth-century America did not foster either mass participation or equality, at least not in the ways these terms would come to be used in the latter part of the twentieth century.

Nevertheless, in the original Constitution, majority and minority rights were matters of considerable concern. The Founders viewed minorities in terms of economic interests first, religious ones second, and racial or ethnic groups not at all. There was, for instance, genuine fear of conflicts between debtors and creditors, and between farmers and merchants. The unique channeling of conflict through the systems of federalism and checks and balances was largely in anticipation of heightened passions among one or more of these groups. At the same time, the Framers of the Constitution showed little concern for the rights of racial and ethnic minorities or the rights of women.

The idea of equality has taken hold and expanded as the United States has become more of a democracy. Most Americans now believe in equality, at least abstractly. Most hold the idea that all citizens should be equal before the law and government. Most Americans also believe in **equality of opportunity**, the idea that people should be given an equal chance to succeed in life. Of course, turning these abstract ideals into policy is difficult and divisive. In making the laws and policies that give concrete meaning to civil rights, citizens must confront the realities of group animosities, social and economic inequalities, and discrimination.

5-1b Two Faces of Discrimination

The term **discrimination** refers to the conscious or unconscious denial of equal treatment to a person based on their membership in some recognizable group. Discrimination can be public or private. This distinction is often of critical importance because a great deal of discrimination is not governmental, but is committed by private citizens pursuing their interests in the private sector. Discrimination by government and discrimination by private citizens must be confronted by very different strategies. Government-sponsored discrimination can be eliminated by laws and constitutional amendments, but discrimination in the hearts and minds of individuals is much harder to identify, limit, and change.

The Question of Private Discrimination

Because it exists outside of the law, discrimination by private citizens is not a constitutional question. The federal and state constitutions prohibit only discrimination that is based on law or public policy, not private discrimination. If a landlord decides that she will not rent a house to an African American family, that decision does not constitute a denial of the constitutional right to equal protection of the laws. The constitutional obligation to provide equal protection applies to government agencies and officials, but not directly to private actors. This reflects the larger principle that constitutions limit government and that constitutional rights are protections against adverse government action. The only way that private discrimination can be fought is by passage of a law that outlaws the discrimination. In other words, the legislature must act before the dispute can become a legal matter. Then, if the discrimination continues to occur, the affected party can obtain relief through the courts. But unless a law specifically prohibits the discriminatory act, the courts can provide little recourse. In the modern era, Congress and the state legislatures have enacted far-reaching legislation to combat the problem of private discrimination. Some have suggested that some of these laws go too far—that they combat discrimination at the expense of civil liberties. In some instances, the courts have agreed.[1] The essential problem is to strike an appropriate balance between people's freedom to express themselves and make their own decisions and everyone else's right to be treated fairly.

5-2 The Struggle for Racial Equality

The development of civil rights in the United States is linked historically with the evolving status of African Americans. The fundamental fact that defined the status of African Americans at the time of the Constitutional Convention was that they had been brought forcibly to this country to work as slaves. As slaves, African Americans were denied the most fundamental of human rights. Chief Justice Roger Taney's majority opinion for the Supreme Court in the infamous Dred Scott case (1857) asserted that persons of African descent "were not intended to be included under the word 'citizens' in the Constitution" and could therefore claim none of the rights and privileges it secures to citizens of the United States. In Taney's view, they were "a subordinate and inferior class

© Ira Bostic, 2013. Used under license from Shutterstock, Inc.

of beings, . . . and had no rights or privileges but such as those who held the power and the Government might choose to grant them."[2] Of course, the racism reflected in the Dred Scott decision was not limited to the Supreme Court, but was also embedded in the political culture of the day, especially that of the South. Even in the North, calls for the abolition of slavery seldom implied the full participation of African Americans in American society.

The dehumanizing and wretched conditions that African Americans endured in the early and mid-nineteenth century are well known. Even freed slaves in northern states were accorded second-class citizenship at best. Although the Civil War and subsequent amendments to the Constitution formally abolished slavery and "guaranteed" the right to vote and equal protection of the law to the citizens who had been slaves, these rights were not readily forthcoming. Having laws is good, but they must be carried out, and African Americans found themselves in a society where both the power of government officials and the actions of private individuals made life incredibly unequal. Before African Americans could begin to enjoy full participation in American society, they had to overcome a vast array of institutions and policies that were geared against them. As minorities in a federal system, they faced both public and private discrimination at the local, state, and national levels. This discrimination took on a multitude of forms. It would be more than a century before the battle could even be fully joined, let alone won.

5-2a Civil Rights Measures Enacted after the Civil War

Slavery was formally abolished by the ratification of the Thirteenth Amendment to the Constitution in 1865. Three years later, the Fourteenth Amendment was ratified. This amendment had a number of important components. First, it effectively overturned the *Dred Scott* decision by announcing, "All persons born or naturalized in the United States, and subject to the jurisdiction thereof, are citizens of the United States and of the State wherein they reside." Second, in a clause that would play a major role in many civil rights cases in the following century, the Fourteenth Amendment provided: "nor shall any State deprive any person of life, liberty, or property, without due process of law; nor deny to any person within its jurisdiction the equal protection of the laws." The Fifteenth Amendment, ratified in 1870, forbade the federal and state governments from denying the right to vote "on account of race, color, or previous condition of servitude." Known collectively as the Civil War amendments, the Thirteenth, Fourteenth, and Fifteenth Amendments provided a constitutional basis for the protection of civil rights. Not for many years, however, would the promise implicit in these amendments begin to materialize.

In addition to outlawing slavery, guaranteeing the right to vote, and prohibiting states from denying persons due process and equal protection of the law, the Civil War amendments granted Congress the power to adopt "appropriate legislation" to protect civil rights. In the decade following the Civil War, Congress passed a number of important civil rights statutes. One of these laws, the Civil Rights Act of 1875, attempted to eradicate racial discrimination in "places of public accommodation," including hotels, taverns, restaurants, theaters, and "public conveyances." This act was an ambitious one that, if enforced, would have represented a direct confrontation to the southern way of life.

The Reconstruction Era effectively ended by the close of the 1870s. By that time, little sentiment existed in the North for continuing what were viewed as punitive measures against the South. The states of the old Confederacy had chafed at the changes wrought in their region by Reconstruction. Southern state legislatures were quickly taken over by politicians who reflected the region's unreconstructed political culture.

5-2b The Cementing of Second-Class Citizenship

With the ratification of the Civil War amendments, African Americans were formally granted citizenship, given the right to vote, and guaranteed "equal protection of the laws." But it is difficult to imagine how any group who had suffered the humiliation of slavery could be expected to participate effectively in American society under the best of circumstances. African Americans were without education, land, and property and certainly were not welcome in white society. It was soon clear, moreover, that any gains made in the post–Civil War period would be short-lived at best. Unfortunately, late-nineteenth-century America was not willing to welcome African Americans as equal citizens. Accordingly, the Supreme Court and the state legislatures rendered decisions that led to a two-tiered society based on race.

The Civil Rights Cases of 1883

In 1883, the Supreme Court struck down the key provisions of the Civil Rights Act of 1875, ruling that the Fourteenth Amendment limited congressional action to only the prohibition of official, state-sponsored discrimination, not discrimination practiced by privately owned places of public accommodation.[3] This interpretation provided an implicit right for private individuals to discriminate against others. Moreover, this decision severely restricted the Equal Protection Clause of the Fourteenth Amendment. It would be eighty years before Congress would again attempt to pass legislation outlawing private discrimination. Meanwhile, individuals were free to discriminate. The white-dominated political culture of the South, and to some degree the rest of the country, fully supported this type of discrimination.

The reality of life for African Americans was a separate and clearly substandard existence. Whatever freedom had been provided by the abolition of slavery was tempered by the social and economic realities of a two-tiered society. Whites would hire African Americans for only the most menial of jobs at the lowest pay. In the unlikely event that African Americans found themselves with any disposable income, they could spend it only at the few inferior establishments open to them. The mainstream of society was closed to African Americans. Not only were private individuals in positions of power allowed to discriminate, but governments also provided active support for this way of life with a whole series of laws that gave the stamp of approval to racial segregation.

The Jim Crow Laws

Beginning in the 1880s, a number of state legislatures passed a series of laws that virtually mandated a dual society based on race. Most southern and border states changed their constitutions to create separate school systems. Laws required African Americans and whites to ride in separate railroad cars, to use separate facilities in public buildings, and even to be buried in separate cemeteries. Courts maintained separate Bibles so that white witnesses would not have to touch the same Bible touched by African Americans. The desire for total racial separation was so strong that segregation became a fundamental state policy enshrined in the state constitutions; as a result, later legislatures were unable to change the policy through simple majority votes.

The southern states did much more than establish a dual society. They also ensured a separate and very unequal society. Public schools provided for black children were clearly inferior. The few black colleges existed mainly for the purpose of training black teachers to work in all-black schools. These institutions were underfunded. No state-run black medical or dental schools existed, and African Americans were not allowed to attend the white professional schools. Thus, there was virtually no way to develop a black middle or professional class. The laws by which this separation was effected were known as **Jim Crow laws**, after a character in a popular minstrel show.

ONLINE 5.2
Life under Jim Crow
https://www.youtube.com/watch?v=7wY-ZZogyJo

In 1896, the U.S. Supreme Court upheld the Jim Crow regime. In *Plessy v. Ferguson*, the Court was asked to review a Louisiana law mandating racial segregation on trains.[4] Homer Plessy, who was one-eighth black, challenged the Louisiana law. Plessy knew he would be arrested for refusing to give up his seat on the whites-only railroad car, but subjected himself to arrest in order to test the law. In the United States, a law cannot just be challenged as unconstitutional—the courts may strike down laws only when necessary to resolve a dispute where one party has shown loss or injury. In the case of a criminal law such as the Louisiana statute at issue in *Plessy*, a person must be arrested or face the real danger of prosecution before the courts will entertain a constitutional challenge.

Plessy was successful in getting the Supreme Court to review the Louisiana law, but he was profoundly disappointed with the Court's decision. The Court would allow separate facilities for African Americans as long as they were "equal." Justice

John Marshall Harlan dissented, arguing that the "arbitrary separation of citizens on the basis of race" was tantamount to imposing a "badge of servitude" on African Americans. The following words from Justice Harlan's dissenting opinion set forth his idea of the "color-blind" Constitution:

> *Our constitution is color blind, and neither knows nor tolerates classes among citizens. In respect of civil rights, all are equal before the law. The humblest is the peer of the most powerful. The law regards man as man, and takes no account of his color when his civil rights as guaranteed by the supreme law of the land are involved.*

The Court's ruling in *Plessy v. Ferguson* would dominate the landscape of civil rights for half a century. The Court had put its blessing on a segregated society. In doing so, it elevated the term **separate but equal** to the status of supreme law. In reality, of course, separate was rarely equal in a Jim Crow society. Not surprisingly, the *Plessy* decision deflated any hope that American political institutions would confront racial injustice. Fifty-eight years would pass before the Court would fully confront the contradictions of separate but equal.

Electoral Disfranchisement

Even though a great many African Americans were registered to vote during Reconstruction, most had been taken off the voting rolls by the end of the nineteenth century. Although the Fifteenth Amendment was supposed to protect against the denial of voting rights by state governments, white-dominated state legislatures found a number of indirect means to keep African Americans from participating in the political process. One of these was the **grandfather clause**, which granted automatic and permanent registration to any person directly descended from someone who had voted before 1865. African Americans, who could not qualify for automatic registration because their ancestors were slaves, were required to take a **literacy test**. The state literacy exams were often high-level constitutional tests rather than simple tests of reading ability. Not surprisingly, whites who took the test were not required to demonstrate similar levels of "literacy."

Another device that kept African Americans (and poor whites) from voting was the poll tax. This tax was literally a fee for the privilege of voting. Finally, another major impediment to the full participation of African Americans in the political process in the South was the one-party system. The Republican party, as the party of Abraham Lincoln and the Union, was virtually dead until the 1950s in the South. Therefore, the Democratic party enjoyed total dominance. Its nominees for state office and Congress were always elected overwhelmingly in general elections. Because the party nominees were chosen in primary elections, the primaries were the real elections. The political parties were private organizations, which could have their own rules. So in the South, the Democrats excluded African Americans. Because they could not run in or vote in Democratic primaries, they were excluded from voting in the general election. The U.S. Supreme Court overturned the **white primary** in 1942.[5]

The electoral situation for African Americans in the South was bleak, to put it mildly. In 1959, 159 counties in eight states had black majorities in their voting age populations. In fifty-one of these counties, fewer than 3 percent of blacks were registered to vote.[6] Registration was next to impossible. In the unlikely event that African Americans could pass the literacy test and pay the poll tax, they were allowed to vote only in a general election that played no role in determining who would be elected. Moreover, beatings and other forms of intimidation were common.

A Failure of Democratic Institutions

At the end of the nineteenth century, most African Americans lived in the South. They were citizens, but this status had little meaning. Southern state governments were dominated by white interests, which structured the rules of participation to keep African Americans out of the decision-making arena. The few African Americans who managed to make their way to northern states did not face the overt legal and political discrimination that plagued African Americans in the South, but in reality the political culture of the North did not provide much more support or opportunity than that of the South.

Before the mid-twentieth century, there was no sign of any national will to confront the South. Congress could do very little, in large part because southern senators, who tended to be reelected repeatedly, held positions of power. Nor did the Supreme Court show any real inclination to confront the states on their obvious violations of the Civil War amendments. Thus, by exploiting existing political institutions and procedures, the white majority was able to use the machinery of government to cement its superior status in society.

The Lack of Protest

From a contemporary standpoint, you might wonder why African Americans seemed to accept their second-class citizenship with minimal protest. For many years, defenders of the status quo were able to point to what appeared to be acquiescence on the part of African Americans. This type of interpretation was highly misleading, however. African Americans simply had no effective way to challenge the status quo. Blacks had no reason to think that they could ever enjoy equality with whites. African Americans were told in a myriad of ways that they should stay in their "place." No institution or politician dared articulate, let alone espouse, their cause. Any African American so foolish as to stray from her place faced a high likelihood of a violent visit from the Ku Klux Klan, which had been formed during Reconstruction as a secret society dedicated to the intimidation of blacks. This intimidation often took the form of murder, with lynching as the preferred mode of execution. African Americans, especially in the South, were virtually without hope.

5-2c The Decline of "Separate but Equal"

It was only a matter of time before state-mandated racial segregation would be challenged in the courts. It is not surprising that most of the major challenges involved the educational system. Most southern states had constitutionally mandated separate school systems, which kept African Americans in a social and economic straitjacket. Through the educational system, the machinery of state government was used to maintain existing social patterns, keep African Americans in low-paying jobs and out of the professions.

The Decline of Legally Mandated School Segregation

The battle against legally mandated segregated education was waged in the courts from the top down. The first successful cases challenged segregated graduate and professional education. Concentrating first on higher education was a sound approach for two reasons. First, the injustices at this level were so clear-cut that they could not be justified under the rather tenuous logic of separate but equal. Most often, a state had only one law school or medical school, and African Americans were not allowed to attend. Second, few whites were affected, and those affected were adults. The number of students and the emotional impact involved in these early cases were thus much less than in later battles involving elementary and high schools.

In 1950, the Supreme Court invalidated an attempt by the state of Texas to establish a separate law school for blacks. The Court found that the newly created law school at the Texas College for Negroes was substantially inferior in both measurable and intangible factors to the whites-only law school at the University of Texas. Consequently, the state had failed to live up to the requirement of the Fourteenth Amendment, which prohibited the states from denying "equal protection of the laws" to their citizens.[7] Of course, Texas argued unsuccessfully that it was entitled to run its educational system as it wanted and that the original intent of the Fourteenth Amendment, as ratified by the states in 1868, had nothing to do with the racial segregation of educational institutions.

The Supreme Court's Texas law school decision and other similar decisions rendered in the early 1950s marked the unraveling of the fabric of *Plessy v. Ferguson*. State educational systems clearly were not equal, and African American plaintiffs increasingly found the federal courts to be sympathetic to their grievances. The courts were willing to take seriously the contention that the states were overstepping their role in the federal system by keeping blacks out of some educational institutions.

The *Brown* Decision

In the 1940s, the National Association for the Advancement of Colored People (NAACP) mounted a major challenge to segregated public schools by instituting lawsuits in a number of southern states. The NAACP's Legal Defense Fund at first concentrated its attack on the inequality of the separate school systems in these states. Then, under the leadership of its chief legal counsel, Thurgood Marshall (who would later be appointed to the Supreme Court by President Lyndon Johnson), the NAACP decided to confront directly the separate but equal foundations of the *Plessy* decision. These cases reached the Supreme Court in 1952, but because of the political magnitude of the issue, the Court asked for the cases to be reargued in 1953. On May 17, 1954, the Court unanimously struck down racial segregation in the public schools. Speaking for the Court in *Brown v. Board of Education*, Chief Justice Earl Warren declared that "in the field of public education, the doctrine of 'separate but equal' has no place. Separate educational facilities are inherently unequal."[8]

The *Brown* decision of 1954 left open the question of how and when desegregation would be achieved. In a follow-up decision in 1955, the Court adopted a formula calling for the implementation of desegregation with "all deliberate speed," but the precise meaning of that phrase was not clear.[9] The Court recognized the magnitude of the task of desegregation in the South and wanted to give lower court judges some flexibility in responding to challenges to segregated schools. In many states, more than a decade passed before meaningful dismantling of segregated school systems was under way.

State Challenges to the Implementation of *Brown*

The political culture of the South in the 1950s harbored tremendous hostility to the idea of court-mandated desegregation. Some southerners saw integration of the public schools as tantamount to the breakdown of the social order. They looked to their state and local officials to fight implementation of the *Brown* decision. Many politicians based their careers on fighting the integration of public schools and universities. In 1956, 101 southern members of Congress signed The Southern Manifesto, in which they expressed their conviction that the Court had erred in the *Brown* decision and pledged to fight for its reversal.

Although the dominant political culture of the South was firmly opposed to school desegregation, the rest of the country was indifferent at best. President Dwight D. Eisenhower remained neutral on the merits of the *Brown* decision, but did say that as president he was obliged to see that the law of the land was enforced.[10] He soon had the opportunity to do so. In 1957, Governor Orval Faubus of Arkansas and other state and local officials sought to block the court-ordered desegregation of Central High School

PROFILES & PERSPECTIVES
Thurgood Marshall
(1908–1993)

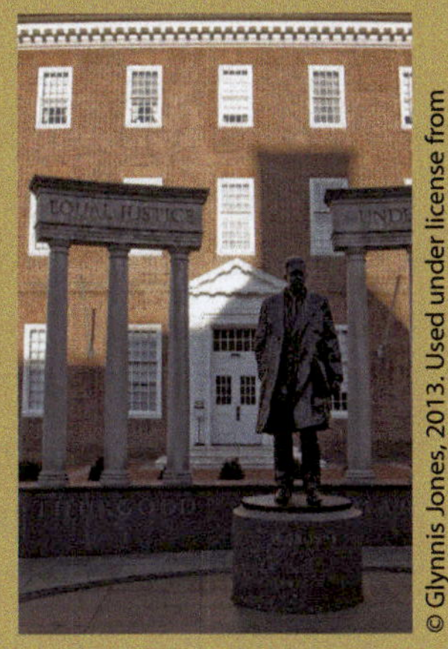

Thurgood Marshall, the first African American to be appointed to the Supreme Court, was born in Baltimore in 1908. After graduating first in his class from Howard University Law School in 1933, Marshall became special counsel to the NAACP. As the most prominent lawyer working in the civil rights movement, Marshall won some thirty legal victories in the U.S. Supreme Court. By far, the most significant was *Brown v. Board of Education* (1954), in which the Supreme Court struck down laws mandating racial segregation in public schools. In 1961, President John F. Kennedy nominated Marshall to a position on the U.S. Court of Appeals. Despite the strenuous opposition of southern senators, Marshall was finally confirmed. In 1965, President Johnson appointed Marshall the U.S. solicitor general, in effect the government's chief advocate before the Supreme Court. Two years later, President Johnson appointed Marshall to the High Court, where he served until ill health forced his retirement in 1991. Marshall died of heart failure on January 24, 1993. His body lay in state in the Great Hall of the Supreme Court building as thousands of Americans turned out to pay their last respects.

For more information, check out these links:
http://www.ai.mit.edu/~isbell/HFh/black/events_and_people/html/001.thurgood_marshall.html
http://www.oyez.org/justices/justices.cgi?justice_id=96&page=overview

in Little Rock. The governor's action caused the Little Rock School Board to petition the federal district court for a delay in the implementation of its desegregation order. In reviewing the case, the Supreme Court refused to allow the delay. In an unusual step, the Court produced an opinion coauthored by all nine justices. The opinion issued a stern rebuke to Governor Faubus, reminding him of his duty to uphold the Constitution.[11]

The events surrounding the desegregation of Little Rock Central High School captured the attention of the nation. Governor Faubus refused to provide protection to the black students who were to attend the school. In fact, he tried to use the Arkansas National Guard to prevent them from entering the school. President Eisenhower took command of the guard and sent federal troops to the city to ensure the students' safety. As they approached the high school, the black students were spat on by a screaming mob of hostile whites. Pictures of the scene made the national news, and the story ran on the front page of magazines and newspapers across the country. The strategy of the white protesters backfired, however. The school was not only successfully integrated, but the scenes of hatred and intolerance also helped build support for the fledgling **civil rights movement** that had begun in earnest a few years earlier.

5-2d THE CIVIL RIGHTS MOVEMENT

The small group of lawyers who petitioned the courts for an end to state-sponsored segregated schools helped set in motion a movement that eventually led to equal citizenship for African Americans. Until the late 1940s, African Americans had had little reason to hope for an end to either private discrimination or the state-mandated segregation that had been sanctioned by the *Plessy* decision. Notably, the courts, the branch of government furthest removed from the passions of the majority, were the initial means of cutting through the laws and customs that supported the South's segregated way of life. As the courts began to strike down state laws as unconstitutional in the late 1940s and the Supreme Court prepared to reconsider the doctrine of separate but equal in the early 1950s, African Americans began to find reason for hope and to seek ways to challenge segregation at its roots.

To succeed, however, the civil rights movement would have to not only attract African Americans but also win white support. The bus boycott of 1955 in Montgomery, Alabama, did much to accomplish both objectives. The boycott began after Rosa Parks was arrested for refusing to move to the back of the bus, as required by a Montgomery city ordinance. Like Homer Plessy sixty years earlier, Parks committed an act of civil disobedience in order to dramatize an injustice. Unlike Plessy, however, Parks did not challenge her arrest in court. But her refusal to move to the back of the bus aroused the black community of Montgomery to institute a boycott of the city's buses. The boycott lasted more than a year, attracted attention across the nation, and sparked a new political movement.

THE ROLE OF MARTIN LUTHER KING, JR.

Rev. Martin Luther King, Jr., first came to prominence in the Montgomery boycott and used its success to help create a national movement to gain basic civil rights for African Americans. King believed in nonviolent protest, which he employed not only to achieve change by inflicting economic hardship on discriminatory organizations but also to gain support among white citizens by demonstrating the justice of the cause and the legitimacy of its methods. King's tactics of civil disobedience became the mainstay of the civil rights movement of the 1950s and 1960s. Its targets were many. Among the first were the segregated eating establishments in many southern towns and cities. Blacks would occupy the stools and chairs at the counter and, after being refused service, would quietly remain seated until they were arrested for violating local ordinances prohibiting disorderly conduct or "refusing to disperse."

During the 1950s and early 1960s, the civil rights movement became a major component of American politics. Whites, who perceived that a politically active black minority would threaten their way of life, sometimes resorted to violence. Some incidents captured national attention. In 1963, a church in Birmingham, Alabama, was firebombed, killing three African American children. Attempts to register blacks to vote were particularly likely to provoke a violent reaction. In 1963, three civil rights workers were slain near Philadelphia, Mississippi. Others were killed trying to register voters in Alabama and in other parts of the South. Again, the national media showed the rest of the country the barbarism of these acts and helped convert an indifferent white population into supporters of equal rights.

Some African Americans did not agree with King's strategy of nonviolent social protest to achieve integration. Leaders such as Malcolm X and H. Rap Brown followed in the tradition of Marcus Garvey in calling for a separate African American community. They had no desire to be integrated into a white society that they perceived as evil and hostile.[12] Although most leaders of the civil rights movement rejected this approach, it remained popular among a significant minority of blacks, especially young men from urban areas.

ONLINE 5.3:
Martin Luther King on His Movement
https://www.youtube.com/watch?v=xDNV8dxYe-g

American Political Culture and the Civil Rights Movement

Ultimately, if the civil rights movement were going to achieve more than momentary or localized success, it would have to secure national legislation to protect the rights of African Americans. As you have seen, the federal courts were able to use the Equal Protection Clause of the Fourteenth Amendment to strike down discriminatory provisions of state law. Although their decisions were often unpopular, the courts were sufficiently removed from politics that they could act counter to public opinion, at least in the short term. Thus, through the courts, the American political system could correct certain fundamental injustices without assembling a majority in favor of change. But the courts could do only so much. As you have seen, a great deal of discrimination was private, and private individuals were not subject to the requirements of the Fourteenth Amendment. Therefore, if African Americans' rights were to be secured, a majority would have to be mobilized in support of national legislation. But the American political culture of the 1950s and early 1960s presented several obstacles to the enactment of civil rights legislation.

First, many southerners believed that their region and its lifestyle were under attack. To succeed, the movement would have to persuade southerners to abandon the racial separatism that had long been a fundamental part of their identity. Second, the movement would have to overcome the indifference of whites in other parts of the country. Although only the South had imposed segregation by law, African Americans throughout the country were often treated as socially inferior and were by no means the economic equals of whites, a situation that had not troubled most whites. Yet whites were the overwhelming majority in the United States, so their support would be needed if civil rights legislation were to be enacted. Would they be willing to limit their own power to discriminate against a minority? There have been few examples of racial and ethnic majorities voluntarily relinquishing power to struggling minorities, yet that would have to happen in the United States if the civil rights movement were to succeed. Finally, African Americans themselves would have to become involved in the political process to a much greater extent than in the past. Above all, as a minority in a fundamentally majoritarian political system, African Americans would have to find a way to demonstrate the injustice of the political culture and the need for change and at the same time avoid frightening whites.

5-2e The Civil Rights Act of 1964

The battle for a national civil rights law that would make private discrimination unlawful proved to be long and difficult. In June 1963, President John F. Kennedy formally asked Congress to pass a civil rights bill. His assassination in November 1963 may have temporarily delayed passage of the bill, but ultimately added momentum to the legislation. More important, however, was the ongoing spectacle of African Americans being subjected to brutal treatment in the South. By the time President Lyndon Johnson signed the Civil Rights Act of 1964 into law, Americans had come to a somewhat uneasy consensus that government action was necessary to prevent private discrimination as well as to cement the federal commitment to racial justice.[13]

The Civil Rights Act of 1964 was a far-reaching, even visionary piece of legislation, and it remains the foundation of national policy on the rights of minorities. The act's most important and controversial section, Title II, prohibited racial discrimination in "places of public accommodations" that affected interstate commerce, including restaurants, stadiums, theaters, and motels or hotels with more than five rooms.

In adopting Title II, Congress relied on its broad constitutional power to regulate interstate commerce (Article I, Section 8) as well as its enforcement powers under the Fourteenth Amendment.

Ironically, Title II reversed the role of the courts and the states in civil rights matters. Before 1964, African Americans had looked to the courts to invalidate state laws that mandated segregation. In these types of cases, laws were the problem. After Congress passed national legislation to make individual acts of discrimination illegal, however, laws became the *solution* for African Americans and the *problem* for individuals who wanted to discriminate. This latter group then turned to the courts to invalidate laws that they felt improperly limited their freedom to discriminate.

In 1964, the Supreme Court upheld Title II, which had been challenged by the Heart of Atlanta motel, which had filed a suit to prevent the new policy from being enforced. The motel owners claimed that Title II was not designed to regulate interstate commerce and that, in any event, the motel should be immune because it was not primarily engaged in interstate commerce. The Supreme Court disagreed, ruling that Title II was a reasonable regulation of interstate commerce because racial discrimination by privately owned places of public accommodation constituted a serious impediment to interstate travel by blacks. The Court also held that the Heart of Atlanta motel was subject to the requirements of Title II because a substantial proportion of its clientele came from out of state.[14] In a related case, the Court held that Title II could be applied to a restaurant in Birmingham, Alabama, that also practiced racial discrimination. Even though most of the patrons of Ollie's Barbecue were locals, its foodstuffs and equipment had moved in interstate commerce.[15] In effect, the Supreme Court gave its blessing to a broad extension of federal power to regulate virtually any business in the country.

Without question, the public accommodations section of the Civil Rights Act of 1964 had an immediate impact on the lives of African Americans, especially in the South, where restaurants, motels, and hotels became available for the first time. In addition, stores removed the Colored and White designations from their drinking fountains and restrooms. The Civil Rights Act did more than ensure equal access to restaurants and hotels. It also addressed these issues:

- *Voting rights* (Title I). The act limited the use of literacy tests. In particular, it made a sixth-grade education sufficient proof of literacy for purposes of voting registration.
- *Employment discrimination* (Title VII). Companies with twenty-five or more employees were forbidden from discriminating on the basis of race or sex in hiring and firing workers and granting pay and benefits.
- *School segregation* (Title IV). This provision allowed the U.S. attorney general to file suit to desegregate schools. Individual citizens then did

not have to sue in the courts. Rather, they could complain to the U.S. Department of Justice, which could initiate legal action.

- *Denial of federal funds* (Title VI). Another important provision of the Civil Rights Act was the requirement that federal funding be withheld from any government or organization that practiced racial discrimination. Because virtually every public school and university system and almost all private colleges depend on federal funding, this provision has had an enormous impact.

Other Important Civil Rights Legislation

Although the Civil Rights Act of 1964 was the most important modern civil rights legislation passed by Congress, other civil rights laws have also contributed to the nation's commitment to equality. Other legislation of the 1960s included the Voting Rights Act of 1965 and the Civil Rights Act of 1968, also known as the Fair Housing Act, which imposed criminal penalties on anyone selling or renting a house or apartment through a licensed agent who refuses to sell or rent on the basis of race or religion. Later legislation, including the Civil Rights Act of 1992, strengthened protection against discrimination in employment. President George Bush signed a compromise bill after first vetoing a similar measure that he had opposed as being too extreme in its demands on employers.

5-2f Dismantling Segregation: An Active Role for Government

State laws mandating separate school systems for blacks and whites were effectively rendered unconstitutional by the *Brown* decision. Although this segregation by law (***de jure* segregation**) soon became a thing of the past, blacks and whites remained largely separated due to long-established housing patterns and economic conditions. The majority of white Americans (not only in the South) resisted the idea of integrated neighborhoods in the 1960s (see Figure 5-1). This ***de facto* segregation**, or segregation in fact, presented much more complex challenges. The demands for the elimination of state-sponsored separation had implied laws that were race neutral. Many people, however, thought that it was unrealistic and naive to expect that the mere elimination of officially sanctioned discrimination would result in real equal opportunity. President Johnson supported this view as he moved to implement the Civil Rights Act of 1964. In his commencement address at Howard University in 1965, Johnson said, "You do not take a person who for years has been hobbled by chains and liberate him, bring him up to the starting line of a race and then say 'You are free to compete with all the others,' and still justly believe you have been completely fair." Johnson was suggesting that government should take an active role in eradicating the vestiges of slavery and segregation. The policies that would flow from this new governmental role would prove to be enormously controversial.

The Busing Controversy

In the 1960s, many people in the civil rights movement came to believe that striking down laws requiring racially segregated schools was not enough. Stronger measures were needed to dismantle dual school systems, which often persisted in the absence of segregation laws. One such measure was to transport children by bus across school attendance zones to achieve a degree of racial integration. Of course, the idea of **busing** was extremely unpopular in white communities, and school boards were not inclined to take this type of action unless ordered to do so by a federal judge.

In the late 1960s, the Board of Education of Charlotte–Mecklenburg, North Carolina, devised a desegregation plan to comply with the Supreme Court's mandate in *Brown v. Board of Education*. A federal district court rejected the plan, however, as not producing sufficient racial integration at the elementary level. The court adopted in its place a plan prepared by an outside expert that called for, among other things, establishing racial quotas, altering attendance zones, and busing students within the district. The Supreme Court unanimously approved the plan, even though it entailed "race-conscious remedies."[16] The Court made clear that a school system which has engaged in discrimination at some point in the past may be ordered to take remedial action to correct a persistent pattern of segregation. These remedies could include the busing of students.

Later, the Court clarified a point of contention, ruling that the court-ordered busing of students across school district lines is permissible only if *all affected districts* had been guilty of past discriminatory practices. If, for example, both city and county school systems had practiced discrimination in the past, students could be bused between the city and county school districts, even though the districts were administratively separate. However, when it was shown that the suburban districts surrounding the city of Detroit had not discriminated, even though Detroit clearly had, the Supreme Court did not allow a cross-district busing remedy.[17]

Busing proved to be quite controversial among both whites and blacks. In many instances, both resented the dismantling of their neighborhood schools. To make matters worse, many whites simply refused to attend schools where African Americans were in the majority and exercised their option of attending private schools. Often, systems where busing was ordered ended up more segregated than they had been previously. By the mid- to late 1980s, the appeal of busing had diminished even within the African American community as a result of these types of problems.

Busing is still in use for the purpose of school desegregation, but to a much lesser extent than twenty or even ten years ago. Around the country, school boards have moved decidedly away from busing as a means of desegregation, opting instead for devices such as magnet schools.[18] In some instances, judges have even ordered school districts to terminate busing.[19] It appears that Americans are now witnessing the demise of this grand social experiment. The busing experience is indicative of both the ambitious nature of desegregation policy and the difficulty of forcing results on a public that offers little support for the process. The public supported an end to segregation by law; it did not support government activism to achieve integration.

5-2g AFFIRMATIVE ACTION

Most commentators agree that Congress did not intend for the Civil Rights Act of 1964 to permit, let alone require, reverse, or correct, discrimination. Since that time, however, the act has come to be interpreted in a way that allows goals for the representation of members of racial minorities to be established. Not surprisingly, this extension of the original act has been extremely controversial. The policies by which federal agencies move to remedy past discrimination through the use of goals, quotas, timetables, and the like are examples of **affirmative action**. These programs usually involve some sort of special efforts to attract applicants for employment or to colleges or universities. Under pressure from federal agencies and/or courts of law, both private and public educational institutions have gradually developed affirmative action programs.

THE *BAKKE* CASE

In the 1970s, the University of California at Davis established a program whose goal was to increase the number of minority physicians in the state. This program was rather typical of those established by many colleges and universities during the mid- and late 1970s. Of course, admitting minority applicants inevitably kept others from being accepted. Not surprisingly, many of these excluded applicants felt that rejection on the basis of their race violated their rights to equal protection under the Fourteenth Amendment.

Allan Bakke, a white male, was not admitted to the Davis medical school, even though his test scores and grades were higher than those of most of the minority students who had been accepted to fill sixteen spaces that had been reserved for minorities. Bakke challenged the program in court, and the Supreme Court heard his case in 1978.[20] Many observers thought the Court would craft a clear ruling that dealt with the constitutionality of programs that allowed race as a consideration. Unfortunately, the Court's decision was not so clear-cut. It did order the University of California to admit Bakke. In addition, it ruled that the program under which he had been rejected was not constitutional because it reserved a fixed number of slots for minorities. In the Court's view, a fixed numerical quota was unacceptable. However, these types of programs would be acceptable if they established *goals* rather than quotas. In other words, a school could consider race as a factor in the decision to admit an applicant, but could not reserve a set number of places for members of a particular group.

Other Important Judicial Decisions

Employment discrimination involves somewhat different issues. Many companies established special hiring or training programs with the goal of increasing the number of minorities in higher-level positions. Kaiser Aluminum and Chemical Corporation had this type of program, which trained existing employees for higher positions in the company. Kaiser reserved half the slots in a training class for blacks. Bryan Weber, a white employee with more seniority than many African Americans who were chosen, filed suit. The Supreme Court held that these types of programs were acceptable because they were voluntarily established by private companies.[21]

In the late 1980s and throughout the 1990s a more conservative Supreme Court manifested a more critical posture toward affirmative action programs. For example, in 1989, the Court struck down a Richmond, Virginia, policy that set aside a certain proportion of city public works contracts for minority business enterprises. The Court based its decision largely on the fact that African Americans constituted a majority of the city population and held a majority of seats on the city council. Moreover, no evidence existed that the city had been discriminating against black-owned construction companies seeking public works contracts.[22] In 1995 the Court indicated that it would strictly scrutinize all affirmative action programs, whether local, state, or federal.[23] Writing for the Court, Justice O'Connor held that "all racial classifications, imposed by whatever federal, state, or local governmental actor, must be analyzed by a reviewing court under strict scrutiny. In other words, such classifications are constitutional only if they are narrowly tailored measures that further compelling governmental interests." This placed a heavy burden on government agencies to justify any sort of preferential treatment afforded to minorities.

Some commentators thought that the Court would move eventually to overturn its 1978 *Bakke* decision, but this turned out not to be the case. In 2003, the Court upheld an affirmative action program employed by the law school at the University of Michigan.[24] The decision made clear that affirmative action programs designed to enhance the diversity of student populations can survive strict judicial scrutiny. Thus, affirmative action remains legally viable, at least for the foreseeable future.

Affirmative Action and Presidential Politics

During the 2000 campaign, the presidential candidates George W. Bush and Al Gore sparred over the issue of affirmative action. Despite certain rhetorical devices designed to mask the candidates' differences on this issue, the two candidates clearly had fundamental disagreements about whether government should consider race as a factor in the distribution of benefits or opportunities. It was also clear that the new president's most profound impact on this issue would be made through his appointments to the Supreme Court, because the affirmative action question would continue to appear on the judicial agenda. In fact, concerns over affirmative action were prominent in the

Senate Judiciary Committee's rejection of Bush's nomination of Charles Pickering to the Fifth Circuit Court of Appeals. In 2004, however, the issue was barely mentioned in the context of the presidential election. By 2004, concern about the war in Iraq, international terrorism, and other national security issues had eclipsed this and many other domestic policy issues.

Public Attitudes toward Affirmative Action

Affirmative action programs have been and remain highly controversial. Although many people feel that such programs are necessary to "level the playing field," others are troubled by any program that provides preferential treatment on the basis of group membership. The public is generally supportive of affirmative action, at least in principle, but a substantial percentage of Americans see it as unfair. Not surprisingly, these attitudes vary significantly by race, as African Americans typically are much more supportive of affirmative action programs.

5-2h Racial Discrimination in Voting Rights

The American electoral system is the vehicle through which much societal discrimination has been buttressed. The systematic exclusion of African Americans from the electoral process was maintained through the early 1960s in many areas. As with the desegregation of the public schools, the process of opening political participation began in the courts. In 1944, the Supreme Court overruled one of its earlier decisions and struck down the infamous white primary as a violation of the Fifteenth Amendment.[25] Fifteen years later, however, the Court refused to invalidate the use of literacy tests.[26]

The Civil Rights Act of 1964 limited the use of literacy tests that had been employed by local officials to keep blacks from voting. In that same year, the states ratified the Twenty-Fourth Amendment, which outlawed the use of the poll tax in federal elections, and in 1966 the Supreme Court struck down the poll tax in state elections as a violation of the Fourteenth Amendment's Equal Protection Clause.[27] Nevertheless, the participation of blacks was still quite limited. To some degree, the low level of voting was due to structural factors, but substantial evidence existed of a pattern of intimidation by local white officials who were unalterably opposed to the idea of blacks voting.

The reason for white intransigence was obvious. African Americans made up a substantial proportion of the population in most southern states—in many counties, they constituted a majority. If blacks were to turn out to vote in substantial numbers, they not only could threaten the political status quo but also might even be elected and take political control in some communities.

The Voting Rights Act of 1965

In 1965, Congress enacted the Voting Rights Act to ensure that African Americans would have access to the ballot box. The act outlawed the use of literacy tests as a condition of voting in seven southern states where black voting had lagged far behind that of whites. In addition, the act had a triggering mechanism by which federal registrars would be sent to any county in these states in which fewer than 50 percent of those of voting age were registered to vote in the 1964 presidential election.

The effect of the Voting Rights Act was dramatic. Black registration and voting increased substantially. By the mid-1970s, blacks were voting in numbers that approached those of whites, and several thousand African Americans had been elected to state and local office (see Figure 5-1). The effects were profound. African Americans became such a force in southern politics that few politicians could afford to risk alienating them. The result was a new breed of white officeholders, epitomized by Governor Bill Clinton of Arkansas, who were sympathetic to the African American community. Perhaps the best example of African American voting power in the New South was the 1989 election of Douglas Wilder as governor of Virginia, the first African American to be elected governor of an American state.

Dismantling Institutionalized Electoral Discrimination

The Voting Rights Act of 1965 was instrumental in increasing the number of African Americans who voted and held public office. But voting rights have come to mean more than the right to cast a ballot. Indeed, if political jurisdictions and institutions are constructed in such a way as to minimize the impact of minority votes, members of these groups risk having the importance of their votes diluted.

The 1965 act did not specifically address actual electoral districts or the problem of **vote dilution**. Nevertheless, some districting practices clearly work to dilute minority

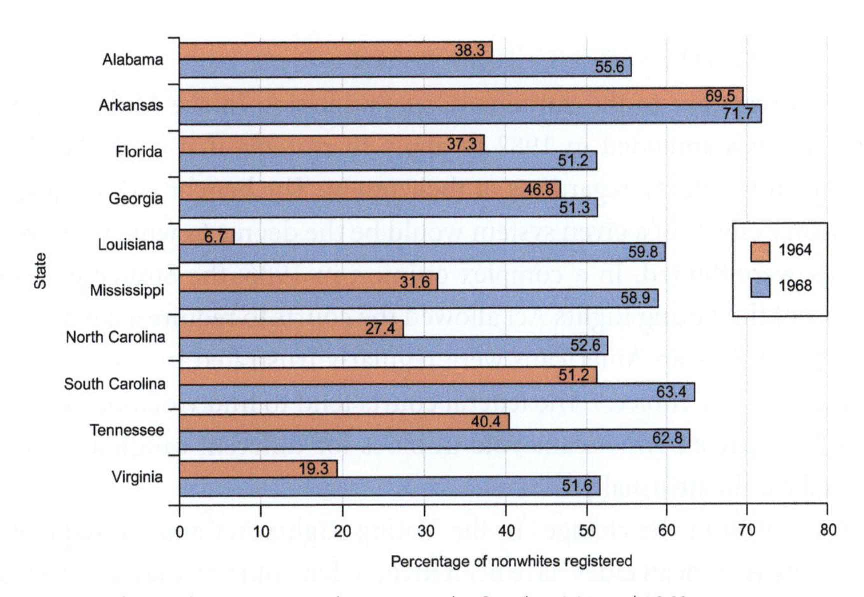

Figure 5-1 *Percentage of Nonwhites Registered to Vote in the South, 1964 and 1968*
Source: Adapted from Herbert Asher, Presidential Elections and American Politics (Chicago: Dorsey Press, 1988), p. 51.

votes in state legislatures, city councils, or congressional districts. This dilution can result from deliberately drawing district lines in such a way that minority voters are dispersed among a number of jurisdictions. The intentional dispersion of minority votes is called **cracking**. In another practice, known as **packing**, all minority voters are placed in one district. Though ensuring one minority representative, this practice dilutes the possibility of minority candidates' effectively contesting two or more seats.

At-Large Elections

Minority votes can also be diluted because of the nature of the electoral system itself, which may or may not have been established with the intent of discrimination. The major culprit in this regard is the practice of electing representatives to city and county commissions and school boards by **at-large voting**. In at-large elections, representatives to a voting body are chosen in a vote from the entire community rather than from districts. For the most part, the intent of these systems was not to discriminate. In fact, at-large elections were established as part of the movement to reform city governments. Nevertheless, their impact has been in many cases discriminatory.

Since 1911, for example, the city of Mobile, Alabama, had used at-large elections to choose its three-member city commission. In the late 1970s, more than 35 percent of the city's residents were black, yet no African American had ever been elected to the city commission, despite several attempts. Local residents brought a suit challenging the at-large system on the grounds that it had the effect of unfairly diluting the voting strength of racial minorities. In 1980, however, the Supreme Court held that unless one can prove discriminatory intent on the part of public officials, at-large voting systems do not violate the Constitution.[28]

Changes in the Voting Rights Act

Largely in response to the Supreme Court's decision in the Mobile case, the Voting Rights Act was amended in 1982 to apply to systems that could be shown to have discriminatory effects, regardless of their intent. The benchmark for judging the discriminatory effects of a given system would be the degree to which the votes of a racial minority were diluted. In a complex opinion in 1986, the Supreme Court held that Section 2 of the Voting Rights Act allowed the courts to require a city to change its voting system if African Americans were regularly frustrated in attempts to elect representatives of their choice.[29] The federal courts tend to find violations in systems where whites and African Americans vote in blocs for different candidates and the white-preferred candidate usually wins.

As a result of the changes in the Voting Rights Act and subsequent court decisions, many American cities have been involved in court cases that have led to changes in their form of government. When courts have found dilution, they have tended to replace at-large systems with districts drawn to ensure that minority voters make up a healthy majority of as many districts as possible. The courts have never recognized any group's right to a certain proportion of seats on any legislative body, however, as the idea of **proportional representation** of minorities is inconsistent with traditional American notions of representation.

The practice of creating districts to maximize the representation of minorities has been extended to state legislative and congressional districts. State houses have long had the responsibility for drawing district lines. Since the reapportionment decisions of the 1960s, redistricting has taken place every ten years—after each census. The redistricting process has long had a partisan political tone because the party controlling the legislature can ensure that the lines are drawn to benefit its electoral chances. This process of drawing district borders to reach a desired political end is called **gerrymandering**. Ironically, in the past, districts were gerrymandered to minimize the impact of minority voters; now, gerrymandering occurs to maximize minority influence! This type of race-conscious redistricting has led to a great increase in the number of African American representatives at the state and federal levels. However, it has also led to an increased ideological polarization and conflict in Congress and the state legislatures.

5-2i Civil Rights for Other Racial and Ethnic Groups

During the latter part of the twentieth century, the United States became increasingly diverse. Increased immigration from Cuba, Mexico, and other Latin American countries, as well as from Asia, has created a different political landscape. To the degree that members of these groups identified with their ethnic heritage and groups were geographically definable, they faced problems of discrimination similar to those faced by African Americans.

Hispanics

Some Hispanics face particular problems because they have entered this country illegally. As a result of their lack of documented citizenship, many are exploited and forced to work in low-paying jobs, such as picking fruits and vegetables. Moreover, many Hispanics, including those who are American citizens, face employment discrimination not unlike that experienced by African Americans.

In many ways, the struggle of African Americans for civil rights set the stage for the emergence of Hispanics as a political force. Faced with exploitation by growers in the Southwest, Cesar Chavez organized the United Farm Workers in 1962. Chavez understood the need to appeal to public opinion throughout the country to bring pressure for change. He developed the tactic of the nationwide boycott of certain farm products to dramatize his cause and create economic hardship for the growers.

In some states—in particular, those in the Southwest—individuals with Spanish surnames represented a strong potential political force. Registering to vote was often difficult, however, because of citizenship problems and language barriers. Hispanics are protected by civil rights and voting rights legislation, however. Under the 1982 amendments to the Voting Rights Act, states and cities must make every effort to see that Hispanic votes are not subject to dilution.

Although Spanish-speaking minorities benefited from legislation intended primarily for African Americans, language and citizenship issues seemed to demand specific legislation. In 1986, Congress passed the Simpson–Mazzoli Act. Under its provisions, individuals who could prove that they had been in the country for five years would be granted citizenship. In addition, American businesses were subject to criminal penalties if they knowingly hired illegal aliens. Fewer persons than expected applied for citizenship, however, and many immigrants, especially those from Mexico, continue to live without the basic protections of American society.

By the 1990s, Hispanic Americans had become a powerful force in American politics. Their influence should continue to increase because Hispanics are the fastest-growing minority group in the United States. The increase in numbers should lead to the continued election of more Hispanic officeholders and increased visibility in positions of power at the national level.

Native Americans

Native Americans have faced unique problems in the American system. Their existence was an impediment to the settlement of the United States, so they were systematically eliminated or forced to migrate westward. As late as the nineteenth century, many Anglo Americans viewed the "Indians," as they were mistakenly labeled, as less than fully human. Consequently, the concept of civil rights had no more meaning for Native Americans than it had for black slaves. As a result, about half the country's approximately 1.4 million Native Americans now live on reservations. These reservations represent the legacy of years of neglect by the federal government.

The federal government has always recognized Native Americans as a group with special status. Technically, reservations are sovereign, with Native Americans controlling their own destiny through separate political and legal systems. Their well-being, however, has been the responsibility of the Bureau of Indian Affairs within the U.S. Department of the Interior, which provides medical care and education to Native Americans on the reservations.

In many ways, Native Americans have endured suffering greater than that of any group in American society. They lag behind other minorities in education, income, and quality of housing. Native Americans also suffer through their lack of political clout. But they too built on the lessons of the civil rights movement. The American Indian Movement (AIM), founded in the late 1960s, articulated many Indian demands and dramatized their plight. Pressure from AIM and other groups helped bring about the passage of the American Indian Self-Determination and Educational Assistance

Act in 1975. Native Americans demanded not only increased aid to the impoverished reservations but also an increased say in how the aid would be spent.

The struggles of Native Americans have left a long legal trail. Virtually every change in the status of Native Americans has been legitimized through a treaty. Many times, the claims of Native Americans are based on the implementation (or the failure of implementation) of treaties. Some treaties exempt a particular tribe from state and federal hunting and fishing regulations. Not surprisingly, others in the area are frequently upset with what they perceive as a dual standard that permits Native Americans to fish and hunt where and when non–Native Americans cannot.

In the early 1990s, many tribes attempted to raise money by experimenting with gambling on the reservations in areas where gambling was not otherwise permitted. In 1992, the federal government attempted to shut down these types of establishments near Phoenix, Arizona, but the courts ruled in favor of the tribes, citing their exemption under earlier treaties. Although operating gambling casinos is controversial, it shows how much Native Americans on reservations desire to improve their standard of living and become more self-supporting and less dependent on the federal government.

Asian Americans

The United States has long been the home of many persons of Asian descent. Many were brought to the West to work on the railroads in the nineteenth century. Following the completion of the major east-west link in 1869, many Asians were subjected to exclusionary laws in San Francisco. The intent of the legislation was to rid the community of Asians, or at least keep them in an inferior economic and political status.

Overall, despite this early exploitation, Asian Americans were not subject to the pervasive discrimination that confronted African Americans. Nevertheless, in a shocking display of national hysteria, if not overt racism, more than one hundred thousand Japanese Americans were placed in internment camps during World War II. This "relocation" was accomplished without any pretense of due process. Nevertheless, the Supreme Court upheld the internment, citing the national emergency of the war.[30] Ultimately, in 1988, Congress recognized the injustice, formally apologized, and paid $20,000 compensation to each survivor of the internment. Yet the clear violation of fundamental constitutional rights by the federal government in the middle of the twentieth century stands as a stark reminder to Asian Americans of their former status as outsiders in American society.

In this century, many Asians have come to this country in search of economic opportunity. As is often the case when racially identifiable minorities share the same urban space, tensions developed between African and Korean Americans during the Los Angeles riots that followed the Rodney King verdict in 1992. Some African Americans claimed that Korean shopkeepers exploited their African American customers, and many Korean businesses were apparently targeted for destruction and looting during the riots. Similar tensions had developed earlier in other cities. In the late 1980s, Asian Americans were the victims of beatings and even murder at the hands of whites who were frustrated with the Japanese domination of the automobile business.

In many ways, Americans of Asian descent have adjusted quite well to American society. Whether as shopkeepers or professionals, by many measures Asian Americans have performed at levels surpassing those of all other groups. Many people credit this situation to the tight-knit family structures of Asian society and the strong work ethic of Asian families. Typically, Asian families place great emphasis on education, hard work, self-discipline, and saving for the future, all of which are values that help minorities achieve integration into the social and economic mainstream.

5-3 Gender Discrimination

Women were not accorded anything resembling equality at the time the American republic was founded. Even with the addition of the Bill of Rights and the Civil War amendments, the U.S. Constitution contained no explicit recognition of women's rights. Indeed, even the right to vote was not guaranteed until 1920, when the Nineteenth Amendment was ratified. Given the lack of women participants in the Constitutional Convention and, until quite recently, the dearth of women holding political office of any kind, there can be no doubt that women were intended to hold second-class citizenship at best. However, it would be simplistic to categorize this sort of systematic discrimination as merely an extension of the racism that defined the treatment of African Americans.

The inferior citizenship status of women in this country was certainly not unique to the United States. It was accepted virtually as a given because of deeply ingrained cultural norms. Western culture was patriarchal in nature. Men had long assumed a superior status within the whole structure of family and religion. Whereas the institution of slavery represented the exploitation of a whole people by another, the institutions surrounding the role of women were tightly woven into a cultural fabric so pervasive that the Founders could hardly be expected to see beyond it. Although one would be hard-pressed to find any race, tribe, or group of people whose cultural roots were grounded in submission to others, most women in the United States and elsewhere accepted their social status outside the political and economic mainstream almost without question.

Cultures evolve, however, and many individuals simply will never accept second-class treatment, regardless of the circumstances. As women began to challenge their status in American politics and the broader society, they faced a dual set of obstacles not unlike those faced by African Americans. First, the law kept women from full participation in society. Second, many individuals discriminated against women for their own reasons. To rectify the former problem, laws would have to be eliminated; to prevent the latter problem, new laws outlawing discrimination would have to be enacted.

Again, the situation is somewhat more complex than was the case for racial minorities. Although few people would accept the idea of basing discriminatory legislation on racial differences, many more might accept discriminatory laws based on gender differences. Some laws that discriminate against women reflect long-standing customs that unfairly recognized men as the only legitimate owners of property. Others are grounded in the belief that biological differences justify discrimination. Some discriminatory laws are intended to protect women against sexual abuse, others regulate the role of women in the military, and still others govern the financial rights of men and women as they dissolve a marriage. Of course, the most visible and controversial laws deal with abortion. These controversies are all the more difficult because people's attitudes toward gender discrimination issues tend to be a function of their religious and/or philosophical beliefs rather than of their gender.

5-3a Women's Struggle for Political Equality

The beginnings of the women's struggle for political equality were rooted in the fight for the vote. Supporters of the vote for women were known as *suffragists*. After women were finally assured of the right to vote through the passage of the Nineteenth Amendment in 1920, however, the movement for women's political rights slowed dramatically. It was as though the vote had been seen as an end in itself rather than as a means of achieving greater societal change. Furthermore, the right to vote did not bring about many substantial changes in policy or a greater acceptance of women as public officeholders.

The modern women's movement took form in the 1960s. The movement adopted many of the tactics that had been employed successfully by African Americans in the civil rights movement, including marches, protests, demonstrations, and boycotts. Perhaps most memorable were public demonstrations in which feminists burned their bras as symbols of the constraints imposed on them by a male-dominated society.

Key Laws Affecting Women's Rights

Congress responded to growing demands for legal equality between the sexes by passing the Equal Pay Act of 1963, the 1972 amendments to Title VII of the Civil Rights Act of 1964, and Title IX of the Federal Education Act of 1972. The first two statutes were aimed at eliminating sex discrimination in the workplace. The third authorized the withholding of federal funds from educational institutions that engaged in sex discrimination. These statutes have been an important source of civil rights protection for women and have given rise to a number of significant court decisions.

The Equal Rights Amendment

Congress began considering a constitutional amendment guaranteeing equal rights for women as early as 1923. In 1972, the Equal Rights Amendment (ERA) had gathered enough support in Congress to be sent to the states, where three-fourths (or thirty-eight) of the state legislatures had to ratify the amendment before it could become part of the Constitution. The ERA was quite concise. It stated:

> *Section 1. Equality of rights under the law shall not be denied or abridged by the United States or by any State on account of sex.*
>
> *Section 2. The Congress shall have the power to enforce, by appropriate legislation, the provisions of this article.*
>
> *Section 3. This amendment shall take effect two years after the date of ratification.*

Initially, the ERA met with much enthusiasm and little controversy in the state legislatures. By 1976, it had been ratified by thirty-five of the necessary thirty-eight states. In the late 1970s, however, opposition to the ERA crystallized in those states that had yet to ratify. The opposition was led by Phyllis Schlafly, a conservative political activist who argued that the ERA and the other items on the feminist agenda would be destructive to the family and ultimately harmful to women. Although Congress extended the period for ratification until 1982, the amendment ultimately failed to win approval by the requisite number of states. However, roughly one-third of the states eventually amended their own constitutions to provide explicit protections against sex discrimination. In our federal system, state laws and constitutions may provide additional civil rights protections beyond those provided by federal laws and the U.S. Constitution.

The demise of the ERA left constitutional interpretation in the field of sex discrimination largely in the domain of the Fourteenth Amendment. In 1976, the Supreme Court articulated a test for judging gender-based policies under the Fourteenth Amendment. According to this test, to be constitutional, a gender-based policy must be substantially related to an important government objective. Applying this test, the courts have reached different results, sometimes upholding and at other times invalidating policies challenged as unconstitutional sex discrimination.

5-3b Women in Military Service

One of the most controversial issues in the area of sex discrimination is the role that women should play in the military. Opponents of the ERA argued that adoption of the amendment would result in women being drafted into combat, a prospect that many people still find unacceptable. In 1981, the Supreme Court upheld the constitutionality of the male-only draft registration law. Writing for the Court, Justice

William Rehnquist stated that the exclusion of women from the draft "was not an 'accidental by-product of a traditional way of thinking about women.'"[31] In Rehnquist's view, men and women "are simply not similarly situated for purposes of a draft or registration for a draft." No doubt many would challenge Rehnquist's assumption, especially in light of the expanded role women played in the current wars in Iraq and Afghanistan. But the question of women's role in the military and, in particular, whether they will ever be subject to the draft appear to have been left to Congress and the president to decide.

5-3c SEX DISCRIMINATION BY EDUCATIONAL INSTITUTIONS

Historically, many state-run colleges were single-sex institutions, but this situation began to change after World War II. By the late 1960s, when the Supreme Court became interested in sex discrimination as a constitutional question, almost all state colleges and universities had become coeducational. Yet some states continued to operate certain specialized institutions on a single-sex basis. In 1984, the Supreme Court required the Mississippi University for Women (MUW) to admit a male student to its all-female nursing school.[32] MUW tried to defend its policy of limiting enrollment to women as a type of affirmative action program. In her opinion for the Court, Justice Sandra Day O'Connor would have none of that, noting that nursing is not a field in which women have been traditionally denied opportunities. Quite to the contrary, it is a profession that has been stereotyped as "female." The Supreme Court could not find any substantial justification for the school's refusal to admit a qualified male applicant.

In 1996, the Court ruled that Virginia Military Institute (VMI), an all-male state-run military college, had to accept women as cadets.[33] Saying that the state of Virginia had to advance an "exceedingly persuasive justification" for the exclusion of women, the Court rejected the state's argument that admitting women would undermine the special character of the institution. The VMI ruling was the final nail in the coffin for single-sex higher education in this country.

An emerging issue of special concern to college students is whether universities can maintain sexually segregated athletic programs. Is the separate-but-equal doctrine appropriate when considering collegiate athletics? Suppose that a young woman wants to play football at a state university. Assuming that the university does not have a women's football program, does the Equal Protection Clause require the school to let the woman try out for the men's team? Although some may feel that these types of issues trivialize the Constitution, these matters tend to be far from trivial in the minds of people who are affected by the policies.

5-3d Women in the Workforce

Traditionally, the socially prescribed role of woman as wife and mother, combined with a protectionist attitude on the part of men, served to keep women out of the workforce in significant numbers, although women were mobilized to fill jobs vacated by men during the two world wars. Now, most adult women are employed, at least part-time. Indeed, roughly half of all women with children under the age of one are employed outside the home.

Despite recent gains, women on average earn only about seventy cents for every dollar earned by men. This discrepancy is partially due to the fact that women are much more likely than men to be employed in relatively low-paying service, clerical, sales, and manufacturing jobs. They are still less likely than men to be doctors, engineers, accountants, lawyers, and the like, although the gender gap in the professions is narrowing. Finally, women have yet to gain access to the top-paying positions in corporations. Some have complained of a *glass ceiling*, an invisible barrier that keeps women out of top managerial positions.

Although women are not a minority—they comprise roughly 53 percent of the population—they have had to struggle as hard as minority groups to gain acceptance in the workplace. Early on, the issue was whether women should be permitted to work at all. Later the issue became which jobs, if any, were unsuitable for women. Then the issue became equal pay for equal work. In the 1980s, the issue came to be defined as equal pay for work of comparable worth. Women's groups argued that women should receive the same pay as men, even if their jobs were different, as long as the jobs entailed similar levels of education and experience. Critics of comparable worth argued that this idea could not be implemented without a massive program of government regulation or numerous lawsuits, either of which would be costly and disruptive to business. In the 1990s, the momentum behind the push for comparable worth declined. Today, the highest-priority issues for working women are access to affordable day care and workplace policies that accommodate childbearing and child-rearing. Although these issues are primarily economic and are not exactly questions of civil rights, they certainly are related to women's search for economic and social equality.

5-3e Affirmative Action on Behalf of Women

To facilitate the integration of women into the economic mainstream, federal, state, and even some local agencies have adopted a variety of affirmative action programs to benefit women. Employers that do business with government, as well as educational institutions that receive public funds, have been encouraged to adopt their own affirmative action programs. Like the policies that grant preferred status to African American applicants, affirmative action programs that benefit women have been controversial and have even been challenged in court.

In 1987, the Supreme Court handed down a landmark decision on affirmative action for women. It upheld a program under which a woman had been promoted to the position of road dispatcher in the Santa Clara, California, Transportation Agency, even though a man had scored higher on a standardized test designed to measure aptitude for the job. The man who had been passed over for the job brought a lawsuit, claiming reverse discrimination, as Alan Bakke had done some years earlier. The Supreme Court rejected the plaintiff's claim, stressing that the affirmative action program was a reasonable means of correcting the sexual imbalance among the Transportation Agency's personnel, who were overwhelmingly male.[34]

In a somewhat different form of affirmative action, some cities and states have required all-male social and civic clubs to admit women. The courts have generally approved these types of measures, even though they are sometimes challenged as violating the concept of freedom of association, which is protected by the First Amendment. In a notable 1984 decision, a unanimous Supreme Court found that the state of Minnesota's interest in eradicating sex discrimination was sufficiently compelling to justify a decision of its human rights commission requiring local chapters of the Jaycees to admit women.[35] Later decisions of the Court extended this ruling to embrace chapters of the Rotary Club as well as private social clubs that served liquor and food to their members.

5-3f Sexual Harassment

In the 1980s, **sexual harassment** appeared on the public agenda as a civil rights issue. The sexual harassment issue has been particularly noticeable on college campuses, where it has entered the debate over questions related to dating, dormitory visitation, and student-teacher relationships.

The issue was aired in a particularly dramatic fashion when law professor Anita Hill appeared before the Senate Judiciary Committee in October 1991 to make allegations of misconduct against Clarence Thomas, who had been nominated by President Bush to a position on the Supreme Court. Hill alleged that Thomas, when he was chairman of the Equal Employment Opportunity Commission, made sexual advances toward her, told off-color jokes in her presence, and generally harassed her in a sexual manner. Thomas categorically denied the charges. Because little supporting evidence existed, the Senate ultimately approved Thomas' nomination to the Supreme Court. Many women believed that the all-male Senate Judiciary Committee had been insensitive to Hill and to the whole issue of sexual harassment. The Clarence Thomas–Anita Hill episode was apparently one factor that led women to run for public office in record numbers in 1992.

One survey conducted in 1991 found that 21 percent of women had experienced sexual harassment on the job.[36] In a 1992 survey, 57 percent of adults said that too little was being done to protect women against sexual harassment in the workplace.[37] It is now generally agreed that sexual harassment is unacceptable, but considerable disagreement exists over what exactly constitutes harassment. That uncertainty will be resolved in the courts.

In 1986, the Supreme Court ruled that sexual harassment in the workplace constituted unlawful gender discrimination in violation of federal civil rights laws.[38] In November 1993, the Supreme Court adopted a legal standard that makes it easier for victims of sexual harassment to sue in federal court.[39] The decision, joined by all nine justices (including Clarence Thomas), came in a case brought by Teresa Harris, who worked for a truck leasing company in Nashville. Harris complained that her boss subjected her to repeated comments and suggestions of a sexual nature. The federal judge who heard the case in Nashville described the boss' behavior as vulgar and offensive, but ruled that it was not likely to have had a serious adverse psychological effect on the employee. He dismissed the case before it could go to a jury trial. The court of appeals in Cincinnati upheld the district court's ruling. In reversing the lower courts, the Supreme Court, speaking through Justice Sandra Day O'Connor, said that it was not necessary for a plaintiff in a sexual harassment case to show "severe psychological injury." It is enough that the work environment would be perceived by a reasonable person as being "hostile or abusive." The Court's decision reinstated Harris' complaint, thus allowing the case to go before a jury in the district court. More important, the decision increased the likelihood that women (and men) who believe that they are victims of sexual harassment in the workplace will file and win federal lawsuits. Thus, the Supreme Court effectively put employers on notice that their conduct would be subject to judicial scrutiny. To avoid litigation, employers must have policies and training programs in place and must take immediate action whenever complaints are filed.

5-4 Other Civil Rights Issues

The concept of civil rights originated in the context of African Americans' struggle for equality. Later, the concept was extended to other racial and ethnic groups and to women. Yet many other groups in society have also experienced discrimination, and they too are seeking a place on the contemporary civil rights agenda. Among these groups are the elderly, the poor, the disabled, and gays and lesbians.

5-4a Age Discrimination

Discrimination against the young is usually not legally problematic because persons below the age of legal majority are presumed not to enjoy the full rights of citizenship. Most questions of age discrimination involve elderly Americans' claims that they have been discriminated against. Federal courts typically employ a "rational basis test" to determine the constitutionality of government policies that discriminate on the basis of age. Under this test, a restriction based on age must be rationally related to a legitimate government purpose in order to be upheld. This test is fairly lenient; most policies reviewed under this standard are ultimately upheld by the court. Most age discrimination cases are not constitutional cases, however. Instead, they are based on provisions of statutes enacted by Congress and the state legislatures. In 1967, Congress enacted the Age Discrimination in Employment Act, which bars companies that deal in interstate commerce or do business with the government from discriminating against their employees on the basis of age. In 1988, Congress enacted a measure that prohibits all organizations that receive federal funds from engaging in age discrimination. A substantial amount of litigation in the state and federal courts now deals with age discrimination by employers. These cases frequently grow out of attempts by companies to save money by dismissing people who are approaching retirement age. As our society ages, and people live and work longer, conflicts involving age discrimination will become more numerous and more intense.

5-4b Discrimination against the Poor

Clearly, neither the Constitution nor civil rights laws mandate anything resembling the equalization of economic conditions. American political culture supports the idea of equality of opportunity, but not the notion of **equality of result**, which is often equated with socialism. Welfare programs are thus seen not as matters of civil rights but rather as entitlements that, at least theoretically, may be terminated by majority rule. On the other hand, the courts have held that in some cases, indigent persons have a constitutional right to public assistance. When a person who is unable to afford legal representation is charged with a serious crime, she is entitled to a lawyer at public expense. Failure to provide counsel to an indigent defendant is considered a violation of due process and equal protection of the law.[40]

Unequal Funding of Public Schools

One of the most litigated civil rights issues since the 1970s has been the question of whether the methods by which many states fund their public schools are constitutional. Many funding systems are based on city or county property taxes and thus allow for tremendous variance among school districts in the amount of funds available to the schools. Critics of these types of inequalities argue that education is a fundamental right and that grossly unequal funding is a denial of equal protection of the law. In1973, the Supreme Court rejected such a challenge to this method of funding public schools in Texas.[41] Note, however, that the Supreme Court's interpretation of the Fourteenth Amendment in this case in no way prevents state courts from adopting a contrary view of the relevant provisions of their state constitutions. Indeed, more than twenty state supreme courts have done exactly that in holding that disparities in funding among school districts violate state constitutional requirements of equal protection. This trend nicely illustrates the principle of **judicial federalism**, under which state courts are free to interpret their state laws in a way that provides additional rights beyond those secured by federal law.

Restriction of Abortion Funding for Indigent Women

Another controversial equal protection issue reaching the courts in the late 1970s was the dispute over legislative efforts to cut off government funds to support abortions. In 1980, the Supreme Court upheld the Hyde Amendment, a federal law that severely limited the use of federal funds to support abortions for indigent women.[42] Writing for the Supreme Court, Justice Potter Stewart noted that "the principal impact of the Hyde Amendment falls on the indigent." Nevertheless, in Stewart's view, "that fact alone does not render the funding restriction constitutionally invalid, for this Court has held repeatedly that poverty, standing alone, is not a suspect classification." As in the case of public school funding, the Supreme Court essentially held that restricting public funding for abortions may not be egalitarian, but that it is not an inequality which offends the U.S. Constitution.

5-4c Discrimination against Persons with Disabilities

Although few laws overtly discriminate against them, persons with disabilities have always faced physical barriers as well as societal prejudice. For the most part, the Congress, not the courts, has taken the lead in recognizing the rights of persons with disabilities. On the other hand, the courts have not been completely insensitive to the rights of persons with disabilities. For example, in 1985, the Supreme Court struck down a zoning law that had been applied to prohibit a home for the mentally retarded from operating in a residential neighborhood.[43] The Court said that no rational basis for the ordinance existed. Rather, it appeared to be based solely on "irrational prejudice against the mentally retarded."

In passing the Voting Accessibility Act of 1984, Congress attempted to increase access to the polls for disabled persons. With the passage of Title V of the Rehabilitation Act of 1973 and the Education for All Handicapped Children Act of 1975, Congress attempted to remove barriers confronting persons with disabilities in employment and education. But the most significant legislation by far in this area is the Americans with Disabilities Act (ADA) of 1990. The ADA requires that

- Businesses provide reasonable accommodations to employees with disabilities (Title I).
- Public services, including public transportation systems, be made accessible to persons with disabilities (Title II).
- Newly constructed or remodeled places of public accommodation (stores, restaurants, hotels, etc.) be made accessible to persons with disabilities (Title III).
- Telecommunications services be reasonably accessible to persons with disabilities (Title IV).

Government agencies and private businesses have been forced to develop policies to comply with the dictates of the ADA. Unlike the Civil Rights Act, the costs of compliance with the requirements of the ADA can be quite substantial. State and local governments have objected to what they see as another set of unfunded mandates from the federal government. Businesses have been given tax breaks to ease the costs of compliance, but these costs remain substantial, and many businesses have been slow to comply. Of course, businesses that fail to comply with the ADA are subject to civil suit.

A person is considered disabled under the ADA if she has a physical or mental impairment that substantially limits her major life activities. Obviously, the ADA provides a fertile field for judicial interpretation because courts must decide what constitutes "reasonable accommodation," "reasonably accessible," "substantially limits," and so forth. Even though the policy originated in the legislative branch, much of the implementation is being done by the courts.

5-4d The Controversy over Gay Rights

Homosexuality has always been taboo in the Judeo-Christian moral tradition. Reflecting this taboo, the criminal laws that this country inherited from England made homosexual activity a serious offense. In the more permissive climate of the 1960s, homosexuals began to "come out of the closet," calling for an end to criminal prohibitions on their activities and for an end to discrimination based on sexual orientation. In the 1970s, gay men and lesbians began to organize and fight for legal rights, in much the same way as African Americans and women had done before them. Organizations such as the Lambda Legal Defense and Education Fund and the Gay and Lesbian Advocates and Defenders went to court to challenge laws they deemed to be discriminatory. They also lobbied Congress and the state legislatures to enact laws to prohibit private discrimination based on sexual orientation. Despite numerous setbacks, these organizations have been reasonably successful in both the legislative and judicial arenas. However, Americans continue to be divided on the issue of "gay rights" and the larger question of homosexuality. Indeed, gay rights was one of the defining elements of the "culture war" that erupted in the 1990s. In the new millennium, gay men and women are out and proud, though not free from discrimination.

California briefly allowed gay couples to marry until a state ballot measure outlawed the practice. Today six states offer gay couples the right to marry or enter into a "civil union" that is basically the same as a marriage. Attitudes towards homosexuality in America are changing, but slowly. Only eight percent more people think homosexuality should be accepted than think it should be rejected as of 2007. In Europe and portions of South America the numbers are much more in favor of acceptance, but in the Middle East, Southeast Asia, and Africa, the numbers in favor of rejection are still very high. Until there is a reasonable consensus within the culture, gay rights advocates will not be completely successful in their legal and political efforts. Of course, it is also true that by and large the mass media and popular culture have been sympathetic to the gay rights cause, and this has had profound effects on American attitudes. As societal attitudes become more tolerant and permissive, the gay rights agenda will continue to advance.

Gay Men and Lesbians in the Military

In the early 1990s, one of the most controversial questions involving gay rights was the policy banning homosexuals from serving in the military. Should a person be disqualified from military service merely because of homosexual orientation, as distinct from homosexual acts? The military justified the ban as necessary to maintain discipline, morale, and good order in the armed forces. Gay and lesbian activists argued that the ban punished persons merely because of their status or orientation, without regard to their personal conduct or the quality of their service. The federal courts reached mixed results in a number of lawsuits challenging the ban, but the Supreme Court has never had the opportunity to rule on the matter.

During the 1992 presidential campaign, candidate Bill Clinton promised that, if elected, he would immediately issue an executive order rescinding the military's ban on homosexuals. Not surprisingly, Clinton received the overwhelming support of gay and lesbian voters in the election. After taking office in January 1993, President Clinton found himself embroiled in a controversy over his campaign pledge. Clinton's initiative met tremendous resistance not only from the military but also from Congress. Critics of the initiative argued that allowing openly gay individuals to serve in the military would damage morale and discipline and would present a host of practical problems. Supporters of the president's plan noted that the objections to gays in the military were strikingly similar to those raised in 1948 when President Harry S. Truman moved to end racial segregation in the military.

In the midst of the controversy, public opinion appeared to side with the military, at least by a slight margin. A poll conducted by *The New York Times* and CBS in January 1993 found that 48 percent opposed permitting gays to serve in the military and 42 percent supported the idea.[44] Facing opposition of unexpected intensity, even from within his own party, President Clinton decided to delay issuance of the executive order for six months. He did, however, immediately order the military to refrain from inquiring into the sexual orientation of new recruits. Eventually, after holding hearings, Congress adopted a "don't ask, don't tell" policy proposed by the Clinton administration as a compromise. The firestorm of controversy that erupted over Clinton's initial proposal showed the lack of societal consensus on the issue of gay rights. But the eventual "don't ask, don't tell" compromise showed how even volatile, emotional issues can be resolved through discussion, debate, and negotiation. However, a series of federal appeals court rulings in 1993, all of which ordered the military to reinstate gays and lesbians who had been discharged, suggested that the ultimate decision on this controversial question would come not from Congress but rather from the Supreme Court. However, the Supreme Court never ruled on the issue. President Obama made repealing Don't Ask, Don't Tell a campaign priority in 2008, and the policy was repealed for good at the end of 2010.[45]

Gay Rights before the Courts

Gay rights advocates did not win any significant victories in the Supreme Court until 1996. In that year, in *Romer v. Evans*, the Court struck down a state constitutional amendment disallowing "any minority status, quota preferences, protected status or claim of discrimination" on the basis of "homosexual, lesbian, or bisexual orientation."[46] Colorado voters had adopted Amendment 2 through a statewide referendum after a controversy erupted over the fact that some of the state's more liberal communities had adopted ordinances prohibiting discrimination on the basis of sexual orientation. In declaring the amendment invalid, the Supreme Court observed

> *It is not within our constitutional tradition to enact laws of this sort. Central both to the idea of the rule of law and to our own Constitution's guarantee of equal protection is the principle that government and each of its parts remain open on impartial terms to all who seek its assistance. . . .*
>
> *We must conclude that Amendment 2 classifies homosexuals not to further a proper legislative end but to make them unequal to everyone else. This Colorado cannot do. A State cannot so deem a class of persons a stranger to its laws.*

In a sharply worded dissenting opinion, Justice Antonin Scalia argued that Amendment 2 was not adopted out of a popular desire to harm gays, but was instead "a modest attempt by seemingly tolerant Coloradans to preserve traditional sexual mores against the efforts of a politically powerful minority to revise those mores through use of the laws." Scalia attacked the reasoning of the majority, saying that the Court's opinion "has no foundation in American constitutional law, and barely pretends to."

Gay Rights versus Associational Freedom

Current federal law does not prohibit discrimination based on sexual orientation with respect to employment, housing, or access to public accommodations.[47] It is important to remember that in a federal system, civil rights are not defined solely by federal law. State and local laws can provide significant protections in this area, and roughly one-third of the states and a number of cities and counties have enacted legislation along these lines. California law, for example, prohibits discrimination based on sexual orientation with respect to education, public accommodations, and public and private sector employment. California law also extends to same-sex "domestic partners" many of the legal rights normally afforded married persons.

One of the difficult questions arising under laws that forbid discrimination by places of public accommodation is defining "public accommodation." Traditionally, the term was used to refer to businesses that opened their doors to the general public, but recently some courts have found this definition to be too restrictive. In an effort to expand existing legal prohibitions against discrimination, gay rights activists have gone to court seeking to have certain private organizations declared public accommodations. One such case gave rise to a controversial Supreme Court decision involving the Boy Scouts of America.[48] James Dale had been dismissed from his position as an assistant scoutmaster after the organization learned that he was gay. Dale successfully sued the Boy Scouts in the New Jersey courts, which ultimately ruled that the Boy Scouts had violated a New Jersey law prohibiting discrimination by places of public accommodation. The New Jersey Supreme Court ruled that the Boy Scout organization constituted a "public accommodation" under New Jersey law, a ruling not subject to review by the U.S. Supreme Court. However, the U.S. Supreme Court took the case and ruled that the application of the state antidiscrimination law to the Scouts violated that organization's rights under the First Amendment. Splitting five to four, the Court held that the Boy Scouts' First Amendment freedom of association trumped the state's interest in advancing the cause of gay rights. Writing for the majority of justices, Chief Justice William Rehnquist opined

> *We are not, as we must not be, guided by our views of whether the Boy Scouts' teachings with respect to homosexual conduct are right or wrong; public or judicial disapproval of a tenet of an organization's expression does not justify the State's effort to compel the organization to accept members where such acceptance would derogate from the organization's expressive message.*

Speaking for the minority, Justice John P. Stevens accused the Court of its prejudices into legal principles:

> *That such prejudices are still prevalent and that they have caused serious and tangible harm to countless members of the class New Jersey seeks to protect are*

established matters of fact that neither the Boy Scouts nor the Court disputes. That harm can only be aggravated by the creation of a constitutional shield for a policy that is itself the product of a habitual way of thinking about strangers.

Critics of the decision, and there were many, argued that the Court was giving a green light to bigotry. But many in the private, not-for-profit sector applauded the Court for protecting a private organization from government control.

The Gay Marriage Issue

As we noted in Chapter 4, "Civil Liberties and Individual Freedom," the Supreme Court in 2003 overturned one of its precedents and struck down a Texas law making private homosexual activity a crime.[49] The Court's decision in *Lawrence v. Texas* came after a number of state courts invalidated their own states' laws prohibiting private homosexual conduct by invoking privacy rights guaranteed by their respective state constitutions. Dissenting in *Lawrence*, Justice Antonin Scalia argued that the decision "dismantles the structure of constitutional law that has permitted a distinction to be made between heterosexual and homosexual unions, insofar as formal recognition in marriage is concerned." Whatever one thinks of Justice Scalia's position on the issue of gay marriage, his observation was borne out by a Massachusetts court decision declaring unconstitutional state laws limiting marriage to heterosexual couples. In a 4–3 decision handed down in November 2003, the Supreme Judicial Court of Massachusetts held that gay and lesbian couples should be entitled to marry in Massachusetts and set a six-month deadline for the state legislature to respond.[50] Chief Justice Margaret H. Marshall began her opinion for the court as follows:

Marriage is a vital social institution. The exclusive commitment of two individuals to each other nurtures love and mutual support; it brings stability to our society. For those who choose to marry, and for their children, marriage provides an abundance of legal, financial, and social benefits. In return it imposes weighty legal, financial, and social obligations. The question before us is whether, consistent with the Massachusetts Constitution, the Commonwealth may deny the protections, benefits, and obligations conferred by civil marriage to two individuals of the same sex who wish to marry. We conclude that it may not. The Massachusetts Constitution affirms the dignity and equality of all individuals. It forbids the creation of second-class citizens. In reaching our conclusion we have given full deference to the arguments made by the Commonwealth. But it has failed to identify any constitutionally adequate reason for denying civil marriage to same-sex couples.

In 1999, the Vermont Supreme Court rendered a similar decision, but the Vermont legislature responded by adopting a statute permitting gay and lesbian couples to enter into "civil unions." Public opinion in Massachusetts opposed gay marriage per se, but was favorable toward the concept of civil unions.[51] However, the legislature was sharply divided and few seemed to be in a mood to compromise. Sponsors of a proposed amendment to the state constitution seeking to overturn the state supreme court's decision were not able to muster the requisite votes. Nor were there enough votes to legalize civil unions as an alternative to marriage. The legislative impasse resulted in the legalization of gay marriage in Massachusetts according to the deadline set by the court. Thus, in May 2004, officials in the Bay State began issuing marriage licenses to gay and lesbian couples.

It was inevitable, given the media attention to developments in Massachusetts, that the issue would erupt into a national controversy. The conflict escalated further in February 2004 when the mayor of San Francisco ordered city officials to begin issuing marriage licenses to same-sex couples in contravention of state law. Ultimately, the California Supreme Court held that the nearly three thousand gay marriages performed in San Francisco were unlawful, but the actions of the mayor helped to nationalize the controversy.

In his 2004 State of the Union address, President George W. Bush called on Congress to "defend the sanctity of marriage." In 1996, Congress had passed the Defense of Marriage Act (DOMA), under which states are not required to recognize same-sex marriages licensed by other states. But conservatives feared that DOMA might be declared unconstitutional by federal courts under the Full Faith and Credit Clause of the U.S. Constitution, which has long been interpreted to require states to recognize marriages licensed by other states. In February 2004, President Bush called on Congress to adopt a federal constitutional amendment defining marriage as "between one man and one woman." According to President Bush, the amendment would "fully protect marriage, while leaving the state legislatures free to make their own choices in defining legal arrangements other than marriage." According to national surveys taken at the time, most Americans opposed the idea of gay marriage, but only a minority supported the idea of amending the U.S. Constitution along the lines recommended by President Bush (see the following "What Americans Think About" feature).

Not surprisingly, this issue made its way into the presidential campaign. John Kerry opposed the idea of amending the Constitution, arguing that Congress should stay out of the matter entirely. Many observers were surprised when, in the late summer of 2004, President Bush's Vice President, Dick Cheney, seemed to echo Senator Kerry's sentiments on the issue. As the campaign entered the stretch run toward the November election, however, the issue was eclipsed by the war in Iraq and other foreign policy and defense issues. However, it should be noted that in 2004, voters in eleven states approved ballot measures to prohibit same-sex marriage. Voters who supported these measures voted by substantial margins in favor of President Bush. Although the issue of same-sex marriage clearly was not a decisive one in terms of the presidential contest in most states, there is reason to believe that the Ohio ballot initiative banning same-sex marriage may have stimulated enough turnout among socially conservative voters to tip the election in Bush's favor in that crucial battleground state.[52]

On May 15, 2008, the California Supreme Court ruled that state-imposed bans on gay couples seeking marriage licenses were unconstitutional and marriage was a fundamental right not to be denied to anyone. Immediately, gay couples from across the country went to California in an effort to get married. Simultaneously, opponents of gay marriage organized a campaign against the decision in a ballot initiative that would restrict marriages to one man and one woman. Designated "Proposition 8," the initiative passed in November of 2008 and effectively returned the ban on gay marriage in California. Showing just how divided and contentious the fight is, on April 30, 2009, a pro–gay marriage group filed a petition to repeal Proposition 8. The repeal effort was unsuccessful, but in 2013 the U.S. Supreme Court struck down Proposition 8.

As noted in Chapter 4, "Civil Liberties and Individual Freedom," homosexuality is an issue on which American culture has changed dramatically in recent decades. No doubt, public attitudes on gay marriage will continue to evolve, most likely in the direction of greater tolerance. Surveys consistently show that younger people are much more liberal on the issue of gay rights generally than are older Americans. However, gay rights should remain a "hot button" political and legal issue for some years to come.

© Jeff Banke, 2013. Used under license from Shutterstock, Inc.

5-5 Conclusion: Evolving Notions of Equality

Legal protection for civil rights can emanate from a number of sources. First and foremost, the U.S. Constitution, as amended after the Civil War, protects the right to vote and prohibits states from denying persons within their jurisdictions the equal protection of the laws. The Fourteenth Amendment also grants Congress the power to legislate in the field of civil rights. Using this power, as well as its broad powers under the Commerce Clause, Congress has enacted a number of important civil rights statutes, most significantly the Civil Rights Act of 1964 and the Voting Rights Act of 1965. Although these statutes are based on the authority of the Constitution, they go beyond the civil rights protections afforded by the Constitution in that they address discrimination by private individuals and corporations.

Many state constitutions contain provisions similar to the Equal Protection Clause of the Fourteenth Amendment. States that do not have these types of constitutional provisions may amend their constitutions to provide for this type of protection. Like Congress, state legislatures may enact statutes that protect civil rights from private discrimination as well as from discrimination by government agencies. Cities and counties may also adopt civil rights ordinances applicable within their jurisdictions. Of course, state and local civil rights laws may not conflict with federal protections. Under our federal system, however, states and localities are free to provide greater, but not lesser, protections to civil rights than are provided by federal law. And, of course, state and local laws may not, for the sake of fostering civil rights, violate individual liberties protected by the federal and state constitutions. When conflicts occur, it is generally up to the courts to sort them out. In doing this, courts attempt to strike a workable balance between equality and freedom, the two core values of our democracy.

Ultimately, though, questions of civil rights, as well as those of civil liberties, are determined not in courts of law but rather in the attitudes and opinions of Americans—in our political culture. The idea of rights is fundamental to American political culture. Our system is founded on the idea that individuals have rights that must be respected by other individuals, by the society generally, and certainly by government. One of the most fundamental rights of individuals is the right to equal treatment before the law and the state. Our society has taken two centuries to evolve to the point that it is willing to extend the right of equal treatment to African Americans and other racial and ethnic minorities, as well as to women. Some would say that the evolution is incomplete—that American society still has a long way to go. Others would argue that we have moved beyond the ideal of equal protection of the law to a system in which preferred status has been institutionalized for certain protected groups and not others. In attempting to foster equality, society must avoid the dangers that can occur when group is pitted against group.

However well-intentioned and committed to civil rights American citizens may be, those commitments and intentions are always tested in times of war. In the wake of the terrorist attacks of September 11, 2001, America found itself again debating the scope and limits of civil rights protections. Under what circumstances, if any, should authorities be permitted to consider race or ethnicity as an element of a terrorist profile? Is it permissible for police or airport security personnel to be immediately suspicious of young, Arabic males? Although many Americans have no problem with **racial profiling**, especially in the context of the war on terrorism, others see this type of stereotyping as a real threat to civil rights. Here, as with many issues of law and policy, reasonable, well-intentioned people can and will disagree. Whatever one's perspective may be, it should be evident that the difficult and complex issues of civil rights will remain on the public agenda for quite some time, especially during America's war on terrorism.

Questions for Thought and Discussion

1. Is affirmative action in hiring a necessary and just corrective to past discrimination, or does it amount to unjust reverse discrimination?

2. Should sex discrimination and race discrimination be judged by the same standards, or are these types of discrimination significantly different?

3. Should the federal civil rights laws be amended to forbid discrimination on the basis of physical or mental disabilities?

4. Does there need to be more legal protection for the rights of gays and lesbians? Should Congress add sexual orientation to the list of prohibited forms of discrimination?

5. What forms of discrimination beyond those mentioned in this chapter have the potential to become political and legal issues in the future?

For Further Reading

Balkin, J. M., and Bruce Ackerman, eds. What Brown v. Board of Education Should Have Said: The Nation's Top Legal Experts Rewrite America's Landmark Civil Rights Decision (New York: NYU Press, 2001).

Chavez, Linda. The Color Bind: California's Battle to End Affirmative Action (Berkeley: University of California Press, 1998).

Finch, Minnie. The NAACP: Its Fight for Justice (Metuchen, NJ: Scarecrow Press, 1981).

Gerstmann, Evan. The Constitutional Underclass: Gays, Lesbians, and the Failure of Class-Based Equal Protection (Chicago: University of Chicago Press, 1999).

Ginsberg, Ruth Bader. Constitutional Aspects of Sex-Based Discrimination (St. Paul, MN: West Publishing Co., 1974).

Glazer, Nathan. Affirmative Discrimination: Ethnic Inequality and Public Policy (New York: Basic Books, 1975).

Davidson, Chandler, and Bernard Grofman, eds. Quiet Revolution in the South: The Impact of the Voting Rights Act 1965–1990 (Princeton, NJ: Princeton University Press, 1994).

Kluger, Richard. Simple Justice: The History of Brown v. Board of Education and Black America's Struggle for Racial Equality (New York: Vintage Books, 1977).

McGlen, Nancy E., and Karen O'Connor. Women, Politics and American Society (Upper Saddle River, NJ: Prentice-Hall, 1998).

Mezey, Susan Gluck. In Pursuit of Equality: Women, Public Policy and the Federal Courts (New York: St. Martin's Press, 1998).

Norell, Robert J. Reaping the Whirlwind: The Civil Rights Movement in Tuskegee, rev. ed. (Chapel Hill, NC: University of North Carolina Press, 1998).

Peltason, Jack W. 58 Lonely Men: Southern Federal Judges and School Desegregation (Urbana, IL: University of Illinois Press, 1961).

Thernstrom, Abigail, and Stephen Thernstrom. America in Black and White: One Nation Indivisible (New York: Simon and Schuster, 1997).

Wolters, Raymond. The Burden of Brown: Thirty Years of School Desegregation (Knoxville: University of Tennessee Press, 1984).

Woodward, C. Vann. The Strange Career of Jim Crow (New York: Oxford University Press, 1968).

Endnotes

1 See, for example, R.A.V. v. City of St. Paul, 505 U.S. 377 (1992), where the Supreme Court struck down a "hate crimes" ordinance on the grounds that it unduly restricted speech protected by the First Amendment.

2 Scott v. Sandford, 60 U.S. (19 How.) 393 (1857).

3 The Civil Rights Cases, 109 U.S. 3 (1883).

4 Plessy v. Ferguson, 163 U.S. 537 (1896).

5 Grovey v. Townsend, 295 U.S. 45 (1927).

6 Wallace Mendelson, Discrimination (Englewood Cliffs, NJ: Prentice-Hall, 1962), p. 170.

7 Sweatt v. Painter, 339 U.S. 629 (1950).

8 Brown v. Board of Education of Topeka, Kansas (first decision), 347 U.S. 483 (1954).

9 Brown v. Board of Education of Topeka, Kansas (second decision), 349 U.S. 294 (1955).

10 Richard Kluger, Simple Justice: The History of Brown v. Board of Education and Black America's Struggle for Racial Equality (New York: Vintage Books, 1977), pp. 753–54.

11 Cooper v. Aaron, 358 U.S. 1 (1958).

12 Alex Haley, The Autobiography of Malcolm X (New York: Grove Press, 1966).

13 Hugh Davis Graham, The Civil Rights Era: Origins and Development of National Policy (New York: Oxford University Press, 1990).

14 Heart of Atlanta Motel v. United States, 379 U.S. 421 (1964).

15 Katzenbach v. McClung, 379 U.S. 294 (1964).

16 Swann v. Charlotte-Mecklenburg Board of Education, 402 U.S. 1 (1971).

17 Millken v. Bradley, 418 U.S. 717 (1974).

18 Stacy Teicher, "Closing a Chapter on School Desegregation," The Christian Science Monitor, July 16, 1999.

19 For example, on September 11, 1999, the Associated Press reported that a federal judge had ordered an end to busing in Charlotte-Mecklenburg, North Carolina, one of the school districts at the forefront of the conflict over busing three decades ago.

20 University of California Board of Regents v. Bakke, 438 U.S. 265 (1978).

21 United Steelworkers v. Weber, 433 U.S. 193 (1979).

22 City of Richmond v. J. A. Croson Co., 488 U.S. 469 (1989).

23 Adarand Constructors, Inc. v. Peña, 515 U.S. 200 (1995).

24 Grutter v. Bolinger, 539 U.S. 306 (2003).

25 Smith v. Allwright, 321 U.S. 649 (1944).

26 Lassiter v. Northampton County Board of Elections, 360 U.S. 45 (1959).

27 Harper v. Virginia State Board of Elections, 383 U.S. 663 (1966).

28 City of Mobile, Alabama v. Bolden, 446 U.S. 55 (1980).

29 Thornburgh v. Gingles, 478 U.S. 30 (1986).

30 Korematsu v. United States, 323 U.S. 214 (1944).

31 Rostker v. Goldberg, 453 U.S. 57 (1981).

32 Mississippi University for Women v. Hogan, 458 U.S. 718 (1984).

33 United States v. Virginia, 518 U.S. 515 (1996).

34 Johnson v. Transportation Agency of Santa Clara County, 480 U.S. 646 (1987).

35 Roberts v. United States Jaycees, 468 U.S. 609 (1984).
36 Why Women are Angry. Newsweek, October 21, 1991, p. 34.
37 University of Michigan, Center for Political Studies, National Election Study 1992.
38 Meritor Savings Bank, FBD v. Vinson, 477 U.S. 57 (1986).
39 Harris v. Forklift Systems, Inc., 114 S.Ct. 367 (1993).
40 Gideon v. Wainwright, 372 U.S. 335 (1963); Douglas v. California, 372 U.S. 353 (1963).
41 San Antonio Independent School District v. Rodriguez, 411 U.S. 1 (1973).
42 Harris v. McRae, 448 U.S. 297 (1980).
43 City of Cleburne, Texas v. Cleburne Living Center, 473 U.S. 432 (1985).
44 "Public Views on Homosexuals in the Military," The New York Times, January 27, 1993, p. A-8.
45 http://www.washingtonpost.com/wp-srv/special/politics/dont-ask-dont-tell-timeline/
46 Romer v. Evans, 517 U.S. 620 (1996).
47 It should be noted that Executive Order 13087, issued by President Bill Clinton in May 1998, prohibited employment discrimination on the basis of sexual orientation by agencies within the executive branch of the federal government.
48 Boy Scouts of America v. Dale, 530 U.S. 640 (2000).
49 Lawrence v. Texas, 539 U.S 558, 578 (2003).
50 Goodridge v. Department of Public Health, 439 Mass. 665 (2003).
51 A Boston Globe poll, reported in that newspaper on February 12, 2004, indicated that 53 percent of Massachusetts' residents opposed gay marriage. However, 60 percent favored creation of "civil unions."
52 See James Dao, "Same-Sex Marriage Key to Some G.O.P. Races," The New York Times, November 4, 2004, p. P4.

Unit 2

POLITICAL CULTURE AND PARTICIPATION

Chapter 6

THE MASS MEDIA

OUTLINE

Key Terms 200

Expected Learning Outcomes 200

6-1 The Development of Mass Media 200

- **6-1a** The Print Media 201
- **6-1b** Electronic Media 203
- **6-1c** News Media Goes Social 207
- **6-1d** The Ubiquitous Media 208

6-2 Mass Media in American Democracy 210

- **6-2a** Mass Media and Political Culture 210
- **6-2b** Ownership and Control of the Mass Media 211
- **6-2c** Are the Mass Media Biased? 212
- **6-2d** The Economic Decline and Media 214

6-3 Freedom of the Press: A Basic National Commitment 215

- **6-3a** The Prohibition against Prior Restraint 215
- **6-3b** Libel Suits 216
- **6-3c** The "People's Right to Know" 216
- **6-3d** Confidential Sources 216
- **6-3e** The Special Case of Broadcast and Online Media 217
- **6-3f** Constitutional Protection of the Internet 220

6-4 Press Coverage of Government 221

- **6-4a** Coverage of the President 221
- **6-4b** Covering Congress 225
- **6-4c** The Media and the Courts 226

6-5 Coverage of Elections, Campaigns, and Candidates 228

6-6 Mass Media and the Making of Public Policy 229

- **6-6a** Agenda Setting 229
- **6-6b** Building Public Support for Particular Policies 230

6-7 Conclusion: The Media—an Essential Part of the American Political System 231

Questions for Thought and Discussion 233

Endnotes 234

KEY TERMS

bloggers
chain ownership
confidential source
electronic media
Web 2.0
citizen journalism
hashtag
fairness doctrine
injunction
leaks
libel
mass media
hyperlocal
pack journalism
paywall
press conference
print media
prior restraint
reckless disregard of the truth
shield laws
SOPA/PIPA
talk radio
tort
trial balloons
vetting
White House press corps
yellow journalism

EXPECTED LEARNING OUTCOMES

After reading this chapter and completing the supplemental online materials, students will:

- Trace the development of American news media
- Describe the media's intermediary relationship in American politics
- Track changes in the media business in America
- Assess the impact of online and social media on political news

6-1 THE DEVELOPMENT OF MASS MEDIA

The **mass media** include the technologies and organizations that disseminate information to the mass public. This broad category can be divided into the print media and the electronic media. Also termed *the press*, the **print media** include newspapers, journals, tabloids, and magazines. The **electronic media** encompass radio, television, and the many news sites on the Internet. Although the media are often referred to as the "fourth estate,"[1] some have gone so far as to call them the "fourth branch of government."[2] A better way to think of the media is as an intermediary institution, like political parties and interest groups. Like these dedicated political organizations, the media help to link government and the public, principally through disseminating political information. Far from being mere conduits of information, however, the media shape public perceptions of issues, candidates, and institutions. Ultimately, the media have a significant effect on American political culture by shaping the values, beliefs, and expectations of the citizenry.

Heap of newspapers with business news

ONLINE 6.1 *The Changing News Landscape*
http://www.youtube.com/watch?v=LvwQqtWOHWo

6-1a The Print Media

During the Revolutionary Era, the media consisted exclusively of print. Consisting of small independent newspapers and pamphlets, pamphlets and papers played a vital role in facilitating political debate and in disseminating information. Indeed, the ratification of the Constitution was vigorously debated in not only the state ratifying conventions but also papers. *The Federalist Papers* first appeared as a series of newspaper articles analyzing and endorsing the new Constitution. Anti-Federalists also made wide use of newspapers in expressing their opposition to ratification.

Newspapers

The first newspapers in America were blatantly political—and partisan. Much like television giants Fox News and MSNBC today, the media a citizen chose was usually a reflection of their ideology. The *Gazette of the United States*, established in 1789, was decidedly Federalist in its political orientation. In contrast, the *National Gazette*, founded in 1791, was a Jeffersonian paper. These papers specialized in defending their partisans and criticizing (often unfairly) their political opponents. In adopting the First Amendment to the Constitution, which, among other things, guarantees freedom of the press, the Framers of the Bill of Rights were keenly aware that newspapers could not always be counted on to report stories fairly, accurately, and objectively. Accusations of media bias are as old as the nation itself. Yet the Framers realized how vital a free press is to a free society and republican government. In 1800, about two hundred small, independent newspapers were operating in the United States. By 1835, the number had grown to more than twelve hundred. In the 1830s, a new style of newspaper appeared: the penny paper. It was cheap, usually costing a cent. The penny papers were independent of political parties and were interested in much more than party politics. James Gordon Bennett's *New York Herald* was an example, serving as the precursor of the modern newspaper. It featured a society column, financial news, and a variety of local human interest stories in addition to political news.

Population growth, westward expansion, and the development of the telegraph and high-speed printing presses all contributed to a nationwide spread of newspapers during the nineteenth century. As the newspaper industry grew, a new profession emerged: journalism. Like any profession, journalism took many years to develop a professional culture that dictated the norms governing how journalists should discover and report the news. By the twentieth century, that culture stressed the need for accuracy, fairness, and impartiality. This professional culture was in part a response to a growing public concern over the press. In the late nineteenth and early twentieth centuries, yellow journalism, which emphasized the sensational with little concern for facts, became a popular style of newspaper reporting. This style of journalism, popularized by such newspapers as Joseph Pulitzer's *New York World*, appealed to the less-educated but functionally literate segments of society: the working class and the masses of new immigrants.

Yellow Journalism

William Randolph Hearst's *New York Journal*, founded in 1885, was the epitome of yellow journalism. Hearst combined extreme sensationalism with political crusades, the most notorious of which was his effort to draw the United States into the Spanish–American War. In 1898, the *New York Journal* helped to whip up war fever by claiming, without solid evidence, that the Spanish had blown up the American battleship *Maine* in Cuba. Most historians now believe that the explosion on the *Maine* was accidental. But Hearst's claim, accompanied by an artist's rendering of the exploding ship, drove the nation into a war frenzy. Reportedly, Hearst sent the following message to artist Frederic Remington, who was on assignment in Cuba: "You furnish the pictures and I'll furnish the war."

The rising middle class, more educated and reform-minded than the masses of workers and new immigrants, found Hearst's yellow journalism obnoxious and eventually it gave way to the more objective, fact-conscious, and dispassionate style of reporting that typified the twentieth century mainstream press. Since 1896, no other paper has represented this style better than *The New York Times*. Although some may find its calm, dispassionate, meticulous style boring, the *Times* is unsurpassed for the depth, breadth, and accuracy. In terms of the extent of its coverage of American government and politics, the *Times* is rivaled only by the *Washington Post*, another of this country's most successful and most respected newspapers. As the Internet became a more common place for Americans to get their news, print newspaper circulation declined. While *USA Today*, *The Wall Street Journal*, and *The New York Times* each sell more than a million papers per day, all of their circulations have declined and all newspapers are suffering from significant loss of readership. In 2008, the Internet surpassed newspapers as the primary news source in America.[3]

The Tabloids

Sensationalism, along with a less-than-fastidious concern for facts, remains the hallmark of the tabloid press. Publishers still find it profitable to appeal to people's appetites for the lurid, the morbid, and the outrageous. Many people buy the "supermarket tabloids," such as the *National Enquirer*, for entertainment; few take them at face value. Nevertheless, from time to time, celebrities who are the victims of false reports in the tabloids successfully sue for defamation of character. The possibility of being sued is evidently little deterrent to the tabloids, however. They can simply make too much money by publishing unflattering, and often untrue, stories about the rich, famous, and powerful. In the summer and fall of 1994, the tabloids feasted on the O.J. Simpson trial—easily the most sensational criminal case in years. A decade later, Scott Peterson's double murder trial supplied similar fodder.

The Contemporary Mainstream Press

In sharp contrast to the tabloids, mainstream newspapers now depend on maintaining public trust. For the most part, journalists do a good job at that, at least by comparison with the yellow journalists of the nineteenth century. Even now, many people question the integrity of the press. Some critics question its impartiality, accusing the press of political bias of one kind or another. Conservatives have been especially vocal in accusing the mainstream press of liberal bias. Others, like Carl Bernstein, who along with fellow *Washington Post* reporter Bob Woodward broke the story of the Watergate cover-up, question the quality of the contemporary mainstream press. In Bernstein's view, "the greatest felony in the news business today . . . is to be behind, or to miss, a major story, or more precisely, to seem behind, or to seem in danger of missing, a major story. So speed and quantity substitute for thoroughness and quality, for accuracy and context."[4] Bernstein suggests that the pressure to hurry the investigation and reporting of a story stems at least partially from the effect of the electronic media—television and radio—on the public's desire for instant information.

6-1b Electronic Media

Radio was invented during the latter years of the nineteenth century. By the 1920s, commercial radio stations were being established in the United States. By 1930, nearly half of all households were equipped to receive their broadcasts. Television was invented during the 1920s and became well established by the 1950s. Today, 98 percent of American households have television sets, and most households have more than one.

Talk Radio

Although radio is the oldest of the electronic media, it has been eclipsed by television in recent decades, especially for news. Many older Americans grew up listening to radio network news before the advent of the network television newscasts. Although the United States now has no widely recognized national radio newscast on this scale, radio has evolved into new forms, most notably **talk radio**, where radio personalities and their guests open the phone lines to callers who become part of the show. Talk radio stations exist in almost every major American city. Most of these stations feature local talk shows in addition to syndicated national shows with hosts such as Rush Limbaugh, Michael Reagan, Sean Hannity, and Dana Loesch. These shows tend toward the conservative viewpoint and have quite loyal listeners. They have become an

important source of news and commentary for people who are distrustful of the mainstream media. Although the medium is predominately conservative, in 2003 a group of unabashedly liberal commentators began a network—Air America—meant to counter this conservative domination. From 2004 to 2010, the network provided an alternative vehicle to many listeners, especially in large markets, breaking liberal commentators into the mainstream like current Minnesota Senator Al Franken and television commentator Rachel Maddow.

The Three Major Television Broadcast Networks

By the 1940s, three major television broadcasting networks had emerged: ABC, NBC, and CBS. As late as the 1970s, these big three networks dominated the coverage of national politics. News anchors such as Walter Cronkite and David Brinkley became household names and were accorded tremendous respect by most Americans. Their images are perpetually associated with the major news stories of the 1960s: the assassination of John F. Kennedy, the Vietnam War, the civil rights movement, the Apollo moon shots, and the 1968 Democratic convention in Chicago. Although the network news programs remain widely watched, they no longer dominate the media landscape.

During the 2004 presidential campaign, the role of the networks, in particular CBS, became the focus of much coverage and debate. In September, the network's popular and highly regarded *Sixty Minutes* aired a segment that relied on questionable documents to buttress the point that George W. Bush had received special treatment during his Vietnam-era National Guard service. Although the documents did not withstand minimal scrutiny, CBS continued to defend the broadcast for days before admitting that it could not vouch for the documents' authenticity. The event seriously undermined the credibility of both the network's main anchor, Dan Rather, as well as that of the network itself. It was a bitter pill for CBS to swallow. In the 1960s, with Walter Cronkite anchoring the evening news, CBS was the paragon of broadcast journalism. The nightly news broadcasts have not recovered from the Rather controversy and have been further supplanted by other forms of news intake, such as cable news channels and the Internet. None of the nightly news broadcasts in 2011 had more than eight million viewers on an average night.[5]

Cable and Satellite TV

The 1960s saw the advent of cable television, which allowed consumers to receive many more channels. Cable TV was greatly spurred by the application of satellite communications in the 1970s and 1980s, making it possible for cable companies to receive and transmit to their subscribers a virtually unlimited number of channels. Of course, satellite technology makes it possible for consumers to bypass cable systems and receive satellite transmissions directly, as many people in rural areas now do with their small "dishes." With many more choices, television viewers are no longer confined to the big three networks for their political information.

Twenty-Four-Hour Television News Networks

Cable television was originally designed to provide service to areas where traditional antennas did not provide adequate reception. The advent of satellite broadcasting, however, radically changed the nature of cable television. Still, the medium was mostly an extension of the entertainment function of television until 1981, when the Cable News Network (CNN) was launched. CNN altered the amount and the nature of politically oriented programming. For example, CNN was the only network to feature gavel-to-gavel coverage of the 1992 Democratic and Republican nominating conventions. CNN's *Crossfire* offered the cable-viewing public a steady diet of liberal-conservative dialogue on the issues and events of the day. Its nightly *Inside Politics* program highlighted breaking developments on the political scene. During the Gulf War, CNN provided almost constant coverage, including unprecedented reports from Baghdad as it was being attacked by the first air strike. Of course, it was not just the American public that had immediate access to these developments. World leaders, including Iraq's Saddam Hussein, tuned to CNN, using it as a source of worldwide information and communication. By 1992, approximately one in four adult Americans reported watching CNN at least "regularly."[6]

By the late 1990s, CNN had been joined by Fox News and MSNBC as the major purveyors of political information on cable and satellite TV. The main strength of the twenty-four-hour news networks is their virtual nonstop coverage during major events and crises, such as the period following the attacks of September 11, 2001. In the days that followed, the major networks joined the cable outlets with nonstop coverage uninterrupted by commercials. Of course, millions of dollars were then in lost advertising revenue. In a week or so, the networks returned to regular programming, and the network news stations continued with almost continual coverage. All stations returned to their regular advertising patterns within two weeks of the incident.

Of course, only so much factual information can be relayed in a given period. This limitation has led to an increased emphasis on opinion-oriented programs modeled after CNN's *Crossfire*. Programs such as *Hardball* on MSNBC and *The O'Reilly Factor* on Fox News became popular in the late 1990s. These shows' ratings skyrocketed in the late 1990s as they focused on President Clinton's scandals and the impeachment saga. Millions tuned in nightly during the 2000 presidential election, especially during the thirty-five-day vote-counting controversy that followed. These shows created a new type of television personality, the "spinner," who appears on one show after another to give one side's perspective on the day's events and issues. The cable networks appeared to evolve into more partisan political vehicles in 2008. Fox News, started by a Republican insider, has always been seen as covertly conservative. By 2008, MSNBC had become Fox's liberal counterweight. Liberal voices Rachel Maddow and Lawrence O'Donnell became MSNBC's answer to Bill O'Reilly and Sean Hannity.[7]

The Internet

Without question, the Internet is the most important development in mass media since the advent of television. The Internet originated in 1969, when the Department of Defense sponsored a project to link mainframe computers at four universities. The proliferation of personal computers in the 1980s led to the creation in the 1990s of new hardware and software, allowing for all computers to be linked on a universal network. Since 1995, Internet connectivity and use have exploded. As of June 30 2012, 2.4 billion people were online, with 273 million in the U.S. and Canada. one firm estimated worldwide Internet use at more than 1.6 billion people, with more than 250 million in the United States and Canada.[8]

ONLINE 6.2 *Another View on News Changes*
http://www.youtube.com/watch?v=vks7gIA2ReQ

Virtually every government agency, media outlet, business, interest group, and political party has a presence on the Internet. What is unique about it is its interactive nature, which allows for information to be disseminated worldwide almost instantaneously. Obviously, the Internet is a tremendous political resource, especially as a tool of political mobilization. Ultimately, the Internet is a boon to democracy and a serious threat to authoritarian regimes. It also poses serious problems relative to national security. Because of its decentralized nature, the Internet is extremely difficult to regulate, much less control.

The Internet has led to the unprecedented availability of a variety of opinions. Every major (and most minor) newspaper's website makes available columnists previously available only to that newspaper's subscribers or those willing to make the trek to the library. Some influential outlets—such as *Salon*, *Slate*, and *Newsmax*—are available only on the web. Likewise, influential media sources, such as Rush Limbaugh, regularly post written and audio files on their sites. Moreover, a number of sites, such as the Drudge Report, contain a wide number of links to newspapers and columns. The Internet has allowed many people who had to rely on one local newspaper for the column of the day to closely monitor thinking from any part of the political spectrum. This monitoring can even occur in real time rather than be delayed by a number of days.

The Bloggers

By 2004, another Internet phenomenon further complicated and democratized the world of news delivery. Just about anyone could create a "web log," commonly known as a "blog," that allowed an individual to make use of readily available programs to easily create and maintain running commentaries about virtually any topic, including politics and world affairs. Thus, **bloggers** provided immediacy to raw, unfiltered news events along with their own running commentary. These blogs serve as yet another outlet for political news. This outlet just about completely eliminated any notion that the major networks could control the dissemination of news. Some bloggers, like Glen Reynolds of Instapundit.com, record hundreds of thousands of hits per day and have achieved virtual mainstream status. Reynolds, a law professor, libertarian, and one of the best-known architects of the "blogosphere," says that his principal interest is "the intersection between advanced technologies and individual liberty."[9] He likens the rise of the blogosphere to "the late 18th century environment of pamphleteers, numerous small ideological newspapers, and coffeehouse debates."[10]

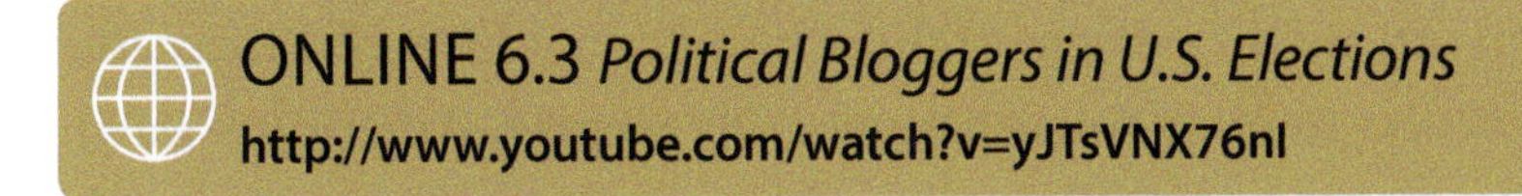
ONLINE 6.3 *Political Bloggers in U.S. Elections*
http://www.youtube.com/watch?v=yJTsVNX76nl

6-1c News Media Goes Social

The true revolution in online media began in 2003, when a new website launched called MySpace. The idea, to give every registered member of the site a free page to post links and updates, was novel. Millions of people signed up, but MySpace was quickly eclipsed by Facebook, which today has more than half a billion members. Other social media, such as microblogging sites Twitter and Tumblr, followed suit. Just as newspapers and television stations moved online, when social media began to soak into the culture reporters and sites established their own presences on those sites, giving a new way to consume news. Consumers can now get their news along with updates about friends' families.

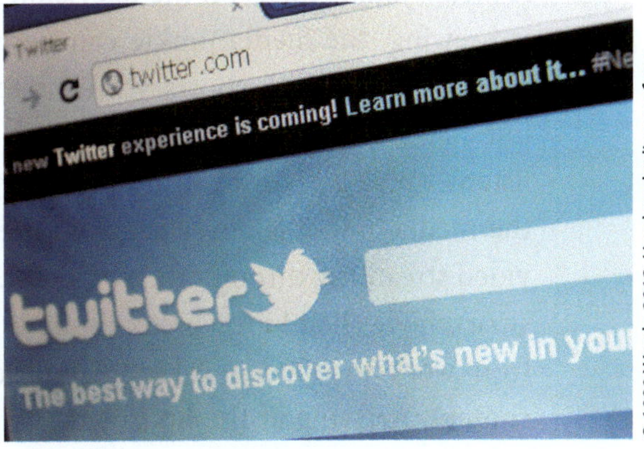

The social media revolution has also brought political figures into a realm where they can interact directly with constituents in a way never before possible. Instead of writing letters to Congresspersons, we can post on their Facebook walls. Reporters often share notes that do not make it into their stories on Twitter to provide insight and context into the working of government. And President Obama moderated two chats on the Reddit link aggregator site during his 2012 reelection campaign.

The ability of news consumers to also create content has spawned a new and vital term, **Web 2.0**. Coined by a new media technology blogger in 2004, Web 2.0 recognizes that online and social media eliminate the cost associated with broadcasting content in televised and printed forms, making content creation easy for the consumer. On Facebook, everyone has their own "channel" in the status updates and wall content they post. Citizens need now to be concerned with the content they create as well as the content they consume.

ONLINE 6.4 *Web 2.0*
http://www.youtube.com/watch?v=6gmP4nk0EOE

6-1d THE UBIQUITOUS MEDIA

The American people are exposed to an amazing barrage of news, information, and entertainment through the mass media. Ninety-eight percent of American homes now have at least one television set, and 67 percent of these homes now subscribe to a cable TV service, giving them access to numerous channels. On average, Americans watch nearly eight hours of television a day.[11] Though watching television may adversely affect reading, most people still manage to at least peruse a newspaper every day.[12] Increasingly, Americans are relying on the Internet, both at home and at work, to stay current on political developments.

THE MEDIA JUNKIE

Many Americans (including the author of this book) have become media junkies. A *media junkie* turns on the television while making coffee at 6 a.m. While the coffee is brewing, the media junkie can peruse five or six channels to get updates on the weather, last night's sports scores, international political developments, local headlines, and the day's outlook for the stock market. Driving to work, the media junkie listens to NPR's "Morning Edition" or one of the many talk radio shows. At work, the media junkie is never far from the Internet, and probably has CNN's audio and video streaming through the computer. In meetings, the media junkie is checking her smartphone, handy for breaking news, stock quotes, and e-mail. On the way home from work, the media junkie again tunes into NPR or more conservative news-driven content. Arriving at the house and sorting through the day's "snail mail," the media junkie simultaneously boots up the home computer and turns on the adjacent TV. Throughout the evening, the media junkie periodically surfs the Net on the phone or tablet, checks e-mail, catches up on Facebook updates and who they follow on Twitter, all while channel surfing cable or satellite TV. The number of media junkies is not really known, but it is at least sufficient to support a number of cable outlets, websites, and technologies that cater to them. The media junkie is addicted to electronic media, which tends to make them much better informed but much less well rested.

ONLINE 6.5 *News Consumption and Mobile Technology*
http://stateofthemedia.org/2012/mobile-devices-and-news-consumption-some-good-signs-for-journalism/

Immediacy of Information

The emergence of satellite and computer technology has given the mass media the capability to report, and often show visually, breaking news around the world with a minimum of lag time. An obvious example was the real-time broadcast of the terrorist attack on the World Trade Center in September 2001. People around the world were able to watch the second hijacked airliner crash into the tower live. Millions of viewers watched in horror as the twin towers burned and occupants of the higher stories who were unable to escape the fire jumped to their deaths. Millions saw the towers collapse as people below ran for their lives. Never has a more horrifying event been captured live by the mass media. There's no doubt that the psychological and political impact of the terrorist attack was amplified by the immediacy of the television coverage. It is one thing to read about this type of event in a newspaper; it is quite another to watch it live on television.

The pervasiveness and immediacy of the electronic media have produced a much greater degree of global awareness among the American people. The revolution in electronic communications has produced more than an "information society," however. It has more or less led to the realization of the global village posited by the mass media guru Marshall McLuhan in the 1960s.[13] A rancher in remote Montana can now receive CNN through a satellite dish and watch live as American planes conduct air raids in Iraq. People can view the same pictures simultaneously on the ground in Iraq, even inside the compound under attack!

The rise of social media has further accelerated this access and immediacy. Three forces have combined to make **citizen journalism**, where reporting is done directly via the populace, a rising trend. The ubiquity of smartphones with still and video cameras, video sharing sites like YouTube and Vine, and the mass dissemination of Facebook and Twitter allow people to shoot video directly, upload it, and share it instantly. Events such as presidential debates or filibusters in the Senate are live-tweeted by

reporters, observers, and other interested parties. Twitter has developed a new lexicon, with the term **hashtag**. For instance, when supporters of Senator Rand Paul wanted to promote his filibuster of a CIA nominee in early 2013, they created the hashtag #standwithrand to group their Twitter posts and provide running commentary of the thirteen-hour event.

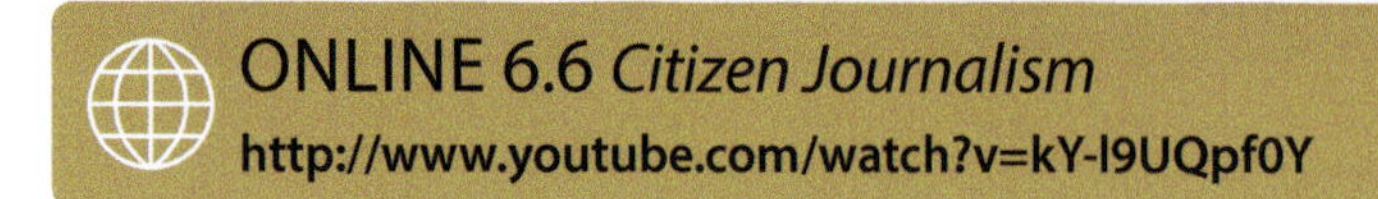

ONLINE 6.6 *Citizen Journalism*
http://www.youtube.com/watch?v=kY-I9UQpf0Y

6-2 MASS MEDIA IN AMERICAN DEMOCRACY

Mass media provide important sources of information about politics and government to the attentive public. Citizens interested in participating in the political process have access to an enormous quantity of information to inform their participation. Potential voters can see and hear candidates discuss issues and pundits discuss the candidates and their strategies. Citizens can observe the actions of their leaders and the workings of their government on a constant basis. To attentive citizens, the mass media provide a gold mine of information, although even the most sophisticated observers can sometimes feel overwhelmed by the sheer volume of information flowing through the media. In addition to their basic role of informing people, the mass media also perform a watchdog function, helping to keep politicians and other elites honest by exposing corruption, waste, deceit, and ineptitude. Hardly a day goes by that does not see some new revelation about an ill-conceived public policy, a poorly administered government program, or a scandal involving public officials in the variety of media available to us.

6-2a MASS MEDIA AND POLITICAL CULTURE

The informational and watchdog functions performed by the mass media are essential in a democracy operating in a mass society. Of course, the mass media do more than inform and expose. They also provide entertainment. Music, movies, television series, and other types of entertainment programming do more than entertain, however. They serve as vehicles for the transmission of popular culture; that is, media reflect and help to shape the basic values, tastes, attitudes, desires, and expectations of the mass public. They even have an impact on political culture. One can argue that

Americans' views of their leaders, and of their political institutions, have been and are being shaped by the mass media. When Vice President Dan Quayle launched his attack on the television series *Murphy Brown* and on the "cultural elite" during the 1992 presidential campaign, he was acknowledging the power of the mass media to shape American culture.

6-2b Ownership and Control of the Mass Media

In this country, the mass media are almost entirely owned and operated by the private sector. The U.S. government has many official publications, but it does not own and operate an official newspaper. The government does contribute money to a public television network, the Public Broadcasting System (PBS), and to a public radio network, National Public Radio (NPR). But these entities are not under the direct control of government officials and cannot fairly be characterized as instruments of government propaganda.

Chain Ownership

Private ownership of the media has generally been regarded as important because private ownership means competition, in both the collection and dissemination of information and the points of view expressed. Although the mass media are almost entirely in private hands, the past several decades have seen a strong trend toward the **chain ownership** of newspapers, magazines, and radio and television stations. For example, *The New York Times* now owns dozens of papers across the country. Moreover, the past few decades have also seen the emergence of large companies that operate or control multiple media outlets. In fact, the New York Times Company is one of these, owning a number of television and radio stations in addition to its family of newspapers. The Gannett Company, which owns more than eighty daily newspapers, also owns sixteen radio and ten television stations. Similarly, the Times Mirror Company controls more than twenty newspapers and fifty cable TV systems or television stations. Some critics of the mass media charge that this concentration of ownership reduces the diversity of information and opinions available to the mass public.

In addition to the issue of ownership and control is the question of the source of news and information available to newspapers and television and radio stations. Although most media outlets rely on reporters for information about local news, these outlets depend heavily on wire services and networks for national and international news. Of the roughly fourteen hundred television stations operating in this country, more than six hundred are affiliated with one of four major national networks: ABC, CBS, NBC, or Fox. Nearly every local newspaper relies on a major wire service, such as the Associated Press or Thomson Reuters, for national and international news, as do many television and radio stations.

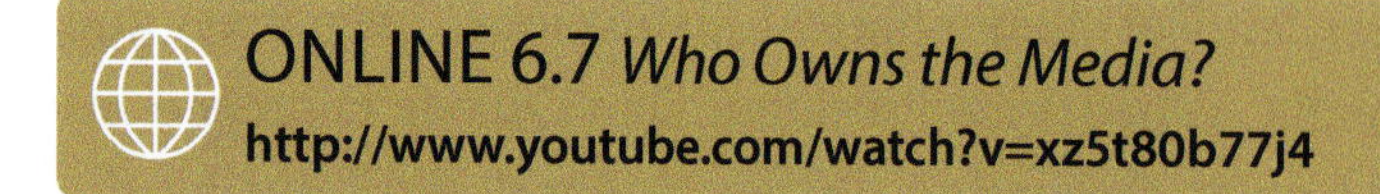

ONLINE 6.7 Who Owns the Media?
http://www.youtube.com/watch?v=xz5t80b77j4

Print in Decline

The Internet revolution has greatly disrupted the oldest and most venerable media institution in the country: print media. The availability of news content from multiple sources, such as new regionally based media sites, has severely undermined the newspaper business that used to see two or more papers existing in even small communities. **Hyperlocal** sites like New England's Forumhome.com undermine the established print news companies that struggled to bring in ad revenue similar to what they had in the print-only days.

Cities with multiple newspapers have seen one paper fold, or two papers merge, as happened with the move to online-only of Seattle's *Post-Intelligencer* in 2009 and the complete closure of Denver's *Rocky Mountain News* that same year.[14] Conglomerate ownership has led to a desire for more revenue streams in the newspaper business, as well. In 2012, *The New York Times* established a **paywall** for its website, where consumers would have to subscribe to the newspaper to access more than twenty articles from the online version of the paper or see content on tablets or smartphones.[15]

6-2c Are the Mass Media Biased?

Conservatives and Republicans have long complained that the mainstream media, especially the major television and cable news networks, are biased in favor of liberal policies and Democratic candidates. In the early 1970s, the Nixon administration went on the offensive against the "liberal media." In the 1980s, Republican presidents Reagan and Bush continued to criticize the media, building a movement that inspired a sea change in modern media: Fox News. Were Republican and conservative suspicions of the media well founded, or were they merely expressions of political paranoia or hypersensitivity? One approach to investigating media bias has been to look at the political affiliations and ideological orientations of reporters and editors. For example, a survey conducted by scholars at Indiana University in 2006 found that only 16 percent of reporters and editors nationwide identified themselves as Republicans, versus 35.9 percent who said they were Democrats.[16]

As citizens, people who work in the media are entitled to their own preferences and affiliations. Most people believe that a strong sense of journalistic professionalism can mitigate the influence of a reporter's biases. The important question is not whether members of the media are biased, but whether their coverage of political issues and events is biased. A survey conducted in October 2004 by the Pew Research Center found that most voters believe that members of the news media let their biases influence their reporting.[17] Of course, the fact that most Americans believe this to be true does not make it so.

In 2012, conservatives and Republicans continued to press the charge of liberal media bias. In particular, these critics focused their attacks on *The New York Times* and the major television networks (save Fox News), all of which were accused of orchestrating their coverage of the elections and other events to support Barack Obama's reelection campaign. In general, the American people have come to believe that there is a liberal bias in the mass media. As of 2004, according to a survey by the Gallup Organization, nearly half the adult population believed that the media were too liberal, while only 15 percent said they were too conservative.[18]

It is important to recognize that not all criticisms of media bias come from the ideological right. Michael Parenti argues that right-wing attacks on the press "help the media maintain an appearance of neutrality and objectivity." In Parenti's view, the media are "complicit with the dominant powers" of society, which he defines as "big business and the executive power of government."[19] According to Parenti, the function of the media "is not to produce an alert, critical and informed citizenry but the kind of people who will accept an opinion universe dominated by corporate and governmental elites, almost all of whom share the same ideological perspective about political and economic reality."[20] Like other critics on the far left, Parenti faults the media for helping to maintain the dominance of the capitalist system. In the national conversation over media bias, Parenti's claims are like voices in the wilderness.

Assuming it exists, the liberal bias in the media is being attenuated by the proliferation of media outlets. After all, most local newspaper editors tend to the conservative side of the spectrum. And the proliferation of cable TV has led to an increasing diversity of views on television. Conservative commentators such as Sean Hannity, George Will, and Fred Barnes are prominently featured on TV talk shows. The rise of talk radio has also contributed to the dissemination of conservative views through the electronic media. The talk-show host Rush Limbaugh, who is decidedly conservative in his orientation, is now (with the possible exception of Howard Stern) the best-known radio personality. In addition, an estimated 10 percent of all radio stations and 14 percent of all television stations are controlled by conservative Christian groups, somewhat offsetting the generally liberal character of the secular media. Finally, one cannot overstate the importance of the Internet as a medium for the dissemination of an amazing spectrum of viewpoints.

ONLINE 6.8 *The Public on Media Bias*
http://www.gallup.com/poll/149624/majority-continue-distrust-media-perceive-bias.aspx

Politically Selective Consumption of Media

With the proliferation of mass media, it is not difficult for a strongly opinionated consumer of mass media to select only those media outlets that conform to his political predilections. One whose orientation is strongly conservative is more apt to watch Fox News, whereas a more liberal individual is likely to be more comfortable with CNN. A survey conducted in October 2004 by the Pew Research Center found that 70 percent of regular Fox News viewers who planned to vote in the presidential election expected to vote for President Bush. On the other hand, 67 percent of regular CNN viewers preferred Senator Kerry. However, the entire sample of regular consumers of media was evenly divided between Kerry and Bush.[21]

A libertarian can set aside time every day to listen to Neal Boortz on the radio. Even extremists of various kinds can find sources of news and commentary that appeal to them, although not through mainstream media. Rather, they go to the Internet. Without question, consumers of mass media, no less than buyers of groceries, benefit from choices in the marketplace. Truly informed citizens, however, draw their information from multiple sources. There appears to be a growing tendency for politically attentive and active citizens to "lock on" to those media outlets that reinforce their point of view. This may be one of the reasons for the greater polarization of politics in recent years, as well as the more overtly partisan commentary in the media.

6-2d The Economic Decline and Media

When the economy worsened in 2008, few institutions were as ill-prepared to weather the storm as the American media. The Internet as a news source (and sites like Craigslist as an alternative avenue for classified ads) was already hitting newspapers and television in their wallets. Declining circulation and viewership were already issues of concern for media owners when the economic troubles hit. By 2009, the situation looked grim for many. Cities with multiple newspapers saw some close their doors completely, such as Denver's *Rocky Mountain News*. Other cities, such as Ann Arbor, Michigan and Seattle, Washington, had papers go online-only. Ad revenues (see Figure 6-1) plummeted for every outlet save cable TV. News outlet stock prices dove 83 percent. CBS devalued its assets by $14 billion. Competing satellite radio providers merged to keep from bankruptcy. The Internet continued to grow, showing no signs of an end to the troubles of traditional media.[22]

The future of media in America is unknown. Online sites have trouble finding revenues, meaning most of the committed news gatherers are either traditional reporters who have found an avenue online or bloggers whose commitment is inconsistent. The only certainty is that the way Americans get their news is changing quickly and drastically, with no assurances of quality news content.

6-3 Freedom of the Press: A Basic National Commitment

In no other country is the press as free from government censorship and control as it is in the United States. The idea of a free press, deeply rooted in Anglo-American legal and political culture, is expressed in the First Amendment to the U.S. Constitution, which explicitly prohibits government from abridging the freedom of the press.

6-3a The Prohibition against Prior Restraint

English common law contributed an important concept to the development of freedom of the press in the United States: the prohibition against prior restraint. **Prior restraint** refers to censorship before the fact—preventing the press from publishing something the government doesn't like. In a landmark 1931 decision, the Supreme Court struck down a Minnesota law that permitted public officials to seek an **injunction** to stop publication of any "malicious, scandalous or defamatory" newspaper or magazine.[23] Officials in Minneapolis had used the law to suppress the publication of a small newspaper, the *Saturday Press*, which had strong anti-Semitic overtones and maligned local politicians. The law provided that after a newspaper was subjected to an injunction, further publication was punishable as contempt of court. The Supreme Court saw this mode of suppression as "the essence of censorship" and declared the law unconstitutional. Though commenting with general approval on the rule against prior restraint, Chief Justice Charles Evans Hughes acknowledged that this restriction is not absolute. It would not, for example, prevent government in time of war from prohibiting publication of "the sailing dates of transports or the number and location of troops." In these and related situations, national security interests are almost certain to prevail over freedom of the press. But where is the line to be drawn? How far can the national security justification be extended in suppressing publication?

The Supreme Court revisited the question of prior restraint on the press in the sensational Pentagon Papers Case of 1971.[24] The Nixon administration attempted to prevent *The New York Times* and the *Washington Post* from publishing excerpts from a classified study about decision making on the Vietnam War. The newspapers had obtained the Pentagon Papers from Daniel Ellsberg, a defense analyst who worked in the Pentagon. In attempting to block the newspapers from publishing these classified documents, the federal government argued that considerations of national security outweighed the First Amendment interests of the press. The Supreme Court disagreed, however. By a 6–3 vote, the Court held that the effort to block publication of the Pentagon Papers amounted to an unconstitutional prior restraint on the press. Apparently, the Court was not convinced that publication—several years after the events and decisions discussed in the papers—constituted a significant threat to national security.

6-3b LIBEL SUITS

Libel consists of injuring someone's reputation by reporting falsehoods about that person. Libel is not a crime, but rather a **tort**, the remedy for which is a civil suit for monetary damages. Libelous publications have traditionally been outside the scope of First Amendment protection. In a landmark 1964 decision, however, the Supreme Court articulated a new rule that afforded far greater protection to published criticism of official conduct.[25] This rule prevents a public official from winning a libel suit unless she can prove that the false statement was made with actual malice or **reckless disregard of the truth** (see Case in Point 6-1). As long as there is an absence of malice on the part of the press, public officials are barred from recovering damages for the publication of false statements about them. The Supreme Court justified the new rule as an expression of "a profound national commitment to the principle that debate on public issues should be uninhibited, robust, and wide-open."

6-3c THE "PEOPLE'S RIGHT TO KNOW"

In a democracy, does the public always have a right to know what its government is doing? Some would argue that our government violates democratic principles to the extent that it maintains secret information or conducts covert activities. According to this view, the proper role of the press is to oppose any government efforts at secrecy. The press thus "represents" the public by scrutinizing and publicizing the actions of government; accordingly, the people are better informed and are better able to evaluate their leaders. An active, adversarial press is therefore vital to democracy. Of course, not everyone shares this view.

Although press freedom is often advocated in terms of democratic principles and "the people's right to know," evidence exists that the American people do not always support the claims of the press against their government. For example, when reporters were excluded from the Grenada invasion of December 1983, an uproar of righteous indignation occurred in the media. However, an ABC News poll taken shortly after the invasion revealed that 67 percent of the public supported censorship of the news media when national security was at stake.

6-3d CONFIDENTIAL SOURCES

The reporter's greatest asset (aside from the First Amendment) is the **confidential source**. The media therefore argue strenuously that the First Amendment gives reporters an absolute privilege to maintain the confidentiality of their sources, a privilege similar to that claimed by lawyers with respect to their clients. On the other hand, prosecutors tend to argue that the public interest in finding the truth in a criminal prosecution outweighs a reporter's interest in maintaining the confidentiality of sources. Although some states have **shield laws** protecting journalists in these types of situations, others permit reporters to be held in contempt of court and confined for refusing to divulge their sources.

In *Branzburg v. Hayes* (1972), the Supreme Court confronted a situation in which a newspaper reporter called to appear before a grand jury refused to identify certain persons he had seen using and selling illicit drugs.[26] The reporter had observed the illegal activities during an undercover investigation of the local drug scene. Citing the First Amendment, he refused to disclose his confidential sources to the grand jury. The Supreme Court sided with the grand jury, saying that "we cannot seriously entertain the notion that the First Amendment protects a newsman's agreement to conceal the criminal conduct of his source, or evidence thereof, on the theory that it is better to write about crime than to do something about it."

Another problem relating to sources of information occurs when a reporter decides to reveal the identity of a source who has given information on the condition that his identity remain confidential. The Supreme Court addressed this problem in a case it decided in 1992. The controversy began when a political campaign worker provided a reporter with damaging information about a rival candidate on the condition that the worker's identity be kept secret. The newspaper made an editorial decision to publish the name of the source, who was fired by his employer as a result. The source sued the newspaper under a state law and won $200,000 in compensatory damages. The Supreme Court rejected the newspaper's argument that these types of suits were barred by the First Amendment, saying that "the publisher of a newspaper has no special immunity from the application of general laws. He has no special privilege to invade the rights and liberties of others."[27]

6-3e The Special Case of Broadcast and Online Media

The Framers of the First Amendment could not have foreseen the invention of radio and television, let alone the prevalence of these electronic media in contemporary society. Nevertheless, because television and radio are used to express ideas in the public forum, most observers would agree that the electronic media deserve First Amendment protection, at least to some extent. Yet since their inception, radio and television have been regulated extensively by the federal government. To operate a television or radio station, a person must obtain a license from the Federal Communications Commission (FCC); broadcasting without a license from the FCC is a federal crime (as operators of pirate radio stations have often discovered). In granting licenses, the FCC is authorized to regulate the station's frequency, wattage, and hours of transmission. To a lesser extent, the FCC also has the power to regulate the content of broadcasts. Station licenses come up for renewal every three years, and the FCC is invested with tremendous discretion to determine whether a given station has been operating "in the public interest."

With no licensure for consumer-created content, the possibility of inappropriate, offensive, and even illegal information being disseminated is greater than ever. People can tweet inappropriate things, make threatening statements on Facebook, and other things that would run afoul of the law if said by a reporter. Prior restraint is not possible with online media because of its instant dissemination. Freedom of speech protections still make the burden of proof fall on law enforcement to punish someone for online speech, but instances of people being punished for their online content are almost nonexistent.

The Fairness Doctrine

Since its creation by Congress, the FCC has required broadcasters to devote a reasonable proportion of their airtime to the discussion of important public issues. Until 1987, the FCC interpreted this statutory mandate to require broadcasters who aired editorials criticizing specific persons to provide notice to those persons and air time for rebuttal. The Supreme Court upheld this **fairness doctrine** in 1969.[28] The Court held that the FCC regulation had struck a reasonable balance between the public interest in hearing various points of view and the broadcaster's interests in free expression. Nevertheless, the fairness doctrine remained extremely controversial. It was finally repealed by the FCC in the summer of 2011.

Editorializing by Public Television and Radio Stations

Electronic media in the public sector have been subject to more restrictive government regulations on editorializing. Based on a 1967 act of Congress, the FCC prohibited public radio and television stations from engaging in editorializing. However, the Supreme Court declared this ban unconstitutional.[29] Writing for a sharply divided Court, Justice William Brennan concluded that the "ban on all editorializing . . . far exceeds what is necessary to protect against the risk of governmental interference or to prevent the public from assuming that editorials by public broadcasting stations represent the official view of government." Nevertheless, most public television and radio stations minimize explicit editorializing, although conservative critics argue that the Public Broadcasting System and National Public Radio tend to offer programming that contains a liberal point of view.

Restrictions on the Content of Programming

For many years, educators, psychologists, and children's advocacy groups have expressed concern about the amount of television that children watch and the kinds of messages they get through TV programs. Some are concerned about the portrayal of sexual conduct, which has become considerably more explicit and provocative over the years. Others object to the extreme commercialism of American television and believe that it fosters excessive materialism in children. In 1993, numerous critics, including the attorney general of the United States, Janet Reno, lashed out at the prevalence of violence on television. Coincidentally, in that same year, the public became alarmed about a rising tide of violence among young people. The year was punctuated with horror stories about toddlers being murdered by teenagers, teenagers bringing loaded guns to school, and, of course, unrelenting gang warfare in the nation's inner cities. Many people saw a connection between the constant barrage of TV violence and the increasingly violent behavior of the country's youth. Some called for restrictions on TV violence. Testifying before Congress, Attorney General Reno suggested that unless television producers and broadcasters voluntarily addressed this problem, the federal government might have to step in. According to a national survey reported in December 1993, about 60 percent of adults said they were offended by the amount of sex and violence on television; 55 percent responded in the affirmative when asked "Should the federal government regulate the amount of violence and sex on television?"[30]

In February 2004, the issue of indecency on the public airwaves reached a national crescendo after singer Janet Jackson experienced a "wardrobe malfunction" revealing one of her breasts during a halftime performance at the Super Bowl. The FCC received numerous complaints and levied a $550,000 fine against CBS for the incident. Two months later, the FCC imposed a fine of nearly $500,000 on Clear Channel Communications for airing sexually explicit content in a program by controversial "shock jock" Howard Stern. For his part, Stern relied on the First Amendment and claimed that the Bush administration was making him a political target. In late 2004, Stern announced plans to move his program to Sirius satellite radio, which is not under FCC jurisdiction. The Janet Jackson and Howard Stern incidents intensified a national conversation about indecency in mass media and popular culture.

To what extent may government regulate the content of television or radio programs without running afoul of the First Amendment? The courts have suggested that government regulation of the broadcasting industry is not necessarily equivalent to restrictions on the print medium. In a broad regulation that would almost certainly be declared unconstitutional if applied to a magazine or newspaper, the FCC has prohibited radio and television stations, whether public or private, from broadcasting "indecent" or "obscene" programs. In a highly publicized 1978 case, the Supreme Court reviewed this regulation as applied to a radio broadcast of a monologue by comedian George Carlin that discussed "seven dirty words you can't say on television." Attorneys for the radio station argued that the monologue in question did not meet the legal test of obscenity and therefore could not be banned from the radio by the FCC. The Supreme Court disagreed, observing that, "when the Commission finds that a pig has entered the parlor, the exercise of its regulatory power does not depend on proof that the pig is obscene."[31]

FCC regulations apply to broadcasters. Cable channels (as distinguished from broadcasts) are not subject to FCC content regulations. Whatever may not be shown on CBS or one of the other broadcast networks, therefore, may be shown on HBO, The Movie Channel, or other channels available exclusively to cable subscribers. Increasingly, there are calls for greater government regulation of pay-TV channels, with regard to both sexual content and violence. The widespread diffusion of new communications technology has thus generated new constitutional questions. However, American political culture has evolved (some might say degenerated) to the point that widespread tolerance now exists for this type of material in the mass media.

6-3f Constitutional Protection of the Internet

As we have already noted, the Internet is by its nature difficult to regulate and impossible for any single government to control. Nevertheless, some people believe that government should attempt to limit certain types of expression on the Net—for example, hardcore pornography and hate speech. Pornography is widespread on the Net, and numerous fringe groups have websites spouting hateful messages aimed at various groups in society. The constitutional question is whether the First Amendment protects this type of expression on the Net. The U.S. Supreme Court weighed in on this question in 1997. The preceding year, Congress passed the **Communications Decency Act**, which made it a crime to display "indecent" material on the Internet in a manner that might make it available to minors. In *Reno v. American Civil Liberties Union* (1997), the Court declared this statute unconstitutional on First Amendment grounds. Writing for the Court, Justice Stevens concluded that, with respect to cyberspace, "the interest in encouraging freedom of expression in a democratic society outweighs any theoretical but unproven benefit of censorship."[32] The decision was widely hailed by Internet users, and Congress has yet to make another attempt to regulate content on the Net.

The online world has also led to an important development in the unlawful use of content. Piracy of copyrighted material is common online, with sites such as the now-closed MegaUpload and Pirate Bay ripping DVDs and scanning books to distribute for free without compensation to creators or distributors. To stem this tide, in 2011 Congress considered the Stop Online Piracy and Protect Intellectual Property Acts (**SOPA/PIPA**). The laws, which would have put greater content control in the hands of Internet service providers and strengthened penalties for violators, were met with instant resistance as a violation of free speech from many across the online world. Online protests, with celebrities shutting their websites down and many others displaying black censorship protest banners, followed the introduction of the bill. When high-profile sites such as Wikipedia went dark for twelve hours, public pressure mounted and the bills failed.[33]

ONLINE 6.9 *SOPA/PIPA*
http://www.youtube.com/watch?v=tzqMoOk9NWc

6-4 Press Coverage of Government

The relationship between the press and government is often marked by confusion and hostility. Much of this can be attributed to the role of the press in a free society. Despite the wishes of those in government that newspapers and television report positive stories, the press has a basic duty to report the activities of government and politicians that are dishonest, inefficient, or corrupt. Members of the press see their role as "keeping the government honest" and providing citizens with enough information to enable them to make informed decisions when voting. The press is also motivated by norms peculiar to its own culture. Journalists advance, and receive the admiration of their peers, by writing stories that have an impact, and the political stories with the most impact are those that expose government officials doing wrong. For example, *Washington Post* reporters Bob Woodward and Carl Bernstein were catapulted to the top of their profession by exposing much of the Watergate scandal that eventually toppled the Nixon administration. Although positive, or at least noncritical, stories may be well received, the vast majority of career-building, breakthrough stories involve the exposure of some wrongdoing on the part of someone important.

Part of the conflict between politics and the press stems from the competitive nature of both institutions. Journalists compete to uncover stories about politicians, and politicians compete for the attention of journalists. Politicians feel that they "win" if they can obtain coverage that places them in a good light. Journalists win if they can claim credit for a good news story. Most good stories, however, do not reflect well on those seeking or holding office. Thus, tension is inevitable. Political officials and journalists need each other, but also try to use each other.

6-4a Coverage of the President

In May 2002, the broadcast and print news media were awash with stories raising questions about what warning President Bush might have had about the September 11 attacks on the World Trade Center and the Pentagon. No person in the world is the subject of as much media scrutiny as the president of the United States. This scrutiny has often angered presidents, some of whom have lashed out, or had others lash out on their behalf, at what they perceive as unfair or biased reporting. Probably the best-known attack on the press came from Richard Nixon's vice president, Spiro T. Agnew. In 1969, after what the administration thought was excessively negative commentary following a televised presidential address, Agnew accused the press of being a small, liberal elite.

The relationship between the president and the press seems to progress through three phases. Many presidents experience what is called the honeymoon period at the beginning of their initial term. The honeymoon phase is characterized by cordial relationships, with the president accorded the benefit of the doubt and the press granted reasonable access to the functioning of government. Cabinet officials and others make themselves available for interviews, and television and newspaper reporters are likely to produce stories that highlight new people and programs. Inevitably, this relationship evolves into another, more hostile, phase. Usually, it occurs after the new government proposes something controversial or makes a decision that is widely unpopular with some major group or interest. After the media focus on the controversy and pose questions that seem to legitimize the criticism, the administration often feels betrayed and unfairly portrayed. Either this hostility evolves further into a state of permanent hostility or both sides become conscious of the need for moderation.[34]

The Presidential News Agencies

Modern American presidents have a complex structure with which to represent their interests with the media. The White House director of communications, formerly known as the press secretary, regularly meets with the reporters assigned to cover the president. These reporters, known collectively as the **White House press corps**, can question the press secretary about policies. In addition, the **press secretary** provides announcements of appointments of new officials, policy initiatives, and other important news from the administration. President George W. Bush started with a former Congressional staffer, Ari Fleischer, and later turned to Fox News commentator Tony Snow. Bush's staff was known for a frosty relationship with the press. President Obama two press secretaries, Robert Gibbs and Jay Carney, have developed reputations as conciliatory and media-friendly. The Office of Media Liaison works with editors from major newspapers and magazines to arrange more in-depth interviews than those provided to the press corps. This method is a favored vehicle by which the president can reward news outlets that are favorable and punish those that are deemed to be overly critical.

The White House Press Corps

Of all the people who cover politics, the most widely recognized are the reporters of the White House press corps who cover the president for major television networks and newspapers. These reporters meet regularly with the press secretary to receive word of the president's schedule and impending policy decisions. Members of the White House press corps have often been accused of practicing **pack journalism**, or deciding which questions to ask and what stories to cover based on what other members of the press corps are doing. Considering the way the press corps routinely meets with the president or press secretary in the small press room at the White House and follows the president around the world, this phenomenon is hardly surprising. Nor is it surprising that members of the press corps sometimes develop confrontational relationships with the president. For example, Sam Donaldson, of ABC News, became well known for his tough questioning style. Although Donaldson is no longer a member of the White House press corps, his style is routinely emulated by others seeking to make a mark on American broadcast journalism, like ABC's Jake Tapper and NBC's Chuck Todd.

THE PRESS CONFERENCE

The most public way the president releases information is the most direct: the press conference. A **press conference** occurs when a president makes himself available for questioning by reporters, usually the White House press corps. The press conference is unique in that it provides the reporter, and usually the public, with unfiltered answers to questions framed by the press. Theodore Roosevelt is credited with the first press conference. Presidents use them to the degree that they feel they can control the agenda and the tone of the meetings. Consequently, presidents have held press conferences with varying frequency, but generally fewer as each new president takes office.

Most press conferences are aired live by the twenty-four-hour networks, but taped and edited on the broadcast networks. The White House now also uses YouTube and other social media to present its public communication directly to the public. Press conferences usually follow a prescribed format. The president begins with a prepared statement regarding recent developments. He has some leeway to choose reporters he feels might be likely to ask friendly questions. He can avoid answering questions and quickly recognize another questioner before any embarrassing follow-up questions can be asked. But no president can completely control a press conference, and some find this format not to their liking. For this reason, President Clinton neglected to hold news conferences during the duration of the Lewinsky scandal and impeachment. A president experiences no real downside by avoiding news conferences because the general public is not particularly interested in them or even aware of their frequency.

Other members of the cabinet and high-ranking officials have briefing or background sessions to give details of an administration initiative. Officials often meet with reporters off the record to provide information. In these types of cases, the news stories cite "informed sources," but do not identify these sources by name. Because the stories are therefore released without attribution, the administration can use "deniability"; that is, the president can deny releasing the information or deny its truth.

Leaks and Trial Balloons

Presidential administrations have long complained about the problem of keeping secret information out of the media. The size of a presidential administration, the prevalence of the media, and the constant interaction between the two contribute to the leakage of information. Presidents and their top advisers often worry about **leaks** and sometimes take extraordinary measures to prevent them. For example, the Nixon White House created a special unit known as the "plumbers" to plug the leaks in its administration. The unit was headed by White House aide Egil Krogh and included H. Howard Hunt and G. Gordon Liddy, both of whom were involved in the notorious Watergate scandal. Unfortunately, Nixon's plumbers went well beyond the confines of the law in trying to protect their president. Although most presidents have not gone to these extremes, all of them have tried, through various methods, to control unwanted leaks to the press.

Most leaks are unintentional and unwanted, but some are used strategically by presidents. Recent administrations have made frequent use of **trial balloons**, or the release, without attribution, of a proposed policy or appointment to the press with the idea of gauging public reaction. The advantage of this approach is that if the reaction is negative, the president can abandon the proposal without having ever officially advanced it. Like all information released without attribution, a trial balloon allows deniability. If the reaction is negative, however, the safer response is merely to abandon the proposal and move on. The Obama administration made great use of the trial balloon method of gauging public opinion for policy options. After the massacre of teachers and children at Newtown, Connecticut's Sandy Hook Elementary in late 2012, President Obama wanted to enact stricter gun control legislation on clip and magazine capacities as well as background checks for all gun purchases. By leaking a draft of his proposal early to the media, Obama was able to gauge that there was public support for most of his ideas, and he issued executive orders to carry out his gun control measures in June 2013.[35]

In many ways, the release of trial balloons is quite rational. Nevertheless, real dangers exist. Policy alternatives may not receive the discussion that formal proposals are accorded, and many complex policies may be abandoned before their advantages can be explained and debated. Moreover, people whose names are floated may be treated quite badly in that they are led to believe that they are to receive a major appointment, only to be passed over while suffering damage to their reputations during the vetting process. **Vetting** is the unofficial airing of a candidacy of an individual before an official nomination. President Obama vetted former Republican Senator Chuck Hagel well before his nomination, to ensure controversial statements made by the Nebraskan would not jeopardize his confirmation by the Senate.[36]

The media play a crucial role in the strategy of releasing trial balloons. One reason the strategy has become more popular in modern presidential politics is that it has become more feasible. The strategy requires a rapid circulation of information among opinion leaders and a quick reaction to the information released. Both would be impossible without modern television news shows, instant newspaper publishing, and radio talk shows. Only in the past two decades has mass communications technology begun to allow the general public to react immediately to a trial balloon.

6-4b Covering Congress

Congress is arguably every bit as important an institution as the presidency, yet it seems to receive substantially less coverage on television, and what it receives is generally negative. This lack of positive coverage has done much to reduce the status of Congress in the mind of the public. Part of the problem is the difficulty the media have in covering Congress effectively. Portraying Congress in understandable terms is not easy, for a number of reasons. First, Congress is an institution of 535 members. The very size of the body makes it hard for the media to cover. Personalities and offices are numerous, and the procedures for making laws are quite complex. Producing understandable stories about isolated aspects of the process tends to be difficult for the media, especially television. In addition, because Congress reacts to and sometimes rejects presidential initiatives, it is often seen as being obstructionist. Although Congress may just be doing its job in the constitutional system, its actions are often portrayed in the media as petty and quarrelsome.

Although it receives less coverage than the presidency, Congress now has much more visibility than it once had. In 1979, the House of Representatives permitted live television coverage of floor proceedings and committee hearings. TV viewers now have unprecedented public access to the proceedings through the cable channel C-SPAN, which also broadcasts interviews and discussions on public policy issues. In 1986, C-SPAN began Senate coverage too. Not many Americans put these broadcasts on their list of favorite programs. Nevertheless, for those few who are interested, the access to the workings of Congress is invaluable. These proceedings are available to all news services that want them.

The television coverage of Congress has been a decidedly mixed blessing for the institution's credibility. The impeachment of President Clinton was televised, beginning with the hearings of the House Judiciary Committee, moving through the debate on the House floor, and ending with the Senate's shutting down its trial and failing to remove the president from office. Throughout the process, the public was treated to harsh rhetoric on both sides, highlighting the confrontational and highly personal nature of some issues.

Congressional Hearings

Although an occasional congressional vote can capture the interest of the American people, the congressional hearing is best suited to television. Perhaps no political event drew the attention of Americans in the 1970s as did the Watergate hearings of 1974. On live television, a relatively small group of members of Congress looked into the break-in of the Democratic National Committee headquarters in the Watergate office building and the subsequent cover-up by the Nixon administration. This hearing attracted Americans for several reasons. First, the issues were clear-cut. Senator Howard Baker (R-Tennessee) repeated the question "What did the president know, and when did he know it?" Second, the committee included several easily recognizable personalities. Third, the events unfolded in a dramatic manner, especially with the news of the secret White House tapes of conversations that occurred in the Oval Office.

In 2004, Americans were highly attentive to the televised hearings of the 9/11 Commission, which had been established by Congress to investigate the breakdowns in intelligence that allowed the plots that led to the terrorist attacks of September 2001 to go undetected. Americans watched as current Bush administration and former Clinton administration officials appeared before the commission to testify. No doubt, avid followers of the hearings were frustrated by the fact that many of the sessions were held in secret, including interviews with President George W. Bush and former President Bill Clinton. Given the magnitude of the terrorist attacks and their consequences for American policy, it was not surprising that much of the testimony became fodder for the presidential campaigns. And given the widespread distrust of government that exists in this country, it was also not surprising that many Americans chose to view the commission as an attempt to cover up rather than reveal the truth of what had taken place prior to September 11, 2001.

The process of passing legislation is perhaps the congressional duty that is hardest to frame to Americans. The problem is not that people lack interest in which laws are passed, but rather that the process just does not lend itself to media coverage. On the other hand, when Congress is performing its investigative role or fulfilling its advise-and-consent function, the media often can portray the process in an interesting and informative manner.

6-4c The Media and the Courts

By the nature of its task, the federal judiciary is the branch of government furthest removed from public access. Though actual trial proceedings are open to the public, judicial deliberations take place behind closed doors. State criminal courts have become less secretive in recent years with the gradual increase in the number of courts that allow cameras. The federal courts still do not permit cameras in the courtroom.

Thus, when a sensational federal trial is reported on the evening news, such as the 1997 case of Oklahoma City bomber Timothy McVeigh, the only available images are courtroom sketches.[37] In many state cases, however, television viewers can see live or tape-delayed television coverage of events in the courtroom.

Commercial television has discovered the entertainment value of sensational criminal trials. Indeed, an entire cable channel, Court TV, is now dedicated to the live coverage and discussion of sensational cases now under way in the judicial system. In 1994, the public was riveted by media coverage of the trial of O.J. Simpson. Seventeen years later it would be the Casey Anthony murder trial. Without question, the public has a serious interest in learning about these types of cases. For the mass media, however, these cases are as much, if not more, about morbid entertainment as about keeping the public informed.

Covering the Federal Courts

Even though the federal courts—in particular, the Supreme Court—produce decisions that have a tremendous effect on society, the judicial process is a mystery to most Americans. Federal judges rarely give interviews. When they do, they do not discuss any substantive matters that might find their way into a decision. For this reason, television coverage of federal judges is not linked to personalities but rather to reporting the outcome of deliberations. The exception occurs when an individual is nominated to a position on the Supreme Court. Then, television and newspaper reporters become aggressive in examining the nominee's personality, ideology, and political affiliations and any potential embarrassing incidents from her past.

The major television networks and newspapers all have reporters and analysts who cover the Supreme Court. They report on, discuss, and analyze major decisions, especially those in which the public has a great interest, such as abortion and school prayer cases. The media are well represented at oral arguments before the Supreme Court. Members of the press pay close attention to the questions that the justices ask the lawyers who are arguing the cases. On the evening news, pundits speculate about how the Court will decide significant cases and how the justices will vote. Months later, when Supreme Court decisions are announced, they are often reported within minutes on CNN. Among newspapers, *The New York Times* provides the most in-depth coverage of the Court's decisions, often printing substantial excerpts from the opinions.

Covering the Supreme Court

The Supreme Court received unprecedented attention during the aftermath of the 2000 presidential election. The Court became involved twice in response to appeals of Florida Supreme Court decisions that had extended deadlines for hand recounts and overturned a circuit court judge who had ruled against further counts contesting the election. In both cases, the United States Supreme Court vacated or reversed the Florida Supreme Court decisions. The oral arguments that preceded these decisions were given unprecedented media attention. Although the justices refused to allow their deliberations to be televised, they did make a historic decision to allow audiotapes to be released soon after the close of the arguments. The tapes were eagerly awaited by all news organizations, including those of the broadcast networks, which interrupted regularly scheduled programming to play them. Americans seemed fascinated with the dialogue between the justices and the attorneys for Gore and Bush.

The Court's decision to stop the recounts and to bring an end to the controversy was released at 10 p.m. on December 12, only two hours before the deadline for states to send slates of electors free from congressional challenge. The complex and confusing decision, replete with a series of concurring and dissenting opinions, proved difficult for the news media to make sense of quickly. Americans were faced with the awkward spectacle of news analysts reading from the decision on live television while trying to decipher the decision's meaning "on the fly" and initially mistaking the decision as supporting further recounts under standards to be set by the Florida Supreme Court.

6-5 Coverage of Elections, Campaigns, and Candidates

Coverage of elections, campaigns, and candidates is a staple in the diet of American journalism, and most Americans follow this coverage to some degree (see Figure 6-1). Nevertheless, a majority of Americans believe that the press has too much influence over elections—in particular, the presidential contest. Moreover, a substantial and growing proportion of the public believes that the media do a poor job in covering the presidential race.

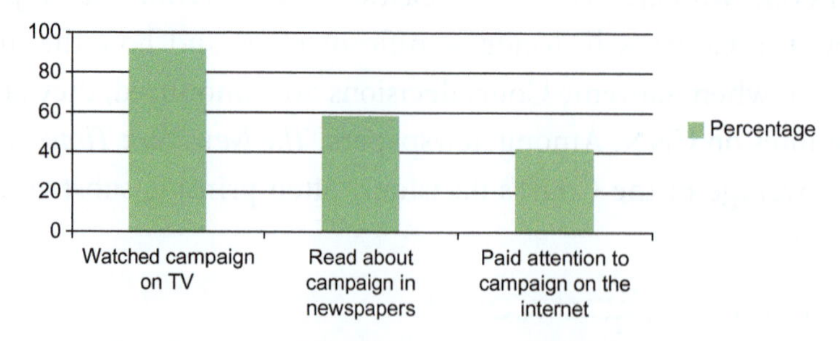

Figure 6-1 *Americans' Attentiveness to the 2008 Presidential Campaign through the Media*
Source: Adapted from Center for Political Studies, University of Michigan, National Election Studies, 2008

Are the Media Preoccupied with Sleaze?

One of the harshest critics of the contemporary media is the journalist Carl Bernstein, one of the *Washington Post* reporters who broke the Watergate story in 1972. Bernstein has written that since the 1970s the press has "been moving away from real journalism toward the creation of a sleazoid infotainment culture." Bernstein chides the "new culture of journalistic titillation," which, he claims, panders to viewers and readers to boost ratings and readerships. Bernstein argues that "it is the role of journalists to challenge people, not merely to amuse them."[38] Defenders of the media counter with the argument that the press only gives the people what they really want as opposed to the idealized preferences they express in responding to surveys. The political scientist Darrell West has said that "people are both turned off by the media and attracted to it at the same time." According to West, if the media ignored scandals and stuck to substance, "it would probably be pretty boring."[39]

When the first hint of a scandal involving a candidate for high office comes to light, the press attacks like a school of sharks smelling blood in the water. The resulting feeding frenzy almost inevitably leads to the ruination of a political career. Talented people with something to contribute to governance can be lost to public life forever. But according to the political scientist Larry Sabato, the greatest impact of media feeding frenzies "is not in the winnowing of candidates but the encouragement of cynicism."[40] Clearly, public cynicism about politics, politicians, and government institutions has been on the steady increase over the past several decades. There is reason to believe that the media contribute to this cynicism, by not only showing the people their leaders "warts and all" but also dwelling on the lurid, the scandalous, and the sensational.

6-6 Mass Media and the Making of Public Policy

The media play a major role in what governments do and how they do it. Newspapers, and especially television reports, help prepare the public for an impending government initiative. Whether the issue is AIDS, the homeless, or starving people in a society far away, the images, especially as portrayed through television or print photojournalism, have a powerful effect on the American public. These images can build support among the public for government policies or lead to pressure from the public to pursue certain policies.

6-6a Agenda Setting

Issues come and go in American politics. In many ways, the most important thing an interest group can do to further its cause is to place an issue on the agenda. Most often, this process involves gaining favorable media coverage, or at least the sort of coverage that dramatizes the issue and frames it in such a way that politicians feel that they must address it. For instance, the issue of illegal immigration is a topic of great importance today. Both sides of the debate try to frame the language to favor their conclusions. Supporters of citizenship rights for illegals cast the issue as one of human rights and dignity, while opponents stress the need for border security and consistent compliance with the law. Depending on which perspective you take, the resulting conclusions are usually foregone. By controlling the terms of debate, a group or side will usually control that debate's outcome.

In American politics, an issue or event can hardly be said to exist unless it receives attention by the media. The central importance of the media in political life is summed up in the following quotation about the need for media coverage of protests: "The first and foremost goal of all political protests is the same: to gain coverage by the media. Like a tree falling in the forest, a protest without media coverage goes unappreciated no matter how much noise it makes."[41]

Often, it is the members of the media themselves who help to place an issue on the public agenda. During 1992, Americans were bombarded with television images from faraway places. One set of pictures was particularly troubling: those showing children starving in Somalia. Few Americans knew where Somalia could be found on a map, and fewer still had any idea about the civil war that had made food distribution impossible. Yet the images were transfixing. The United States, as the world's single remaining superpower, seemed in a position to do something to help. Some people argued that the United States had no real national interest in Somalia. Nevertheless, President Bush ordered troops to the African country to restore enough order that relief could be provided. This decision had widespread bipartisan support. Nevertheless, it is doubtful that the intervention would have taken place if the American people, and their elected representatives, had not seen the horrible images of starving Somalis on television.

When Bill Clinton became president, he continued the American policy of providing security so that humanitarian organizations could feed the starving people of Somalia. However, that policy was soon complicated by the United Nations' effort to capture the warlord Mohammed Aidid. In what is widely referred to as Blackhawk Down, American troops were caught in a deadly battle with Aidid's forces, and seventeen Americans died. One dead GI was dragged through the streets. Soon, this image was beamed to startled and disgusted TV viewers in the United States. Again, images guided policy. This time, the message was different: "Get out."

6-6b Building Public Support for Particular Policies

In the days following the terrorist attacks on September 11, the major television networks broadcast nonstop coverage with few commercial interruptions. Weeks later, the cable news stations had developed regular coverage of the "war on terrorism." Many reporters and some anchors wore flag lapels. Clearly, the media supported the war effort and supported, in a general sense, the military response to the terrorist attack.

There was nothing novel about the approach the television networks took, although the intensity may have been heightened. In November 1991, an adviser to President George H.W. Bush said that television was "our chief tool" in building public support for the war against Iraq.[42] Bush had moved rapidly to send American troops to Saudi Arabia after the Iraqis had invaded Kuwait. Having been invited by Saudi King Fahd, Bush sought to stem any further advance by Iraqi forces. This effort was known as Operation Desert Shield. The operation evolved into Desert Storm, when the mission shifted from a defensive to an offensive posture with the goal of driving the Iraqis out of Kuwait. Following a passionate debate in January 1991, Congress voted to support military action against Iraq, providing President Bush with the authority to act militarily if the forces of Saddam Hussein did not leave Kuwait by January 15.

By all accounts, President Bush was extremely effective in using television to build the national consensus necessary to obtain the support of the Democratic-controlled Congress. By the time the United States engaged in military action in late January 1991, the president's approval rating exceeded 90 percent and support for military action was widespread. A major factor in rallying this support was the president's effective use of television. The president used the media at various stages of the process. In his first televised address to the nation, he explained the seriousness of the Iraqi invasion of Kuwait. His message was unequivocal, when he said that the invasion "will not stand." Thus, he quickly let the American public know that the conflict was serious and that he was committed to resolving it. In later speeches, Bush was clear on why the United States was involved and what the options were and that he was committed to using force to achieve his objectives. When the build-up, and later the war, began, Americans had been informed and involved at every step of the process.

For the first time, Americans were able to witness a historic congressional debate over whether to authorize the use of force, as the president requested, or continue economic sanctions with the hope that military force would not be necessary. The issues were debated openly for the American people, along with the rest of the world, to see. Although most Democrats voted to continue economic sanctions rather than approve the immediate use of force, President Bush was able to put together a majority in favor of using military force.

6-7 Conclusion: The Media—An Essential Part of the American Political System

It is generally acknowledged that the mass media have had and are having an important effect on American politics, but considerable disagreement exists over exactly what the effect is and whether it is desirable or undesirable. Surely one effect of mass media is to greatly accelerate the pace of political change. Events are reported instantaneously.

Information flows back and forth from the mass public to decision makers and from one decision maker to another with amazing speed. Although everyone, including the attentive citizen, wants good information as soon as he can get it, a danger exists that the decision-making process may speed up to the point that human beings cannot cope with the pressures of making rapid decisions. Arguably, the quality of political decision making can suffer if individuals are not afforded enough time to digest facts, frame options, and calmly consider the consequences of adopting one alternative over another.

Mass media have become an integral part of the American political system. Our national political conversation is carried on through the mass media. It is impossible to imagine contemporary politics without television and radio and the Internet. Ever since the Kennedy–Nixon debate during the 1960 campaign, political actors who have not understood the media have eventually suffered for it. This understanding must be fluid. The mass media of today differ greatly from the media of the 1960s. Over the next several decades, media will probably take on forms that are difficult to imagine now.

Questions for Thought and Discussion

1. Generally speaking, is the American press too critical of government or not critical enough?

2. Does violence on television merely reflect violence in society, or does it encourage violent behavior? Should the government regulate the amount of violence on television? What constitutional problems might be raised by government regulation of TV violence?

3. Generally speaking, are the mass media biased against conservative ideas, policies, and politicians?

4. Would the government be justified in preventing a television network from reporting about an impending military operation if the report would jeopardize the success of the mission? Would this type of prohibition raise a constitutional problem?

5. Do the modern electronic media promote the candidacies of "outsiders," such as Ross Perot? Or does the cost of a modern media campaign prevent unconventional candidates from mounting serious challenges?

Endnotes

1. This reference stems from eighteenth century England: The "three estates" were the nobility, the commons, and the clergy.
2. Some commentators characterize the media as the fifth branch of government; the bureaucracy, the fourth.
3. Pew Research Center, "Internet Overtakes Newspapers as News Source," December 23, 2008, http://www.people-press.org/2008/12/23/internet-overtakes-newspapers-as-news-outlet/
4. Carl Bernstein, "The Idiot Culture," *The New Republic*, June 8, 1992, p. 24.
5. Emily Guskin and Tom Rosenstiel, "Network: By the Numbers," accessed July 30, 2013 at http://stateofthemedia.org/2012/network-news-the-pace-of-change-accelerates/network-by-the-numbers/
6. "The American Media: Who Watches, Who Listens, Who Cares," Times Mirror Center for People and the Press, Washington, D.C., 1992, p. 40.
7. James Joyner, "MSNBC Rebranding as Liberal News Network," November 6, 2007, http://www.outsidethebeltway.com/archives/msnbc_officially_liberal_news_network/
8. Internet World Stats, accessed July 30, 2013 at http://www.internetworldstats.com/stats.htm
9. Glenn H. Reynolds, "About Me," May 24, 2002, http://instapundit.com/about.php
10. Glenn H. Reynolds, http://www.instapundit.com/, blog posted October 14, 2004, 1:31 p.m.
11. See Harold W. Stanley and Richard G. Niemi, *Vital Statistics on American Politics 2003–2004* (Washington, D.C.: CQ Press, 2003), p. 173.
12. A 1992 study found that roughly 60 percent of adults read at least one newspaper daily. See *Multimedia Audiences Report* (New York: Mediamark Research, Spring 1992).
13. See Marshall McLuhan, *Understanding Media: The Extensions of Man*, 2d ed. (New York: New American Library, 1964); Marshall McLuhan and Quentin Fiore, *The Medium Is the Message: An Inventory of Effects* (New York: Bantam Books, 1967).
14. Dan Richman and Andrea James, "Seattle P-I to Publish Last Edition Tuesday," *Seattle Post-Intelligencer*, March 16, 2009, http://www.seattlepi.com/business/article/Seattle-P-I-to-publish-last-edition-Tuesday-1302597.php; Dealbook, "Rocky Mountain News Is Shutting Down," *The New York Times*, February 26, 2009, http://dealbook.nytimes.com/2009/02/26/rocky-mountain-news-to-shut-down/
15. Ryan Chittum, "The Paywall Prevents a Deeper Downturn at the NYT," *Columbia Journalism Review*, October 26, 2012, http://www.cjr.org/the_audit/the_paywall_prevents_a_deeper_1.php
16. David Hugh Weaver, *The American Journalist in the 21st Century* (New York, NY: Erlbaum, 2006).
17. "Voters Impressed with Campaign, But News Coverage Gets Lukewarm Ratings," The Pew Research Center for People and the Press, October 24, 2004, retrieved from http://people-press.org/2004/10/24/voters-impressed-with-campaign/
18. http://www.gallup.com/poll/149624/majority-continue-distrust-media-perceive-bias.aspx
19. Michael Parenti, *Inventing Reality: The Politics of the News Media*, 2d ed. (New York: St. Martin's Press, 1993), p. 6.
20. Ibid., p. 8.
21. "Voters Impressed with Campaign, But News Coverage Gets Lukewarm Ratings," The Pew Research Center for People and the Press, October 24, 2004, retrieved from http://people-press.org/2004/10/24/voters-impressed-with-campaign/
22. http://stateofthemedia.org/2009/overview/executive-summary/
23. *Near v. Minnesota*, 283 U.S. 697 (1931).

24 *New York Times Co. v. United States*, 403 U.S. 713 (1971).

25 *New York Times Co. v. Sullivan*, 376 U.S. 254 (1964).

26 *Branzburg v. Hayes*, 408 U.S. 665 (1972).

27 *Cohen v. Cowles Media Co.*, 111 S. Ct. 2513 (1992).

28 *Red Lion Broadcasting Co. v. FCC*, 395 U.S. 367 (1969).

29 *FCC v. League of Women Voters of California*, 468 U.S. 364 (1984).

30 National survey of 1,025 adults conducted by Scripps-Howard News Service and Ohio University. Results reported in Thomas Hargrove and Guido H. Stempel III, "Poll: TV Sex, Violence Irk 60 Percent," *Knoxville News-Sentinel*, December 26, 1993, p. A1.

31 *FCC v. Pacifica Foundation*, 438 U.S. 726 (1978).

32 *Reno v. American Civil Liberties Union*, 521 U.S. 844, 117 S.Ct. 2329, 138 L. Ed. 2nd 874 (1997).

33 http://www.wired.com/threatlevel/2012/10/dodd-says-sopa-dead/

34 Michael Grossman and Martha Kumar, "The White House and the News Media: Three Phases of Their Relationship," *Political Science Quarterly*, vol. 94, Spring 1979, pp. 57–73.

35 David Kravets, "MPAA Chief Says SOPA, PIPA 'Are Dead,' But ISP Warning Scheme Lives On," *Wired*, December 3, 2012, http://www.washingtonpost.com/wp-srv/special/politics/obama-gun-proposals/index.html

36 Jeremy Peters, "Hagel Approved for Defense in Sharply Split Senate Vote," *The New York Times*, February 26, 2013, http://www.nytimes.com/2013/02/27/us/politics/hagel-filibuster-defense-senate-confirmation.html?pagewanted=all

37 CNN.com, "The McVeigh Trial: After 28 days of 'overwhelming evidence,' the jury speaks: Guilty," accessed July 30, 2013 from http://www.cnn.com/US/9706/17/mcveigh.overview/

38 Bernstein, "The Idiot Culture," pp. 24–25.

39 Kolbert, Elizabeth, Quoted in Kolbert, "As Political Campaigns Turn Negative, the Press Is Given a Negative Rating Published in the New York Times, May 1, 1992."

40 Larry Sabato, *Feeding Frenzy: How Attack Journalism Has Transformed American Politics* (New York: Free Press, 1991), p. 207.

41 Jeffrey Berry, *The Interest Group Society*, 2d ed. (Glenview, IL: Scott, Foresman, 1989), p. 110.

42 Richard Haas, quoted in *The New York Times*, November 5, 1991.

Chapter 7

PUBLIC OPINION IN AMERICAN POLITICS

OUTLINE

Key Terms 237

Expected Learning Outcomes 238

7-1 The Nature of Public Opinion 238

- **7-1a** Public Opinion in a Democratic Society 240
- **7-1b** Public Opinion and the U.S. Constitution 240

7-2 Public Opinion and American Political Culture 242

- **7-2a** Individualism and Equality 242

7-3 The Opinions of Individuals 244

- **7-3a** Values and Beliefs 244
- **7-3b** Attitudes and Opinions 245
- **7-3c** Ideology 246
- **7-3d** Political Socialization 251
- **7-3e** The Effect of Other Socioeconomic Factors 256
- **7-3f** Opinion Dysfunction 261

7-4 Measuring Public Opinion 263

- **7-4a** The Dangers of Unscientific Polling: The Literary Digest Poll and the 1936 Election 264
- **7-4b** The Scientific Measurement of Opinion 265

7-5 Public Opinion and Public Policy 268

- **7-5a** Models of Public Opinion in the Policy Process 269
- **7-5b** Means of Communicating Public Opinion to Policy Makers 269
- **7-5c** Television and Radio Talk Shows 270

7-6 Conclusion: The Dimensions of Public Opinion 270

Questions for Thought and Discussion 271

Endnotes 272

KEY TERMS

attitudes
balanced response sets
beliefs
cognitive dissonance
cognitive response
demagogue
defining events
double-barreled question
exit poll
gender gap
nonresponse bias
opinions

party identification
political alienation
political efficacy
political values
pollsters
population
priming
propaganda
public opinion
pundits
random-digit dialing
random sample
reliability
sample
sampling frame
sampling plan
social desirability bias
straw poll
systematic sample
validity

EXPECTED LEARNING OUTCOMES

After reading this chapter and completing the supplemental online materials, students will:

- Define public opinion
- Identify the role of public opinion in a democracy
- Compare long- and short-term political opinions
- Describe the process of creating a poll
- Analyze a poll for validity, reliability, and overall quality
- Trace the development of individual opinions

7-1 THE NATURE OF PUBLIC OPINION

Public opinion is the aggregation of individual opinions on issues of concern to the public. Normally, people think of public opinion in the context of political issues, such as abortion, gay rights, or euthanasia. But anything that people think about or talk about or are interested in can become the stuff of public opinion. In a sense, public opinion is simply what **pollsters** measure through their surveys—whether it's people's approval or disapproval of the president's performance or their perceptions of what kind of person Michael Jackson really was.[1]

In a democratic system, public opinion is vital. If a government is designed to follow the preferences of the populace, then there must be some way for regular communication of citizen preferences to their elected leaders. How can elected representatives give the people what they want if the only feedback they get from their constituents is a vote every two years? By polling, elected officials have a better idea of what the peoples' preferences are and can decide to vote as true representatives of the public will.

Barely a day goes by that the American people are not presented with the results of some public opinion survey. Television networks and newspapers often collaborate on national surveys (for example, CBS/*New York Times*, ABC/*Washington Post*, NBC/*Wall Street Journal*, and CNN/*USA Today*). Hundreds of other, smaller television stations and newspapers conduct their own polls from time to time. And, of course, thousands of surveys are performed each year by universities, public agencies, and research corporations. Survey research is now a major industry in this country. We, the people, are fascinated with what we, the people, think. Realizing the degree of this interest, the mass media provide us with a steady diet of polls and **pundits** explaining, analyzing, and interpreting polls. Thus, it was not at all surprising that immediately after the first Romney-Obama presidential debate in 2012 the discussion quickly shifted from the debate itself to speculation regarding what the next polls would show.

Public opinion polls play a major role in political campaigns and elections. Potential candidates use these polls to "test the waters." Actual candidates use surveys to test messages, determine areas of support, and elicit voter concerns. The mass media use polls to track the public's preferences and perceptions and thereby enliven their coverage of campaigns. During a presidential campaign, television viewers and newspaper readers are treated to a steady diet of polling data. Media also use a particular species of survey, the **exit poll**, to "call" elections within minutes after the polls have closed and before all the returns have come in. Exit polls involve interviews with voters as they exit the voting place. Correctly done, this type of poll can provide an accurate assessment of who is winning the race before the votes are counted. However, in a close race, like the 2000 election, exit polls can be quite counter-productive.

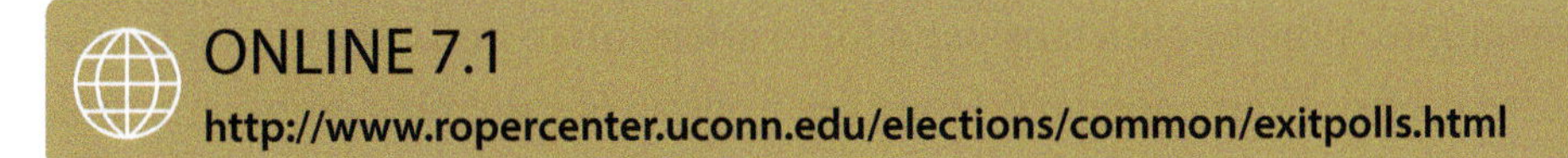

ONLINE 7.1
http://www.ropercenter.uconn.edu/elections/common/exitpolls.html

In the 2000 election, elements of the mass media used exit polls in Florida to call the election for Vice President Gore. Unfortunately, the polling places had not yet closed in the Florida panhandle, which is located in the central time zone. Anecdotal evidence indicates that some people (nobody knows how many) were dissuaded from voting because they thought that the election was over in their state. The race in Florida was actually much closer than predicted. Is it possible that George Bush might have received significantly more votes in Florida had the media not prematurely called the race for Gore? Certainly, many Bush partisans believed so.

Public opinion is critical in any time of national emergency, especially war. Most presidents have enjoyed strong levels of support at the initial stages of military conflict. George W. Bush's approval ratings soared to about 90 percent after the terrorist attacks of 9/11, but declined dramatically throughout the rest of his presidency. Americans usually rally around their president during wartime, unless the war bogs down with no successful conclusion in sight, like Vietnam. The first President Bush enjoyed very high levels of support before, during, and immediately after the Gulf War in 1991, but just like his son saw his approval ratings slide following the war's successful conclusion, as Americans refocused on domestic issues. Presidential approval ratings are fluid and highly dependent on current events.

7-1a Public Opinion in a Democratic Society

Public opinion plays a special role in a democratic society because the essential democratic idea is that government should respond to the popular will. A democratic regime must be constantly aware of the demands and supports coming from the public. Yet even the most authoritarian of governments must be ever conscious of what its citizens think. A democracy exists to *respond* to the public, and an authoritarian system exists only if it can *control* opinion by limiting the spread of ideas that the regime considers dangerous or subversive. This control can be accomplished through some combination of **propaganda** and fear. Thus, any authoritarian system, whether it's Iran or Cuba, pays a good bit of attention to public opinion.

A democracy, on the other hand, is interested in responding to, rather than controlling, public opinion. That is not to say that leaders in democratic societies never engage in propaganda or fear mongering, for they certainly sometimes do. But that behavior is clearly at odds with the ideals of democracy. When a politician arouses anger or action among the people by appealing to their fear, hatred, or greed, he or she is called a **demagogue**. When politicians pay a lot of attention to polls, they open themselves up to accusations of demagoguery. However, polls are a valuable democratic tool, so every politician walks a very fine line when deciding how much attention to pay to a poll. During his eight years as president, Bill Clinton was often accused of governing by focus group because of the attention he paid to public reactions to his proposed policies.

7-1b Public Opinion and the U.S. Constitution

The Founders of the American republic realized the importance of public opinion. The campaign for the ratification of the Constitution was, in essence, a battle for public acceptance of a stronger central government. *The Federalist Papers* represented an effort to persuade the public of the need for structures of federalism, separation of powers, and checks and balances. Yet the Founders also maintained a healthy fear of public opinion run amok. They foresaw dangers in the popular will, and their concern over government responding to momentary surges in public opinion inspired them to create governmental institutions to blunt popular passions. In short, the Founders knew that any democracy could devolve into demagoguery.

The very constitutional structures that have come to be celebrated by the public were designed to temper the influence of variable popular majorities on public policy while allowing policy to reflect a societal consensus. The Framers of the Constitution wanted to prevent government from acting under the pressures of fleeting popular passions, and they certainly wanted to protect the rights of individuals from what Alexis de Tocqueville called "the tyranny of the majority." The Presidency was even designed to have no popular voting input, using the electoral college as an insulation of politics from the public's passions. The Founders probably never imagined that popular opinion could be gauged in any kind of systematic way or that the daily ebbs and flows of opinion would be of consequence to the system. Communication was so limited that only fundamental, lasting divisions in society could become issues among the mass citizenry.

Despite the intentions of the Founders, the American political system has become significantly more democratic over the more than two hundred years since America proclaimed its independence. The electoral franchise has been broadened to include all adults. Channels of political participation not envisioned (or desired) by the Founders have been opened up to the average citizen, such as voting for president. Multiple sources of information (newspapers, magazines, radio, television, and online) have become available to the mass public. The expansion of channels of political participation and the proliferation of mass media have led to increased interest in public opinion, as candidates, journalists, and elected officials have all developed an urge to take the public's pulse. Whether attempting to predict election results or anticipating public support for a government initiative, analysts, journalists, and politicians now routinely seek the most current and accurate measure of public opinion. Public opinion has become a science as well as an industry, and shaping public opinion has become an art.

"I'm neo-undecided."

7-2 PUBLIC OPINION AND AMERICAN POLITICAL CULTURE

One way to think of public opinion in the United States, or in any liberal democracy, is as a marketplace of ideas. If American political institutions are functioning properly and tempering majority rule with mechanisms to promote deliberation and protect minority rights, public discussion of issues should involve a free intellectual exchange. In the free marketplace, opinions compete for public acceptance. No opinion is automatically excluded from consideration merely because it is new, different, or unfamiliar. But, although this marketplace metaphor may be useful as an expression of the classical liberal ideas of tolerance and intellectual experimentation, it hardly describes the reality of American public opinion.

In the real world of public opinion, some opinions are taken much more seriously than others. The political culture of any society, by definition, places some limit on the range of alternatives that are subject to serious discussion. This situation is not the result of some sort of conspiracy. Rather, the degree to which human beings want to consider complex political alternatives is finite, limited by their experience. This statement does not mean that a political culture cannot evolve to make other alternatives legitimate; it just means that not every opinion or idea competes on a level playing field.

Contemporary public opinion in the United States must be understood in reference to fundamental shared American values. These values are a product of our history, religion, and geography. When Alexis de Tocqueville came to the United States in 1831, he was struck by Americans' efforts to reconcile two fundamental values, liberty and equality, which Europeans tended to view as being mutually exclusive. European societies were saddled with age-old divisions based on social class. The value of liberty usually applied only to the resource-rich upper classes, who wanted to be free from government restraint. They tended to see equality as a threat to their liberty.

7-2a INDIVIDUALISM AND EQUALITY

The long journey to America and the subsequent movement westward greatly reduced the importance of social class as a meaningful concept of societal organization. Alexis de Tocqueville saw the "frontier" experience as crucial in the development of the values of individualism and social equality. Clearly, much of what is unique about American folklore and myth is related to the efforts of the pioneers who settled the continent and relied on family and friends to get through hard times. In the United States, individualism came to take on a meaning somewhat different from what it had meant in Europe. American individualism as a core value stresses self-reliance and individual responsibility. It seeks to minimize the role of the government, especially in matters related to private property. Every society differentiates what belongs in the public sphere from what belongs in the private sphere. Americans tend to stress the latter. For instance, few other societies seriously question the government's right to limit firearms. But many Americans still profess a constitutional right to possess handguns with minimal government regulation. They have been successful at articulating and defending this perspective largely because of the core value structure that values the individual over the society.

Social equality is also a core American value. With rare exceptions, Americans have never had any use for royalty or titles of nobility. American popular culture—including music, magazines, movies, and TV shows—has always glorified the "common person" as opposed to the privileged. At the same time, this social equality has had meaning only within the multitude of groups accorded status within the society. Although the settlers had no use for the social stratification that served as a reminder of the European class system, they did not include African Americans among the constellation of groups whose members would be accorded social equality.

Individualism and self-reliance in the world of commerce have led to a commitment to capitalism as an economic system and an even stronger commitment to the institution of private property. In a capitalistic economic system, individual corporations rather than the government control the major means of production. Socialism, a system in which the government owns and operates major industries, has never had much appeal in the United States. Although Americans in the twenty-first century have come to accept a degree of government control of the economy, the basic structure of the American economy remains distinctly capitalist. The strong attachment to private property has led to many disputes over such issues as zoning, land-use planning, the regulation of signs, and the conservation of natural resources. Again, most Americans have come to accept the idea that government has a role to play in regulating the use of private property for the sake of the public interest. Still, whenever government proposes a specific project or policy that interferes with the private control of land, conflict is inevitable.

American individualism has led to a tenuous popular commitment to civil liberties. Yet particular claims of personal freedom are often more contentious than individualism in the abstract. To many people, individualism implies self-reliance, hard work, personal initiative, and responsibility. To others, personal freedom may involve behavior that is outside the social mainstream. The discussion of civil liberties in Chapter 4, "Civil Liberties and Individual Freedom," centered around the difficulty of protecting the expression of unpopular opinions in a majoritarian system. Nevertheless, most Americans remain committed to the ideals, if not always the application, of personal freedom.

The Internet has opened up new avenues for personal expression. Personal weblogs, or blogs, evolved from Internet bulletin boards and discussion forums in the early 2000s. Free sites and software such as Blogger.com and WordPress allow people to freely discuss politics, recipes, sports, or whatever topic they're interested in with anyone in the world with Internet access and the address to their blog. Today, bloggers are even considered legitimate news sources, with sites such as HuffingtonPost.com and DrudgeReport.com adding straight news coverage to personal analysis of political events.

7-3 The Opinions of Individuals

As you have seen, public opinion is the aggregation of what citizens think and feel about the people and policies associated with their government. These thoughts and feelings, which are conditioned by the society's core values, may or may not be expressed. To this point, we have treated public opinion from the perspective of the system as a whole. To understand how public opinion works in a system, however, we must first examine how individuals structure their thoughts and feelings about political objects.[2]

7-3a Values and Beliefs

People's opinions are built on their values, beliefs, and attitudes. **Political values** are basic sets of feelings about what ought to be and how people ought to behave. Values emerge from our upbringing, including our religious beliefs and sense of right and wrong. People hold a few basic values that form the foundation of other feelings and preferences about politics. An example of a political value is the fundamental "rightness" of equality.

Beliefs are less fundamental to individuals than their values. **Beliefs** can best be thought of as propositions about what is true or false. For example, some people believe that the death penalty deters crime; others do not. Although some people believe that private ownership of guns increases personal security, others believe that gun ownership is more likely to put a person in jeopardy. Beliefs are more specific-policy related, but they are manifestations of those big-picture beliefs. Most people now believe that smoking is detrimental to one's health. This widespread belief has developed as scientific evidence about the dangers of smoking has accumulated over the years. A person who sees limited government as a value may not like smoking, but oppose a local government imposing a smoking ban based on their belief that such policies are not government's responsibility in a society.

ONLINE 7.2
http://www.people-press.org/2012/06/04/partisan-polarization-surges-in-bush-obama-years/

Although science (including, supposedly, political science) is ideally based on a sharp distinction between what is true or false and what is right or wrong, the opinions of individuals in the real world are usually not based on a clear fact–value distinction. Indeed, beliefs about what is true or false are often based somewhat on values. For example, the extent to which people believe that "Democrats are better than Republicans for working people" depends on how they define better and worse, as well as on their assimilation of facts about Democratic and Republican behavior over the years.

Beliefs are more numerous than values, but they are still the basic building blocks of a person's opinion system. Whereas values may not be stated or realized by the individual, beliefs almost always are. Beliefs are not quite as enduring as values. Few people experience a fundamental shift in what they hold dear. Beliefs, on the other hand, may change with new information.

7-3b Attitudes and Opinions

Political attitudes are built on both values and beliefs. Political **attitudes** are "more or less enduring orientations toward an object or situation and predispositions to respond positively or negatively toward that object or situation."[3] That is, a person can have an attitude toward a particular minority group, toward the Republican party, or toward conservatives, for example. An attitude is a feeling that is not tied to a specific policy or situation. These types of feelings can stem from values and beliefs, but also from other nonpolitical areas of one's life. For instance, one's attitudes toward women's rights could stem from political values (for example, equality) and beliefs (for example, that women can do any job as well as men). However, a person's attitudes can also be affected by her experience with discrimination while attempting to establish a career.

Opinions are people's preferences and judgments about public issues and political candidates. One's opinions tend to be mixtures of thoughts and feelings toward persons and policies. They may directly reflect values, beliefs, and attitudes. People's fundamental religious values may be directly reflected in their opinions. For instance, opponents of legalized abortion often rely on and refer to religious precepts and symbols. But many pro-life advocates also state beliefs about the beginning of human life, which may or may not have a basis in a particular religious creed. Another person might express the belief that human life does not begin at conception in arriving at a pro-choice position. That person might also hold a negative attitude toward government involvement in

people's private lives. These types of values, beliefs, and attitudes, taken in the aggregate throughout society, make up the contours of public opinion on the issue of abortion.

Individuals and groups of individuals who make up the multitude of publics in America create the base that gives rise to demands for government action. This base is continually changing, but the change is slowed by the relative stability of basic values. The nature of demands is complicated by the fuzzy boundaries that separate political attitudes from attitudes formed in nonpolitical areas of people's lives.

7-3c Ideology

Most people hold beliefs, opinions, and attitudes on a wide variety of issues and about a large number of political personalities. When someone's beliefs, attitudes, and opinions are organized into a coherent logical structure, we say that this person possesses an ideology. Political culture refers to the values, expectations, and ideas that are broadly shared in society. Ideology, on the other hand, refers to those ideas, or systems of ideas, that are in conflict in society. Moreover, ideology involves an agenda for action—a set of prescriptions for public policy making. Not everyone employs an ideology. Indeed, evidence indicates that most people's beliefs, attitudes, and opinions are not highly constrained to any kind of logical order.[4] To the degree that individuals' beliefs have discernible patterns, however, they display some evidence of ideological thinking.

The Liberal-Conservative Continuum

Let's revisit the ideology section of Chapter 1 for a moment. We used a left-to-right scale as a map of ideologies. On the left-hand side of the continuum were ideologies supporting more government control over society. As we moved to the right, legitimate governmental authority declined. The most common way of conceptualizing ideological differences is the one-dimensional liberal-conservative scale. The continuum ranges from the radical label on the "far left" to the reactionary label on the "far right." Those in the middle are called *moderates* or *centrists*. The more familiar terms *liberal* and *conservative* apply to those whose ideologies are left and right of center, respectively.

Radicals believe that the established order is fundamentally corrupt or unjust. They would like to see an altogether new political and economic system, brought about by a revolution if necessary. Reactionaries are equally unhappy with the status quo, but they would like to return to an imagined bygone golden age, or at least to a time when they believed things were better. Both radicals and reactionaries tend to be impatient with or frustrated by the dominant political dialogue and with conventional forms of political participation. They often find ideological companionship by associating themselves with a fringe political group or even a religious cult. Blogs and online resources have provided a place for people on the fringe to find community, however, and those minority groups now have a voice far beyond their numbers. The Internet can act as a megaphone, raising the volume of a small group's political voice. Not surprisingly, they find themselves "outside the conversation" on most issues, furthering their sense of isolation and lessening their identification with the political system.

The political dialogue in America is fairly moderate. If we think about the left-right political ideology continuum like a football field, we play our politics between the forty yard lines. Not many influential groups or spokespersons are on the far left or far right. Those that do exist seldom have access to the mass media to state their positions. However, the Internet has proven to be a perfect medium for dialogue among those on the fringes of the political system. However geographically isolated people may find themselves, most now have access to a computer and the Internet. The ability of people with minimal financial resources to communicate and organize over a wide geographic area gives just about any group, no matter how small, the opportunity to communicate, not only with each other but also with potential converts to their cause.

The liberal-conservative continuum has the advantages of simplicity and widespread familiarity. Not only political scientists but also commentators in the media and everyday citizens routinely use the terms *liberal* and *conservative* in describing people's views on issues. And, when surveyed, most people are able to place themselves on the spectrum. But what do liberal and conservative mean? These terms have been with us since their origin in the political philosophy of the late eighteenth and early nineteenth centuries. But so many different varieties of liberalism and conservatism exist, and their public policy connotations have changed so much over the past two centuries, that defining them with any degree of precision is difficult.

The Role of Government in the Economy

In late nineteenth- and early twentieth-century America, the liberal-conservative debate centered around the role of government in the economy. Conservatives strongly defended the doctrine of *laissez-faire*, even though pure market capitalism had never really existed in this country. Liberals argued that in order to survive, capitalism had to evolve to permit the formation of labor unions, the creation of public welfare programs, and the government regulation of key industries. Conservatives accused liberals of embracing socialism; liberals chided conservatives for their insensitivity to the plight of workers and the poor. This debate was largely resolved by widespread popular acceptance of the New Deal and the welfare state created in the aftermath of the Great Depression. Although liberals and conservatives still argue about government's proper role in the economy, that debate is not now the principal component of liberal-conservative conflict.

Foreign Policy and Military Issues

Historically, foreign policy has been another important dimension of the liberal-conservative debate. After World War II, America's primary adversary became the Soviet Union and its communist allies. The United States established a policy of stopping the spread of Communism, by military force if necessary. In the early 1960s, this policy brought America into the ill-fated Vietnam War. Liberals and conservatives were divided over the war. Liberals, often called doves in the foreign policy context, argued first for limited involvement and later for withdrawal of our forces. Conservatives, or hawks, argued for a total commitment to win a clear military victory. Liberals and conservatives also divided over the issue of the growing antiwar movement. Liberals argued for tolerance of dissent and in many cases applauded the tactics of the protesters. Conservatives were outraged by what they perceived to be assaults on both patriotism and law and order.

In the 1970s and early 1980s, liberals and conservatives continued to argue about America's posture toward the Soviets and communism in general. The specific issues were many and varied: the nuclear arms race, aid to anticommunist military dictatorships in Latin America, aid to rebels fighting Marxist governments in Nicaragua and Angola, and military intervention in Grenada, for example. Conservatives argued that the United States should continue building its military capabilities and confront Soviet expansionism and Communist insurgency wherever they threatened American interests. Liberals countered that America was investing too much in weapons and not enough in education, social programs, and environmental protection. The end of the Cold War and the demise of the Soviet Union muted this aspect of the liberal-conservative debate, at least for a time. During the 1990s, liberals argued for swifter and deeper reductions in military spending; conservatives insisted that it was "still a dangerous world out there." The terrorist attacks of 9/11 seemed to vindicate the conservative position.

Civil Rights

Another historic element of the liberal-conservative debate has been civil rights. In the 1950s and 1960s, many conservatives opposed efforts to end segregated schools and other types of discrimination against blacks. Other, more moderate conservatives argued that although these types of practices were wrong, reform had to move at a pace slow enough for the American people to adapt. Liberals, on the other hand, championed the civil rights claims of African Americans and, later, of women, the poor, people with disabilities, and gays and lesbians. One major argument between liberals and conservatives is over affirmative action programs to aid minorities. Liberals argue that these types of programs are needed to remedy present and past discrimination. Conservatives see affirmative action programs as reverse discrimination.

Crime and Criminal Justice

Crime and criminal justice have been another point of division between liberalism and conservatism. Conservatives firmly believe in law and order. They believe that criminals should be punished harshly to drive home the message that society disapproves of their behavior. Finding conservatives who oppose capital punishment is difficult. Moreover, conservatives are highly critical of legal rules that hamper police and prosecutors in ferreting out crime and punishing criminals. The exclusionary rules that forbid the fruits of illegal searches and improperly obtained confessions from being used as evidence have been frequent targets of conservative ire.

Liberals, on the other hand, as champions of the underdog, have tended to portray criminals as victims of an unequal and unjust society. They have called for the rehabilitation of criminals rather than harsh punishment. Liberals have tended to oppose the death penalty as barbaric and as racist in its application. As advocates of individual rights, they have looked to courts of law to maintain strict constraints on law enforcement. The mass public has tended to favor the conservative perspective on criminal justice. As crime rates rose in the 1970s and early 1980s, the public became impatient with the criminal justice system, which many regarded as excessively hampered by rules created by liberal judges. Consequently, many liberals backed away from their traditional positions on crime and punishment. This situation was certainly evident in 1994, when many liberal Democrats running for Congress ran TV ads stressing law-and-order themes. A number of liberals in Congress made a big show of their support for President Clinton's crime bill, which passed Congress in August 1994. The idea behind this legislation was to take the crime issue away from conservatives and Republicans.

Traditional Values and Institutions

To a great extent, the contemporary liberal-conservative debate is over the legitimacy of traditional values and institutions. In what they sometimes characterize as a cultural war, conservatives find themselves defending monogamy, traditional marriage, the nuclear family, and heterosexuality against what they perceive as a rising tide of societal decay. Liberals counter that they are not attacking these institutions per se, but rather advancing social progress and change. In the liberal mind, such choices are to be made freely by individuals, not imposed by society.

The ground is continually shifting beneath this "cultural war." By the year 2000, voters in Vermont were embroiled in a controversy regarding the state's recognition of civil unions between same-sex partners. Churches were considering whether to ordain openly gay ministers and bishops. Gay and lesbian couples were having greater success in adopting children. In 2003, the Supreme Court held that private, consensual homosexual activity is protected by the Constitution.[5] By 2009, six states had legalized gay marriage in some form or another. The context will shift from time to time, as issues come to the fore and are resolved, but the underlying attitudes remain the same.

Ideology and Public Policy

Most public arguments about issues, from abortion to the role of women in society, have fairly well-recognized liberal and conservative positions. Box 7-1 compares the attitudes of liberals, moderates, and conservatives in the year 2008 on abortion, global climate change, and civil rights. The tables show significant differences between self-identified liberals and conservatives on all three issues. On abortion, more than half of liberals believe that abortions should be allowed in all instances save when the child is not the gender the mother wants. Conservatives are much more likely to favor restrictions except for cases of rape and where the mother's life is in danger. On the issue of climate change, though, the differences between liberals and conservatives are small. More than three-quarters of all respondents believe climate change is occurring, though conservatives are less likely than liberals to support higher gas taxes as a method of combating climate change. Significant differences return in civil rights where almost half of conservatives favor a gay marriage prohibition, 30 percent more than liberals. Conservatives also are 40 percent more likely to believe that the War on Terror has prevented more terrorists from attacking the United States.

In general, liberals tend to favor government spending (other than military spending) more than do conservatives. However, a difference in degree exists, with a good deal of consensus that spending on poor people should not be cut back. On the other hand, more pronounced differences become obvious when the subject is abortion, as indicated in Box 7-1. Liberals are much more likely to feel that the decision regarding abortion should be a personal choice. Conservatives believe that abortions undermine the sanctity of life and thus should only be allowed in the direst of circumstances. These questions represent the two dimensions of the liberal-conservative basis of ideology. Liberals are more likely to favor a more active government in dealing with economic disparities, but are less likely to favor government involvement in personal decisions.

People who identify themselves as liberal or conservative do not necessarily take consistently liberal or conservative positions on issues. There is no doubt that many people are confused about the labels and may identify themselves incorrectly in a survey. But many others simply don't fit neatly into a liberal-conservative dichotomy. A simple illustration suffices to explain why. A devout Roman Catholic may oppose legalized abortion and the death penalty on the grounds that both involve an immoral taking of human life. In her mind, the two positions are logically consistent, yet one of the positions (opposition to abortion) is conventionally seen as a conservative viewpoint, and the other (opposing the death penalty) is usually defined as a liberal perspective. The woman is not confused about her positions, but may be uncertain about which label, liberal or conservative, best applies to her. To answer the question, you would need to know where she stands on a whole range of issues. Of course, even after obtaining that information, she may not fit into the standard liberal-conservative framework. That would not, in itself, mean that she doesn't have an ideology, however.

Issues often become framed in different ways over time, and liberal and conservative positions become reversed on what would appear to be the same issue. A good example is the issue of American support for Israel. Although both parties have been strong supporters of the Jewish state, persistent strains of opposition to this support arose among many more conservative voters, especially those in the rural South. However, with President Bush's strong support of Israel during and following the suicide bombings of 2002, the strongest support for Israel came from traditionally conservative writers, while many liberals expressed a great deal more sympathy for the Palestinians. Moreover, southern Protestants were the segment of the American electorate expressing the most support for the Israeli cause.

The invasion of Iraq in 2003 likewise confounded the usual ideological divisions. Most liberals were uneasy at best about the conflict and its conduct and were critical of the Bush administration's approach. The war revealed some divisions among conservatives, some of whom attributed the administration's policy to "neoconservatives" in the administration. Some traditional conservatives, like Rep. John Duncan (R-Tennessee), even voted against the resolution authorizing President Bush to go to war in Iraq.

7-3d Political Socialization

Political socialization is the process by which people learn about their political world. Through this process, individuals develop patterns of attitudes and beliefs, which help shape the way they view the political world. Through political socialization, important facts, values, and processes of decision making are transmitted to new generations of Americans. Most political socialization occurs before adulthood. By the time people complete their education, they have probably acquired a **party identification**, meaning that they identify with a political party or consider themselves Independents. They may have formed a conscious ideological orientation, a set of attitudes about various groups and issues, and a basic orientation toward authority. Moreover, by the time they reach adulthood, most people have developed their sense of commitment to community and likelihood of participating in politics.

Political socialization explains much of the diversity that is fascinating about American politics. The incredible variation of opinion, belief, attitude, and participation

Box 7-1 *Issue Positions by Ideological Self-Identification, 2008*

	LIBERAL	MODERATE	CONSERVATIVE	ALL
Abortions should be allowed if giving birth would harm the mother's health	69.0%	40.6%	36.0%	48.1%
Abortions should be allowed if giving birth could be fatal to the mother	88.0%	68.6%	64.7%	73.4%
Abortions should be allowed in the case of incest	63.3%	34.9%	29.2%	41.9%
Abortions should be allowed in the case of rape	83.5%	66.4%	57.9%	68.4%
Abortions should be allowed where the child would have a serious birth defect	73.6%	50.5%	43.8%	55.3%
Abortions should be allowed where the child is not the gender the parent wanted	22.9%	10.7%	8.2%	13.7%
Abortions should be allowed where the parent cannot financially care for the child	51.4%	21.4%	19.5%	30.7%
World temperature has been rising the last 100 years	97.0%	87.4%	76.9%	85.9%
Favorability toward power plant emissions restrictions	88.7%	69.9%	66.5%	74.7%
Favorability toward higher gasoline taxes	35.2%	10.5%	13.2%	20.1%
Favorability toward a constitutional amendment banning gay marriage	12.7%	29.3%	47.4%	31.5%
Favorability toward affirmative action in employment	17.5%	7.3%	5.6%	10.0%
The Iraq war has decreased the likelihood of terrorist attack on the United States	8.6%	23.2%	48.9%	29.5%

Source: Adapted from 2008 National Election Study, Center for Political Studies, University of Michigan, http://www.electionstudies.org.

is in large part a reflection of the myriad ways in which we all come to experience the political world. Of course, people's learning about politics is closely related to their social class, religion, and ethnicity. Each of these factors has its own effect on opinions and conditions the ways in which people are socialized. This conditioning effect can be seen in the ways the primary agents of political socialization operate: the family, the school, and one's peer groups.

FAMILY

The family plays the most important role in transmitting political values and orientations across generations. One way that parents teach children about politics is through explicit reference to and identification with various groups. No object of political orientation is more crucial to the political system than the political party. Children tend to take on the political party identification of their parents. Partisanship is learned in much the same way as religion is: children soon learn that "we are" Catholic, Baptist, Methodist, Jewish, Muslim, or some other faith. On the other hand, some children may not hear anything about religion, and others hear only negative references about various religious groups. These messages help the child form a religious orientation that will likely last a lifetime. In the same way, many children hear that "we are" Democrats, Republicans, or Independents. In a sense, party identification is something like an attachment to a sports team. A child in New York City may grow up liking the Yankees and hating the Mets (or vice versa). This affinity may be inherited from the parents or perhaps from an older sibling. The attachment is never really pondered; that's just the way it is.

The family transmits values in both affective and cognitive ways. The specific information a child hears about political parties usually forms the base for later cognitive thinking. Thoughts such as "Democrats are good for the working person" and "Republicans are better in foreign affairs" may be somewhat simplistic, but they provide a *cognitive* basis for receiving and processing political information. Likewise, the child may hear statements about a political party, such as "They do not like people like us, and I can't stand them." These statements can make up the foundation for later *affective* reactions to politics.

The family communicates cognitive and affective information about liberals and conservatives in much the same ways it transmits party affiliation. Although ideological identification is certainly a less-enduring orientation than is party identification, with the decline in the importance of party labels, ideological labels have taken on added significance. Although children typically do not think of themselves as liberals or conservatives, they tend to hear more about these terms as they become teenagers.

Children learn from their families much more than affective and cognitive orientations toward various political individuals and groups. In many ways, their broader personal socialization can have an indirect effect on their later political opinions. A child's first experience with authority is with her parent or parents. Children are taught either to obey authority figures without question or perhaps to question and challenge any attempt at discipline. Societies vary greatly in the way authority is treated in the family. To some degree, societal patterns of child rearing explain different societies' attitudes toward government authority. The tradition of unquestioning obedience to authority figures in German families is one explanation for the widespread acceptance of Hitler's policies during the Holocaust period in Nazi Germany.[6] Attitudes learned in childhood toward authority can have an effect on later attitudes and beliefs toward civil liberties and proper police conduct. The lack of a relationship with one's father can apparently also lead to a low sense of **political efficacy**, the feeling that one can make a difference in politics.[7]

Children first learn about politics through their perception of key personalities. At an early age, they become aware of—and usually have positive feelings toward—the president. This early view then evolves to one that mirrors the parents' position, with children of Democrats becoming somewhat critical of Republican presidents, and Republican children likewise being critical of Democratic presidents. Children growing up in homes without political dialogue miss much of this early adjustment. To some degree, the parents in these apolitical homes tend to have lower levels of income and education, and the father tends to be absent. Thus, the role of the family cannot be viewed in isolation from the effect of social class.

Considerable evidence indicates that lower-class families socialize their children differently than do middle- and upper-class families. The eminent political sociologist Seymour Martin Lipset has observed that the typical lower-class individual "is likely to have been exposed to punishment, lack of love, and a general atmosphere of tension and aggression since early childhood."[8] In Lipset's view, these experiences tend to foster, among other things, racial prejudice and political authoritarianism. Political scientists Thomas Dye and Harmon Zeigler have written that "the circumstances of lower-class life...make commitment to democratic ideas very difficult."[9] One must remember, however, that these are only generalizations. Not all lower-class families share these characteristics, and not every citizen of lower-class origins develops antidemocratic attitudes. Nor are middle- and upper-class families devoid of racial prejudice and authoritarian inclinations.

School

Although parents play the primary role in transmitting party identification and attitudes toward authority, the school is responsible for teaching the rules and rituals of democracy and the specifics of the American political system. At first, much of the teaching is affective. Students learn the myths of the American Revolution and Civil War, developing positive attitudes toward individuals such as George Washington and Abraham Lincoln. Their earliest exposure to the symbols of American democracy may be through the pledge of allegiance to the flag.

For many children, the teacher is the first real authority figure outside the home. She may provide the first real discipline that many children have ever experienced. The teacher can therefore have a profound effect on learning, both directly, through teaching the symbols of nationhood, and indirectly, in her role as an authority figure. Depending on the nature of the class and the teaching style employed, children can develop different views of authority. At one time, schoolchildren in lower-income areas were likely to be taught a more structured obedience to authority, and middle-class children were encouraged to question and challenge authority figures. All schools are now experiencing great difficulty in teaching respect for authority. To some degree, this situation represents a change in educational philosophy. But this difficulty also reflects the more fundamental breakdown of authority in society. Schools can reinforce, at most, only what is transmitted through the family and the broader culture. They cannot, in and of themselves, teach values that are not being taught in the home or that are being contradicted in the popular culture.

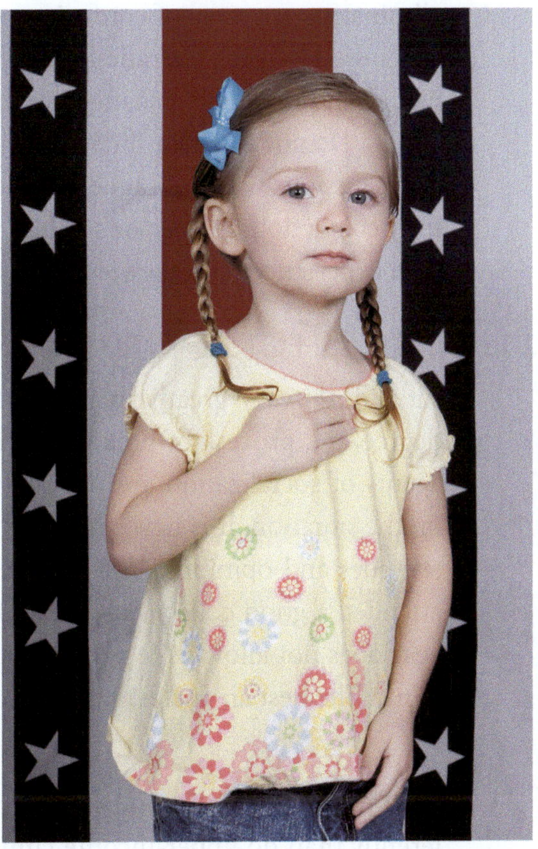

In middle or junior high school, children learn about democratic institutions, through both classroom instruction in American history and repeated exposure to elections. Students there learn the basic institutions of American politics. In addition, virtually all classrooms and schools regularly hold elections to various posts. In high school, most students become comfortable with voting machines, with many holding mock elections corresponding to those held among their adult counterparts.

Many students who attend college take political science courses, which are required for graduation in a number of state college and university systems. In these courses, students learn fundamental notions of tolerance and acquire skills for evaluating various public policy alternatives. Moreover, college usually exposes students to a wide variety of ideas and cultures. This exposure is important in developing tolerance for diversity, which is not only imperative in contemporary pluralistic America but also essential for amassing intellectual capital to invest in one's later political life.

Peer Groups

The groups with whom individuals associate provide the third major agent of socialization in American politics. Although the family and the school have had their major effect by the time a child reaches adulthood, peer groups continue to affect political attitudes and opinions well into adulthood. Those who were raised in Democratic families, but work in groups that are largely Republican, such as investment bankers, are likely to change to become more like the groups they join. Likewise, children of Republicans who end up working in Democrat-dominated professions, such as the news media, are also likely to switch their partisan allegiance.

Peer groups have a major influence on political attitudes for a number of reasons. First, people generally strive to reduce **cognitive dissonance**, which is the psychological discomfort, or dissonance, a person feels when trying to process contradictory feelings or thoughts.[10] Most people naturally come to terms with contradictory information by eliminating a source of confusion or discomfort. For instance, a young woman who was raised in a Democratic family but now works for a heavily Republican company would find it easier to change her party orientation than her career. Even the change from a Democrat to an Independent would lessen the stress she feels when involved in discussions with colleagues. That statement does not mean that she would not have firm convictions. A person's values and beliefs about the world evolve based on her own experiences and the viewpoints she develops.

7-3e The Effect of Other Socioeconomic Factors

Individuals vary greatly in their attitudes, opinions, beliefs, and values. To a great degree, the process of political socialization explains these differences. Though the agents of socialization are not particularly numerous, their effect varies depending on the situation. It is never possible to explain completely all the variation in political attitudes and opinions. Just knowing that Megan was raised by Republican parents, attended a good college, and now works at a public relations firm making $75,000 a year does not allow us to predict her attitudes or opinions with a high degree of certainty. The best an analyst can do is discern tendencies among different groups.

Social Class

Working-class families and schools in northern industrial cities socialize children differently than do upper-income families and schools in California suburbs. But social class has its own effect on attitudes apart from the socialization process. People of lower income and education make different demands on government. Those who are unemployed or employed in low-paying jobs are likely to place little value on the concept of minimal government. They likely look to government to create jobs and provide social services. On the other hand, those in the most-educated social class are much more likely to support civil liberties and government funding for the humanities. Of course, lower-income and less-educated people tend not to participate in politics as frequently as people of higher income and more education. Their demands on the system are therefore likely to have less effect.

Religion

Religious affiliation can have a major effect on particular values and beliefs. A fundamentalist Christian in the rural South may feel that his religion implies values that lead him to demand that the local school board eliminate its sex-education program. Catholics traditionally opposed birth control and abortion, although American Catholics are now moving away from the church's official position on these issues. Many of the more mainline Protestant denominations have taken rather liberal stands on some social issues. In this area, some variance has occurred between the elites and the masses. The leaders of religious organizations of Methodists, Presbyterians, Lutherans, and Episcopalians have held more activist positions on many social issues than the membership as a whole.

Religion has always played a major part in shaping political values in America. Many people explicitly ground their political values in religious values; others make a point of keeping the two separate. Organized churches have often inspired their members to live in a way consistent with their teachings. At other times, churches have remained silent, preferring to concentrate on the private lives of members rather than take stands on public issues. Churches have had a major effect on both the nature and the expression of opinion. Black clergy played a major role in the civil rights movement, and they are still the most trusted leaders among African Americans.[11] In the 1980s, fundamentalist Protestants mobilized, often at the urging of ministers, to fight legalized abortion, gay rights, feminism, and other manifestations of secular humanism. Certainly, the power of religious leaders to inspire movements is indisputable, as is the practical value that a network of churches provides to a mass movement. Nevertheless, the tremendous variety of denominations and creeds in the United States makes the relationship between religion and political values a complex one. People of sincere religious feelings can be found on all sides of any given public issue.

Region

For the greater part of this country's existence, a person's region provided the best clues to her political attitudes. The unique history of the South, especially in regard to slavery and connected economic issues, meant that many national issues were viewed in terms of their effect on the region. Into the latter half of the twentieth century, southerners were especially conscious of their regional identity, which, in many cases, had as much effect on their political opinions as social class and education did. Regional identity was especially pronounced during the civil rights movement of the 1960s.

Many issues have taken on a regional slant, and individuals often view policies in terms of the effect on their region. For instance, energy policies have different effects on oil-producing states in the Southwest than on oil-consuming states in the Northeast. Likewise, western states have a particular interest in water policy. Despite these lingering regional interests, the United States has become less a society of pronounced regional differences and more a society of different groups that cut across regions. The reason for this situation is quite simple: Technological advances have made this country so interconnected that communication is instantaneous and travel is forgiving of great distance. The nationalization of television has made regional isolation less and less a factor in shaping opinion. Public opinion and the underlying political culture have become much more homogeneous throughout the country.

AGE

If region has lost much of its political clout, age seems to have taken on increased importance as a reference for public opinion formation. This factor parallels the rise in the proportion of the population that is over age sixty-five. Every generation of Americans has a distinct political history marked by certain **defining events**. Many younger adults do not fully appreciate the impact of the Great Depression or World War II on the attitudes of the oldest Americans. Older Americans may not fully appreciate the impact of Vietnam or the civil rights movement on the baby boomers. The Great Depression likely made an entire generation of Americans more supportive of government programs designed to ensure old-age income security. The Vietnam War led a later generation to question authority, especially when the issue arises of committing American troops to conflicts overseas. Perhaps the events of September 11, 2001, will have their own effect on another generation. This effect could be manifested in a number of ways, including a greater likelihood of turning to government institutions as problem solvers or using pressure to limit immigration.

On the other hand, some evidence exists that all generations experience similar changes in attitudes as they age. As people acquire property, have children, and pay more taxes, they tend to become more conservative. Property owners and taxpayers feel that they have a greater stake in the system and tend to be suspicious of proposals for major economic change, especially if they think that it will cost them money. Parents tend to be protective of their children and, consequently, become more concerned about crime, violence, drugs, promiscuity, and other social problems that may threaten their children's well-being. Baby boomers who experimented with drugs and held negative attitudes toward the police in the 1960s and 1970s may find themselves sounding like their parents as they attempt to raise their own families. As a result, both generational and aging effects have an effect on the formation of political attitudes.

Race

In many ways, race has become the dominant factor in the formation of political attitudes and opinions. Although this statement is true among all groups, it is especially true for minority groups. African Americans are much more likely than whites to self-identify as liberals and Democrats. They are more likely to adopt liberal positions on civil rights and liberties issues, social welfare issues, and the rights of workers. They are much more likely to see government in positive terms—as a force for good in society rather than a nuisance. Yet, when it comes to social issues, such as abortion, gay rights, and the role of women, African Americans tend to be somewhat more conservative than whites. Box 7-2 compares attitudes across racial lines on three public issues in the year 2008. As suggested, African Americans are somewhat more conservative than whites on the issues of abortion and gay marriage. But they are three times as likely as whites to believe that the federal government should see to fair treatment in matters of employment.

Gender

Although the United States has had a history of women's political activism since the nineteenth century, few issues were defined as women's issues before the women's movement of the late twentieth century. Today, differences in attitudes between men and women have led to something of a **gender gap** in voting, especially in presidential elections. In recent elections women have tended to be more supportive of Democrats; men have tended to favor Republicans. Box 7-2 compares attitudes across gender categories on three public issues in the year 2000. Interestingly, men and women do not differ all that much on the question of abortion. Not surprisingly, women are more likely than men to favor an equal role for women in society, but it is important to note than the great majority of men also take this position.

Marital Status

As suggested earlier in section 7-3e, evidence indicates that married people with children are significantly more conservative than others in society. This group is potentially powerful on a whole range of social and economic issues, especially those that can be subsumed under the umbrella of family values. In the 1992 election, the Republicans tried to exploit their advantage on these types of issues to the married-with-children group. Most observers, however, thought that the Republicans failed to present a coherent appeal to this group while managing to alienate many women and single parents.

Box 7-2 *Issue Positions by Sex and Race, 2008*

	MALE	FEMALE	WHITE	BLACK	ALL
Abortions should be allowed if giving birth would harm the mother's health	44.20%	48.60%	48.80%	34.80%	46.60%
Abortions should be allowed if giving birth could be fatal to the mother	74.70%	74.20%	75.00%	69.60%	72.80%
Abortions should be allowed in the case of incest	52.60%	41.40%	47.10%	47.80%	46.60%
Abortions should be allowed in the case of rape	66.30%	67.90%	68.20%	69.60%	67.10%
Abortions should be allowed where the child would have a serious birth defect	62.10%	57.70%	60.50%	52.50%	59.70%
Abortions should be allowed where the child is not the gender the parent wanted	20.00%	10.70%	15.60%	13.00%	15.00%
World temperature has been rising the last 100 years	87.40%	85.60%	86.00%	91.30%	86.40%
Favorability of power plant emissions restrictions	78.90%	80.20%	79.10%	79.30%	79.60%
Favorability of higher gasoline taxes	29.80%	17.10%	22.20%	13.00%	22.90%
Favorability of a constitutional amendment banning gay marriage	33.60%	25.70%	27.40%	38.70%	29.40%
Favorability of affirmative action in employment	10.90%	9.20%	6.40%	42.10%	10%

Source: Adapted from 2008 National Election Study, Center for Political Studies, University of Michigan, http://www.electionstudies.org.

7-3f OPINION DYSFUNCTION

Any system of representative democracy is designed to process demands for government action. One gauge of the health of a political system is the degree to which its citizens believe what government officials say. Another is whether citizens trust that the system is in fact what it purports to be: Is a Communist system truly the "vanguard of the workers" that its leaders claim? Is the American system as representative of the wishes of the majority and protective of the rights of the minority as our national and state leaders assert? If individuals do not trust their government or have little faith in the integrity of their system, they will fail to provide the level of support necessary to maintain its institutions over succeeding generations.

ALIENATION

A lack of trust in government can be both a cause and, to some degree, a product of political alienation. **Political alienation** is a feeling of distance from and hostility toward the political process. More than mere dislike of a particular political leader or policy, it is a deep-seated negative feeling about the entire political process. Although one can be actively alienated and freely express these types of feelings, alienation can exist without explicit realization or expression. Every society has some politically alienated individuals. Some people are generally alienated from all social institutions and would probably feel apart from any governmental system. For the most part, however, the level of political alienation in a society is reflective of the state of that society's political institutions. And most people would agree that high levels of political alienation do not reflect well on a given system. An alienated individual does not trust her government.

Political alienation increased dramatically in the United States between the 1960s and the 1990s. In the early 1960s, more than 70 percent of American adults felt that they could trust the national government most of the time. By 1996, only 32 percent felt that way. Despite some increase in recent years, trust in the government has clearly diminished greatly (see Figure 7-1).

LACK OF EFFICACY

Democratic institutions presuppose that citizens will support the basic rules by which decisions are made and that they will participate at least minimally in making demands on the system. When individuals feel that the system "does not listen to people like me" or that "people like me cannot make a difference," they suffer from a lack of political efficacy. A significant proportion of the American public could be categorized as lacking efficacy.

Clearly, someone who feels a lack of efficacy in his daily life is likely to feel the same toward political institutions (see Figure 7-2). Someone who feels powerless on the job, or powerless to obtain a job, will find it hard to feel much power in the political arena. Likewise, an individual who feels a lack of power and influence with people in personal settings may transfer that perspective to politics. It would be misleading, however, to automatically conclude that an individual's lack of political efficacy necessarily reflects deeper personal problems. In the aggregate, it may reflect a true state of affairs in some systems. Most citizens of Castro's Cuba may well feel that the government does not pay much attention to people like them, and, from all indications, their perception is correct. Feelings of a lack of efficacy could reflect on the individual, the system, or both.

INTOLERANCE

A democracy cannot work without an efficacious citizenry to make demands and provide support. Although the threat of opting out may endanger democratic institutions, the threat of those who make demands that would opt *others* out is every bit as dangerous. If a political culture does not support a reasonable degree of tolerance for others, it is doubtful that political institutions can do much more than stave off a majority who would use their power to limit the rights of a minority.

An abundance of evidence indicates that falling levels of efficacy are often followed by rising levels of intolerance among the same people. No better example exists than the rise of the Nazis in Germany following World War I. Working-class Germans felt dispirited and outside the political system in the Weimar Republic. They were brought back into politics through the appeals of Adolph Hitler. Unfortunately, those who would appeal to the downtrodden usually do so by providing a scapegoat. In the case of the Nazis, the principal scapegoat was the Jews. In this country, politicians looking to appeal to persons of low political efficacy have also been prone to scapegoating. African Americans, Jews, Asian Americans, and many other ethnic minorities have been the targets of

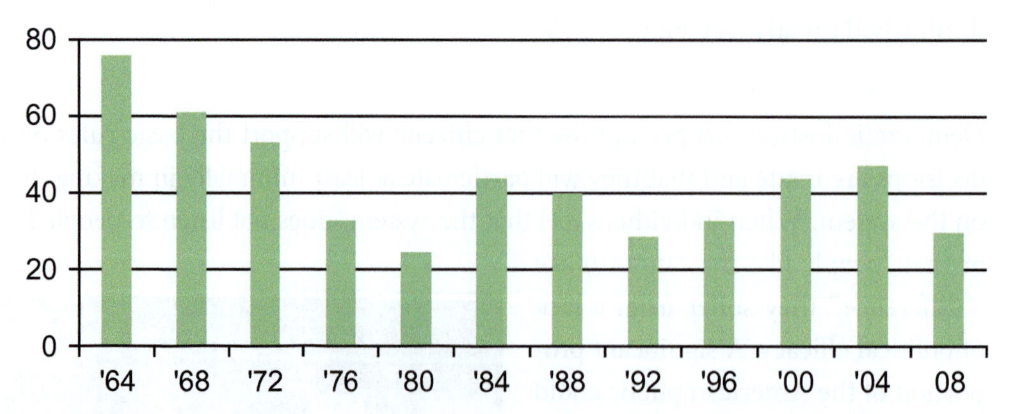

Figure 7-1 *Percentage of Respondents Agreeing that they Trust Government in Washington "All of the Time" or "Most of the Time," 1964–2008*

Source: Adapted from Center for Political Studies, University of Michigan, National Election Studies, electionstudies.org.

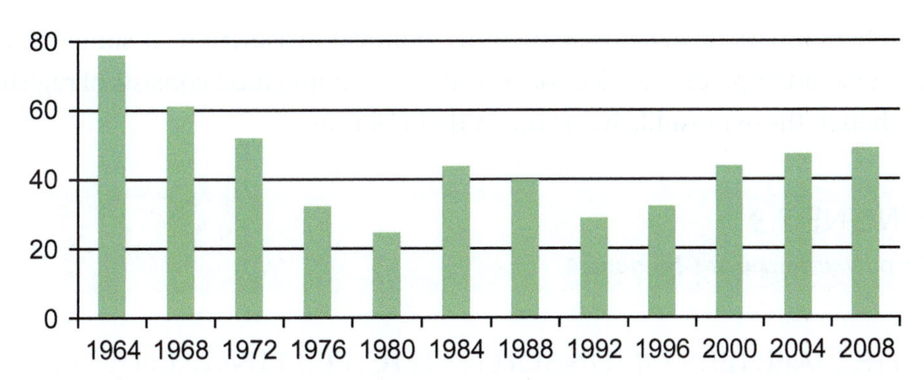

Figure 7-2 *Percentage of Respondents Agreeing or Strongly Agreeing with the Statement "People Like Me Don't Have Any Say about What the Government Does," 1964–2008*

Source: Adapted from Center for Political Studies, University of Michigan, National Election Studies, electionstudies.org.

these types of efforts. Following the attacks on the World Trade Center and the Pentagon in 2001, many people feared a wave of attacks on Muslim Americans along with intolerance for the expression of the Muslim religion. Surprisingly few attacks of this type or expressions of religious or cultural hostility occurred. American political culture has evolved to the point that the public expression of this type of animus is discouraged.

7-4 Measuring Public Opinion

For centuries, leaders have tried to know the will of their people. For the most part, these attempts have been haphazard and thus prone to error. Most nonscientific measurement of public opinion has been through key informants. A member of the state legislature may go to a certain coffee shop when he is back in his district. His conversations may touch on issues before the general assembly. Although these types of conversations may indeed provide insight into people's feelings on a given issue, the legislator would be wise to avoid generalizing beyond the folks at the diner. In all likelihood, they are not at all typical of the general population. Even if they do represent an accurate cross section, the tone and tenor of the dialogue could have as much effect on the attitudes they express as do their underlying beliefs and values.

Both politicians and nonpoliticians are continually observing what people say about politics. A member of a country club may find that she and her friends feel the same way about increasing income taxes on the wealthy. However, it would be a mistake to generalize these feelings into a statement such as "Everyone seems to oppose that proposed income tax increase."

Other attempts at measuring opinion may appear to be systematic and scientific, but may in fact be just as misleading. Consider a straw poll at a state fair. A **straw poll** is a survey in which the respondents decide whether to participate. The problem with a straw poll is the same as that encountered by a state legislator. The respondents are not necessarily typical of the rest of the population of interest. A **population** is the group of people about whom an analyst wants to generalize. Usually, that population includes adults in a nation, state, or some other political jurisdiction. If someone is trying to understand or predict an election, however, the population consists of registered voters or, better, those most likely to vote in that election.

ONLINE 7.3
http://www.ncpp.org/?q=node/4

7-4a THE DANGERS OF UNSCIENTIFIC POLLING: THE LITERARY DIGEST POLL AND THE 1936 ELECTION

The people whose opinions or attitudes are measured in any given attempt comprise the **sample** of a particular population. Virtually any attempt at public opinion measurement involves some sort of sampling. Measurements of opinion in which no attempt is made to ensure that the sample is representative of the population as a whole are nonscientific. Although nonscientific sampling can provide some insights, the danger of making patently incorrect statements about the population is always present. Drawing incorrect conclusions about what a given population thinks can be risky—to a business looking to market new products, for example, or to a politician trying to get elected to public office.

Perhaps the most infamous example of the hazards of unscientific polling is the *Literary Digest* debacle of 1936. *Literary Digest* had been polling the American people by mail and using the results to correctly predict presidential elections since 1916. Essentially, the magazine used telephone directories and lists of automobile owners to construct its sample. This method automatically biased the sample against the working class and poor because, in those days, few people who were not at least middle class could afford telephones and cars. After selecting a sample, the *Digest* mailed out millions of ballots. In 1936, based on a sample of nearly 2.4 million potential voters, the *Digest* predicted that the Republican challenger, Alf Landon, would defeat the incumbent, President Franklin D. Roosevelt, by a margin of 57 percent to 43 percent in the popular vote. Of course, FDR won the election handily, receiving almost 63 percent of the vote. Why was the *Digest*'s prediction so wrong? First, despite its tremendous size, the sample was unrepresentative of the electorate. The response rate was a meager 22 percent, which exacerbated the problem of **nonresponse bias** (those who respond to a survey may hold different opinions from those who do not). Moreover, the survey was done in September, many weeks before the election. It had no way of detecting late shifts in voters' inclinations. The magnitude of the error in the *Literary Digest*'s prediction convinced uninformed observers of the futility of polls. To more sophisticated observers, it only demonstrated the necessity of scientific survey research.

7-4b THE SCIENTIFIC MEASUREMENT OF OPINION

One could say that George Gallup invented the modern polling industry. In 1935, Gallup founded the American Institute of Public Opinion at Princeton University. Although his background was in journalism and advertising, he had become interested in polling during the 1932 elections. He made a national reputation for himself by correctly predicting the outcome of the 1936 election. Even though his sample size was only a few thousand people, Gallup constructed a reasonably representative national sample by focusing on demographic traits, such as age, sex, region, and party affiliation. Over the years, Gallup refined his techniques, and the Gallup poll became a mainstay of American public opinion research. The Gallup poll continues under the direction of George Gallup, Jr., and is one of the most respected and influential survey research organizations.

Public opinion research has come a long way since its establishment by George Gallup, Elmo Roper, and a few others in the 1930s. Two major technological developments have been telecommunications and computers. Researchers can now gauge public opinion instantly using a computer. Electronic voice programs can read questions to the respondent over the phone, and when respondents press particular keys on their phones, the data can be automatically recorded. While it is easy to gather data this way, it has no value if it is incorrectly or improperly analyzed. Research is worthless unless someone pays careful attention to the methodological requirements of scientific polling.

SAMPLING

The first task in conducting a survey is choosing respondents. Those chosen to be questioned must be representative of the population about whom one wants to generalize. In virtually all cases involving the general population, interviewing every member of interest would be impossible or quite difficult. For instance, if a researcher wants to measure public opinion on an issue for Americans over the age of eighteen, she could hope to interview only a small proportion of that group.

The list of potential respondents from which respondents are chosen is the **sampling frame** for a particular survey. It could consist of listings of registered voters, students at a particular college, or published phone numbers. Often the survey researcher does not work from a true list, but rather from a list that theoretically exists. For example, in **random-digit dialing**, the last four digits in a phone number are randomly assigned to lists of telephone prefixes in a given area. This common practice allows a researcher to tap a broader sampling frame (the list of all phone numbers) than would be possible with listed numbers. A sampling frame should ensure that the sample that is eventually drawn will be representative of the population as a whole.

After a sampling frame is developed, the next step is creating a sampling plan. A **sampling plan** is the method of choosing a subset of the sampling frame that is representative of that frame. The best way to do that is by taking a **random sample**, or one in which every member of the sampling frame has an equal chance of being selected. An alternative is to take a **systematic sample**, or one in which every third, fourth, fifth, or whatever member of the sampling frame is selected. This method produces a good sample unless something is systematic about the sampling frame that makes every third, fourth, fifth, or whatever member different from others in the frame. In a case of this type, a random selection process is essential.

Controversy

The Use of Exit Polls to Call Elections

As we noted in the Introduction to this book, tremendous controversy arose over the use of exit polls in leading the television networks to make early calls on the 2000 presidential election. Based partially on findings gleaned from people interviewed as they left the voting place, the Voter News Service (VNS), an organization funded by a consortium of news networks, projected that Al Gore had won Florida. This projection later was withdrawn, causing great concern, partly because at the time of the call, residents in Florida's central time zone had not yet finished casting their ballots. In 2004, the exit polls suggested that John Kerry was going to defeat President Bush in a number of so-called battleground states. As the returns came in, it was obvious that the exit polls were wrong. Why that was the case was a major topic of conversation in the media in the days following the election.

Why do exit polls fall short as a technique? The principle of "every voter has an equal chance of being selected" is violated, to a degree, and the chance of error increases. Analysts choose representative precincts at which to administer surveys to those who leave. To the degree that the representative precincts are not representative, the outcomes might be likewise not representative. But each "error" is compounded because each nonrepresentative precinct brings about a number of respondents. In a traditional phone survey, respondents are selected singly. One nonrepresentative respondent is likely to balance another. Much less chance for error exists with precincts as the unit. Moreover, the selection of respondents at a polling place depends to some degree on the interviewer. Interviewers have less discretion and less opportunity to color responses in a phone survey.

Exit polls have two advantages. First, only voters are interviewed, as opposed to likely voters in a phone survey. Second, the surveys occur on Election Day and tap the timeliest information. They have one related and important disadvantage: They miss completely those people voting early, by absentee ballot, or by mail. The numbers in these excluded categories have been growing rapidly in the past ten years.

Question Writing

The wording of questions is, of course, crucial to a successful public opinion survey. In writing questions, analysts confront a fundamental challenge. They must construct a question that mirrors the phenomenon of interest, and they must provide the respondent with a set of alternative responses that mirror the range of opinions that exist in the population. The survey process must be as transparent as possible in translating attitudes into tabulated survey responses.

A good survey question measures only one attitude or opinion. Consider the question "Do you approve or disapprove of the way President Obama is handling the economy?" The response alternatives are balanced. **Balanced response sets** are desirable because they give no subtle cues that might lead the respondent. The question asks about one specific aspect of performance. This question would appear to be valid. An indicator has **validity** if it measures what it should measure. Another consideration is **reliability**. An indicator is reliable if it would produce the same response if it were asked again. You would have no reason to doubt the reliability of this question unless respondents really had no opinion, but felt obliged to provide one. For that reason, an interviewer should always make clear to the respondent that "Don't know" is an acceptable response.

Sometimes the wording of a poll undermines its validity. During the investigation into an affair between then-President Bill Clinton and intern Monica Lewinsky, the *St. Louis Post-Dispatch* conducted a poll asking respondents what the outcome of the investigation should be. The survey response set provided the following options: impeach the president, censure or fine him, Clinton should resign, leave the president alone, other, and don't know. When a plurality of voters said that Clinton should be left alone, the *Post-Dispatch* ran with the story under the headline "Most people don't want Clinton forced out of Presidency, poll shows." However, the multiple options for punishment naturally divided those who believed the president should have been held accountable for his actions. When one added up the impeachment, resignation, other, and censure/fine responses, more people wanted Clinton punished than not. But putting all responses on one side into one option but giving the other side multiple options, the poll was predetermined to produce the response reported.[12]

Problems in Question Writing and Interpretation

Although selecting respondents is the necessary first step in producing a valid survey, the construction of questions to ask members of the sample is equally important. Unclear questions yield uninterruptible results. Biased questions lead to biased results. Let us return to the presidential approval rating question discussed in section 7-1, "The Nature of Public Opinion." Consider this question: "Do you approve or disapprove of the way President Obama is handling taxation and jobs?" A respondent certainly might think that the president is doing a good job on one issue and a bad job on the other. This type of respondent might well say "Disapprove." But someone who disapproves of the president's performance on both issues would give the same answer. The analyst would be unable to reconstruct the original attitudes from the responses that are given. The overall figures in this type of case would provide artificially low evaluations. Asking about two phenomena in one question is using a **double-barreled question**. This type of question is certainly not valid, nor is it likely to be reliable.

The cardinal rule of question writing is a simple one: *Measure what you purport to measure*. The responses to a question should indicate what people really think, not something about the question itself. Consider the question "Do you favor increasing taxes so that the homeless could be provided with a place to stay?" Opposing an increase in taxes when the issue is framed in this way would be hard. A great many respondents would feel that they *should* answer in the affirmative. A question framed or phrased so that it seems to imply that a particular answer is preferred suffers from **social desirability bias**. A question is biased if it produces a response that is not a true indicator of the underlying opinion, attitude, belief, or value that it seeks to measure. In this example, an analyst using this type of question might report that the American people are more willing to pay taxes for programs for the homeless than they really are.

The most obvious example of social desirability bias is that of the intention to vote. When asked, almost all respondents say that they intend to vote in almost any election. At most, however, only about half the adult population casts ballots. People feel that they should vote and may intend to vote. These feelings and intentions are so bound up in the "ought to" of voting that responses to that question are useless in predicting a true vote. Asking for whom a person intends to vote does not present this problem. There is no socially desirable response that the respondent would feel compelled to provide to a neutral interviewer.

Another type of bias is subtler but just as likely to lead to false inferences. Responses to a question can be affected by its placement in the survey. Responses to any question can be biased by those questions asked previously, in a process called **priming**. That is why a survey about the presidential election usually begins with the key question of vote intention. If the vote intention question is asked after a series of questions on presidential job performance, respondents might be primed to match their vote intention to the candidate they had indicated was superior at the tasks presented in the survey. Respondents do not like to appear to give contradictory or irrational answers to questions. But a survey is an artificial process that may not replicate the respondent's own thought processes. She might decide to vote on the basis of other criteria than are measured in a survey.

7-5 PUBLIC OPINION AND PUBLIC POLICY

Clearly, public opinion is of fundamental importance in a democratic polity. Unless public policy bears some, albeit indirect, relationship to public opinion, a political system can hardly be called democratic. This statement does not mean, however, that public opinion determines public policy directly. In every democracy, policy is made by leaders who respond to and shape public opinion.

7-5a MODELS OF PUBLIC OPINION IN THE POLICY PROCESS

Consider the two alternative models of the policy-making process (see Figure 7-3). In Model A, which you might call the *traditional democratic theory model*, public opinion prompts policy makers to adopt policies to which, in turn, the public reacts. Although some might consider this model to be a good *prescription*, it is hardly a good *description* of how public policy is made in the United States—or in any of the world's democracies, for that matter. Model B is much more realistic. In this model, which you might call the *elite-pluralist model*, the policy process is initiated by activists, which are usually interest groups. These "policy initiators" get issues on the public agenda and help to frame the discussion of these issues. The activities of the initiators have direct influence on policy makers as well as on public opinion. Public opinion has a direct effect on policy makers. The policies that emerge from the process have a feedback effect on all the other elements of the model. Even though public opinion is not the prime mover, as it is depicted in Model A, it is still a crucial element of the process. Without public approval, policy decisions are not made or, if they are, do not survive over the long run.

7-5b MEANS OF COMMUNICATING PUBLIC OPINION TO POLICY MAKERS

Policy makers learn of public opinion in a number of ways. Most pay close attention to the results of public opinion polls now routinely reported in the mass media. But they also heed phone calls and letters they receive from citizens directly. Policy makers tend to assume, with some justification, that those who take the time and trouble to contact them directly feel more intensely about an issue than most people who

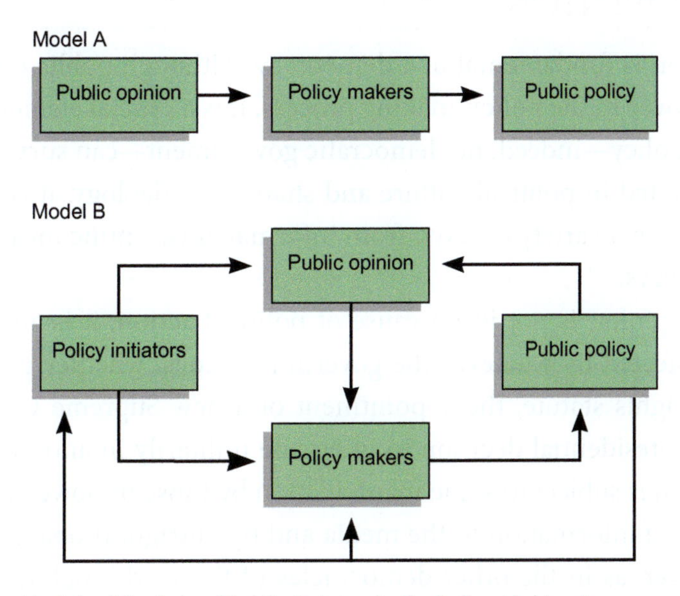

Figure 7-3 *Alternative Models of the Role of Public Opinion in the Policy-Making Process*

respond to a public opinion poll. Of course, that is why interest groups often mount phone-call and letter-writing campaigns. That is also why presidents in recent years have asked citizens who support their initiatives to contact their representatives in Congress. Presidents understand that members of Congress have staffs who tally the phone calls, cards, and letters their bosses receive.

7-5c TELEVISION AND RADIO TALK SHOWS

In the 1980s, a new programming format took hold in the American media: the call-in show. Millions of Americans watch *Larry King Live* on CNN or listen to Rush Limbaugh's syndicated radio show. These and other similar shows allow viewers or listeners, as the case may be, to call in and register their opinions. Often, the callers get into an argument with the host of the program or a guest. The format makes for lively television or radio. In the 1990s, these types of shows, especially talk radio, became a sort of ongoing national town meeting in which issues are discussed. Politicians have learned to pay attention to these programs as sources of information on the public mood. Though certainly not scientific measures of public opinion, these programs do provide politicians and other elites with an opportunity to learn what average people are thinking about politics. They also provide a channel of communication from the average person to the political elites. (This theme is explored further in Chapter 8, "Popular Participation in Politics.")

7-6 CONCLUSION: THE DIMENSIONS OF PUBLIC OPINION

Public opinion is fundamental in a democracy. Although public opinion may not be the prime mover in the policy-making process, it is a crucial element. Without public support, no policy—indeed, no democratic government—can survive for long. Public opinion is rooted in political culture and shaped by ideology. It is communicated to policy makers in a variety of ways, from informal, unscientific means to sophisticated scientific surveys.

Public opinion is not just a cause of political action; it is also an effect. Public opinion is affected by whatever the government does, whether it is the adoption of a new civil rights statute, the appointment of a new Supreme Court justice, or the making of a presidential decision to intervene militarily in another country. Indeed, public opinion is subject to some manipulation by those in power, through the strategic "leaking" of information to the media and by outright propaganda. In the United States, however, as in the other democracies of the world, public opinion has more influence over leaders than leaders have over public opinion.

Questions for Thought and Discussion

1. In general, do you think that people in government pay too much or too little attention to public opinion?

2. Does a preoccupation with public opinion mean that a government official or political candidate will ignore the interests and views of minorities?

3. In covering polls, do the mass media reflect or create public opinion?

4. How do politicians try to manipulate public opinion?

5. Is the study of public opinion an art, a science, or both? Why?

ENDNOTES

1 http://www.harrisinteractive.com/harris_poll/index.asp?PID=438

2 For an excellent survey of contemporary political science literature dealing with political attitudes and opinions, see Barbara Norrander and Clyde Wilcox, *Understanding Public Opinion*, 2nd ed. (Washington, D.C.: CQ Press, 2001).

3 William Lyons and John M. Scheb II, "Ideology and Candidate Evaluation in the 1984 and 1988 Presidential Elections," *Journal of Politics*, vol. 54, May 1992, pp. 573–84.

4 See, for example, Philip E. Converse, "The Nature of Belief Systems in the Mass Public." In *Ideology and Discontent*, ed. David Apter (New York: Free Press, 1964).

5 *Lawrence v. Texas*, 539 U.S. 558 (2003).

6 Gabriel Almond and Sidney Verba, *The Civic Culture* (Princeton: Princeton University Press, 1963).

7 Robert Lane, *Political Ideology* (New York: Free Press, 1962).

8 Seymour Martin Lipset, *Political Man* (Garden City, NY: Doubleday, 1963), p. 114.

9 Dye and Zeigler, *The Irony of Democracy*, p. 152.

10 Leon Festinger, *A Theory of Cognitive Dissonance* (Stanford, CA: Stanford University Press, 1957).

11 A survey of 1,211 African American adults conducted by Gordon S. Black Co., November 11–25, 1992, found that black churches were tied with the NAACP for first place in a ranking of groups effectively representing the interests of African Americans. Results reported in *USA Today*, February 19, 1993, p. 6A.

12 "Most people don't want Clinton forced out of presidency, poll shows," *The St. Louis Post-Dispatch*, October 18 1998.

Chapter 8

Popular Participation in Politics

OUTLINE

Key Terms 274

Expected Learning Outcomes 274

8-1 Mass Participation in a Democracy 274

- **8-1a** Are People Political by Nature? 275

8-2 Levels of Individual Participation 275

- **8-2a** Political Apathy 276
- **8-2b** Spectator Activities 276
- **8-2c** Political Activism 277
- **8-2d** Deciding How Much to Participate 278

8-3 Participation through Voting 279

- **8-3a** Trends in Voting Turnout 280
- **8-3b** Who Votes? 283
- **8-3c** The Individual Decision to Vote 284
- **8-3d** Explanations for Nonvoting 285
- **8-3e** Reforming the System 285
- **8-3f** Evaluating Nonvoting 286

8-4 Extraordinary Forms of Political Participation 287

- **8-4a** Demonstrations, Marches, and Mass Protests 287
- **8-4b** Riots 287
- **8-4c** Strikes and Boycotts 288
- **8-4d** The Question of Civil Disobedience 290
- **8-4e** Martin Luther King, Jr., and Civil Disobedience 291

8-5 Social Movements 292

- **8-5a** Abolitionism 293
- **8-5b** Agrarian Populism 293
- **8-5c** The Labor Movement 294
- **8-5d** The Civil Rights Movement 295
- **8-5e** The Antiwar Movement 296
- **8-5f** The Women's Movement 297
- **8-5g** The Gay Rights Movement 297

8-5h The Christian Right 300
8-5i The Pro-Life Movement 301
8-5j The Antiglobalism Movement 302
8-6 Conclusion: Participation and Political Culture 302
Questions for Thought and Discussion 304
Endnotes 305

KEY TERMS

active and attentive class
boycott
charismatic leader
civil disobedience
general strike
modern pluralist theory
political activists
political apathy
political resources
social movement
spectator activities
strike
traditional democratic theory
turnout
voting registration

EXPECTED LEARNING OUTCOMES

After reading this chapter and completing the supplemental online materials, students will:

- Understand the role of participation in a democracy
- Theorize about human tendencies toward participation
- Describe trends in U.S. voter turnout
- Identify nonvoting forms of participation
- Trace the relationship between social movements and political participation

8-1 Mass Participation in a Democracy

Time magazine went so far as to call it "The Year of the Youth Vote."[1] The 2008 election featured a significant increase in the number of young people casting a vote, to almost half of people aged 18 to 24 casting a ballot.[2] Every four years, a presidential election occurs that inspires the most people to go to the polls. But every day there are opportunities to participate in a democratic society. We may not take advantage of them, but at least occasionally it is vital to involve ourselves in politics.

In a democracy, citizens are expected to engage in their nation's civic life, although democratic theorists differ about the degree to which the mass public should be expected to get involved. The classical Greek ideal suggests that citizens participate voluntarily and with the expectation that their involvement will have some effect on what government does. Democratic institutions demand some minimal level of participation if they are to survive. Nevertheless, some upper limit seems to exist on the amount of participation that democratic institutions can process. Even assuming that this type of limit exists, though, it clearly has not been reached in the United States. Suffice it to say that a representative democracy—dependent on the orderly functioning of parties and interest groups and the actions of Congress, the presidency, and the courts—must inspire a healthy but manageable degree of popular participation beyond the exercise of the ballot.

Of course, any democratic system must channel participation through legitimate structures. In the United States, writing letters to public officials, contributing money to causes and campaigns, and assembling to conduct peaceful protests are all legitimate expressions of political preferences. Rioting, harassing one's opponents, and bribing public officials are also forms of political participation in that they serve to communicate preferences to those in politics, but these activities are outside the law and are almost universally regarded as illegitimate forms of political action. To the degree that people feel they must use illegitimate forms of participation to get their point across, democratic systems face serious crises.

8-1a Are People Political by Nature?

The ancient Greek philosopher Aristotle described man as a "political animal." For Aristotle, participation in politics was essential to make people fully human. The political scientist Robert Dahl, however, argues that citizens are not by nature political animals. Rather, Dahl maintains that citizens tend not to participate in politics to any extent until issues directly touch their lives.[3] Whether people are "political" by nature is of key importance to any discussion of political participation because much of the criticism of low levels of participation in the United States has at its core the belief that the system can be changed to bring about greater involvement. If people are naturally disinclined to participate, any such changes are doomed to failure.

Even if governmental politics are not involved, politics is in everything. As "reality" television has come to dominate the airwaves, we see how people behave in political ways. The show *Survivor*, with its shifting alliances and attempts by contestants to manipulate each other to achieve their goals, is a perfect example of how people act politically regardless of their goals. Politics is, after all, a way for people to participate in a process that will produce an outcome. If you do not participate, you have no say in the outcome.

8-2 Levels of Individual Participation

The fundamental form of participation in any democracy is voting. For many people, voting is the only form of participation. At the least, most people in a democracy should vote in most elections. The vote is the "official" input to the system, the device by which those who staff government are chosen. Political participation involves much more than voting, however. The political scientist Lester Milbrath has described political participation as a hierarchy ranging from

Maximum Participation
(Highest resource demands)

Holding public office
Becoming a candidate for office
Raising money for a candidate or cause
Attending a caucus or strategy meeting
Becoming an active member of a political party or interest group
Contributing time to a political campaign
Attending a political meeting
Contributing money to a party, candidate, or PAC
Contacting a public official
Wearing a button or putting a sticker on a car
Calling a talk radio discussion show
Attempting to convince another to vote a certain way
Voting
Initiating a political discussion
Listening to political dialogue
Ignoring all political messages

Nonparticipation
(Lowest resource demands)

Figure 8-1 *The Continuum of Political Participation*

the noninvolvement of the apathetics, or those who do not participate, to gladiatorial activities, such as running for office and working in campaigns (see Figure 8-1).[4]

8-2a Political Apathy

Approximately 25 percent of the American electorate could be classified as apathetic.[5] These individuals essentially remove themselves from possible participation by failing to register to vote or registering but rarely, if ever, casting a ballot. **Political apathy** can stem from many causes. First, apathetics could be pleased with the status quo, and their lack of political involvement could reflect their satisfaction. Robert Kaplan has written that "apathy, after all, means that the political situation is healthy enough to be ignored."[6] But because most people in this category have lower levels of income and education, this explanation would seem to be insufficient. More likely, the vast majority of people in this category are alienated or lacking in political efficacy, or both (see Chapter 7, "Public Opinion in American Politics").

The apathetics have long been of interest to political candidates. If apathetics were to mobilize, they would be a powerful force in today's evenly split environment. Ten percent of the public is a rough estimation of the apathetic, and that ten percent could have changed the results of every election between 1992 and 2004. Many candidates have made explicit appeals to those outside the mainstream of American politics, hoping to persuade them to participate. In 1972, George McGovern, the Democratic presidential nominee, made a series of appeals to those who had traditionally felt left out of American politics. His strategy failed, however, for one simple reason: apathetics do not follow politics, and they have low levels of trust and efficacy. Therefore, any message targeted to apathetics is not likely to be heard or, if heard, not likely to be believed.

ONLINE 8.1
http://www.people-press.org/2012/09/28/youth-engagement-falls-registration-also-declines/

8-2b Spectator Activities

With few exceptions, a person who decides to play an active role in politics begins by voting. Voting is the fundamental act that separates those who are involved in politics from the apathetics, who are not. Thus, voting serves as the common denominator for all those who are active in the political community. It also serves as the base of the hierarchy of political participation. With voting at the base of the hierarchy are other activities that Milbrath has called **spectator activities.**[7] (Although voting might not seem to be a spectator activity, it is certainly less active than running for office or working for a political campaign.) Like voting, the other activities at the base of the hierarchy are simple—they demand a minimum of effort, time, and political resources. Talking to other people about politics, wearing a campaign button, and putting a bumper sticker on a car are other examples of spectator activities. Note that none of these activities by themselves can have much effect on a political contest, but in the aggregate their effect can be significant.

Moving up the hierarchy of political participation, the number of people participating in each category declines. At the same time, however, a person who engages in an action partway up the hierarchy is likely to participate also in the lower activities. In other words, a person who votes may not participate in any other, more demanding activities. However, a person who writes to a member of Congress is quite likely to have participated in less demanding activities, such as voting and discussing politics with others.

8-2c POLITICAL ACTIVISM

Other political activities demand much more effort than do spectator activities. Attending meetings or working for a campaign requires a considerable investment of time in the political process. Some people are **political activists** and participate in depth in the political arena by contributing large amounts of time and money either to a single cause or across a variety of causes. To the degree that these persons possess political resources, they can begin to have an effect on outcomes in a policy area. These persons become part of the attentive public for that issue. Others become involved across a number of issue areas. They may become associated with a political party and may even decide to seek public office.

Relatively few Americans decide to participate in politics at high levels. Perhaps only one in fifteen could be classified as "active and attentive" (see Figure 8-2).[8]

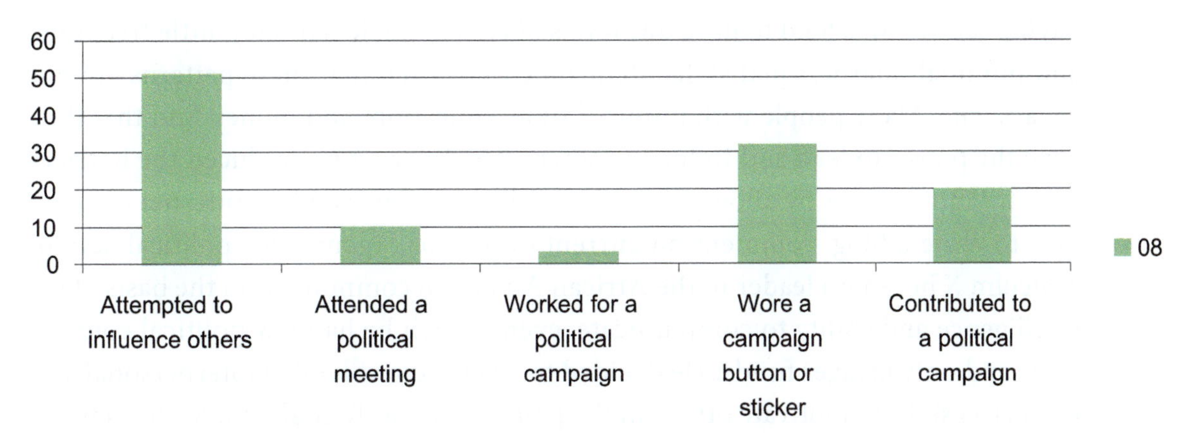

Figure 8-2 *Levels of Political Participation in 2008*
Source: Adapted from Center for Political Studies, University of Michigan, National Election Study 2008.

Thus, any given American has only about a 7 percent probability of being a member of the **active and attentive class**. From the perspective of the individual, that percentage may seem like relatively few (and it is), but in numbers, 7 percent of the American public means more than twenty million people. These 7 percent are active in political parties, provide leadership in civic organizations, join interest groups, and attend public meetings. During the 2008 presidential election campaign, almost a third of the American public put a political bumper sticker on their car or wore a campaign button. Just over 10 percent made a political campaign contribution. Ten percent attended a political meeting, and less than 5 percent actively worked in a campaign. The numbers for 2008 represent a hopeful trend in American politics, as the numbers of people participating has increased for two consecutive elections.

8-2d Deciding How Much to Participate

Deciding how much to participate in the political process is a complex decision. In making it, people consider not only the amount and type of political resources they possess but also the perceived costs and benefits of participation. This decision is not necessarily conscious. In fact, it may be more of a "nondecision" arrived at by default. That is, when individuals glance past a report of candidates' stands on complex political issues while skimming local newspapers, they may, in effect, make a decision not to follow that election and not to care about the eventual winner. They are then much less likely to vote.

Political resources are the means of exercising influence that an individual or group can bring to bear in the political arena. In general, individuals' main political resources are much the same as their personal resources: money, time, communication skills, and personal connections. Of course, these resources tend to be cumulative; that is, people with one resource usually have others. Individuals holding important positions in society usually are highly educated and have many personal connections in addition to high incomes. On the other hand, those holding low-paying service jobs tend to have low levels of education, less money, little free time, and minimal interpersonal skills. Remember, however, that these patterns are not always true. Many people with minimal time, education, and money find that they have the power to lead and influence others. The Internet has reduced the barriers to entry into politics by allowing anyone with a computer and an Internet connection to write a blog, comment on current events, or organize for political action. Malcolm X became a leader in the African American community on the basis of his intelligence and ability to communicate, even though he had few political connections and only meager funds. He decided to use his considerable interpersonal and rhetorical skills to motivate others in the political arena. To Malcolm X, the benefits of participation were obvious. He saw participation as essential to changing the conditions African Americans faced in the United States. Likewise, his decision to enter politics had obvious costs: politics dominated and eventually cost him his life.

Of course, most people do not have the charisma or communications skills of Malcolm X. Most people do behave rationally, however; that is, they decide to use their resources in the political arena if the benefits of doing so exceed the costs. The benefits of participation are many and varied. The most obvious benefit is that of fulfilling one's perceived citizen duty. Americans are socialized to vote, at the very least, and to take an active part in community affairs. Other benefits include the sense of helping to further a cause. A person who believes strongly that the natural environment is endangered may enjoy considerable personal benefits from contributing time and money to an interest group such as the Sierra Club or working to elect a candidate who strongly supports environmental causes. In addition, other, more tangible benefits can be obtained. Many people participate because they think that they will fare better economically if their preferred party or candidate wins or if a certain policy is implemented. A wealthy industrialist may spend a lot of her resources in a presidential election because of the perception that her industry would fare better under one administration than another.

Every political act involves some costs. Although voting would seem to be a fairly low-cost activity, a voter must make the decision to register and invest time in following the issues or candidates in an election. Other activities cost considerably more in both time and money. Attending a meeting or playing a major part in a campaign takes considerable time and, in the latter case, requires a great deal of money. Many people who participated in Ross Perot's 1992 presidential campaign made significant commitments of time and money because they believed that they were part of a major movement to change the face of American politics.

8-3 Participation through Voting

Voting is the means by which political preferences are formally expressed in a democracy. Indeed, voting is, at least potentially, the most democratic of all forms of participation. For this to be the case, two essential conditions must be met. First, there must be universal suffrage; that is, all citizens must have the right to vote. Second, all votes must count equally. In *Gray v. Sanders* (1963), the Supreme Court observed, "The conception of political equality from the Declaration of Independence, to Lincoln's Gettysburg Address, to the Fifteenth, Seventeenth, and Nineteenth Amendments can mean only one thing—one person, one vote."[9] Writing for the Court in *Reynolds v. Sims* (1964), Chief Justice Earl Warren elaborated on this theme:

> *The right to vote freely for the candidate of one's choice is of the essence of a democratic society, and any restrictions on that right strike at the heart of*

representative government. And the right of suffrage can be denied by a debasement or dilution of the weight of a citizen's vote just as effectively as by wholly prohibiting the free exercise of the franchise.[10]

In addition to being a means of expressing one's preferences, the act of voting seems to have intrinsic value for the voter. It increases one's sense of efficacy, encourages volunteerism, and strengthens citizenship.[11] Yet despite the essential character of voting in a democracy, and despite the intrinsic value of voting, many Americans choose not to vote. Certainly, Americans have a right not to vote if that is their preference. In the United States, the right to vote implies the right *not* to vote, and few commentators have suggested that voting should be compulsory.[12] Although few would insist that everybody should be required to vote, there is a growing sense that political participation through voting is lower than it ought to be in the United States.

8-3a Trends in Voting Turnout

Voter **turnout** can be defined as the number of people voting expressed as either a percentage of those registered to vote or a percentage of the voting-age population (VAP). Turnout has always been low in the United States compared to the other democracies of the world (see "Comparative Perspective"). Turnout peaked in 1960, when almost 63.1 percent of eligible Americans voted in the Nixon–Kennedy presidential election (see Box 8-1). Several factors contributed to this increase. Registration became somewhat easier over the first half of the twentieth century, and as more and more Americans completed high school, more had the background to understand the issues and follow campaigns. Finally, the trend toward a more urban society with an increasingly participatory culture and better communications also played a part. Nevertheless, the way elections are conducted and the necessity of formal registration kept voter turnout lower than in most other democracies.

Between 1960 and 1996, turnout for presidential elections declined by about 11 percentage points, from 65 percent to 54 percent. Had it not been for an increase in voting in the South, the decline would have been even greater.[13] Most of the change in the southern states was in response to the passage of the Voting Rights Act of 1965 and the tremendous increase in African American registration and voting that ensued. By the end of the 1960s, virtually all the structural impediments to registration and voting had been removed. Ruy Teixeira lists eight major changes in the registration system that occurred between 1960 and 1988:

1. The abolition of the poll tax
2. The abolition of literacy tests
3. Formal prohibitions against discrimination in registering voters
4. The increased availability of bilingual registration materials
5. The increased number of states allowing registration by mail
6. A decline in residency requirements
7. The moving of registration deadlines closer to elections

The implementation of national standards for absentee registration

The removal of structural impediments, such as the outlawing of the poll tax and the easing of residency requirements, made voting much easier in the United States. Nevertheless, between 1972 and 1988, a steady decline in voter turnout occurred. In 1972, turnout was at 55.2 percent of VAP; by 1988 it had declined to 50.1 percent.

In the 1992 presidential election, turnout spiked dramatically to 55.1 percent of VAP. In fact, the percentage of Americans voting in the 1992 election was greater than in any presidential election since 1972. Because no structural changes occurred between 1988 and 1992, this significant increase in turnout must reflect unique characteristics of the 1992 election. An obvious factor that made 1992 different was the independent candidacy of Texas billionaire H. Ross Perot. Perot's candidacy greatly increased interest in the election. For one thing, he offered an alternative to the two traditional parties. Second, his well-funded campaign, which drew heavily on his immense personal wealth, brought more people into the process. Finally, Perot's entry into the race made the outcome less predictable than it would have been otherwise.

In 1996, turnout fell to 49.1 percent, the first time that voter turnout shrunk below half of the voting age population since universal suffrage was adopted. In 2000, there was an increase, with turnout at 51.3 percent of VAP. In 2004, a high-stimulus campaign produced a significant spike in turnout—55.3 percent of voting-age Americans cast ballots in the race between George W. Bush and John Kerry.[14] Both Democrats and Republicans worked hard to get their voters to the polls. However, the most interesting phenomenon in that election was the degree to which evangelical Christians turned out, not only to vote for President Bush, but also to support initiatives in eleven states to ban same-sex marriage. The 2008 campaign produced a further increase in voter turnout over 2004, again largely due to mobilization efforts.[15] Democratic nominee Barack Obama used online tools to collect, train, and mobilize supporters across the country, especially among younger people. The result was a 56.8 percent VAP turnout, the third consecutive election with a voting increase. The 2012 election saw a more than 3 percent decline, down to 53.8 percent of all voting age citizens.[16]

Comparative Perspective

Levels of Voting Turnout in Presidential Elections around the World, 2012

Voter turnout in the United States is among the lowest in the developed democracies, regardless of how turnout is defined. In the 2012 presidential election, only 55 percent of voting-age Americans turned out to vote. Here are the comparable turnout rates in other countries for presidential elections held in the United States, Germany, Britain, India, and Japan during the last fifty years. What factors explain why countries vary so much in participation in elections?

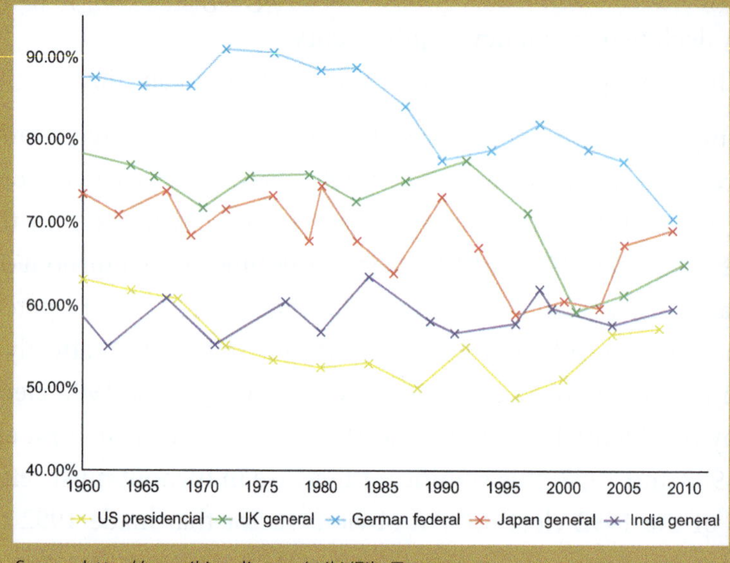

Source: http://en.wikipedia.org/wiki/File:Turnout.png

Box 8-1 *Turnout for Presidential Voting in the United States, 1960–2008*

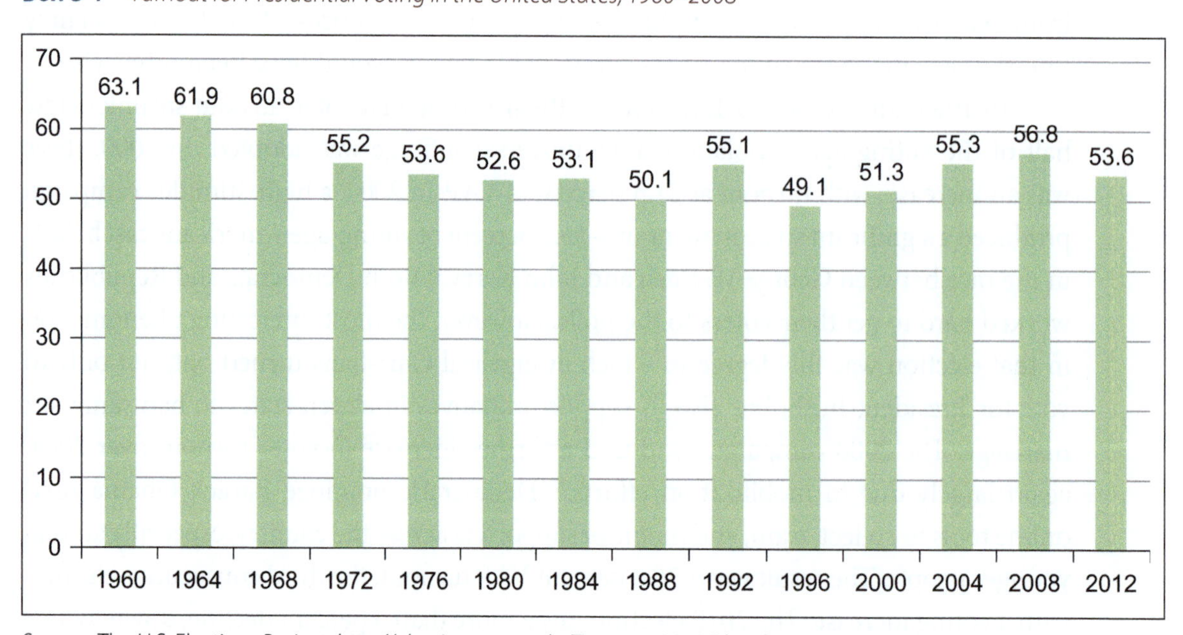

Sources: The U.S. Elections Project. http://elections.gmu.edu/Turnout_2012G.html

8-3b WHO VOTES?

Voting turnout varies somewhat by social group. For example, people with more education tend to vote more frequently than people with less education. The same is true of income: higher income is positively associated with higher turnout. Young people (those in the 18–24 age bracket) are the least likely to vote of any age category. People in the 45–70 age bracket tend to vote the most.

In the 2000 election, roughly 38 percent of voters in the 18–29 age bracket turned out to vote. Because research suggested that younger voters would be more likely to support a Democratic alternative to President Bush, Democrats made tremendous efforts to mobilize younger voters in subsequent elections. The Obama campaign made extensive efforts to reach out to younger voters using social media and mobile applications in 2008 and 2012, and turnout rose to nearly 50 percent in each of those elections among 18–29 year olds.[17]

Historically, women and minority groups voted in much lower proportions than white males. To a great extent, this disparity occurred because at one time women and minorities were not eligible to vote. Even after these groups were enfranchised, closing the gap took some time. No significant gap now exists between women and men—if anything, women are slightly more likely to vote than men. Something of a gap still exists between whites and nonwhites, but it is narrowing. The difference between whites and nonwhites is mainly attributable to differences in income and education. For example, middle-class blacks are just as likely to vote as middle-class whites. Partisanship also has an effect on turnout. People who strongly identify with a political party tend to vote more than Independents or weak partisans. Of the two major parties, Republicans tend to vote at higher levels than Democrats. These, of course, are only group tendencies. Individuals have to decide for themselves whether to vote.

By far the greatest barrier to vote is the requirement of **voter registration**. All citizens who want to cast a ballot in an election must register in advance of the election. Registration is the most significant reason most people do not cast ballots in a given election. In fact, when one only considers those who have registered to vote, turnout increases from the voting age population numbers we present here. In 2012, for instance, 58.2 percent of all eligible voters turned out compared with 53.6 percent of voting-age citizens. As a result, many states have experimented with same-day voter registration. But recently many states have gone the other way, putting more requirements in place that make it more difficult for new aspiring voters to register.

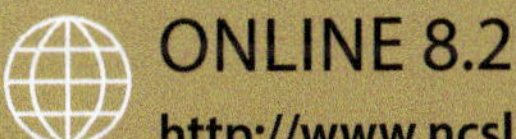

http://www.ncsl.org/legislatures-elections/elections/voter-id.aspx/

8-3c The Individual Decision to Vote

The decision of whether to vote is a two-phase process. The first choice is whether to register. The second choice, open to those who have registered, is whether to go to the polls on election day and cast a ballot. Most states have made it much easier to register over the years. Much of this situation can be attributed to the Voting Rights Act of 1965, which made many restrictive practices illegal. Moreover, an unmistakable change in American political culture has occurred away from the perspective that only informed, supposedly "responsible citizens" should be allowed the privilege of voting to the perspective that all Americans have a right and responsibility to vote, regardless of their political knowledge or level of civic responsibility. Nevertheless, researchers estimate that even through the 1980s, the mere existence of registration laws depressed actual voting turnout by 14 percent.[18]

Current registration laws may not present much of a barrier to those who do intend to vote. Nevertheless, more than one in four Americans just do not register. Most states require some sort of waiting period, typically thirty days or so, although four states permit registration on election day. Many states now permit postcard registration or registration at locations other than the election commission or the courthouse. In addition, many groups, particularly African Americans, have worked quite hard to assist in registering voters, including many who would not have been likely to do so on their own.

In the 1990s and early 2000s, states experimented with mail-in ballots and early voting in an effort to make voting easier and thus increase participation. To date, these efforts have met with only limited success. For a variety of reasons that we discuss in section 8-3d, "Explanations for Nonvoting," many Americans simply do not want to be bothered by the simple act of voting. Recently, thirteen states have trended towards limiting access to registration and voting, claiming the need to reduce voter fraud, especially among illegal immigrants. Kansas Secretary of State Kris Kobach wrote laws in his state as well as five others requiring proof of citizenship to register as well as photo identification requirements at the polling place.[19]

Reasons for Failing to Register

Why do so many people choose not to register? Registration takes some forethought. No matter how simple the act may have become, it still involves a commitment of time and attention, even if only briefly. And many people believe that the cost of expending that amount of personal resources is still not worth the benefits they would derive from voting. Of course, few people make these cost/benefit calculations explicitly. Rather, whatever information they have received and digested about the political system, especially an upcoming contest, has not convinced them to go to the trouble of registering. Their reasons probably are related to their low sense of efficacy and civic duty. The political socialization process simply did not work for these people. The combination of family, school, and peer group influences failed to instill a feeling that voting is something a person "ought to do." Other people may not register because they distrust the whole political system or may lack the skills and interest needed to consume the information necessary to follow the political process.

8-3d Explanations for Nonvoting

As noted in section 8-3b, "Who Votes?" education is a major predictor of turnout. A person with a college degree is almost twice as likely to vote as a person without a high school diploma. We would expect, then, that as Americans generally become more educated, voting turnout would increase. In 1960, only about half of all adult Americans had graduated from high school, and fewer than one in ten had graduated from college. By 1988, more than three in four had graduated from high school, and two in ten had earned a college degree. Yet turnout has declined since 1960. Coupled with the increased ease in registration and the enfranchisement of the African American electorate in the South, the observed decrease is even more dramatic. Clearly, an explanation is required.

As we discussed in Chapter 6, "Public Opinion in American Politics," Americans have become more cynical and alienated since the 1960s. The United States has seen a decline in levels of political trust and efficacy. People do not trust government as much as they used to, nor do they feel that their participation can make a real difference. People today are less likely to feel that they are members of a political community. The breakdown of community is related to many things, including the decline of cities, the increase in social mobility, the breakdown of the traditional family, reduced membership in labor unions, and the decline of organized religion. Society has become, to a great extent, a collection of disconnected individuals who lack interest in public affairs and do not feel a duty to participate in them.[20] For evidence that this affects voting behavior, one has only to consider the fact that individuals who have strong organizational affiliations, whether with churches, labor unions, civic groups, or political parties, are much more likely to participate in elections than those who do not have such ties.

8-3e Reforming the System

In 1993, Congress passed the Motor Voter Act, which requires states to register voters when they renew their driver's licenses. Because 90 percent of adults have licenses to operate motor vehicles, Congress anticipated that many more Americans would register to vote. The expectation was that turnout would increase by about 5 percent.[21] President George Bush had vetoed an earlier version, but during the 1992 campaign, Bill Clinton said that passage of the bill would be a high priority. The act that was finally adopted represented a compromise of sorts. Republicans fought to remove sections that would have also allowed registration at welfare offices. The Republicans felt that the legislation was an attempt to increase participation among those who were most likely to vote for Democrats. The actual long-term effects of the Motor Voter Act, if any, remain to be seen. However, Democratic hopes (and Republican fears) that the act would result in a massive influx of new Democratic voters into the electorate have not been realized.

In the incredibly close 2000 presidential election, many who thought that they had registered to vote through the program were indeed not registered because of breakdowns in communications among registrants, departments of motor vehicles, and county election commissions. This confusion was a by-product of the (until recently) widely unrecognized decentralized electoral system in the United States. Much of the decisions involving the mechanics of voting take place at the county level, by county officials working within the constraints of county budgets. Until 2000 the fact that one jurisdiction might have opted for touch-screen voting machines while others had punch cards did not seem to have any consequence for the outcome of elections. The 2000 election brought intense public and media scrutiny to an area of governmental administration that had long been ignored.

8-3f EVALUATING NONVOTING

Some would argue that a society in which a majority of citizens opt out of the political process is not a genuine democracy. Others worry about the stability of a political system characterized by widespread nonvoting. Seymour Martin Lipset, a well-known political sociologist, has argued that a society in which most citizens do not vote "is potentially more explosive than one in which most citizens are regularly involved in activities which give them some sense of participation in decisions which affect their lives."[22] Thomas Patterson, a distinguished political scientist, is among those who worry about the long-term impact of widespread nonparticipation on the system. Patterson questions whether self-government can be maintained when most citizens do not vote. In his view, "No stone should be left unturned in the effort to bring Americans back to the polls."[23]

Since younger citizens are the least likely to turn out, since 2003 the American Association of State Colleges and Universities has sponsored the American Democracy Project, a four-hundred-plus campus effort to build civic skills and knowledge among college students to prepare them for active citizenship. Through service learning, voter registration and mobilization events, social media, and campus events, ADP schools have been an integral part of reducing the nonvoting tendencies of college students nationwide.

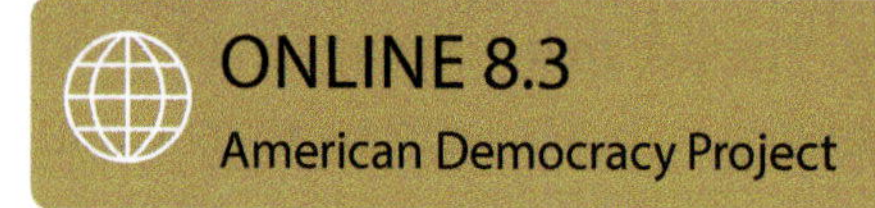

8-4 Extraordinary Forms of Political Participation

Traditional democratic theory considers voting, political party affiliation, working in campaigns, and even running for public office to be the proper means of political participation in a democracy. **Modern pluralist theory** stresses interest group affiliation and activity. But numerous other activities can also be classified as political participation. Some may be regarded as unconventional, and others may be considered altogether illegitimate.

8-4a Demonstrations, Marches, and Mass Protests

Demonstrations, marches, and protests have become more or less conventional elements of American politics, in large part because of their role in the civil rights and antiwar movements of the 1960s. Although some people find these activities objectionable, most realize that they are protected by the First Amendment guarantees of free expression and free assembly.

Groups that perceive themselves as "outsiders" in the political system typically use demonstrations, marches, protests, and other extraordinary forms of political action. Quite often, demonstrations are a means of not only making a point about a public policy issue but also gaining public recognition for a group that has been ignored. An extraordinary event like a march or protest is likely to capture the attention of the mass media, especially television, and thereby have some effect on public opinion. In the 1950s and 1960s, for example, the civil rights movement successfully used extraordinary activities—marches, demonstrations, and protests—to raise white Americans' consciousness of the injustices of racism and discrimination.

8-4b Riots

Sometimes, demonstrations, marches, and protests arise spontaneously in response to some decision or event. When no planning or leadership occurs, however, these activities carry a considerable risk of erupting into violence such as rioting and looting. The World Trade Organization Ministerial Conference in Seattle of 1999 is an example. More than 40,000 people showed up to protest globalization, willing to block and prevent the WTO meetings if necessary. Activists blocked traffic, keeping the delegates from arriving at the conference. Police tried to push the protestors away, and when they refused, responded by firing tear gas, pepper spray, and rubber bullets into the crowds. Protesters reacted violently, demolishing storefronts, setting dumpsters on fire and pushing them into busy intersections, slashing the tires of police cars, and causing general havoc in the city. More than 600 people were arrested, and the damage caused was estimated at $20 million. Few would argue that riots are a legitimate form of political expression. Yet citizens must recognize that they are a powerful means of influencing public opinion and, ultimately, the government. Certainly, the race riots of the 1960s drew national attention to the conditions of the nation's inner cities and led to the enactment of public policies to alleviate those conditions.

On the other hand, riots can have a counterproductive effect. One can credit the urban riots of the 1960s with helping to build support for the law-and-order–oriented candidacy of Richard Nixon in 1968. By 1968, many Americans had come to feel threatened by the rising tide of crime in the cities and by the general atmosphere of turmoil that pervaded the society. The riots certainly contributed mightily to this sense of uneasiness. The Nixon administration produced policies that many saw as contrary to the interests of urban minorities. Furthermore, the riots contributed to the phenomenon of "white flight" to the suburbs that ultimately worsened the problems of the cities by reducing their tax bases and making it more difficult for them to meet the needs of their residents.

Although no political system can tolerate rioting, most elites recognize rioting as an indicator that the system is not working. Rioting is certainly a collective political act that makes demands on the political system. At the least, it signals the participants' lack of faith in legitimate forms of political action. Elites respond to riots by demanding either more social control or increased aid to the cities. Conservatives typically call for law and order; liberals propose social programs. Government may do either or both of these things—they are not mutually exclusive. The urban riots of the 1960s led the federal government to enact tough new laws, such as the Anti-Riot Act of 1968. But they also led to more federal funding of programs designed to reverse urban decay.

8-4c Strikes and Boycotts

A **strike** is a collective decision by a large number of people to refuse to work in order to dramatize a situation or force those who are adversely affected to make some concession. In the United States, we associate strikes with labor unions. Strikes are not nearly as common now as they were fifty years ago, when the labor movement was in its infancy. Then, strikes were a means of forcing corporations merely to acknowledge and tolerate unions. Strikes now occur only when labor leaders and management teams are unable to settle on the wages and benefits to be provided under a collective bargaining agreement.

Unknown in this country is the **general strike**, in which a large segment of the population refuses to work for a day to dramatize opposition to the government. This type of strike can paralyze a country—shops close, factories shut down, and transportation systems grind to a halt. This type of dramatic display of opposition can set in motion forces that bring down a regime. For example, in the Philippines in 1986, supporters of the presidential candidate Corazon Aquino staged a general strike to protest the reelection of President Ferdinand Marcos, who had been reelected in an atmosphere of pervasive fraud and corruption. Ultimately, after the Reagan administration shifted its support to the challenger, Marcos relinquished power and Aquino was declared president. Fortunately, in a democratic society with mechanisms for the orderly and periodic transfer of power, these types of extraordinary actions are seldom necessary.

A **boycott** is a collective refusal to purchase a particular good or service. Consumer groups unhappy with the safety or quality of certain products sometimes ask consumers to boycott particular companies. Groups displeased with the amount of sex and violence on television have been known to call for boycotts of companies that advertise during objectionable programs. Labor unions sometimes ask consumers to boycott companies with which they have grievances.

Perhaps the best-known example of an effective boycott took place in Montgomery, Alabama, in 1955. Rosa Parks, a black woman, was arrested for refusing to give up her seat in the whites-only section of a municipal bus. The Rev. Martin Luther King, Jr., the son of a well-known black minister in Atlanta, went to Montgomery and organized a boycott of the bus system by local blacks. The boycott, which lasted more than a year, was highly successful in dramatizing to the nation the issue of racial segregation. Eventually, the federal courts declared the segregated bus system unconstitutional.

8-4d THE QUESTION OF CIVIL DISOBEDIENCE

Certain forms of political actions are regarded as illegitimate by nearly everyone. Terrorism, assassination, extortion, and intimidation all may be politically motivated. Yet only the most militant radicals and reactionaries consider these types of actions to be an acceptable means of making a political point. Does political participation have to be confined to the boundaries of the law to be considered legitimate? **Civil disobedience** refers to the intentional breaking of the law to make a political point. Civil disobedience does not include actions that directly harm individuals. An assassination is not an act of civil disobedience; nor is bombing a building. Sometimes, civil disobedience does involve damage to property. More commonly, it entails one or more of these behaviors:

- Trespassing on government or corporate property
- Minor crimes against public order, such as disturbing the peace, disorderly conduct, unlawful assembly, or obstruction of vehicular traffic
- Refusal to pay taxes or perform military service
- Interference with public officials' performance of official duties

Civil disobedience has a long tradition in the United States, going back to the Boston Tea Party and other lawless actions by the American colonists to protest British rule. In the 1840s, the writer Henry David Thoreau refused to pay his poll taxes to protest American involvement in the Mexican War and the institution of slavery, both of which Thoreau considered immoral. Thoreau's act of civil disobedience became an icon in American political culture and has been invoked by successive generations of political activists who felt compelled to break the law for a perceived higher good.

In the 1960s, college students occupied campus administration buildings and refused to leave in order to protest the Vietnam War. In the 1970s, antinuclear activists trespassed on the grounds of power plants and government research facilities. In the early 1990s, members of Operation Rescue, a militant antiabortion group, violated court orders forbidding them from interfering with the operations of abortion clinics. All these activities are examples of civil disobedience. In each case, people broke the law on the ground that they were obeying a "higher law," whether it was the law of God or their own moral codes.

The question of civil disobedience is as old as politics itself. St. Paul believed that governments were ordained by God and that "whoever resisteth them, resisteth the ordinance of God."[24] On the other hand, St. Peter argued that people should "obey God rather than men."[25] Thomas Hobbes, rejecting the ability of human beings to know transcendental truth, argued that the duty to obey government was absolute. At the other extreme, anarchists deny the duty to obey any and all laws. Democratic thinkers have tended to argue for a duty to comply with the law if, and only if, the law is enacted by democratic procedures (see Case in Point 8-1).

John Locke and Thomas Jefferson certainly believed that people have a right to overthrow government by force when that government no longer respects their inalienable rights. In fact, Jefferson wrote: "The tree of liberty must be refreshed from time to time with the blood of patriots and tyrants."[26]

8-4e Martin Luther King, Jr., and Civil Disobedience

The best-known exponent of civil disobedience in the twentieth century was Mohandas Gandhi, who used the technique of nonviolent resistance by the masses to win India's independence from British colonial rule. Gandhi's philosophy and methods of nonviolent civil disobedience influenced the American civil rights movement of the 1950s and 1960s, and especially the leader of that movement, Rev. Martin Luther King, Jr. In 1963, King led a protest march in Birmingham, Alabama. He and a number of civil rights leaders were arrested and jailed because they violated a court order prohibiting them from marching without a permit. Organizers of the march had, in fact, attempted to obtain a permit from Birmingham officials, but were denied. Believing that they had a constitutional right to assemble in a public forum to express their grievances, the organizers went ahead with the march. In a letter written from the Birmingham jail, King defended his group's exercise of civil disobedience. Like Thoreau and Gandhi before him, King argued that civil disobedience is proper when the law being violated is itself unjust, as long as the violator is willing to suffer the penalty for the act of disobedience. It is this willingness to accept punishment that dramatizes the sincerity of the belief in the injustice of the law. Breaking a law without being willing to face the consequences is not civil disobedience, it is merely lawlessness.

Anyone can easily understand civil disobedience in an authoritarian society where someone has no means of redressing grievances through democratic procedures. But how can anyone justify violating a law that has been adopted democratically? King's answer to this question was that black Americans had been denied the opportunity to participate in the political process. As far as blacks were concerned, the laws requiring racial segregation and other forms of discrimination had not been established democratically; hence, they had no obligation to obey them.

In his letter from the Birmingham jail, King justified civil disobedience in part on the ground that blacks in the South had been locked out of the political process. More recently, antiabortion protesters have frequently employed civil disobedience. How can these groups, who are not locked out of the political process, justify their violations of the law? They do so only on the basis of the moral rightness of their cause and the gravity of the evils they are fighting. To the committed environmentalist or antinuclear activist, trespassing or committing an act of vandalism to save the world from contamination or annihilation may seem necessary. To the committed pro-life activist, violating a court order prohibiting interference with the activities of an abortion clinic may appear necessary to save the lives of unborn children. These committed activists may find it puzzling that others do not share their zeal or their willingness to flout the conventions of the law. Of course, if everyone did, anarchy would be the rule.

8-5 SOCIAL MOVEMENTS

A **social movement** refers to the purposeful, directed actions of a large number of people attempting to achieve some collective purpose. Usually, that purpose is to bring about a major societal change that cannot be achieved through the ordinary channels of political participation. Social movements tend to attract people who feel disaffected and alienated. Perhaps they have been formally excluded from participating in politics, as women and African Americans once were. Or perhaps they feel that those in power are simply not interested in them or in what they have to say. Whatever the cause, social movements tend to be populated by "outsiders."

A social movement is distinguishable from a political party or an interest group in that a movement is not a formal organization, nor is it limited to conventional forms of political participation. Social movements typically use unconventional tactics: demonstrations, marches, strikes, boycotts, and even civil disobedience. Some of the more militant elements of social movements may go even further, inciting riots, harassing opponents, and even committing acts of terrorism. Yet most people who join social movements are peace-loving, law-abiding citizens who believe strongly in something and feel that extraordinary effort is required to advance the cause.

Social movements are often grassroots uprisings. Yet although emphasizing mass action, movements tend to need charismatic leaders to galvanize people into action, to attract new adherents, and to bolster people's faith and courage when things go badly. In the United States, the best example of a **charismatic leader** of a social movement is the Rev. Martin Luther King, Jr. Grassroots uprisings can build slowly over time, or they can erupt spontaneously as massive popular reactions to certain events. For example, the incident at Three Mile Island nuclear power plant in 1979, when an accidental leak of radiation led to the evacuation of more than one hundred fifty thousand residents, helped to galvanize the antinuclear movement in the 1980s.

ONLINE 8.4

Charismatic Leaders **http://www.psychologytoday.com/blog/naturally-selected/201203/charismatic-leadership-the-x-factor-in-politics**

To understand social movements and their place in American politics, consider a number of the more significant movements that have taken place historically. Our examination begins in the early nineteenth century with the movement to abolish slavery and includes a number of recent movements, some of which are still important on the contemporary political scene. The survey is not intended to be exhaustive, but merely to highlight some of the more important social movements that have shaped American politics.

8-5a Abolitionism

Slavery was a point of contention in American society as early as the late eighteenth century. Abolitionist sentiment was particularly strong among Pennsylvania Quakers, who regarded slavery as an affront to their Christian ideals. At the Constitutional Convention of 1787, northern and southern delegates managed to reach a compromise on slavery for the sake of forming "a more perfect union." But the slavery issue would not go away. Congress struggled with the issue and managed to fashion a series of legislative compromises to hold the Union together. But the abolitionists, who regarded slavery as morally intolerable, would not be satisfied by anything short of total destruction of the "peculiar institution."

Early on, abolitionists were not popular even in the North, where they were regarded as troublemakers and extremists. In the face of public opposition, they persisted, holding public rallies, giving speeches, writing essays, and publishing pamphlets and newspapers. Some even adopted more extreme tactics. In 1859, John Brown led a group of radical abolitionists in a raid on the federal garrison at Harper's Ferry, Virginia. Brown's plan was to obtain a large supply of arms to lead an uprising of slaves. The plan failed, and Brown was hanged for his actions. But John Brown began to be seen as a martyr within the abolitionist movement. Eventually, most people in the North began to agree that slavery was an evil that had to be eradicated. Ultimately, the question was resolved in favor of abolition by the bloody Civil War of 1861–1865. After more than fifty years of struggle, the abolitionists had prevailed.

8-5b Agrarian Populism

After the Civil War, farmers in the South, Midwest, and West experienced a long period of economic distress. At the same time, American industry was experiencing tremendous growth. By the 1880s, many farmers began to believe that they were being exploited by banks, railroads, and grain storage companies. The populist movement sought government control of these institutions and a number of other egalitarian policies, such as a progressive income tax and an expanded supply of cheap paper money. Out of this movement emerged the short-lived Populist party. Its leader, William Jennings Bryan, garnered 47 percent of the popular vote in the 1896 presidential election, but was narrowly defeated by the better-financed Republican candidate, William McKinley. Although by 1900 the Populist party had been subsumed by the Democratic party, the populist movement had a tremendous effect on American politics. Because it was instrumental in moving the country away from a *laissez-faire* economic policy to one of active government intervention, it helped pave the way for the New Deal of the 1930s and the creation of the modern welfare state.

8-5c THE LABOR MOVEMENT

In the late nineteenth and early twentieth centuries, the United States witnessed a colossal legal and political battle over the right of workers to form labor unions, organizations of workers that bargain collectively with management over the terms and conditions of employment. Corporate America vehemently, and in some cases violently, opposed the labor movement, which was sometimes characterized as a precursor to socialism. One of the first labor unions, the Knights of Labor, formed in 1869, embraced an extreme variety of socialism. Some early labor leaders, such as Eugene V. Debs, the president of the American Railway Union, adopted more conventional socialist views. But most unions have been more pragmatic than ideological. Samuel Gompers, the first president of the American Federation of Labor (AFL), embodied this pragmatism. According to Gompers, "Unions, pure and simple, are the natural organization of wage workers to secure their present material and practical improvement."[27]

The principal tactic of the labor movement was the strike, in which workers would walk off the job. In response to strikes, corporations would bring in nonunion workers, known disparagingly as *scabs*, to replace the strikers. Quite often, violence would erupt as scabs crossed picket lines to get to the workplace. Before workers obtained the legal right to form unions, to collectively bargain with management, and to strike if their demands were not satisfied, corporations would often enlist the aid of law enforcement authorities to arrest strikers or break up picket lines. Sometimes, the confrontations between the police and the strikers turned violent.

During the Great Depression of the 1930s, the labor movement grew in numbers and influence. The New Deal enacted under the leadership of President Franklin D. Roosevelt formally recognized the place of labor unions in the American economy. By the late 1930s, laws were adopted guaranteeing the rights of workers to unionize and collectively bargain with management over wages and other terms of employment. Although the right to unionize had been won, unions still had a major national agenda to advance. Foremost among these was the elimination of right-to-work laws, which made union membership optional in organized industries.

Since the 1930s, labor unions have been politically active, primarily, but not exclusively, through the vehicle of the Democratic party. That affiliation was strained in 1993, however, when President Clinton, a Democrat, led the fight for Congressional approval of the North American Free Trade Agreement (NAFTA). Organized labor had fought hard against NAFTA, and most Democrats in Congress voted against it. But President Clinton prevailed by relying on a coalition of Republicans and conservative

Democrats. Despite hard feelings among leaders of the labor movement, most of which were directed at President Clinton, organized labor has maintained its longstanding relationship with the Democratic party.

Union membership has been in decline except for the segment of government employees. Teachers' unions and state employee representation organizations have grown in recent years while traditional manufacturing-base union jobs have been in decline. Republicans, who tend to see the unions as counterproductive and impeding factors in balancing state budgets, have moved to limit or strip public employee unions' collective bargaining rights recently. Most notably, Wisconsin Governor Scott Walker completely stripped state employees of unionization rights in 2011, causing a backlash that led to an unsuccessful recall election against him the following year. Two more states, Indiana and Michigan, have followed suit with right-to-work laws since Walker's successful effort in Wisconsin. In late 2012, after the other states had passed their similar laws, a state judge ruled Walker's law unconstitutional.[28]

8-5d The Civil Rights Movement

It is hard to say exactly when the civil rights movement began. In the early twentieth century, the NAACP mounted a campaign of litigation challenging racial segregation in the courts. *Brown v. Board of Education* (1954), which invalidated segregated public schools, was the most significant political victory in that campaign. But the struggle for civil rights as a mass movement did not really begin until the latter part of the 1950s. Arguably, the modern civil rights movement began when Rosa Parks refused to give up her seat in the whites-only section of a Montgomery bus in 1955. The Montgomery bus boycott was the first in a series of mass political actions that began to typify the civil rights movement. Boycotts, demonstrations, marches—all were effectively employed by the movement. Even civil disobedience, principally in the form of sit-ins at segregated facilities, was successfully employed.

The civil rights movement had a tremendous effect on American politics and social life. The adoption of the Civil Rights Act of 1964, the Voting Rights Act of 1965, and many other civil rights laws since then can be credited to the fact that the civil rights movement galvanized the conscience of America. Were it not for the movement, politicians—even liberal Democrats like President Lyndon Johnson, who pushed the Civil Rights Act through Congress— are unlikely to have manifested nearly as much concern for the civil rights of black Americans.

Before the mid-1960s, the civil rights movement employed strictly peaceful means, although opponents of the movement often practiced terrorism. The charismatic leadership of Martin Luther King, Jr., who embraced Gandhi's philosophy of nonviolent resistance, was instrumental in maintaining the peaceful character of the movement. By the mid-1960s, however, many black citizens began to believe that nonviolent protest was not enough—that more dramatic action was necessary. New, more militant voices began to be heard in the African American community. After Dr. King was assassinated in Memphis in 1968, the militant voices began to appeal to an increasing number of black Americans. Radical groups, like the Black Panther party, went so far as to stage bank robberies and jailbreaks in an attempt to bring about revolution against the white-dominated society.

8-5e The Antiwar Movement

Another major contributor to the upheaval of the 1960s was the anti–Vietnam War movement that sprang up on college campuses in the mid-1960s. What started as a series of peaceful demonstrations and protests soon escalated into acts of civil disobedience, principally burning draft cards and refusing military service. Like the civil rights movement, the antiwar movement became more violent and militant as the 1960s progressed. Student protesters occupied university administration buildings, burned American flags, and even torched ROTC facilities. On some campuses, students clashed with police in violent riots.

One of the most memorable, and bloodiest, episodes in the chronicles of the antiwar movement was the massive clash between demonstrators and police on the streets of Chicago during the Democratic National Convention during the summer of 1968. The Vietnam War had become the political issue of the year and threatened to tear the Democratic party apart. The protesters, led by the activists David Dellinger and Tom Hayden, assembled in Chicago in an attempt to persuade the Democrats to repudiate the war. When they learned that the convention attendees had rejected an antiwar plank in the party platform, the protesters marched to the convention hall, where they encountered legions of police officers. The ensuing battle was broadcast to the nation on live network television.

The antiwar movement helped solidify public opposition to the Vietnam War. Although the movement subsided after American forces left Vietnam, some of the more radical elements of the movement persisted throughout the 1970s. To some extent, the participants—and to a greater extent, the tactics—of the antiwar movement of the 1960s were revived by the antinuclear, environmental, and disarmament movements of the 1980s.

In late 1990, as America debated its response to Iraq's surprise invasion of Kuwait, many of the images of the 1960s antiwar movement were rekindled as the more vocal opponents of military intervention assembled in America's cities to make their views known. Although the mass media gave these protests considerable attention, at least early on, the protesters had little effect on public opinion. If the Persian Gulf War of 1991 had dragged on into 1992 or 1993, and had the war bogged down into a Vietnam- or Korea-style stalemate, the number of antiwar protests, and their impact, would surely have grown markedly. Similarly, antiwar demonstrations on college campuses during the fall of 2001 had little effect on public support for America's "war on terrorism." Operations Enduring Freedom and Iraqi Freedom began in 2002 and 2003, with public sentiment beginning strongly in favor and fading quickly. In 2008, Barack Obama's promise to remove U.S. troops from Iraq represented a massive change in opinion at home that had started to oppose our presence there from 2005.

8-5f The Women's Movement

People tend to think of the women's movement as a recent phenomenon, but women have a long history of organized political activity in this country. Women played an important role in the movement to abolish slavery. Many would trace the formal origin of the women's movement to the Seneca Falls Women's Rights Convention of 1848, which called for women to have equal rights in property ownership, trades, and educational opportunity. Most notably, the convention initiated the movement to secure the right to vote for women. In their struggle to achieve the right to vote, the suffragists engaged in a variety of political acts, not all of which were legal. In the early twentieth century, women played an important role in the temperance movement that led to the national prohibition of alcoholic beverages.

In the 1970s, a new wave of feminism swept the country. Feminists demanded liberation from a male-dominated society that they believed kept them in a position of subservience. It was in this climate that the Equal Rights Amendment, which had been proposed originally in 1923, was finally passed by Congress and sent to the states for ratification. The ultimate failure of the ERA to win ratification was not simply the result of male resistance, however. Many women evidently agreed with Phyllis Schlafly, who led the campaign against the ERA, that feminism is detrimental to the interests of women.

Despite the demise of the Equal Rights Amendment, women's groups in the 1980s and 1990s continued to push for policies to benefit women working outside the home. These groups demanded, and received, legal protection against sexual harassment on the job. Women's groups played a major role in the enactment of the Family and Medical Leave Act of 1992, which requires employers to permit workers to take as many as twelve weeks of unpaid annual leave to deal with births, illnesses, and other family emergencies.

8-5g The Gay Rights Movement

One of the hallmarks of the 1960s was the sexual revolution, a broad cultural revolt against traditional sexual values and mores. Traditional values of modesty and chastity came under attack, both in popular culture (books, movies, plays, and music) and in everyday social life. To many people, virginity began to be viewed as a sign that a person was hopelessly old-fashioned, or even socially inept. Tolerance and experimentation became the watchwords of the times.

Out of the sexual revolution emerged a new openness with regard to homosexuality, which had long been taboo in Western culture. In the 1970s, people who were homosexual began to "come out of the closet," and heterosexuals began to express sympathy or tolerance rather than revulsion and condemnation. A new term, *gay*, was coined to replace more negative terms for being homosexual. That is not to say that animosity toward, or discrimination against, homosexuals disappeared. To the contrary, many gay men and lesbians who come out of the closet are still met by hostility and discrimination.

By the 1980s, gay men and lesbians had become politically aware and activated. They had even organized a number of interest groups to push for policy changes in the legislative and judicial branches of government at the local, state, and national levels. In particular, gays sought the repeal of sodomy laws that, although seldom enforced, technically made their sexual practices illegal. In the 1960s, 1970s, and 1980s, many states did do away with these types of laws, not so much as a result of political activity by gays, but rather because these statutes were widely regarded as outmoded.

In a setback to the gay rights movement, however, the U.S. Supreme Court ruled in 1986 that state sodomy laws, as applied to homosexual conduct, did not violate the U.S. Constitution. In what gay rights activists regarded as an affront, the High Court said that gays have no right under the Constitution to engage in homosexual sodomy.[29] Subsequently, however, many state courts invalidated their own state sodomy laws based on state constitutional privacy protections. In 2003, the Supreme Court, likely influenced by state court decisions as well as changing public attitudes, overturned its 1986 decision and declared unconstitutional a Texas law criminalizing homosexual conduct.[30]

More important than the demise of sodomy laws, however, is the effort by gay men and lesbians to acquire specific protection under civil rights laws. Some cities (for example, New York and San Francisco, where gays represent substantial voting blocs) have adopted ordinances specifically prohibiting discrimination on the grounds of sexual orientation. But gays have been less successful at the state and national levels. As of 1994, little sentiment seemed to exist in Congress or state legislatures to extend civil rights protections to gays. Indeed, in 1992, voters in Colorado adopted an amendment to the state constitution prohibiting the state legislature and courts from extending civil rights protection to gays. In 1996, however, in a major victory for gay rights, the U.S. Supreme Court struck down the amendment on the basis of the Equal Protection Clause of the Fourteenth Amendment.[31]

The other major objective on the gay rights agenda has been to persuade the government to put more effort into finding a cure for AIDS, not only because homosexuals disproportionately suffer from the disease but also because the disease exacerbates people's fears of homosexuality. One especially militant gay rights and anti-AIDS group, ACT UP, made headlines in the late 1980s and early 1990s by staging disruptive demonstrations and engaging in acts of civil disobedience. Whether these types of militant actions help or hinder the causes of gay rights and the fight against AIDS is debatable. But what is not debatable is that attitudes toward homosexuality have changed dramatically over the past several decades. The gay rights movement certainly is responsible for much of that attitudinal change.

By 2004, the agenda of the gay rights movement focused on the issue of marriage. Gay rights activists saw the legalization of homosexual marriage as a critical test of public acceptance of gays and lesbians. In November 2003, the Massachusetts Supreme Court ruled that the Massachusetts state constitution required that the legislature rewrite its statutes to provide marriage rights for gay couples. This set off a national discussion of gay marriage that led some local officials to perform weddings for gay couples. Although these marriages were later overturned, the "right to marry" a person of the same sex further widened the discussion of rights for gay and lesbian couples. In Chapter 5 we explored the changes across the country in 2008, with California's on-again, off-again allowance for gay marriage and other states' acceptance of it, like Iowa. Gay men and women will continue their fight until gay marriage is allowed in all states. Though the issue of gay marriage is still very much in flux, it is clear that there has been tremendous cultural change in this area over the last three decades.

ONLINE 8.5

Gay Marriage Laws in the U.S. **http://gaymarriage.procon.org/view.resource.php?resourceID=003980**

8-5h The Christian Right

Periodic upsurges of political activity have occurred among fundamentalist Christians throughout American history. The most recent of these upsurges, which began in the late 1970s and continues now, has been referred to as the Christian Right. Most modern social movements—including the gay rights, environmental, antiwar, civil rights, and women's movements—have been oriented toward the ideological left, that is, participants in these movements have tended to be liberal or even radical in their overall political orientations. The Christian Right stands in sharp ideological contrast to these liberal-to-radical movements. The Christian Right is a conservative movement concerned primarily with socio-moral issues and "family values." Its agenda includes restoring prayer to the public schools, maintaining social and legal taboos on homosexuality, censoring pornography, and, above all, prohibiting abortion. Indeed, the Christian Right as a social movement overlaps considerably with the pro-life movement, which is focused almost exclusively on the abortion issue.

The Christian Right is built on a network of fundamentalist preachers who exhort their congregations to become politically active. The movement has become adept at the arts of conventional politics: voter registration drives, lobbying, litigation, running candidates for public office, and fundraising. In the 1980s, the leadership of the Christian Right succeeded in mobilizing a large segment of the population that had been politically inactive. The Christian Right played an important role in the 1980 election and 1984 reelection of Ronald Reagan. In the late 1980s, the movement fragmented somewhat. Some conservative Christians supported Pat Robertson, a TV evangelist, for the Republican nomination in 1988. Others, including the Rev. Jerry Falwell, the founder of the Moral Majority and one of the leading spokespersons for the Christian Right, supported the more moderate candidate, George H. W. Bush. In 1992, many in the Christian Right looked to Pat Buchanan, a conservative TV commentator, who challenged incumbent President Bush for the Republican nomination. Buchanan's insurgency was eventually defeated, but at the price of some bitter feelings within the Republican party.

In the 1992 general election, most conservative Christians supported George H. W. Bush, but some defected to the Independent Ross Perot, and still others voted for Bill Clinton, who was not shy about exploiting his "Christian credentials" as a member of the Baptist church. In the wake of the Democratic victory in 1992, the leadership of the NCR (New Christian Right) turned its attention to the local level, running candidates for school boards, city councils, and county commissions across America.

During the mid- to late 1990s, the Christian Right faded somewhat, but it certainly played an important (if not decisive) role in the election of George W. Bush in 2000. Bush's presidency was marked by two significant victories for cultural conservatives. First, Bush issued an executive order banning the use of federal funds to support embryonic stem cell research.[32] Second, Bush pushed for (but could not achieve) a constitutional amendment to prevent the legalization of gay marriage in any state. Bush, himself a born-again Christian, believed strongly against stem cell research (as an extension of his views on abortion) and gay marriage. Bush's commitment to their cause was rewarded by strong mobilization and support of the Christian Right throughout his Presidency.

8-5i The Pro-Life Movement

The pro-life movement draws much of its support from the Christian Right, although it is a distinctive phenomenon unto itself. The movement embraces a number of organized groups, such as Right to Life, Operation Rescue, and Rescue America. Right to Life is a conventional interest group, committed to lobbying, litigation, and influencing elections. Rescue America and Operation Rescue are direct action groups that picket and sometimes blockade abortion clinics. Critics charge that these groups harass women going to clinics seeking abortions and try to intimidate doctors and other clinic personnel. Randall Terry, a leader of Operation Rescue, argues that most of his group's actions are specifically protected by the First Amendment. Of course, those on the other side of the issue believe that these actions constitute an interference with a woman's constitutional right to obtain, and a doctor's right to provide, an abortion.

In March 1993, the nation was shocked when Dr. David Gunn was shot and killed by an antiabortion protester outside a clinic in Pensacola, Florida. The killing was the most publicized of a number of lawless actions by fringe elements in the pro-life movement. In other incidents, clinics have been bombed or vandalized, clinic staff members and doctors have been harassed—even stalked—and women seeking abortions have been confronted. Indeed, antiabortion activities have been successful in closing down many abortion clinics throughout the country. Although most people on both sides of the abortion issue deplore the violence that has infected the struggle over abortion rights, the very nature of the issue increases the likelihood that protest will become violent.

In 2001, the pro-life movement focused on a new issue: stem cell research. Pro-life activists opposed the use of stem cells obtained from human embryos, as they regard the destruction of a human embryo to be tantamount to homicide. In August 2001, President George W. Bush issued an executive order limiting the use of federal funds to support research in this area to the seventy-eight embryonic stem cell lines then in existence. Opponents of the order insisted that new stem cell lines had to be created in order for research to progress. Stem cell research again became a national issue during the 2004 campaign as candidate John Kerry (as well as a number of celebrities) criticized President Bush's stand on the issue.

In 2009, Wichita, Kansas abortion doctor George Tiller, known nationally as one of the few doctors willing to perform late-term abortions, was shot and killed by a pro-life activist while he was ushering at his church. Tiller had long been a touchstone in the abortion fight, having been shot in both arms during an attempt on his life in 1993. Scott Roeder, a pro-life activist, was apprehended by police and admitted to killing Tiller. After a long period where little to no violence accompanied the abortion debate, the Tiller homicide brought the issue to the fore once again.[33]

8-5j The Antiglobalism Movement

The changes in the communications and economic infrastructure during the last quarter of the twentieth century led to an increasingly global economy. This situation invariably led to a rise in business among multinational corporations and a host of treaties and agreements among nations to deal with this trade. By 2001, it had become difficult for any organization, such as the World Trade Organization or the International Monetary Fund, to hold meetings in Europe or the United States without massive protests staged by people convinced that the new global economy threatened the jobs or cultures of many people across the world in addition to the natural environment. Many involved in these protests saw themselves in the vanguard of what they hoped would become a new social movement. The protestors were a diverse mix, including black-masked anarchists, union members, socialists, communists, environmentalists, human rights activists, and self-styled radicals and activists of various bents and persuasions.

The largest and most destructive protest of the institutions of the global economy took place in Seattle in 1999 at the time of the meeting of the World Trade Organization. More than fifty thousand protestors managed to keep many meetings from taking place. Their methods were not always peaceful. On the contrary, a good deal of property damage occurred, and many arrests were made. Some protestors manifested little understanding of the issues and institutions of globalization. For them, participation in the protest was a chance to experience some 1960s-style activism.

8-6 Conclusion: Participation and Political Culture

People can participate in politics in many ways, ranging from minimal spectator activities to active involvement in parties, campaigns, and interest groups to involvement in grassroots social movements and direct mass political action. The challenge to any democracy is twofold. First, the system must stimulate enough popular participation in politics so that it may continue to function as a legitimate "government by the people." Second, the system must maintain effective, legitimate channels of participation to avoid a groundswell of unconventional (and potentially violent) action that threatens to push the system into chaos. Although American democracy has struggled from time to time with the second of these challenges, for the most part political participation in the United States has been both conventional and peaceful. Many people would argue, however, that its citizens have been less successful in meeting the first challenge—engendering sufficient participation to be considered a true and vital democracy.

Americans tend to be quite proud of their political system. They are certainly proud of the Constitution and the freedoms enshrined in the Bill of Rights. They are convinced that America stands at the forefront of the world's democracies. Many Americans would be surprised to learn that the Founders did not intend for the political system to be a democracy and that many of the Framers of the Constitution equated democracy with mob rule. Most Americans now are not comfortable with the elitism that typified the Founders. Contemporary Americans are more comfortable with Abraham Lincoln's characterization of our political system as a "government of the people, by the people, and for the people." Certainly, that is what most Americans believe that our government should be. Yet, ironically, most Americans do not bother to vote in most elections. Even presidential elections generate barely a 50 percent voter turnout.

Part of the reluctance to register and vote stems from a cynicism about government. When polled, a majority of Americans are apt to say that they think the government is run by a "few big interests" that are more concerned with "looking out for themselves" than for the good of the people. Of course, when people do not participate in elections, they can hardly expect that their views will be taken into account. This is one of the paradoxes of American politics: Americans believe that their system was intended to be, and ought to be, a democracy. Yet they are reluctant to participate in the most basic of democratic institutions: the election. Two powerful elements of political culture are in conflict. Americans feel that they ought to vote. Thus, participation is fundamental to American political folklore. People often hear how Americans have fought and died to protect the right to vote. But Americans are also skeptical about the role of government and somewhat cynical about politicians. In many ways, this cynicism is becoming as ingrained in the American character as is the obligation to participate. It is not surprising, then, that this discord in the culture has led to a relatively low level of voting.

Questions for Thought and Discussion

1. Why do Americans turn out to vote at lower rates than citizens in other democracies?

2. Does the right to vote include the right to have one's vote counted, even if the voter fails to follow instructions in the completion of the ballot?

3. With regard to forms of participation other than voting, is there an upper limit of mass participation beyond which a democracy cannot function?

4. Is it legitimate for a person to trespass on private property or block government buildings to draw attention to a political issue?

5. Has the environmental movement reached its peak in the United States? Is environmentalism likely to be more or less politically significant in the future?

6. Should people feel obligated to vote if they know nothing about the candidates or issues in an election?

7. Is there a minimal level of voter turnout for an electoral system to be considered democratic?

8. What social movements have been most effective in reshaping the American political agenda?

Endnotes

1 David Von Drehle, "The Year of the Youth Vote," *Time*, January 31, 2008, http://www.time.com/time/politics/article/0,8599,1708570,00.html

2 U.S. Census Bureau, "Voter Turnout Increases by 5 Million in 2008 Presidential Election,"U.S. Census Bureau Reports, July 20, 2009.

3 Robert Dahl, *Who Governs?* (New Haven, CT: Yale University Press, 1961), p. 225.

4 Lester Milbrath, *Political Participation: How and Why Do People Get Involved in Politics?* (Chicago: Rand McNally, 1965), p. 18.

5 Sidney Verba and Norman Nie, *Participation in America* (New York: Harper & Row, 1972), p. 119.

6 Robert Kaplan, "Was Democracy Just a Moment?" *Atlantic Monthly*, vol. 280, no. 6, December 1997.

7 Milbrath, *Political Participation*, p. 18.

8 J. R. Neuman, *The Paradox of Mass Politics* (Cambridge, MA: Harvard University Press, 1986), p. 11.

9 *Gray v. Sanders*, 372 U.S. 368, 380 (1963).

10 *Reynolds v. Sims*, 377 U.S. 533, 555 (1964).

11 Robert Putnam, *Bowling Alone: The Collapse and Revival of American Community* (New York: Simon and Schuster, 2000), p. 35.

12 In many democracies, from Australia to Uruguay, voting is viewed as an essential obligation of citizenship and is legally compulsory. In Australia, for example, citizens who fail to vote can be fined unless they can produce a satisfactory explanation for not voting.

13 Ruy Teixeira, *The Disappearing American Voter* (Washington, D.C.: Brookings Institution, 1992), p. 7.

14 Michael McDonald, The United States Elections Project, http://elections.gmu.edu/Turnout_2008G.html

15 Peter Dreier, "Obama's Youth Movement," *The Huffington Post*, September 17, 2008, http://www.huffingtonpost.com/peter-dreier/obamas-youth-movement_b_127169.html

16 United States Elections Project, "2012 General Election Turnout Rates," July 22, 2013, http://elections.gmu.edu/Turnout_2012G.html

17 U.S. Census Bureau, "Voting-Age Population—Reported Registration and Voting by Selected Characteristics: 1996 to 2010," retrieved July 27, 2013 from http://www.census.gov/compendia/statab/2012/tables/12s0399.pdf

18 G. Bingham Powell, Jr., "American Turnout in Comparative Perspective," *American Political Science Review*, vol. 80, March 1986, p. 17.

19 John Milburn, "Kobach Touts Success of Photo ID Law," *Topeka Capital-Journal*, November 23, 2012, http://cjonline.com/news/2012-11-23/kobach-touts-success-photo-id-law

20 Teixeira, *The Disappearing American Voter*, p. 37.

21 Estimate by Thomas Mann, of Brookings Institution, as reported in *The New York Times*, March 18, 1993, p. 1.

22 Seymour Martin Lipset, *Political Man* (Baltimore: Johns Hopkins University Press, 1981), p. 164.

23 Thomas E. Patterson, *The Vanishing Voter* (New York: Vintage Books, 2003), p. 186.

24 Romans 13:1–10.

25 Acts 5:29.

26 Thomas Jefferson, letter to William Stevens Smith, November 13, 1787.

27 Samuel Gompers, quoted in John M. Blum, et al., *The National Experience* (New York: Harcourt Brace & World, 1963), p. 438.

28 Kevin Cirilli, "Scott Walker's Wisconsin Anti-Union Law Struck Down," September 14, 2012, *Politico*, http://www.politico.com/news/stories/0912/81244.html

29 *Bowers v. Hardwick*, 478 U.S. 186 (1986).

30 *Lawrence v. Texas*, 539 U.S. 558 (2003).

31 *Romer v. Evans*, 517 U.S. 620 (1996).

32 Scott Rosenberg, "Bush's Stem Cell Fumble," Salon.com. August 21, 2001. http://dir.salon.com/story/politics/feature/2001/08/10/stem_cell/index.html

33 Karen Ball, "Tiller's Murder," *Time*, June 1, 2009, http://www.time.com/time/nation/article/0,8599,1902077,00.html

Unit 3

The Political Process

Chapter 9

CAMPAIGNS AND ELECTIONS

OUTLINE

Key Terms 310

Expected Learning Outcomes 310

9-1 The Importance of Elections 310

- **9-1a** Types of Elections 312

9-2 Presidential Campaigns and Elections 313

- **9-2a** The Nomination Process 313
- **9-2b** The General Election Campaign 323
- **9-2c** The Electoral College Vote 334

9-3 Individual Voting Behavior 337

- **9-3a** Party Identification 337
- **9-3b** Issues 338
- **9-3c** Ideology 340
- **9-3d** Candidate Image 341
- **9-3e** A Model of the Voting Decision 342

9-4 The 2000 Cliffhanger 342

- **9-4a** Florida's Post-Election Contest 344
- **9-4b** The Counting 345
- **9-4c** The Contest Period: The Courts Take Over 347
- **9-4d** The U.S. Supreme Court Ends the Process 348

9-5 The 2004 Election 348

9-6 The 2008 Election 349

- **9-6a** The Candidates 349
- **9-6b** The Issues 350
- **9-6c** The Voters Decide 350

9-7 The 2012 Election 350

- **9-7a** The Candidates 351
- **9-7b** The Issues 351
- **9-7c** The Voters Decide 351

9-8 Congressional Campaigns and Elections 352

- **9-8a** Financing Congressional Campaigns 353
- **9-8b** National Trends and Local Context 356

9-8c Congressional Elections: The Earthquakes of 2006 and 2010 358
9-8d The Perennial Campaign 358
9-9 Conclusion: Campaigns, Elections, and American Political Culture 358
Questions for Thought and Discussion 360
Endnotes 361

KEY TERMS

bundling
candidate image
coattails
consultants
expectations game
general election
incumbency advantage
Iowa caucus
issue voting
New Hampshire primary
nomination
party image
photo opportunity
primary election
prospective voting
retrospective voting
seed money
sound bite
spin control
SuperPAC
tracking polls

EXPECTED LEARNING OUTCOMES

After reading this chapter and completing the supplemental online materials, students will:

- Understand the role of elections in democratic government
- Analyze the decision-making process for candidates
- Map the elections process from primary through general
- Describe the role of money in a campaign
- Trace trends in recent presidential and congressional elections

9-1 THE IMPORTANCE OF ELECTIONS

For the second time in as many elections, there was little uncertainty about who would win the 2012 presidential election. Predictive models, polls, and a collection of blogs all came to the same conclusion: Barack Obama would retain the presidency with a 100 electoral vote or more margin. The electoral vote prediction website Five Thirty Eight correctly predicted that Obama would beat Mitt Romney with at least 330 electoral votes, well more than the 270 needed to become president. Just like in 2008, the outcome was decided relatively early on election night. After two consecutive elections that were in dispute until the end of election night (or a month longer, as in the case of 2000) the uncertainty of the winning candidate's identity was gone in 2008. Obama had a strong win in both the popular and electoral vote, a topic that was on the forefront of voters' minds after the split election of 2000.

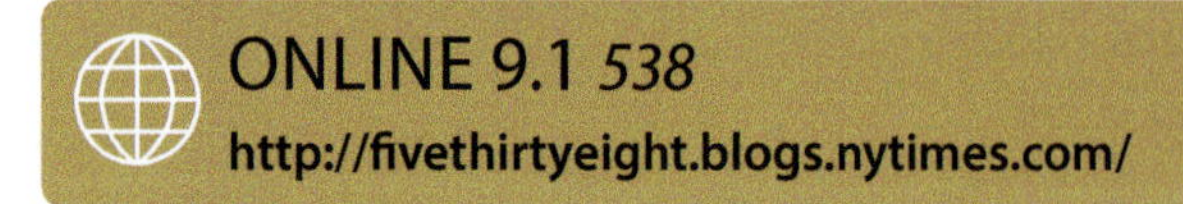

ONLINE 9.1 *538*
http://fivethirtyeight.blogs.nytimes.com/

© Rena Schild, 2013. Used under license from Shutterstock, Inc.

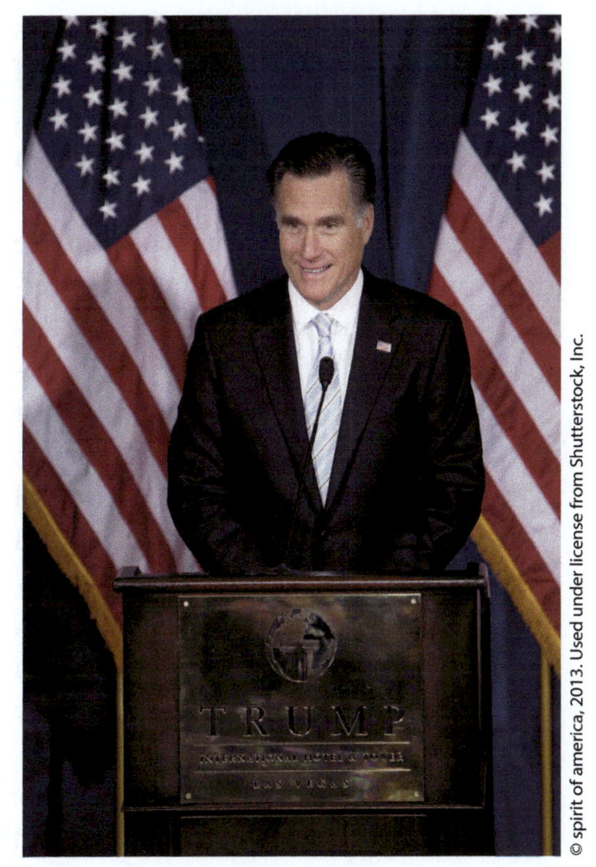

© spirit of america, 2013. Used under license from Shutterstock, Inc.

In between victories, a very different series of elections made Obama's 2012 reelection look unlikely. The midterm elections for Congress turned control of the House of Representatives over to Republicans and closed the gap in the Senate, taking the Democratic seat advantage from eighteen to six. The election also ended the conversation debating if the Republican party was in freefall. President Obama's ambitious agenda would not be so easily passed by Congress anymore. As quickly as can happen in the American electoral system, the pendulum of power swung from strongly in the Democrats' favor to Republican momentum.

Even when elections are not volatile, they are fundamental to any democracy. The essence of any democratic government is to give the public the opportunity to turn an entire government out through peaceful means. Elections are like scheduled revolutions: if the public wants to change their entire government, they get the chance to do so at regular intervals. Thomas Jefferson suggested after the War for Independence that no more than twenty years should pass before another revolution happens. With elections, Jefferson gets his revolution every two years. More to the point, elections provide the mechanism through which the electorate communicates its preferences to government. Elections allow those who make the effort to vote to select those who will hold office. Moreover, elections hold public officials accountable to the people they govern.

If officials do not perform their jobs to the satisfaction of a majority of the electorate, they are not reelected. Finally, elections perform the function of conferring legitimacy on the political system. If rulers are chosen in free and fair elections, they are widely perceived as having the right to rule. This perception of legitimacy is of critical importance. It is no wonder that shortly after George W. Bush's narrow, controversial victory in the electoral college in 2000, many Democrats and media commentators began to question the legitimacy of his presidency. In 2004 and 2008, there was no such dispute because of the large victory margin each winner earned.

Anyone considering running for office, as well as anyone considering running a political campaign, must be aware of the variety of forces that converge during an election. One must consider a number of questions: Who will turn out to vote? What will the overall level of turnout be? What is the ideology of the two candidates, and whose ideology is more appealing to the voters? What are the key issues in the race, and how are these issues reflected in public opinion? What interest groups have a stake in the contest, and how will they seek to influence the outcome? How will the race be portrayed in the media? Indeed, will the media even take notice? Will the media be able to portray events in the lives of the candidates as scandals, thereby diverting attention from the substantive issues of the race? Finally, how will the political party organizations regard the campaign? How crucial is this election to the parties' overall national strategies? Will the parties provide assistance? The answer to each of these questions has a bearing on the outcome of the race.

9-1a TYPES OF ELECTIONS

There are two basic types of elections: primary and general. In a **primary election**, a political party selects one candidate from a field of contenders to run against the nominees of other parties in a general election. A primary narrows the field of contenders basically into a two-candidate race (minor parties also nominate candidates but rarely win). In a **general election**, voters make the final choice of who will hold office. Parties can use a variety of methods to select the person to get their **nomination**.

The most common are the primary election and the caucus. In a primary election, voters are asked to go to the polls to choose among the contenders for a party's nomination. In a caucus system, people affiliated with a party hold a meeting to select the party's nominee.

The complexity of the American federal system produces a great number of elections, held at different times, for different offices. In a given year, a citizen may be asked to vote in nomination contests and general elections for offices at the local, state, and national levels. These elections are often held at different times throughout the year. Thus, it is not surprising that turnout, especially for state and local elections, tends to be quite low. If as many as 50 percent of those who are eligible turn out to vote in a state or local election, commentators are likely to describe the turnout as "high."[1]

In addition to voting for people for public office, Americans also participate in other types of elections, including *referenda*, elections in which voters make policy directly by changing laws, constitutions, or charters. This process takes place at the state level under guidelines set by the states. Many states do not have the referendum process. The states which do allow for referenda are often criticized as being nearly ungovernable because the constant flow of citizen initiatives handcuffs the government and makes it less responsive to the peoples' needs.[2] The U.S. Constitution does not contain any provision for a referendum at the national level. Two elections are held at the national level: presidential and congressional.

9-2 Presidential Campaigns and Elections

The presidential contest has two major phases. The first phase is the race for the Democratic and Republican parties' nominations. A candidate cannot reasonably expect to be elected president without first being nominated by one of the two major parties. Most people seeking the presidency are eliminated at this stage. The nomination phase culminates with the national conventions held by the two major parties during the summer of the election year. The second phase of the presidential contest is the general election, in which the party nominees are pitted against each other. Normally, the general election focuses on the Democratic and Republican nominees, but on occasion, as in Ross Perot's 1992 candidacy, a major third-party candidate receives a significant share of the vote. In 2000, some argued Green party candidate Ralph Nader pulled votes from Democratic nominee Al Gore, costing Gore the election.

9-2a The Nomination Process

The modern presidential nomination system is a long process that formally begins with the Iowa caucuses and New Hampshire primary in February of an election year and does not end until the party conventions in the summer. In 2008, the Democratic nomination was not secured by Barack Obama until June. The possibility existed until close to the time the convention was about to start that the Obama and Clinton campaigns might go into the convention not knowing who would be chosen as the party's nominee. Candidates, however, must begin laying the groundwork for a campaign well before the month of February. Some candidates make informal visits to potential voters in the states of Iowa and New Hampshire at least a year or more before the event. Fundraising must start early, and an organization must be put together. Political parties provide minimal help to candidates during this phase. For all intents and purposes, the candidates are on their own. Despite the year or more of preparation and campaigning, most of the declared candidates in each party are eliminated less than a month after the first primary.

Getting Started

One of the more fascinating aspects of politics is observing which potential candidates decide to begin a campaign. Soon after a presidential election has taken place, political pundits begin mentioning people who might be likely candidates for the next presidential election. These political analysts are usually looking for several features in a potential candidate. First, the candidate must have some national or regional stature. Since 1960, four presidents have been state governors (George W. Bush, Clinton, Reagan, and Carter), three were former vice presidents (Johnson, Nixon, and George Bush), and two (Kennedy and Obama) were senators when they ran for president, although several others also had congressional experience earlier in their careers. Of course, Al Gore was vice president when he ran against Texas Governor George W. Bush in 2000. The 2004 and 2008 elections were a significant break with recent history, with the Democratic nominees for both president and vice president as well as the Republican presidential nominee being members of the U.S. Senate.

Another important consideration is the party of the current president. If the incumbent president is popular, few people from his own party may challenge him, and the best possible challengers from the other party may shy away from the race. Therefore, the incumbent's popularity at the midpoint in his term, after the midterm congressional elections, may be a decisive factor in who will consider a race. The other announced candidates can also influence whether someone will consider a bid for the presidency. Al Gore sought the presidency in 2000 in an unusual situation. The incumbent president, Bill Clinton, enjoyed high job performance ratings. However, his personal approval ratings were quite low, due in large part to the scandals that plagued him for several years. The Clinton factor caused confusion for the Gore campaign. Gore had to separate himself from Clinton personally but embrace his policy performance.

Several other factors influence the decision to enter the contest. What are the strengths of the candidate? Does the candidate have a good television appearance? Is the candidate a good public speaker? Does the candidate enjoy much name recognition outside her home state? Does the candidate have access to a good base of financial resources? A candidate must have access to, or the ability to fundraise, hundreds of millions of dollars to campaign through a primary and into a presidential contest. Although resources can be developed over time, a strong position at the beginning improves the candidate's chances. Others, such as party leaders, potential opponents, and the media, must recognize these strengths so that the candidate can make a fast start from the gate.

At the same time, potential candidates have to consider their liabilities. Job performance and political failures are certainly relevant. In addition, has the potential candidate made any major blunders or had any personal problems that would provide the media with an opportunity for a "feeding frenzy" of "attack journalism"?[3] Thomas Eagleton's psychiatric counseling quickly ended his bid for the vice presidency in 1972. Gary Hart's alleged affair with Donna Rice and Joe Biden's supposed plagiarism of others' speeches became sources of intense, negative media attention in 1988 and effectively ended each candidate's campaign for president. The possibility that these types of failings will end a campaign may have diminished somewhat because of Bill Clinton's survival and eventual triumph in 1992 despite feeding frenzies over an alleged affair, an allegation of pot smoking during his college years, and a charge that he dodged the draft during the Vietnam War. The late revelation that George W. Bush had a decades-old conviction for driving while intoxicated caused a disruption during the final week of the 2000 campaign. Controversy over the validity of Barack Obama's birth certificate and his citizenship dogged the candidate in 2008 and led to a new movement among conservatives, called the "birthers." Birthers believe that Obama was not born in the United States, and thus not eligible to be president. While widely discounted, the birther movement remains intact and inspired proposed laws in 2011 that would require presidential candidates to provide their birth certificates when running for office.

The constant presence of scandal has led to a new strategy, evident in the 2008 presidential election. Barack Obama released a memoir, *Dreams from My Father*, well before he ran for president in 2008. In the memoir, Obama admitted to having used cocaine as a younger man, as well as smoking marijuana. In other times, Obama's candor might have cost him a shot at the nomination, let alone the presidency. However, Obama's strategy was what political insiders refer to as "getting in front of the story." By admitting a scandalous event occurred the campaign does not have to respond to allegations from opponents and the press, allowing that campaign to stay on message.

As a result of the admission being in the public sphere well in advance of his candidacy, Obama's drug use became a nonstory.[4]

Ultimately, the individual must decide whether to pursue the nomination. The party cannot draft nominees, and the national committee does not have enough central organization or political clout to recruit and nominate a candidate. Potential candidates must launch their own campaigns without much assistance from the party. Often, potential candidates float the possibility of a campaign as a trial balloon to test public reaction, but they must commit early enough in the process to begin raising funds.

Raising Money

Raising money for a campaign is the most crucial aspect of a candidate's nomination strategy. It is sometimes called the first primary because the candidate with the most money at the time of the first primary typically wins the nomination. The candidate must begin with a base of money called seed money. **Seed money** is obtained from individuals and groups that are already closely associated with the candidate. For example, a cattle rancher from Texas is likely to rely on other ranchers to provide money early in the process to help jump-start the campaign. Members of Congress and national party leaders have already won other elections, and they usually have an established network of contributors who can help provide seed money. The seed money is used to form an organization, rent office space, buy office supplies, hire staff, contract with professional consultants, conduct surveys, and raise more funds.

In particular, seed money is mostly used to develop more resources through direct mail. Direct mail fundraising involves buying or developing a list of potential contributors. The campaign then sends out to the targeted individuals as many requests as it can afford. The letter typically makes a dramatic appeal describing the candidate's strengths and explaining how he can correct the country's problems. It then asks for money. Even if a small proportion (2 or 3 percent) of the targeted group responds, the method can pay off well enough that the candidate can begin another mass mailing. This process can continue for some time. The candidate is also likely to go back to previous contributors after some time has passed. Millions of dollars can be raised in this fashion.

Candidates rely on other methods too. Fundraising events—such as thousand-dollar-a-plate dinners, cocktail parties, and celebrity galas—can be helpful, as can direct appeals after a speech by the candidate or at a reception for the candidate. The candidates can also use donations from interest groups, but it is important to note that political action committees (PACs) are not as important in presidential campaigns as they are in congressional campaigns. Candidates have also used paid advertising to ask potential donors to send in contributions. In the 1992 Democratic nomination process, Jerry Brown used an 800 number to bring in donations. George W. Bush raised in excess of $100 million for his successful bid for the presidency in 2000.

His early success clearly discouraged many potentially strong opponents. For example, Elizabeth Dole pulled out of the race early while citing the difficulty of raising enough money. By 2004, the newest method of money raising, the Internet, had matured to the point that one candidate, Howard Dean, used it to tremendous advantage to have by far the best-funded primary campaign among those seeking the Democratic party presidential nomination. Websites such as MoveOn.org likewise helped raised substantial sums of money for John Kerry, the eventual nominee.

The 2008 election saw the first real media attention to the phenomenon known as **bundling**. Candidates know that individual donors exist in networks of friends, family, and work associates who are also potential donors. Therefore, candidates enlist well-connected supporters to serve as bundlers. A bundler solicits contributions from donors to whom they are connected and collects (or bundles) those contributions together. George W. Bush termed his bundlers the "Bush Rangers" if they committed to raising $100,000 apiece through friends for his campaigns. But not all bundlers are reputable. Hillary Clinton's 2008 campaign struggled to respond to news that prominent Clinton bundler Norman Hsu had warrants out for his arrest in connection with pyramid schemes.[5]

Overall, fundraising is the single most important activity for a presidential candidate in the modern era. The adage that it takes money to make money certainly applies to the need for seed money in a campaign. To do well in the early contests, the candidate must have enough money to hire a staff and pay for advertising. Early success can then be translated into momentum that will generate more press coverage and increase the number of people willing to contribute to the campaign. Because the government's public funding program matches individual contributions up to $250, a large number of donations in that category can be quite rewarding when the check from the government arrives after each new nomination contest.

Putting Together a Staff

The campaign staff includes four main groups. At the top are the candidate's closest advisers. They may be family members, personal friends, business associates, or previous campaign supporters. Often, these advisers are not paid, but some may be. They are usually part of the candidate's team from the beginning. Second, modern presidential campaigns rely heavily on paid **consultants**, who include media relations experts, pollsters, advertising specialists, campaign strategists, and fundraising experts. These professionals have a particular expertise that they make available to different candidates in all kinds of elections. One of the first competitions is to see which candidate hires the best team of consultants. Because the candidate with the most money can pay for the best help and the best consultants want to continue their image of being winners, the reputation of the consultant team can serve as an early indicator of which candidate has the best chance of winning.

The other two groups involved in the campaign are the paid campaign staff and the volunteers. Though candidates increasingly rely on professional consultants for guidance at the highest levels, an extensive network of paid staffers still conducts much of the campaign's organizational tasks. The number of paid staffers may be quite small during the early stages of the campaign, and many of the workers travel from state to state as the primaries and caucuses take place. The volunteers are more likely to work for the local branch of the campaign during the period before their own state's primary or caucus. After the caucus or primary, the local office quickly goes dormant.

The Use of Polls

One of the first steps taken by a campaign is to assess the candidate's popularity and name recognition. Surveys are used to see what kinds of voters are aware of the candidate. They also examine what issues appeal to different voters. Typically, pollsters divide the population into groups according to whether they will participate in the nomination process and how likely they are to vote. This analysis can be used to determine which voters should be targeted by the candidate, what types of messages should be used in communicating with certain groups, what forms of media time should be purchased, and which opponents are most likely to provide the toughest competition. Most campaigns take several early polls to determine the viability of the candidate and to map a strategy. Then, throughout the campaign, **tracking polls** are conducted by the campaigns and the media. The campaigns look to see how well the candidate performs over time and with different messages and the media look for the ability to predict the winner of the contest. It is important to remember that tracking polls simply trace opinion changes over time and that there is a big difference between the unreleased internal tracking polls and those administered for news outlets.

Finally, as a primary or caucus approaches and the polls provide an idea of how well the candidate will do, the campaign begins **spin control** on the **expectations game**. Through spin control, the candidate's aides try to control the message that the media communicate to the voters. The expectations game is a matter of perception. Before a primary, political experts and the media predict how well the candidates will do, and a candidate who wins by a narrow margin may be characterized as a loser for failing to do as well as expected. Consequently, spin control is used to reduce expectations so that the media will positively report the results, whatever they are.

By 2000, the number of tracking polls had reached record levels. Each major network regularly released results of the horse race between the candidates, and each candidate relied on his own, more detailed surveys. The Bush campaign "leaked" internal numbers showing him with a lead in key states and close in others thought to be strong for Gore. Subsequently, Bush spent critical campaign time in California, and Gore campaigned hard in the critical state of Florida, where most independent polls showed a dead heat. Pundits questioned the wisdom of Bush's strategy, which appeared to be an effort to create a climate of impending victory. The later easy victory for Gore in California, along with other results, cast doubt on Bush's numbers. After the campaign was over, it appeared that Bush's strategy did not work. The national media polls had created the impression that Gore had pulled to a virtual dead heat. Meanwhile, Gore concentrated his efforts in an all-night blitz that ended in Tampa, Florida.

Building Momentum

The first major event of the nomination process is the **Iowa caucus**. Consequently, in most presidential election years, potential candidates practically live in Iowa. Because many candidates begin canvassing the state months before the caucus, active party members in the state have an excellent opportunity for meeting at least one candidate. Until the last few weeks before the caucus, candidates rely mainly on personal appearances as the main method of contacting voters. Because Iowa is the first test of the political viability of the candidates, the results can be important. A poor showing can eliminate a candidate from serious consideration.

The expectations game depends largely on where the candidates are from and their name recognition. Generally, the established front-runner and any candidates from nearby states are expected to do better than others. In 1992, Senator Tom Harkin from Iowa was in the race, so the Democratic results were considered less important than usual. Harkin was expected to win a majority of votes, and he did. In 2000, Republican John McCain made a controversial decision to skip the Iowa caucuses. McCain did not feel that he had the resources to mount a credible campaign in Iowa. This break with conventional wisdom later worked to McCain's advantage because he remained a viable candidate in later primaries. In 2008, McCain was again a contender for the GOP nomination, but after losing in 2000 McCain contested the Iowa caucuses. Former Arkansas Governor Mike Huckabee won the 2008 Iowa caucuses, with McCain a distant fourth. McCain's lack of luck in Iowa did not prevent him from winning the nomination in 2008, however, as he pulled ahead of the rest of the Republican pack after Super Tuesday.

ONLINE 9.2 *How the Iowa Caucuses Work*

The second major test is the **New Hampshire primary**. Its results may be more important than the Iowa caucus because it is a primary with more citizens participating. Usually held a week after the Iowa caucuses, the primary also receives tremendous media coverage. A dismal performance in both events effectively ends the chances of almost all candidates. Between 1972 and 1996, every Republican winner in the New Hampshire primary had gone on to win the party's nomination. However, in 2000, the ultimate winner, George W. Bush, lost to John McCain in New Hampshire. Bush's advantages in organization and money, though, ultimately overcame the McCain effort in New Hampshire. Nonetheless, McCain was able to extend the race with far fewer resources than Bush largely on the strength of the exposure in the free media that came with a New Hampshire victory. Hillary Clinton ensured that the 2008 Democratic nomination race would be close when she won New Hampshire shortly after Obama's Iowa victory.

Although the Democrats have had more exceptions, five of the last seven New Hampshire winners, including John Kerry in 2004, have gone on to win the nomination. Jimmy Carter's victory in 1976, when many analysts saw him as a long shot, gave his campaign tremendous momentum that eventually led to the Democratic nomination. If a candidate does not win, he must perform better than was expected by the political experts. Winning the expectations game can occasionally be enough for a candidate. Bill Clinton, for example, did not win in either Iowa or New Hampshire in 1992, but he won the expectations game. Early in the 2004 campaign, many people thought that former Vermont Governor Howard Dean would win the Democratic nomination for president. However, after he failed to win in Iowa and went on a televised rant in front of supporters, press reports centered on a man and a campaign coming unraveled and Dean faded quickly.

Narrowing the Field

Almost immediately after the New Hampshire primary, the candidates experience the effect of how well they performed. If they win in either state or beat the expectations game, they may receive a bounce in the national polls. More importantly, candidates with momentum can garner more contributions to keep their campaigns afloat. Contributors like to see that they are not wasting their money on a loser, so money flows toward the front-runners. The media also begin to focus attention on the candidates who appear to have a chance to win the nomination. Of the candidates chasing the front-runners, only the more controversial candidates, such as Al Sharpton in 2004 and 2008, continue to receive significant media attention. Several small states have caucuses and primaries in the week or so after the New Hampshire primary, and these events allow some previous losers to shine more brightly or front-runners to tighten their grip on the lead, but most of the attention then turns to Super Tuesday.

Super Tuesday

Super Tuesday is the second Tuesday in March. With a large number of delegates at stake on a single day, it was designed to be the most pivotal event in the nomination process. The original purpose of holding so many primaries on one day was to make the South more important in the Democratic nomination process, and Super Tuesday is generally seen as an excellent opportunity for a more conservative or moderate Democrat, such as Bill Clinton in 1992, to emerge with a large number of delegates. Typically, the race in each party is narrowed down to either one or two candidates after Super Tuesday. Because the large population of African American voters in the South is mostly Democrats, it also rewards a candidate who appeals to those voters, such as Barack Obama in 2008. In 2000, however, Super Tuesday was not so important. Al Gore had already locked up the race for the Democrats, and John McCain did not have the resources to contest many primaries. In 2004, Super Tuesday was again decisive, as John Edwards withdrew from the race after John Kerry all but locked up the nomination by winning nine of the ten primaries held on that day.

The Home Stretch

Shortly after Super Tuesday come the primaries in three large states with hundreds of delegates available: Illinois, Michigan, and New York. Because Super Tuesday is so crucial, most candidates have spent almost all their financial resources on advertising and campaigning in those states. After Super Tuesday, only the front-runners are generally able to replenish their campaign funds quickly. Consequently, even though hundreds of delegates are still at stake, the challengers have difficulty competing evenly with the front-runner in each party. Many challengers may have formally withdrawn by this point, and the rest are likely to be strapped for cash. Few second-place campaigns since 1972 have been able to continue after the New York primary in a seriously competitive mode. Even though California has the most delegates available in both parties, it has rarely had an effect on the nomination since 1972 because its primary comes at the end of the nomination season. Generally, the front-runner attempts to avoid any major embarrassments in the final few contests and begins to plan for the convention. Although a competitive nomination contest through the last few weeks is possible, one has not taken place recently.

Frontloading

The 2012 primaries saw the most tightly compacted calendar of primaries and caucuses in history. Iowa and New Hampshire's importance in building early momentum lead to candidates spending significant amounts of time and resources in each state. Candidates would basically move themselves and their staffs to Iowa and/or New Hampshire for a year leading up to their contests. Both states would receive massive infusions of cash from hotel rooms, food purchased, and televised campaign ads. Candidates would promise significant policies that would benefit those states, such as promoting ethanol made from Iowa corn as the dominant alternative energy source.

Other states saw the benefits of Iowa and New Hampshire's placement on the primary calendar and began to move their primaries forward. In 1960, for example, the primary calendar was stretched out from the end of January until early July. By 2008, almost every primary was over by the beginning of April, leaving a primary season of less than three months. The process of compacting the primary schedule is known as **frontloading**, and there is widespread agreement among scholars that frontloading leads to higher costs of campaigning, less candidate interaction with the voting public, and less usable political information for the voters.[6]

ONLINE 9.3 *Frontloading*
https://www.youtube.com/watch?v=VmpjnV2rJU8

The Convention: Culmination of the Nomination Process

At a national convention held during July or August, each party nominates its candidates for president and vice president. The conventions also determine the party platforms in addition to the rules by which the parties will govern themselves for the next four years. Both parties use majority rule among the delegates to make most decisions, including the selection of the nominee. Theoretically, with more than two candidates, a number of ballots could be needed before one candidate gets a majority. Indeed, in the past, numerous ballots were often required before the convention settled on a nominee. This multiple balloting made for a great deal of excitement and intrigue at the convention. But, in the modern era, the majority of delegates have already been pledged to vote for a particular candidate before the convention. No convention since 1968 has featured a wide-open contest that created any suspense. Because the eventual nominee controls the majority needed to win before the convention, the most important function of the convention is to provide the party with a tremendous advertising opportunity. The government provides the financing for the convention for both the major parties, and the major networks provide hours of free prime-time coverage.

As the party displays how it has rallied around the candidate, the convention can provide a significant public opinion boost to the party's nominee. That was apparently the case for Michael Dukakis in 1988, but the "bump" was short-lived and did not carry him through the election. In 1992, on the other hand, Bill Clinton's campaign orchestrated the convention to serve as a public relations coup that greatly boosted his public prestige and gave him considerable momentum heading into the general election contest. In 2004, support for incumbent president George W. Bush surged after the Republican convention, and Bush was able to sustain this momentum through the November election. After the 2008 conventions, Barack Obama had a slight lead on John McCain that would grow when serious economic crises became public. McCain would never lead Obama in the polls.

9-2b THE GENERAL ELECTION CAMPAIGN

The nomination process eliminates almost all the serious presidential candidates. Few third-party or Independent candidates have had much of an effect on the general election (Ross Perot in 1992 was a notable exception), so the race generally comes down to the Democratic and Republican nominees. The acceptance speech by each candidate at the national party convention serves as the first official act of the general election campaign. This speech highlights the issues that the nominee intends to focus on throughout the campaign, communicates the candidate's vision for the country, and attempts to bring together the various elements of the party again after the nomination battles. Typically, the Democrats have held their convention first, and the Republicans have stayed out of the limelight during this time. The Republicans hold their convention later in the summer, and the Democrats let the Republicans take center stage during this time. Late August is regarded as the last opportunity for each campaign to plan its general election strategy. Labor Day weekend marks the beginning of an exhaustive fall campaign.

THE ELECTORAL ENVIRONMENT

The political environment influences how the candidates prepare for the campaign. First, is the president running for reelection, or are both candidates hoping to fill an open seat? The incumbent president has the power of the entire administration at his disposal to influence voters, but he also has a record that must be defended. Generally, incumbents have done well. Sixteen incumbents have won reelection, whereas Bill Clinton was only the tenth challenger to beat an incumbent president.

The performance of the current administration is also important. Citizens consider the health of the economy, whether any scandals have taken place, and how well the president has protected national security. The incumbent president or the nominee of the incumbent president's party is likely to be held accountable by the voters for the economy, the ethical and moral conduct of the administration, and the maintenance of peace and security.

Another concern is the degree to which the president's party has been fractured. Because parties are loose coalitions of diverse factions with differing ideologies and issue positions, a party can easily experience disunity. Depending on how the dissatisfaction manifests itself, it can be devastating for the party's nominee in the general election. The causes of the split may be many. The nomination battle may have pitted one side against another. A particularly divisive issue may have become more salient. Poor performance by an incumbent president may have caused some to become dissatisfied. Many looked at the 2008 presidential race as a referendum on unpopular (and term-limited) President Bush. Or, personality problems between two individual party leaders may be at the source of a party break.

A party fracture can lead to three possible results. First, party supporters may abandon the party and vote for the opponent. For example, southern Democrats, who had supported the party since the Civil War, began voting for Republican presidential candidates in 1964 after the Johnson administration passed civil rights legislation and proposed further initiatives in that area. Second, voters may simply decide not to vote in a particular election. For example, disgruntled conservatives saw an unappealing moderate in 2008 Republican nominee John McCain and thus may have stayed home.

Third, a splinter group from a party may break off after the nomination process and support a candidate other than the original party nominee. For example, after having served as a Republican president from 1901 to 1909, Teddy Roosevelt became frustrated with the Republican nominee, William Howard Taft, in 1912. Consequently, Roosevelt decided to form a third party, the Bull Moose party, which was able to capture 27 percent of the vote. Because most of Roosevelt's supporters were Republicans, he took more voters away from Taft than from the Democratic nominee, Woodrow Wilson, who won the election. Many would argue that Ross Perot served a similar function in 1992. Though Perot was not as closely identified with the Republican party as Roosevelt had been in 1912, Perot's mostly conservative ideas tended to appeal more to Republican identifiers and Independents (who had voted for Bush in large numbers in 1988) than Democratic supporters. The result was that Republican George Bush received ten million fewer votes in 1992 than he had in 1988 and lost the election.

After these types of factors are taken into consideration, a campaign must consider several questions. First, what strategy will it use for campaigning in the states? Second, how can its financial resources best be used? Third, how can the campaign influence the image of the candidate that is presented in paid advertising and in the news? Finally, what issues are going to be most effective, and what positions should the candidate take on those issues?

State-by-State Strategies

Because of the time and energy required to visit every state during the campaign, few modern campaigns send a candidate to every state. Instead, the campaigns target certain states for the vast portion of personal attention by the candidate, her running mate, and their families. Two factors influence the choice of states to be visited and the number of trips to each one. First, how many electoral votes does the state have? Because the electoral college reflects the number of people in a state, the most populous states have the most electoral votes. For example, California has 55 electoral votes; New York, 29; Texas, 38; and Florida, 29. Meanwhile, Alaska, the District of Columbia, Montana, North Dakota, South Dakota, Vermont, and Wyoming have only three electoral votes apiece. Considering that only 270 votes are needed to win in the electoral college, a candidate who takes just the four most populous states (with 151 votes) would have more than half the votes necessary for victory. Consequently, both candidates tend to devote a large share of their resources to the ten largest states.

Second, what is the likelihood of winning a given state? Each party carefully scrutinizes the past results of presidential, congressional, and gubernatorial elections to determine whether a state is a likely win, a potential win, or a likely loss. For example, Arizona, Kansas, and Utah have been conservative stalwarts for decades. Few Democratic presidential candidates would consider any of them a potential target for a win. On the other side, the District of Columbia, Massachusetts, and Minnesota have been steady supporters of the Democrats for decades. Though neither side completely writes off a state, no candidate wants to waste valuable resources on a lost cause. The result is that populous states receive much attention, but an average-size state may also garner attention if it is considered competitive.

The formulation of a state-by-state campaign strategy can be complicated by the presence of a strong third-party candidate, such as Ross Perot in 1992. In a two-way race, each candidate knows the strengths of the other, and both know that a vote gained is a loss for the other side. A third actor complicates the situation by allowing disgruntled members of the opposite party to choose someone else. Attacking just one opponent may not be enough. States assigned to the definite loss category could even become victories. For example, in 1992 Clinton was able to capture nine states that had voted Republican in at least the past six presidential elections. It is difficult to attribute all this showing to Perot's presence in the race, but it is interesting to note that Perot received a greater-than-average share (at least 20 percent) of the vote in six of the nine states.

In 2004, it was clear from the polling data which states would be the "battlegrounds" going into the general election. Thus, it was no surprise that both President Bush and his challenger, Senator John Kerry, spent most of their time on the campaign trail in Florida, Ohio, Pennsylvania, Michigan, Wisconsin, and a handful of other states. Ultimately, the 2004 election came down to Ohio, which opted for President Bush by a very narrow margin. The fact that the GOP put so much effort into GOTV (get out the vote) in Ohio was one of the reasons Bush was able to carry the state. The Democrats were also very successful in their GOTV efforts in Ohio. John Kerry received more votes in Ohio than either Al Gore or George Bush had received in 2000. Still, it was not enough.

In 2008, Barack Obama was generally seen as the better candidate to respond to the economic crisis that began in September. The election contest with John McCain was never close, and Obama even won states that traditionally vote Republican, like Indiana. Obama's campaign centered around an eighteen-state strategy. Those eighteen states were chosen by the Obama campaign based on their ability to win them and the electoral college impact they would have.[7] For 2012, the game had changed. Nascent use of database technology since 2004 had bloomed into what was commonly called the "Big Data" election. The Obama campaign used sophisticated algorithms over massive databases to try to target, down to the neighborhood and in some cases the individual, the most likely voters that had not been activated in previous elections. Moving forward, any campaign that does not have a sophisticated data-driven campaign will lag behind those that understand the importance of voter data.[8]

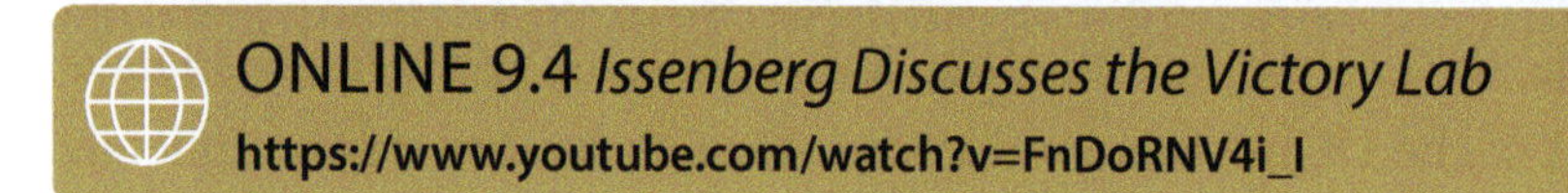

ONLINE 9.4 *Issenberg Discusses the Victory Lab*
https://www.youtube.com/watch?v=FnDoRNV4i_I

Financing the General Election Campaign

Before the 1976 election, candidates could spend as much money as they could raise. From 1860 through the election of 1972, the winner of the election outspent the loser twenty-one of the twenty-nine times.[9] Fundraising was dominated by "fat cat" contributors who could give hundreds of thousands or even millions of dollars. Solicitors, or individuals with excellent personal connections that helped them raise millions, were vital to any presidential campaign.

A new era of campaign financing began in the 1970s. In a series of three major pieces of legislation, Congress created a new public funding system for presidential elections. The new system, which took effect for the 1976 election, provides candidates with millions of dollars of public funds during the general election; in exchange, the candidate must agree to forgo contributions from any other sources during the general election. In 1992, Clinton and Bush each received $56 million in public funds for the general election. This money goes directly to the candidate's campaign committee to spend on travel, advertising, staff salaries, consultant fees, and other necessary items.

Advertising usually takes the largest share of the resources. The spending limit has two exceptions. First, the candidate's party can spend more than $10 million on behalf of the candidate during the election (or two cents per American of voting age). Second, the candidate can receive private donations to offset certain legal and accounting expenses that do not count against the limit. Otherwise, the candidate cannot receive any money from PACs, individuals, or even family members during the general election campaign.

Candidates are not required to accept the public money. If they do not, they can spend as much money as they can raise. They still must abide by the $1,000 limit on individual contributions and the $5,000 limit on PAC contributions, but they can spend as much of their own money as they want. Ross Perot, for example, did not attempt to qualify for public funding in 1992 and spent tens of millions of dollars from his own resources to pay for his campaign. In 2008, while noted campaign finance reform advocate John McCain accepted the $85 million public funding subsidy, Barack Obama relied on private fundraising using an aggressive Internet strategy. Obama's campaign raised more than $600 million bypassing the federal funding option.

Perot's case also illustrates another key feature of the public funding laws. Both major parties automatically qualify for public funding on the basis of their performance in the preceding election. Third-party and Independent candidates, however, do not automatically qualify for funding. To qualify, a candidate must receive at least 5 percent of the total popular vote and be on the ballot in at least ten states. In addition, a third-party candidate receives the money after the election, which makes it rather difficult to run a successful campaign. Even if third-party candidates qualify for public funds, they are eligible for only part of the funding provided to the major-party candidates. After third-party candidates qualify, they become eligible for public funding in the next election.

The campaign laws in effect in 2000 also had two key exceptions. First, there were no limits on soft money. State party committees can raise unlimited funds for the purpose of party-building activities, such as party bumper stickers, get-out-the-vote drives, and party mailings. Because the presidential campaign tends to save its precious resources for advertising focused on the candidate rather than on the party in general, the law is designed to enhance the parties. In practice, however, it has become a loophole in the campaign finance regulations. The candidate and the national party committee actively seek unlimited contributions from individuals, which are then earmarked for the state parties. For example, in both 1988 and 1992, George Bush appeared at dinners where large contributors received more prestigious seats and were able to have their picture taken with the president. Many contributions were in the hundreds of thousands of dollars. Though this type of money is not under the direct control of the presidential candidate; it can be used for activities that generally help the party but also benefit the candidate.

Political action committees also enjoyed a loophole in the election laws. PACs could not donate money to a presidential candidate during the general election, but they could spend as much as they wanted on independent expenditures. Thus, a PAC could spend millions of dollars on advertising that attacked or supported a candidate as long as the PAC did not work with the campaign in developing the advertising. For example, in 1988, the National Security PAC spent more than $7 million on negative advertisements attacking Democrat Michael Dukakis; among the ads was the Willie Horton advertisement, which has been described as the low point in one of the nastiest presidential campaigns ever. In this case, Bush benefited from the advertising, but was able to avoid responsibility for it because of the legal separation between his campaign committee and the PAC.

The campaign legislation of 1973 changed presidential elections in four ways. First, the campaigns operated on more equal financial footing. Because Republicans had traditionally appealed to wealthier individuals, they usually enjoyed financial advantages over the Democrats until 1976. On the other hand, the increasing use of soft money had allowed the old inequality to reappear to some extent. The Republicans were the first to exploit the loophole, and they maintained sizable advantages over the Democrats in soft money until the 1992 election. In 1984, Reagan received $16 million to Mondale's $1 million, but Clinton and Bush were more equal in 1992. By the 2000 election, the parties had reached virtual parity in spending.

Second, in the first elections under the new laws, spending was reduced. The soft money loopholes, however, have allowed campaign spending to rise faster than the rate of inflation. Third, the limits on individual contributions severely constrained the "fat cat" contributors and initially somewhat reduced their role. The trend toward soft money, though, has allowed the fat cats to become major players again. Finally, the limits on spending have forced candidates to use campaign funds more carefully. Consequently, candidates are much more likely to focus their efforts on their own campaigns rather than on the party. Again, soft money has mitigated this effect by forcing the national committees to work with the state parties to raise and spend soft money. Thus, on one hand, the new restrictions have tended to separate the presidential campaign from the campaigns of other party members, including members of Congress and state officials; on the other hand, soft money has had the effect of increasing party cooperation.

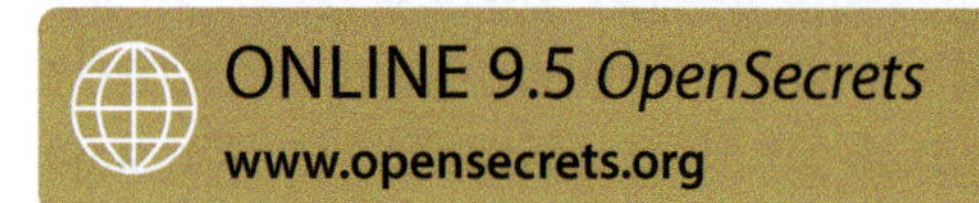

Campaign Finance Reform of 2002

In May 2002, Congress passed, and President Bush signed, major campaign finance legislation. Campaign finance reform appeared on the national agenda during the 1996–2002 and throughout the nomination process and, to some extent, the general election in the 2000 presidential elections. Senator John McCain of Arizona mounted a strong challenge to the front-runner George W. Bush during the primaries. This challenge was largely built around McCain's commitment to campaign finance reform—in particular, around the bill he had cosponsored with Democratic Senator Russ Feingold of Wisconsin. Bush opposed the McCain–Feingold legislation. During the campaign, the issue again arose, with Al Gore favoring the McCain–Feingold bill.

President Bush took office in January, 2001, still expressing grave doubts about his old nemesis John McCain's finance reform package. The Republican House leadership helped delay consideration of the bill until 2002, when, following indications that President Bush would not veto the legislation, the House followed the Senate in passing legislation to restructure the regulation of contributions to candidates in federal elections.

The finance legislation signed into law in 2002, eventually titled the Bipartisan Campaign Reform Act (BCRA), targets the use of soft money in campaigns. The soft-money process allows moneyed interests a mechanism for circumventing the limits on contributions by supposedly allowing unlimited contributions to "party building" activities. The legislation did increase the amount of hard money that can be contributed directly to candidates and to the party's local and national committees. However, its most controversial element is that it limits the ability of corporations and labor unions to run election ads for specific candidates during the last portion of campaigns. Many people speculated that the Supreme Court might invalidate this restriction on what many regard to be protected political speech, but that proved not to be the case.[10]

The 527s

In the wake of BCRA, a new species of political creature evolved—the *527 group*, so called because they are governed by Section 527 of the federal tax code. Because they were not specifically covered by BCRA, 527s came to serve as vehicles for independent expenditures on behalf of candidates. Although they cannot endorse candidates, they render assistance by attacking opponents. These attacks are legal as long as there is no coordination between the group and a political campaign organization.

Two such groups played a prominent role in the 2004 presidential campaign. A liberal 527 known as MoveOn.org received a $5 million contribution from billionaire George Soros and proceeded to run television ads that were extremely critical of President Bush. On the other side of the fence, the Swift Boat Veterans for Truth attacked John Kerry's record of service in Vietnam and subsequent antiwar activities. Both MoveOn.org and the Swift Boat Veterans leveled charges against President Bush and Senator Kerry, respectively, that many people (including the candidates themselves) considered to be scurrilous and irresponsible. Bush, Kerry, Senator John McCain, and political notables across the land called for legal action to rein in these independent groups. But others argued that what these groups were doing was nothing more than exercising their First Amendment rights, albeit in a way that many Americans found offensive.

Despite a significant presence in 2004, 527 organizations were not as active in the 2008 cycle. In particular, federal 527 groups raised and spent half of what they did in 2004. The closeness of the 2004 campaign led to a late push by the groups attempting to alter the balance, but with the 2008 election nowhere near as close, the groups had little incentive to become more involved.[11]

SuperPACs

A new development after 2010 altered the campaign finance landscape even more. In *Citizens United vs. FEC*, the Supreme Court undermined BCRA by allowing unlimited and undisclosed donations from and to corporations, unaffiliated groups, and labor unions in response to an FEC ruling that a conservative group could not distribute a movie critical of then-candidate Hillary Clinton. The Citizens United case created a new class of **SuperPAC** that could collect large sums of money from anonymous donors and spend it in any way that did not expressly advocate for the election or defeat of a candidate. In effect, SuperPACs return us to the era of soft money, but now political parties cannot be involved as middlemen.[12]

ONLINE 9.6 *Souter on Citizens United*
http://www.youtube.com/watch?v=VcXQ-BHmfbk

The National Media Campaign

Two elements are essential in controlling the image of the candidate that is conveyed to the voting public. First, the campaign must manage the news media. Second, the campaign must develop a paid advertising schedule that allows the candidate to reveal personal strengths, attack the opponent's weaknesses, focus on a few issues, and provide a general theme of what the candidacy is all about. Today, a successful campaign requires a skilled team of consultants who assist the candidate in managing the media. Because the mass media—including the television and radio networks, national news magazines, and major newspapers—send reporters and photojournalists to all campaign stops of both major candidates, the candidates can receive hours of free advertising throughout the campaign. In addition to being free, this advertising appears to be more unbiased and credible to the voters than paid advertising.

The Nixon campaign of 1968 was perhaps the first to effectively utilize media and advertising experts to manage the news. Now campaigns devote daily attention to the media. The candidate's schedule is designed so that the campaign stops on a given day are coordinated to develop a theme. The campaign staff carefully plans the events so that each one provides a suitable visual setting to reinforce the theme. For example, a factory might serve as the backdrop for a speech on the economy, and an aircraft carrier would be used for a defense policy theme. Because the campaign even controls the angle and position of the media's cameras at these types of events, any pictures that appear in the news present the image the campaign wants the viewer to see.

A major criticism of the modern media campaign is that it encourages simple messages that can be easily edited by television news producers. As a result, voters receive only a sound bite. A **sound bite** is a short clip, maybe ten to fifteen seconds long, that consists of a catchy phrase (such as "Change we can believe in") conveying a simple message. Candidates are not rewarded for providing the details of a complex policy or explaining why they think changes are necessary. A sentence or two attacking the opponent or a witty one-liner is more likely to make the news. Often, an attack is launched late in the afternoon so that it is aired on the evening network news and the opponent does not have time to respond. Though the strategic advantage of this type of move cannot be questioned, it falls somewhat short of the democratic ideal of an exchange of ideas that enables voters to make real choices between candidates.

Radio advertising has been around since Franklin D. Roosevelt's campaigns in the 1930s, and television has been a part of presidential campaigns since Eisenhower's first election in 1952. Since the enactment of the campaign finance legislation, paid advertising has become the main campaign tool, taking up most of the candidates' public funding. Typically, candidates spend as much as 90 percent of the public funds for television advertising, and as much as half of that amount may be saved for the last month or so of the campaign. Internet campaigning has become an integral part of any candidacy. Any candidate hoping for success must have a website, social networking presence, YouTube channel, Twitter feed, and an army of online content providers and commenters.

Advertising campaigns have increasingly adopted the best techniques Madison Avenue has to offer. Candidates work extensively with public speaking experts, acting professionals, makeup experts, hair stylists, and advertising consultants. Typically thirty seconds long, the advertisements carefully blend music and visually stimulating video clips with a simple theme. Expansive discussions of policy are avoided. Though the brief television ad or web video provides slightly more time than the average sound bite, the candidate must still keep the message simple and focus on one theme. Strong campaigns coordinate the images and messages of the sound bites and the paid advertising.

Campaign consultants have developed a variety of techniques to assess how a message is being received by the public. The consultants usually test the potential effect of an ad before airing it by showing it to a group of viewers who are similar to the voters the campaigns are hoping to reach. After an ad has been shown on television, the consultants use surveys to assess its effect. Early in the campaign, the consultants try to find the "hot button" issues that are important to voters and develop the image and message that work well for the candidate. In the last weeks of the campaign, when there is little time for careful preparation, the consultants can move quickly with their advertising to respond to the opponent or even the media.

The Role of Issues in the Campaign

Though media campaigns tend to focus on personality and symbolism, issues still matter. Most voters are at least somewhat interested in a candidate's views on the issues, though they tend to react negatively to candidates who take extreme positions. Generally speaking, American political culture has fostered a preference for more moderate candidates than is the case in most other democracies. Americans have rejected the more extreme political ideologies, such as communism and fascism, and tend to elect moderate members of the two moderate parties that dominate American elections. Furthermore, from a strategic standpoint, if a candidate needs a majority to win (as is the case in the usual two-candidate election), the middle ground is most advantageous. With only two candidates, if candidate A places herself at the exact center of the ideological mainstream, her opponent is forced to choose a position to the left or right of center. After the opponent does so, all the voters on the other side (half the voters) plus the middle voter will choose candidate A. Candidate A will now have 50 percent plus one vote, the amount needed to win.

During the nomination process, a candidate has to please the voters in his party. Because the participants in primaries and, especially, caucuses tend to be more extreme than the average voter, candidates must often take more extreme positions during the nomination process. After the nomination is won, however, the candidate must attempt to appear more moderate to have a chance to win. Often, a candidate focuses on different issues in the nomination battle and the general election campaign. Occasionally, a candidate is caught by an opponent or the media in an attempt to soften or change a position. Becoming more moderate without appearing to "flip-flop" on the issues or seeming too "slick" can be difficult. Yet a candidate who does not appear moderate may be branded as an extremist. For example, in 1988, Republican George Bush made Michael Dukakis look unpatriotic by attacking him for opposing a policy that would require children in the public schools to recite the pledge of allegiance. In 2008, Barack Obama was able to successfully describe a possible McCain presidency as four more years of the unpopular incumbent George W. Bush.

Presidential Debates

The nationally televised debates that have become common in the past few elections provide a forum for greater depth than is possible in sound bites and thirty-second ads. Although debates are not required, a tradition has developed that the two major candidates should participate. One problem, however, is that no neutral organization exists that both parties will allow to conduct debates. Consequently, the rules, time, date, place, and number of debates are determined solely by negotiations between the two candidates' organizations. Typically, the front-runner is somewhat concerned about giving the opponent too many opportunities. Therefore, the incumbent, usually a Republican over the past thirty years, has been reluctant to take on the challenger in debates. Because he was behind in the polls, George H.W. Bush was the exception in 1992. He agreed to three presidential debates and one vice presidential debate that included both major-party candidates and Ross Perot's ticket. In 2000, candidate George W. Bush was eager to debate Vice President Gore. In 2004, incumbent President Bush was not so eager to debate John Kerry. Given Bush's lackluster performance in the three debates that did take place in 2004, the president's reluctance was easy to understand.

Though personality and style are important, the debates also provide a forum in which candidates can present their views on the issues. Winning candidates tend to be more moderate, or at least appear more moderate to a larger number of voters, than losing candidates. Though issues may not be the main focus of the modern American campaign, the positions that candidates take affect their chances of victory, and the art of position-taking is an important part of developing a winning image.

The three presidential debates between Al Gore and George W. Bush played a pivotal role in the 2000 elections. Before the debates, Gore had built a formidable lead in the polls, and most observers figured that his command of detail and experience in debate would serve him well against Bush, who lacked substantial debate experience or command of the details of policy. Bush's main advantage was that he faced minimal expectations. At the end of the three debates, most observers believed that Bush had helped himself considerably, not so much by displaying competence or expertise, but by force of personality, much like Ronald Reagan in the 1980s. Certainly, the narrowing gap in the polls and the extremely close vote on election day strongly suggest that the debates helped Bush.

In 2004, the situation was reversed. By most accounts, Senator John Kerry outperformed President Bush in the three debates between them. Even President Bush's supporters expressed dismay at how poorly he had performed, especially in the first debate. Still, Kerry's strong performance in the debates was not enough to secure victory in the November election. The 2008 debates were "split" between Obama and McCain. Neither candidate outshone the other or embarrassed himself, nor did either candidate really change the course of the election with their performance. In 2012, Mitt Romney looked to have momentum, emerging from the first debate as the resounding winner. However, in the subsequent two debates Obama won, nullifying that momentum.

ONLINE 9.7 *2012 Debates*

1. http://www.youtube.com/watch?v=NAi4wCfcCPU
2. http://www.youtube.com/watch?v=9b1VQdHNvfY
3. http://www.youtube.com/watch?v=n0LhytVWsmA

9-2c THE ELECTORAL COLLEGE VOTE

On the first Tuesday in November, voters go to the polls to cast their votes for the presidential candidate of their choice. If these voters look carefully at the ballot, they notice that they are not voting directly for candidates for president. Rather, voters in each state are asked to choose a slate of individuals who will represent their state in the electoral college (see Figure 9-1). The electoral college is composed of electors who are chosen by each state. The method of choosing electors is determined by each state's legislature. Until 1800, in ten of the fifteen states, electors were chosen by state legislatures rather than elected directly by the people. By 1832, only South Carolina did not use a direct election. Since 1864, all states have chosen electors by direct elections.

Almost all states (except Maine and Nebraska) use a winner-take-all system to determine the results. Under a winner-take-all system, all the electors from a state are awarded to the party that receives the most popular votes in the state. If two million persons vote for candidate X and two million and one voters choose candidate Y, candidate Y wins all the electoral votes from that state. Note that a majority of votes (50 percent plus one vote) is not needed to win. A plurality, or the most votes, is all that is necessary. Consequently, a close race in the popular vote may translate into a large margin of victory in the electoral college.

The number of electors from each state is equal to the number of its members of Congress. If a state has four House members and two senators, for example, it receives six electors. (The electors are not the same individuals as the congressional delegation, however.) Because the Congress consists of 435 House members and 100 senators, and the District of Columbia receives three electors, the electoral college is composed of 538 electors.

The electoral college system worked as planned in the first two presidential elections. As you have seen, however, the emergence of political parties, which had apparently not been envisioned by the Framers of the Constitution, revealed flaws in the system. After the contentious election of 1800, in which both Thomas Jefferson and his running mate, Aaron Burr, received the same number of votes in the electoral college, thereby throwing the election into the House of Representatives, Congress adopted the Twelfth Amendment, requiring electors to vote separately for president

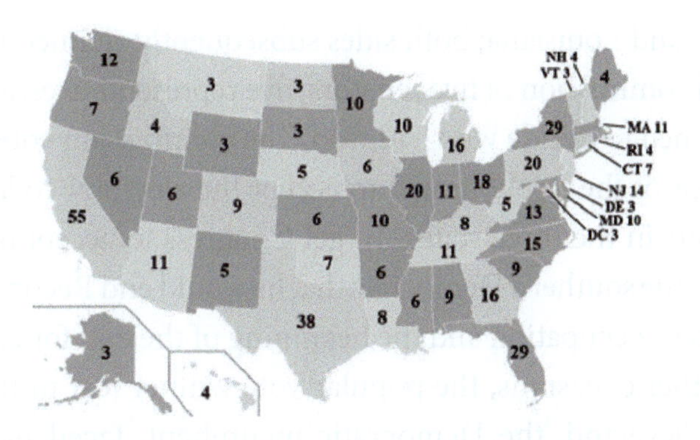

Figure 9-1 *Electoral Votes per State for the 2012 Election*
Available at http://www.ourwhitehouse.org/gettingthevotes.html

and vice president. If a presidential candidate does not receive a majority (270 votes now equals 50 percent plus 1 of the 538 electors) in the electoral college, the decision goes to the House, where each state delegation has one vote in choosing from the top three finishers. If a vice presidential candidate does not receive a majority of electoral votes, the Senate selects the vice president from the top two finishers.

On several occasions, the electoral college has either thwarted the national public's preference for a candidate, come perilously close to negating the outcome of the popular election, or has sent the election to the House of Representatives. The crucial election of 1860, which sent Abraham Lincoln to the White House and plunged the country into the Civil War, was one of these situations. The Democrats were divided over the issue of slavery. Consequently, four major candidates ran for president: Lincoln for the Republicans, Stephen Douglas for the main wing of the Democrats, John Breckenridge for a southern offshoot of the Democratic party, and John Bell for the Constitutional Union party, which drew its support from southerners committed to the preservation of the Union. Lincoln received less than 40 percent of the popular vote, but he carried eighteen northern states that enabled him to win the electoral college by twenty-eight votes. This pivotal election in our history was decided by only 25,000 popular votes. Lincoln won by 25,000 votes in New York, and its electors gave him a majority in the electoral college.

The election of 1876 also tested the limits of the system. The contest was between Rutherford B. Hayes, the Republican, and Samuel Tilden, the Democrat. Tilden had a 3 percent margin over Hayes in the popular vote (or 250,000 more votes), but Hayes beat Tilden by one electoral vote. Because the electoral college decides the winner, Hayes became the new president. The manner in which Hayes got that crucial vote was as important as the fact that the popular vote was circumvented by the electoral college. During the election, the Republicans had made massive attempts at voting fraud, and the Democrats had intimidated black voters in three hotly contested races in Florida,

South Carolina, and Louisiana; both sides subsequently claimed the electors from those states. A special commission of five senators, five representatives, and five Supreme Court justices was formed to decide who had won. The commission voted along party lines (an 9–7 split in favor of the Republicans) to accept the electoral college votes submitted by Hayes' supporters in the three states. To get Congress to accept the commission results, Hayes promised the southern Democrats that he would end Reconstruction, which meant the end of military occupation and the beginning of the end for civil rights in the South.

On two other occasions, the popular vote winner lost in the electoral college. In 1888, Grover Cleveland, the Democratic incumbent, faced Benjamin Harrison, the Republican challenger. Cleveland had a 1 percent lead in the popular vote (a 95,000-vote advantage), but he lost in the electoral college. Slim victories in two states—15,000 votes in New York and 3,000 in Indiana—gave Harrison the electoral college votes he needed to win. Finally, in one of the most controversial outcomes in American history, George W. Bush won the electoral college vote with a margin of two votes (271) but lost the popular vote by more than 300,000 votes to Al Gore.

Although Gore could have won in 2000 if only 500 people in Florida had voted differently, the country has often faced close electoral college calls. On several recent occasions, a small change in the votes in a few states could have thrown the election into the House of Representatives. In 1948, Truman won the election, but a shift of 12,500 votes in California could have prevented him from reaching a majority in the electoral college. Similarly, Kennedy in 1960 could have been denied an electoral college majority if just 9,000 votes had been different in Illinois and Missouri. In 1968, Republican Richard Nixon received only 43.4 percent of the popular vote, but he garnered 301 electoral votes of 538 possible (56 percent), which was nearly 31 more than he needed to win (270). However, a 55,000-vote shift in New Jersey, New Hampshire, and Missouri would have thrown the election into a Democratically controlled House that might have chosen his Democratic opponent, Hubert Humphrey. In 1976, a switch of 3,687 votes in Hawaii and 5,559 votes in Ohio would have prevented Carter from achieving an electoral college majority.

One of the most significant issues with the electoral college is that it seems to undermine the popular will. The popular vote was never intended to be the sole determinant of the president, but when a candidate can win the popular vote and lose in the electoral college, the effect is to threaten the legitimacy of the elected candidate and make members of the public feel that their votes do not count. A Republican in Massachusetts, which has voted Democratic in presidential elections every cycle but 1984 for a century, knows that his vote will have no bearing on the outcome of the election. One-party dominant states will therefore provide no incentive to vote for members of the out-party or voters unaffiliated with either party. Critics of the electoral college fear that it suppresses voter turnout and have called for changes, even going so far as to advocate eliminating the college altogether and replacing it with a nationwide popular vote.

The main reason why some voters feel they have no say is the winner-take-all nature of all save two states' electoral college votes. A candidate who wins a simple majority of the popular votes in a state doesn't win a percentage of electoral votes equal to their percentage of the popular vote: they win every vote in the state. A narrow winner in California wins every one of that state's 55 electoral votes, even if they only win 51 percent of the vote. A fairer distribution of the votes would give 28 electoral votes to the winner with 51 percent and the remaining 27 to the second-place candidate with 49 percent of the vote. The winner-take-all nature of state electoral college distribution means that winning big states has a huge advantage for the winner.

Another option is the Maine and Nebraska plans. Each state allocates only two electoral votes to the statewide winner. The other votes are distributed based on the winner of each Congressional district. Voters in the districts have a much greater chance of influencing the outcome of the election in that district or at least being closer to having their voice heard. A number of proposals such as the direct popular vote, proportional distribution, and congressional district distribution were publicized after the 2000 election, but no national support has developed for electoral college reform as of yet.

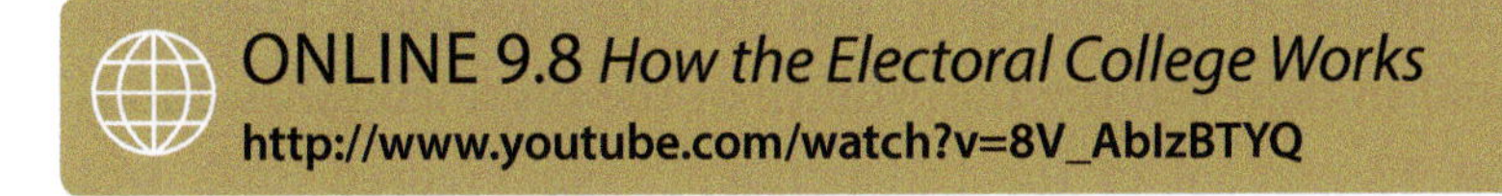

ONLINE 9.8 *How the Electoral College Works*
http://www.youtube.com/watch?v=8V_AbIzBTYQ

9-3 Individual Voting Behavior

In any election, a candidate faces two fundamental challenges: to get potential supporters to register to vote, follow the campaign, and heed the candidate's message, and to convince voters to make "the right choice." In developing strategies to achieve these goals, campaigns must take into account the forces that underlie the vote decision.

9-3a Party Identification

Party identification, the feeling of attachment that individuals have for a political party, is the major long-term force in American politics.[13] Most people develop party identification early in life, usually through parental influence. Though some people do change the party with which they identify, most keep this identification as a predisposition to vote for a certain party's candidates. For example, a Democrat is most likely to vote for the Democratic candidate in any given election. Other forces, of course, can cause this person to vote for the Republican candidate.

Party identification allows citizens to make sense of politics from a particular point of view. As a result, people do not have to process the vast amount of political information that comes to them in a campaign.[14] For instance, a woman who is committed to the Democratic party because of its stand on organized labor may feel that she does not have to pay close attention to all that the candidates say unless the Democratic candidate takes a different stand on labor issues. Likewise, a man who strongly agrees with Republican tax policy may not feel any need to reconsider his vote on a day-to-day basis.

Party identification tells us more about how people will vote than any other indicator. In any presidential campaign, the candidates must mobilize voters from their own parties. In 1992, on the other hand, 10 percent of Democrats voted for George Bush, and 10 percent of Republicans voted for Bill Clinton. In 2000, 8 percent of Democrats cast ballots for George W. Bush, and only 8 percent of Republicans voted for Al Gore. Likewise, in 2004, more than 90 percent of Republicans voted for President Bush, and more than 90 percent of Democrats voted for John Kerry. Despite two-thirds of the electorate holding a party identification, a full third has no party affiliation. That pivotal third usually makes the difference between the winning and losing candidate. In 2008 and 2012, those swing voters moved from choosing Republican Bush in 2004 to Democrat Obama.

Since the 1960s, the number of Independents has steadily increased. This group has been quite instrumental in determining the winner of the presidential elections. In 1992, Bill Clinton won 42 percent of the Independent vote, George Bush won 31 percent, and Ross Perot won 27 percent. This was the first time in more than a quarter of a century that the Democrat captured more of the Independent vote than the Republican. In 2000, however, Independents again preferred the Republican candidate, albeit by a narrow margin (see Table 9-1). In 2008, Independents strongly favored Obama over McCain.

9-3b Issues

In any contested election, the voter is offered a choice between or among candidates. With rare exceptions, these competing candidates support different policies and take different positions on the issues. Moreover, even in cases in which the candidates do not take clear or differing stands on various issues, their party label gives important issue cues to the voter. Nevertheless, the role of issues in arriving at the vote decision is not clear, and political scientists have disagreed over the importance of issues in voting behavior.

Most observers agree that issues have played a major role in recent presidential elections. Ronald Reagan's victory in 1980 was widely viewed as a clear message from the electorate that a change in basic public policy was expected. A majority of voters

TABLE 9-1 Presidential Voting among Various Groups, 2012

	OBAMA	ROMNEY	OTHER
Male	45	52	3
Female	55	44	1
White	39	59	2
African American	93	4	3
Latino	71	27	2
Asian American	72	25	3
18–24	60	36	4
25–28	60	38	2
30–39	55	42	3
40–49	48	50	2
50–64	47	52	1
65+	44	56	0
60+	47	51	2
No High School	71	25	4
High school graduate	51	48	1
Some college	49	48	3
College graduate	47	51	2

Source: CNN http://www.cnn.com/election/2012/results/race/president#exit-polls

had lost faith in the ability of the federal government to solve social problems. The electorate seemed to prefer a strong national defense and less government involvement in the economy. Clear differences existed between Reagan and the incumbent Democrat, Jimmy Carter. The electorate perceived these differences and acted accordingly.

Likewise, the 1992 election was widely seen as having been affected by economic issues. In fact, the Clinton campaign staff operated under the motto "It's the economy, stupid!" Issues have played a key role in many other presidential elections also. In 2000, Al Gore and George W. Bush disagreed on a number of domestic policy items. However, in many ways their differences were about details on an agenda with relative agreement on broad strokes. For instance, when Gore proposed a prescription drug benefit under Medicare, Bush responded with his own program. Both candidates put forth proposals for tax reduction. The difference was in the details, and the difference highlighted the historic themes of each candidate's party. In 2004, the war in Iraq and "values" issues such as same-sex marriage were uppermost on the list of salient issues. The 2008 and 2012 elections hinged on the voters' faith in Obama to handle the crisis of 2008 and continuing economic challenges. Social issues gave way to talk of ending the two-front war and reviving a flagging domestic economy.

Prospective and Retrospective Issue Voting

Issue voting can take place in two ways. With **retrospective voting**, voters look back at how well a candidate has done. In contrast, with **prospective voting**, voters look forward and predict how each candidate will perform in the future. Obviously, this type of voting is difficult to do, especially given the tendency of politicians to make campaign promises that are hard to keep. In 1976, Democratic challenger Jimmy Carter asked voters whether they were better off than they had been four years earlier. Obviously, Carter was asking voters to use retrospective voting to remove his opponent, Gerald Ford, from office. Unfortunately for President Carter, challenger Ronald Reagan turned the tables by asking the same question four years later. In each case, the incumbent lost. In both cases, many voters concentrated on the incumbent's performance on economic issues.

On the other hand, a successful incumbent or a candidate closely associated with the incumbent often wants to put the discussion of the issues in retrospective terms. Both Ronald Reagan's 1984 reelection campaign and George Bush's 1988 campaign against Michael Dukakis called for a retrospective evaluation of the Reagan presidency. In 2008, once the economic troubles surfaced, so did troubles for the incumbent party. Despite his being term-limited out of office, the 2008 election was widely seen as a referendum on Bush's performance on the economy. Voters were in the mood to punish the incumbent administration, and absent the opportunity to do that directly to President Bush they judged his successor, John McCain, as the candidate to bear responsibility for the economic problems facing the nation.

9-3c Ideology

Although voters' evaluations of a particular issue may vary, a citizen's ideology is a more enduring framework that helps her reach voting decisions. An ideology is an abstract view of the political world, with an underlying belief or set of beliefs that ties together various attitudes and opinions. The authors of *The American Voter*, which has become a classic in voting behavior research, found that few Americans could articulate an ideological position on politics.[15] Nevertheless, later research found that most voters could make some use of the liberal-conservative continuum in evaluating issues and candidates. The most educated and sophisticated voters do, in fact, use liberalism and conservatism as devices to order their positions on issues, which in turn influence their voting decisions.[16]

Though few Americans think in ideological terms, most Americans are familiar with ideological labels. Barack Obama effectively described John McCain, a moderate Republican, as a virtual clone of conservative George W. Bush, putting McCain in a difficult position during the course of the campaign. The Obama reelection campaign used the same strategy against Mitt Romney in 2012, painting the middle-of-the-road former Republican governor of Massachusetts as a hard-right conservative to magnify the differences between the candidates.

9-3d Candidate Image

American politics has become increasingly about image. Much of this phenomenon can undoubtedly be attributed to television. A candidate can more easily project an image of what he is about in a thirty-second spot than describe complex policy positions. Many images do successfully embody issue positions, however. One of the more successful television spots used during the 1988 election was the Willie Horton ad. It showed a rather unflattering picture of an African American along with a long line of prisoners entering and leaving prison through a revolving door. The narrator explained that Michael Dukakis had supported weekend passes for some felons, which gave them the opportunity to commit horrible crimes like the rapes and murders that Horton had committed. The ad was widely condemned as appealing to racial prejudices. Nevertheless, for many people, the ad symbolized a wide range of domestic issue positions that came together to form an image of a Democrat who was "soft on crime."

In 2004, John Kerry suffered somewhat from an image of being aloof and out of touch with ordinary Americans. The Kerry campaign attempted to counter this by having the candidate go on a widely publicized goose-hunt a few weeks before the election. The image of Senator Kerry, an extremely wealthy liberal Democrat from Boston, dressed in camouflage and toting a shotgun was designed to connect with millions of hunters and gun owners across the country. Unfortunately for the Kerry campaign, the incident merely provided more fodder for the late-night comedians. Candidates must always take care not to be seen as trying to project a spurious image. Even without the assistance of the late-night comics, most voters are not taken in by such charades. For John McCain, overcoming Barack Obama's image as a young, charismatic, and energetic leader was a significant problem. The McCain campaign tried to point out Obama's lack of experience in national politics and his growing celebrity status in ads, but McCain's strategy merely reinforced positive images of his opponent already held by the public.

Party Image

Party image is the reaction people have toward a political party. Typical party images might be "The Republicans are the party of the rich" or "The Democrats are the tax-and-spend party." The party image is separate from that of the candidate. In the 1950s, party image was a powerful force in determining how Americans voted. The force of these images has faded somewhat as the parties have become less important in American politics. Still, the Republican party suffers somewhat from its white, Anglo-Saxon, Protestant image. The image is slowly changing, however, as Hispanics, Asian Americans, and Catholics are increasingly identifying themselves as Republicans.

Candidate Image

Although party image has waned somewhat as a short-term force, **candidate image** has become more and more important since the 1950s.[17] More than anything else, television is responsible for this change. Communicating an image of a candidate is much easier than projecting an image of a political party. Creating a negative image of the opposing candidate is also easier. Because of the advantages of projecting a candidate image as opposed to a party image, modern presidential campaigns have become candidate centered. Nixon's 1972 campaign for president, for example, was run totally independently of the Republican party structure. Calling itself the Campaign to Re-Elect the President, and known by its critics as CREEP, this organization was at least partially responsible for some of the excesses that led to the Watergate scandal.

Candidates establish their own images and try to paint unflattering images of their opponents in a number of ways. First, candidates can purchase advertisements, usually on television, to project themselves in positive terms and their opponents in negative terms. Second, they can make use of the existing news media by using photo opportunities and sound bites. A **photo opportunity** is an event staged with the hope that it will be photographed or filmed by the news media. If successful, photo opportunities and sound bites reflect positively on the candidate. Moreover, they appear in the news without cost to the candidate.

Candidate image has been crucial in most recent presidential elections. These images have been negative as well as positive. One of the most enduring images of the 1988 presidential campaign was that of Michael Dukakis riding in a tank. The Dukakis campaign originally arranged the filming as a photo opportunity, but the attempt backfired. Dukakis appeared ill at ease, and the Republicans soon used the image to ridicule Dukakis and highlight his lack of foreign policy experience. As mentioned above, Barack Obama's 2008 campaign featured his charisma and youth as centerpieces. By contrast, John McCain was older and less engaging with the public, making for a serious contrast of imagery between the two campaigns.

9-3e A Model of the Voting Decision

Figure 9-2 depicts a simplified model of the vote decision. The darker line represents a stronger link. Party identification has a strong, direct effect on the vote. It also affects the vote decision indirectly; that is, a voter's party identification has an effect on his image of the party, which in turn has an effect on the vote. Ideology, issues, and candidate image also play a role in the vote decision.

9-4 The 2000 Cliffhanger

The presidential election of 2000 was the closest and perhaps most controversial in modern American history. The turnout of 51 percent represented a slight increase over the turnout in 1996, but fell short of the 1992 election, in which Ross Perot's candidacy had injected more interest in the process. Before election night, much discussion occurred regarding the closeness of the election. On the eve of the election, most publicly released tracking polls showed George Bush with a slight lead over Al Gore, although the difference was within the margin of error, making the election too close

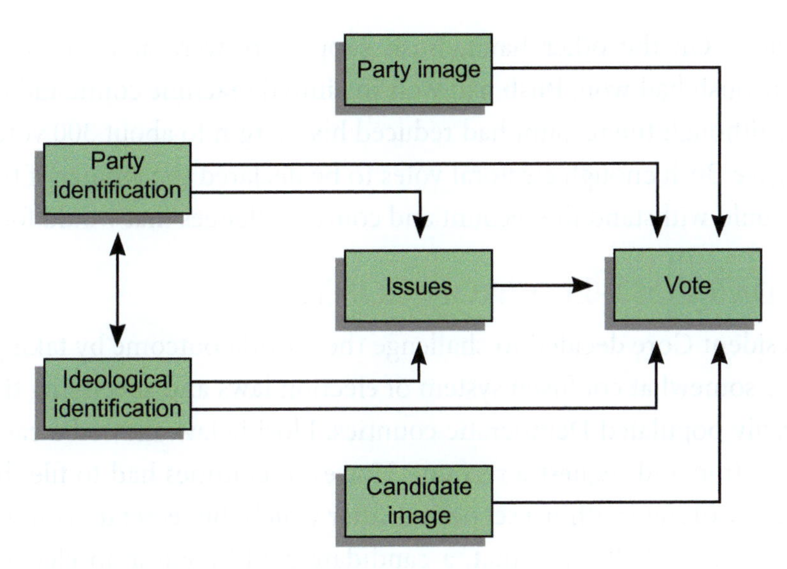

Figure 9-2 *A Model of Voting Behavior*

to call. Most projections regarding the electoral college were likewise close or "too close to call." In the last weeks of the election, both campaigns shifted to a massive get-out-the-vote campaign directed at their supporters.

The controversy over the eventual outcome was presaged by the earlier returns and exit poll projections from the Voter News Service (VNS), a company funded by the major television networks along with the Associated Press. When most of Florida's polls closed at 7 p.m. Eastern, VNS soon provided data that led the networks to project that Gore had won the state's twenty-five pivotal electoral votes. When combined with the projections of a Gore victory in Pennsylvania and Michigan, the Florida call could not have contributed to any enthusiasm among Bush supporters. However, as the vote counting proceeded in Florida, it became obvious that the projection was premature, and Florida was termed too close to call. As the evening progressed and electoral votes spread evenly between Bush and Gore, Florida loomed as the state whose electoral votes would ensure victory for either candidate.

Early the next morning, the networks declared Bush to have won Florida and the presidency. However, as the last precincts reported, the race tightened dramatically, with the final unofficial count indicating fewer than 2,000 votes separating the two. Moreover, in Palm Beach County, a growing cry was heard of widespread voter frustration with a "confusing" ballot. The networks again classified Florida as too close to call, and an amazed and confused American public still did not know who their next president would be.

The weeks that followed were unique in American politics, highlighting the federal nature of the system. Gore had won the national popular vote. He led in the electoral college without the Florida vote. He and his campaign leaders were convinced that they had really won Florida if people who turned out to vote had their intentions measured, but that many were "disenfranchised" by confusing ballot procedures involving punch card ballots. On the other hand, Bush supporters were at least as convinced that Governor Bush had won. Bush had won the initial machine count and the subsequent recount, although the recount had reduced his margin to about 300 votes. The Florida victory gave Bush enough electoral votes to be declared the winner, if the results from Florida could withstand the recount and court challenges that would follow.

9-4a Florida's Post-Election Contest

Vice President Gore decided to challenge the Florida outcome by taking advantage of the state's somewhat confused system of election laws and specifying the challenge in four heavily populated Democratic counties. Florida law allowed a candidate to protest an election and request a recount. However, counties had to file their votes with the secretary of state within a set period, after which the secretary could accept returns at her discretion. Following that, a candidate could contest an election outcome in state court in the capital city of Tallahassee.

Florida law did not anticipate anything like the situation that existed in November of 2000. As in most states, the laws were a patchwork of sometimes-contradictory elements that had evolved in response to isolated problems rather than a comprehensive integrated package. The laws left great power to various state and county officials, all of whom had been elected on a partisan ballot. In this case, the official most under the spotlight was the governor, Jeb Bush, the brother of George W. Bush. The governor immediately recused himself from the process. However, others remained, including Katherine Harris, the Republican secretary of state, who had cochaired George W. Bush's campaign in Florida and served as a delegate to the Republican National Convention. The state attorney general, Democrat Bob Butterworth, who played a lesser role, had held a similar position with the Gore campaign. At the county level, where the decision whether to recount had to be made in the protest phase, the three-member canvassing boards all were elected on a partisan ballot.

The partisanship inherent in the process created a climate of distrust among all involved. Democrats dominated the boards, especially in three of the larger counties Gore chose to protest. Thus, the request for this type of recount lost Gore a potential upper hand in the battle for public support during the protest. The Bush team decided to avoid this type of challenge and to instead work to avoid any further hand recounts as unnecessary and unwarranted. The tone was then set for a five-week war of words, with the Democrats' "count every vote" mantra countered by the Republicans' "the legal votes have been counted" version.

Most of this verbal warfare centered on ballots that the machine counts missed that would have to be counted by hand if "voter intent" could be determined. The voter could have voted for more than one candidate in an election, thus invalidating the ballot as an overvote. Officials had no way to discern voter intent from this type of ballot. The real battle of the ballots regarded "undervotes," in which machines were unable to register a voter preference. Many in Palm Beach County had claimed that they had been confused by the ballot and cast these types of overvotes in attempts to vote for Gore. Likewise, many African Americans in Duval County claimed to have likewise mistakenly overvoted, also in an attempt to vote for Gore. These types of voter errors could not be legally addressed after the fact, and apart from a failed attempt to force a revote in Palm Beach County, were not the subject of much of the legal wrangling in the election aftermath.

Many of Florida's counties, including the three challenged by Gore, used punch card ballots that exacerbated the many problems with improperly cast ballots. All voters were instructed to punch the holes, or chads, corresponding to their preference all the way through and to make sure that any hanging chads were removed. However, many voters did not follow these instructions and left their punch cards with partially removed chads that machines did not count. Other ballots often had mere indentations, called dimpled chads, or pregnant chads. No consensus in law or in practice stated whether this type of mark reflected the clear intent of the voter. A person could make a good case that this type of mark might just as well reflect a voter's change of mind after thinking that she might cast a vote for one person and later deciding to abstain from making a choice. Many wanted to count any mark, or crease, observable by a candidate's name, but others felt that counting dimples and creases was in fact creating votes rather than counting them.

The post-election drama in Florida came to a head with the request for hand recounts in four heavily Democratic counties. The canvassing boards in all the counties decided to move ahead with recounts. Only one, Volusia County, finished recounting by the November 14 legal deadline. The law did allow the secretary of state to accept later returns at her discretion. The legal teams then brought in another set of players, members of the Florida Supreme Court. All seven members of the Court were appointed by Democratic governors (one jointly appointed by the Republican Jeb Bush). Following a lower-court decision that would allow Secretary of State Harris to use discretion that was not arbitrary, the Florida Supreme Court ruled that Ms. Harris must accept all vote totals turned in by Sunday, November 26. The Court ordered her not to certify a winner in the election until after this date.

9-4b The Counting

The next ten days were among the most bizarre in American political history. Three counties had the task of deciding whether to conduct their hand recounts and, if so, how. Two counties, Palm Beach and Broward, began their counts with different and somewhat shifting criteria, and Dade stopped and started its count before later deciding not to continue. Florida law did mandate that recounts in the protest period consider all votes cast. Each of the counties' canvassing boards faced the task of examining hundreds of thousands of ballots. This task was performed in full public view under the watchful eyes of not only partisan observers but also the constant gaze of millions of viewers on national cable news channels.

Of course, the rules for counting were the key element, and local canvassing boards decided these rules with Democratic majorities. Given the overwhelming Democratic majorities in Broward and, to a lesser degree, in Palm Beach, a more liberal counting standard would clearly work to Gore's advantage. That is, if the canvassing boards considered any discernible mark as a vote, a greater chance existed that any uncounted ballot would yield a vote for Gore rather than for Bush. Moreover, all were operating with full knowledge of the running total. The Gore team was confident that it would find the votes it needed, and the Bush team was upset over a process that centered in such a Democratic enclave in possibly determining the outcome of the election in not only Florida, but also, by extension, the country. The 2000 presidential election showed every prospect of being determined by a small number of actors with their own political agendas.

Not surprisingly, the counting process was fraught with controversy. Broward's board was the most partisan of the three and soon began to consider that almost any discernible ballot perforation be counted as a vote. In one widely broadcast memorable scene, two members of the board indicated that they could not discern a preference. A third member, however, a Democrat, indicated that she could see a prick of light coming through next to Gore. The chairperson, another Democrat, first could not see anything, but after some alternative views, agreed. The Republican buried his head in his hands, and the ballot was counted as a vote for Gore. Gore picked up more than 500 votes from the Broward recount. The process did little to convince many observers of the possibility of those involved from either side of operating free from unconscious bias.

One other issue surfaced while the counties scurried to complete their recounts. Florida allowed citizens living overseas or serving in the military to request ballots and, as long as the ballots were sent by election day, to be counted for up to ten days after the election and before counties filed them with the secretary of state for inclusion with the statewide totals. Considering that these ballots play no part in the determination of most outcomes, little attention has traditionally been paid to these votes. However, for obvious reasons, the two to three thousand ballots that were expected could have been critical in 2000. There was fairly widespread agreement that these votes would tend to favor George W. Bush. In a public relations disaster, Gore campaign attorneys sent memos to Democratic observers in each county to challenge military ballots for a variety of reasons, including the lack of a postmark. However, people serving overseas often do not have a way to see that a postmark is applied. Many ballots were challenged and eliminated. Bush gained another 600 votes from overseas ballots, giving him a lead of 930 votes before any hand recounts.

When the deadline approached, Secretary of State Harris announced that she would not accept the results from Palm Beach County that missed the five o'clock specification even though the count was on target to be completed within hours. This decision angered Democrats who thought that she had it within her discretion to accept the results, further exacerbating the partisan ill will on both sides. The final numbers, including the controversial hand recounts from Broward County, left Bush in the lead by approximately 500 votes. This total was certified, and Ms. Harris convened the state canvassing board to pronounce Bush the winner of Florida's twenty-five electoral votes and to certify Bush's electors to the electoral college.

9-4c The Contest Period: The Courts Take Over

The entire recount procedure had taken place under the extension of the protest period mandated by the Florida Supreme Court. The Bush campaign asked the United States Supreme Court to review the Florida Supreme Court's decision. To the surprise of many, the Supreme Court decided to hear the case. The U.S. Supreme Court vacated and remanded the earlier Florida Supreme Court decision pending clarification.[18] Considering that Gore still trailed following the hand recount done under the now-vacated ruling, the issue appeared to be closed. However, the contest period still remained.

In Florida, a candidate who trailed after the protest period and certification could contest the outcome of the election in circuit court in Tallahassee if he or she could bring into doubt enough questionable ballots as to put the final outcome in doubt. As was the case in most of the litigation in this highly unusual situation, the law was not clear, having developed through court interpretation of scattered cases around limited statutory language. Gore contested the failure of Dade County's canvassing board to count the undervotes as well as the criteria used to hand count ballots in Palm Beach County. In addition, he contested a questionable use of original rather than machine-recounted votes in another county.

Judge Sanders Sauls ruled that all ballots from Dade and Palm Beach counties be trucked to Tallahassee. Millions followed the ballots' progress on a moving truck as the trial began. The Gore team called voting experts and statisticians to demonstrate problems with the punch card ballot system that could have led to voters having difficulty registering their preferences and leading to less-than-fully-punched ballots that machines would not count. Judge Sauls ultimately did not agree, and ruled that the Democrats had not made their case in justifying further recounts of the questionable ballots. Again, the issue appeared to be settled. The only way for Gore to get further recounts was through an appeal to the Florida Supreme Court to overrule Judge Sauls. Not many observers thought that this appeal was likely. Sauls' decision seemed to leave few avenues for appeal.

The drama would not end so soon. In a surprising and contentious 4–3 decision, the Florida Supreme Court overruled Judge Sauls and ordered a statewide recount of all undervotes in each Florida county, with the exceptions of Palm Beach and Broward, to begin immediately. There, they ordered the secretary of state to accept the late figures from Palm Beach County along with those from Broward. However, the court provided no direction regarding what standards should be used, again leaving that major decision to canvassing boards in each county. The counting of Dade ballots got under way in Tallahassee, and other counties' canvassing boards met to develop a process for counting undervotes in their counties.

9-4d The U.S. Supreme Court Ends the Process

The Bush campaign attorneys immediately sought relief from the United States Supreme Court to stop the new wave of hand recounts. On December 9, five Supreme Court members agreed to order the recounts stopped immediately pending a full hearing of the case. The halt was ordered on the basis of "irreparable damage" that could occur to the Bush campaign if counting continued without clear standards that produced an outcome that could later be determined to have been based on an improper process.

The Court later heard oral arguments in the case known simply as *Bush v. Gore*. The Court ruling that followed late on the evening of December 12 brought an end to the five-week post-election battle, but not to the controversy. In a complicated split decision, the Court ruled that the Florida Supreme Court decision specifying the recounts without standards violated equal protection standards under the U.S. Constitution and that the case should be remanded to the Florida Supreme Court so that consistent standards could be applied. Seven of the nine justices agreed with that proposition. However, by a 5–4 margin, the Court also agreed that Florida law mandated that electors be chosen by December 12 and that there was no time for the Florida Supreme Court to use appropriate due process, specify standards, and allow for recounts to occur to meet that deadline.[19] The effect of the ruling was to end any recounting, leaving Bush in the lead, with electors already certified and with no further options for Gore. The election was decided. When the electors cast their votes on December 18, Bush had 271 electoral votes, one more than the 270 he needed to win. Bush was the winner, but the controversial resolution to the 2000 campaign would follow him throughout his presidency.

9-5 The 2004 Election

The 2004 campaign was the most engaging, and also the most divisive, that the country had experienced since 1968. Throughout the campaign, polls showed that public interest in the campaign was very high and that Americans had strong feelings about the incumbent president, George W. Bush. The media coverage of the campaign was extensive, if not always impartial; the political rhetoric on both sides was often vitriolic; and the race went down to the wire. In 2004, more than $600 million was spent on political ads on radio and TV, more than twice as much as in 2000. Because both sides worked so hard to mobilize voters, and because Americans were more engaged in the campaign than they had been in many years, voter turnout was significantly (though not dramatically) higher. Contrary to widespread expectations and conventional wisdom, the higher turnout helped the Republican candidate. Fortunately, the election was decided by the next day, and the nation was spared a protracted and stressful post-election challenge.

9-6 THE 2008 ELECTION

The 2008 election was a historic one. The United States chose its first African American president in a race that was not at all close after two narrowly split contests in 2000 and 2004. Young people, who had been considered disengaged from politics, were more active in advocating for candidates and voting than in previous elections. The issue dynamics of the election had changed as well. The war on terror was not front and center in peoples' minds the way it had been in 2004, replaced by a concern much closer to home: serious economic crisis that threatened America's long-term stability.

9-6a THE CANDIDATES

With George W. Bush term-limited out of office, the only certainty in 2008 was that the sitting president would not return to office. Unlike previously term-limited presidents Reagan and Clinton, though, Bush's vice president would not seek election to the presidency. Dick Cheney's absence meant a series of Republican hopefuls emerged. Former Massachusetts Governor Mitt Romney, most famous for helping the 2002 Salt Lake City Winter Olympics after a bribery scandal, emerged early as the front-runner. Former Arkansas Governor Mike Huckabee entered, as did Senator John McCain in his second bid for the GOP nomination after losing to George W. Bush in 2000. After a divided series of primaries, McCain emerged dominant after Super Tuesday and proceeded to pull away to the Republican nomination.

The Democratic primary was much more contentious. Senator Hillary Clinton of New York established a presence early, as did Illinois Senator Barack Obama. A field of nine Democratic hopefuls emerged, but Clinton and Obama would be the only two candidates with any chance at the nomination. Former Senator John Edwards of North Carolina was briefly part of the top tier of candidates, securing a few delegate commitments that could have brokered the Democratic convention. Clinton and Obama would fight until the very end, splitting primaries with Obama taking a slight lead. Democratic conventions feature unpledged party insiders, called superdelegates, who could have turned the nomination over to Clinton. Obama continued to build a lead and brokered a deal with Clinton who agreed to support him in the convention.

9-6b The Issues

Early in the campaign the war on terror was a significant issue. McCain advocated for wider actions in the military's activity, including suggesting that Iran should be next. Obama, on the other hand, stressed withdrawal of U.S. troops from Iraq on a short timetable. The election changed to a domestic issue–based campaign when a series of frightening economic events occurred in succession. Mortgage lenders and underwriters were exposed for making risky investments which were bankrupting them. Investment brokerage houses were going out of business or being bought by larger, more solvent companies. Employers began shedding jobs at a massive rate. The American economy looked to be on the verge of collapse. Once the economic crisis set in, it became the dominant issue in voters' minds.

9-6c The Voters Decide

Democratic nominee Obama went from a slight lead to an insurmountable one as the effects of the financial crisis became more widespread. After the close uncertainty of the previous two elections, voting day was rather uneventful in 2008. States that George W. Bush had won in the previous two elections, like North Carolina and Florida, went to the Democratic side. Even strongly trending Republican states like Indiana chose Obama, who ended the night with a commanding victory of 365 electoral votes to McCain's 173.

The spike in youth voting was significant in 2008, but it was not enough to put Obama over the top alone. Women voted strongly for Obama, as did African Americans and first-time voters. Partisanship, geography, and social class were also important in the contest, but McCain lost on a variety of fronts and Obama won on them. The win was not necessarily a mandate for Obama, as older voters, whites, and men preferred McCain. The American public is not at the same voting stalemate it was in 2000 and 2004, but the public has not also made one of the historic shifts that occasionally happens.

9-7 The 2012 Election

After dramatic turns and twists for three consecutive elections, the 2012 election was rather straightforward. President Obama headed his Republican rival, Mitt Romney, from the very beginning and was eventually reelected with a large electoral vote margin. Romney only came close to challenging once, after the first debate between himself and Obama. However, despite an economy that had not recovered as promised during the 2008 campaign, Americans voted in large numbers for the president, and he won reelection with a 332–206 electoral vote margin. While close, Obama won fewer states in his reelection effort than he did when first running in 2008.

9-7a THE CANDIDATES

President Obama sought reelection in 2012 and had no primary opposition. On the other hand, a wide-open Republican primary was promised when John McCain declined to run again versus Obama. Having performed well in 2008, Romney was seen as the likely Republican nominee but a number of challengers laid before him. First, a popular conservative, Tim Pawlenty of Minnesota, entered the primary. Soon after, so did Texas Governor Rick Perry. Perry immediately took control of the pre-primary season, even forcing Pawlenty out. But when Perry faltered during debates, other hopefuls such as Michele Bachmann, Herman Cain, and Rick Santorum all led preference polls for brief periods. After every other Republican primary candidate had led momentarily, Mitt Romney became the last candidate standing and cruised to the Republican nomination.

9-7b THE ISSUES

With the death of Osama bin Laden, voter thoughts shifted primarily to economic ones. The U.S. economy was struggling to recover and improve from the dire straits of the 2008 campaign, but there was a stable if slight improvement. Thus President Obama entered his reelection campaign with uncertainty but the ability to run on those improvements and his success in passing the Affordable Care Act. Ads, debate questions, and news coverage all focused nearly exclusively on economic issues. Romney attempted to leverage his business experience as a reason he would manage the economy better into recovery than Obama would, but Romney had a charisma and credibility gap to the president that left his campaign messages unheard or discounted.

9-7c THE VOTERS DECIDE

Pundits such as Nate Silver were nearly ready to call the election in August, but fearful of Dewey-defeat-Truman-style gaffes, they instead expressed great confidence that President Obama would win reelection handily. Using state-by-state polls, Silver correctly predicted that the president would win reelection and again correctly predicted the winner. Silver accurately predicted how all fifty states would vote in 2012.[20] While not the mandate he received in 2008, Obama's reelection victory was strong and suggested a more aggressive stance in the final four years of his presidency.

9-8 CONGRESSIONAL CAMPAIGNS AND ELECTIONS

A comparison of congressional and presidential elections reveals both differences and similarities. The format is the same in that it has a nomination process and a general election. Candidates for the U.S. Senate are nominated through statewide primaries; House candidates are nominated though primaries held in each House district. The Republican and Democratic nominees who emerge from these primaries face off in the general election. The two major parties tend to dominate almost all congressional elections, as they do most presidential elections. Name recognition and public approval are just as important to congressional candidates as they are to presidential candidates. On the other hand, the political environment, membership turnover, effect of incumbency, and nature of campaign financing are quite different.

All House members must run for reelection every two years. The two senators from each state have six-year terms that start and end at different times so that they usually do not come up for reelection at the same time. The two-year cycle of House elections overlaps with the four-year presidential term and the six-year senatorial term so that every even-numbered year has a congressional election. The 1992 election year was known as the presidential election year, but all 435 House members and at least 33 senators were also up for election. The 1994 election year was known as a midterm election because it occurred at the midpoint between presidential elections. Consequently, the president was not up for election, but 435 House members and at least 33 senators were. Every two years, a House member must withstand the possibility of a nomination battle against a fellow party member and then survive a general election against a challenger from the opposing party.

One of the most salient features of congressional elections in the past five decades is the surprising lack of turnover from year to year. On average, since 1950 more than 90 percent of the House members who have desired reelection have been successful. The Senate has been a bit more volatile, but since 1960 senators have enjoyed an average reelection rate of more than 75 percent. The various factors contributing to the high rates of electoral success and low rates of turnover for members of Congress are known as the **incumbency advantage**. Members of Congress have a variety of resources available for improving their name recognition and public approval. The government provides free mail, free travel to the district, free long-distance telephone calls, district offices, staff to assist the legislators with constituent service, and the power to secure government projects that provide jobs and money for their districts. Because the features that contribute to the incumbency advantage are so much a part of the nature of Congress as an institution, this topic is discussed in detail in Chapter 12, "Congress."

9-8a FINANCING CONGRESSIONAL CAMPAIGNS

A potential challenger faces a formidable task in squaring off against an incumbent member of Congress. The government has provided at least two years, and in many cases decades, of funding to the incumbent for activities that increase name recognition and good feelings with voters. If this advantage is not enough to drive away most people, they must also consider the huge advantage the incumbent usually has in raising money for campaigns.

Because so much of the average campaign is conducted over the television or radio airwaves, running for Congress is enormously expensive. The average amount spent per candidate in 1992 was $197,000 in the House. This figure, however, is misleading in that winners of a House seat spent $550,000 on average. The average Senate candidate spent $1.1 million. The total amount spent represents a 52 percent increase in campaign spending since 1990. By 2000, Congressional candidates had raised more than $800 million, greater than a 39 percent increase over 1998. In 2000, the New Jersey Senate candidate David Corsine spent a record $45 million on his successful campaign.[21]

Incumbents enjoy five main advantages in raising campaign funds:

1. Interest groups want access to power, and incumbents are already in power and likely to stay there.
2. An incumbent member of Congress has been a winner at least once. People like to know that they are not wasting their money on someone with no chance of winning, and incumbents quickly pass this test.
3. Because incumbents have already been winners, they have been able to develop a successful fundraising organization.
4. An incumbent's previous contributors can be canvassed again for money.
5. Incumbents usually have money in the bank well before the campaign has even begun.

Money is important to all candidates, but challengers have the greatest need for money and the most difficulty in raising it. Because challengers must overcome the incumbency advantage, they must spend hundreds of thousands of dollars even to be considered serious candidates. The ability to raise money is probably the best indicator of a challenger's chances of winning. For example, from 1984 to 1990, only 45 House challengers on average in each election were able to raise as much as $300,000. Of these well-funded challengers, 20 percent (or 35 of the total 180 in the four elections) were able to win against an incumbent. On the other hand, only seven of the hundreds of challengers who raised less than $300,000 won an election. Successful challengers spent an average of $500,000.[22]

Sources of Money

Members of Congress have four sources of campaign funds:

1. Individuals
2. PACs
3. Party organizations
4. Their own personal finances

Members of Congress are not eligible for the public funding that presidential candidates receive. The Federal Election Campaign Act of 1974 placed a limit of $1,000 on the amount individuals can contribute to a campaign for each election and a $5,000 limit on PAC contributions per candidate per election. Many more individuals than PACs give money to candidates, but PACs tend to give more money each time they contribute and donate money to many more candidates in any one election year. Individuals give a larger total amount of money to all congressional candidates than PACs, but PACs are much more important for the average incumbent. In 1992, 44 percent (or $263,500) of the total funds raised by incumbents came from PACs, versus only 26 percent (or $149,700) for the successful challengers.[23] For the election cycles 1975 through 1998, PACs contributed between 40 and 50 percent of their total receipts to congressional campaigns. During this period, total PAC contributions to congressional candidates increased more than ninefold, from about $23 million to nearly $200 million per election cycle.

Party money tends to be not that important in most races. On the other hand, family money and loans can be quite important. Personal finances tend to make up a much larger share of a challenger's funds than they do for the average incumbent. Often, challengers must rely on family money and loans to get their campaigns started. If they lose, they may never be able to pay off the loans. The winning challengers in 1992 averaged $65,500 of debt in the House and $266,073 in the Senate.[24] After winners are successful, however, they quickly begin to accrue the benefits of being an incumbent. PACs almost immediately turn their attention to the new members and begin making contributions (see Table 9-2). In 1992, from election day until the end of December, PACs donated $1.2 million to new members.[25]

PACs and Congressional Campaigns

Members of Congress have experience and access to power that people, particularly interest groups, want. Well before the campaign starts in the summer of an election year, the member must start raising money. PACs provide the most readily available funds at this time. As you have seen, the more than four thousand PACs are organizations that exist solely to raise and spend campaign money on behalf of some issue of interest to the donors. PACs with a specific economic interest, such as the American Medical Association's concern about legislation affecting the healthcare industry, are the most common and best-funded groups. Therefore, most PAC money available to legislators is tied to a particular economic interest.

TABLE 9-2 Cost of Federal Political Campaigns, 1998-2012

CYCLE	TOTAL COST OF ELECTION	CONGRESSIONAL RACES	PRESIDENTIAL RACE		
2012*	$6,285,557,223	$3,664,141,430	$2,621,415,792		
2010	$3,643,942,915	$3,438,675,910	N/A		
2008*	$5,285,680,883	$2,485,952,737	$2,799,728,146		
2006	$2,852,658,140	$2,852,658,140	N/A		
2004*	$4,147,304,003	$2,237,073,141	$1,910,230,862		
2002	$2,181,682,066	$2,181,682,066	N/A		
2000*	$3,082,340,937	$1,669,224,553	$1,413,116,384		
1998	$1,618,936,265	$1,618,936,265	N/A		

*Presidential election cycle

Source: Opensecrets.org http://www.opensecrets.org/bigpicture/

This PAC money tends to flow to members who can be most influential on bills affecting that economic interest. Because Congress assigns bills to various committees based on their subject matter, interest groups know which legislators are most likely to be able to help or hurt their cause. Consequently, PAC money tends to be concentrated on members of the relevant committees. For example, members of the Agriculture Committee would receive, on average, more PAC money from farming interests than from other members. Although the wealthier PACs, such as the American Medical Association, can spread their money around, most focus their money on the better investments available in certain committees.

Because the jurisdiction of congressional committees does not change significantly from year to year, the PACs can concentrate on certain members, and committee members know that they have a steady source of funds from a core group of PACs. One outcome of this relationship is that PACs tend to shower much more money on incumbents than on challengers. This statement is especially true for economic interest groups, which tend to donate much more money to incumbents than do ideological interest groups. Of the $659 million spent by all congressional candidates in the 1992 election, $180 million of it came from PACs. Most of the PAC money, $127 million, went to incumbents. Of the top twenty recipients of PAC money in the Senate, eighteen were incumbents, and fifteen of them won reelection. All the top twenty PAC recipients in the House were incumbents, and fifteen of them also won reelection.

Another advantage of incumbents is that they can stockpile their campaign funds over time. If a member has a relatively easy campaign one year, it would be wise to save some of the money raised that year for the next campaign. Because individuals and PACs are limited in how much money they can give a candidate in any one election ($1,000 for an individual and $5,000 for a PAC), a member can receive only so much help from any one source in a given year. Therefore, members take contributions every year and build up a war chest for future tough campaigns. Some members have amassed war chests of more than a million dollars. For example, at the end of 1992, David Dreier, a Republican representative from California, had $2,026,019 cash on hand, and Dan Rostenkowski, a Democrat from Illinois, had $1,245,721 in his war chest.[26] When you consider that the House candidate who ranked fortieth in total spending in 1992 spent $1,086,152, you can easily see how valuable a large war chest can be. Potential challengers know that they will have a difficult time raising as much money as the incumbent during the campaign, and few can match funds with a large war chest.

The large advantage that incumbents have in campaign financing scares off many qualified potential challengers. Most challengers are aware that they have to either spend large sums of their own money or borrow heavily to start a campaign. Of the $659 million spent in the 1992 elections, $54 million was either lent to or contributed by the candidate personally. Almost all this personal funding was done by challengers or candidates in open races with no incumbent. These financing advantages combined with the other benefits of incumbency, such as the franking privilege which allows legislators to send free mailings to their constituents and congressional staff, help explain why reelection rates of more than 90 percent have been routine in recent decades.

9-8b National Trends and Local Context

Thomas P. "Tip" O'Neill, a former speaker of the house, once stated that "all politics is local." The tremendous attention that legislators give to local problems through constituency service is clear evidence that they understand this maxim. Members spend as much time as possible in their district speaking to groups, such as the Kiwanis and Rotary Club, visiting local schools, and attending public functions of all types to enable constituents to get to know them. Members must develop a unique "home style" that fits both their personality and the local culture. This home style is used to develop trust between the constituents and the member so that the legislator can effectively communicate with the district and rely on the trust she has built up to survive tough elections.[27] Sometimes, despite the member's best efforts, the partisanship and political ideology of the local culture make it impossible for her to retain the seat.

National Events and Congressional Elections

The effect of national events on congressional races has been extensively studied by political scientists. Three factors stand out as most important:

1. *Bad economic conditions generally hurt the party of the president.* A recession (when economic income growth falls and unemployment rises) in the months before an election generally results in a loss of seats in Congress for

the president's party. Alternatively, average or even strong economic growth may not help the president's party. Voters seem more willing to punish poor performance than to reward good results.

2. *The popularity of the president.* Many factors contribute to the president's job approval ratings, including the economy, foreign policy, scandal, relations with Congress, and personal factors. Typically, the president's party loses congressional seats in the midterm election. In the ten midterm elections between 1954 and 1990, the party that controlled the White House lost an average of twenty-three seats in the House and three in the Senate. The president's popularity affects how badly his party performs in the midterm election. In fact, many observers see the midterm election as a referendum on the president's job performance. That was certainly the case in 1994, when President Clinton's sagging approval rating cost the Democrats control of both the House and Senate.
3. *In presidential election years, the president's own political survival not only depends on his popularity but also influences whether the president has coattails.* Presidents are said to have strong **coattails** if they can bring several new party members into Congress in a presidential election year. Because of the decline in partisanship, recent presidents have had weaker coattails than their predecessors. In fact, the Republicans controlled the presidency for twenty of the twenty-four years from 1969 to 1993, but the Democrats dominated the House throughout the entire period and controlled the Senate for eighteen of those years. This period of divided government suggests that congressional elections are no longer tied as closely to the popularity of presidents as they were for most of the first two centuries of the republic.

SCANDALS

Scandals can also influence congressional elections. The 1972 Watergate scandal involving the Republican administration of Richard Nixon led to a massive infusion of 91 new members in Congress in 1974 with the Democrats taking 49 of the 55 House seats that changed from one party to the other. Some would argue that the House bank scandal contributed to the large number of new legislators elected in 1992. Many members had written checks that would have bounced because of insufficient funds had they been deposited in an ordinary bank. In similar circumstances, most citizens would have to pay large fees and possibly suffer damage to their credit ratings, so some people saw the special treatment as proof that Congress is out of touch with the American public. Of the 46 members with more than a hundred overdrafts, 54 percent retired or lost. Of the 269 members who had any rubber checks, 77 (or 29 percent) retired or lost.

9-8c Congressional Elections: The Earthquakes of 2006 and 2010

After fifty years of stable one-party control of Congress, the 1994 elections not only changed party control of the legislature but ushered in an era of instability in party control. At least one chamber of Congress has changed party control five times since 1994. In 2006, Congressional elections were seen as a referendum on an increasingly unpopular Bush presidency, leading to both the House and Senate switching to Democratic control. The election of 2008 added not only a Democratic president but a Democratic majority in the Senate not seen for six decades, enough to marginalize Republicans in the chamber that gives the minority party the most power of any branch of the federal government. Indeed, some called 2008 the GOP's death knell. However, the Tea Party and a strong slate of Republican challenger candidates emerged during the early Obama presidency, and by 2010 had a message of fiscal conservatism that resonated with voters as economic uncertainty continued to grip the nation. Republicans swept Democrats out of control of the House and nearly took control of the Senate at the same time.

Recent congressional selections reveal a nation closely divided between Democratic and Republican voters, with a substantial bloc of Independent voters willing to swing back and forth in their support of Republican and Democratic congressional candidates. The political landscape in the first decade of the twenty-first century is such that neither party can expect to maintain firm control of Congress over the long term.

9-8d The Perennial Campaign

Because members of the House of Representatives are up for reelection every two years, they always seem to be running for office. The public gets tired of congressional races and tends to be more interested in presidential contests, which occur only once every four years and involve major national issues. Not surprisingly, then, voter turnout tends to be quite low in most midterm elections, when no presidential race is taking place to stimulate interest. On the other hand, interest groups pay close attention to all congressional races. Members of Congress are continually in search of money from PACs. The public is more or less aware of this phenomenon, and it contributes to the low public regard for Congress as an institution.

9-9 Conclusion: Campaigns, Elections, and American Political Culture

Americans have been faulted for their low turnout in elections. Citizens in other democracies tend to turn out to vote at much higher levels. To some extent, the relatively low level of turnout in the United States reflects the alienation and cynicism of voters. But it is also a function of the complexity of the American electoral process and the sheer number of elections in which citizens are asked to participate. The American system of elections places a great burden on the average citizen, a burden that many are not willing to bear. Most observers would agree that the process by which our leaders are chosen is too complicated and time-consuming. Furthermore, the immense sums of money required to wage a successful campaign deter many potentially qualified candidates from seeking office. Proposals for reform are made from time to time, but few have much chance of being adopted. The current structure is deeply embedded in American political culture.

American political culture is committed to the idea of representative democracy. No matter how bitter the campaign, Americans are taught to accept the outcome of an election and respect the legitimacy of the process. If more and more people become disaffected and choose not to vote, however, or if people participate begrudgingly, believing that the process is corrupt, it is only a matter of time before the system faces serious challenge. Thus, it came as a great relief to many when the 2004 presidential election was decided in a timely way, was widely perceived as fairly contested, and most Americans accepted the outcome.

QUESTIONS FOR THOUGHT AND DISCUSSION

1. Should the United States have a national presidential primary in which each party chooses its presidential nominee? If this type of primary were instituted, what would the consequences be for the two major political parties?

2. How much weight should Americans give to the "character issue" in deciding whether to vote for a presidential candidate? Do the mass media give too much or too little attention to the character issue?

3. Considering that more Americans identify with the Democratic party than with the Republican party, why have Republicans been so successful in winning the presidency?

4. Should the electoral college be abolished? What would have to happen to bring about a movement to do away with it? Who might support this effort? Who would be likely to oppose it?

5. Should congressional campaigns be reformed to give incumbents less of a financial advantage than they now enjoy?

Endnotes

1 Voting turnout in a local primary election can run as low as 10 percent. Normally, turnout in local elections is in the 20 to 30 percent range.

2 Peter Schrag, "Take the Initiative, Please: Referendum Madness in California," *The American Prospect*, December 19, 2001, http://www.prospect.org/cs/articles?article=take_the_initiative_please

3 Larry Sabato, *Feeding Frenzy: How Attack Journalism Has Transformed American Politics* (New York: Free Press, 1991).

4 Lois Romano, "Effects of Obama's Candor Remains Uncertain," *The Washington Post*, January 3, 2007, http://www.washingtonpost.com/wp-dyn/content/article/2007/01/02/AR2007010201359.html

5 Tom Hamburger, Dan Morain and Robin Fields, "Candidates' Reliance on 'Bundlers' Let Hsu Thrive," *The Los Angeles Times*, September 14, 2007, http://articles.latimes.com/2007/sep/14/nation/na-hsu14

6 William G. Mayer and Andrew Busch, *The Front-Loading Problem in Presidential Nominations* (Brookings Institution Press, 2003).

7 Mark Blumenthal, "Plouffe on Obama and Polling," Pollster.com, August 27, 2008, http://www.pollster.com/blogs/plouffe_on_obama_and_polling.php

8 Sasha Issenberg, *The Victory Lab* (New York: Crown, 2012).

9 Herbert A. Asher, *Presidential Elections and American Politics*, 5th ed. (Pacific Grove, CA: Brooks/Cole, 1992).

10 *Federal Election Commission v. Beaumont*, 539 U.S. 146, (2003).

11 OpenSecrets.org, "527s: Advocacy Group Spending in the 2008 Elections," March 4, 2013, http://www.opensecrets.org/527s/

12 *Citizens United v. Federal Election Commission*, 558 U.S. 310 (2010).

13 Angus Campbell, Phillip E. Converse, Warren E. Miller, and Donald E. Stokes, *The American Voter* (Chicago: University of Chicago Press, 1960).

14 Asher, *Presidential Elections and American Politics*, p. 61.

15 Campbell, Converse, Miller, and Stokes, *The American Voter*.

16 William Lyons and John M. Scheb II, "Ideology and Candidate Evaluation in the 1984 and 1988 Presidential Elections," *Journal of Politics*, May 1992.

17 Samuel A. Kirkpatrick, William Lyons, and Michael Fitzgerald, "Candidates, Parties and Issues in the American Electorate: Two Decades of Change," *American Politics Quarterly*, July 1975.

18 *Bush v. Palm Beach Canvassing Board*, 531 U.S. 98 (2000).

19 *Bush v. Gore*, 531 U.S. 98 (2000).

20 Forbes.com, "How Accurate Were Nate Silver's Predictions for the 2012 Presidential Election?" November 7, 2012, http://www.forbes.com/sites/quora/2012/11/07/how-accurate-were-nate-silvers-predictions-for-the-2012-presidential-election/

21 Federal Election Commission (www.fec.gov).

22 David Price, *The Congressional Experience: A View from the Hill* (Boulder, CO: Westview Press, 1992), p. 28.

23 Beth Donovan and Ilyse J. Veron, "Freshmen Got to Washington with Help of PAC Funds," *Congressional Quarterly Weekly*, March 27, 1993, p. 723.

24 Ibid., p. 724

25 Ibid., p. 723.

26 Michael Barone and Grant Ujifusa, *The Almanac of American Politics 1994* (Washington, D.C.: National Journal, 1993), pp. 1453, 1461.

27 Richard Fenno, *Home Style: House Members in Their Districts* (Boston: Little, Brown, 1978).

Chapter 10

POLITICAL PARTIES

OUTLINE

Key Terms 364

Expected Learning Outcomes 364

10-1 The Role of Parties in a Democracy 364

10-1a Functions of Parties 365

10-2 The Development of the American Party System 366

10-2a Parties in the Early Republic 367

10-2b Slavery and Party Realignment 369

10-2c The Populist Revolt 370

10-2d The Great Realignment of 1932 371

10-3 The Contemporary Party System 373

10-3a Why Only Two Parties? 374

10-3b The Fate of Third Parties 375

10-4 Parties and the Governing Process 380

10-4a The Party in Government 380

10-4b The Party in the Electorate 381

10-5 The Structure of the National Parties 384

10-5a The National Office 385

10-5b State Party Systems 385

10-6 The National Party Conventions 388

10-6a A Brief History of the Conventions 388

10-6b The Rise of the Primaries 389

10-6c Party Reform: 1968–2000 391

10-6d The Convention Delegates 395

10-6e The Functions of the Conventions 396

10-7 Decline and Revitalization of the Parties 397

10-8 Conclusion: Parties and Contemporary Political Culture 399

Questions for Thought and Discussion 400

Endnotes 401

KEY TERMS

Australian ballot
candidate-centered campaigns
caucus
closed primary
coalition
congressional caucus
dealignment
direct primary
grassroots party politics
interest aggregation
interest articulation
linkage institutions
loyal opposition
majority party
McGovern–Fraser Commission
minority party
multiparty systems
national conventions
Occupy Wall Street
open primary
partisan realignment
party in Congress
party in government
party in the electorate
party machines
party out of power
party platform
progressive movement
proto-party
realigning election
secret ballot
single-issue politics
soft money
spoils system
superdelegate
Tea Party
Super Tuesday
third-party candidate
two-party system
war chest
winner-take-all

EXPECTED LEARNING OUTCOMES

After reading this chapter and completing the supplemental online materials, students will:

- Describe the parties' role as a linkage institution
- Compare American and international political parties
- Place parties in eras of party dominance
- Define dealignment relative to the role of political parties
- Analyze the power of American parties today

10-1 THE ROLE OF PARTIES IN A DEMOCRACY

A political party is "any continuing organization, identified by a particular label, that presents candidates for public office at mass elections."[1] Parties perform crucial functions in a democratic political system. They recruit political leadership, simplify and stabilize the political process, promote governmental organization, and foster coherent policy making. Without parties, it would be difficult for democratic systems to choose their leaders and even more difficult for those chosen to implement the will of the people expressed through elections.

In the early 1940s, E. E. Schattschneider wrote that "political parties created democracy and modern democracy is unthinkable save in terms of the parties."[2] Perhaps he overstated the case, but contemporary political scientists tend to believe that democracies are *unworkable*, if not *unthinkable*, in the absence of political parties.[3] Schattschneider knew that parties served a necessary role in American politics, one that connects the people to their political system. Any intermediary organization that connects people with politics is called a **linkage institution**.

When a country has two major parties, as in the United States, and one establishes clear dominance, that party is the **majority party**. The majority of citizens who express a party preference identify with this party. The majority party usually, but not always, has a majority of seats in the legislature. A party attains majority status by appealing to, and structuring programs for, a wide variety of interests. The **minority party** is the party that does not claim the allegiance of a majority of party identifiers. American politics has always had a major minority party that is striving to become the majority party. Basically, a minority party becomes a majority party whenever large groups defect from the majority. Many people who had previously not identified with a party may join these defecting groups. Whenever a massive, long-term shift occurs in voter allegiance from one party to another, a **partisan realignment** has occurred. A realignment suggests that an important change has taken place in the political culture and signals that the country is embarking on a new direction in public policy.

10-1a FUNCTIONS OF PARTIES

Political parties serve both to aggregate and to articulate interests. **Interest aggregation** is the process of bringing together various interests under one umbrella, and **interest articulation** is the process of speaking on behalf of these issue positions. Parties engage in both activities with the goal of winning elections.

In the United States, a person does not "join" a party. To be considered a Republican or Democrat, you do not need to pay dues or carry a card. Rather, you simply identify with the party you prefer. Your preference, and therefore your party identification, might change from day to day. A political party consists of those who hold office, seek office, and support those seeking office who identify with a common party label. These people all have the common purpose of winning office for themselves and/or other party members. The party label has meaning to these party identifiers, although the meaning is not necessarily the same for all identifiers. Although parties often stake out opposing policy positions and disagree over major issues, parties usually do not allow themselves to be identified in terms of a single issue. Rather, in order to win, they put together shifting coalitions of voters attracted to various issues. A **coalition** is a loose collection of groups who join together to accomplish some common goal. Thus, parties provide a vital function in any democratic system. They promote compromise and cooperation among various interests. They allow the multiplicity of interests to find their voices, even though those voices may be somewhat muted.

The parties' tendency to promote compromise helps to ensure stability within the political system. In the United States, the Democratic party has traditionally represented a loose aggregation of diverse interests that might otherwise have little in common. For years, southern whites, Catholics, Jews, union members, African Americans, and various other ethnic groups were able to coexist in the party despite disagreements over social issues. The desire to achieve electoral victory enabled these groups to tolerate each other and find common interests. When this coalition fell apart, as it did during the Reagan era of the 1980s, the Republican party was able to win presidential elections convincingly, even though it remained the minority party.

Although parties structure alternative sets of public policy preferences on many issues, they can be expected to come together in any time of national emergency. Following the September 11, 2001 attack on the United States, leaders of both parties embraced the president and quickly acted in almost total unanimity to provide President George W. Bush and his administration the legislation he needed to fund the military response and the increases in domestic security.

10-2 The Development of the American Party System

The Constitution does not mention political parties. This omission may be due to the Founders' fear that parties were a version of "factions," which they considered disruptive. Political parties "were widely regarded as hostile to the pursuit of a harmonious society and were seen as the agents of all manner of special interests."[4] Indeed, some thought that, by exacerbating political conflict, parties could place at risk the very survival of the new republic.[5] John Adams went so far as to assert that the emergence of political parties should be "dreaded as the greatest political evil under our Constitution."[6] One of the Constitution's greatest supporting documents, Federalist Paper #10, went so far as to design the government to prevent political parties from forming. However, political parties are as much a part of government as elections. The authors of Federalist #10 even realized the futility of their desire to keep parties from forming—they knew that the only way to prevent them was to sacrifice freedom of speech and assembly, which they termed "a cure worse than the disease."[7]

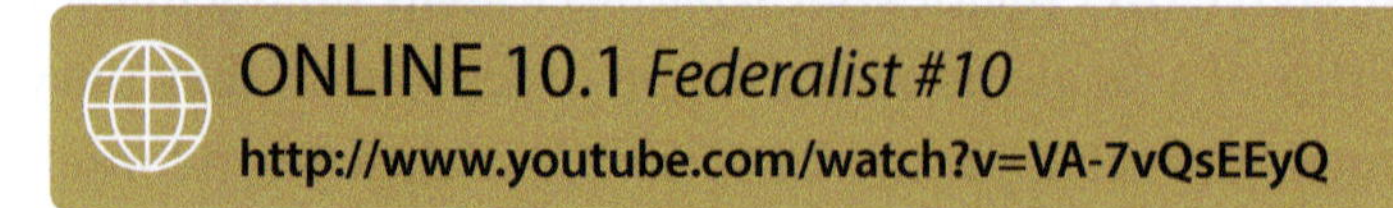

ONLINE 10.1 *Federalist #10*
http://www.youtube.com/watch?v=VA-7vQsEEyQ

The first two articles of the Constitution addressed how members of Congress and the president, respectively, should be elected, but left organizing the campaigns to develop on their own. Likewise, although Article I outlines the powers of and limits on the Senate and House of Representatives, it says little about the organization of either chamber. Yet both the elective and legislative processes strongly implied the development of parties. In fact, it is difficult to imagine any but the smallest of nations conducting elections and passing legislation without political parties. Thus, even though the parties were basically inevitable in American politics, they have existed outside the formal constitutional framework. Parties are shortcuts to governing. Parties allow coalitions to form around ideologies and issues, providing information shortcuts to voters.

As we noted, the Founders were wary of the influence of any organized group on the political process. Nevertheless, the first real attempt at organizing various interests for the purpose of affecting an election was to secure the ratification of the Constitution. The Federalists, including John Adams, George Washington, and Alexander Hamilton, strongly supported ratification. Those who opposed the ratification of the Constitution were known as Anti-Federalists. The Anti-Federalists represented a diverse set of interests and were united only by opposition to the Constitution. In four states—Virginia, New York, Pennsylvania, and Massachusetts—they came close to blocking ratification. Although the Anti-Federalists were too loosely organized to merit description as a political party, their opposition to the Federalists foreshadowed party competition and the emergence of the **two-party system**.

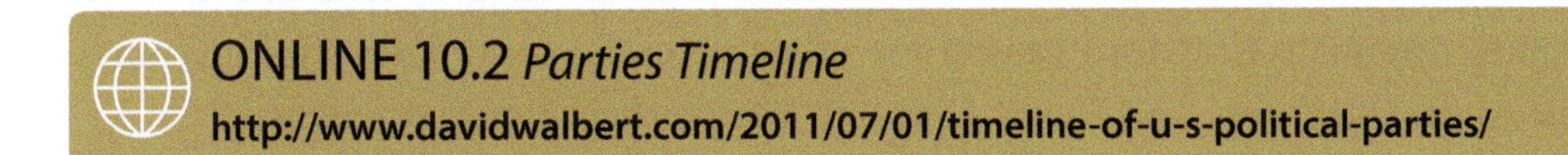

ONLINE 10.2 *Parties Timeline*
http://www.davidwalbert.com/2011/07/01/timeline-of-u-s-political-parties/

10-2a Parties in the Early Republic

The first president, George Washington, sought to avoid the formation of political parties by including diverse interests in his administration. What he got instead was severe factionalism *within* the administration. Alexander Hamilton, Washington's secretary of the treasury, was a major proponent of Federalist ideas. The Federalist program strongly supported banking and business and, by extension, the interests of the major cities. The centerpiece of the program was a national bank, which was desired by the business and banking interests.

Thomas Jefferson, whose views were sharply divergent from those of Hamilton's, was Washington's secretary of state. Jefferson became the spokesman for opposition to Hamilton's program within the administration. James Madison, who also opposed Hamilton's policies, led the opposition in Congress. Within a few years, the followers of Jefferson and Madison organized a political party under the name Democratic Republicans. By 1796, both Federalist and Democratic Republican candidates were presenting themselves to voters as members of opposing political parties. These party labels provided a cue to the voters. The voters could quickly determine the candidates' basic approach to government by their party affiliations. These early parties greatly simplified the task of voting in the fledgling republic by reducing complex issues to a simple choice. This reduction was vital if major issues were to be subject to rational decision making by government.

The Federalists won the presidential election of 1796, but Jefferson and the Democratic Republicans won the election of 1800. The Federalists would not win another presidential election. After Alexander Hamilton was fatally shot by Aaron Burr in 1804, the Federalist party went into a serious decline. The Federalists' opposition to America's involvement in the War of 1812, which proved to be both popular and successful, sealed their doom.

The Era of Good Feelings

After the disintegration of the Federalists, a brief period known as the Era of Good Feelings took place, when factionalism appeared to decline. During this period of one-party dominance, the Democratic Republicans relied on a **congressional caucus** to choose their nominees for the presidency. A **caucus** is a meeting of all members of a legislature from a particular political party. This method ensured that the nomination decision would be dominated by party insiders. King Caucus, as it was called, was used to nominate Democratic Republican presidential candidates from Jefferson in 1804 until the controversial decision to nominate William H. Crawford in 1824. The decision to nominate Crawford caused the other potential candidates—John Quincy Adams, Andrew Jackson, and Henry Clay—to launch their own campaigns.

Adams and Jackson emerged as the eventual front-runners in the popular election, but no one earned a majority in the electoral college, throwing the election into the House of Representatives. Under the Constitution, the House can consider only the top three vote recipients in the electoral college. Henry Clay, who finished fourth in the electoral college, threw his support to John Quincy Adams, who had come in second. With Clay's support, Adams was able to win the election. The fact that Crawford, the caucus nominee, did not win the election, in addition to the perception of political corruption within Congress, led to the demise of King Caucus.

Andrew Jackson and the Origin of the Democratic Party

In the aftermath of the election of 1824, the Democratic Republicans split into the National Republicans, championed by John Quincy Adams, and the Democratic Republicans, who were led by Andrew Jackson. The Jackson wing, which would later evolve into the Democrats, became the dominant party, and supporters of Adams continued to offer competition. This period helped to redefine cleavages in the country. Jackson had appealed to working persons, exploiting class divisions and establishing the Democratic party as the party of the "common man." In addition, the Democrats took on a regional base in the South and the West and became the "majority party." This party began to develop an organizational base as candidates ran under its banner for state and local offices throughout the country. This party base was strengthened to some degree by the spoils system that Jackson championed. The **spoils system** is a system of staffing government that rewards supporters with jobs and contracts.

Democrats and Whigs

© Aquir, 2013. Used under license from Shutterstock, Inc.

After Jackson came back to beat Adams in the election of 1828, the former Democratic Republican party underwent a permanent split, which opened up an opportunity for other parties to join the fray. Many Democratic Republicans who did not join the Jackson wing, along with people from other parties, created what became known as the Whig party. Its leaders were Daniel Webster and Henry Clay. Although the Whigs managed to elect William Henry Harrison in 1840 and Zachary Taylor in 1848, they continued to struggle as the minority party because of, in large part, their inability to unify their northern and southern branches. The Whig party was a viable minority party, however, in that it strongly contested major elections. The Whigs came to represent the interests of business and the eastern cities. In contrast, the Jacksonian Democrats directed their appeals to the "common man" and made structural changes to open up the party to wider participation.

10-2b Slavery and Party Realignment

The slavery issue split the parties in much the same way as it divided the nation. By the 1830s, those who were committed to ending slavery in the United States became organized under the abolitionist label. Under the leadership of William Lloyd Garrison, who wrote persuasively against slavery in his newspaper, *Liberator*, the nation confronted the issue on moral as well as economic and practical political terms.[8] The ensuing divisions led to the first great party realignment, which began in 1852 and continued for more than twenty-five years. The Democratic party had included both northerners and southerners. Andrew Jackson was unwavering in his insistence that slavery was allowed under the Constitution and that those who wanted to abolish it were suggesting changes that the Democrats found unacceptable. Later, his successor, Martin Van Buren, continued the Democrats' commitment to permitting slavery in the South.

The Whigs were less unified on slavery during the 1830s, when they were the **party out of power**. They were therefore less committed to the status quo and more likely to take the risk of establishing a new image.[9] In the 1840s and 1850s, first the Whigs and then the Democrats became increasingly split over the slavery issue. Out of the conflict emerged two parties dedicated to the abolition of slavery: the Liberty

party and the Free Soil party. Slavery had effectively redefined the parties. The Whigs collapsed under the pressure, and the Democrats were weakened to a degree sufficient to make them vulnerable to the newly constituted Republican party.

The Founding of the Republican Party

The Republican party was established in Ripon, Wisconsin, in 1854. It represented the interests of northern Whigs and Free Soil party members. This new party was clearly committed to the end of slavery. The Republicans nominated John C. Frémont for the presidency in 1856, but he received only 33 percent of the popular vote and lost the general election to Democrat James Buchanan. In the years after Buchanan's victory, however, the Democratic party broke into rival factions over the slavery issue. By drawing support from antislavery Democrats, the Republicans soon became the majority party. Lincoln's election in 1860 and the ensuing Civil War left the Democrats as the minority party. They had split into southern and northern wings, and although the party survived, it was badly damaged.

The Republicans and Democrats have remained the two major political parties ever since the Civil War. For the most part, the Republicans have maintained their identity as the party of business. However, major shifts among great blocs of voters have periodically changed the nature of the parties. These shifts, or realignments, have come when the parties have reacted to major problems in society.

10-2c The Populist Revolt

The next great realignment of the parties came in the 1890s, when widespread unhappiness with the economy was exploited by Democrat William Jennings Bryan. The farmers, particularly hard hit, faced declining prices for their crops. The country was divided over monetary policy. The merchants of the East wanted to protect the price of gold. A new group, the Populists, led by Congressman Bryan of Nebraska, wanted to move to the silver standard, which they felt would benefit the farmers and other western interests. The election of 1896 split both parties around economic interests. Since the end of the Civil War, few major substantive issues had divided the two parties. This situation changed in 1896, with the Democrats' nomination of Bryan. Although the Republican candidate, William McKinley, won the election and the Republicans retained majority status, the interests that the parties aggregated and articulated shifted somewhat. In 1896, as in 1860, many voters shifted their allegiances. This was the second great **realigning election**. The cleavages in support were regional, with many states becoming one-party states.

10-2d The Great Realignment of 1932

The two-party system remained stable from 1896 until the onset of the Great Depression in 1929. During this period, both parties mirrored the dominant political culture, which stressed minimal government intervention in the economy. Before the Great Depression, most Americans were not inclined to consider a large government role in the economy. But the depression changed the political culture and the political landscape for decades to come. The political parties changed to reflect the new political environment.

The depression of 1929 put millions of Americans out of work. Both in cities and on the farm, immense human suffering took place, and many feared that they would have no way to provide food or shelter for their families. President Herbert Hoover was constrained by the traditional ideology of the Republican party and was thus unable to offer the voters a reason to keep him in office to deal with the economic crisis. The Democratic candidate for president, Franklin Delano Roosevelt, offered a program that seemed radical at the time. Labeled the New Deal, it included a greatly increased role for government. Such programs as the National Recovery Administration (NRA), the Works Progress Administration (WPA), the Tennessee Valley Authority (TVA), and Social Security cast the federal government in the role of protecting citizens against economic ruin. The New Deal agenda also included price supports to help farmers, bank reform, and improved conditions for the nation's workers.

Beginning in 1932, the Democrats were able to assemble a viable coalition of voters. The elements of the New Deal coalition included southern whites, blacks and other ethnic groups, Catholics, and Jews. The party had the support of labor unions and residents of many large cities in addition to small farmers. The grand scope of their programs enabled the Democrats to appeal to a wide variety of constituencies. Roosevelt's appeal to the coalition was so strong that he was reelected to office in 1936, 1940, and 1944.

Holding the Democratic Coalition Together

Since the death of Roosevelt and the end of World War II, the Democrats have had much difficulty holding together their wide array of constituencies. For the most part, the Democratic party has remained the majority party, although it has experienced a number of serious challenges from the Republicans. Despite being the minority party, the Republicans won the presidency in 1952, 1956, 1968, 1972, 1980, 1984, 1988, 2000, and 2004. Significantly, they gained control of both houses of Congress in 1994, leading some observers to speculate that the Republican party was on the verge of becoming the majority party in the United States. That, of course, has not happened. The election of Barack Obama to the presidency and the Republicans' loss of enough members to filibuster in the Senate meant that some pundits were referring to the marginalized GOP as part of a new emerging Democratic majority. However, due to the rise of the Independent voter, it is unlikely that either party will maintain long-term political dominance in the future in the way that the Democratic party did in the decades following the great realignment of 1932.

The first shock to the New Deal coalition came from the civil rights movement. Roosevelt's successor was Harry Truman, whose Fair Deal reached out to blacks in a way that concerned many southern whites. In 1948, many southerners voted for a **third-party candidate** for president, Strom Thurmond, of South Carolina, whose party was called the Dixiecrats. Although Thurmond polled only about 2.5 percent of the popular vote nationally, his strong showing in the South earned him thirty-nine electoral votes. The Democrats were faced with a quandary that has concerned them ever since: How were they to appeal to southern whites and minorities at the same time? This tension produced another third-party candidate, George Wallace, who ran for president in 1968 and 1972. Both Wallace and Thurmond were southern Democrats who appealed to whites frightened by the civil rights movement.

The civil rights movement and its challenge to what was perhaps the strongest base of the Democratic party, southern voters, increased the tension between the national and the state and local elements of the party. The national Democratic party was increasingly liberal, although at the grassroots level in many areas the party remained conservative. **Grassroots party politics** are those activities that originate at the local level and work their way up through the party. They can be contrasted with policies that begin at the national level. The upshot of this conflict was that many Democratic voters chose to vote for Republicans and third-party candidates in presidential elections in which the national party seemed to them to be "out of touch."

The Democratic coalition has faced challenges beyond those connected with civil rights. Many in the party felt challenged by the lifestyle issues with which the party was forced to grapple in the 1960s. Writing in the late 1960s, analyst Kevin Phillips foresaw an "emerging Republican majority" stemming from the dissatisfaction of many Catholic and working-class voters with the "intellectual" wing of the Democratic party, which seemed to be "soft on crime" and supportive of various nontraditional lifestyles.[10] Although most such voters did not change their party identification, many did, in fact, vote for Republican presidential candidates from the late 1960s to the late 1980s.

In fact, the Democrats were able to elect only three presidents between 1968 and 2008. The candidacies of Hubert Humphrey in 1968, George McGovern in 1972, Walter Mondale in 1984, Michael Dukakis in 1988, Al Gore in 2000, and John Kerry in 2004 failed to some extent because they were perceived to be "too liberal" on social issues. Much of the New Deal coalition deserted the Democrats during these elections, in large part because of uneasiness with the party's social policies. In fact, during this period the only successful presidential candidates were Jimmy Carter, of Georgia, and Bill Clinton, of Arkansas, southern governors who were able to keep southern and ethnic voters without alienating minorities and union members.

The Republican Coalition Since 1932

With a brief notable exception, the Republican party has been the minority party since Roosevelt's victory in 1932. It has a more loyal constituency because the elements of its coalition have not been nearly as diverse or as quarrelsome as have the members of the Democrats' coalition. The Republican party has drawn its strength from white, suburban voters, Protestants, and small business. But divisions have also occurred among Republicans. In particular, the conservative elements of the party have been at odds with more mainstream views. Issues such as abortion have often divided these groups. George W. Bush's presidency focused mostly on the divisive cultural conservative issues that divided his party. As attention turned from domestic social policy to wars overseas and the economy at home, Bush's core issues mattered less to everyone but his most conservative base. The result, in 2008, was a Republican party split in two: one more fiscally conservative and the other more culturally so. Republican party insiders and activists have taken to the Internet to determine what direction they need to lead the party in, and sites like The Next Right have emerged as a town hall discussion for the GOP's next steps.[11]

The Republicans have always had a smaller but more closely knit coalition than the Democrats. This coalition can tolerate little shrinkage. When battles over core social issues, such as abortion, split the party, they almost always mean defeat in presidential elections. In 2000, the Republican candidate, George W. Bush, did his best to downplay the abortion issue, not only to hold his party together but also to avoid alienating pro-choice Independents, who might otherwise be favorably disposed to a Republican candidate. In 2004, the dominant social issue was gay marriage, and this played well for the Republicans. President Bush was able to take a conservative position on the issue without alienating many Republicans and also attracting some conservative Democrats and Independents.

10-3 The Contemporary Party System

The American party system is a loosely constructed two-party system built around a structure that mirrors the federal system. Most of the world's democracies have **multiparty systems**. In Great Britain, the major parties—Conservative and Labour—in some ways parallel the American Republican and Democratic parties. The British political parties are much more disciplined, however, with few party members voting against the leadership of the party in Parliament. Likewise, the British parties have more cohesive constituents. To some degree, the British pattern can be attributed to its unitary system of government as opposed to the U.S. federal system. In a unitary system, the national party does not need to be constructed on a base of state or local systems. Moreover, the British parliamentary system, in which the prime minister is chosen from the majority party in the legislative branch, has no counterpart to our "checks and balances."

The Founders constructed American national government to limit the power of factions. The party system reflects in many ways that desire to limit power. Just as the federal system retains states as policy-making units in government, the American party system retains state parties as policy-making units in party affairs. Just as the separation of powers diffuses power between Congress and the president, the party system likewise diffuses the power of the parties to function as unified organizations. Also important to note is the persistence of American political culture. Unlike other nations, the founding of the American Republic was unified in support of free-market capitalism. With the economic framework for the United States basically decided, there were fewer arguments, such as whether or not capitalism should be the framework for our economy. With that argument off the table, there was no place or need for a corresponding political party. Thus, our culture of individualism and capitalism also helped keep other parties from forming.

10-3a WHY ONLY TWO PARTIES?

With rare exceptions, two political parties have always existed at the national level in the United States. This two-party system does not result from any direct design on the part of the Founders, who did not mention parties in the Constitution. The two-party system was not even consciously planned. Rather, it has flowed from other structural characteristics of American government as well as from American political culture.

The major reason for the two-party system has to do with the **winner-take-all** electoral system for president and Congress. In a winner-take-all electoral system, a party must capture the most votes in a district to obtain any representation in the government. For instance, a presidential candidate must win the most votes in a state before obtaining any electoral votes. In a winner-take-all system, a new party must win entire districts in a race for the House of Representatives before it has any representation in the House. It must win entire states before obtaining any Senate seats or accumulating any electoral votes for president. Thus, if a new party were to form and get 15 percent of the votes nationwide, it could easily end up with no House seats and win no electoral votes in a presidential contest. This system makes it hard for any new party to grow.

Another structural explanation for the two-party system is the difficulty third parties have experienced in getting on the ballot. Although the last two third-party candidates, John Anderson and Ross Perot, were listed on all fifty state ballots, the task continues to be quite difficult in some states. Indeed, in 1980, John Anderson had to sue election officials in some states to get his name on the ballot.[12]

Recently, the two-party system has been further cemented by the federal funding of presidential elections, established by the Revenue Act of 1971 and the Federal Election Campaign Act of 1974.[13] Since the 1976 election, the candidates representing the two major parties have received millions of dollars in federal funds to conduct their campaigns. A third party has difficulty obtaining the federal funding that the Democratic and Republican parties routinely receive. For example, in 1980, Independent John Anderson barely obtained the 5 percent of the popular vote in the general election that is needed to qualify for federal funds. Even if a third-party candidate qualifies for federal funds, the amount of funding is a fraction of what the major candidates receive. The major-party candidates' funding advantage makes it all but impossible for a third-party candidate to mount a viable campaign unless he has enormous personal resources, as did Ross Perot in the 1992 election.

In the 2000 presidential election, the 5 percent goal became of paramount importance in regard to Ralph Nader's candidacy. As the campaign drew to a close, surveys indicated an extremely tight race between Vice President Gore and his Republican opponent, George W. Bush. Moreover, Nader supporters came disproportionately from those who would otherwise have voted for Al Gore. Democrats, along with many in the media, began to put pressure on Ralph Nader to withdraw so as not to cost Gore the election. Meanwhile, many Nader supporters indicated that they were wavering in their support and considering a Gore vote. Nader steadfastly refused to ease up on his campaign, indicating that he was focused on building the Green party, under whose banner he ran. Clearly, to build a viable third party, the federal funding that would accompany the 5 percent total would be a crucial element. Nader supporters then faced a dilemma: Either vote for their first choice, Ralph Nader, and risk having their second choice, Al Gore, lose; or vote for Al Gore and risk an outcome in which Ralph Nader would not receive enough votes to provide federal funding to the Green party in future elections. When the votes were cast, Nader did not get 5 percent. In many ways, the Nader dilemma underscores the almost impossible position of third parties in America's winner-take-all system.

10-3b The Fate of Third Parties

Third parties have never won a presidential election in the United States. Nor have third parties remained a powerful force for more than a few years. The candidates and their supporters who have entered politics under the banner of a third party have usually done so out of frustration with the two major parties. For example, consider the Progressive party. Three totally different organizations were active under that name during the 1912, 1924, and 1948 presidential campaigns. The first Progressive party was also known as the Bull Moose party. Its candidate was the popular

Theodore Roosevelt, who left the Republican party to oppose William Howard Taft in 1912. Roosevelt's platform contained many reforms that were later implemented by the major parties, including the right of women to vote and the direct election of U.S. senators. Though Roosevelt was not successful, his candidacy led to the election of Democrat Woodrow Wilson. In 1924, another Progressive party was led by the Wisconsin senator Robert LaFollette. It too placed many items on the national agenda, including the recognition of labor unions. LaFollette carried only his home state of Wisconsin. Later, in 1948, Henry Wallace ran as a Progressive, but did not fare as well as Roosevelt or LaFollette.

Third parties have been for the most part closely identified with charismatic leaders. That was certainly the case with Teddy Roosevelt in 1912. It was also true in 1968, when the Alabama governor George C. Wallace led the American Independent party in a national crusade against racial integration and other manifestations of modern liberalism. Decried by many as a demagogue, Wallace managed to earn nearly 14 percent of the popular vote in the 1968 presidential election. The Wallace candidacy was quite successful in foreshadowing the concern that many Americans felt about social issues. Many of these themes were later used with great success by Richard Nixon, Ronald Reagan, and George Bush.

The Rise and Fall of the Reform Party

In 1992, another charismatic individual, Texas billionaire H. Ross Perot, stepped onto the stage of American politics. His "party," originally named United We Stand, was little more than a hastily assembled organization to promote Perot's bid for the presidency. Perot's party was much more of an individual-centered organization than were any of the incarnations of the Progressive party. Nevertheless, with 19 percent of the popular vote in the 1992 election, Perot's candidacy was the most successful third-party bid for the presidency since Teddy Roosevelt received 27 percent in 1912. Like Roosevelt in 1912, Perot forced the major parties and candidates to address issues and concerns that they might otherwise have chosen to ignore. Among Perot's priorities were balancing the budget, reforming the tax code, and strengthening campaign finance laws. In particular, Perot's 1992 campaign did much to put the federal budget deficit at the top of President Bill Clinton's priority list in 1993 and 1994. To some extent, the budget surplus of the late 1990s resulted from policies advocated by Ross Perot.

In 1995, Perot attempted to institutionalize his contribution to the American political dialogue by founding the Reform party. In 1996, the Reform party nominated Perot as its presidential candidate, to no one's surprise. However, Perot received only 8 percent of the popular vote in 1996, causing the party to fall into obscurity for nearly two years. In 1998, however, the Reform party scored a major success when one of its candidates, the former professional wrestler Jesse "The Body" Ventura was elected governor of Minnesota. After that, Ventura became the Reform party's de facto leader, although the party soon degenerated into factionalism. In 1999 and 2000, as the party prepared to nominate a candidate for president, it lacked any clear ideological direction. Rather, it was a hodgepodge of disaffected citizens and mavericks ranging from the billionaire Donald Trump to the Hollywood star Warren Beatty. In 2000, after a struggle for control of the party (and its federal matching funds), Pat Buchanan secured the Reform party nomination and barely registered in the presidential election. In the wake of this debacle, most observers declared the Reform party dead.

The Green Party

Green parties appeared in Europe in the 1970s and 1980s and in some countries, such as Germany and France, have had considerable success. Green parties are basically political parties centered around an environmentalist platform. In the United States, the Green party espouses, according to its own publications, "ecological wisdom," grassroots democracy, social justice, feminism, and nonviolence.[14] It is an agenda well to the left of the Democratic party. The Green party first appeared on the ballot in the United States in Alaska in 1990. In 1996, the longtime consumer activist and corporate critic Ralph Nader assumed leadership of the Green party and in 2000 mounted a serious presidential candidacy. Although the Green party has real ongoing appeal to a segment of Americans, Ralph Nader's successes in 2000 were more attributable to his strong name recognition and dissatisfaction among some liberal Democrats with their party's candidate, Al Gore. In 2004, the Green party and Nader parted company, and neither fared very well politically. Together, Nader and Green party nominee David Cobb received less than 1 percent of the popular vote nationwide.

The Libertarian Party

The Libertarian party was founded in 1971 and held its first national convention one year later. In 1980, the Libertarian presidential candidate, Ed Clark, appeared on the ballot in all fifty states. By the 1990s, the party was firmly established on the American political scene. By 1996, the Libertarian party had become the first third party in American history to field a presidential candidate in all fifty states in three consecutive elections. In 2000, the Libertarian candidate, Harry Browne, again appeared on all fifty state ballots, although he garnered less than 1 percent of the popular vote nationwide. The Libertarian party has found a niche in American politics mainly because its ideologically consistent message calling for less government interference resonates

with a significant segment of the electorate. The Libertarian party espouses free-market capitalism, advocates a noninterventionist foreign policy, and maintains a strong commitment to personal liberty.

Lesser Third Parties

Regardless of their limited potential to gather votes (see Table 10-1), the minor parties add a bit of spice to the political process. Most exist only at the presidential level and have no organizational structure. With the exception of the Libertarians, minor parties raise and spend little money. Although a few third parties manage to have a major effect in a particular election, many more linger for decades while capturing little interest or support. Many are on only a few state ballots. These parties come into existence outside the mainstream as a somewhat natural consequence of the fact that the two parties tend toward the center. Because "winning" is so unlikely, these third-party candidates are able to argue in favor of ideas that the major parties are afraid to touch. Later, these ideas often become part of the platforms of the major parties. Third parties fail to last, both because they are associated with individual candidates and because the system is so weighted in favor of two parties. But they do provide a valuable vehicle for protesting the status quo.

TABLE 10-1 Major Third Parties' Share of the Presidential Vote, 1832–2012

YEAR	PARTY	PRESIDENTIAL CANDIDATE	PERCENTAGE OF VOTE
1832	Anti-Masonic	William Wirt	8
1856	"Know-Nothings"	Millard Fillmore	22
1856	Secessionist Democrats	J.C. Breckenridge	18
1860	Constitutional Union	John Bell	13
1892	Populist	James B. Weaver	9
1912	Progressive (Bull Moose)	Theodore Roosevelt	27
1912	Socialist	Eugene Debs	6
1924	Progressive	Robert LaFollette	17
1948	States' Rights	Strom Thurmond	2
1948	Progressive	Henry Wallace	2
1968	American Independent	George Wallace	14
1980	Independent	John Anderson	7
1992	United We Stand	Ross Perot	19
1996	Reform	Ross Perot	8
2000	Green	Ralph Nader	3
2004	Libertarian	Michael Badnarik	<1
2008	Libertarian	Bob Barr	<1
2012	Libertarian	Gary Johnson	<1

The Rise of the Proto-Party

A new development in the party system is important to note here as well. The most recent developments in American party politics have involved groups that are loosely affiliated with one ideological wing of the existing parties, but are neither breakaway groups nor officially sanctioned parts of existing parties. While they are a powerful bloc within their respective parties, they could break away and undermine their currently affiliated party in important ways. Their status leads to a new term, the **proto-party**.

Starting on April 15, tax day, in 1999, a group of reformers calling themselves Taxed Enough Already (TEA) began protesting Washington D.C. spending. Inspired by conservative groups and the presidential candidacy of Ron Paul, the group developed into the **Tea Party**. Not technically a party itself, but a powerful faction that grew within the Republican party, Tea Party–affiliated candidates like Marco Rubio (R-FL) won big in 2010. While not as successful in 2012, the Tea Party continues to wield significant power inside the Republicans. The group, which is actually made up of a number of separate factions, does not have the national organization or structure to qualify as a party, nor do they have candidates who run with the Tea Party label.

In 2011, a Tea Party response emerged on the left as a social movement known as **Occupy Wall Street** began protests across the country against what they saw as unfair and unequal distributions of wealth in the country. Occupy Wall Street has struggled to build themselves into the national force the Tea Party has, but look to be the same kind of powerful intra-party force that the Tea Party has become on the right.

Third parties now tend to be narrowly ideological, basing their appeal on a fairly strict set of beliefs about government. Most are on the left side of the political spectrum. The parties arouse some interest, but they have a difficult time being taken seriously, mostly because their views are so far outside the mainstream. The Socialist and Socialist Workers parties are typical of these parties. The limited American appetite for socialism has greatly restricted their appeal, but they continue nevertheless. Other fringe parties represent conservative interests. These, too, have a difficult time being taken seriously, along with the potpourri of other parties, such as the Natural Law party and the Prohibition party.

ONLINE 10.3 *Mapping Third-Party Voting in the United States*
http://www.youtube.com/watch?v=e8y2C82NFDE

10-4 PARTIES AND THE GOVERNING PROCESS

The parties have tremendous responsibility for government in the American system. When Bill Clinton was elected president in 1992, he campaigned as a New Democrat who could work with Congress to pull the federal government out of "gridlock." After the election was over, the parties were charged with the responsibility of governing rather than campaigning. For the first time in more than a decade, the Democrats held the presidency and a majority in both the House and the Senate. In this new political landscape, the Republican party had a complementary role, that of the **loyal opposition**. The role of the loyal opposition is to criticize the majority party, provide useful debate on legislation, and block the more extreme policies of the majority party. In 1994, however, the political landscape changed again. Republicans gained control of Congress, thus restoring divided-party government.

Divided-party government slows the policy-making process dramatically. A president has great difficulty getting his legislative agenda through a House or Senate controlled by the other party. When the opposition party controls the Senate, the consequences can be especially aggravating for a president; the Senate must approve judicial and other high-level appointments. Bill Clinton experienced frustration with the Republican-controlled Senate during his administration. Likewise, George W. Bush found himself facing a Senate controlled by Democrats early in his presidency. Slow Senate action, and often inaction, led to a tremendous backlog of judicial appointments. George W. Bush was unquestionably greatly relieved when the Republicans recaptured the Senate in the 2002 midterm elections. With Republicans in charge of both houses of Congress, President Bush had reason to believe that his agenda would be enacted. However, the war in Iraq and the 2004 election proved to be massive distractions for both the president and Congress. But Bush's victory over John Kerry in 2004 and the Republicans' solidifying majorities in both houses of Congress gave new life to the president's agenda in 2005.

10-4a THE PARTY IN GOVERNMENT

Elected officials are part of the **party in government**. The party in government consists of those officeholders from a particular party. Although party affiliation is crucial to the way the president and cabinet operate in office, they do not have to contend with members of the other party in day-to-day internal operations. At the same time, however, the president and cabinet have to be ever aware of their party in Congress and how it and the opposition in Congress will react. They also have to be sensitive to party identifiers in the electorate, most of whom were their supporters during the election.

Members of Congress are even more aware of their membership in the party in government. Congress is organized along party lines. The congressional Democrats and Republicans must take positions as party members. Above all, they must decide whether they will support positions of their party that are not in line with their own views or the views of their constituents in their district. Representatives and senators are also conscious of their role as supporters or opponents of the president's legislative proposals. Usually, members of the president's party in Congress are expected to support the president. However, this support cannot be assumed. For instance, in 1993, President Clinton could not persuade most Democrats to support the North American Free Trade Agreement (NAFTA). In fact, Richard Gephardt, the Democratic majority leader in the House of Representatives, and David Bonior, the House Democratic whip, led the opposition to NAFTA in Congress. Clinton won congressional support for NAFTA only by relying on a coalition of conservative Democrats and Republicans. Had the trade agreement not been negotiated principally by the Bush administration, Republican support might not have been forthcoming. The Democratic **party in Congress** did not deliver support for what the president wanted.

The party in government functions in a rather loose manner in modern American politics. Parties have weakened as institutions, and elected government officials face many pressures from organized interest groups. Pressures from party leaders to function according to a party agenda often are outweighed by perceived pressure from important groups and interests in a representative's state or district. For example, in early 1993, President Clinton proposed a complex British thermal unit (BTU) energy tax. The plan eventually was scrapped when Democratic senators from energy-producing states refused to go along with the Democratic leadership in the Senate, which was supporting the president. Clinton's later abandonment of the plan bothered many Democrats in the House of Representatives who had supported the president and the party despite their own misgivings about the plan's popularity in their district. In this case, the Democratic party in government was unable to operate with enough discipline to deliver a Democratic president's legislative program.

10-4b The Party in the Electorate

The **party in the electorate** refers to all those voters who identify with a party. In the United States, individuals do not formally express their party preference. The closest Americans come to making this type of declaration is when they register as Democrats or Republicans in those states that require voters to state a party preference to vote in a party primary. Most Americans express their party identification merely as a feeling. Thus, the Democratic and Republican parties in the electorate consist of those who say that they are Democrats or Republicans when asked "Are you a Democrat, a Republican, or an Independent?"

The party in the electorate refers to those voters who in national elections generally identify with a particular party. The term takes on less meaning between elections. The party in the electorate is mostly about electing candidates. Its official role is to nominate candidates for president. In that process, people participate as representatives of their parties, doing a party's main business: choosing who will run for office under its banner. Unofficially, the party in the electorate is the base on which the candidate hopes to build a winning electoral coalition.

Trends in Party Identification

Because Americans identify with, rather than join, political parties, the best way to determine the support for each party is to ask people "Do you consider yourself a Democrat, a Republican, or an Independent?" This measure, called party identification (see Table 10-2), is probably the best indicator of the status of the party in the electorate. When Americans answer this question, they are not necessarily indicating their voting preference in any particular election. Rather, they are expressing their affinity with one or the other party or, of course, a lack of affinity with either party. In many elections, voters choose a candidate from the opposite party. Over the long term, however, party identification is the best available indicator of how a person would vote in any election.

ONLINE 10.4 *Pew Center on Partisanship Today*

The University of Michigan has regularly asked Americans about their party identification since 1952. The biggest change over the more than forty-year period has been the decline in those identifying with the Democratic party. The Republicans have remained the minority party throughout the period. The biggest increase has been among Independents. These changes in the party in the electorate have not only influenced the outcomes of elections, but have also both reflected and changed the ways in which campaigns are conducted.

Party identification is a relatively stable and enduring force in American politics. With the exception of the 1964 election year, when Barry Goldwater pulled the Republican party further to the conservative end of the spectrum than many Americans were prepared to go, year-to-year changes in party identification have been minor.

The Rise of the Independent Voter

The most notable trend in party identification over the past four decades is the rise of the Independent voter—the voter who identifies with no particular party. This is true not only in the United States, but also in most democracies around the world. "In almost all the advanced industrial democracies . . . the proportion of the population identifying with a particular party has declined in the past quarter-century, as has the strength of party attachments."[15] One reason for this phenomenon is the rise of mass media. Citizens no longer depend on parties for cues about issues and candidates.

TABLE 10-2 Trends in Party Identification, 1952–2008

Strong Democrat :
Weak Democrat :
Independent Democrat :
Independent Independent :
Independent Republican :
Weak Republican :
Strong Republican :
Apolitical :

	'80	'84	'88	'92	'96	'00	'04	08
STRONG DEMOCRAT	18	17	17	18	18	19	17	26
WEAK DEMOCRAT	23	20	18	18	19	15	16	17
INDEPENDENT DEMOCRAT	11	11	12	14	14	15	17	20
INDEPENDENT INDEPENDENT	13	11	11	12	9	12	10	12
INDEPENDENT REPUBLICAN	10	12	13	12	12	13	12	6
WEAK REPUBLICAN	14	15	14	14	15	12	12	8
STRONG REPUBLICAN	9	12	14	11	12	12	16	10
APOLITICAL	2	2	2	1	1	1	0	1

Rather, they get this information directly through the media. The prevalence of mass media has elevated the importance of a candidate's image while lessening the importance of that candidate's party affiliation. If voters have less need for partisan cues, they are less likely to form attachments to parties. Although the decline in partisan identification has affected both major parties, it has come more at the expense of the Democrats than the Republicans. It is important not to overstate this trend. Even in 2000, only 12 percent of the electorate identified themselves as straight Independents, that is, not leaning toward either party.

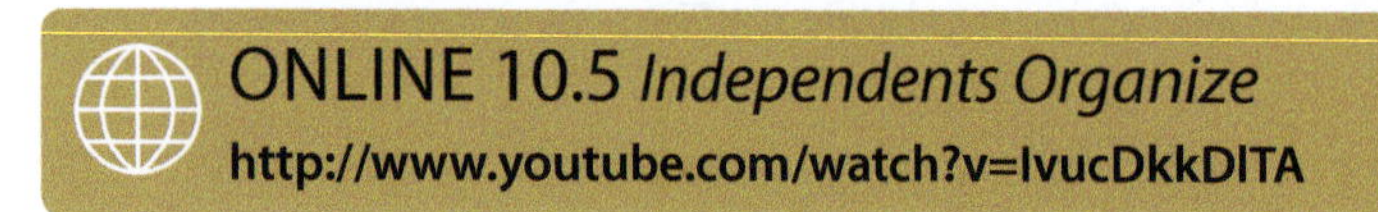

ONLINE 10.5 *Independents Organize*
http://www.youtube.com/watch?v=IvucDkkDITA

10-5 The Structure of the National Parties

The political parties are organized around the American federal model. Unlike the federal system of government, however, the federal party system leaves much power at the state level. In fact, the national party offices are quite limited. There is little the national party offices can force the state or local parties to do. The national party has no control over who is nominated to run for an office under the party's name. Each state party controls the method of candidate nomination within the state. The national party also has little control over campaign finance. The national parties can provide assistance to the state parties or individual candidates, but the total amount of national party money spent in state and local races is a small fraction of all spending. Furthermore, after an individual is elected under the party banner, the party can do little to force that person to comply with the party's policy preferences.

The two major parties are organized with the national party at the top of the federal structure, but neither functions as a hierarchy, in the manner of the military or a business organization. Party leaders cannot issue commands that will be followed by the party members. A party is composed of individuals who are free to leave at any time. In fact, much of the party structure is composed of volunteers. Increasingly, the two major parties have hired professional staff members to perform organizational tasks on a day-to-day basis, but volunteers fill most of the decision-making positions. For the most part, not much of a party is in existence between elections. The party in most states has a small staff, and the national party has a somewhat larger staff, but most of the party organization lies dormant from election to election. In addition, the parties experience a great turnover in personnel from one election to another as volunteers choose to join or drop out because of their affection for a party's candidates.

10-5a The National Office

Both the Republican and Democratic parties conduct most of the national party's effort through the Washington offices of the national committee chair and the professional staff. The national chairperson is elected from among the members of the national committee. The national party chair appears regularly on television and radio news shows, defending the party's position or the position of major people within the party. Because the president acts as party leader, the chair of the president's party has less responsibility for maintaining party visibility, unity, and organization. The opposition party chair must provide a greater leadership role; several competitors within the party may be vying for power, so in the absence of a president from the party, the chair must protect the party's interests. In addition, the chair travels among the states, supporting candidates for state and national office, raising money for those campaigns, and building a **war chest** of funds for the next election. The party leader must have a complex set of skills, including being able to raise funds and assist in campaigns for important offices. In recent years, Terry McAuliffe, the chairman of the Democratic National Committee from 2001 to 2004, best exemplified these traits.

10-5b State Party Systems

Although the national parties garner much of the media attention, the state and local parties have historically been the most important element of each party. Each party has tremendous diversity across the states in terms of ideology and the issues that matter most to voters. For example, white Democrats in the South are much more likely to favor military spending and much less likely to support civil rights, gay rights, or social welfare than Democrats in the northeastern states or on the west coast. Republicans are more homogeneous than Democrats, for the most part, but they also experience serious differences on issues such as abortion rights, school prayer, and other moralistic causes. Therefore, you cannot assume that all Democrats or all Republicans are the same.

Party Machines

The state parties also differ in history, party organization, and rules. Two of the historical factors that have been most influential in shaping state parties have been the presence of party machines and the progressive movement. **Party machines** are local party organizations that dominate elections in an area over a long period through a variety of both legal and illegal means. By distributing government jobs and contracts to loyal voters, the machines were able to keep many voters dependent on the party for their job security. Others received access to city services or direct assistance from the party. In some cases, machines resorted to illegal means of influencing elections, such as allowing loyal voters to cast more than one ballot, keeping dead voters on the voter registration lists so that others could use their names to vote more than once, or buying the votes of citizens. Two of the most notorious party machines were the Tammany Hall Democratic machine, in New York, and the Cook County machine, in Chicago, Illinois.

Party machines were most prevalent and most powerful at the turn of the twentieth century but then slowly began to lose their power. The expansion of the federal government since the Great Depression of the 1930s has taken away the machine's role of providing social service programs to loyal voters. The federal government is now involved in unemployment compensation, welfare, Social Security, and aid to families with dependent children, and anyone is eligible to receive the benefits regardless of party. Therefore, parties could not use the role of service provider as persuasively as they could before the New Deal programs. This loss made it difficult to hold voters in the fold.

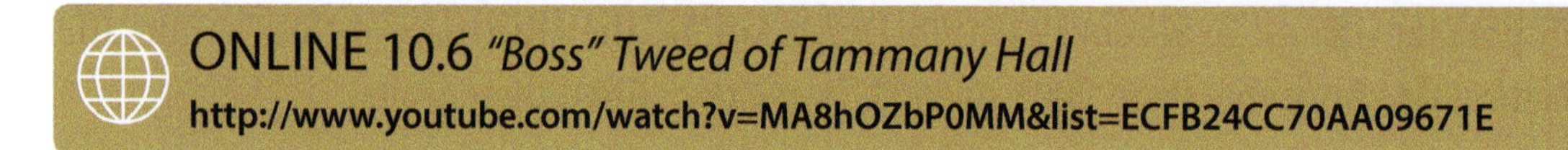

ONLINE 10.6 "Boss" Tweed of Tammany Hall
http://www.youtube.com/watch?v=MA8hOZbP0MM&list=ECFB24CC70AA09671E

The **progressive movement** also had an impact on the party machines. The progressive movement was an effort to reform government by eliminating fraud, corruption, and inefficiency. Like the founding generation, the Progressives were deeply suspicious of parties and sought to minimize their influence. The Progressives envisioned "a national community, in which new political institutions . . . would forge a direct link between public opinion and government representatives."[16]

Many government reforms favored by Progressives were direct assaults on the party machines. The **Australian ballot**, now used in American elections, allows voters to vote in secret and to choose between individuals of each party for each office. Because parties could no longer observe whether a voter cast a party ballot, the introduction of the Australian ballot made it more difficult to enforce party loyalty. The primary election is another reform that took power away from party leaders. Most state and local parties had used caucuses (party conferences) to determine the candidates the party would nominate for an office. Because the caucuses did not use secret voting, a well-organized machine could easily dominate the process. Primaries, however, take the decision out of the hands of the party leaders by allowing voters to choose party nominees through a **secret ballot**. Depending on the rules of the state, the primary may even allow Independent voters to participate in a party's primary. Furthermore, in most states, the party cannot even control who is allowed on the ballot; the state establishes the rules for how a candidate is placed on the ballot.

Differences in Partisan Strength in the States

The strength of each party varies greatly from state to state. To understand partisanship in any state, one must examine its industrial development, urbanization, migration patterns, and the impact of historical events, such as the Civil War. The heavily industrialized states of the Midwest and Northeast have long had strong labor unions, so they also have had strong Democratic parties. Urban areas tend to have more minorities, which tend to be Democratic, so more urbanized states are more likely to have strong Democratic parties.

A large influx of new voters can affect a state's partisan orientation. For example, the migration of wealthy elderly people and Cubans into Florida has radically altered the state's politics. Wealthy senior citizens moving into the state from the North have made it more Republican. Because of their opposition to Fidel Castro, Cuban Americans are likely to be conservative voters. Both groups contributed to the emergence of the Republican party in Florida during the 1970s and 1980s. In 2000, these Cuban Americans supported by a large margin the candidacy of Republican George W. Bush.

Historical events affecting partisanship can be either local or national. The Civil War is an example of a historical event that still influences partisanship in this country, particularly in the South. For most of the period from 1876 to the 1980s, the South was dominated by the Democratic party. Because Lincoln and the presidents during the Reconstruction period were all Republicans, the vast majority of white southerners were Democrats. Black southerners were mostly Republican until the 1930s, when Roosevelt's New Deal legislation brought African Americans into the Democratic party. The Democrats' dominance in the South began to erode only as the Democrats in Washington began to push for civil rights legislation and social welfare programs in the 1960s. In the 1964 presidential election, the Republicans captured the majority of southern electoral votes for the first time in almost ninety years.

The South has continued to vote Republican at the presidential level since 1964, but until 1994 it remained heavily Democratic in state races and congressional elections. For example, the Democrats controlled a majority of the Congressional seats from the South, winning 90 of 147 seats in the 1992 election. In 1994, however, the Republicans won 77 of the southern seats (13 of 22 in the Senate and 64 of 125 in the House). The Republicans recently made great strides in states such as Florida and Texas, with Texas, Mississippi, and North Carolina each having two Republican U.S. senators for the first time since Reconstruction. By 2000, the Senate was evenly split at 50 for each party and the Republicans enjoyed a narrow 221–212 margin in the House of Representatives, with two members elected as Independents. The 2002 midterm elections saw the Republicans retake control of the Senate and extend their margin in the House. And in 2004, Republicans made additional gains, extending their margins to 55–45 in the Senate and 232–203 in the House. Most of these gains came in the South. By 2004, the once solidly Democratic South had become solidly Republican.

ONLINE 10.7 *Party Strength in the States*
http://www.gallup.com/poll/114016/state-states-political-party-affiliation.aspx

10-6 The National Party Conventions

The major political parties come alive at their **national conventions**, held every four years in the summer before the election for president takes place. These conventions are in many ways the only time the parties have a chance to present themselves to the American people. Since the 1950s, conventions have been televised. On occasion, they have provided viewers with excitement and entertainment. A successful convention is regarded as essential to the later electoral success of the party's candidate.

10-6a A Brief History of the Conventions

The first political convention was held in 1831 in preparation for the 1832 election. The Anti-Masonic party (a short-lived minor party) held the first national convention in 1831 in a Baltimore saloon and nominated a candidate to oppose Andrew Jackson, the incumbent Democratic president. Months later, the Whigs met in the same Baltimore saloon to nominate another opponent to Jackson. The Democrats held their first national convention in 1832 to confirm Jackson as their presidential nominee. In 1836, the Democrats met to confirm Jackson's chosen successor, Vice President Martin Van Buren. The Whigs chose not to have a convention but instead ran several candidates from different regions in the hope that they would prevent Van Buren from attaining a majority in the electoral college, thereby throwing the election into the House of Representatives. The Democrats prevailed, and Van Buren was elected.

Since 1836, the major political parties have routinely used conventions to choose the party's presidential nominee for the general election. The national party establishes rules for how many delegates are allowed from each state, the District of Columbia, and the territories. Generally, each state is allotted delegates in proportion to its percentage of the nation's population. Consequently, California, with nearly thirty million residents, received almost sixty times as many delegates to a convention in the 1990s as Wyoming, with less than half a million residents. The state party organizations determine how convention delegates from each state are chosen.

From 1832 to 1968, party leaders exerted much greater control over the conventions than has been the case since the 1970s. Indeed, state party leaders were crucial to the nomination of a presidential candidate. Two factors contributed to the power of the state leaders:

1. *Most delegates were chosen by means of political caucuses, so they were part of the mainstream party organization.* The process of choosing convention delegates through a caucus system involves a complex organizational structure that begins with party supporters gathering in a series of local meetings all across a state. These local groups send a small number of delegates to a series of ever-higher-level meetings that culminate in a statewide convention. The state convention determines the party rules for that state and selects its delegates to the national convention. Caucuses tend to be dominated by a small number of party activists. Because most states used caucuses until the 1970s, the vast majority of convention participants were professional politicians or party workers who had faithfully supported important political leaders. Furthermore, most delegates sent by a caucus system were not legally bound to support any particular candidate at the national convention. Therefore, the delegates could "shop around" at the convention to choose either a preferred candidate or the one with the greatest chance of defeating the other party's candidate.
2. *The delegates from most states were generally more committed to the state's leaders than they were to the national party.* Patronage, a system that uses political support rather than merit as the basis of government hiring, was particularly useful in maintaining party loyalty. Because state leaders could command a large number of votes, presidential candidates had to bargain with them for the nomination. Most negotiations took place behind closed doors. At many conventions during these years, several ballots were needed to determine who would be the party's nominee.

10-6b The Rise of the Primaries

Wisconsin introduced the **direct primary** in 1903 as a device to involve more people in the nomination process. In a direct primary, party members vote for their preferred party nominee in a primary election that is held in the winter or spring before the party's national convention. Of course, the nomination of a presidential candidate reflects the federal system, with states having a good bit of discretion in how their convention delegates are chosen. Thus, it is not surprising that the state legislatures began to consider the primary as an alternative. By 1912, the Democrats were using presidential primaries in twelve states, and the Republicans were using them in thirteen states.

The high point for primaries during this period came in 1916. More than 50 percent of all the Democratic delegates and almost 60 percent of the Republican delegates were chosen by primaries. But from 1920 through the election of 1968, fewer than 50 percent of the delegates were chosen by primaries in any given contest. Primaries fell from favor because of low voter turnout, their high cost, and the party leaders' desire to reassert their power over the nomination process. Discusses the white primary, which is a system that excluded African Americans from party membership. The white primary was later struck down by the Supreme Court.

Types of Primaries

Primaries differ on a number of dimensions. Perhaps the most important distinction is between open and closed primaries. In an **open primary**, any voter can choose to participate in either primary merely by declaring her intention after entering the voting place. This system allows voters to cross over, or vote in the primary in which they sense the most excitement or in which they have the most interest. Most important, Independent voters or voters from the other party can have as much effect on a party's nominee as that party's own voters. In contrast, in a **closed primary**, a person must be registered as a Democrat or Republican to participate in the election. Primaries also differ in the type of ballot voters confront after entering the voting booth. In some states, voters vote for delegates representing a candidate rather than vote for the candidate. In other states, the vote for the preferred candidate is a "beauty contest" that does not have any role in selecting delegates. In these states, party activists at a state convention choose delegates.

Advantages and Disadvantages of Primaries versus Caucuses

The primary system offers several benefits over the caucus system:

- Voters can maintain the secrecy of their preferences for individual candidates in a primary, although doing so in a caucus is more difficult.
- A primary requires less time and energy for an individual to participate, so more people vote in primaries than attend party caucuses.
- A wider variety of people participate in primaries than in caucuses.

Because caucuses tend to be dominated by party activists, caucus participants are more extreme ideologically than primary voters. On the other hand, primaries are much more costly: the state has to pay for the election workers, voting booths, ballots, and other costs, and the candidates must pay for a campaign that reaches the millions of potential voters participating in a primary. Primaries also strip party leaders of their control over the nomination process. In some state and local elections, candidates have won the nomination even though state party leaders refused to endorse them. Delegates selected by primaries are also more likely to be required by law to vote in accordance with the results of the primary. This arrangement reduces the flexibility of the state's delegation at the convention. State party leaders no longer have as much opportunity to bargain with potential candidates.

10-6c Party Reform: 1968–2008

As late as 1968, most delegates to the national conventions were chosen by caucuses rather than through the primary system. That was the last year, however, that the caucus system delivered the nomination to the candidate of the party establishment. A number of dramatic events produced tremendous conflict within the Democratic party and led ultimately to a series of reforms that changed the nature of the party's nomination process. Early in the year, President Lyndon Johnson, beleaguered by protest against the Vietnam War and a poor showing in the New Hampshire primary, decided not to seek reelection. A number of candidates emerged to seek the Democratic nomination, including Hubert H. Humphrey, the incumbent vice president; Eugene McCarthy, a U.S. senator from Wisconsin; and Robert F. Kennedy, who represented New York in the Senate. Contrary to the Johnson administration, both Kennedy and McCarthy opposed continued American involvement in Vietnam. Kennedy and McCarthy tried to take their messages to the people directly by actively campaigning in state primaries. Many young people and others dissatisfied with traditional politics participated in these campaigns. These newcomers provided tangible assistance but also created an image of a new type of campaign that was not beholden to party insiders. In contrast, Humphrey decided to forgo the primaries and rely instead on his close ties to the party leadership throughout the states.

In the spring of 1968, both Martin Luther King, Jr., and Robert Kennedy were assassinated, creating turmoil throughout the nation, but especially inside the Democratic party. Some of Kennedy's support went to Senator McCarthy; some went to a new candidate, Senator George McGovern, of South Dakota. In any event, Humphrey won enough delegates to secure the nomination. The Democratic National Convention of 1968 was held in Chicago, where Mayor Richard Daley was determined to control the convention and deliver the nomination to Humphrey with a minimum of difficulty. The convention was a nightmare for the Democrats, with thousands of outraged protesters convinced that the party had ignored the wishes of the people in choosing Humphrey. Many saw the party nomination system as closed and even corrupt. Pressure to open up the process to more popular participation followed.

The Democratic party found itself in a precarious condition after the 1968 convention. Its traditional base had been shattered. Many union and blue-collar voters had bolted to the Republican candidate in response to the antiwar, pro-civil rights, and perceived radical direction of the Democratic party. Humphrey had run third during a good bit of the campaign, trailing both the eventual winner, Richard Nixon, and George Wallace, an Independent candidate from Alabama. Southerners, most of whom had voted Democratic since the Civil War, were now defecting from the party. The once "solid South" appeared to have been lost.

In 1968, the party formed a commission, headed by George McGovern, to recommend changes in the rules of delegate selection.[17] Congressman Donald Fraser chaired the committee after McGovern resigned to seek the presidency. It issued its report in 1970 and has since been referred to as the **McGovern–Fraser Commission**. In essence, the McGovern–Fraser rules were designed to open the Democratic party to wider participation by women, minorities, and young people (see Figure 10-1). The rules also loosened the grip of traditional party bosses.

The rules suggested by the McGovern–Fraser Commission took effect in the 1972 presidential election. The major way the rules were enforced was by the convention's ability to judge the credentials of any delegation sent by a state. Any state whose delegation did not pass muster risked having an alternative delegation seated in its place. Rather than risk these types of challenges, the state parties pressured state legislatures to change the law determining the basis of selection. The easiest way to meet the McGovern–Fraser requirements was to institute a delegate selection primary. More and more states opted for primaries, and the majority of delegates to the national convention are now chosen by primaries.

Somewhat ironically, the first Democrat to benefit from the rules changes was George McGovern. His nomination as the Democratic candidate for president in 1972 came from a convention that better reflected the racial and gender diversity of the country. Few party professionals were in attendance. The nomination, however, was doomed from the outset, because the American public was put off by the party it observed on television.

The Superdelegate System

The Democrats have repeatedly reformed their nomination process since the dismal showing of 1972. Nearly every convention has reformed the process in some way. One

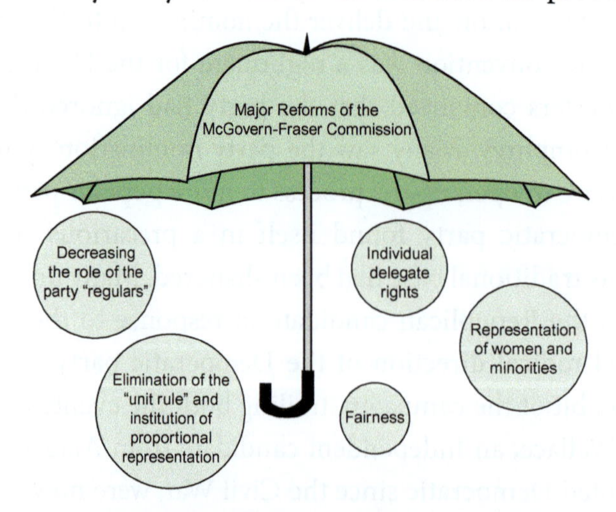

Figure 10-1 *Major Reforms of the McGovern–Fraser Commission*

of the more significant changes was the introduction of the **superdelegate** system in 1984. Concerned that few party leaders had attended the 1976 and 1980 conventions, the party set aside a certain number of delegate spots for elected party officials. These superdelegates can be members of Congress, governors, or mayors. The superdelegates provide three main benefits for the party:

3. Because of their name recognition, their presence brings the party more media attention.
4. The support of a wide range of Democratic leaders gives a strong display of party unity.
5. Because the superdelegates are not determined by primary elections and are not legally bound to vote for any particular party nominee, the superdelegates allow the national leaders of the party to have more control over the party than they had during the 1976 and 1980 conventions.

In 1986, the Democrats created another commission, the Fairness Commission, to study complaints that the convention was not allowing minority views to be truly reflected among the delegates who were selected. Jesse Jackson had won about 18 percent of the Democratic vote in 1984 but only 10 percent of the delegates to the convention. This phenomenon occurred because states had been required by party rules to ensure that a candidate who received 20 percent of the popular vote in a primary also received at least an equal percentage of the delegates. This percentage was changed to 15 percent for 1988, which had the effect of increasing the clout of second- or third-place candidates.

The Democratic Leadership Council and Super Tuesday

The increase in the number of primaries weakened the hold of the party professionals on the nomination process. Moreover, as the nominations of McGovern, Mondale, and Dukakis demonstrated, the process had become dominated by the more liberal states. For instance, Iowa, with its caucus, and New Hampshire, with its primary, are the first two states to begin the delegate selection process. This arrangement gives the Democrats of these states tremendous power in determining the nominee. Especially in Iowa, where only a small percentage of the party's voters even take the trouble to attend caucus meetings, moderate and conservative candidates seemed to be at a pronounced disadvantage.

In 1986, a group of southern Democrats decided to push for reforms that would give the South more clout in the nomination process and thereby increase the likelihood of a more moderate, and hence more electable, Democratic nominee. Their idea was to have the southern states hold their primaries on one day, early in the primary season. This idea proved popular with state legislatures throughout the South. In 1988, fourteen southern and border states moved their primaries to **Super Tuesday**.

Super Tuesday did not work as planned in 1988. Jesse Jackson received most of the votes of African Americans, offsetting to a large degree the strong showing of Tennessee Senator Al Gore, the more moderate of the candidates. Meanwhile, Michael Dukakis did well in Florida and Texas. Super Tuesday had little effect on the 1988 election. It did, however, play a major role in the nomination of Bill Clinton in 1992. Clinton emerged from Super Tuesday as the clear front-runner. Shortly thereafter, Clinton's main rival, former Senator Paul Tsongas, of Massachusetts, suspended his campaign because contributions were drying up. Even though Super Tuesday did not give Clinton enough delegates to clinch the nomination, it effectively delivered a knockout blow to the other candidates.

By 2000, Super Tuesday had declined dramatically in importance. Rather, the nominations of each party rested on issues peculiar to various states after the end of the New Hampshire primary. For instance, George W. Bush had to fight off a stronger than expected showing by John McCain, who had won in New Hampshire. The battle centered on two states, South Carolina and Michigan. In South Carolina, the issues centered around the confederate flag and its place in the state capitol building as well as around Bush's appearance at Bob Jones University. Michigan had changed its rules to allow any voter to vote in any party's primary. Although McCain won Michigan, largely with the help of Democrats who crossed over, Bush ultimately prevailed in securing his party's nomination. In 2004, George W. Bush's nomination by the Republicans was never in doubt, and John Kerry's nomination as the Democratic standard-bearer was all but assured before Super Tuesday.

The 2008 contest saw the controversy over ever-earlier primaries compacted into the first months of the process, the phenomenon known as **frontloading** (see Chapter 9). The parties' rule that Iowa's caucus be the first nominating event was challenged by Florida and Michigan, who scheduled primaries before Iowa in an attempt to get more attention and clout. For a time, the Democratic party intended to deny the Florida and Michigan delegations voting rights at the convention, but a late deal was struck which allowed the states to both participate.

Republican Reforms

Most reforms in the nomination process have taken place at the instigation of the Democratic party, mainly because the Democratic party includes a more diverse array of interests than the Republican party does. Thus, more interests are fighting for influence and representation. Republicans have not appointed commissions to study reform. Nevertheless, they have adopted many of the changes the Democrats have championed. Of course, new state laws, such as those creating primaries and Super Tuesday, have also affected them.

10-6d The Convention Delegates

The national convention held every four years during the presidential campaign serves as the supreme governing body for each national party. The conventions are composed of delegates from each of the fifty states, the District of Columbia, and the territories. In 2004, the Democrats had 4,353 delegates at their convention in Boston, and the Republicans had 2,509 delegates at their convention in New York City. The Republicans determine the number of delegates representing each state-by-state population. The Democrats employ a rule that apportions delegates on the basis of a combination of state population and how well the party performed in the last presidential election in the state. The two major parties vary greatly in their rules, structure, and method of choosing delegates to the convention.

In general, the delegates of both parties tend to be more extreme than the general electorate in their ideological persuasion. The Republican delegates tend to be more conservative and the Democratic delegates more liberal than those who identify with the parties. For example, in 1992, 24 percent of the self-described Democrats in a national survey identified themselves as being conservative, although only 5 percent of Democratic convention delegates self-identified as conservative. On the other hand, 8 percent of Republicans nationally identified themselves as liberals and only 1 percent of Republican convention delegates adopted the liberal label.[18]

Profiles Democratic and Republican convention delegates in five presidential elections: 1968, 1976, 1992, 1996, and 2000. These numbers are really not surprising. Party activists enter politics because they tend to care about issues. Those who become delegates take these commitments to the convention. Those who run the conventions must take care, however, that the convention rhetoric is not too extreme for the tastes of the general public. That was apparently the case at the 1992 Republican National Convention, where right-wing elements of the party made speeches that were not well received by the general public. This situation may have hurt George H.W. Bush somewhat in the 1992 general election.

In the 2000 campaign, Republican candidate George W. Bush did not allow an intolerant image to emerge. Quite to the contrary, he helped present an image of softness and inclusiveness—his so-called compassionate conservatism. A significant number of African Americans and women graced the podium, with nary a word about the cultural warfare alluded to in 1992. Although Bush's attention to this image ultimately did little to increase his share of the African American vote, his softer approach did apparently ease the concerns of many moderate voters, especially women, who had helped lead to Republican defeats in the preceding two elections. Seeking reelection in 2004, Bush talked less of compassionate conservatism and instead stressed his leadership in the global war on terrorism and the need to stay the course in Iraq. Despite Democratic efforts to paint him as a right-wing extremist, Bush was able to maintain sufficient support from women, moderates and, significantly, from Hispanics. To a great extent, Bush's warm and friendly style helped offset negative characterizations in the media.

One issue that resonated during the primaries in 2000 but much less so during the general election that followed was campaign finance reform. Although there were no significant differences between the two parties' identifiers in the public, substantive differences existed between the two parties' delegates. Democratic delegates were much more likely to support reform than were those to the Republican convention.[19]

10-6e THE FUNCTIONS OF THE CONVENTIONS

The national convention chooses the party's candidates for president and vice president, determines the party platform, and establishes the rules governing the party for the following four years. Both parties use majority rule among the delegates to make most decisions, but in the modern campaign the presidential nominee of each party orchestrates much of what happens. Because the majority of delegates have already been pledged to vote for a particular candidate before the convention, no convention since 1968 has featured a wide-open contest that created any suspense. Because the eventual nominee controls the majority needed to win before the convention, the most important function of the convention is to provide the party with a tremendous advertising opportunity. The government contributes the financing for the convention for each of the two major parties, and the major networks provide hours of prime-time coverage. Each party uses its convention to demonstrate how it has rallied around the candidate, and the nominee usually enjoys a public opinion boost.

WHAT NATIONAL PARTY CONVENTIONS DO

1. Determine the rules for conducting party business.
2. Bring together diverse groups in the party.
3. Develop and provide exposure for upcoming party leaders.
4. Debate and write the party platform.
5. Showcase the party's image.
6. Nominate the president and vice president.
7. Launch the campaign.

Another function of the convention is choosing a national committee to run the party in the period between conventions. The national committee organizes the next convention, helps conduct the presidential campaign, formulates and publicizes party policies, and appoints a national chair. It can also fill any vacancies that may occur in the nominations for the office of president and vice president before the general election. The Republican National Committee is composed of a male and female member from each state, the District of Columbia, American Samoa, Guam, Puerto Rico, and the Virgin Islands. The Democratic National Committee is much larger; each state is allowed committee members in proportion to the number of its convention delegates. In addition, the committee includes the party leader in the U.S. House, the party leader in the Senate, the president of the Young Democrats, the president of the National Federation of Democratic Women, and the chair of the Conference of Democratic Mayors. The national committees meet at least once a year. The Democrats also have a smaller executive committee, composed of members from the national committee, which meets more often throughout the year.

The **party platform**, a document that is developed at a party's national convention, establishes what the party stands for. Usually, the party's presidential candidate controls the process that creates the platform, but the final document is typically a compromise that may contain elements that are not even fully supported by the presidential candidate. Party members in Congress, the state legislatures, and the electorate are free to choose which aspects of the platform they support. The national party cannot force public officials to enact policy consistent with the platform. Many people scoff at party platforms. No expectation exists in American political culture that parties should be bound by their platform promises. Indeed, cynicism about the platform has itself become a staple of the culture. Nevertheless, the platforms have tremendous symbolic importance for those who are intensely interested in the issues the platforms address. With the advent of various single-issue groups, some issues, such as abortion, generate tremendous interest.

The Republican and Democratic platform planks concerning abortion in 1992 showed the clear differences between the parties on this issue. The Republican plank, which was adamantly pro-life, represented a victory for the conservative wing of the party. The president's wife, Barbara Bush, distanced herself from the plank, and the president never committed himself to pushing a "human life" amendment to the Constitution.

ONLINE 10.8 *2012 Convention Highlights*

Republicans: **http://www.youtube.com/watch?v=zctzWxXS7g8**

Democrats: **http://www.youtube.com/watch?v=HAQShkB3JeY**

10-7 Decline and Revitalization of the Parties

As partisanship in the electorate eroded over the past few decades, most scholars lamented the slow death of political parties in America. Because political parties are seen as stabilizing forces within the political system that can make politicians more accountable to the voters and produce more coherent policies, the **dealignment** of our party system was seen as detrimental to democracy. Throughout the 1960s and 1970s, parties declined in importance as a voting cue for most citizens and as a defining theme of most campaigns. Increasingly, candidates rather than parties were the focus of campaigns. These **candidate-centered campaigns** were seen as lacking in accountability but overflowing with special-interest money, slick advertising campaigns, and too much mudslinging. The increasingly important role of television, political consultants, and large amounts of money made parties less influential. In addition, the Watergate scandal, which involved Republican President Nixon's administration, devastated the Republican party and caused declining levels of trust in government and both political parties.

To make matters worse, the campaign finance reforms of the early 1970s further eroded the parties' influence on campaigns, and the restrictions on party spending made many observers wonder why the parties themselves were not more visible actors in the 1976 presidential election between Republican Gerald Ford and Democrat Jimmy Carter.[20] This combination of factors seriously undermined the influence of parties, and many observers questioned whether parties could be revived.

The Watergate scandal and the resulting loss of the presidency in the 1976 election forced the Republicans to revamp the party by improving the resources and facilities needed to influence future campaigns. The Republicans became much more proficient at raising money, distributing money to candidates, and spending money on media resources and technology. The new forms of campaigning that developed during the 1980s required expensive equipment and expertise. The Republicans were the first to invest heavily in media support facilities, direct mail advertising, computer targeting of voters, and polling. The Republican national party had a technological advantage over the Democrats in terms of the assistance it could provide candidates. The Democrats had only begun to narrow this gap during the late 1980s and early 1990s.

In response to the limited role of parties in the 1976 presidential election, Congress changed the federal campaign finance rules so that parties could raise and spend more money independently of the candidates. Because candidates were spending the money they raised on developing their own name recognition rather than communicating party interests, the parties had to fend for themselves. The campaign finance change that had the most effect was the creation of a legal loophole that allowed **soft money**. This change in the campaign finance laws permitted parties to raise and spend money for general political activities—such as bumper stickers, mass mailings supportive of the party but not a particular candidate, and phone banks urging potential party supporters to get out and vote—that are not covered by the limits on contributions to presidential or congressional candidates. As a result, individuals can give as much money as they want to the party, either state or national. Together, the two parties raised more than $168 million in soft money in the 2001–2002 election cycle.

As a result of both parties' efforts to modernize and the legal change allowing soft money, the national parties of the 1990s were more influential than they were in the 1970s. The resurgence of the parties was threatened, however, when President Bush signed the campaign finance reform bill in 2002. Under campaign finance reform, parties are restricted in their ability to raise soft money. The effect it will have on the role of the parties remains to be seen, but the 2004 presidential campaigns suggest that the reforms weakened somewhat the ability of the parties to control campaign messages. In 2004, independent groups like MoveOn.org and the Swift Boat Veterans for Truth greatly eclipsed the role of the parties in supporting their preferred candidates.

10-8 Conclusion: Parties and Contemporary Political Culture

Many, if not most, Americans view political parties with suspicion, even scorn. This negative reaction is deeply rooted in American political culture. Most of the Founders were not fond of political parties even though many of them joined parties after they appeared on the scene around the turn of the nineteenth century. Most of George Washington's contemporaries agreed with him when he decried parties for provoking the "mischiefs of faction." Washington's view is still widely shared now because many people are turned off by partisan bickering and maneuvering. Americans seem to regard parties as, at best, a necessary evil.

With the advent of the media age, voters depend less on parties to structure their participation and guide their political choices. With the development of open primaries, party regulars have a rough time controlling the nomination process. At the November elections, Americans have little difficulty splitting their tickets and voting for candidates of different parties for different offices. All these factors conspire to weaken the parties and, some would say, debilitate government.

American parties have been slow to respond to changing conditions. Their structure has remained essentially the same since the 1950s, when parties were the main vehicles many Americans had for participating in politics. On the other hand, interest groups (see Chapter 11, "Interest Groups") have been more creative in gaining members and in communicating with them. Unfortunately, this situation has led to an increase in **single-issue politics** and worked against forces that promote consensus in society.

Despite the loose and often contentious nature of the party coalitions, the American two-party system has been remarkably stable. The American party system does not always offer voters a clear policy choice, nor does it ensure that a coherent set of government policies will be pursued after the elections are over. Although the two-party system does not bring discipline to the governing process, it does act as a force for stability. As long as the two-party system exists, parties will be forced to bring together many groups if they hope to win elections. As American political culture strains under forces that isolate and separate groups of citizens, the much maligned two-party structure provides one of the few forces capable of drawing together groups of citizens.

Questions for Thought and Discussion

1. Why did the Framers not mention political parties in the Constitution?
2. Why have third parties not been more successful in the United States?
3. Are political parties necessary in a democracy? Are they desirable? Are they inevitable?
4. Why have so many states chosen to select delegates to the national party conventions through primaries rather than through party caucuses or state conventions? Is this trend good for American democracy?
5. What changes in the laws governing campaigns and elections would strengthen political parties?

ENDNOTES

1 John Crittenden, *Parties and Elections in the United States* (London: Prentice-Hall, 1982), p. 3.

2 E. E. Schattschneider, *Party Government* (New York: Holt, Rinehart & Winston, 1942), p. 1.

3 John H. Aldrich, *Why Parties? The Origin and Transformation of Party Politics in America* (Chicago: University of Chicago Press, 1995), p. 3.

4 Jules Witcover, *Party of the People: A History of the Democrats* (New York: Random House, 2003), p. 3.

5 Joel H. Silbey, "From 'Essential to the Existence of Our Institutions' to 'Rapacious Enemies of Honest and Responsible Government': The Rise and Fall of American Political Parties, 1790–2000." In *The Parties Respond: Changes in American Parties and Campaigns*, 4th ed., ed. Louis Sandy Maisel (Boulder, CO: Westview Press, 2002), p. 4.

6 Quoted in Richard Hofstadter, *The Idea of a Party System: The Rise of Legitimate Opposition in the United States, 1789–1840* (Berkeley, CA: University of California Press, 1969), p. 2.

7 James Madison, "Federalist #10," November 22, 1787, http://www.constitution.org/fed/federa10.htm

8 James L. Sundquist, *Dynamics of the Party System* (Washington, D.C.: Brookings Institution, 1973), p. 39.

9 Ibid., p. 44.

10 Kevin Phillips, *The Emerging Republican Majority* (New Rochelle, NY: Arlington House, 1969).

11 The Next Right, http://www.thenextright.com/

12 See *Anderson v. Celebrezze*, 460 U.S. 780 (1983).

13 For elaboration on this theme, see Micah L. Sifry, *Spoiling for a Fight: Third-Party Politics in America* (New York: Routledge, 2003).

14 See the Green party website, located at http://www.greens.org/na.html

15 Larry Diamond and Richard Gunther, *Political Parties and Democracy* (Baltimore, MD: Johns Hopkins University Press, 2001), p. ix.

16 Sidney M. Milkis, *Political Parties and Constitutional Government: Remaking American Democracy* (Baltimore, MD: Johns Hopkins University Press, 1999), p. 5.

17 William J. Crotty, *Political Reform and the American Experiment* (New York: Thomas Y. Crowell, 1977), pp. 241–47.

18 The national survey results are from the 1992 National Election Study conducted by the Center for Political Studies at the University of Michigan. Ideological profiles of the 1992 convention delegates are reported in Harold W. Stanley and Richard G. Niemi, *Vital Statistics on American Politics*, 4th ed. (Washington, D.C.: CQ Press, 1994), p. 149.

19 Marjorie Connelly, "Delegates Out of Step with Public on Issue of Fund Raising," *The New York Times*, August 17, 2000.

20 See Beth Donovan's article "Much-Maligned 'Soft Money' Is Precious to Both Parties," *Congressional Quarterly Weekly*, May 15, 1993, pp. 1195–98, for a discussion of reporters who made such comments about the political parties in the 1976 election. These comments, allegedly made by David Broder in the *Washington Post*, are considered one of the motivating factors influencing the 1979 legislation allowing soft money.

Chapter 11

INTEREST GROUPS

OUTLINE

Key Terms 404
Expected Learning Outcomes 404
11-1 What Are Interest Groups? 404
- **11-1a** Interest Groups and Political Parties 405
- **11-1b** Interest Groups and American Society 406

11-2 Interest Groups and American Democracy 406
- **11-2a** Interest Groups and the Constitution 407
- **11-2b** Pluralism 408
- **11-2c** Hyperpluralism? 409
- **11-2d** The Public Interest 409

11-3 Organized Interests in the United States 410
- **11-3a** Economic Groups 411
- **11-3b** Noneconomic Groups 419

11-4 Why Do People Join Interest Groups? 421
11-5 What Do Interest Groups Do? 423
- **11-5a** Influencing Elections 424
- **11-5b** Fundraising 429
- **11-5c** Lobbying 430
- **11-5d** Grassroots Lobbying 431
- **11-5e** Influencing Public Opinion 432
- **11-5f** Targeting Political Opposition 433
- **11-5g** Building Coalitions 434
- **11-5h** Litigation 434

11-6 Subgovernments: Iron Triangles and Issue Networks 436
- **11-6a** Iron Triangles 436
- **11-6b** Issue Networks 438

11-7 Conclusion: Interest Groups and Political Culture 438
Questions for Thought and Discussion 440
Endnotes 441

KEY TERMS

direct mail
free riders
grassroots lobbying
gridlock
hyperpluralism
interest
interest groups
interest-group liberalism
iron triangle
issue network
lobbying
pluralism
political action committee
political entrepreneurs
professional associations
public interest group
right-to-work laws
selective benefits
selective incentives
single-issue groups
tariff
trade associations
union density

EXPECTED LEARNING OUTCOMES

After reading this chapter and completing the supplemental online materials, students will:

- Compare the political roles of interest groups with political parties
- Trace the development of interest groups in American politics
- Describe the representational role of interest groups
- Compare types of membership incentives used by interests

11-1 WHAT ARE INTEREST GROUPS?

People are often judged not just by their own selves but the company they keep. People and groups to whom we are loyal can bring us embarassment along with their support. The American political environment is no different. The groups with which political figures affiliate bring them supporters, but also notoriety. One of Barack Obama's core support groups in 2008 was the Association of Community Organizations for Reform Now (ACORN) a liberal group that worked with community organizers like Obama in his early days out of college. ACORN brought thousands of supporters to Obama's campaign, but when a conservative videographer set up an undercover sting operation that appeared to show ACORN endorsing prostitution and human trafficking, the president was forced to back away from a group that he had been involved with from the very beginning of his political life.

Interest groups are private organizations formed to advance the shared interest of their members. In political science, an **interest** is simply something that someone wants to achieve—a goal or desire. Often, the shared interest that brings people together is economic—a desire to get a larger slice of the pie. But the interest of the group may be purely ideological—a wish to see public policy in a given area move in a liberal or conservative direction. To qualify as an interest group, an organization must have a political objective and be able to articulate that objective publicly.

Interest groups can be permanent or ephemeral. They can exist for many decades, like the American Bar Association, or for mere months, like the Swift Boat Veterans for Truth. The latter group emerged in the late summer of 2004 to play a major role in changing the tenor of the presidential election campaign. Interest groups attempt to advance their members' interests by influencing the policy-making process. As we shall see, they do this by lobbying decision makers, attempting to influence public opinion, and even engaging in litigation. Politics, from the perspective of interest groups, is basically a struggle to determine "who gets what, when and how."[1]

Although they have existed in one form or another since the founding of the Republic, interest groups have proliferated in recent decades. One explanation for this is the increasing diversity of American society and the increasing complexity and specialization of the American economy. The American people can be divided into so many different groups based on age, sex, race, ethnicity, language, religion, ideology, economic status, occupation, lifestyle—the list goes on and on. Each of these cleavages gives rise to different political interests and hence to organizations created to further those interests.

© Ryan Rodrick Beiler, 2013. Used under license from Shutterstock, Inc.

11-1a Interest Groups and Political Parties

At the outset it is important to distinguish interest groups from political parties. As we saw in Chapter 9, political parties exist to recruit political leaders, mobilize voters in elections, and guide governance. Parties in the United States are large, undisciplined, ill-defined organizations that stand for broad, even vague, notions of what public policy ought to be. In their respective platforms, the two major parties address a wide range of policy issues, from abortion to health care to tax policy. Moreover, the parties bring together vast numbers of people who more or less support what the party represents.

By nominating candidates for public office and developing platforms that cover the spectrum of public policy questions, parties present themselves to the electorate as virtual "governments in waiting." When a party does come to power, it must deal with all the issues of public policy, not merely those it finds convenient or feels strongest about. Moreover, the party in power expects that the voters will hold it responsible for the policies it enacts. Interest groups, on the other hand, are much more sharply focused in their objectives. Interest groups exist to get government to do what they want it to do. They are typically concerned with a fairly narrow range of issues. To a person interested only in the environment or in the issue of abortion or in preserving Social Security benefits for the elderly, for example, the appropriate interest group may hold considerably more appeal than becoming active in one of the major parties. Although political parties are responsible to all citizens, interest groups are responsible only to their members.

In recent years, the functional differences between parties and interest groups have become somewhat muddied. Increasingly, interest groups pursue their policy objectives indirectly by supporting candidates who share their objectives or philosophy. An excellent example of this is MoveOn.org, a liberal organization that focuses its efforts on securing electoral victories for Democratic candidates. In 2004, MoveOn.org played a major role in the political process by running television ads highly critical of President George W. Bush and his policies. Of course, other interest groups, such as the Swift Boat Veterans for Truth, engaged in the same strategy, but for the other side. Indeed, the role of these independent groups in the campaign and their alleged connections to the political parties and presidential candidates became an issue of public concern during 2004.

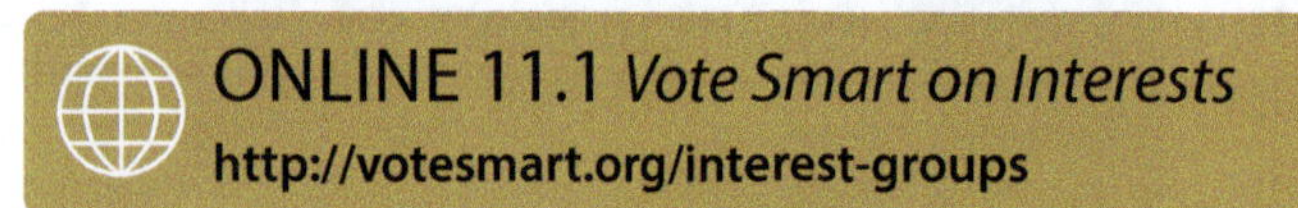

ONLINE 11.1 *Vote Smart on Interests*
http://votesmart.org/interest-groups

11-1b Interest Groups and American Society

Interest groups now occupy center stage in American politics; indeed, some would argue that they have replaced political parties as the primary institutions that mediate between the American people and their government. But interest groups are nothing new; they have a long history and are deeply rooted in American political culture. Writing in the 1830s, Alexis de Tocqueville noted that "Americans of all ages, all conditions, and all dispositions constantly form associations."[2] From the early days of the Republic, America was a nation of "joiners."

The tendency of Americans to join associations has lessened in the post-modern age. The average American today is less likely to join a civic group or a bowling league than was the case thirty or forty years ago. Today, most Americans live lives that are more private, more isolated, and more anonymous. Americans, on the whole, are less "public regarding" than they used to be, and few citizens have any real sense of community.[3] At the same time, the number of interest groups has proliferated, as Americans have learned how participation in such groups can be an effective means to advance their interests politically.

11-2 Interest Groups and American Democracy

The Founders referred to interest groups (as well as political parties) as "factions." According to James Madison, writing in *The Federalist* No. 10, a faction is "a number of citizens . . . who are united and actuated by some common impulse of passion, or of interest, adverse to the rights of other citizens or to the permanent and aggregate interests of the community." Madison observed that "the latent causes of faction . . . are sown in the nature of man." Yet Madison also noted that "the most common and durable source of faction has been the various and unequal distribution of property." Madison also believed that factions would thrive under a republican form of government, writing that "liberty is to faction what air is to fire, an aliment without which it instantly expires." Nevertheless, in Madison's view, it would be foolish to try to prevent factions by restricting freedom. Madison wrote that "it could not be a less folly to abolish liberty, which is essential to political life, because it nourishes faction than it would be to wish the annihilation of air, which is essential to animal life, because it imparts to fire its destructive agency." Rather, in Madison's view, a constitution should be designed to prevent one faction from gaining control of the government. The fundamental design principles of the Constitution—federalism and separation of powers—were adopted to disperse power and ensure that no single faction could achieve dominance. Interest groups, just like political parties, were seen as dangerous but not so dangerous that the liberty which allows them to exist should be taken away.

11-2a Interest Groups and the Constitution

The United States Constitution implicitly guarantees the right to form interest groups. The courts have long recognized that the First Amendment protects the right to join political associations for the purpose of petitioning government for a redress of grievances. In 1957, Chief Justice Earl Warren noted:

> *Our form of government is built on the premise that every citizen shall have the right to engage in political expression and association. This right was enshrined in the First Amendment of the Bill of Rights. Exercise of these basic freedoms in America has traditionally been through the media of political associations. Any interference with the freedom of a party is simultaneously an interference with the freedom of its adherents. All political ideas cannot and should not be channeled into the programs of our two major parties. History has amply proved the virtue of political activity by minority, dissident groups.*[4]

A year later, a unanimous Supreme Court recognized:

> *Effective advocacy of both public and private points of view, particularly controversial ones, is undeniably enhanced by group association, as this Court has more than once recognized by remarking on the close nexus between the freedoms of speech and assembly. . . . It is beyond debate that freedom to engage in an association for the advancement of beliefs and ideas is an inseparable aspect of . . . liberty.*[5]

Similarly, Justice William Brennan, speaking for the Supreme Court in 1984, observed that "implicit in the right to engage in activities protected by the First Amendment [is] a corresponding right to associate with others in pursuit of a wide variety of political, social, economic, educational, religious, and cultural ends."[6] Of course, the reason that the courts have been called upon to make such pronouncements is that from time to time government agencies and officials have sought to suppress or interfere with unpopular advocacy groups.

11-2b Pluralism

Early in the twentieth century, political scientists began to develop a theory of American politics that came to be known as **pluralism**.[7] Pluralism stands in sharp contrast to classical republicanism and traditional democratic theory. Classical republicanism stressed the need for virtuous elites that would pursue the public interest. Traditional democratic theory stressed the need for elected officials to respond to the will of the majority. In contrast to these earlier theories, pluralism conceived of politics as the struggle among competing interest groups.

Pluralism presupposes that "all the active and legitimate groups in the population can make themselves heard at some crucial stage in the process of decision."[8] Public policy is thus nothing more than the government's response to group demands. Whereas the Founders saw factions as potentially mischievous and in need of regulation, the pluralists conceived of interest groups as necessary, desirable, and even virtuous. Their principal virtue was that they provided a vehicle for political participation beyond the formal and often insignificant exercise of voting. Pluralists viewed the perpetual interest-group struggle as having a stabilizing effect on the political system. Because people belong to multiple groups with overlapping interests, the intensity of conflict is reduced. The system tends toward a stable equilibrium that maximizes the greatest good for the greatest number. Moreover, the policy-making process is enhanced by the fact that policy makers have been exposed to multiple competing solutions to problems.

Many political scientists have questioned the assumptions and conclusions of pluralism.[9] Some have suggested that lurking behind the pluralist façade is a "power elite" that makes the important decisions.[10] Others have stressed the fact that not all groups in society are represented by organizations and that not all organizations are taken seriously by policy makers. As one scholar has observed, "the fact that some citizens by dint of their superior representation by organized interests seem to have a louder voice than others strikes many Americans as undemocratic."[11]

ONLINE 11.2 *Pluralism in America: Has Its Time Passed?*
http://www.youtube.com/watch?v=nGdo3hOGqYo

11-2c HYPERPLURALISM?

Some commentators believe that the American political system is suffering from **hyperpluralism**, a condition in which the prevalence of group demands makes it impossible for government to plan, deal with long-term problems, and make policies that further the public interest. Moreover, the constant barrage of interest-group demands undermines the rule of law. Perhaps the best-known exponent of this perspective is Theodore J. Lowi, whose book *The End of Liberalism* argues that pluralism, or **interest-group liberalism**, as Lowi calls it, has corrupted our politics and undermined our government. According to Lowi, "interest group liberalism has sought to solve the problems of public authority in a large modern state by . . . parceling out to private parties the power to make public policy."[12] Some critics of pluralism would go even further, arguing that the existence of numerous powerful interest groups causes the political system to bog down.[13] **Gridlock**, the inability of government to make or implement any decision, may be one of the consequences of hyperpluralism.

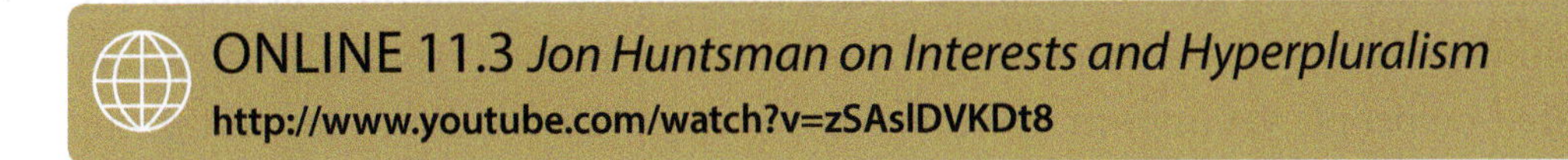
ONLINE 11.3 *Jon Huntsman on Interests and Hyperpluralism*
http://www.youtube.com/watch?v=zSAsIDVKDt8

11-2d THE PUBLIC INTEREST

Classical republican thinkers believed that the objective of government was the furtherance of the public interest. The *public interest* is one that is shared in common by all members of the society. The theory of pluralism rules out the idea of a public interest. It "portrays society as an aggregate of human communities, rather than as itself a human community; and it equally rules out a concern for the general good in practice by encouraging a politics of interest group pressures in which there is no mechanism for the discovery and expression of the common good."[14] In discussing the problem of the public interest, two questions must be posed. First, does such a thing as the public interest really exist, or is it merely an idealistic notion without any basis in reality? Second, assuming that the public interest does exist, what political mechanisms will allow it to be discovered and pursued?

Protection of the natural environment is often cited as a good example of a public interest. Obviously, everyone has an interest in preserving the environment. But not everyone agrees on how seriously the environment is threatened or on how it can best be preserved or restored. Certainly, groups are sharply divided over who should pay the price to clean up the environment. Business? The consumer? The taxpayer? Education provides another example. Most Americans agree in the abstract that education is a good thing. But what kind of education? Should it be compulsory? Again, who should pay to improve the educational system—the taxpayers or those directly benefiting by receiving an education? Of course, any group advocating any particular course of action with respect to education is likely to claim that its proposal is consistent with the public interest. What may be more accurate is to say that the proposal is in keeping with the group's perception of the public interest.

Is it meaningful, then, to talk about the public interest *as distinct from* the interest of one or more groups? If the public interest is defined as that good in which each member of society shares equally, whether he realizes it or not, we would be hard-pressed to give a concrete example of the public interest. On the other hand, most people in society share certain interests—interests that transcend the narrow claims of particular groups seeking immediate gratification of their desires. Most people recognize the need to protect the environment, educate their children, and train workers to be more competitive in the global economy. Increasingly, people are aware of the long-term consequences of running a government that is ridden with debt. These interests may or may not be public interests in the truest sense of the term, but they are surely closer to the ideal of the public interest than, for example, an effort by a particular industry to gain a lucrative exemption from a regulation that applies to other similar industries. Unfortunately, these broader interests, especially when they are shared by people yet unborn, are often drowned out in the din of interest-group politics. Politicians looking to maintain power are most likely to listen to those who do the most to affect the outcome of the next election, whether by giving (or withholding) campaign funds or by mobilizing (or failing to mobilize) voters directly. It is difficult to get politicians to pay attention to issues that everyone regards as important but no one is organizing to articulate.

11-3 Organized Interests in the United States

Although obtaining an exact count is difficult, at least ten thousand interest groups exist in the United States. These groups may be divided into two basic categories: economic and noneconomic. This distinction reaches to the heart of interest articulation in a democracy. Economic groups exist mainly to use the political process to secure financial gains for their members. Other than supporting the basic economic philosophy of capitalism within the context of a market, economic groups do not have ideological preferences. Their members do not share core political values that drive their action. Rather, they share economic interests, which may indeed transcend ideological feelings. In contrast, noneconomic groups exist to articulate their values, not to advance material interests. Both economic and noneconomic groups are formed to advance the common interests of their members by influencing government policy. For the most part, leaders of interest groups do not seek government office.

11-3a Economic Groups

Economic interest groups include business organizations, trade associations, professional groups, and labor unions. These groups vary considerably in terms of their specific objectives, general ideological orientation, and political affiliation. Their number and importance reflect the major role that government at all levels plays in the regulation of economic activity. The role the federal government should play in regulating business has been debated since the founding of the Republic. Indeed, the "regulation of interstate commerce" clause of Article I, Section 8 of the Constitution made an active federal role a possibility that the Supreme Court's decision in *Gibbons v. Ogden* (1824) cemented as a reality.[15] In *Gibbons*, one of the key decisions of the nineteenth century, the Supreme Court took a broad view of Congress' power to regulate interstate commerce.

The first major economic issue facing the federal government, and one that is still important, was the **tariff**, a tax charged on products imported into a country. American industrial interests have often favored various tariffs because of the protection they provide. A tariff makes foreign goods more expensive relative to domestic products that are not subject to the tariff. Consumers or those needing to import goods for their businesses do not benefit from tariffs. In the late 1980s, many American interest groups, including those representing the troubled automobile and steel industries, fought for protective legislation. With few exceptions, these groups did not get what they wanted. The Bush administration and its successor, the Clinton administration, proved to be fairly committed to the concept of free trade.

Business Interests

Most businesses are set up as corporations. Legally, the corporation has an existence beyond the individuals that comprise it. Large corporations, such as General Motors, AT&T, and IBM, have many strategies for attempting to influence public policy that may have an effect on their interests. Hiring a lobbying firm or creating a political action office within the company is the most expensive strategy, but it also allows the firm to make individual decisions on the political issues most crucial to its interests. Many large corporations hire their own lobbyists to represent their interests. Estimates indicate that business groups account for more than half of all interest groups with offices in Washington, D.C.

In 2002, Enron Corporation declared bankruptcy and came under tremendous scrutiny for unsound business practices and possible securities fraud. Democrats in Congress questioned the role that Enron executives had played in helping the Bush administration craft its energy policy during 2001. Vice President Dick Cheney came under pressure to release details of any role that Enron officials might have played. The Bush administration decided not to release these details, making the argument that this type of release would harm future administrations' ability to get advice to inform policy making. The role of business interests will always be controversial in a democracy.

A second strategy is to join interest groups that advance either general business interests or narrower issues related to a particular industry. In the general category are such interest groups as the Chamber of Commerce and the National Association of Manufacturers. Examples of narrower groups are trade associations, such as the American Bankers Association or the National Beer Wholesalers Association. A firm incurs some costs of membership in these types of organizations, but the overall cost is less than individual political action by the corporation. Another option that may be available is membership in professional associations, which are usually composed of individuals (although sometimes institutions also join) who have a common occupational interest. The National Realtors Association, the American Medical Association, and the American Bar Association (lawyers) are examples of professional associations. Because the membership is usually in the name of the individual worker, the firm may have only indirect input into the political goals of the organization, although it still receives at least some representation of its interests.

By combining memberships in the various types of economic groups, a corporation can greatly expand its ability to have its voice heard in Washington. For example, a large pharmaceutical company may be a member of the Chamber of Commerce and the National Association of Manufacturers for general business reasons, the National Association of Pharmaceutical Manufacturers for industry-specific representation, and the American Medical Association through the doctors it employs. Each organization may represent different interests of the company, use different means of influencing policy, and monitor different types of legislation or regulatory policy. The multiple layers of membership provide greater access to the system.

General Business Organizations

Among the oldest business groups in the United States is the Chamber of Commerce. Founded in 1912, the Chamber of Commerce is a national organization that embraces thousands of local Chambers of Commerce across America. The Chamber, which has become synonymous with the national business community, is dedicated to protecting the free enterprise system from government interference. In the 1980s and early 1990s, it worked hard to defeat efforts to have the national government mandate that businesses provide their employees with various benefits, such as family medical leave. Almost every community in the country has its own local Chamber of Commerce. Consequently, the national Chamber can mobilize a very large network of supporters who can influence local elected officials. Rather than have a stranger from a D.C. lobbying firm drop by the office of a member of Congress, a business leader from the member's hometown can personally deliver the Chamber's message. This personal touch makes it easier to gain access to influential political leaders.

The Chamber, as well as other business interests, has usually supported Republican presidential candidates over Democrats, and consequently, Republicans, such as Presidents Reagan and both Bushes, have been more sympathetic to the interests of the business community. When Bill Clinton was elected president in 1992, the Chamber of Commerce and other probusiness interest groups expressed concern about the direction that public policy would take under the new administration. These concerns were heightened on February 4, 1993, when Congress, at the urging of the Clinton administration, enacted a law requiring companies to give their workers as many as twelve weeks of unpaid leave per year to deal with births, adoptions, and serious illnesses within a worker's immediate family.

The Chamber of Commerce purports to represent the entire business community. It therefore takes stands on broad, business-related issues. These issues often involve an employer's relationship with its workers. The Chamber usually opposes (or at least seeks to weaken) legislation that increases the cost of hiring workers, such as increases in the minimum wage or mandatory health insurance. These issues typically pit the interests of business directly against those of labor. Taxes are another major Chamber concern. It almost always opposes increases in corporate taxes and other taxes that affect business operations across a wide variety of industries, such as the energy tax proposed by President Clinton in 1993. Although President Clinton was generally perceived as hospitable to the interests of business, probusiness interest groups opposed many of the regulatory initiatives that emerged from the Clinton administration, especially from the Food and Drug Administration, the U.S. Forest Service, and the Occupational Safety and Health Administration. By and large, probusiness groups were pleased when Republicans took over the presidency in 2001 and were successful in securing various favorable policy changes.

Trade Associations

Of course, most business interests are not so universal. In fact, most business and corporate interests are relatively narrow. For example, the steel industry faced stiff competition in the 1970s and 1980s from foreign producers that had much lower labor costs and other overhead. Therefore, it was in the steel industry's interest to pursue tariffs on imported steel. Other American businesses took a different position on this issue. Higher prices on steel might help the steel industry, but the American auto industry, which uses large amounts of steel, wanted lower steel prices so that it could produce inexpensive cars to compete with foreign automakers. Consequently, general business organizations, such as the Chamber of Commerce and the National Association of Manufacturers, could not take a stance on this issue without alienating one set of members or the other. On the other hand, an organization with a narrower focus and a smaller membership that shares the same interest could pursue protective tariffs for the steel industry. **Trade associations** fill this important need for industries. American industries and businesses make most of their efforts to affect government through trade associations of companies producing the same type of goods or services.

Professional Associations

Professional associations are organizations of individuals employed, or self-employed, in a variety of skilled enterprises, such as medicine, law, accounting, and engineering. Professions generally limit their membership by granting licenses to practice. By state law, certain professional organizations are allowed to control their membership so that the public is protected against unqualified, incompetent individuals. Typically, the main task confronting any professional association is securing state action that confers professional status on its members. Often, major battles in state legislatures ensue between competing professional groups. For example, ophthalmologists, who have medical degrees, and optometrists, who are trained in colleges of optometry, are continually at odds over the degree to which the latter should be allowed to perform medical procedures or prescribe drugs to their patients. Each group makes major contributions to candidates for state legislatures.

Although professional associations operate mostly at the state level on questions of licensing, they have an abiding interest in federal legislation that might affect the economic well-being of their members or the advancement of their professional agendas. Consider the Association of Trial Lawyers of America. In the first six months of 1992, this organization received more than $2.5 million in contributions.[16] One might wonder what interests trial lawyers have that would lead them to commit these types of resources to politics. But 1992 was an election year, with the presidency, one-third of the Senate, and all of the House up for election. The subject of legal reform was on the electoral agenda, with tremendous potential consequences for trial lawyers. For instance, imposing limits on the amounts that juries in civil cases can award for damages could have a substantial effect on the fees attorneys receive.

The best-known professional organizations are probably the American Bar Association (ABA), which represents lawyers, and the American Medical Association (AMA). During the 1950s and 1960s, the AMA raised tremendous amounts of money, which it used to successfully fight the passage of national health insurance legislation and to delay and change the provisions of medical insurance for the elderly (Medicare). Since the introduction of Medicare in 1965, the AMA and other associations of medical specialties have devoted great resources to its implementation by seeking to expand the definition of covered illnesses (such as adding mental illnesses or addiction treatments), working to increase compensation for services, and removing restrictions on the individual doctor's decisions about medical care for patients.

The health insurance and medical cost reduction plan proposed by President Clinton in 1993 was another policy struggle with a potential impact of billions of dollars on the medical industry. The AMA, medical specialty organizations, hospital associations, insurance companies, and pharmaceutical manufacturers were actively involved in the policy debate, from the inception of the public hearings conducted by Hillary Rodham Clinton through the legislative debates in Congress.

In recent decades, public education has been an increasingly contentious national issue. By the 2000 presidential election, the appropriate role of public education and the desirability of limited publicly funded vouchers were at the forefront of the campaign and a major point of contrast between George W. Bush and Al Gore. The issue was clear: Democrat Al Gore opposed any use of public money for vouchers for private education, and Republican George W. Bush advocated providing vouchers to pupils in failing public schools for use in the school of their choice, including private schools. The Gore position closely paralleled that of the National Education Association (NEA), the oldest, largest, and most influential of any organization dedicated to advocating for public education. This organization, which has more than 2.5 million members, has become one of the most critical organizations supporting the Democratic party. In fact, it sent 350 delegates and alternates to the 2000 national convention in Los Angeles.

The prominent role of the NEA in Democratic party politics has led many Republicans to refer to it and its state subsidiaries as teachers' unions. Not surprisingly, the NEA tends to see itself as a professional organization that advocates not only for the benefit of its members but also for broader public interest. The differences between the characterizations of the organization are important in affecting public opinion and, possibly, public support for NEA positions. Clearly, NEA opponents would like to dismiss its support of any position as merely self-serving and to undercut any perception of a position as stemming from professionals stating their best view of the public interest. Likewise, the NEA would rather be perceived as a professional association than as merely another labor union.

Organized Labor

This country experienced an epic battle in the late nineteenth and early twentieth centuries over the right of workers to form labor unions. The labor movement eventually won the battle, and in 1935 Congress adopted legislation that guaranteed the rights of workers to unionize and collectively bargain with management over wages and other terms of employment. The American Federation of Labor (AFL) was created in 1881 as a means of unifying diverse trade unions. The Congress of Industrial Organizations (CIO) was created in the late 1930s to provide representation for less-skilled industrial labor. In 1955, the AFL merged with the CIO to form an umbrella organization that, at its peak, represented more than 80 percent of union employees in this country.

After the right to unionize had been won, unions still had a national agenda to advance. Foremost among their goals was the elimination of **right-to-work laws**, which prevent labor agreements from requiring all workers to join the union. Because labor leaders know that some workers will choose not to get involved in the union, but will nevertheless profit from the higher wages and improved safety or other benefits won by the union, they prefer a system that requires all nonmanagement workers in a unionized company to join the union as a condition of employment. Therefore, unions have continuously fought to remove or prevent the passage of right-to-work laws. Most of this battle has taken place in the states. The main rival to the AFL–CIO has been the Teamsters, who have broken with most of organized labor by occasionally supporting Republican candidates. In 1992, the Teamsters raised more campaign money than any other lobbying organization. They generally represent truck drivers and those involved in the transportation sector, although they also have organized other workers. The Teamsters, along with the United Mine Workers, have had to overcome a history of violence and corruption that has tarnished their image.

Since their inception, labor unions have been politically active. Generally, the unions have supported Democratic candidates, and Democrats have, by the same token, supported the interests of organized labor. Indeed, organized labor was a key element of the New Deal coalition assembled by President Franklin D. Roosevelt in the 1930s and maintained by the Democratic party for decades thereafter. In the 1960s, however, the close relationship between organized labor and the Democratic party began to break down, largely over the Democrats' liberal positions on social issues. Unions even compete with each other for political clout. During the 2008 Democratic primaries, two competing unions backed the two leading candidates and engaged in a mobilization and fundraising contest as much about promoting their own stature as their affiliated candidate. The government union American Federation of State, County, and Municipal Employees (AFSCME) backed Hillary Clinton, while the Service Employees International Union (SEIU) supported Barack Obama.[17] The rank-and-file members of labor unions tend to be liberal—in fact, extremely so—on economic issues, and they tend to be somewhat conservative on social issues. In fact, the term *populist* may be a better description of the ideological orientation of organized labor.

The interests of workers, like those of business, are often specific to particular industries or trades. These unions attempt to influence legislation that might affect their industries or their relationship with their employers. For instance, the United Auto Workers (UAW) have long raised a large amount of money, much of which was used to try to influence Congress on issues related to the regulation of the automobile industry. Often, the UAW and American industry have the same interests. For example, both favor legislation limiting the number of cars that Japan can ship to the United States. In seeking legislation that is in their own economic interest, however, the UAW may be hurting the economic interests of other union members who must pay higher prices for cars. The UAW's influence was significantly expanded in 2009 when General Motors and Chrysler were close to complete failure. The federal government initiated a multi-billion-dollar bailout of both companies. Chrysler's assets were sold to numerous investors, mostly Italian carmaker Fiat. However, 30 percent of Chrysler's assets and almost half of General Motors' were turned over to the United Auto Workers in the deal. Economic observers pointed out that union salary and benefit demands had contributed to the high costs of American cars, the manufacturer's inability to respond to market demands, and inability to manage money. Never before, though, has a union had a controlling interest in a business.[18]

Union density, the proportion of the nonagricultural workforce belonging to unions, peaked in the mid-1940s at about 36 percent. Since then, union density has declined to around 13 percent.[19] However, the political influence of organized labor has not diminished. The 1980s saw a low period for unions. The landslide reelection of Ronald Reagan as president in 1984 was a particular defeat. The AFL–CIO endorsed and worked hard to elect Reagan's Democratic opponent, Walter Mondale, who was widely perceived as an old-fashioned prolabor Democrat. Because Mondale was negatively perceived as having been captured by special interests, many observers regarded the AFL–CIO endorsement as a liability rather than an asset to his campaign. Worse yet from the labor leaders' perspective, polls showed that only 52 percent of union families voted for Mondale in 1984.[20]

In the 1990s, the Democratic party worked hard to recapture the support of organized labor, but this effort was complicated by President Clinton's support of NAFTA and other free trade policies opposed by labor unions. NAFTA is an acronym for the North American Free Trade Agreement, which became effective on January 1, 1994. Essentially, the agreement reduced trade barriers that had limited commerce among the United States, Canada, and Mexico. Unions opposed NAFTA (as they oppose such agreements generally) because they believe that maintaining tariffs and other barriers to imports is necessary to preserve jobs in America. President Clinton, who styled himself as a New Democrat, generally supported the idea of free trade, much to the chagrin of organized labor.

The negotiations that led to NAFTA were begun under President George H.W. Bush in the late 1980s, but were finalized by Bush's successor, Bill Clinton. Because NAFTA changed many American trade laws, it had to be approved by both the House of Representatives and the Senate. Labor unions fought hard to get Congress to reject NAFTA, which they argued would cause American jobs to be exported to Mexico. Union spokespersons let it be known that they would work to defeat any member of Congress who voted in favor of NAFTA.

At first, it appeared that the unions would succeed. They found an unlikely ally in H. Ross Perot, the Texas billionaire who had run for president in 1992 as an Independent candidate and had put together an impressive political organization named United We Stand. Throughout 1993, Perot spoke out against NAFTA at rallies around the country. As late as early November, public opinion was negative toward the agreement, although many people had not made up their minds. Perot's claim that NAFTA was dead in the House of Representatives appeared to be right. But a tremendous last-minute effort by the White House and other supporters of NAFTA resulted in a decisive shift in public opinion. Ultimately, NAFTA passed both the House and Senate by comfortable margins. Most Republicans in Congress supported NAFTA; indeed, their support was never really in doubt. The battle over NAFTA was really a struggle within the Democratic party, over which organized labor traditionally exercised strong influence. The fact that President Clinton, a Democrat, supported NAFTA and was able to get it through Congress showed the degree to which union influence over the Democratic party and the political process in general had declined.

Despite the decline of the labor membership, unions and their lobbyists remain quite active in politics, supporting measures to increase workers' benefits and improve workplace safety. Union efforts tend to be successful only when their positions are supported by a substantial segment of the nonunion workforce. That was the case with the Family and Medical Leave Act, adopted in 1993. Unions supported the measure, and so did most nonunion employees. Unions also continue to be significant sources of financial support for Democratic candidates. Between 1992 and 2008, 92 percent of all labor contributions went to Democratic candidates or party committees.

While union power has experienced a resurgence, union membership continues to decline. Less than a quarter of the workforces in manufacturing, construction, transportation, and information are union members. The largest unionized sector of the economy is government employees, with more than a third of all government workers a union member. As part of an effort to increase membership, unions encouraged President Obama to introduce **card check** legislation in 2009. Card check legislation changes existing law so that unions can organize in a new business more easily, but also take away existing secret ballot votes. Supporters of card check laws say that management can intimidate workers into not voting to empower a union, while opponents believed that card check laws would encourage intimidation by unions, coercing workers into joining.[21]

ONLINE 11.4 *The Future of Unions?*

http://www.nytimes.com/2012/07/18/business/economy/unions-past-may-hold-key-to-their-future.html?pagewanted=all&_r=0

11-3b NONECONOMIC GROUPS

Over the past thirty years, the most rapidly growing segment of interest groups has been the noneconomic sector. The 1960s and early 1970s witnessed an explosion in single-interest, ideological groups and public interest groups that were largely liberal in nature. Conservative ideological groups responded with tremendous growth in the late 1970s and early 1980s. Certainly, groups of both ideological types multiplied throughout both periods, but it is fair to say that the earlier period was characterized by the growth of liberal groups and the later period by the expansion of conservative groups. Nevertheless, a survey of the directory *Washington Representatives* shows that lobbyists working for economic interests still outnumber those working for noneconomic groups by nearly a four-to-one ratio. Noneconomic groups are interested in a range of topics, including the environment, school prayer, civil rights, abortion, and homelessness. Despite this range of issues, noneconomic interests can be loosely grouped into three categories: single-issue, broad ideological, and public interest groups.

SINGLE-ISSUE GROUPS

As their name suggests, **single-issue groups** are organizations focused on one particular policy area. Rather than push for a broad policy agenda, these types of groups may be concerned about only a few legislative proposals or regulations. Groups exist for almost every conceivable policy area. Although most are organized for action at the national level, many act only in certain states or local areas.

Two of the most prominent categories of single-issue groups in the 1980s were the abortion groups on both sides of the battle and the environmentalists. The National Abortion Rights Action League, on the side protecting legalized abortions, and the National Right to Life group, dedicated to the restriction and eventual criminalization of abortion, are two of the most influential groups in the abortion debate. Though the discussion may include religious issues, social welfare, and the state of the American education system, the fundamental issue for both groups is the legal availability of abortions in the United States.

The environmental movement has greatly expanded since the 1960s, and a bevy of groups have formed to cover a variety of specific issues within the overall concern for the environment.[22] Some national groups, such as the National Wildlife Federation and Greenpeace, are concerned about a wide range of environmental issues both inside and outside this country. Other national groups focus on only a certain portion of the environment: the Sierra Club is organized to promote the protection of scenic areas, and People for the Ethical Treatment of Animals demands political action to protect animals from use in product testing and confinement in zoos and circuses. In addition, numerous groups form around local or even temporary issues, such as the ad hoc group of entertainment stars who tried to save Walden Pond in Massachusetts from development in the early 1990s. These various groups form coalitions from time to time to seek political action, and they also maintain their own, separate identities and causes.

Ideological Groups

Ideological groups promote a broader array of interests than do the single-issue groups. Civil rights groups, religious organizations, and broad political ideological groups are in this category. Several different types of civil rights groups exist. Some groups, such as the National Association for the Advancement of Colored People (NAACP) and Jesse Jackson's Rainbow Coalition, fight for legislation promoting racial equality in all facets of American life. Others, such as the National Organization for Women, fight for gender equality. More recently, groups such as ACT UP and Queer Nation have been formed to promote gay rights. The civil rights groups seek action in a wide variety of ways from the legislative, judicial, and administrative bodies at the national, state, and local levels of government.

Religious groups seek government action that fits their beliefs about how society should be organized. Religious fundamentalists, represented by such organizations as the Christian Coalition, have pushed for a more conservative ideological agenda, including outlawing abortion, allowing prayer in public schools, and preventing gays and lesbians from gaining protection under civil rights laws. Although the fundamentalist groups received more attention throughout the 1980s and 1990s, the Catholic Church and the mainline Protestant churches have always been active in a wide variety of issues. The Catholic Church has pushed for outlawing abortion (in agreement with the fundamentalist Protestants), but has also opposed the death penalty and advocated more liberal social welfare policy (in agreement with the more liberal and moderate Protestants). The Catholics and more liberal Protestants have also pushed for the United States to take a more aggressive stance in promoting human rights in other countries.

Other ideological groups exist just to advance a particular policy agenda. Groups such as the Americans for Democratic Action and the National Committee for an

Effective Congress support a liberal agenda. The National Conservative Political Action Committee and the Fund for a Conservative Majority advocate conservative causes. Some members of these types of groups may have religious motivations, but the groups themselves are not specifically religious in nature.

Public Interest Groups

Ideally, a **public interest group** is "one that seeks a collective good, the achievement of which will not selectively or materially benefit the membership or activists of the organization."[23] Whereas the ideological and single-issue groups are mass membership organizations, a public interest group may not be as concerned about having members. Often, charitable foundations or a few wealthy benefactors subsidize its actions. A key feature of public interest groups is that they are nonprofit organizations, so contributors receive tax deductions for contributions. This nonprofit status prevents the groups from maintaining political action committees (PACs) to support their causes, however. (PACs are discussed in detail in section 11-5a, "Influencing Elections.")

Public interest groups are usually composed of a small number of professionals who perform research on the topic, provide expert testimony at congressional hearings, and work to influence public opinion on an issue that is of no direct benefit to them. An example of this type of group is the League of Women Voters. The league promotes efforts to increase voter turnout. Other groups, such as Common Cause, seek reform in government. Recently, Common Cause has been heavily involved in the movement to limit the influence of PACs, curtail the perks received by government officials, and eliminate the wasteful pet projects of legislators. Other groups are less concerned about specific political battles and focus more on societal issues, such as homelessness, child welfare, and drug abuse.

11-4 Why Do People Join Interest Groups?

The simple answer to why people join interest groups is that they have a common interest. Farmers join an agricultural group because they have a stake in keeping commodity prices high and the costs of producing crops low. As you have read, groups serve a wide variety of economic and noneconomic interests—so many, in fact, that a group seems to be available for every conceivable common interest. Shared interests alone do not seem to explain all types of interest groups, however. For example, more than ten thousand interest groups are in Washington, but almost none of them represent the interests of homemakers, students, the homeless, or sports fans. Furthermore, even some of the largest interest groups, such as the American Medical Association and the National Association of Realtors, cannot persuade all potential members to join. Considering the importance often attached to the influence of interest groups in our political system, why don't all Americans participate in interest groups?

The Free-Rider Problem

In his classic book *The Logic of Collective Action* (1965), Mancur Olson argued that groups that pursue benefits for society at large, as opposed to **selective benefits** for their members, are not likely to succeed. These types of groups have difficulty recruiting and retaining members because anyone can benefit from the group's activities without joining. If individuals were to act purely on the basis of self-interest, they would prefer to be **free riders**, or persons who enjoy the benefits of an organization's activity without having to pay the costs.

For example, most Americans might agree that clean air is an important public policy, but a relatively small proportion of Americans are members of interest groups, such as the Sierra Club and the National Wildlife Foundation, that push for environmental legislation. Any individual can evaluate the situation and realize that one person's $25 contribution to the organization will not affect the group's ability to influence politics. Furthermore, an individual knows that if the group is successful in affecting public policy, free riders cannot be prevented from taking advantage of the cleaner air that results from the group's activity. Thus, the individual has no incentive to join. If everyone reaches the same conclusion, however, the interest group will be either quite weak or nonexistent.

Despite the free-rider problem, people do join Common Cause, the Sierra Club, and other public interest groups. Indeed, the emergence and proliferation of these types of groups since the 1980s is one of the more interesting features of the political system. Why do people join these groups? Are they irrational? One answer is that interest groups may provide selective incentives to members. **Selective incentives** can be any private benefit that induces a potential member to join or a current member to stay in an organization. Clean-air legislation may not be enough of an incentive to get an individual to join the National Wildlife Federation, but selective incentives, such as a glossy calendar of wildlife scenes, a newsletter on wildlife preservation, bumper stickers displaying the member's support of a public good, or a T-shirt featuring an endangered species, may provide an individual with a tangible benefit that a nonmember could not receive. The benefit must be relatively inexpensive, or else it costs the interest group more than it receives from the individual.

Occasionally, however, selective incentives may be quite important to a potential member. For example, individuals in certain industries may not be able to obtain local government contracts unless they belong to a labor union. Similarly, an accountant who is not certified as a CPA will have a difficult time finding a job or obtaining clients. Therefore, economic groups may have selective incentives that are quite powerful in inducing potential members to join. This is one reason that narrow economic interests typically have an easier time forming interest groups than broad, public interests of a more ideological nature.

Not all selective incentives are economic in nature, however. Most political scientists understand that people do not act solely on the basis of immediate self-interest. Many people seem to have a need to be involved, to participate, to make a contribution, and to try to mold society to what they believe is right. Interest groups may provide intangible benefits associated with social interaction with other like-minded individuals or allow individuals to enhance their own sense of political efficacy by supporting a worthy cause. Although these individuals may be extremely important in providing much of the funding and political activity for ideological groups, such as the pro-life or pro-choice movements in the abortion battle, political participation is fairly low in the United States.

The low rate of political participation in noneconomic interest groups tends to confirm Olson's concerns about the free-rider problem. In turn, the free-rider problem reduces the effect that many public interest or noneconomic interest groups could have on the system. At the same time, the free-rider problem is reduced by two other factors that influence the formation of interest groups. First, some individuals may be willing to take on enormous personal costs that exceed the personal benefits they obtain from a desired change in public policy. Through their willingness to take political action, these individuals, sometimes called **political entrepreneurs**, allow others to receive political benefits at a lower cost. Ralph Nader is an example; he was willing to spend thousands of dollars from his own pocket in the 1970s to form a consumer-protection interest group.

A second way in which the free-rider problem may be overcome is through the use of sponsorship. Many public interest groups do not have a large membership base, but they can rely on a relatively small number of benefactors, such as charitable foundations, wealthy individuals, or even the government, to maintain a staff of professional activists who pursue some political aim. For example, Marian Wright Edelman heads the Children's Defense Fund, an organization devoted to lobbying on behalf of children on health and social issues. The sixty million children in the United States are not members of the interest group. Instead, most of the group's funds come from a small number of large donors. Organizations that rely on sponsorships rather than on individual memberships are not as influenced by the free-rider problem. Rather than provide selective incentives to induce individuals to join, they are concerned about receiving grants and other large donations.

11-5 What Do Interest Groups Do?

In a nutshell, interest groups try to influence public policy. They do that in a variety of ways—some direct, some indirect. The groups may contact policy makers directly to try to persuade them to take a certain action or cast a vote in a desired direction. Or, they may try to influence the public to bring pressure on government to achieve a desired goal. Much of the activity of interest groups now has to do with supporting and opposing candidates for public office. Most activities undertaken by interest groups can be grouped into these categories:

- Influencing elections
- Fundraising
- Lobbying
- Influencing public opinion
- Targeting opposition
- Building coalitions
- Engaging in litigation

11-5a INFLUENCING ELECTIONS

Increasingly, interest groups seek to influence campaigns and elections at all levels of government. They try to influence the positions that candidates take on issues and even the platforms that parties adopt at their conventions. Sometimes they even recruit political candidates. At the same time, candidates and campaign officials are paying more attention to interest groups. The reason is that interest groups can mobilize significant numbers of voters and can make substantial campaign contributions.[24]

POLITICAL ACTION COMMITTEES

Political action committees (PACs) are legal mechanisms through which interest groups funnel contributions to candidates for public office. For example, the MoveOn Political Action Committee, affiliated with the liberal group MoveOn.org, contributed more than $2 million to congressional campaigns in 2000, and more than $3.5 million in 2002. This money came from more than ten thousand individual contributors.[25] By concentrating and targeting money raised from individual contributors, PACs can have a significant effect on the political process.

During the 1940s, labor unions created organizations to funnel their contributions to candidates, often with such names as the United Automobile Workers' Committee for Political Education. Corporations could not form similar organizations until the enactment of the Federal Election and Campaign Act of 1971 (FECA). This legislation was supposed to be a reform. Its intent was to regulate the influence of business and labor interests, but the act had the unintended consequence of expanding the role of interest groups in the political process. Since the 1971 law went into effect, PACs have proliferated (see Figure 11-1).

In popular usage, the terms *PAC* and *interest group* are often used interchangeably; however, many interest groups do not have PACs. More than 10,000 interest groups are in Washington, D.C., and fewer than 4,200 PACs are registered with the

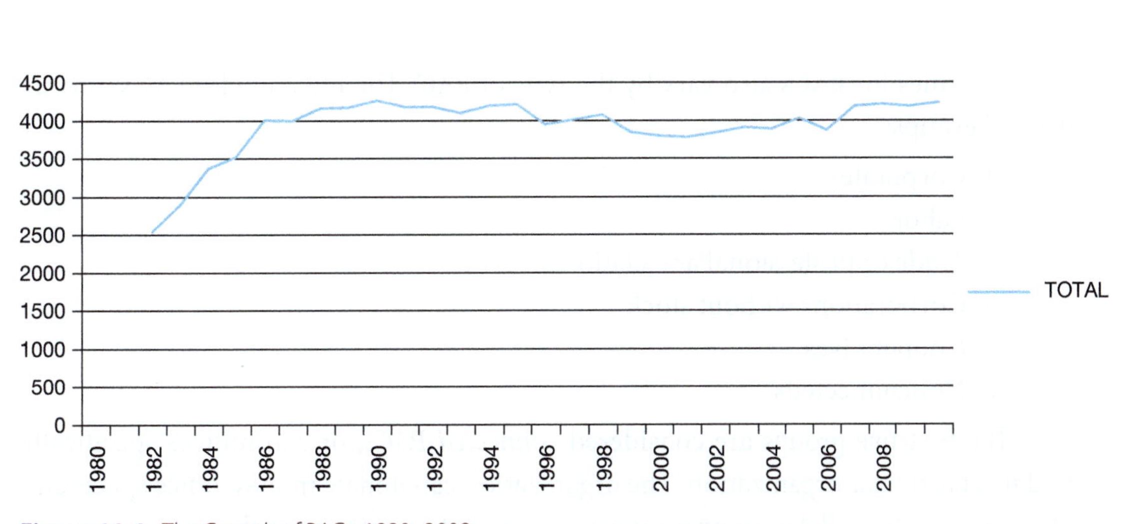

Figure 11-1 *The Growth of PACs, 1980–2008*
Source: Adapted from the Federal Election Commission.

Federal Election Commission (FEC). Most interest groups attempt to influence the political system without the benefit of a PAC. A PAC performs two activities: distribute funds to candidates for campaign purposes and spend money, separate from any candidate's campaign, to influence voters on an issue. The FEC defines a multicandidate PAC (which most PACs are) as one that has been registered for at least six months, has received contributions from more than fifty persons, and has made donations to at least five candidates for federal office. A multicandidate PAC cannot be formally tied to a political party, but, of course, most PACs have an ideological preference for the issues and candidates of one party or the other.

Any group of individuals can form a PAC by filling out the forms required by the FEC, filing the necessary quarterly reports, and following the FEC rules. These rules are numerous, but two in particular are important for all PACs. First, no PAC may contribute more than $5,000 to a candidate's campaign in any election (with a primary and general election considered separate elections). Also, no individual can donate more than $5,000 to any one PAC in a year. On the other hand, no limits exist on how much a PAC can spend independently from any particular candidate's campaign to influence voters. In 1976, the Supreme Court ruled in *Buckley v. Valeo* that it is unconstitutional to regulate independent expenditures by PACs.[26] Independent expenditures can be used to advertise support for or opposition to an individual. For example, in 1988 the National Rifle Association (NRA), which opposes gun control, advertised its opposition to the Democratic presidential candidate Michael Dukakis because of his support for legislation to control handguns. The NRA could not give the advertising money directly to the Bush campaign, but it could spend as much as it wanted to buy its own advertising.

The rules for PACs also vary by the type of PAC. The FEC divides PACs into six general groups:

1. Corporate
2. Labor
3. Trade or professional associations
4. Corporations without stock
5. Cooperatives
6. Nonconnecteds

The first five groups are considered *connected PACs*, or committees specifically tied to a particular organization. The organization can donate money, office space, and other support to the PAC for operating expenses, but cannot give to the PAC any money that will eventually go to candidates. Corporations and labor unions are forbidden from donating any money to presidential or congressional campaigns either directly from the organization's treasury or through contributions to a PAC. The money that a PAC gives to candidates or spends independently must be obtained from individuals in the organization. For example, the Teamsters union cannot donate money to DRIVE-PAC, the Teamsters' PAC. All funds the PAC donates to campaigns or spends independently on an election must come from the individual members of the union.

You can easily tell the affiliation of the connected PACs by their names. For example, corporate PACs are specifically tied to a particular company, such as General Motors or AT&T, and the PAC must use the name of the company. Other connected PACs are similar in that labor PACs use the name of the supporting union and trade PACs use the name of the supporting trade association. Nonconnected PACs are quite different in that they have no supporting organization. As their name suggests, these types of PACs cannot be connected (in a financial sense) to any other organization. The nonconnected category, therefore, has the widest range of possible ideological preferences and types of interest groups. Almost all the PACs of noneconomic interest groups are in this category. Examples of nonconnected PACs include the National Abortion Rights Action League PAC and the National Committee to Preserve Social Security PAC. Because nonconnected PACs do not have a parent organization providing operating expenses, many are strapped for funds. Often, all the money raised by a nonconnected PAC goes to meet operating expenses with none left over to make contributions to candidates.

Of the approximately 4,200 PACs in existence in 2008, the largest category was corporate. There were 1,601 corporate PACs, 1,300 nonconnecteds, 925 trade and professional association PACs, 273 labor PACs, 97 corporation-without-stock PACs, and 38 cooperatives.[27] Since 1980, the nonconnected category has been the fastest growing by far (see Figure 11-1). The number of nonconnected PACs has more than tripled since 1980, whereas the labor and trade categories grew by only 23 percent and the corporate by 75 percent. Because nonconnected PACs are usually single-issue groups with a narrow ideological focus, some observers have been alarmed by the rapid growth in the number of nonconnecteds.

Political action committees' overall spending in the 2008 election cycle provide a good measure of the activities of various interests in the election, including congressional elections (see Table 11-1). In recent years, the National Association of Realtors has become a significant player in elections, and in 2008 their contributions exceeded those of traditional powerhouse the National Rifle Association, which was not even in the top twenty contributing PACs. Ten of the top donors were labor unions. Very few businesses contributed enough to the 2008 campaign, with only AT&T and Honeywell making the top twenty contributors.

TABLE 11-1 Top 20 PAC Contributors to Candidates, 2011–2012

PAC Name	Total Amount	Dem Pct	Repub Pct
National Assn of Realtors	$3,960,282	44%	55%
National Beer Wholesalers Assn	$3,388,500	41%	59%
Honeywell International	$3,193,024	41%	59%
Operating Engineers Union	$3,186,387	84%	15%
National Auto Dealers Assn	$3,074,000	28%	72%
Intl Brotherhood of Electrical Workers	$2,853,000	97%	2%
American Bankers Assn	$2,736,150	20%	80%
AT&T Inc	$2,543,000	35%	65%
American Assn for Justice	$2,512,500	96%	3%
Credit Union National Assn	$2,487,600	47%	52%
Plumbers/Pipefitters Union	$2,395,150	94%	5%
Northrop Grumman	$2,353,900	41%	58%
American Fedn of St/Cnty/Munic Employees	$2,279,140	99%	1%
Lockheed Martin	$2,258,000	41%	59%
Blue Cross/Blue Shield	$2,177,898	33%	67%
Machinists/Aerospace Workers Union	$2,173,500	98%	1%
American Federation of Teachers	$2,171,644	99%	0%
MINT PAC	$2,138,229	0%	100%
Every Republican is Crucial PAC	$2,086,000	0%	100%
Teamsters Union	$2,053,410	96%	4%

Although some groups, such as the NRA, have long played a major role in electoral politics, the contours of group activity ebb and flow as the parties probe the limits of the law's limitations on soft money and various interests decide to invest more in the political process. The Realtor's PAC increased its spending more than any other political action committee between 1998 and 2000. However, the second- and third-greatest increases were shown by committees representing the political parties. The Democrats' PAC to Our Future and the Republicans' Keep Our Majority contributed a large amount to various candidates during the 2000 election cycle. In many ways, this phenomenon represented a strengthening of the parties as they flexed their money-raising abilities. These increases almost certainly paved the way for legislative passage of the 2002 campaign finance law (see Figure 11-2).

Other interests undoubtedly decided that they needed to play a much greater role in politics. Probably the most obvious among them was Microsoft, which almost quadrupled its candidate expenditures between 1998 and 2000. During this time, executives at Microsoft certainly must have rethought their earlier decisions to stay fairly removed from the political arena as they found themselves embroiled in a lengthy, expensive trial following the Justice Department's filing of a lawsuit alleging that the company practiced anticompetitive business practices.

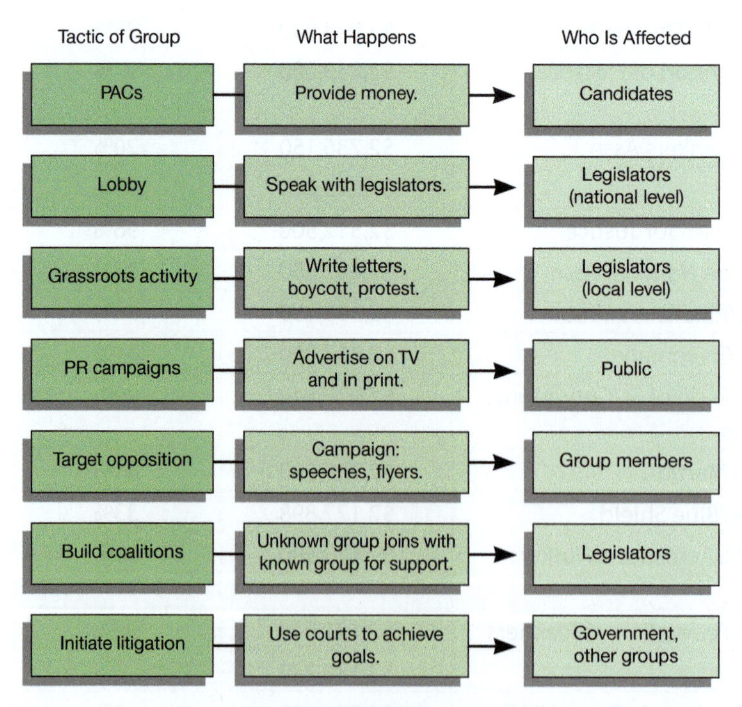

Figure 11-2 *Greatest Increase in PAC Spending for Candidates (1998–2000)*
Source: Adapted from the Federal Election Commission.

11-5b Fundraising

Fundraising is the most crucial activity undertaken by an interest group or PAC. To contribute to candidates or advertise its preferences through independent expenditures, a PAC must have money. The wealthiest PACs spend millions of dollars in each election cycle. Other interest groups must also raise money for the various activities they use to influence policy. Generally, economic interest groups have an easier time raising funds than do ideological groups or public interest groups. For one thing, the free-rider problem is much more severe for noneconomic groups. Noneconomic groups are also more likely to depend on individuals for their funding than economic groups are. For example, the National Association of Manufacturers depends on businesses to contribute funds. On the other hand, Common Cause (a consumer protection public interest group) refuses to accept business donations to avoid the appearance of being "bought off" by the companies it is supposed to be watching.

There are as many fundraising techniques as there are interest groups and innovative leaders. Historically, the most common method has been **direct mail**. Before the internet, direct mail dominated. Most successful groups used direct mail for their fundraising. As more electioneering tactics moved online, so did fundraising. Now, direct mail means sidebar ads on websites and direct e-mail appeals.[28] Direct mail is popular for several reasons. First, finding potential donors is easy—numerous mailing lists that provide detailed information about consumer preferences are available for purchase. Second, the wide availability and low cost of computers make it easy to produce sophisticated, targeted appeals. Third, through pictures, highly inflammatory language, and dramatic appeals that may stretch the truth ("Without you, we will have no rain forests in twenty years!"), groups can plead for money and also spread the word on their political positions. Fourth, after a donor has been found, continuing to send further solicitations to the same person is easy. On the other hand, direct mail entails high costs at the beginning until donors are found, and the response rate is often extremely low. For ideological interest groups, however, direct mail may be the only way to contact potential members. Conversely, economic interest groups have the advantage of knowing where potential donors conduct business or are employed; thus, they can avoid sending mass mailings to millions of people, only a small percentage of whom will be interested in the issue.

Other methods of fundraising depend on the type of interest group. Groups with a geographically concentrated membership frequently use face-to-face, personal requests for funds. For example, it would be feasible to make personal appeals to union members who are concentrated in a few factories. On the other hand, a national interest group would have a difficult time personally contacting all its members. Likewise, locally based groups may use seminars, rallies, special entertainment events, dinners, and other special events requiring attendance by their members. These methods are usually appropriate for labor and corporate PACs and may be used by professional associations if professional conventions are a regular feature of the occupation. On the other hand, nonconnected PACs, public interest groups, and other noneconomic, widely dispersed groups typically cannot use these methods.

Some wealthy interest groups may be able to use telephone solicitation or even media advertising for fundraising. These methods are expensive, however, and may be effective in only special cases. For example, the National Rifle Association may find it cost-effective to advertise nationally in magazines such as *Soldier of Fortune* because a large number of gun enthusiasts would see this type of advertisement. On the other hand, most groups would find that advertising in a weekly newsmagazine, such as *Time* or *Newsweek*, would be quite costly and reach such a diverse audience (with a low percentage of potential responses) that the money would be wasted.

In the late 2000s, online fundraising is the new dominant method of soliciting contributions to groups. Direct mail still dominates fundraising, but since 2004 campaigns and groups have been aggressively recruiting small fund donations from specific segments of the population very successfully.[29]

11-5c LOBBYING

The most basic, but also the most controversial, activity undertaken by interest groups is lobbying. **Lobbying** is any action taken by an interest group to let the government know how the members of a group feel about proposed or existing regulations or legislation. Today's interest groups commonly form coalitions to support or oppose policies in which they have a mutual interest. Thus, lobbying is often a cooperative enterprise. As one scholar of interest groups noted recently, "Organized interests fight their battles today largely in coalitions. Lobbying coalitions are also the building blocks out of which consensus within the Washington Beltway is built."[30]

Most interest groups have someone on staff who regularly watches both Congress and the administration to see whether any action is being taken on an issue affecting the common interests of the group. Many public interest and smaller ideological groups cannot afford to hire professional lobbyists to keep tabs on the government, although most economic groups and the larger noneconomic groups can. Typically, they either employ their own full-time lobbyist (or lobbyists) or contract with a public relations company or law firm that specializes in political activity. Often, these firms work for a number of interest groups with different concerns—a necessity if conflicts

between clients are to be avoided. These firms can spread some costs among their clients, such as the salary paid to a former government official "with connections" or the cost of buying and thoroughly evaluating all publications with information on congressional activity. Consequently, many corporations and trade groups find it more efficient to contract with these political "guns for hire" than to pay for their own staff.

The cost of obtaining information on what government is doing can be quite expensive. Congress passes hundreds of legislative bills every year out of the thousands that are proposed. In addition, the administrative agencies add thousands of pages of regulations every year to the *Federal Register*, a daily government publication of all new regulations. Although numerous publications, such as the *Congressional Quarterly Weekly Report* or the *Roll Call* newsletter, offer information on what has happened, often the most valuable information on what *may happen* cannot be obtained from publications. Then the experience and connections of a lobbyist come into play. That is also the reason that so many former members of Congress, administrative staffers, and White House assistants are employed by these political action firms. Concern over the "revolving door" between government service and employment by interest groups has caused both Congress in 1991 and President Clinton in 1993 to invoke rules barring their respective employees from taking jobs as lobbyists immediately after leaving either Congress or the White House.

Lobbying takes on many forms. The popular image of the lobbyist coercing a member of Congress into voting a particular way on a piece of legislation over a drink is largely false. The heavy demand on the average member's time, media scrutiny, and various ethics rules make such overt "arm twisting" less likely to occur in the modern Congress. The lobbyist's job is much more subtle and diverse. The most basic function is to transmit information to government officials in the legislative or executive branches. This transmitting may be done in several ways: direct conversations with a member of Congress, presentations to congressional or administrative staff members, publications in the media, or testimony in congressional committee hearings.

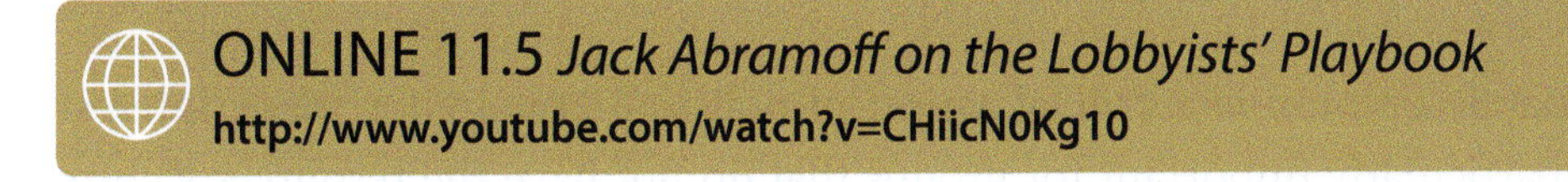
ONLINE 11.5 *Jack Abramoff on the Lobbyists' Playbook*
http://www.youtube.com/watch?v=CHiicN0Kg10

11-5d Grassroots Lobbying

One other important category of lobbying is **grassroots lobbying**, a fairly broad category of activity which can be defined as "any type of action that attempts to influence inside-the-beltway inhabitants by influencing the attitudes or behavior of outside-the-beltway inhabitants."[31] Typically, grassroots lobbying involves orchestrated personal contacts between constituents and a member of Congress. The most common grassroots tactic is the letter-writing campaign. Its aim is to flood the offices of targeted members of Congress, such as party leaders or committee chairpersons, with an overwhelming amount of mail or to have each individual write to the member representing her home district. Many interest groups routinely provide in their direct mail or regular publications some samples of letters or actual postcards that individuals can use. This way, individuals are spared the trouble of finding out bill numbers and names, congressional committees considering the bill, and the addresses of members of Congress.

When members of Congress agree with an interest group, the large volume of mail may provide a cover for the action they take. Members of Congress even occasionally explain a vote by mentioning that they received bags of mail or that the mail on one side of an issue outnumbered the mail on the other side. Thus, they treat the mail as an expression of public opinion even though only one side may have made a concerted effort. If a silent majority does not counteract the efforts of a determined minority on an issue, these types of campaigns can be effective.

If other, more formal means of lobbying are not effective, a group may turn to a different form of grassroots activity: political protest. Protests can take a number

ONLINE 11.6 *Andy Paul on the Tactics of Grassroots Lobbying*
http://www.youtube.com/watch?v=8owNCm-TTus

of forms: economic strikes, boycotts, marches, picketing, and sit-ins. Any activity that involves a number of people and will draw the media's attention can be used. The civil rights protests of the 1960s may be the most successful example of the use of this political tactic by a group that was largely denied access to the formal means of political influence. The sit-ins, boycotts, and marches forced the issue on the national agenda, and the brutality witnessed by television viewers helped mobilize public opinion to support the passage of the Civil Rights Act of 1964 and the Voting Rights Act of 1965.

11-5e Influencing Public Opinion

Influencing public opinion is a crucial aspect of political strategy for many interest groups. It is particularly important for groups that do not have the resources to hire lobbyists or fund a PAC. When a group believes that its point of view would attract popular support if presented properly, it may adopt a public relations strategy. Ideological groups whose messages may have an effect on a large number of people are particularly likely to face this situation.

Formulating a public relations campaign can be quite difficult. The most direct approach is to buy media advertising. However, this option is expensive, it may appear to be biased, and sustaining interest in an issue through advertising is difficult. Most groups cannot afford even a limited advertising campaign. Therefore, most groups look for ways to obtain free media coverage. Some interest groups choose to fund research on the topic and later publish the results to make a point. For example, the Consumers' Union regularly tests various products for safety and then publicly releases the information. Another indirect method is to publicize the voting records of members of Congress. The Americans for Democratic Action (ADA), a liberal group, has issued a rating of all members of Congress each year since the 1960s. Using a scale from 0 to 100, the rating shows how often each member agreed with the group's position. Voters can assume that an ADA score of 100 indicates a liberal legislator. Finally, a group can provide the media with film footage, photos, or interviews of persons suffering from a situation that the group thinks should be remedied by government action. For example, an environmental group, such as Greenpeace, might provide the networks with footage of whales being killed or seal pups being clubbed. This type of graphic footage may be more effective at moving public opinion than a written argument would. Consequently, air time on the television news is a valuable commodity.

11-5f Targeting Political Opposition

One of the more important elements of any political strategy is to know one's opposition. In addition to observing government activity, a successful lobbyist must keep track of what the political opposition has been doing and planning. You can find several good potential sources of information on the opposition: members of Congress and their staffers, other lobbyists, members of the interest group, the media, government hearings, administrators, and various people at social functions. For many groups, the opposition may change from one issue to another. For example, in the same year, the United Auto Workers might oppose several different groups, such as the auto manufacturers, consumer safety groups, and even other unions, for different reasons. The union might oppose the auto manufacturers on worker safety issues, work with industry representatives against a consumer safety group to avoid new safety features on American cars that would raise the cost of American cars versus imports (and therefore possibly cost them jobs), and oppose the steel unions' efforts to obtain higher tariffs on steel (which would also raise the price of a car).

Groups often feed off their opposition. The actions or words of the opposition may be useful in motivating potential members to join or current members to become more active. The direct mail solicitations sent by ideological groups commonly highlight the words or actions of some well-known politician on the other end of the ideological debate. Senator Edward Kennedy is a favorite target of conservative groups, just as the religious right is a frequent target of liberals. For example, the debate over gay marriage provides "counter-fundraising" opportunities for groups on both sides. The National Organization for Marriage [32] website asks for donations to prevent gay marriage as a threat to traditional marriage. Pro-gay marriage groups such as the Human Rights Campaign[33] then solicit from their members not just for the issue at stake but to prevent the opposing groups from gaining political power.

11-5g Building Coalitions

Just as important as targeting the opposition is building coalitions with other interest groups. One interest group testifying at a congressional hearing does not suggest a strong current of public opinion on the issue, but if several lobbyists with different points of view, diverse constituencies, and a wide set of connections to the members of Congress appear, the issue is likely to be taken more seriously. Likewise, a coalition of groups is more likely to gain access to congressional offices, the media, and the administration. Different groups will also have diverse resources and abilities. For example, Greenpeace, one of the more radical environmental groups, has a unique talent for drawing media coverage. Greenpeace does not have a PAC, however, and tends not to use traditional channels of lobbying in Congress. Conversely, the Sierra Club, an older and more moderate organization, does have access to Congress and administrators. Thus, although the groups might agree on a particular environmental issue, they would use different tactics.

The coalitions that form among interest groups are often temporary and rather narrowly focused. The groups may have different goals and tactics that prevent permanent coalitions. Also, similar groups are competing for the same set of potentially interested citizens. For example, the National Committee to Preserve Social Security and the American Association of Retired Persons (AARP) both depend on senior citizens for most of their funds. Although both would oppose any proposal to reduce Social Security benefits, they would be rivals in claiming responsibility for defeating the legislation. Of course, the level of competition varies widely.

11-5h Litigation

The courts have increasingly become a focus for interest groups. One of the first interest groups to employ litigation to affect public policy was the NAACP. Through its Legal Defense and Education Fund, headed by Thurgood Marshall, the NAACP brought, and usually won, lawsuits challenging racial segregation and other civil rights violations. More recently, environmental and consumer groups have found litigation to be an effective means of advancing their interests. Quite often, interest groups may not be direct parties to lawsuits because they lack standing to sue. The courts require the party who brings a lawsuit to have standing—that is, to be directly and adversely affected by the policy or situation being challenged in the suit. This requirement means that interest groups frequently have to find someone to serve as the plaintiff of record. After a suitable plaintiff is located, the interest group can provide legal representation and financial assistance. For example, in *Brown v. Board of Education*, the landmark school desegregation decision of 1954, the NAACP recruited the parents of Linda Brown to challenge school segregation in Topeka, Kansas. The Browns were the plaintiffs of record, but the NAACP was the driving force behind the lawsuit. Evidence indicates that more than half of all important constitutional law cases are sponsored in this way by interest groups.[34]

Amicus Briefs

Another way in which interest groups use the courts to advance their interests is by filing *amicus curiae* briefs in cases in which they have a stake. Literally meaning "friend of the court," an *amicus* brief is filed by a person or group that is not a direct party to a case but wants to inform the court of its views on how the case should be decided. In a case involving a major social, political, or economic issue, many different groups may file *amicus* briefs (see Figure 11-3). Interest groups filed *amicus* briefs in more than half the noneconomic cases decided by the Supreme Court in the 1970s,[35] and this trend continues now.

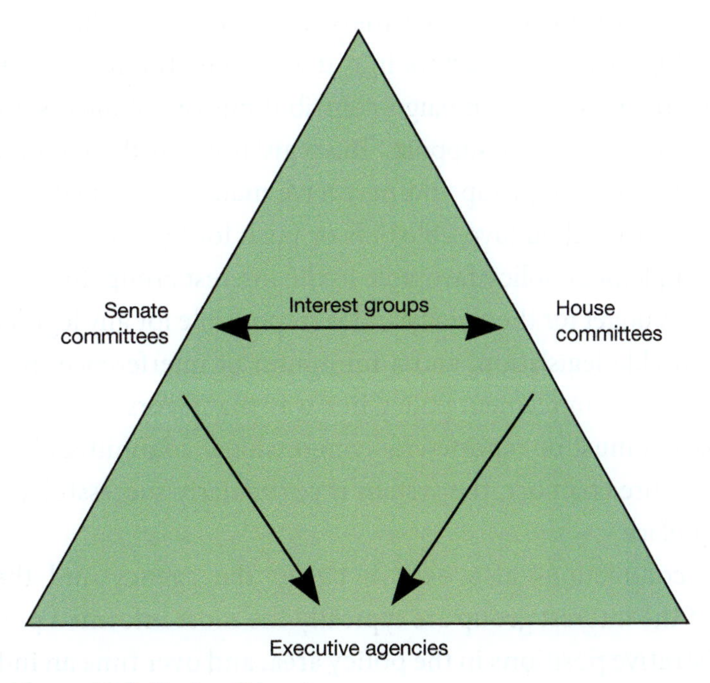

Figure 11-3 *The Iron Triangle*

11-6 Subgovernments: Iron Triangles and Issue Networks

The term **subgovernment** refers to an informal arrangement between private parties and public officials that operates "under the table," or to use a more prevalent metaphor, "off the radar screen." Such arrangements are and have always been controversial in that they may provide largely unknown and unaccountable parties undue influence over public policy. Subgovernments may take a number of forms. The two most common terms to describe subgovernments in the United States are "iron triangle" and "issue network."

11-6a Iron Triangles

An **iron triangle** is a three-way relationship involving a legislative committee (or subcommittee), an executive agency, and an interest group (see Figure 11-3). Because Congress parcels out bills to committees with set jurisdictions over policy areas, interest groups, particularly economic groups, usually find that most bills affecting their interests pass through one congressional committee in each chamber. Similarly, policy is implemented by various cabinet departments and agencies, depending on the issue. Therefore, an interest group typically directs its lobbying efforts at one or two administrative units—one committee in the House and one in the Senate.

The iron triangle theory suggests that in the long run an interest group will dominate the subsystem that produces policy for a certain issue. Each of the three sets of actors gets something from the system, so no one has a reason to break up the relationship or let other actors into the system. The interest group provides the member of Congress with campaign contributions or volunteers, information on the policy, and other means of support. The legislators on the committee, who may be members of the interest group and may have many constituents who are involved in the group, either block unfavorable bills or push for legislation that the agency needs in order to implement policy favorable to the interest group. In addition, the committee passes the budget for the agency and is responsible for any legislative oversight. Big budgets, favorable legislation, and a minimum of interference from outside sources allow the agency to implement policy in a way that favors the interest group. Because most legislation must be reported by congressional committees before being considered by the entire chamber, the system is particularly successful at preventing action from taking place.

Other connections also exist between the agency and the interest group. Members of the interest group are typically the most informed potential appointees for administrative positions in the policy area, and over time an individual may hold various jobs in an industry, in the government agencies regulating the industry, in the economic interest groups representing the industry, in congressional or White House staff positions, or in the law and public relations firms that serve the interest groups.

Consider the case of subsidies for tobacco farmers. The agriculture committees in the House and Senate are responsible for agricultural policy, including subsidies. The Agriculture Department is the administrative body responsible for implementing farm policy. Senator Jesse Helms was the committee chairman from 1981 to 1986 and again assumed a leadership role in 1994 until his retirement in 2003. Senator Helms represented North Carolina, a state that relies on both tobacco farming and the manufacture of tobacco products. He received PAC money from several sources related to tobacco, such as the RJR corporate PAC and tobacco farming interests. In response to his state's economic interest and his connection to the interest groups supporting tobacco farming, Helms continued to push for tobacco subsidies and large budgets for the Agriculture Department. The Agriculture Department responded by working closely with tobacco farmers to help them qualify for subsidies. The tobacco interests may also have provided the senator or the Agriculture Department with research that supports subsidies (such as the number of people employed in the industry, the volume of tobacco exports, and the plight of small farmers).

The issue was further muddled by the 1998 settlement between the tobacco companies and the states that provided for payouts to the states to compensate them for smoking-related healthcare costs. The states agreed to drop lawsuits that had threatened to bring financial ruin to the tobacco industry in exchange for a twenty-five-year series of multimillion-dollar payouts that began in 2000. Moreover, tobacco companies agreed to spend almost $2 billion on programs to discourage youth smoking and to eliminate advertising on billboards and displaying their logos on T-shirts and other merchandise. The entire settlement could exceed more than $200 billion. In a sense, this agreement expanded the arena beyond the usual players, and the conflict was resolved in an unusual way.

Other interests, such as legislators concerned about health issues or the surgeon general, are not included in the policy subsystem. If a member of Congress is not on the committee that handles the policy, he is not likely to have much opportunity to affect it, particularly in the House, where more rigid rules prevent members from taking the initiative on matters outside the jurisdiction of the legislator's own committee. The surgeon general is excluded because that person has no say over the Agriculture Department's budget or the legislation that provides the subsidies. Even the president may be frustrated in his attempts to fight the entrenched interests in an iron triangle. Because members of Congress, lobbyists, and career civil servants are in Washington for so long, they can usually wait out any temporary intrusions into the policy subsystem. A president has so little time to devote to a wide range of issues that no single administration can ensure that policy is implemented as it intended. The media and the public are even less likely to stay focused on an issue long enough to counter the iron triangle. Over time, an iron triangle can be quite effective at implementing policy in a favorable way and blocking any new initiatives.

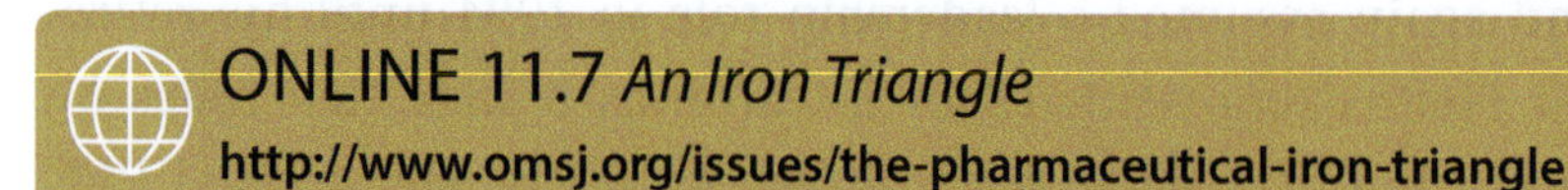

ONLINE 11.7 *An Iron Triangle*
http://www.omsj.org/issues/the-pharmaceutical-iron-triangle

11-6b Issue Networks

An **issue network** is a conglomeration of decision makers, activists, and experts in a particular policy area.[36] It is typically larger, more diverse, and more dynamic than the iron triangle. In the issue network, relationships change, participants come and go, and roles and levels of influence likewise change. An issue network in a particular policy area may involve governmental actors from several branches and several levels of government; activists and lobbyists representing numerous diverse interests; and experts from think tanks, consulting firms, and academia. Because it is more inclusive and less insular than the iron triangle, the issue network is less objectionable to those who object to the undue influence of private actors over public policy. Today, the issue network may be a more realistic model of interest group influence in most policy areas.

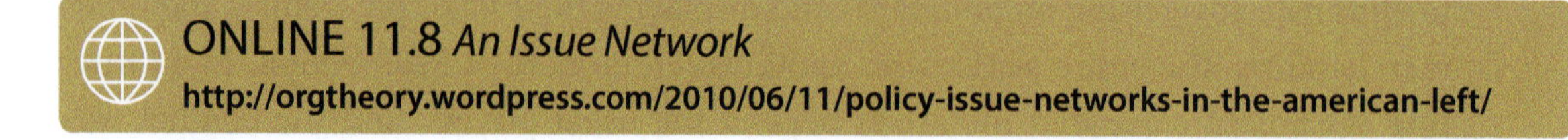

ONLINE 11.8 *An Issue Network*
http://orgtheory.wordpress.com/2010/06/11/policy-issue-networks-in-the-american-left/

11-7 Conclusion: Interest Groups and Political Culture

Interest groups are a subject of as much controversy as any phenomenon in American politics. Many believe that they foster and enhance political participation and are a desirable mechanism for ensuring representation and citizen involvement. Becoming involved in an interest group does not require an inordinate amount of time, energy, or money. By affiliating with an interest group, an individual can promote a particular cause directly. Unlike voting or getting involved in a political party, joining an interest group ensures that people's energies are focused on subjects that matter to them personally. Joining an interest group is an eminently practical form of political participation that appeals to America's pragmatic culture.

American political culture has become increasingly supportive of the articulation of individual demands through interest groups. At the same time, some commentators worry that the political system is becoming fragmented into small, narrowly defined groups that are increasingly unable or unwilling to compromise. Increasingly, critics of American politics lament that our political culture seems to place no emphasis on the needs of the community as opposed to the interests of the individual or small group. Others believe that a political system built around interest groups, as the American system increasingly appears to be, is incapable of rational policy making that meets the long-term needs of society. Still others object to what they believe to be the conservative, probusiness bias of the interest group system. Regardless of one's evaluation of pluralist politics, interest groups clearly are playing an increasingly important role in this country's governance. Interest groups do not seek to govern, but in influencing those who do, interest groups can have a substantial impact on governance.

Questions for Thought and Discussion

1. Do interest groups have too much influence in the political process? What reforms might lessen their influence?

2. What effect has the proliferation of interest groups had on political parties in this country?

3. Why are some interest groups more successful than others in influencing policy making?

4. Does the proliferation of interest groups suggest changes in the underlying political culture?

5. What effect do political action committees have on congressional elections? What reforms, if any, are needed in the way that PACs operate?

Endnotes

1 Harold D. Lasswell, *Politics: Who Gets What, When and How* (New York: McGraw-Hill, 1938).

2 Alexis de Tocqueville, *Democracy in America*, vol. 2 (New York: Vintage Books, 1954), p. 114.

3 Robert D. Putnam, *Bowling Alone: The Collapse and Revival of American Community* (New York: Simon & Schuster, 2001).

4 *Sweezy v. New Hampshire*, 354 U.S. 234, 250–251 (1957).

5 *N.A.A.C.P. v. Alabama*, 357 U.S. 449, 460 (1958).

6 *Roberts v. United States Jaycees*, 468 U.S. 609, 622 (1984).

7 Pluralist theory is generally thought to have begun with the publication of Arthur Bentley's seminal book, *The Process of Government* (1908).

8 Robert A. Dahl, *A Preface to Democratic Theory* (Chicago: University of Chicago Press, 1956), p. 137.

9 One of the best-known and most trenchant critiques is Grant McConnell, *Private Power and American Democracy* (New York: Knopf, 1966).

10 The classic exposition of this view is found in C. Wright Mills, *The Power Elite* (New York: Oxford University Press, 1956).

11 Anthony J. Nownes, *Pressure and Power: Organized Interests in American Politics* (Boston: Houghton Mifflin, 2001), p. 220.

12 Theodore J. Lowi, *The End of Liberalism*, 2d ed. (New York: W. W. Norton, 1979), pp. 43–44.

13 See, for example, Jonathan Rauch, *Demosclerosis: The Silent Killer of American Government* (New York: Times Books, 1994).

14 Robert Paul Wolff, "A Critique of Pluralism: 'Beyond Tolerance.'" In *The Dissent of the Governed: Readings on the Democratic Process,* eds. John C. Livingston and Robert G. Thompson (New York: Macmillan, 1972), p. 89.

15 *Gibbons v. Ogden*, 22 U.S. 1 (1824).

16 Information provided by the Federal Election Commission, on the web at www.fec.gov.

17 Jay Newton-Small, "Behind Obama's Union Comeback," *Time*, March 3, 2008, http://www.time.com/time/politics/article/0,8599,1718918,00.html

18 David Welch, "Chrysler, GM, and Union Ownership," *Business Week*, May 1, 2009, http://www.businessweek.com/autos/autobeat/archives/2009/05/chrysler_gm_and.html

19 According to the AFL-CIO website, "the 16.3 million U.S. workers who belonged to unions in 2001 represented 13.5 percent of the total wage and salary workforce."

20 Harold W. Stanley and Richard Niemi, *Vital Statistics on American Politics*, 3d ed. (Washington, D.C.: CQ Press, 1990), p. 106.

21 "The New Old 'Card Check,'" *Wall Street Journal*, July 21, 2009, http://online.wsj.com/article/SB124804413309863431.html

22 See Ronald G. Shaiko, *Voices and Echoes for the Environment: Public Interest Representation in the 1990s and Beyond* (New York: Columbia University Press, 1999).

23 Jeffrey M. Berry, *Lobbying for the People* (Princeton, NJ: Princeton University Press, 1977), p. 7.

24 For an excellent study of these trends, see Mark J. Rozell and Clyde Wilcox, *Interest Groups in American Campaigns: The New Face of Electioneering* (Washington, D.C.: Congressional Quarterly Books, 1998).

25 Information obtained from MoveOn.org website, http://www.moveon.org.

26 *Buckley v. Valeo*, 424 U.S. 1 (1976).

27 Harold W. Stanley and Richard Niemi, *Vital Statistics on American Politics 2003–2004* (Washington, D.C.: CQ Press, 2003), p. 102.

28 http://www.fundraising123.org/files/groundspring-handbook.pdf

29 Fredreka Schouten, "Internet Critical for Political Cash," *USA Today*, December 12, 2008, http://www.usatoday.com/news/washington/2006-12-17-internet-cash_x.htm

30 Kevin W. Hula, *Lobbying Together: Interest Group Coalitions in Legislative Politics* (Washington, D.C.: Georgetown University Press, 1999), p. 2.

31 Kenneth M. Goldstein, *Interest Groups, Lobbying and Participation in America* (Cambridge, UK: Cambridge University Press, 1999), p. 3.

32 http://www.nomblog.com/33191

33 http://www.hrc.org/

34 Karen O'Connor and Lee Epstein, "The Role of Interest Groups in Supreme Court Policy Formation." In *Public Policy Formation*, ed. Robert Eyestone (Greenwich, CT: JAI Press, 1984).

35 Karen O'Connor and Lee Epstein, "Research Note: An Appraisal of Hakman's 'Folklore,'" *Law and Society Review*, vol. 16, 1982, pp. 701–11.

36 See Hugh Heclo, *Issue Networks and the Executive Establishment* (Washington, D.C.: American Enterprise Institute, 1978).

Unit 4

Institutions of Government

Chapter 12

CONGRESS

OUTLINE

Key Terms 446
Expected Learning Outcomes 446
12-1 The National Legislature 446
- **12-1a** The Congressional System versus the Parliamentary System 447
- **12-1b** Congress and the Two-Party System 448

12-2 Functions of Congress 448
- **12-2a** Representing Constituents 449
- **12-2b** Making Laws 452
- **12-2c** Controlling the Government's "Checkbook" 453
- **12-2d** Maintaining the System of Checks and Balances 456

12-3 The Institutional Development of Congress 457
- **12-3a** An Evolving Institution 459

12-4 The Members of Congress 462
- **12-4a** Female Representation 462
- **12-4b** Minority Representation 463

12-5 How Congress Is Organized 464
- **12-5a** Leadership 464
- **12-5b** Committees 471
- **12-5c** Staff 473
- **12-5d** Agencies Providing Assistance to Congress 475

12-6 How Congress Makes Laws 476
- **12-6a** Bill Referral 478
- **12-6b** Committee Action 478
- **12-6c** Getting a Bill to the Floor 478
- **12-6d** Dislodging Bills from Committees 479
- **12-6e** Calendars 479
- **12-6f** Floor Procedure 480

12-7 An Institution under Scrutiny 481
- **12-7a** The Advantages of Incumbency 482
- **12-7b** The Constant Campaign 483
- **12-7c** Proposals for Reform 483

12-8 Conclusion: Assessing Congress 486
Questions for Thought and Discussion 487
Endnotes 488

KEY TERMS

casework
Committee of the Whole
conference committee
delegate style of representation
descriptive representation
electronic voting
franking privilege
joint committees
majority leader
majority whip
markup session
multiple referral system
ombudsman
oversight
particularism
party caucus
perks
policy representation
pork barrel
quorum
rider
Rules Committee
safe seat
select committees
seniority
sequential referral system
service representation
single-member districts
special committees
standing committees
subcommittees
symbolic representation
trustee style of representation
unanimous consent agreements

EXPECTED LEARNING OUTCOMES

After reading this chapter and completing the supplemental online materials, students will:

- Describe the Constitutional design of Congress
- Trace the development of Congress as an institution
- Critique the process by which bills become law
- Describe the leadership structure of Congress
- Analyze reform efforts in Congress

12-1 THE NATIONAL LEGISLATURE

In a democracy, the governmental institution that enacts the laws is referred to as the legislature. In the United States, the national legislature is the Congress, which is made up of two chambers: the House of Representatives and the Senate. In addition to adopting laws governing the nation, Congress has the responsibility to see that the laws it passes are administered by the executive branch in the ways that Congress intended when it passed them. Moreover, members of Congress represent the citizens who live in the areas that elect them and are expected to provide service to their

constituents. Congress is also occasionally required to act in a judicial fashion, such as when considering whether to impeach and remove the president or a federal judge. Finally, Congress has certain electoral powers because it is required to choose the president and vice president if no candidate secures a majority of the electoral college vote.

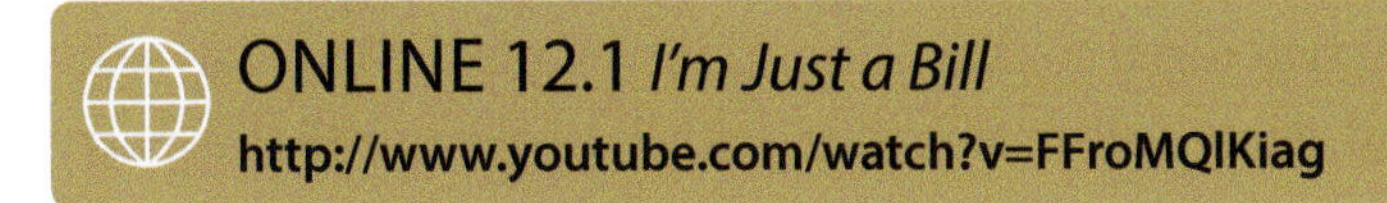
ONLINE 12.1 *I'm Just a Bill*
http://www.youtube.com/watch?v=FFroMQIKiag

12-1a THE CONGRESSIONAL SYSTEM VERSUS THE PARLIAMENTARY SYSTEM

The American system of government differs considerably from the parliamentary system of most European countries. A parliamentary system is organized around more centralized and disciplined political parties, and the legislative branch is clearly superior to the executive. In England, a person runs for Parliament as a candidate of the Labour, Conservative, or Liberal party. The candidates are chosen and assigned to districts by their parties, and members of Parliament are expected to vote with their parties when laws are being considered. The majority party in Parliament chooses the prime minister, who along with the cabinet wields executive power. Unlike the American president, the prime minister and the cabinet are directly accountable to the Parliament. Thus, no separation of powers (or checks and balances) exists between the lawmaking and administrative branches in a parliamentary system. This system stands in stark contrast to the American congressional system (or presidential system, as it is sometimes called). In this country, congressional candidates seek office as Democrats or Republicans, but they may run in a geographic district they live in, with or without the blessing of the official party structure. After members of Congress are in office, they vote with their parties most of the time, but they are in no way bound to do so. Presidents need the support of Congress to get legislation passed, but presidents, unlike prime ministers, do not rely on members of the legislature to stay in office. In fact, a politically astute president can sometimes increase his status by opposing the actions of a Congress controlled by the opposition party. President Clinton enjoyed his greatest popularity when Republicans held majorities in both the House and the Senate, especially when the House impeached him.

Although presidents and Congress are not bound together as are the chief executive and legislature in a parliamentary system, they often act very much in concert in times of national emergency. For instance, following the September 11, 2001, terrorist attacks, Congress voted almost unanimously to support President Bush in approving the use of military force against Osama bin Laden's al Qaeda terrorist network. These eras of cooperation are often short lived. By May 2002, many Democrats were openly questioning the way in which the president and his administration had dealt with information about potential terrorist threats before September 11.

12-1b Congress and the Two-Party System

Many parliamentary systems are structured so that minor political parties can win seats in the legislature. Typically, candidates run nationwide with a provision that a party will win a number of seats in proportion to its share of the popular vote. In the United States, the electoral system is quite different. All members of the U.S. Congress are elected from **single-member districts**, that is, only one person represents a particular geographic area. This statement is certainly true of the House of Representatives, where each member represents a district carved out of a state. The number of districts in a state depends on its population. In the Senate, of course, two senators represent each state, but the two senators' terms in office are staggered. Thus, states are single-member districts in the sense that only one candidate wins a Senate seat in each election. It is virtually impossible for candidates from minor political parties to win seats in Congress. With rare exceptions, all members of Congress are from either the Democratic or Republican party. The two-party system in Congress frustrates certain voters, who may wish for clearer alternatives to the Democrats and Republicans. Most observers agree, however, that the two-party system promotes stability in politics and policy making.

12-2 Functions of Congress

The delegates to the Constitutional Convention of 1787 had two purposes in mind while structuring the new Congress. First, they wanted a forum in which legislators could deliberate on the national condition, policy alternatives, and the government's general direction. Second, the Founders intended for the legislators to represent the people who elected them. To allow members to pursue the policy aspect of the job, the Constitution gives Congress broad powers over the economy and taxes, oversight of the bureaucracy, and some partnership with the president in foreign affairs. To ensure that members could feel free to express their opinions, the Constitution prevents the executive branch and the judiciary from prosecuting members for their debate on the floor of Congress. The Constitution also allows members to devise their own rules for conducting business in Congress. Combined with the power to develop a budget, this self-governance feature later resulted in Congress providing itself with staff members, a library, offices, research agencies, and other resources necessary for conducting legislative business.

In addition to this deliberative function, Congress is also charged with representing the people. Because the judicial branch and the bureaucracy are appointed and the president is elected by the entire nation, the only way local interests are heard in the national government is through the members of Congress. The Constitution provides for this relationship through the method of frequent elections. A House member is elected every two years from a district that elects only one legislator to the House. Senators are chosen every six years by states, but each state has two senators whose terms in office are staggered. Before the ratification of the Seventeenth Amendment in 1913, senators were chosen by the state legislatures, but they have since been chosen in statewide popular elections. Because of the longer span of time between elections for senators versus representatives, it is generally thought that the Founders intended for the representatives to be closer and more responsive to the people than senators.

The problem, however, is that these two functions—deliberation and representation—often are not compatible. Policy deliberation requires lots of time. Good policy making requires careful research, much debate, input from concerned citizens and those affected by the policy, and the development of substantial expertise. This activity keeps the legislators in Washington. On the other hand, representation of the people can also be quite demanding. A member must spend time visiting constituents in the district (which may be thousands of miles from D.C.), responding to inquiries (including letters, phone calls, and personal visits), and, to secure reelection, campaigning actively in the district. The representation function claims much of the legislator's time and energy. Therefore, a member must make trade-offs between these two functions in terms of time and energy.

12-2a Representing Constituents

Representation is a central issue in considering the functions of Congress, but this concept has multiple dimensions. One dimension is referred to as **descriptive representation**. In other words, does the membership of Congress look like the American people in terms of gender, race, religion, age, education, and occupation, for example? Do all identifiable social groups have a member in the legislature? Members of Congress are overwhelmingly white, male, Christian, highly educated, wealthy individuals. A large number are lawyers, and most have been politicians for years or even decades. Females, ethnic minorities, religious minorities, and blue-collar workers have fewer legislators (in percentage terms) than their share of the population. This situation leads many people to question whether Congress is good at providing descriptive representation. Because representation is an abstract concept that involves an individual's own subjective feelings, descriptive concerns may have a powerful effect on how people feel about the government and the American system. Therefore, the look of Congress may influence the levels of political trust and participation in the system.

Recent decades, although not altering the preceding description, have certainly seen a more diverse Congress. The 113th Congress that took office in January 2013 was the most diverse in the nation's history. Voters chose 98 women, 43 African Americans,

31 Latinos, 12 Asian American and Pacific Islanders, and 7 gay and bisexual members to Congress in 2012. Religious diversity is also on the rise, as there are now Muslims, Buddhists, and Hindus in the two chambers.[1] There is every reason to believe that the diversity of Congress will continue to increase, although not at the pace that many critics of the current Congress would prefer.

Symbolic Representation

Representation also involves a symbolic component. People must believe that they are being represented, and symbolism can be used to increase the likelihood that people will feel this way. Televised sessions of Congress, public discussions of issues on television talk shows, and newsletters from members to their constituents are examples of activities that may cause voters to feel that they are being represented. For others, elections and campaigns for office may provide enough symbolic reassurance of the representation function. Members of Congress are quite aware of the importance of symbolism, and they take every opportunity—such as giving speeches at high schools or providing a flag that has flown over the Capitol to a school—to encourage the voters' belief that they are being represented. These activities come under the heading of **symbolic representation**.

Service Representation

The process of making government services available to the people and allowing individuals to believe that government is there for them is referred to as **service representation**. Because the federal bureaucracy is so large, embracing hundreds of agencies and thousands of programs, the rules can be overwhelming. Accordingly, legislators help individuals and organizations (such as businesses, schools, or even city governments) in obtaining government services. Members of Congress routinely handle a variety of requests. High school students may ask for help in obtaining information for a research paper. An injured person may ask for assistance in obtaining disability insurance payments from the Social Security Administration. A business owner may need help in obtaining a check from a government agency for services performed for the government. The process of providing this type of help is known as **casework**.

ONLINE 12.2 *Casework in Congress*

http://www.nytimes.com/2012/09/09/opinion/sunday/a-congress-for-the-many-or-the-few.html?pagewanted=all

When a member of Congress intercedes with an administrative agency on behalf of a citizen, the member is performing the role of an **ombudsman**. Because the demand for constituency service has increased so dramatically in this century, the members themselves cannot possibly handle all the requests. Nevertheless, the members recognize that providing these services can have potential electoral benefits. Voters may be opposed to a member's policy decisions, but few will be angry and some will be extremely happy if the member helps a senior citizen get her Social Security check. Because the members of Congress control the federal budget, they have chosen to take this opportunity to please voters by providing funding for staff and district offices for each member. The large personal staff that each member receives free of charge from the government performs almost all the casework, but the member reaps the benefits of performing the service role.

Competing Models of Policy Representation

Policy representation requires that a legislator make policy decisions that are best for her constituents. But what does "best for constituents" mean? A legislator who adopts the **trustee style of representation** is one who makes policy decisions based on what she thinks is best. The member can be removed from office if the voters do not agree with her view of what is best, but as each vote occurs, the member makes an independent decision. Conversely, a legislator who embraces the **delegate style of representation** acts on what he thinks the constituents in the district want. The delegate is not worried about making the best decision in terms of how well the policy will work or how much it costs or whether the president wants it; rather, the delegate is nothing more than a translator of citizen preferences into final congressional votes.

Some people would argue that a delegate is not capable of providing any kind of leadership; only a trustee has the kind of leeway to make difficult votes on issues that may not be politically popular. For example, the civil rights bills of the 1960s were not favored by a majority of Americans, so a legislature full of delegates would not have passed these antidiscrimination laws. Because some legislators chose to do what they personally thought was best for the country, the Civil Rights Act of 1964, the Voting Rights Act of 1965, and the Fair Housing Act of 1968 were passed in the face of contrary public opinion polls. Of course, few legislators would subscribe to either view of representation in the purest sense. Legislators, because they are pragmatists for the most part, choose whichever style they think is best for a given occasion.

Overall, each form of representation contributes to an understanding of how Congress works, although service representation stands out for the pervasive manner in which it influences the way members shape the institution and their own time. Policy representation, however, may be the most important in understanding how well Congress governs the country. If Congress appears to do no more than what is now popular with the people calling in to radio talk shows, it appears to lack leadership. On the other hand, if Congress forces too much unpopular policy onto the electorate through the trustee role, it appears out of touch with the people. Either extreme leaves members of Congress vulnerable to attack.

12-2b Making Laws

The Framers of the Constitution wanted a strong legislature to be the keystone of the new national government. Thus, the Constitution gave the new Congress much broader powers than the legislature that existed under the Articles of Confederation. These constitutional powers may be divided into two broad categories:

- *Enumerated powers* include those powers mentioned specifically in the Constitution.
- *Implied powers* include those powers inferred from general language in the founding document.

Enumerated Powers

Although the enumerated powers of Congress are spelled out in a number of provisions scattered throughout the Constitution, most of the key powers are provided in Article I, Section 8. They include the powers to

- Lay and collect taxes
- Borrow money
- Provide for the U.S. defense and general welfare
- Declare war
- Raise and support an army and navy, and regulate the state militias
- Regulate commerce among the states
- Control immigration and naturalization
- Coin money
- Establish post offices and post roads
- Grant patents and copyrights

The Constitution did not confer on Congress police power—the general authority to make laws for the protection of the public welfare. Under our country's federal system, this responsibility was vested in the state and local governments. But over the years, the enumerated powers of Congress, especially its power to regulate interstate commerce, have been broadened substantially by congressional action and judicial acceptance. For example, Congress is not specifically empowered to regulate the Internet, but it may make certain online transactions across state lines a crime by drawing on its broad power to regulate interstate commerce.[2] Congress has invoked the commerce power to make policy in many areas ranging from environmental protection to organized crime to civil rights. In recent years the Supreme Court has imposed some boundaries around Congress' use of the Commerce Clause. In one important case, by a 5–4 margin the Court struck down the 1990 Gun-Free Schools Act, which had made it a federal crime to take a gun within one thousand feet of a school.[3] Still, Congress' power under the Commerce Clause remains broad.

Constitutional Amendments Conferring Power on Congress

Several constitutional amendments confer additional powers on Congress. Importantly, the Sixteenth Amendment permits Congress to "lay and collect taxes on incomes from whatever source derived, without apportionment among the states." This amendment nullified an earlier Supreme Court decision striking down an income tax imposed by Congress. A number of constitutional amendments endow Congress with the power to legislate in support of civil rights and liberties. For example, the Thirteenth, Fourteenth, and Fifteenth Amendments permit Congress to enforce civil rights through "appropriate legislation." The Nineteenth Amendment removes gender as an impediment to voting, and the Twenty-Sixth Amendment lowers to eighteen the voting age in state and federal elections. Both amendments contain clauses permitting Congress to enforce their terms by "appropriate legislation."

Implied Powers

Congress obviously now exercises far more powers than are specifically enumerated in the Constitution. The Necessary and Proper Clause (Article I, Section 8, Clause 18) permits Congress to "make all laws which shall be necessary and proper for carrying into Execution the foregoing powers, and all other powers vested by this Constitution in the Government of the United States." This clause has been interpreted to provide Congress with a vast reservoir of implied powers. Under the doctrine of implied powers, there is scarcely any area in which Congress is absolutely barred from acting because most problems have a conceivable relationship to the broad powers and objectives contained in the Constitution. Thomas Jefferson, an opponent of the doctrine of implied powers, perceived as much in 1790 when he wrote a memorandum to President George Washington, saying "To take a single step beyond the boundaries thus specially drawn around the powers of Congress is to take possession of a boundless field of power, no longer susceptible of any definition." The constitutional powers of Congress, although not exactly "boundless," are now certainly far greater than most of the Founders could have imagined.

12-2c Controlling the Government's "Checkbook"

The single most time-consuming issue on the legislative calendar in any year is the federal budget. In Article I, Section 7, the Constitution requires that all "bills for raising revenue shall originate in the House of Representatives; but the Senate may propose or concur with amendments as on other bills." As with any other bill, the president may veto appropriations bills, and Congress may override the veto. In addition, Congress has important powers over the budget and economy through such powers as the ability to lay and collect taxes, pay the debts and provide for the common defense and welfare of the United States, borrow money, coin money, and pay for a navy and an army. Without this power over the purse, Congress would not be effective in its struggles with the president, the bureaucracy, or the states.

By custom, the president sends an annual budget proposal to Capitol Hill, and Congress has also established its own complex organizations and rules for dealing with the federal budget. Each year, the president's staff in the Office of Management and Budget provides a detailed plan that numbers in the tens of thousands of pages, and Congress has its own set of estimates, established by the Congressional Budget Office. Congress considers the president's recommendations, and it may choose to alter the president's proposal, reject it, or pass its own alternative.

The Budgetary Process

Congress divides its budgetary process into three parts. The Appropriations Committees in the House and Senate consider how the money will be spent for each executive department and program. The Ways and Means Committee in the House and the Finance Committee in the Senate decide how the revenue will be raised (or, in other words, who will pay the taxes). Finally, the budget committees in each chamber establish the overall spending and revenue levels. All details, however, are still worked out in the Revenue and Appropriations Committees. Consequently, you can easily imagine that the money committees are the most influential and desirable of all legislative committees. Of course, the full chamber (House or Senate) must approve all proposals made by its committees. Ultimately, both chambers must pass the identical budget before it can be sent to the president for approval.

Particularism and the Pork Barrel

The annual budget deficits that occurred from 1969 to 1997 focused much more attention on this function of Congress. One result is that the congressional budgeting procedures became increasingly controversial. Despite four major overhauls of the budget process since 1974, some critics still maintain that the major problem is that members engage in **particularism**, where a member of Congress considers legislation only in terms of how it affects his or her home district. Particularism means that rather than consider whether the nation needs something, such as a permanent space station, members vote for it only if they can get some of the contracts in their districts.

The **pork barrel** is a pejorative term suggesting that an expenditure is not only particularistic but also wasteful. The term refers to a government project or spending measure that benefits a certain legislator's constituency. Most people would agree that a Coast Guard station in the middle of a desert would be wasteful spending, but most of the time it is difficult to get people to agree on what is "pork." A congressional district's new six-lane highway through a town of only ten thousand people may appear to be pork barrel spending to an outsider, but to the residents of the community the new highway means jobs and economic growth in addition to enhanced public safety and convenience. During the 2000s, pork barrel spending requested by specific legislators took on a new name: **earmarks**. While they were the same particularized spending programs, the name changed. When defense spending was used to balloon earmark-related spending after September 11, 2011, calls for an end to such particularized spending increased. Earmark reform first came to Congress in 2007, when majority Democrats required public disclosure of all earmarks. When Republicans retook control of the House in 2011, they supposedly banned earmarks, but members still attempt to get around the ban.[4]

ONLINE 12.3 *The Trouble with Earmarks*
http://www.youtube.com/watch?v=5QcvQ7P86iU

Any efforts to curtail pork barrel expenditures are particularly difficult in times of budget surplus. Even though the Republicans controlled both the House and Senate during the 106th Congress, they found themselves adding many questionable items to the final appropriations bill at the end of the session in late 2000. In a speech on the Senate floor, Senator John McCain (R-Arizona), a longtime critic of pork barrel spending, claimed that "tens of billions in pork barrel and special-interest spending have been packed into these appropriations bills, as well as numerous provisions pushed by Capitol Hill lobbyists that the American public will not know about until after these bills become law." McCain complained that "all of this maneuvering and horse trading has been conducted behind closed doors, away from the public eye, bypassing a process whereby all of my elected colleagues could evaluate the merit of each budget item." McCain's comments were not so much directed at the pork barrel spending for fiscal year 2001, but rather at the underlying particularism engaged in by his colleagues, including many who had been critical of excessive spending. McCain was especially critical of further pork barrel spending in the spending bills for fiscal year 2002 that were added following the September 11, 2001 terrorist attacks.

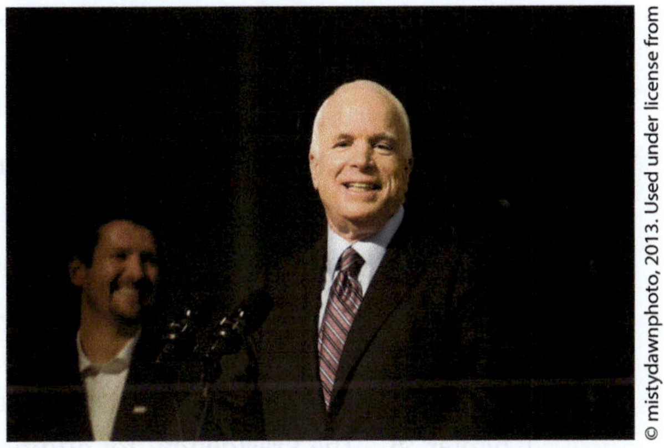

One must understand that some degree of particularism is the inevitable consequence of how representation in Congress (especially the House) is structured. A member's first concern is for the well-being of his district (or state in the case of the Senate). Members show their concern by obtaining federal money for projects and programs that benefit their constituents. In an age of fiscal surpluses, little pressure exists (other than condemnation from mavericks like Senator McCain) to control pork barrel spending.

12-2d Maintaining the System of Checks and Balances

The principle of separation of powers, which is a fundamental part of the philosophy underlying the Constitution, is designed to prevent tyranny. Because of the abuses experienced throughout the period of British rule, the executive branch was particularly suspect of being capable of tyrannical acts. Therefore, the Founders were quite concerned with providing Congress with the ability to place checks on executive power. Despite this effort to provide the principle of separation of power with some teeth, each branch has the responsibility to maintain the balance. Historically, Congress has had to hold its ground against persistent encroachment by the executive branch. Typically, presidents have asserted their powers most vigorously during times that demanded stronger and more decisive government leadership. Thus, the Civil War and the Great Depression provided Abraham Lincoln and Franklin D. Roosevelt, respectively, with the greatest opportunities for expanding the powers of the president at the expense of the Congress.

The Constitution has provided several methods for Congress to maintain checks on the other two branches. The most powerful check has already been discussed: the power of the purse. Neither the judiciary nor the executive branch is capable of doing anything without money. Of course, Congress does not have complete control over the budget because of the presidential veto.

Checking the Chief Executive

Congress can check presidential powers by several means. First, it can override a presidential veto by a two-thirds vote in each chamber. Second, all presidential appointments to either executive or judicial positions are subject to confirmation by the Senate, where a simple majority must vote to confirm. Third, the Senate must approve of all presidential treaties with other nations by a two-thirds vote. Fourth, Congress is responsible for oversight of the bureaucracy. Congress performs **oversight** when it examines the actions of the various departments and agencies to see whether they are executing the laws in a manner consistent with the intent of the legislature. Finally, Congress can impeach the president or any executive officer. The term *impeachment* technically refers to the action of the House of Representatives in adopting one or more articles of impeachment by a majority vote. To be removed from office, the impeached official must be convicted of "high crimes or misdemeanors" by the Senate. Only twice in our history have presidents been impeached, but both Andrew Johnson and Bill Clinton were acquitted by the Senate (see Chapter 13, "The Presidency," for additional discussion).

Checking the Court

The legislature spends much more time maintaining checks on executive power than judicial power, but its contacts with the judiciary can be quite dramatic, as evidenced by the Harriett Miers nomination controversy in 2005. Miers, a close confidant of President Bush, was his nominee to succeed Justice William Rehnquist, who had passed away. When members of the president's own party questioned Miers' capacity and training to serve on the court, the nomination was withdrawn.

Congress influences the judiciary in a number of ways. One way is through the judicial appointment process. All presidential nominations to the federal courts must be approved by the Senate. Usually, the confirmation hearings held in the Senate Judiciary Committee are less than sensational. The Senate is mainly interested in the qualifications and ideology of the person nominated. The Senate is unlikely to approve a nominee whose qualifications are seriously questioned or whose ideology is unacceptable to the majority of senators. This confirmation function, which the Constitution refers to as "advise and consent," helps shape the judiciary and, ultimately, the decisions that emerge from it.

Congress can attempt to undo judicial decisions in two ways. Court decisions based on the interpretation of a statute can be countered by amending the statute. Judicial decisions based on interpretation of the Constitution can be nullified by amending the Constitution itself. The latter is difficult to accomplish because it requires not only passage by a two-thirds vote in both chambers of Congress but also ratification by three-fourths of the states. Nevertheless, four times in our country's history, particular Supreme Court decisions have been reversed through the adoption of a constitutional amendment.[5]

The ultimate weapon that Congress may use against the judicial branch is impeachment. No justice of the Supreme Court has ever been removed from office by Congress. In 1801, Justice Samuel Chase was ordered to be impeached by the House, but he was narrowly acquitted in the Senate. The Chase proceeding set quite an important precedent: Federal judges are not to be impeached unless they are guilty of "high crimes or misdemeanors." Political differences between the Court and the Congress are not a proper basis for impeachment.

12-3 The Institutional Development of Congress

The first Congress in 1789 was composed of sixty-five House members and twenty-six senators. Each House member represented thirty thousand citizens. After a majority of legislators arrived in New York City, the first capital, legislative business began. Indeed, the First Congress began working before the inauguration of President Washington in April 1789. Some of its first concerns were the internal organization of each chamber, the issue of tariffs, the organization of the federal courts, and what title to use when addressing the president. Vice President John Adams, in his dual role as president of the Senate, pushed for discussion of the presidential title. Some of the suggested titles were His Mightiness the President of the United States of America and Protector of Their Liberties, His Highness, or His Mighty Highness. Several legislators scoffed at such pretensions. They referred to Adams as His Rotundity in mocking his proposals and eventually settled on a simpler title suggested by James Madison: the President of the United States.[6]

In the first few sessions of Congress, few formal rules or institutions constrained the legislators. Most of the action took place on the floor of each chamber. There were no permanent committees, and most of the debate on each bill was conducted on the floor. Ad hoc, or temporary, committees were formed as they were needed to work out the details of a bill. In one session, there were 350 ad hoc committees. Not until Thomas Jefferson's presidency, from 1801 to 1809, did Congress establish permanent, standing committees. The committees did not have fixed jurisdiction over a policy area, however, so they had little opportunity to block legislation or radically change proposals. Most committee chairs were considered close allies of President Jefferson. Through his "lieutenants" in the legislature, the president was able to dominate congressional actions.

Another important characteristic of the early Congress was that legislators were amateur politicians who would spend only a few years in Congress and then return to their district and continue their chosen professions. After the capital was moved to the new town of Washington, few people were interested in spending much time in a little town full of mosquitoes, high temperatures, and high humidity during the summer. Membership in Congress changed quite frequently. About half the House members in the second Congress were new. The average tenure of a member in the first ten Congresses was only four years. The legislative session was just a few months long, and by today's standard, few bills were discussed. Typically fewer than two hundred bills were considered in each of the first ten sessions of Congress.

Important differences also existed between the two chambers. Senators were chosen by state legislatures at that time, so they also differed somewhat in their attitudes. The Senate was much more of a "gentleman's club." It kept most of its meetings secret, and it was viewed as somewhat of an executive council in that it conferred more directly with administrative officers. By 1794, the Senate had removed the secrecy rule, but it still remained a much less active organization than the House. Senator John Quincy Adams wrote in his diary that "the year which this day expires has been distinguished in the course of my life by its barrenness of events."[7] The Senate proposed less legislation, spent less time in committees, and received less public attention than the House.

12-3a An Evolving Institution

Throughout the nineteenth century, the legislature changed from a largely disorganized body with few committees, no parties, and little stability in membership into a more professional, organized assembly. In 1810, the War Hawk faction, led by Henry Clay, won the congressional elections. Consequently, Clay was elected Speaker, and he quickly asserted himself by expanding the powers of the office. He was the first Speaker to make appointments to permanent committees independently from the president. He also established five House committees to oversee expenditures in the federal bureaucracy. One author notes that by 1814 "the committee system had become the dominant force in the chamber."[8] The committees became the congressional workhorses slogging through the grudging details of legislation. But the Speaker retained tight control over appointments to committees and their jurisdictions. From 1810 to 1910, the Speaker exerted tremendous control over the House.

The legislative workload also changed dramatically. In the Twelfth Congress, about 400 measures were introduced, but by the Twenty-Fourth Congress in 1835, more than 1,100 measures were being proposed. In the Sixtieth Congress, which met from 1907 to 1909, more than 38,000 proposals were introduced. Until the 1820s, Congress usually passed more than 50 percent of the proposals. But, as the total number of measures introduced grew, the percentage of bills that were passed dropped quite dramatically. By the twentieth century, fewer than 10 percent of the proposals, on average, were passed in Congress.

Differences between the House and the Senate also became more important politically from 1810 to 1910. Because of the equal representation of the states in the Senate and the rising tensions between the North and the South over the issue of slavery, the Senate became the primary battleground for legislative disputes over regional differences. Also, because it had no single leader as powerful as the Speaker of the House, the Senate maintained a bit more independence from tight leadership control. The Senate's committees evolved a bit more slowly than the system in the House, but the Senate also never had to experience a battle between its members and leaders like the one the House experienced in 1910.

The Strong Committee System

Until the twentieth century, most Speakers of the House had been relative amateurs. Of the thirty-three Speakers before 1899, twenty-five had fewer than eight years of service in the House before moving into the top position. None had more than fourteen years of service before being elected Speaker. Between 1899 and 1999, however, no Speaker was elected who had fewer than fifteen years of experience.[9] Almost all of them had at least twenty years of service before being chosen as Speaker. Because of the powerful position that Speakers had assumed in the House, the position became more prestigious. But as Speakers increasingly centralized their control over the House, other members became frustrated with the system. In 1910, House Republicans revolted against their leader, Speaker Joe Cannon. Cannon had been Speaker since 1903 and had wielded strong powers. He appointed committees, picked committee chairs, set the legislative calendar, decided who would get to speak on the floor during debate, and determined who would get to reconcile legislative differences with the Senate on conference committees. The Speaker's readiness to punish members who did not agree with him precipitated the revolt. In some cases, he had either failed to promote to a chair a member with the greatest seniority or had stripped a chair of his position.

The outcome of the insurgency against Cannon was a committee system that was much more independent of the Speaker. The committees would now enjoy a fixed jurisdiction over a particular policy area no matter how the Speaker felt about the issue. Furthermore, **seniority** on a committee (the number of years served continuously on the committee) would determine the ascent to leadership regardless of the member's relationship with the Speaker. Committees would also have more power over their own, internal rules of organization. Finally, the Speaker would no longer control appointments to the committees. The Ways and Means Committee, the committee responsible for tax policy, would now decide committee appointments. The overall effect of the revolt was that committee chairs became power brokers within the system who could make or break a bill.

Decentralization and Fragmentation

The strong committee system continued to control the House of Representatives until the 1970s. By that time, however, an undercurrent of dissent had been developing over the abuses of power by committee chairs. Because seniority determined who received the chair, members from safe seats were more likely to serve enough time to become a chair. A **safe seat** is a representative's district that is so one-sided that it always elects a member of the same party to the House. These types of seats were especially common in the South from the 1870s until the 1960s. Because the Republicans were the party of Abraham Lincoln and the Union in the Civil War, the South had few Republican politicians until the Democrats became involved with the civil rights movement in the 1960s. Consequently, many chairs in both chambers were southern Democrats who were quite conservative, particularly on civil rights issues. Many northern Democrats who were elected in the 1960s and 1970s felt stymied by a system that prevented them from pushing for civil rights, social welfare policy, and other liberal reforms. These new members were aware of the need to establish their own leadership credentials for election purposes. Also, these members were influenced by the political culture of the time, which was one of change and of questioning authority.

This influx of new members conspired against the power structure and brought on the most important reforms of Congress since 1910.

A series of reforms were instituted in the 1970s, but the three most important for congressional procedure were the elimination of the automatic seniority rule for becoming a chair, the institution of multiple referral, and the establishment of the so-called Subcommittee Bill of Rights. The Democrats in the House determined that seniority would still matter in determining rank within a committee, but they now ruled that a majority of votes among just the Democrats in the House could remove a chair. Though this rule has been used on few occasions, it has provided a powerful tool for constraining the power of chairs.

The **multiple referral system** also undermined the power of the chairs. Before the 1970s, a bill would go to only one committee to be considered. If the committee chair chose to ignore the bill, it would simply die in committee. If the bill was complex enough that it involved more than one issue area and another committee might be interested in influencing the legislation, there was no way for more than one committee to consider the bill. Multiple referral, however, allowed more than one committee to influence a piece of legislation. This move decentralized power in Congress by allowing more members access to legislation. Although this practice arguably made the process more democratic, it was also much more chaotic and inefficient. The practice was abolished in 1995 in favor of a **sequential referral system**, under which the Speaker can refer a bill to another committee after one committee has finished with it. Alternatively, the Speaker can refer parts of bills to separate committees, but cannot send an entire bill to more than one committee at a time.

The final major reform of the 1970s was the Subcommittee Bill of Rights. House Democrats also brought about this change. It removed several powers from the committee chair and secured certain powers and resources for the subcommittee. The subcommittees, or smaller units of the full committee, are responsible for considering one segment of the broad range of issues considered by the full committee. Subcommittees allow a small group of members an excellent opportunity to become experts in a particular policy area and to become influential on that issue. By guaranteeing them the right to their own rules, staff, jurisdictions, and funding, this reform allowed these small groups to have much greater leeway than was previously possible under the strong committee chair system. Combined with the other changes of the 1970s, these reforms decentralized power in Congress substantially. Pushing legislation through the House would become much more difficult for party leadership and the president.

Because senators have always enjoyed more access to debate and policy changes on the floor of the chamber, they have never felt compelled to make such massive changes in the Senate's rules. Because all senators have equal standing in amending a bill, what happens in committees is not as crucial as it is in the House. Therefore, the

Senate's rules have not undergone such dramatic reform. Subcommittees became more important in the Senate in the 1970s, but they still do not play the prominent role that they do in the House. Although the Senate's system of committees and subcommittees is less decentralized than that of the House, it has always provided greater opportunity for individual members to influence policy.

ONLINE 12.4 *Committees in Congress*
http://www.govtrack.us/congress/committees/

12-4 THE MEMBERS OF CONGRESS

In our discussion of descriptive representation in section 12-2a, "Representing Constituents," we posed this question: How closely does Congress resemble America? Throughout its history, members of Congress have been wealthier and better educated than the average American. The two most prominent professions throughout the years have been law and business. Most members have also been older than the average citizen, and most have been Christians. The average age of all representatives elected in 1994 was 52 years old, while the average age of senators was 58. Some commentators talked about the new blood that was injected into Congress after the 1992 and 1994 elections, but the average age dropped by less than half a year. Of the 535 representatives and senators elected in 1994, all except about 10 percent were Christians. Most of the rest were Jewish. In 1993, Roman Catholics formed the largest single religious group, with about 30 percent of the members.

Considering the restrictions on any type of political participation by females throughout most of the nineteenth century and the denial of political participation to most minorities in this country until the 1960s, it is not surprising that most members have been white males. Female representation has increased steadily since women gained the right to vote in 1920. The representation of African Americans has witnessed two distinct periods of involvement, and other minorities have only recently seen an infusion of members.

ONLINE 12.5 *Diversity in Congress*

12-4a FEMALE REPRESENTATION

During the 2000 New York senatorial campaign, many observers commented on the fact that Hillary Rodham Clinton could become New York's first female senator. Her≈subsequent victory over Republican Rick Lazio did propel her into a small but growing group of female senators. Although more than half the population is female, women never made up more than 10 percent of Congress until 1993. In 1973, it had fourteen female representatives and no female senators. By 1983, it still had only twenty-one female representatives and two female senators. The number of women on the ballot changed dramatically in 1992, however. In an election year dubbed the Year of the Woman, more than one hundred females won their party's nomination for a congressional seat. After all the elections in November 1992 and the races to fill vacant seats in 1993, a total of forty-eight women were in the House and six were in the Senate. The 1994 elections resulted in victories for forty-nine female representatives and eight female senators. By 2008, seventeen females represented their states in the Senate along with 78 in the House. Obviously, women have made substantial progress in penetrating this elite realm, but they still have a long way to go to reach parity with men.

12-4b Minority Representation

When Barack Obama (D-Illinois) was overwhelmingly elected to the U.S. Senate in November 2004, he became the only African American in that body. African American representation has experienced two distinct eras. The first was in the Reconstruction period, after the Civil War. The Thirteenth, Fourteenth, and Fifteenth Amendments to the Constitution passed in the years immediately after the war abolished slavery, conferred citizenship on all persons regardless of race or color, and guaranteed the right to vote regardless of race. Because the black population was heavily concentrated in the South, blacks were able to win seats in states where their voting rights were traditionally denied. Two African American senators, both from Mississippi (one ironically filling the seat abandoned by Confederate President Jefferson Davis before the war) were elected during the Reconstruction period. Twenty black representatives were elected from the South between 1870 and 1901. Because Lincoln and his party opposed slavery and southern secession, all African American representatives throughout this period were Republicans.

Despite the gains made during Reconstruction, discriminatory practices—such as the poll tax, literacy tests, and grandfather clauses—eventually prevented any new black representatives from being elected to Congress between 1901 and 1929. From 1929 until the 1960s, Congress had no more than five African Americans, and all were from outside the South. The Voting Rights Act of 1965 and the Twenty-Fourth Amendment, which banned the poll tax in federal elections, radically improved black turnout in the South, and the number of black legislators slowly began to rise. By 1973, fifteen African Americans were in the House and one was in the Senate. By 1983, the numbers had only improved slightly to twenty in the House and zero in the Senate. In 1982, however, an amendment to the Voting Rights Act made a radical change in the way districts could be drawn after the 1990 census. In effect, a state legislature had to increase the number of minority seats in the state no matter how the lines had to be drawn. If a state with ten House members had a 20 percent African American population, the state would have to make every effort to produce two districts that had a majority of African Americans. The law was at least partially responsible for raising the total from twenty-five House members in 1992 to forty voting members and one nonvoting member from the District of Columbia in 2008.

Other minorities did not experience the same rise and decline of representation during the Reconstruction period. All their gains have occurred in this century (see Table 12-1). Hispanics have had less than two hundred legislators in this country's history, but seventeen were elected in 1994, and two nonvoting members are from the territories of Puerto Rico and the Virgin Islands. Hispanics enjoyed the same benefits as African Americans in the application of the 1982 Voting Rights amendments to the redistricting process. Although two Hispanics served as senators in the past, the Senate has none now. The proportion of Hispanics in the Congress is 3.9 percent, but 9 percent of the general population is Hispanic. Asian Americans, the third-largest minority in the United States, are also underrepresented.

12-5 How Congress is Organized

The Constitution is largely silent on how Congress should conduct its business. It says that the House has the right to "choose their speaker and other officers" and "the Vice President of the United States will serve as the President of the Senate, but shall have no vote, unless they be equally divided." Indeed, the Senate that took office in January 2000 found itself in that predicament, with incoming Vice President Dick Cheney the potential tie-breaking vote.

The Senate can choose other officers, including a president pro tempore, who presides over the Senate "in the absence of the Vice President." The Constitution also states that each chamber must publish a "journal of its proceedings" and that each chamber "may determine the rules of its proceedings." How a bill passes in each chamber is not explained. No mention is made of committees or subcommittees. As is the case on many constitutional issues, the Founders provided a great deal of flexibility to allow future generations to shape the Constitution to their needs. Consequently, the organization of Congress has changed dramatically over time.

12-5a Leadership

Exerting leadership in either chamber of Congress is difficult in the modern age. Individual senators have always had a great deal of freedom to frustrate leaders trying to get legislation passed, but increasingly the House has also become a complex environment for leadership. The gradual breakdown of partisanship in the electorate that has increasingly caused members to run candidate-centered campaigns has also

TABLE 12-1

HOUSE	FEMALE	BLACK	HISPANIC
97th (1981-82)	19	16	6
98th (1983-84)	21	20	10
99th (1985-86)	22	19	11
100th (1987-88)	23	22	11
101st (1989-90)	25	23	11
102nd (1991-92)	29	25	10
103rd (1993-94)	48	38	17
104th (1995-96)	49	39	18
105th (1997-98)	51	37	18
106th (1999-2000)	58	39	19
107th (2001-02)	59	36	19
108th (2003-04)	59	37	23
109th (2005-06)	70	44	22
110th (2007-08)	71	44	23
111th (2009-10)	78	41	22
112th (2011-2012)	110	41	26
113th (2013-2014)	180	43	34
SENATE	**FEMALE**	**BLACK**	**HISPANIC**
97th (1981-82)	2	0	0
98th (1983-84)	2	0	0
99th (1985-86)	2	0	0
100th (1987-88)	2	0	0
101st (1989-90)	2	0	0
102nd (1991-92)	2	0	0
103rd (1993-94)	6	1	0
104th (1995-96)	8	1	0
105th (1997-98)	9	1	0
106th (1999-2000)	9	0	0
107th (2001-02)	13	0	0
108th (2003-04)	14	0	0
109th (2005-06)	12	1	1
110th (2007-08)	14	1	2
111th (2009-10)	17	1	3
112th (2011-2012)	16	1	4
113th (2013-2014)	20	2	4

Source: Adapted from Harold W. Stanley and Richard Niemi's *Vital Statistics on American Politics 2003-2004*, http://www.diversityinbusiness.com/dib2006/dib20611/News_HispanicVote.htm, http://baic.house.gov/historical-data/representatives-senators-by-congress.html?congress=109, and http://womenincongress.house.gov/historical-data/representatives-senators-by-congress.html?congress=111 allowed members greater freedom from the party leadership. When parties were the dominant factor in campaigns, the party leaders could use more coercion to force the rank-and-file members to stay in line with the party. The modern Congress, however, is composed of 535 individual enterprises who are in the business of getting reelected. Toeing the party line for a president or Speaker who cannot do much to influence one's reelection opportunities is not the highest priority for the modern member of Congress, who is most interested in the game of survival. The modern congressional leader cannot be a tyrant. Rather, the modern leader is forced to negotiate, compromise, and work to form coalitions to get legislation passed. One member has stated, "Once in a while we need more than good leadership—we also need good followership."[10]

Leadership in each chamber is divided along party lines. Each party in each chamber has its own caucus. The **party caucus** is an organization composed of the members of one party in each chamber, although the organization is not formally part of the legislature. The caucus is used to determine how leaders will be chosen and how committee assignments will be made. Soon after an election and before the next session of Congress has met, each party in each chamber convenes a meeting of its caucus to choose its leaders and form a committee to determine party choices for the standing committees of Congress. The actual committee assignments and the election of the Speaker or president pro tempore must occur on the floor of each chamber, but the party decisions are routinely approved by the majority on the floor. Practically, though not formally, each party makes the decisions on committee assignments of its own members. The majority party, by virtue of its numerical dominance, always wins a floor vote on the position of Speaker of the House and president pro tempore in the Senate.

House Leadership

The Speaker is the most important leadership position in the House. The Constitution does not require that the Speaker be a member of Congress. However, that has always been the case. The Speaker's power peaked at the turn of the twentieth century, but it is still a powerful position. Through the party leadership on the Rules Committee, the Speaker controls the schedule for all House business. The Speaker also has the power to recognize members during debate. Perhaps most important in the media age, the Speaker has become the spokesperson for the majority party in the House. When the president has been of the opposite party (as was the case from 1981 to 1993, when Democrats controlled the House and Republicans were in the White House, and from 1994 to 2000, with a Democratic president and a Republican Congress), the role of the Speaker has been particularly important. Although Newt Gingrich was unquestionably the key player in the Republican victory in 1994, his stewardship of the Republican majority was not nearly so effective. Indeed, the leadership's miscalculation in confronting President Clinton on the shutdown of the government in 1995 played a key role in rebuilding Clinton's popularity for his successful reelection bid in 1996.

Next to the Speaker, the two highest-ranking leaders of the House are the majority leader and the majority whip. The **majority leader** is the second-highest-ranking leader of the majority party. While the Speaker presides over floor debate from the podium at the front of the House, the majority leader controls the party's efforts on the floor. Like the Speaker, the majority leader and majority whip are elected by the party caucus. Typically, a member moves from one job to another as positions become vacant, but it is possible for other party leaders to contest the election. The **majority whip** is responsible for closely watching party members to determine how they plan to vote and whether they will be in attendance for a vote. The whip is the "eyes and ears" of the party leadership. The whip is also responsible for notifying members in advance of important legislation. Each bill has a floor manager who controls debate for just that bill. The floor manager works closely with the majority leader in pushing the legislation through the chamber. This job calls on strong persuasive skills and a keen ability to count votes. In the late 1990s, these types of skills earned the Republican whip Tom Delay the nickname "the hammer."

The minority party also has its own leader and whip. Because the majority party controls floor debate, the minority leadership has less effect on legislation. The minority leadership works with the majority leadership in arranging the legislative calendar, but it also works against the majority party in attempting to defeat the majority's legislative agenda.

One can easily underestimate the importance of which party is the majority party. The Democrats controlled both Houses of Congress for the better part of a half-century before the Republicans captured the House and the Senate in the important 1994 midterm election. During their decades of control, the Democrats were able to staff and run important committees and support functions. In many ways, their control over day-to-day congressional functions helped bring about their demise. One example, the Congressional post office, often served as a no-interest "bank" for many (mostly Democratic) members. The ensuing scandal greatly scarred the Democratic party. After the Republicans' ascendance, they pledged a more open administration of the House.

ONLINE 12.6 *Leadership in Congress*

The Rise and Fall of Newt Gingrich

The nature of the presidency has always highlighted the personality of the person holding the office. If anything, this phenomenon has been heightened in the age of television. Ronald Reagan personalized the office in a unique way. Bill Clinton was in many ways a "celebrity president," viewed by many almost as a movie or rock star.

But Congress, by its nature, a mass institution of 535 members, is not usually framed in personal terms. Even its leaders have not traditionally been well known by the general public. However, the campaign of 1994 changed all that.

The Democrats controlled the House of Representatives for a half-century before the Republicans won a landmark majority in 1994. The landmark victory could be attributed to many factors. Voters were apparently dissatisfied with the direction of the first two years of the Clinton administration, which had struggled with a failed national healthcare proposal. The Republican leader, Newt Gingrich, of Georgia, successfully challenged the maxim that "all politics is local" by nationalizing the campaign around a Contract with America. The vast majority of Republican Senate and House candidates signed on to this commitment to bring change to the way Congress worked and to support specific legislation in a number of areas. This national strategy captured the attention of Republican supporters, who turned out in greater numbers than their Democratic counterparts. The victory catapulted Newt Gingrich into the job he had always wanted—Speaker of the House of Representatives. He was *Time* magazine's 1995 Man of the Year. A historian by training, Gingrich saw himself as a major historical figure.

Yet by 2000 the Republicans were struggling to hold on to their majority. Bill Clinton had resurrected his image in 1996 in large part on the basis of his epic budget battle with Gingrich, whose strategic decision to play a high-stakes poker game with the president proved to be his undoing. Gingrich, so successful in his behind-the-scenes role in creating the 1994 victory, had become a visible public figure and, in many ways, the best thing that happened to Bill Clinton. Gingrich became a symbol of Republican "excess" and "extremism" against which Clinton and the Democrats could position themselves. Soon, Gingrich was more of a political liability than a benefit. He was censured for mishandling the finances of his own political action committee (PAC).

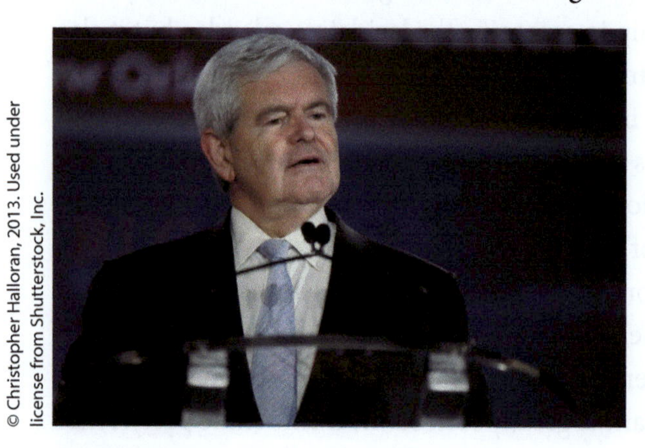

Newt Gingrich

Gingrich's political demise was as much personal as it was ideological. Ironically, his downfall came in the midst of another classic conflict between the Republicans and Clinton: the impeachment battle of 1999. The president was under attack for behavior stemming from personal, moral shortcomings. Yet Gingrich was strangely silent. He had been having a relationship with an aide, and his marriage had ended. Bill Clinton retained his presidency buttressed by continuing high levels of public support, while

Gingrich resigned as Speaker and also from Congress. To replace Gingrich as Speaker, the Republican caucus chose a much less visible and controversial figure, Representative Dennis Hastert, of Illinois. The contrast could not be more stark. While Gingrich is visionary, pugnacious, and confrontational, Hastert is pragmatic, reserved, and more conciliatory. Whereas Gingrich sought the national spotlight, Hastert is more content to stay behind the scenes. Whereas Gingrich was an easy target for Democrats, the personable Hastert does not inspire partisan rancor.

Leadership in the Senate

The Senate is quite different from the House in that it has no Speaker. The vice president officially serves as the presiding officer of the Senate, but vice presidents rarely perform this role except at the beginning of a session, at the president's State of the Union address to Congress, or in the case of a tie vote. Otherwise, the president pro tempore, a member elected by the rest of the Senate, serves as the presiding officer on a day-to-day basis. Often, the president pro tempore passes the power of the chair over to another senator on a temporary basis. The powers of the president pro tempore are in no way similar to the Speaker's in the House, and they never have been. The position is not even considered the most powerful in the Senate.

The majority leader is the most powerful figure in the Senate, but still has less power than the Speaker of the House. Because the rules of the Senate allow individual legislators considerable freedom to propose legislation or speak on a bill, the majority leader cannot push a bill through the Senate as easily as the Speaker can in the House. The majority whip in the Senate performs much the same role as the whip in the House.

The minority party leader has more leeway to frustrate the majority in the Senate than the minority leader has in the House. Therefore, when the House, Senate, and presidency are all controlled by one party (as was the case in 1993), the Senate minority leader becomes the "point person" for the opposition. For example, during the first Clinton term, the Senate minority leaders Bob Dole (R-Kansas) and Trent Lott (R-Mississippi) assumed the role of leading the Republican opposition, not just in Congress but also in the country. Dole resigned to run for president in 1996. Although he lost, Republicans gained control of the Senate, allowing Trent Lott to become the majority leader.

The 2000 Election and the Jeffords Defection

The election of 2000 left the Senate split evenly—fifty Democrats versus fifty Republicans. It was the first time in more than one hundred years that the Senate had been split down the middle. The even split necessitated a "power sharing" arrangement between the Republican and Democratic leadership. Because ties in the Senate are broken by the president of the Senate (who is also the vice president of the United States), and because the president of the Senate was Republican Vice President Dick Cheney, Republican leader Trent Lott remained as majority leader; Democrat Tom Daschle remained as minority leader. However, the two leaders agreed to have equal committee memberships and equal staff payrolls. Senator John Breaux, a conservative Democrat from Louisiana, observed, "Power sharing was the first real test of bipartisanship in the new fifty-fifty Senate, and we passed."

The power sharing arrangement did not last long enough to allow an assessment, however. In May 2001, Senator James Jeffords, of Vermont, miffed at some of President Bush's legislative agenda and clearly angry at what he regarded as pressure from the leadership, announced that he was switching from the Republican party to Independent status. In making this switch, he also decided to vote with the Democrats on organizational matters. The upshot was an unprecedented change in control from the Republicans to the Democrats. As a result of the Jeffords defection, Democrats were in a position to exert considerable control over the legislative process. They chaired committees, and, as we have noted, the prerogatives of chairmanship are considerable. For instance, Senator Edward M. Kennedy's (D-Massachusetts) leadership of the Judiciary Committee enabled him to have a major effect on confirmation hearings for President Bush's nominees to the federal bench.

The 2006 Exchange of Power

As President George W. Bush's second term was starting, so was the end of his time as president. Term-limited from running a third time, Bush was a lame duck. Beyond Bush's status, the tide of public opinion had turned against the War on Terror and Republicans who had supported the president leading up to and through the invasion of Iraq suffered at the polls. Bush had also expended significant political capital unsuccessfully attempting to get a partial privatization of Social Security. Finally, the public looked at the administration's response to Hurricane Katrina as a major failing of Bush's leadership. Without Bush on the ticket, the 2006 Congressional elections became a proxy for voters, punishing Bush's party when they could not punish him. Democrats won 31 seats in the House of Representatives to take control of the chamber after twelve years out of power. In the process, American voters elected the first female Speaker of the House in history, California's Nancy Pelosi. Democrats also took control of the Senate, with forty-nine Democrats and two Independents who caucused with the party, giving them a 51–49 majority.[11]

The 2008 Landslide

After taking control of Congress in 2006, Democrats looked to build on their successes in 2008. A number of factors helped. Most importantly, Republicans were retiring from Congress at rates comparable to those of Democrats in 1994.

Twenty-seven Republicans decided to run for other seats or end their time in office in 2008. Only six Democrats retired. Fourteen Republicans were defeated in the general election, along with three others who lost their primaries. Of the thirteen open seat elections, Democrats won them all. In the Senate, the gains were even more significant. Democrats gained eight seats in the Senate, including comedian Al Franken, who won narrowly after a five-month recount process was contested in court, beating incumbent Minnesota Senator Norm Coleman. Franken's election gave Democrats sixty seats in the Senate, enough to invalidate any Republican filibusters. Effectively, the Democratic win in the 2008 cycle gave Democrats absolute power over Congress.[12]

The Tea Party and the Obamacare Referendum of 2010

Just as Bill Clinton learned during his first two years in office, having both chambers of Congress controlled by your partisans is a double-edged sword. First, it is still difficult to get things accomplished because of the lack of party discipline in the presidential legislative system. Second, you have nobody else to blame if you struggle or overstep your authority. President Obama carefully navigated a controversial healthcare reform through Congress, the Patient Protection and Affordable Care Act of 2010, now commonly referred to as "Obamacare." The provisions of the bill, which required all Americans to have some form of health insurance or pay a fine to be included in indemnity insurance pools, touched off anger from the growing Tea Party movement. Town hall meetings with legislators were contentious affairs the summer leading in to the election. Using concern over the costs and expanding federal government reach of the law, conservative Tea Party candidates won in districts across the country and Republicans retook control of the House of Representatives.

12-5b Committees

Although most of the leadership's influence over legislation is exerted on the floor of each chamber, most of the actual work that goes into making legislation occurs in the standing committees of Congress. Though never mentioned in the Constitution, temporary committees for working out the details of legislation were routinely used in the early Congresses. By Jefferson's presidency, some committees were made permanent. After the revolt against Speaker Cannon in 1910, committees were given fixed jurisdiction over particular issues and control over their own rules for conducting business. The committee system had always been important, but since 1910 it has been the dominant institutional feature of Congress.

Four types of committees are in Congress. By far the most important are the standing committees. **Standing committees** possess authority to consider legislation within a fixed policy domain. For example, the Ways and Means Committee in the House considers all tax legislation proposed in the House. Although there are some exceptional means of passing legislation that has not been through the proper committee, almost all major pieces of legislation must pass in committee before reaching the floor of the House. That is not true for the Senate, however. Some bills never pass through the Senate committee system. See Table 12-2 for the list of standing committees of Congress.

Another important type of legislative committee is the conference committee. A **conference committee** exists only temporarily when the two chambers need to reconcile differences between two versions of the same bill. Both chambers must pass exactly the same version of a bill before it can go to the president to be signed into law. If the House and the Senate have passed different versions, they may agree to form a conference committee composed of an equal number of representatives and senators who will work out the differences. If the two sides cannot agree, the bill dies. Sometimes, the conference committee agrees, only to find that the compromise will

TABLE 12-2

SENATE COMMITTEES	HOUSE COMMITTEES
Aging	Agriculture
Agriculture, Nutrition, and Forestry	Appropriations
Appropriations	Armed Services
Armed Services	Budget
Banking, Housing, and Urban Affairs	Education and the Workforce
Budget	Energy and Commerce
Commerce, Science, and Transportation	Ethics
Energy and Natural Resources	Financial Services
Environment and Public Works	Foreign Affairs
Ethics	Homeland Security
Finance	House Administration
Foreign Relations	Intelligence
Health, Education, Labor, and Pensions	Judiciary
Homeland Security and Governmental Affairs	Natural Resources
Indian Affairs	Oversight and Government Reform
Intelligence	Rules
Judiciary	Science, Space, and Technology
Rules and Administration	Small Business
Small Business and Entrepreneurship	Transportation and Infrastructure
United States Senate Caucus on International Narcotics Control	Veterans' Affairs
Veterans' Affairs	Ways and Means

Source: http://www.govtrack.us/congress/committees/

not pass the House or Senate. That was the case in 1994 with President Clinton's crime bill. House Republicans objected to the increased social spending added to the bill by the conference committee. The bill passed the House only after this spending was scaled back. Later, the revised compromise bill faced considerable opposition in the Senate, but it eventually passed there too.

The other kinds of committees are less important to the passage of legislation. **Select committees**, or **special committees**, are temporary panels that allow members to investigate a problem and make recommendations for legislation. The special committees do not have the power to propose or pass legislation, however. Likewise, **joint committees** have no legislative authority. Members from each chamber sit on joint committees that deal with special topics of interest to Congress as a whole. For example, a joint committee oversees the Library of Congress. Joint committees are more administrative in nature and do not propose or pass legislation.

Subcommittees have become an increasingly important part of the committee system in Congress, particularly in the House. **Subcommittees** are units that exist within a full standing committee to consider one narrow issue within the overall policy area considered by the full committee. For example, the Foreign Affairs Committee has a subcommittee for each different region of the world, and the Agriculture Committee has subcommittees for different sectors of the farming economy, such as livestock, commodities, and crops. Subcommittees play a more important role in the House than in the Senate. Because representatives sit on fewer committees than senators and more people are on each full standing committee, representatives are more likely to focus attention on subcommittee work. Almost all the House committees make extensive use of their subcommittees, but some Senate committees spend little time in subcommittee consideration of a bill.

12-5c STAFF

Congress employs more than twenty-five thousand people (see Figure 12-1). The functions performed by these employees include security, maintenance, research, clerical help, and assistance with casework. The Capitol Police Force and Architect's Office hire more than three thousand workers to provide physical support of the Capitol grounds, and the four agencies that provide general legislative support have more than ten thousand employees. The remainder work either directly for members on their personal staffs or on committee or leadership staffs.

Each member of Congress, regardless of party affiliation or seniority, receives an allowance for personal staff. In 2012 allowances ranged from $1,270,129 to $1,564,613, with an average of $1,353,205. The total amount available to a senator is the sum of two personnel allowances (administrative and clerical assistance and legislative assistance) and the office expense allowance. In fiscal year 2013 the Senate allowance figures varied

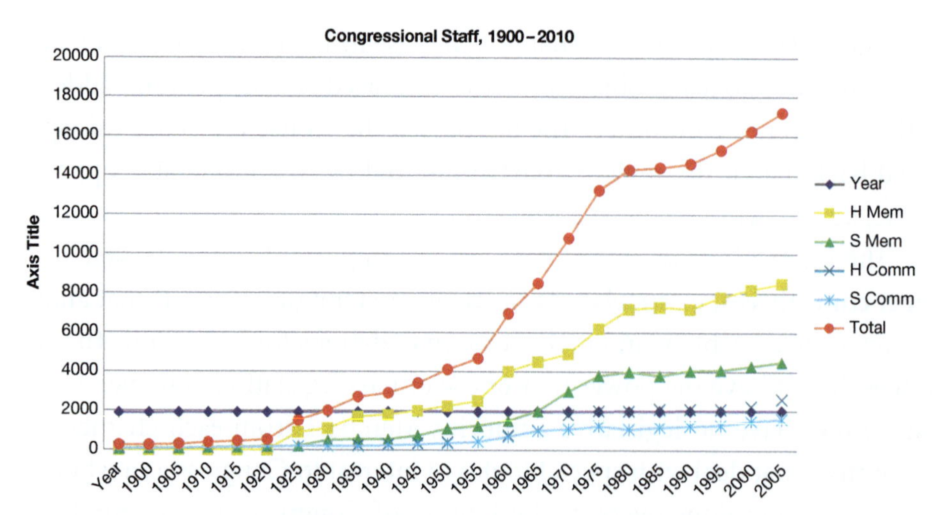

Figure 12-1 *Increase in Congressional Staff, 1930–2005*

Source: Adapted from Norman J. Ornstein, Thomas E. Mann, and Michael J. Malbin, Vital Statistics on Congress 1999–2000 (Washington, D.C.: AEI Press, 2000), pp. 130–31. and from OpenCRS Reports at https://opencrs.com/document/R40056/2008-10-15/

from $2,361,820 for a senator representing a state with a population under 5 million to $3,753,614 for a senator representing a state with a population of 28 million or more.[13] Based on the role that a staffer fulfills, their salary can vary widely. A U.S. Representative's district caseworker takes in just over $31,000 a year, while the district director makes more than twice that much. Chiefs of staff make the most money, at $97,000 in the House and $116,000 in the Senate. The member may use these employees for many activities, including scheduling, handling mail, performing clerical work, answering phones, helping to formulate policy, meeting with administrators, dealing with lobbyists, or helping to negotiate with other legislators. On the whole, however, the personal staff members devote most of their time and attention to helping the legislator deal with constituents. Staff members handle most casework requests. The House has more than 6,000 full-time personal staff members, and the Senate employs more than 3,400.

Personal staff members provide a wide range of services, such as organizing the member's schedule, handling the mail, answering the phones, assisting with legislation, and representing the member at an assortment of meetings. Their most important function is working to maintain good relations with the constituents in the district. Considering that the member can hire more than twenty persons in either Washington or the home district, you can easily see how a large amount of casework can regularly be provided to the district. Of course, each member's fondest hope is that all assistance provided to a constituent will be rewarded in the future with a vote.

In addition to staff allowances, each member also receives funding for an office in Washington and at least one office in the home district. The allocation for the home office depends on local cost factors and the number of people the member represents. Senators tend to get more money because they represent more people and have larger districts, in terms of physical space, than representatives. The allowance provides for office rental, furnishings, communication equipment (such as telephones and fax machines), stationery, and other office necessities. The total cost per House member now approaches $200,000. In the Senate, the cost ranges from $127,000 to $470,000.[14]

Of the personal staff provided to members, about 45 percent in the House and 30 percent in the Senate, on average, work in the district rather than in Washington.[15] Although it is difficult to evaluate how much the constituent service role affects the job of the average Washington staffer, the vast majority of the time spent by the district staffers is clearly devoted to the continuous care of the legislator's constituents. Most members, however, are not willing to rely exclusively on staff resources for maintaining voter contact. Because the maxim among congressional candidates is that all politics is local, members want to spend time in the district personally. To allow this, the members have provided themselves with travel allowances. In the early 1970s, the rules allowed reimbursement for a set number of trips back to the district, although members now have an overall budget allowance that does not limit the number of trips. Most members, if they care to do so, can fly home to the district on the government's tab every weekend during the session. Considering that few official meetings take place on Monday mornings or Fridays, many legislators spend only Tuesday, Wednesday, and Thursday in Washington. The rest of the week can be spent in the district, making public appearances that look good to voters or raising money for the next campaign.

Committee and Leadership Staff

In addition to members' personal staff, each chamber provides staff for the committees, the leadership, and officers of the chamber. Because most of the personal staff members are busy helping the legislator with constituents in the district, the committee staff must provide most of the assistance on research and policy formulation. The House has approximately fourteen hundred full-time committee staffers, and the Senate employs just fewer than one thousand. In addition, the leadership needs extra assistance in establishing the legislative schedule, arranging party caucuses, and organizing the party's legislative strategy. The House and Senate each have more than one hundred leadership staff positions. Each chamber also hires officers of the chamber, such as the parliamentarian, the doorkeeper, and the clerk. These officers perform the administrative tasks of keeping the institution running.

12-5d Agencies Providing Assistance to Congress

Three main agencies assist Congress in investigating the bureaucracy, providing research on legislation, producing a budget, and assessing technological advances. For the most part, the thousands of workers in these agencies allow the legislature to be less reliant on the executive branch for sources of information.

The Library of Congress has nearly five thousand employees who provide the legislature with one of the most complete library collections in the world. The library is open to the public, and it specializes in providing research to Congress through the Congressional Research Service (CRS). The CRS was founded in 1914, as the Legislative Reference Service, to provide nonpartisan research to members of Congress. Any member can make almost any kind of request. The CRS provides long-term research on policy, but it does not make recommendations. It also spends time responding to smaller requests by members for historical or statistical references for a speech or letter to a constituent. CRS reports on most topics are available to the public through members of Congress.

The General Accounting Office (GAO) performs oversight of the bureaucracy for Congress. In particular, the GAO investigates how money appropriated by Congress has been spent. Many scandals on excessive government spending, such as five hundred dollar toilet seats on a military plane or one hundred dollar screwdrivers, have been uncovered by GAO studies. The GAO, developed in 1921, is the largest congressional support agency, with more than five thousand employees.

The Congressional Budget Office (CBO) was also a product of the 1970s reforms (see Figure 12-2). The 1974 Budget and Impoundment Control Act was passed in response to what the Democrats in Congress viewed as an abuse of power by President Nixon in his handling of the budget. As part of an effort to assert greater influence on the budget process and to rely less on the executive branch for the details needed to form budget policy, Congress formed the CBO. The CBO, which has about 225 employees, provides Congress with assessments of the economic and budgetary effect of policy proposals. The assumptions developed by the CBO for assessing the budget are often in conflict with the president's numbers, which are developed by the Office of Management and Budget (OMB). One of the annual rituals of the budget process is a battle over whose numbers (the CBO's or the OMB's) should be used. During the 1980s, the Democrats controlling Congress became increasingly reliant on the CBO numbers rather than trust the Reagan or Bush OMB numbers. Beginning in 1993, Congress and President Clinton agreed to use a common set of assumptions for developing budgets.

12-6 How Congress Makes Laws

Over the years, the process by which Congress passes a bill has become increasingly complex. In the first few Congresses, most debate on legislative details took place on the floor of each chamber, with few formal rules and no permanent committees. Since the 1990s, however, most bills must pass through a complicated maze of committees, subcommittees, and legislative calendars just to reach the floor of one chamber. If a bill passes on the floor, it must begin a similar process in the other chamber. Then differences between the House and Senate versions of the bill must be ironed out. Finally, the bill must pass the scrutiny of the president, who must either accept or reject the bill in its entirety.

Before describing the policy process, we must point out how much the rules and institutions of the two chambers differ. In general, the House is much more structured than the Senate. Because of a tradition of more deliberation on the floor of the Senate, the fact that representatives are more numerous than senators, and the absence of a filibuster in the House, a senator has much more freedom to debate, amend, and vote on all parts of a bill. The House restricts who can speak on a bill, how long someone can speak, and whether someone can propose any changes in the bill through amendments. Unless a representative is a party leader, she will have few chances to speak during floor debate. The most likely opportunity will come during the consideration of a bill that was originally debated in a committee of which the representative is a member. Otherwise, a representative has access to the floor only during the period when noncontroversial measures are considered or during the hours after the rest of the legislature has gone home. At this point, the floor is open to any member who cares to speak to a couple of cameras in front of an empty room. Conversely, all senators have equal access to speak, propose amendments, or even talk a bill to death by using a filibuster. No rules exist to control speech on the Senate floor.

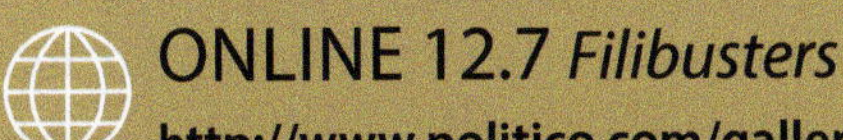

ONLINE 12.7 *Filibusters*

http://www.politico.com/gallery/2012/12/longest-filibusters-in-history/000608-008553.html#.UTeyy0C_KQQ.email

In addition, bypassing the committee system in the House is difficult, but a senator can do so quite easily by adding a rider at any time. A **rider** is an amendment to a bill that is not directly related to the policy issue in the original bill. The Senate allows this, but the House permits only amendments that are germane (or related to the same topic). Senators may use riders to attach to a bill that is certain to become law a favorite pork barrel project or a piece of legislation that is opposed by the president.

Because of these differences, no senator has an excuse for not "speaking his mind" on a bill or amendment. Therefore, senators must be prepared to speak on a wider variety of issues than most representatives. Furthermore, because only a hundred senators deal with as many issues as the House, discuss almost as many bills as the House, and participate in nearly as many committee and subcommittee meetings as the House, senators spend less time on formulating details than representatives do. Representatives are much more likely to specialize in a particular policy area that is considered in their committee or subcommittee assignments. Because of their limited access to most bills on the floor, representatives must become experts in a particular policy area to gain influence in the chamber.

12-6a Bill Referral

The first step in enacting legislation is to have a member of Congress place a copy of a bill in the hopper. Though the media often speak of the president proposing legislation, only a member of Congress can introduce a bill. On average, about ten thousand bills are proposed in each two-year Congress. Before any action can be taken, the bill must be referred to one of the standing committees. In the House, the Speaker has control over this process, but the parliamentarian, a staff person responsible to the Speaker, routinely handles most referrals. In the Senate, the presiding officer formally controls referral, but the Senate parliamentarian handles most cases. Because committees have a fixed jurisdiction over bills in a particular policy area, there is not much discretion on most bills. After a bill has been referred, the committee chair is responsible for deciding whether it will receive any action. Most bills simply die of neglect in committee. Of the 7,732 bills proposed in the 105th Congress (1997–1999), only 394 were enacted into law.[16] The overwhelming majority of these bills died in committee.

12-6b Committee Action

In most House committees and some Senate committees, a subcommittee of the full committee first considers the bill. For example, all bills relating to agriculture are referred to the House Agriculture Committee; a bill on subsidies to tobacco farmers goes to a subcommittee on farm commodities. The subcommittee likely holds a public hearing in which experts from government, think tanks, industry, and interest groups can testify on the bill and discuss any problems with current regulation or the absence of government intervention. Next, the subcommittee holds a **markup session** in which members of the subcommittee revise the bill—sometimes drastically and sometimes only slightly. The reason they call it a markup is that they literally cross out the sections they do not like. The subcommittee then sends the bill to the full committee, where the bill may again receive a hearing and markup. The final step in the committee process is the committee report on the bill. The committee expresses its sentiments in the report, which may be as long as a thousand pages. The committee issues a majority report that usually provides reasons for passing the legislation, a minority report, and additional or supplemental views.

12-6c Getting a Bill to the Floor

Bills take different paths to get to the House and Senate floors. The House uses a **Rules Committee** to establish when a bill will be placed on the legislative calendar, how much debate will be allowed, and whether amendments will be permitted. The resolution specifying this type of information is forwarded from the Rules Committee to the House floor. A majority on the floor must approve the rule. In contrast, the Senate uses negotiations between the majority and minority party leadership to determine when a bill will be debated. There are no limits on debate or the number of amendments. Often, the Senate uses **unanimous consent agreements** as a means of establishing some format for considering a bill, but these types of agreements are quite fragile. Any senator may block this type of agreement to expand debate or add an amendment. Because of the Senate's more open rules, it is much more difficult for party leadership or the president to steer a bill through that chamber.

12-6d Dislodging Bills from Committees

Both the House and Senate have procedures whereby bills can be dislodged from committees that have taken no action on them. In the House, 218 members (50 percent plus one) must sign a discharge petition. In the Senate, dislodgment can be effected through an ordinary floor motion, which of course requires a majority vote. These dislodgment rules are seldom invoked. In the House, the Speaker often brings a bill to the floor when the number of members signing the petition approaches the necessary majority. In the Senate, there really is no need to move for dislodgement because Senate rules allow a bill to come to the floor as an amendment to another bill already under consideration.

12-6e Calendars

After a bill reaches the floor in the House, it is placed on a particular calendar. The calendars are used to divide legislation into noncontroversial minor bills and major bills. Each calendar has a set schedule during the month, and each has its own rules. Note that much of the legislation that Congress passes ends up on the minor bills' calendars. More than one-third of all public laws are commemorative in nature. They could include bills naming a certain date to be National Cheese Day or congratulating the New York Yankees for winning the World Series (again). Administrative actions include electing a Speaker or determining a date of adjournment. Of the substantive bills, fewer than twenty-five would be considered major pieces of legislation, such as the Clean Air Act or the welfare reform bill.

The Senate uses only two calendars to divide up its workload. The Executive Calendar deals with treaties that must be ratified and presidential nominations, such as cabinet secretaries and federal judges, who must be confirmed. The Calendar of Business is the general calendar that can be used for any other legislation. The leadership does not have to provide advance notice of the agenda for the following week, but it has become customary for the majority party leadership to notify other members. The agenda is discussed on the floor, a notice is printed in the *Daily Digest* and the

Congressional Program Ahead, and the party whips are responsible for sending out whip notices, whip advisories, and whip issue papers on forthcoming legislative action.

12-6f Floor Procedure

House consideration of a bill entails five basic steps. First, the floor must accept the resolution that lays out the rule granted by the Rules Committee. Second, the House places itself into the Committee of the Whole. The **Committee of the Whole** is a device used by the House to expedite consideration of a bill. In essence, the full House can then act as though it were a committee. The advantage is that the House can then follow several rules that are more lenient than the full-chamber rules, such as a smaller number of legislators who must be present for business in order to proceed (called a **quorum**), a five-minute rule on debate of any amendment, and an easier process for closing debate.

After taking itself out of the Committee of the Whole, the floor moves into general debate. Generally, one hour of debate is allowed. Each party has a floor manager, usually a member from the committee with original jurisdiction over the bill, who controls the time for the party. For the most part, committee members dominate the time set aside for debate. The floor manager is extremely important to the passage of the legislation because consideration of the bill can be obstructed or delayed in numerous ways. A hostile member can propose numerous amendments, require recorded votes for every amendment, demand quorum calls so that time must be taken for each member to check in, or ask for a complete reading, word for word, of the bill and its amendments. Because time is such a precious commodity in a tightly packed schedule, delays can cause the party leadership to abandon a bill.

After general debate, the amendment process occurs. What happens at this stage is determined largely by the rule that was passed for the bill. The Rules Committee could have established a closed rule that allows no amendments. A modified rule is also possible. The modified rule may determine who can amend a bill or what sections may be amended or how many amendments are allowed. An open rule allows all proposed amendments to be considered. Each section of the bill is announced, and each amendment affecting that section is considered. Each amendment receives only five minutes for the proponent to speak and five minutes for any opponents. The amendments can vary in importance and in the level of change being proposed. Some amendments change only a few words of minor consequence. Others may be designed to kill the entire bill. The floor manager has the responsibility to fend off the more hostile amendments.

The final consideration of the bill divides the amendments into recorded and nonrecorded blocs. The nonrecorded amendments are usually not controversial and are passed with a voice vote. All members present simply yell out their voting preference, and the chair determines whether the ayes or nays have won. A standing vote, in which each member stands to be counted for one side or the other, is also possible. The recorded votes on more controversial amendments have been cast by **electronic voting** since 1973. Each member has a personalized card (somewhat like a bank ATM card) that allows access to one of the voting machines in the chamber. The member inserts the card and pushes a button for Yes, No, or Present But Not Voting. The vote on the final bill also uses the electronic voting method. In the 106th Congress (1999–2000), the House recorded 603 total votes, and the Senate cast 298.

Overall, the legislative process includes a series of obstacles that can prevent the passage of a bill. Many observers have noted that the process provides a number of veto points at which any opponent can try to kill a bill. Indeed, in the 106th Congress, only 580 passed both chambers of Congress and were approved by the president so that they could become public laws.

12-7 An Institution under Scrutiny

The most salient feature of congressional elections is that most members, if they want, are returned to Congress after every election. The trend over the past twenty years has been that more than 90 percent of House members seeking reelection have been returned to Congress. Senators have experienced slightly lower reelection rates, but the vast majority are also reelected. Many observers have found these turnover rates disquieting, particularly in light of public opinion polls showing a relatively poor rating for Congress as an institution. Even most members of Congress make fun of the institution when they are talking to constituents in the district.

Congressman Les Aspin once quipped, "I don't care what my district thinks of Congress as long as fifty-one percent of it likes me."[17] Americans do tend to distinguish between Congress as an institution and their own particular representatives. A *New York Times*/CBS News survey conducted in 1994 found that while only 25 percent of people surveyed approved of Congress' performance as an institution, 56 percent approved of the performance of their own representative.[18] There are two main reasons for this paradox. First, an institution that requires compromise for any action to take place will naturally frustrate many observers without dimming their view of a particular member of the organization. Citizens may think that their representative is doing the right thing but that she is being stymied by all the other "no-good" politicians in Washington.

A second reason that individual members emerge unscathed from the criticism of the institution is that they work hard to create a good image of themselves to their constituents. One main feature of the modern campaign is that candidates run their own enterprises in getting elected. The parties are not nearly as active in campaigns as they once were, and candidates must raise their own money, create their own campaign organizations, and determine their own positions on policy. The move from a party-centered campaign system at the turn of the twentieth century to a candidate-centered campaign system during the 1960s has dramatically altered the electoral process. Elections are no longer quite as easy to interpret in terms of national partisan trends. Each congressional election year is composed of 435 individual House elections and 33 or 34 Senate elections rather than one broad statement on national partisan preferences. Members have learned how to survive in Washington even when Congress as an institution is berated, the presidency changes from one party to the other, or policy failures, such as the savings-and-loan crisis of the early 1990s, occur. Members rely on two main methods for survival: using the advantages of incumbency and raising large sums of money. (For a discussion of campaign finance as it relates to congressional elections, see Chapter 9, "Campaigns and Elections.")

12-7a The Advantages of Incumbency

Because of the constitutional requirement that Congress control the purse strings, members of Congress have been able to use government funds for a variety of expenditures that have become quite useful to individual members in their quest to stay in office. The institutional support—such as the franking privilege, paid personal staff, travel allowances, and government-funded offices in Washington and the home district—that each member receives regardless of party, age, or experience is known as the incumbency advantage. However, this incumbency advantage cannot always overcome a damaged candidate. Following his admission that he had an extramarital relationship with a missing Congressional intern, Congressman Gary Condit (D-California) found his popularity sinking amid devastating national media attention. In December 2001, he declared that he would seek reelection the following year despite criticism by his party leader, Dick Gephardt, and the Democratic governor of California, Gray Davis. He was defeated in the Democratic primary by one of his former staff members.

The Franking Privilege

The **franking privilege** is the power of any member of Congress to sign (or to have the printer reproduce his signature on) any piece of mail and have it delivered without cost to the member. The use of this power is limited in that members cannot mail campaign materials on the frank, but they can send letters, public opinion polls, or newsletters about policy discussions or what the member has been doing in Washington or the district. Although the member's literature cannot directly say "vote for me," one would have difficulty finding any comments in a newsletter that would not make the legislator's parents proud. The use of this privilege has grown dramatically. In the 1950s, fewer than 45 million pieces of mail were sent, but by the 1980s an average of more than 600 million deliveries were made; the high was 925 million pieces in the 1984 election year. In 1994, more than 363 million pieces of franked mail were sent at a cost of nearly $53 million.[19] In recent years, however, public concern over the privileges of Congress and electronic newsletter and website delivery have led to a reduction in the amount of franked mail. Still, the franking privilege remains a major aspect of incumbency advantage.

12-7b The Constant Campaign

The main purpose of all this institutional support is to allow the member to maintain continual contact with her constituents. A politician never wants to be accused of "not being in touch with the people." To survive in a political system that lacks strong party ties, relies heavily on mass media, and requires large amounts of money to win elections, the average member of Congress must run a continual campaign from the minute one election ends until the next. Because voters do not pay close attention to politicians or elections, members must do everything possible to keep their names before the public. Name recognition is difficult to attain through a few advertisements during a campaign, when so many other politicians are blanketing the airwaves, so a legislator must engage in a continual effort throughout his or her two- or six-year term. Travel home, personal staff, and district offices help maintain name recognition through casework and personal contact.

12-7c Proposals for Reform

Public confidence in Congress is undeniably at an all-time low. One reason is the widespread perception that members are interested only in getting themselves reelected and raising money for that purpose. But Congress has a poor public image for several other reasons, including the intractable federal debt, the gridlock of the late 1980s and early 1990s, and a series of scandals that rocked Capitol Hill during the same period. Particularly damaging were revelations in 1991 that some representatives had badly abused their privileges in the bank and restaurant that the House operated exclusively for its members.

Curtailing Members' Perks

Widespread dissatisfaction with Congress has led to several proposals for reform, some of which have come from within the institution itself. But Congress has a difficult time coming to grips with reform. The reasons for this difficulty are numerous, but the most obvious is that members do not want to take steps that will reduce the benefits of holding office and, most importantly, their electoral advantage over challengers. One thing that is most irritating to the public are the **perks** that members of Congress receive: their expense allowances, travel budgets, subsidized life and health insurance, free tax preparation, subsidized restaurants, free health club, free parking, free haircuts, free office decorations, free use of photography and recording studios, discounts on official merchandise, and so on. Although some perks have been curtailed in recent years, they have helped foster the impression that members of Congress are out of touch with the people they represent. Moreover, they lend credence to the perception that the entire institution is corrupt.

Campaign Finance Reform

Critics argue that it is unseemly for members of Congress to have to continually raise money for reelection—money that tends to come from wealthy contributors and political action committees who clearly expect something in return. Whether or not this obsession with fundraising is a corrupting force, the public certainly perceives it that way. In addition, few quality challengers can raise the funds to compete with incumbents, thus contributing to the low rate of turnover in Congress. A variety of proposals have been put forth, including public financing of campaigns, prohibiting contributions from PACs, placing spending limits on candidates, mandating free media access to challengers, and restricting contributions from outside the candidate's district. All these options are controversial, and none can be assumed to have the desired effect. Moreover, under the present circumstances, a majority of incumbents in either chamber or party is highly unlikely to be mustered to support any of these measures. Furthermore, even presidents feel somewhat limited in pushing for reform. For example, President Clinton favored campaign finance reform in 1994, but he was reluctant to push it for fear of alienating key members he needed to support his crime bill and healthcare agenda. The bipartisan McCain–Feingold bill introduced in the 106th Congress would put serious limitations on the use of soft money in all federal races.

During the 2000 presidential election campaign, Republican candidate Senator John McCain chose campaign finance reform as his signature issue. Although he ultimately was defeated by George W. Bush, McCain promised to introduce legislation at the onset of the 107th Congress. Clearly, the issue had reached the political front burner, if not among the general public, then certainly among many in the media and those holding public office. In 2002, however, the backlash against soft money led to the passage of the Bipartisan Campaign Reform Act (BCRA), or as it is commonly known, McCain–Feingold (see Chapter 9). Despite numerous attempts at capping or limiting the amount of money that flows into politics, most campaign finance reforms simply make candidates be more creative in finding money sources, since advertising and other forms of campaign outreach continue to be prohibitively expensive without hundreds of thousands of dollars in campaign war chests.

Term Limits

During the early 1990s, there was considerable interest in the idea of limiting the number of terms that members of Congress can serve (see Case in Point 12-1). A variety of proposals surfaced calling for various limits on the number of consecutive terms that members of the House and Senate would be eligible to serve. All these proposals had a common purpose: to remove the professional politician and restore the concept of citizen-legislator. More than twenty states adopted measures that would in some way limit the terms of members of their congressional delegations. Typically, these measures limited senators to two terms (twelve years) and House members to three, four, or six terms (six, eight, or twelve years). However, none of these measures prevented any member of Congress from seeking reelection, because in 1995 the Supreme Court struck down the state-by-state approach to term limits for members of Congress in *U.S. Term Limits v. Thornton*.[20] In his opinion for the Court, Justice Stevens claimed that the Framers of the Constitution intended "that neither Congress nor the states should possess the power to supplement the exclusive qualifications set forth in" Article I. He further observed that "allowing individual states to craft their own qualifications for Congress would...erode the structure envisioned by the framers."

In dissent, Justice Clarence Thomas argued that "nothing in the Constitution deprives the people of each state of the power to prescribe eligibility requirements for candidates who seek to represent them in Congress.... And where the Constitution is silent, it raises no bar to action by the states or the people." In its majority opinion, the Court recognized cogent arguments on both sides of the term limits issue. It concluded, however, that an issue of this magnitude must be referred to the formal process by which the Constitution is amended. Immediately after the *Thornton* decision was rendered, supporters of term limits pledged renewed efforts to achieve a constitutional amendment to limit the tenure of members of Congress. That, of course, has not transpired.

Presumably, imposing term limits on all members of Congress would require a constitutional amendment along the lines of the Twenty-Second Amendment, which limits presidents to two consecutive terms. Political scientists often question the wisdom of attempting to limit congressional terms, citing the need for stable political leadership. On the other hand, regular turnover in Congress would likely enhance public trust in that beleaguered institution.

In 1994, Republicans effectively nationalized congressional races by having their candidates sign a Contract with America that called for Congress to consider the question of term limits, among other things. With the resounding Republican victory, the advocates of term limits were optimistic that the issue would finally make it to the congressional agenda. Ironically, though, the magnitude of the Republican victory in 1994 was itself an argument for the electorate's ability to impose term limits through the ballot box.

12-8 Conclusion: Assessing Congress

Congress is a complex institution that has changed dramatically since its founding. The idea of the citizen-legislator has long been abandoned for the professional legislator, with a staff and support system that rival those of a corporate executive. As Congress has evolved as an institution, however, it has come into difficult times. Congress is unloved and unappreciated by the American people, who see it as constantly bickering and unable to rise above in-fighting.

During the twelve years of the Ronald Reagan and George H.W. Bush presidencies, Congress was often accused of contributing to gridlock. Many people were pleased to see divided-party government end when the Democrats won the presidency in 1992. However, divided government returned when the Republicans gained control of both houses of Congress in the dramatic midterm elections of 1994. Yet President Clinton and the Republican Congress managed to achieve some major policy accomplishments, most notably in the realms of fiscal policy, foreign trade, and welfare reform.

Though Congress as an institution is still held in relatively low regard, individual members of Congress tend to have reasonably good relationships with their constituents. Those who want to be reelected usually are. The incumbency advantage comes at a steep price, however. The money it brings to the incumbent inevitably commits him to special interests. Even if the commitment is only to grant some access to hear the interest's point on an issue, the appearance of corruption has done much to convince many Americans that the institution is not deserving of their respect. Paradoxically, although it was designed to be "closest to the people," Congress remains the least loved and respected of the institutions of government.

Questions for Thought and Discussion

1. Should members of Congress vote according to what they think is best for the country, or should they follow what they think their constituents want?

2. How can a member of Congress accurately determine what her constituents want? Should all constituents' opinions count equally?

3. Are term limits for members of Congress a good idea? If so, what limits should be imposed?

4. Why is Congress less trusted and respected than the other two branches of the national government? What reforms might improve Congress' public image?

5. What changes in the ways Congress operates would create more party discipline in voting on legislation? Is more party discipline desirable?

6. How did Republican control of Congress from 1994 to 2004 affect the way in which the institution is perceived by the mass public?

ENDNOTES

1 Jim Acosta, "Meet the 113th Congress: More Diverse Than Ever," CNN.com, January 3, 2013, http://inamerica.blogs.cnn.com/2013/01/03/meet-the-113th-congress-more-diverse-than-ever/

2 *Hoke v. United States*, 227 U.S. 308 (1913).

3 *United States v. Lopez*, 514 U.S. 549 (1995).

4 Ron Nixon, "Congress Appears to Be Trying to Get Around Earmark Ban," *The New York Times*, February 5, 2012, http://www.nytimes.com/2012/02/06/us/politics/congress-appears-to-be-trying-to-get-around-earmark-ban.html?pagewanted=all

5 *Chisholm v. Georgia* (1793) was overturned by the Eleventh Amendment; *Scott v. Sandford* (1857) was overturned by the Thirteenth and Fourteenth Amendments; *Pollock v. Farmer's Loan and Trust Co.* (1895) was overturned by the Sixteenth Amendment; and *Oregon v. Mitchell* (1970) was overturned by the Twenty-Sixth Amendment.

6 Paul Boller, *Congressional Anecdotes* (Oxford: Oxford University Press, 1991), p. 4.

7 As quoted by Ross K. Baker, *House and Senate* (New York: W. W. Norton, 1989), p. 35.

8 William N. Chambers, *Political Parties in a New Nation* (New York: Oxford University Press, 1963), p. 194.

9 In 1999, Representative Dennis Hastert (R-Illinois) was elected Speaker of the House after serving in the House for only thirteen years, but this occurred only after his predecessor, Newt Gingrich (R-Georgia), resigned his leadership position and gave up his seat in the Congress after the Republican party's disappointing performance in the 1998 midterm elections.

10 Quoted in the *Congressional Record*, 100th Congress, first session, December 3, 1987, p. 3.

11 "CNN Election Night 2006 Coverage: Democrats Retake House," November 7, 2006, http://www.cnn.com/ELECTION/2006/

12 "CNN Election Night 2008 Coverage," November 7, 2008, http://www.cnn.com/ELECTION/2008/

13 Ida A. Brudnick, "Congressional Salaries and Allowances," Congressional Research Service, January 15, 2013, http://www.senate.gov/CRSReports/crs-publish.cfm?pid='0E%2C*PL%5B%3D%23P%20%20%0A

14 Roger H. Davidson and Walter J. Oleszek, *Congress and Its Members*, 7th ed. (Washington, D.C.: CQ Press, 2000), p. 154.

15 Norman J. Ornstein, Thomas E. Mann, and Michael J. Malbin, *Vital Statistics on Congress 1999–2000* (Washington, D.C.: AEI Press, 2000), p. 126.

16 Davidson and Oleszek, *Congress and Its Members*, 7th ed., p. 233.

17 Quoted in the *Washington Post*, June 22, 1975.

18 *New York Times*/CBS News national survey of 1,161 persons, conducted September 8–11, 1994. Margin of error is ±3 percentage points. Results reported in *The New York Times*, September 13, 1994, page A-8.

19 Davidson and Oleszek, *Congress and Its Members*, 7th ed., p. 156.

20 *U.S. Term Limits v. Thornton*, 514 U.S. 779 (1995).

Chapter 13

THE PRESIDENCY

OUTLINE

Key Terms 490

Expected Learning Outcomes 490

13-1 The President: Personification of American Government 490

- **13-1a** The Many Roles of the President 491

13-2 The Constitutional Basis of the Presidency 495

- **13-2a** Creating the Presidency 495
- **13-2b** Presidential Terms 496
- **13-2c** Removal of the Chief Executive 498

13-3 The Scope and Limits of Presidential Power 500

- **13-3a** Competing Theories of Presidential Power 500
- **13-3b** The President's Powers to Limit Congress 502
- **13-3c** The Powers of Appointment and Removal 507
- **13-3d** The Power to Grant Pardons 508
- **13-3e** Executive Privilege 509
- **13-3f** The Power to Make Foreign Policy 510
- **13-3g** The Specifics of Conducting Foreign Affairs 512
- **13-3h** Presidential War Powers 514
- **13-3i** Domestic Powers during Wartime 518

13-4 The Structure of the Presidential Office 520

- **13-4a** The White House Staff 521
- **13-4b** The Executive Office 522
- **13-4c** The Cabinet 523

13-5 The Functioning Presidency 524

- **13-5a** The President's Legislative Agenda 524
- **13-5b** Power and Persuasion 529
- **13-5c** The Budget 532

13-6 Evaluating Presidential Performance 533

- **13-6a** Assessing George W. Bush's Presidency 535
- **13-6b** Initial Assessments of the Obama Presidency 535

13-7 Conclusion: Assessing the Presidency as an Institution 536
Questions for Thought and Discussion 537
Endnotes 538

KEY TERMS

amnesty
chief of staff
constitutional theory
executive agreements
executive privilege
honeymoon period
impoundment
inherent power
lame duck
landslide
legislative agenda
line-item veto
mandate
pardons
pocket veto
stewardship theory
treaty

EXPECTED LEARNING OUTCOMES

After reading this chapter and completing the supplemental online materials, students will:

- Describe the constitutional design of the executive branch and its differences from other branches
- Compare the multiple roles the president serves
- Analyze the powers of the president
- Contrast the president's domestic and foreign powers

13-1 THE PRESIDENT: PERSONIFICATION OF AMERICAN GOVERNMENT

When President Barack Obama took the oath of office on January 20, 2009, the event was more significant than simply one new chief executive stepping behind the desk of his predecessor. Obama, the nation's first African American president, became a symbol of the American people. In international affairs, the personification of American government is the president. Barack Obama is therefore the "face of America" to the rest of the world.

Obama spoke with the eloquence that had earned him a reputation as an orator, both in the Senate and while campaigning for president. The nation whose leadership he inherited was nervous, in a financial crisis unknown for generations. As the nation's top elected official, Obama sought to allay fears of a collapse, saying "that we are in the midst of crisis is now well understood. Our nation is at war, against a far-reaching network of violence and hatred. Our economy is badly weakened, a consequence of greed and irresponsibility on the part of some, but also our collective failure to make hard choices and prepare the nation for a new age. Homes have been lost; jobs shed; businesses shuttered. Our health care is too costly; our schools fail too many; and each day brings further evidence that the ways we use energy strengthen our adversaries and threaten our planet." Obama's words were meant to invoke a sense that a new age of American society had begun, all because of one new person sitting behind a very old desk.

ONLINE 13.1: *Obama's 2009 Inaugural Speech*
https://www.youtube.com/watch?v=VjnygQ02aW4

This personalization of politics and the use of presidential images to denote political eras are not surprising. Of the three branches of government, only the executive branch can be so easily captured in an image. This image has taken on even more political clout with the advent of the electronic media. It is hard to imagine any American who could not recognize a picture of the president. In fact, the American president is probably the most recognizable presence in the world. Hence, despite its coequal constitutional status with Congress and the Supreme Court, the executive branch has in many ways become the "first among equals" in national government.

13-1a The Many Roles of the President

The realities of international affairs and the United States' role as a major world power have inevitably tended to strengthen the presidency. Yet major areas of disagreement still occur over the proper scope of the president's power. Nevertheless, Americans invariably look to the White House for leadership and action when they want government to act. Because Americans expect their president to be a problem solver, they tend to judge presidents harshly when problems linger unresolved. Accordingly, despite President George H.W. Bush's overwhelming popularity at the close of the Gulf War, he was defeated for reelection a little more than a year later, in part because he was perceived as not being sufficiently engaged in solving domestic problems.

Head of State

The American president has tremendous resources with which to attack problems, but these resources have to support the president in an ever-increasing number of roles. The president is, of course, the head of state who represents this country symbolically at home and abroad. It is in this role, which is most like that of a monarch, that the president appears most impressive and majestic. This is why Americans were so distressed when they saw television coverage of President Bush becoming ill at a state dinner in Japan in 1992. When the president is on stage representing this country, we like to think of him as being superhuman.

Chief Executive

The president is the chief executive, which means that he is responsible for running the massive federal bureaucracy. That means putting together a team of people, called the administration, who occupy the top positions in the executive departments and agencies. It also means putting together a White House staff to help the president manage the government.

The tremendous growth of government in the twentieth century, especially since the 1930s, has greatly increased the resources of the presidency. But it has also increased the difficulty and complexity of being the nation's chief administrator. No single human being, no matter how much staff she is provided, can stay on top of what the federal government is doing at any given time. A president must strive for some reasonable middle ground.

President Carter was criticized for trying to micromanage the executive branch. On the other hand, President Reagan was often characterized as being out of touch with what was going on in his administration. After assuming the presidency in January 2001, George W. Bush gave the impression that he would not be overly detail-oriented, but rather would work with the Cabinet with Vice President Cheney more involved in legislative and administrative matters. Of course, this arrangement changed dramatically in September 2001, when President Bush took on the details of military and diplomatic policy while Cheney assumed a clearly subordinate, even barely visible role.

Crisis Manager

The president also now plays the role of crisis manager. The president must be able to act quickly and effectively when events around the world dictate an American response. When Saddam Hussein's Iraq annexed its tiny neighbor Kuwait in August 1990, thereby threatening the world's oil supply, world leaders looked to the United States, and ultimately to George H.W. Bush, to respond to the crisis. Sometimes, crises at home require immediate action. The president is expected to lead the government's response to national disasters, such as Hurricane Andrew, which devastated much of south Florida in 1992. Although President Bush was given high marks by most commentators for his quick, decisive action in response to the crisis in Kuwait, he received a less positive assessment for the federal government's response to Hurricane Andrew. Most observers gave President Clinton high marks for his response to the Oklahoma City bombing in 1995. Perhaps the highest grade for crisis management would be reserved for George W. Bush's response to the terrorist attacks of September 2001. Perhaps his most memorable single act was his appearance at the scene of the fallen trade towers, when in response from a person in the crowd yelling "I can't hear you," he yelled back, "I can hear you, and the world can hear you," while draping his arm over the shoulder of a firefighter standing next to him. Often, these spontaneous actions are the most effective in sealing a bond between a leader and the rest of us.

Commander-in-Chief

The Constitution makes the president commander-in-chief of the armed forces. Obviously, in time of war, the president is "first among generals." In a development probably not foreseen by the Framers of the Constitution, the role of commander-in-chief has come to mean that the president has the power to initiate war and to direct its progress. But being commander-in-chief means much more than that. The president has the primary responsibility for setting the military policy of the United States and governing its massive military establishment. For example, President Harry S. Truman issued an executive order desegregating the military after World War II. In 1993, President Bill Clinton tried to fulfill a campaign promise by issuing an executive order lifting the ban on gays in the military, but he soon discovered that key members of Congress had other ideas. Ultimately, the president was forced to compromise with those who wanted to maintain the ban.

Chief Diplomat and Chief Foreign Policy Maker

By virtue of both constitutional text and history, the president is the nation's chief diplomat. He is under unrelenting pressure to represent the United States effectively on the world stage. Moreover, he is accorded primary responsibility for both making and implementing this country's foreign policy. And since the demise of the Soviet Union, the United States is the only superpower in the world. As the chief diplomat and principal foreign policy maker of the world's greatest power, the president is necessarily cast in the role of the leader of world leaders. He is expected to lead the way in finding solutions to problems such as the civil war in the former Yugoslavia. George Bush felt extremely comfortable in this role. Bill Clinton, on the other hand, struggled with the complexities and dilemmas of foreign policy and world leadership during his first two years in office. He later developed a comfort level with foreign policy, but left office without the clear foreign policy legacy that he would have liked to achieve.

George W. Bush's journey to Europe in May 2002 represented some of his first major actions as chief diplomat and foreign policy maker. He negotiated an agreement with Russian president Vladimir Putin to drastically cut back on nuclear arms. While in

Russia, President Bush made clear that he wanted Congress to overturn legislation that put Russia in a disadvantaged trading position with the United States. On that same trip, President Bush met with other European leaders to shore up support for American policy in the Middle East and, in particular, toward Iraq.

Chief Legislator

Although the Constitution formally places the legislative power of the national government in Congress, the president has come to be regarded as the chief legislator. Even though the president does not formally participate in the legislative process, Congress looks to him to set the legislative agenda. Americans expect the president, not Congress, to initiate major policies. Unlike George H.W. Bush, who was faulted by his critics for failing to provide leadership in domestic policy, Bill Clinton came to Washington with an ambitious legislative agenda that spanned health care, welfare, crime, and the economy. He failed in his signature legislative goal—healthcare reform—in 1993 despite having Democratic majorities in both houses of Congress. He later embraced some of the policies enunciated by the Republican Congress that took over in 1994, the most notable being welfare reform. However, Clinton's most skillful performance in the role of chief legislator may well have been his active role in marshalling bipartisan support for the North American Free Trade Agreement (NAFTA) in 1993. Barack Obama, like Clinton before him, began his presidency with a proposal to provide government-run health insurance to the uninsured.

Party Leader

Finally, the president is the symbolic leader of his party. Though others run the party organization, the electorate tends to think of the party in terms of the president's policies, appointments, decisions, and leadership style. Failure to lead effectively, with the attendant loss of popularity, can potentially harm members of his party significantly, especially as they seek election or reelection. At the same time, the president is expected to limit his partisan activities. Being party leader thus presents the president with a dilemma. But facing dilemmas—and finding a way to resolve them—is what being president is all about.

When the president appears every January to report to Congress on the "state of the Union," as required by the Constitution, he is acting as head of state, chief legislator, and party leader. When the president enters the House chamber for the speech, everyone, regardless of party affiliation, stands to applaud the leader of the country. During the speech, the president sets forth the broad outlines of his legislative agenda. Media pundits watch carefully to see how Democrats and Republicans, who sit on opposite sides of the main aisle, are responding to the president's message. After the speech is over, the networks provide time for a leader of the opposing political party to respond. Presidents generally dislike this practice because they do not want their State of the Union messages to be viewed in such partisan terms.

13-2 THE CONSTITUTIONAL BASIS OF THE PRESIDENCY

Perhaps the most glaring weakness of the Articles of Confederation was that they did not provide for any real leadership in the national government. All members of Congress represented individual states. No one represented the nation as a whole. No one provided leadership. Clearly, some type of chief executive was needed if the United States was to function effectively as a nation.

13-2a CREATING THE PRESIDENCY

The delegates to the Constitutional Convention of 1787 agreed on the need for an executive authority in the new national government they were creating. They were also in agreement that the executive should be a separate, independent branch of government—they did not want a parliamentary system. As with other matters at the convention, though, the delegates disagreed over the nature, structure, and powers of the executive branch (see Figure 13-1). Some delegates preferred a weak administrator, whose main function would be to faithfully execute the laws passed by Congress. Others, most notably Alexander Hamilton, wanted an executive endowed with significant independent powers and capable of providing vigorous national leadership. Writing in *Federalist* No. 70, Hamilton articulated his view of the presidential office:

> *There is an idea, which is not without its advocates, that a vigorous executive is inconsistent with the genius of republican government. ...Energy in the executive is the leading character in the definition of good government. It is essential to the protection of the community against foreign attacks; it is not less essential to the steady administration of the laws, to the protection of property...; [and] to the security of liberty against the enterprises and assaults of ambition, of faction and anarchy.*

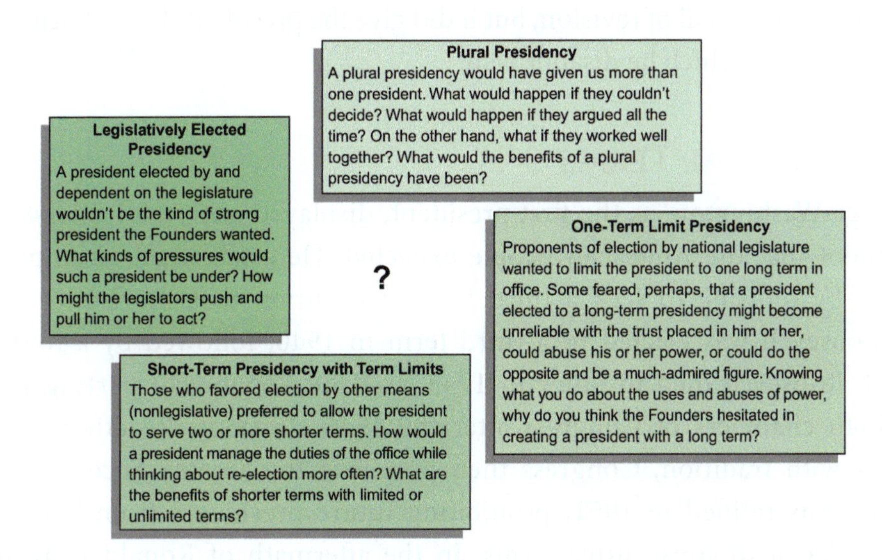

Figure 13-1 *Potential Presidencies*

The Framers of the Constitution opted for a middle ground. The Constitution they drafted seemed to contemplate a president who would be capable of acting independently, but who would also be answerable to Congress. The president would be endowed with significant constitutional powers, but these powers would be well defined and limited. In the more than two hundred years since the Constitution was ratified, the presidency has changed more dramatically than either the legislative or the judicial branch of the national government. The presidency has grown in size, scope, and power beyond anything ever contemplated in the late eighteenth century. But even with these changes, the president is no king and must still answer to Congress, the courts, and, ultimately, the American people.

A Single Executive?

A number of delegates at the Constitutional Convention of 1787 favored a multiple executive in which presidential power would be shared by three or more individuals. The delegates, who had recently participated in a successful revolution against the British Crown, were reluctant to create an institution that could degenerate into a monarchy. But the knowledge that George Washington would assume a central role of leadership greatly reduced these fears. Ultimately, the delegates opted for a single executive.

Of course, a single executive is more likely to become a tyrant. This fear motivated many people to suggest limiting the president to a single term of seven years or to two three-year terms. Still others maintained that the president, in concert with the Supreme Court, should function as a "council of revision," which would decide on the constitutionality of acts of Congress. Neither of these proposals was adopted. In the end, the Constitution prescribed a four-year term for the president, with no limit on the number of terms that one individual could serve. The Constitution said nothing of a council of revision, but it did give the president the authority to veto acts of Congress of which he disapproved.

13-2b Presidential Terms

George Washington, as the first president, displayed both the leadership and self-restraint that the American people expected. He established an important precedent by refusing to seek a third term, a tradition that survived until Franklin D. Roosevelt was elected to a third term in 1940, followed by a fourth term in 1944. Roosevelt died in office in 1945, and the Republican party gained control of both chambers of Congress after the 1946 elections. Reacting to Roosevelt's break with tradition, Congress then proposed the Twenty-Second Amendment, which was ratified in 1951, prohibiting future presidents from being elected to more than two consecutive terms. In the aftermath of Ronald Reagan's popular first term and landslide reelection in 1984, Republicans began to urge the repeal of the Twenty-Second Amendment. This consideration was short-lived, however. The nation soon became preoccupied with the Iran–Contra affair and other problems during Reagan's second term.

Presidential Succession and Disability

The constitutional problem of presidential succession has troubled generations of Americans. The problem first arose in 1841 when President William Henry Harrison died after only a month in office. The immediate question was whether Vice President John Tyler would assume the full duties and powers of the office for the remaining forty-seven months of Harrison's term or serve merely as acting president. Unwilling to settle for less than the full measure of presidential authority, Tyler set an important precedent, which has been followed by the eight other individuals who have succeeded to the office because of the death or resignation of an incumbent president.

The related problem of presidential disability has proved more perplexing. Several presidents have been temporarily disabled during their terms of office, giving rise to uncertainty and confusion about the locus of actual decision-making authority. For example, President Woodrow Wilson was seriously disabled by a stroke in 1919 and for a number of weeks was totally incapable of performing his official duties. No constitutional provision existed at that time for the temporary replacement of a disabled president. The result was that Wilson's wife, Edith, took on much of the responsibility of the office, an arrangement that evoked sharp criticism.

The problem of presidential disability is addressed by the Twenty-Fifth Amendment, ratified in 1967. This amendment, proposed in the aftermath of the assassination of President Kennedy in 1963, establishes, among other things, a procedure under which the vice president may assume the role of acting president during periods of presidential disability. The amendment provides alternative means for determining presidential disability. Section 3 allows the president to transmit to Congress a written declaration that he is unable to discharge the duties of the office, after which the vice president assumes the role of acting president. The vice president continues in this role unless and until the president can transmit a declaration to the contrary. If, however, the president is unable or unwilling to acknowledge his inability to perform the duties of the office, the vice president and a majority of the cabinet members are authorized to make this determination.

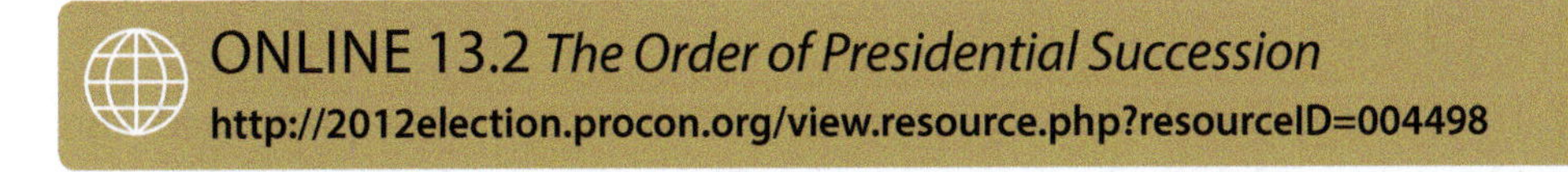
ONLINE 13.2 *The Order of Presidential Succession*
http://2012election.procon.org/view.resource.php?resourceID=004498

13-2c Removal of the Chief Executive

The ultimate constitutional sanction against the abuse of presidential power is impeachment and removal from office. *Impeachment* refers to an action of the House of Representatives in which that body adopts, by at least a majority vote, one or more articles of impeachment accusing a sitting president of "high crimes and misdemeanors." An impeached president is then tried before the Senate, at least two-thirds of which must so vote in order to remove the president from office.

Only twice in U.S. history have presidents been impeached, but in neither case was the president removed from office. President Andrew Johnson was impeached by the House of Representatives in 1868 but narrowly escaped conviction by the Senate. President Richard M. Nixon almost certainly would have been impeached and convicted had he not resigned the presidency in 1974. Nixon's role in the Watergate cover-up had become clear; he had even been named by a federal grand jury as an "unindicted co-conspirator." In 1998, the House of Representatives impeached President Clinton, charging him with perjury and obstruction of justice. After trial, the Senate acquitted him of both charges, and he remained in office to fill out his term.

The Andrew Johnson Impeachment

President Andrew Johnson was impeached solely for political reasons, stemming from his clash with Congress over Reconstruction policy. His ultimate acquittal can be attributed to the fact that he had not committed indictable offenses, although many in Congress were willing to interpret quite broadly the "high crimes and misdemeanors" language in the Constitution. As America matured through the twentieth century, however, it became clear that American political culture set certain guidelines for the impeachment of a president, who would have to commit some serious breach of ethics or law to be impeached. The public would not support the removal of a popularly elected president by a Congress inspired by purely political motives.

The Impeachment of Bill Clinton

In January 1998, the nation became immersed in one of the most prolonged and intense presidential scandals in American history. The events leading to the eventual impeachment of President Clinton in 1998 began to unfold behind the scenes in a sexual harassment lawsuit filed by Paula Corbin Jones, a former worker in Arkansas state government during Clinton's tenure as the governor of that state. Jones' attorneys sought to query President Clinton about other alleged sexual relationships. The Supreme Court, in *Clinton v. Jones*, allowed this questioning to take place, accepting Jones' lawyers' arguments that the president could answer questions in this civil suit without interfering with his presidential duties.

On January 17, 1998, Clinton submitted to questioning and became the first president to testify in a civil lawsuit while serving as president. During this testimony, the president was asked specifically about having had an affair with Monica Lewinsky. Clinton denied a sexual relationship with Lewinsky, who had also denied an affair during an earlier deposition. However, word of a relationship had begun to spread. A Lewinsky friend and confidant, Linda Tripp, approached the independent prosecutor Ken Starr with tape recordings. Starr, who had long been involved in investigating alleged wrongdoings in the Whitewater case, sought and received approval from Attorney General Janet Reno to launch an inquiry into the Lewinsky matter.

The story of a sexual relationship between the president and a young White House intern, Monica Lewinsky, first appeared on the Internet in the *Drudge Report*, which had become aware of a story about to break in *Newsweek*. The story soon became the focus of massive media and public attention. President Clinton addressed the nation on January 26 with the following statement:

> *I want to say one thing to the American people. I want you to listen to me. I'm gonna say this again. I did not have sexual relations with that woman, Miss Lewinsky. I never told anybody to lie. Not a single time. Never. These allegations are false. And I need to go back to work for the American people. Thank you.*

Not surprisingly, many Republicans and some Democrats pointed to the Lewinsky mess as indicative of President Clinton's lack of moral fiber. The president's defenders, while decrying the president's apparent lack of judgment, sought to frame the issue as a private one between the president and his family. Many defenders sought to exploit the president's continuing high approval ratings by shifting the focus to the independent counsel Ken Starr. First Lady Hillary Rodham Clinton, appearing on NBC's *Today* program, blamed a "vast right-wing conspiracy" bent on destroying her husband.

Ken Starr convened a grand jury to look into the matter, especially whether the president had committed perjury in his testimony in the Paula Jones case. By the summer, many had testified before the grand jury, including President Clinton, who eventually testified from the White House on August 17. By this time, Judge Susan Webber Wright had dismissed the original Jones lawsuit and Ms. Lewinsky had admitted the affair. Following his testimony, the president addressed the nation to admit the affair and to seek forgiveness.

The president's problems grew worse in September when Ken Starr prepared a lengthy, detailed report and submitted it to the House Judiciary Committee. The committee conducted somewhat acrimonious debate before large television audiences before voting along party lines to recommend that the House vote to impeach on all counts. Meanwhile, the country remained divided. Although most citizens condemned the president's behavior, a clear majority did not favor impeachment. To many, the true villain was Ken Starr, who was vilified for his relentless pursuit of the Clintons and excessive concentration on the more prurient aspects of the Lewinsky affair. The House eventually voted to impeach on two counts: perjury and obstruction of justice. On December 20, 1998, William Jefferson Clinton became the second president to be impeached.

In many ways, the trial in the Senate the following January was anticlimactic. It was clear from the beginning that the Republican leadership in the Senate saw impeachment as a losing political proposition in the climate of high approval ratings for the president. Facing almost no chance of mustering the necessary two-thirds to convict, the trial was short-lived. Ultimately, the House impeachment managers failed to achieve a majority on either count, allowing President Clinton to serve out the remainder of his term. The president was hardly vindicated, however. In April, Judge Wright held the president in contempt for giving misleading testimony in the Jones case. Finally, in his last day in office in January 2001, President Clinton agreed to a plea bargain with the new special prosecutor, Robert Ray. In this agreement, Clinton admitted to providing misleading testimony and agreed to surrender his license to practice law in Arkansas.

ONLINE 13.3 *The Clinton Impeachment*
https://www.youtube.com/watch?v=oRA0_o4Eq6Y

13-3 The Scope and Limits of Presidential Power

Article II, Section 1 of the Constitution provides that the "executive power shall be vested in a President of the United States." Sections 2 and 3 enumerate specific powers granted to the president. They include the authority to appoint judges and ambassadors, veto legislation, call Congress into special session, grant **pardons**, and serve as commander-in-chief of the armed forces. Each of these designated powers is obviously a part of "executive power," but that general term is not defined in Article II.

13-3a Competing Theories of Presidential Power

In the early days of the Republic, James Madison and Alexander Hamilton engaged in the first of what was to be a long series of sharp disagreements among constitutional theorists about the proper scope of presidential power. Madison argued that presidential power is restricted to those powers specifically listed in Article II. By contrast, Hamilton argued that the president enjoyed broad power. He believed that "the general doctrine of our Constitution...is that the executive power of the nation is vested in the President; subject only to the exceptions and qualifications which are expressed in that instrument." Madison maintained that if new exercises of power could be continually justified by invoking inherent executive power, "no citizen could any longer guess at the character of the government under which he lives; the most penetrating jurist would be unable to scan the extent of constructive prerogative." These competing theories correspond to quite different notions of the proper role of the president in the newly created national government. Although Madison envisaged a passive role for the president, who would faithfully execute the laws adopted by Congress, Hamilton viewed the presidency in more activist terms.

The Stewardship Theory of Presidential Power

The debate over the scope of presidential power was by no means confined to the early years of the Republic. A vigorous debate took place early in the twentieth century between those who espoused the **stewardship theory** and those who embraced the **constitutional theory** of presidential power. The constitutional theory, derived from Madison's ideas, finds its best and most succinct expression in the words of President William Howard Taft. In his view, the president can "exercise no power which cannot be fairly and reasonably traced to some specific grant of power or justly implied and included within such express grant as proper and necessary to its exercise." The stewardship theory, the modern counterpart to Hamilton's perspective, was best encapsulated by President Theodore Roosevelt. In his view, the Constitution permits the president "to do anything that the needs of the nation [demand] unless such action [is] forbidden by the Constitution or the laws." According to this perspective, the president is a steward empowered to do anything deemed necessary, short of what is expressly prohibited by the Constitution, in the pursuit of the general welfare for which he is primarily responsible.

American constitutional history has, for the most part, vindicated the views of Hamilton and Roosevelt. Although some observers advocate scaling down the modern presidency, few truly expect this type of diminution to occur. The problems of modernization, the complexities of living in a technological age, and the need for the United States as a superpower to speak to other nations with a unified voice and respond quickly to threats to the national security have forced us to recognize the stewardship presidency as both necessary and legitimate. The inherent vagueness of Article II has facilitated this recognition.

The Supreme Court and Presidential Power

The Supreme Court has been, for the most part, willing to allow the expansion of executive power. But on occasion the Court has invalidated particular exercises of executive power that it found excessive under the Constitution. For instance, in 1952, the Court disallowed President Truman's effort to have the government take over and operate the steel industry to prevent a stoppage of production caused by a steelworkers' strike.[1] In a dramatic decision during the summer of 1974, the Court unanimously ruled against President Nixon's claim that he had a right to withhold his tape recordings from Congress during the Watergate crisis.[2]

Another important instance in which the Court imposed limits on the stewardship presidency was in the Pentagon Papers Case of 1971.[3] In the most celebrated case arising from the Vietnam controversy, the Court refused to issue an injunction against newspapers that had come into possession of the Pentagon Papers, a set of classified documents detailing the history of American strategy in Vietnam. Basing his position on inherent executive power and not on any act of Congress, President Richard M. Nixon sought to restrain the press from disclosing classified information that, he argued, would be injurious to the national security. The Court, obviously skeptical of the alleged threat to national security and sensitive to the values protected by the First Amendment, refused to defer to the president.

13-3b The President's Powers to Limit Congress

Under the Constitution, the American president has substantial powers to provide a check on congressional action. These checks can become the subject of considerable testiness, especially when the president is from one party and Congress is controlled by the other. This phenomenon, known as divided-party government, has occurred with regularity since 1968 (although in 2000 the Republicans captured the presidency and kept a slim lead in the House of Representatives while having to rely on Vice President Cheney's potential tie-breaking vote to maintain control of the Senate). American political culture has created the term *gridlock* to denote both the division and the resulting frustration. Many people, and not just Democrats, were relieved when Bill Clinton won the presidential election of 1992. To many, this victory meant the end of gridlock because Democrats would control both the executive and legislative branches of government. But President Clinton soon discovered, much to his chagrin, that Congress has a mind of its own. To some extent, gridlock is a function of the constitutional design as the president and Congress respond to their differing constituencies.

The Power to Veto Legislation

Under Article I, Section 7 of the Constitution, "every bill" and "every order, resolution or vote to which the concurrence of the Senate and the House of Representatives may be necessary" must be presented to the president for approval. This "presentment" requirement has only three exceptions. It does not apply to

1. Actions involving a single chamber, such as the adoption of procedural rules.
2. Concurrent resolutions, such as those establishing joint committees or setting a date for adjournment.
3. Proposed constitutional amendments adopted by Congress.

The president has ten days (not counting Sundays) in which to consider legislation presented for approval. The president has several options:

- Sign the bill into law, which is what usually occurs.
- Veto the bill, which can be overridden by a two-thirds majority of both chambers of Congress.
- Neither sign nor veto the bill, thus allowing it to become law automatically after ten days.

A major exception applies to the third option, however: if Congress adjourns before the ten days have expired and the president still has not signed the bill, it is said to have been subjected to a pocket veto. The beauty of the **pocket veto** (at least from the president's standpoint) is that it deprives Congress of the chance to override a formal veto. This device was first used by President James Madison in 1812.

The veto was rarely used until after the Civil War. President Andrew Johnson (1865–1869), who was at odds with Congress over Reconstruction, vetoed more bills than any of his predecessors. In fact, Johnson vetoed twenty-nine bills in four years, whereas all previous presidents combined had vetoed only fifty-nine bills. Johnson's use of the veto power was one of the reasons the House of Representatives impeached him. He survived his Senate trial because there was no clear evidence of wrongdoing on his part. Using the veto, even using it unwisely, is not an impeachable offense!

Franklin D. Roosevelt used the veto more frequently than any other president in history. During his almost thirteen years in office, Roosevelt issued 635 vetoes. Amazingly, only 9 of these were overridden by Congress. By contrast, Gerald Ford had 12 of his 66 vetoes overridden. Of course, Ford, a Republican, was facing a hostile Congress in which the Democrats controlled both chambers, whereas Roosevelt, a Democrat, had the luxury of having a Congress controlled by the Democrats throughout his tenure. More recently, President George H.W. Bush used the veto 46 times and was overridden only once, even though he faced a Democratic Congress. Bush's Democratic successor, Bill Clinton, did not veto any bills passed by Congress during his first year in office. In this respect, Clinton's first-year experience was similar to that of Jimmy Carter's, who vetoed only one bill during his first year. See Table 13-1 for a listing of the presidential vetoes from 1789 to 2009.

TABLE 13-1 Presidential Vetoes, 1789–2009

REGULAR	VETOES	POCKET	TOTAL		
YEARS	PRESIDENT	VETOES	OVERRIDDEN	VETOES	VETOES
1789–1797	Washington	2	0	0	2
1797–1801	Adams	0	0	0	0
1801–1809	Jefferson	0	0	0	0
1809–1817	Madison	5	0	2	7
1817–1825	Monroe	1	0	0	1
1825–1829	J. Q. Adams	0	0	0	0
1829–1837	Jackson	5	0	7	12
1837–1841	Van Buren	0	0	1	1
1841–1841	Harrison	0	0	0	0
1841–1845	Tyler	6	1	4	10
1845–1849	Polk	2	0	1	3
1849–1850	Taylor	0	0	0	0
1850–1853	Fillmore	0	0	0	0
1853–1857	Pierce	9	5	0	9
1857–1861	Buchanan	4	0	3	7
1861–1865	Lincoln	2	0	5	7
1865–1869	A. Johnson	21	15	8	29
1869–1877	Grant	45	4	48	93
1877–1881	Hayes	12	1	1	13
1881–1881	Garfield	0	0	0	0
1881–1885	Arthur	4	1	8	12
1885–1889	Cleveland	304	2	110	414
1889–1893	Harrison	19	1	25	44
1893–1897	Cleveland	42	5	128	170
1897–1901	McKinley	6	0	36	42
1901–1909	T. Roosevelt	42	1	40	82
1909–1913	Taft	30	1	9	39
1913–1921	Wilson	33	6	11	44
1921–1923	Harding	5	0	1	6
1923–1929	Coolidge	20	4	30	50
1929–1933	Hoover	21	3	16	37
1933–1945	F. Roosevelt	372	9	263	635
1945–1953	Truman	180	12	70	250
1953–1961	Eisenhower	73	2	108	181
1961–1963	Kennedy	12	0	9	21
1963–1969	L. Johnson	16	0	14	30
1969–1974	Nixon	26	7	17	43

REGULAR	VETOES	POCKET	TOTAL		
YEARS	PRESIDENT	VETOES	OVERRIDDEN	VETOES	VETOES
1974–1977	Ford	48	12	18	66
1977–1981	Carter	13	2	18	31
1981–1989	Reagan	39	9	39	78
1989–1992	G. Bush	29	1	17	46
1993–2000	Clinton	36	2	1	37
2001–2009	G. W. Bush	11	1	12	4

Source: Adapted from Harold W. Stanley and Richard G. Niemi, Vital Statistics on American Politics 2003–2004 (Washington, D.C.: CQ Press, 2003), p. 260.

However, after the Republicans captured Congress in 1994, President Clinton was no longer in the position of working with a friendly Congress unlikely to pass legislation leading to a veto. The new Speaker, Newt Gingrich, had an activist conservative agenda for Congress stemming from the Contract with America that Republicans used successfully to gain control of the House. Bill Clinton was not shy about using, or threatening to use, his veto power, and, although the Republicans had control, they did not have the supermajority they needed to override presidential vetoes. During his eight years in the White House, Bill Clinton used the veto thirty-six times; Congress overrode his veto only twice.

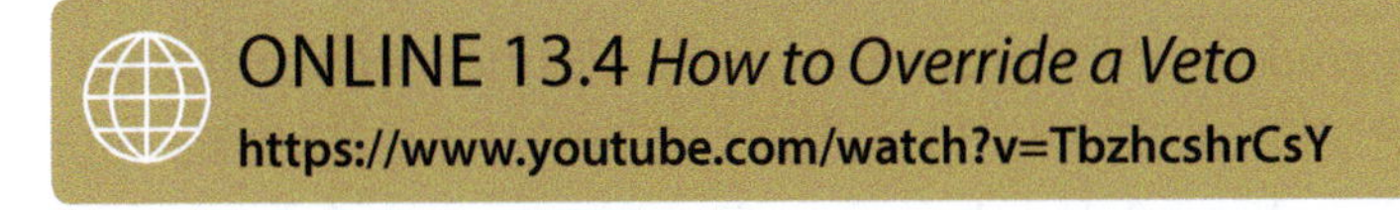

ONLINE 13.4 *How to Override a Veto*
https://www.youtube.com/watch?v=TbzhcshrCsY

An Item Veto?

The veto is a blunt instrument of presidential power, in that presidents must accept or reject a piece of legislation as a whole. Recent presidents—most notably, Ronald Reagan and George Bush—called for a constitutional amendment providing the president with a **line-item veto**, a power exercised by many state governors. A line-item veto is a veto of only part of a particular bill as opposed to a veto of the entire piece of legislation. Supporters of the line-item veto argue that it would allow the president to control the swelling federal budget more effectively. Arguably, a line-item veto would also allow the president to defeat the congressional tactic of attaching disagreeable riders to bills the president basically supports. In 1994, Republican Congressional candidates called for the line-item veto in their Contract with America. In 1996, Congress passed it into law. However, it was short-lived. Six members of Congress challenged it as an unconstitutional surrender of Congress' authority and violation of the separation of powers (see Case in Point 13-2). In a 6–3 ruling, the Supreme Court struck down the item veto, noting that the Constitution allows the president to exercise only the options of signing legislation or vetoing it, but not the authority to strike specific items with legislation approved by Congress.[4] The ruling upset both the president and key Republicans in Congress who saw the line-item veto as necessary to control Congress' propensity to spend.

Many observers believed that the idea of a presidential line-item veto died with the Supreme Court's decision in 1998. Yet, in his first press conference after winning reelection in 2004, President George W. Bush resurrected the idea. "I do believe there ought to be budgetary reform in Washington. I would like to see the president have a line-item veto again, one that (can pass) constitutional muster."[5] Exactly how a statute could be drawn to "pass constitutional muster" remained unclear, but a Democratic spokesman for the House Appropriations Committee said, "It's probably something that some real clever lawyers can get around."[6]

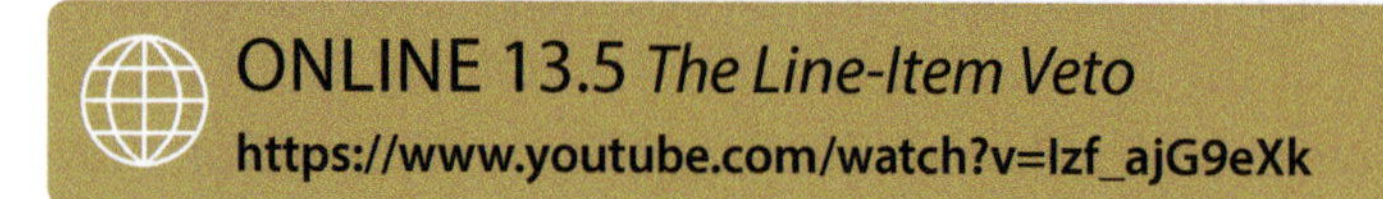

ONLINE 13.5 *The Line-Item Veto*
https://www.youtube.com/watch?v=Izf_ajG9eXk

Impoundment

Another controversial presidential check on the legislative branch is **impoundment**, or the refusal to allow the expenditure of funds appropriated by Congress. The first instance of impoundment occurred in 1803 when President Thomas Jefferson withheld $50,000 that Congress had allocated to build gunboats to defend the Mississippi River. Jefferson's purpose was merely to delay the expenditure, primarily because the Louisiana Purchase, completed shortly after Congress appropriated the money for gunboats, minimized the need for defenses along the Mississippi. During the remainder of the nineteenth century, presidents rarely invoked Jefferson's precedent. In 1905, Congress gave the president statutory authority to engage in limited impoundments to avoid departmental deficits. In 1921, Congress extended this authority to allow the president to withhold funds to save money in case Congress authorized more than was needed to secure its goals. Although Congress provided for a limited power of impoundment, these concessions to the president did not significantly undermine Congress' basic power of the purse.

Richard Nixon, however, extended the power of impoundment beyond acceptable limits. Nixon not only used impoundment to suit his budgetary preferences but also attempted to dismantle certain programs of which he disapproved. The most notorious example was the Office of Economic Opportunity (OEO), which Nixon tried to shut down by refusing to spend any of the funds Congress had designated for the office. (Congressional and public pressures forced Nixon to capitulate on the

OEO issue.) In one of his far-reaching uses of the impoundment power, Nixon ordered the head of the Environmental Protection Agency (EPA), Russell Train, to withhold a substantial amount of money allocated for sewage treatment plants under the Water Pollution Control Act of 1972. Particularly disturbing to some members of Congress was that Nixon had originally vetoed the act and Congress had overridden the veto. Thus, Nixon was seeking to have his way by impounding funds despite the wishes of a two-thirds majority of Congress.

Largely in response to the Nixon administration's unbridled use of impoundment, Congress adopted the Congressional Budget and Impoundment Control Act of 1974. Although the act recognizes a limited presidential power to impound funds, it requires the president to inform Congress of the reasons for an intended impoundment and provides for a bicameral legislative veto to prevent the president from proceeding.

13-3c The Powers of Appointment and Removal

Long before the advent of the modern stewardship presidency, it was obvious that presidents could not be expected to fulfill their duties alone. As presidential power has expanded, so too have the size and complexity of the executive branch. Originally, Congress provided for three cabinet departments—State, War, and Treasury—to assist the president in the execution of policy. The executive establishment now has fifteen cabinet departments in addition to a plethora of agencies, boards, and commissions in the executive establishment. In 1790, fewer than a thousand employees worked for the executive branch; that number now has grown to approximately three million. Almost all these are civil service employees, however, the president directly appoints some two thousand upper-level officials.

Although the Constitution permits some upper-level officials in the executive branch to be selected solely at the discretion of the president and some to be appointed solely by the heads of departments, the more important federal officials are to be appointed by the president with the advice and consent of the Senate. In the case of appointments requiring senatorial consent, the president nominates a candidate, awaits Senate approval by majority vote, and then commissions the confirmed nominee as an "officer of the United States." The Constitution is reasonably clear on the subject of the presidential appointment power, but the issue of removal of an appointed official has been rather problematic. Obviously, the president has a strong interest in being able to remove those appointees whose performance displeases him. However, the Constitution addresses the question of removal only in the context of the cumbersome impeachment process. It is unlikely that the Framers intended that an administrative official whose performance is unacceptable to the president be subject to removal only by impeachment. Given the difficulty of this method of removal, this type of limitation could paralyze government.

Most observers agree that officers of the United States can be removed by means other than impeachment—except for judges, whose life tenure (assuming good behavior) is guaranteed by the Constitution. The problem is the role of Congress in the removal of executive officers. Given that the Constitution requires senatorial consent for certain presidential appointments, is it not reasonable to expect Congress to play a role in the removal of these officials? The Supreme Court's decisions in this area suggest that the legality of presidential removal of an official in the executive branch depends on the nature of the duties performed by the official in question. Officials performing purely executive functions may be removed by the president at will; those performing quasi-legislative or quasi-judicial functions can be removed only for cause. Legitimate cause includes malfeasance (wrongful conduct) or abuse of authority.

13-3d THE POWER TO GRANT PARDONS

President Gerald Ford's full and unconditional pardon of former President Richard Nixon following the Watergate affair may have been politically unwise, but it was unquestionably constitutional. Article II, Section 2 states that the president shall have the power to "grant reprieves and pardons for offenses against the United States, except in cases of impeachment." Although impeachment proceedings were initiated against President Nixon, his sudden resignation foreclosed any possibility of impeachment, let alone conviction by the Senate. Whether or not they liked the idea, most observers agreed that President Ford acted constitutionally in issuing the pardon to Nixon.

The pardoning power came under tremendous scrutiny in early 2001 following outgoing President Clinton's controversial pardons issued in the last days of his administration. Although many pardons raised eyebrows, one was particularly troubling—that of the fugitive billionaire Marc Rich. Although the power to pardon is absolute and unconditional, both the House and the Senate held hearings to investigate the circumstances surrounding the pardon, including the failure of the president to consult with the prosecuting attorneys in the case and, most especially, the role of Mr. Rich's ex-wife, Denise Rich. Ms. Rich had played a major role in fundraising for the president, Hillary Clinton for her senate campaign, the Democratic National Committee, and the Clinton Library. President Clinton's impolitic use of the pardoning power met with substantial public disapproval. According to a Gallup poll, 62 percent disapproved of the pardon, and only 20 percent approved of it. Worse, 58 percent believed that the pardon was made in "return for financial contributions."[7] The Rich pardon scandal further damaged former President Clinton's public image and helped to ensure that his legacy would be defined primarily in terms of scandal. The important point is that just because a president has the constitutional authority to take a certain action does not mean that the action is immune to criticism.

Amnesties

Although the presidential pardon was traditionally thought to be a private transaction between the president and the recipient, it did not prevent President Jimmy Carter from granting **amnesty**—in effect, a blanket pardon—to those who were either deserters or draft evaders during the Vietnam War. President Carter's amnesty was not challenged in the courts; neither was it criticized on constitutional grounds, although many considered it to be an insult to those who had fought and died in Vietnam. Note that Congress has traditionally granted amnesty to those who deserted or evaded service in America's wars.

13-3e Executive Privilege

Beginning with George Washington, presidents have asserted a right to withhold information from Congress and the courts. Known as **executive privilege**, this "right" has been defended as inherent in executive power. Indeed, it must be defended as such because it is mentioned nowhere in the Constitution. Scholars are divided over whether the Framers foresaw this type of power in the presidency, but the point is moot in light of two centuries of history supporting executive privilege and explicit Supreme Court recognition.

Although the term *executive privilege* was coined during the Eisenhower administration of the 1950s, the practice dates from 1792. In that year, President Washington refused to provide the House of Representatives with certain documents it had requested relative to the bewildering defeat of military forces under General St. Clair by the Ohio Indians. Washington again asserted the privilege in 1795 when the House requested information dealing with the negotiation of a peace treaty with Great Britain. A few years later, President Thomas Jefferson, once a sharp critic of Washington's approach to the presidency, would rely on inherent executive power in defying a subpoena issued during Aaron Burr's trial for treason in 1807.

Later presidents invoked executive privilege primarily to maintain the secrecy of information related to national security. Presidents Truman, Eisenhower, Kennedy, and Johnson all found occasion to invoke the doctrine to protect the confidentiality of their deliberations. Nevertheless, the power of executive privilege did not become a major point of contention until the Nixon presidency.

President Clinton's claims of executive privilege in limiting evidence in the Lewinsky matter was later the basis of one of the charges in his impeachment hearings. Ken Starr and House Republicans on the Judiciary Committee concluded that Clinton's privilege claims amounted to an abuse of power. However, the full House did not concur and failed to impeach Clinton on that count.

The Watergate Controversy

During his first term (1969–1973), President Richard M. Nixon invoked executive privilege on four separate occasions; others in the Nixon administration did so in more than twenty instances. But after his landslide reelection in 1972, Nixon and his appointees routinely employed executive privilege to evade queries from Congress regarding the Watergate break-in and subsequent cover-up. Although Nixon was able to use executive privilege to withhold information requested by Congress, he was unable to avoid a subpoena issued by the federal courts at the request of the Watergate special prosecutor Leon Jaworski. Earlier, Nixon had fired Archibald Cox, Jaworski's predecessor, when Cox refused to back down in his efforts to subpoena the infamous tapes on which Nixon had recorded conversations with other people involved in the Watergate scandal. In an episode that became known as the "Saturday night massacre," Nixon fired Attorney General Elliot Richardson and Assistant Attorney General William Ruckelshaus, both of whom refused to follow the president's order to dismiss Cox. Ultimately, Cox was dismissed on the order of Robert H. Bork, who was the solicitor general at the time. Although there was no question of Nixon's constitutional authority to dismiss Cox—who was, after all, an employee of the Justice Department—the dismissal was politically disastrous: the Saturday night massacre led Congress to consider the possibility of impeaching the president. Succeeding Archibald Cox, Leon Jaworski pursued the Watergate investigation with just as much enthusiasm as his predecessor. When the federal district court denied Nixon's motion to quash a new subpoena obtained by Jaworski, the question of executive privilege went to the Supreme Court.

In a severe blow to the Nixon administration, the Supreme Court ruled unanimously that the tapes had to be surrendered.[8] Recognizing the legitimacy of executive privilege, the Court nevertheless held that the needs of criminal justice outweighed the presidential interest in confidentiality in this case. The Court refused to view executive privilege as an absolute presidential immunity from the judicial process. Thus, the Court asserted the primacy of the rule of law over the power of the presidency. Although Nixon reportedly was tempted to defy the Court's ruling, wiser counsel prevailed and the tapes were surrendered. Shortly thereafter, recognizing the inevitable, Richard Nixon resigned the presidency.

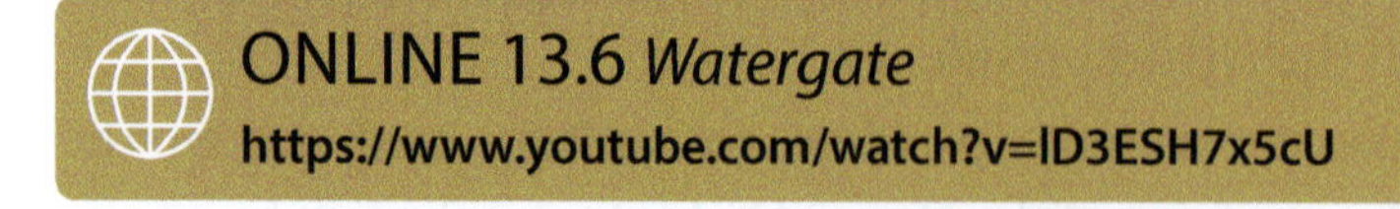
ONLINE 13.6 *Watergate*
https://www.youtube.com/watch?v=lD3ESH7x5cU

13-3f The Power to Make Foreign Policy

Scholars have written of the "two presidencies."[9] One aspect of the presidency, concerned with domestic affairs, is severely limited by the Constitution, the courts, and Congress. The other aspect of the presidency, involving foreign affairs and international relations, is less susceptible to constitutional and political constraints. Although the thesis may have been overstated, the basic point is valid. Throughout American history, Congress, the courts, and the public have been highly deferential to the president in the conduct of foreign policy. While some commentators suggest that a serious reading of the Constitution indicates that the Framers intended for Congress to play a greater role in foreign policy, the demands of history, more than the intentions of the Framers, determine the roles played by the institutions of government.

Another factor contributing to presidential dominance of foreign policy inheres in the distinctive structures of Congress and the executive branch. Congress is composed of 535 members, each representing either a state or a localized constituency. In contrast, the president represents a national constituency. American political culture supports the idea that the president alone should speak for the nation in the international arena.

The "Sole Organ" in the Field of International Relations?

In *United States v. Curtiss-Wright Export Corporation* (1936), the Supreme Court placed its stamp of approval on the primary power of the president in the realm of foreign affairs, referring to the president as the "sole organ of the federal government in the field of international relations."[10] Many would challenge the Court's sweeping endorsement of presidential power to make foreign policy; few would argue that the president should be subject to no constitutional limitations in making and executing the foreign policy of this nation. Clearly, though, the degree of freedom afforded the president in the field of foreign policy has been substantial indeed.

In the wake of Vietnam and Watergate, and fueled by revelations about covert activities by the Central Intelligence Agency (CIA) during the 1960s, Congress in the 1970s adopted a series of laws limiting presidential power to employ covert means of pursuing foreign policy objectives. Moreover, during the 1980s, members of Congress began to get personally involved in diplomatic affairs by making trips to foreign countries that were not approved by the White House. For example, Speaker of the House Jim Wright (D-Texas) launched his own "peace mission" to Central America during the mid-1980s, when the Reagan administration was actively supporting rebels fighting the Marxist government of Nicaragua. Needless to say, President Reagan and his advisers were not amused by what they saw as an encroachment on the role of the executive.

Similarly, Reagan was irritated when Senator Richard Lugar (R-Indiana) went to the Philippines in 1986 to investigate allegations of fraud in the elections that kept President Ferdinand Marcos, a longtime ally of the United States, in power. The White House had originally supported Marcos' claim to a legitimate electoral victory, but it had to retreat from its support of Marcos based in part on statements made by Senator Lugar. Clearly, the president had been upstaged and embarrassed by a U.S. senator acting on his own in the foreign policy arena. Although nothing is illegal about these types of activities on the part of members of Congress, they are not likely to curry favor with the White House and in fact may generate considerable political ill will.

The Iran–Contra Scandal

In the 1980s, when Congress learned of CIA efforts to support the Contras battling to overthrow the Marxist government of Nicaragua, it adopted the Boland Amendments, a series of measures restricting the use of U.S. funds to aid the Contras. The Reagan administration attempted an "end run" around the Boland Amendments by secretly selling weapons to Iran and using the profits to aid the Contras. When the operation was uncovered, an outraged Congress conducted an investigation that included the testimony of Lt. Col. Oliver North, a staff member of the National Security Council who was heavily involved in the covert operation. North was convicted of perjury and obstruction of justice, but his conviction was overturned on appeal in 1991.

Although the Iran–Contra affair was a blow to the credibility and prestige of the Reagan administration, it remains shrouded in legal uncertainty. It is not clear whether the administration violated the Boland Amendments, although little doubt exists that it sought to undermine the policy objective behind the amendments. Second, given the Supreme Court's pronouncements in *United States v. Curtiss-Wright* (1936), a serious question exists about the extent to which Congress may exercise control over presidential actions in the foreign policy sphere. Clearly, Congress may impose restrictions on the expenditure of government funds because Congress possesses the "power of the purse." May Congress prevent the president from carrying out a foreign policy objective through "creative enterprises," however, such as the deal to sell weapons to Iran?

Troubling constitutional questions involving the allocation of powers in the field of foreign policy are unlikely to be resolved in the courts of law. Rather, as "political questions," they are apt to be resolved in the court of public opinion. As the underwhelming public response to Iran–Contra demonstrates, the American people are not particularly troubled by broad presidential latitude in the foreign policy arena. Indeed, American political culture has always glorified the heroic individual who leads the community out of crisis.

13-3g The Specifics of Conducting Foreign Affairs

Although presidential authority in international relations rests in large part on inherent executive power, the Constitution also enumerates specific powers important in the everyday management of foreign affairs. Article II, Section 3 authorizes the president to receive ambassadors and emissaries from foreign nations. In effect, it provides the president the power to recognize the legitimate governments of foreign nations. This power is of obvious importance in international relations, as attested by Franklin Roosevelt's recognition of the Soviet government in the 1930s, Truman's recognition of Israel, Kennedy's severance of ties with Cuba, and Carter's recognition of the People's Republic of China.

Treaties

In addition to the authority to recognize foreign governments, the president is empowered by Article II to make treaties with foreign nations, subject to the consent of the Senate. A **treaty** is an agreement between two or more nations, in which they promise to behave in specified ways. The atmospheric nuclear test-ban treaty negotiated under President Kennedy's leadership, the SALT I treaty reached with the Soviets during the Nixon presidency, and the Panama Canal treaty negotiated during the Carter administration illustrate the importance of the treaty-making power.

In the early 1990s, treaties dealing with issues of international trade emerged as more important than agreements dealing with strategic issues or arms control. The North American Free Trade Agreement (NAFTA) and the General Agreement on Tariffs and Trade (GATT), both of which were negotiated in 1993, dramatically altered the climate for international business. In essence, these treaties lowered barriers to imported goods and services, thus facilitating trade among nations. Most economists predicted positive economic consequences for the world community. President Bill Clinton, whose first year in office was marred by a number of foreign-policy problems, gained considerable stature as a world leader by presiding over the successful conclusion of these treaties. This success abroad also had a positive effect on Clinton's approval rating at home, which rose to 56 percent in December 1993, a level of public support that Clinton had not enjoyed since he took office the preceding January.[11]

Executive Agreements

Like treaties, **executive agreements** require certain national commitments. These types of agreements, however, are negotiated solely between heads of state acting independently of their legislative bodies. Most of these agreements involve minor matters of international concern, such as specification of the details of postal relations or the use of radio airwaves. In recent years, however, the executive agreement has emerged as an important tool of foreign policy making. It enables the president to enter into an agreement with another country without the need for Senate approval, as is constitutionally required in the case of treaties.

Perhaps the most dramatic recent use of the executive agreement was President Jimmy Carter's agreement with Iran that secured the release of fifty-two American hostages in early 1981. The agreement negated all claims against Iranian assets in the United States and transferred claims against Iran from American to international tribunals. In 1981, the Supreme Court upheld the validity of Carter's executive agreement.[12] The Court found in the Emergency Powers Act of 1977 sufficient presidential authority to cancel claims against Iran. Finding no statutory authority for the transfer of claims to an international tribunal, the Court held that Congress had tacitly approved the president's actions by its traditional pattern of acquiescence to executive agreements. Thus, merely by being used, a power that is thought by some to conflict with the Constitution can gain legitimacy.

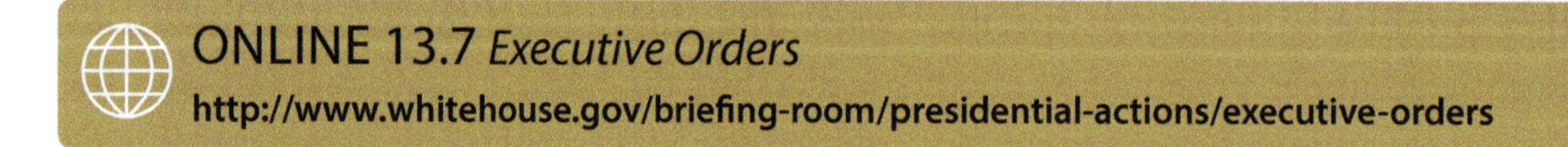

ONLINE 13.7 *Executive Orders*
http://www.whitehouse.gov/briefing-room/presidential-actions/executive-orders

13-3h Presidential War Powers

Presidential dominance in international affairs is not limited to or based on the formalities of recognizing and striking agreements with other governments. Essential to the president's foreign policy role is the tremendous power of the American military, over which the Constitution makes the president commander-in-chief. Force is often threatened, and sometimes used, to protect American allies and interests, maintain national security against possible attack, or defend the nation against actual attack. The success of American foreign policy would be severely limited if the Constitution curbed the nation's ability to respond effectively to threats against its interests or security. On the other hand, the Constitution was designed as a limitation on the power of our government.

The Framers of the Constitution attempted to provide some limitation on the war-making power, as they did with government power in general, by dividing power between the president and Congress. Although Article II recognizes the president as commander-in-chief, Article I provides Congress with the authority to declare war. Does this mean that a formal declaration by Congress is the only way the United States can get into a war? Evidently not. The military conflicts in Vietnam and Korea qualify as wars, yet in neither case did Congress issue a formal declaration of war. When the United States was attacked by Islamic terrorists in September 2001, President George W. Bush rhetorically declared that the United States would wage a "war on terrorism." President Bush did not seek, and Congress did not pass, a declaration of war. But Congress did adopt a resolution authorizing Bush to use military force against the terrorists and those states that harbor them.

Presidential power to commit military forces to combat situations in the absence of a formal declaration of war has a long-standing heritage. It was first exercised in 1801, when Thomas Jefferson sent the U.S. Marines to "the shores of Tripoli" to root out the Barbary pirates. In 1846, James K. Polk sent American troops to instigate a conflict with Mexico that Congress formally approved by declaring war. In 1854, Franklin Pierce authorized a show of American force that led to the total destruction of an entire city in Central America. During the Civil War, Abraham Lincoln exercised broad war powers to prevent the dissolution of the Union.

The Vietnam War

Lacking a formal declaration of war by Congress, the Johnson administration maintained that inherent presidential power essentially included the power to make war. In the Gulf of Tonkin Resolution of 1964, Congress gave limited authority to the president to take whatever actions were necessary to defend the government of South Vietnam and American interests and personnel in the region. The resolution was adopted in response to an alleged attack on American ships operating near North Vietnam. Later evidence indicated that the attack was at least exaggerated and was perhaps contrived to force Congress to sanction the growing American involvement in Southeast Asia. It was not long before the war expanded far beyond anything envisioned by Congress in 1964. In a later development in the Vietnam conflict, President Nixon's covert war in Cambodia certainly fell beyond any authority granted the president by the Gulf of Tonkin Resolution. Amidst the harsh strains of sometimes violent anti-war protest, calmer voices began to be heard questioning the legality of the war effort.

During the Vietnam era, the Supreme Court had ample opportunity to rule on the constitutionality of the war, but it declined to do so, viewing the issue as a "political question."[13] The Court drew some criticism for this deferential posture. However, the Court likely would have also been attacked if it had chosen to review the constitutionality of the Vietnam War. It certainly would have been criticized more harshly if its ruling had been adverse to the president. In any event, the influence of the courts over the conduct of wars, foreign or domestic, is minimal at most. The reason in large part is that the courts really do not have any way to make presidents abide by their decisions.

The War Powers Resolution

In the waning days of the Vietnam War, Congress began to question the unbridled conception of presidential war powers. In 1973, Congress adopted the War Powers Resolution over the veto of President Nixon. The act was designed to limit the president's unilateral power to send troops into foreign combat. It requires the president to make a full report to Congress when sending troops into foreign areas, limits the duration of troop commitment without congressional authorization, and provides a veto mechanism whereby Congress can force the recall of troops at any time.

Serious questions have arisen about the constitutionality of the War Powers Resolution. Yet because Congress has not yet invoked the resolution, the courts have had no occasion to address the question of its constitutionality. The War Powers Resolution is unlikely to ever be subjected to judicial review because it is unlikely to ever be invoked against the president. Even if the resolution were invoked and litigation resulted, the courts probably would view the matter as a political question. In 1982, a federal judge dismissed as "political" a lawsuit brought by members of Congress against President Reagan. The members were attempting to get the courts to invoke the War Powers

Resolution to prevent the Reagan administration from providing military aid to the government of El Salvador.[14]

Aside from the question of its constitutionality, the War Powers Resolution is probably not an effective constraint on the presidential war power. Indeed, it can be viewed as little more than a symbolic gesture of defiance from a Congress displeased with the conduct of the Vietnam War. The existence of the War Powers Resolution did not prevent President Reagan from employing military force in pursuit of his foreign policy objectives. Reagan sent the U.S. Marines into Beirut and even used naval gunfire against the rebels in the Lebanese civil war. Reagan employed U.S. troops to topple the Marxist government of Grenada. And he ordered an air strike on Libya to punish the Gadhaffi regime for its support of international terrorism. Although Reagan chose to comply with the War Powers Resolution in all three cases by notifying Congress of his actions, it was still the president who made the decisions to send troops into hostile situations. Congressional disapproval would have made no difference in the cases of Grenada and Libya; the hostilities had practically ceased by the time Congress was notified. In the case of Lebanon, when the ninety-day time limit expired, Congress chose to extend the deadline rather than face an embarrassing and probably futile confrontation with the president over the removal of the troops.

The 1991 Persian Gulf War

Soon after Saddam Hussein's Iraq invaded and annexed Kuwait in August 1990, President George H.W. Bush ordered military forces into Saudi Arabia in a defensive posture. When it became clear that Iraq had no intention of leaving Kuwait, Bush ordered a massive buildup of forces in the region and began to threaten the use of force to remove Iraqi troops from Kuwait. Bush's critics soon suggested that the War Powers Resolution had been triggered because American troops were in a situation of imminent hostility. Yet Congress did not attempt to "start the clock" under the resolution.

When the president did finally decide to move against Iraq in January 1991, he first obtained a resolution from Congress supporting the use of force. Had Bush refused to obtain congressional approval, it would have been interesting to see whether and how Congress would have asserted itself. Little question exists, however, of whether Bush's decision to seek congressional approval ultimately enhanced political support for the war. The war was executed with overwhelming force, resulting in minimal losses to allied forces. Iraq, which suffered enormous losses in both life and property, capitulated quickly. In the wake of the war, President Bush's approval ratings soared to levels not seen since the end of World War II. Presidential popularity is a volatile phenomenon, however, and Bush's approval ratings dropped steadily during the remainder of 1991, culminating in his defeat in the presidential election of 1992.

Afghanistan and the War on Terrorism

When Islamic militants flew hijacked airplanes into the World Trade Center and the Pentagon in September 2001, they were continuing a series of terrorist acts aimed at the United States. In the 1990s, these acts included attacks on American embassies in Africa and military housing in Saudi Arabia and the suicide attack on the USS Cole in Yemen. President George W. Bush responded to the 9/11 attacks by assembling a worldwide coalition and demanding that the Taliban government in Afghanistan turn over Osama bin Laden, the leader of the terrorist effort, to the United States. When the Afghan leader Mullah Omar refused, the United States began a relentless bombing campaign that led to the victory of the opposition Northern Alliance and other groups in overthrowing the Taliban. This effort was clearly the beginning of a new era in U.S. policy. This war, unlike those in Bosnia, Kosovo, and the first Gulf War, was supported by the vast majority of the American people and by an overwhelming majority in Congress.

The war in Afghanistan was, by most accounts, a success. The Taliban was defeated and al Qaeda forces dispersed. A new transition government was installed in Kabul. In the fall of 2004, Afghans went to the polls in that country's first-ever democratic election. A fledgling democracy had taken root in a country with no history of democracy. On the other hand, Mullah Omar and bin Laden evaded capture, and many of the Taliban and al Qaeda operatives escaped into the lawless areas of northwest Pakistan.

Of course, no one (including President Bush) knew in 2002 what the scope of the war on terrorism would be. After the Taliban was overthrown, what other states might come under military attack? The president argued that Iraq was a terrorist state, and many people speculated on imminent military action to remove Saddam Hussein. Meanwhile, major conflicts between Israel and the Palestinians further strained the United States' ability to focus on any one conflict. How long would the war on terrorism last? Clearly, it would be a war unlike any other.

The war on terrorism raised other questions. In November 2001, President Bush announced that the United States would make use of military tribunals to try noncitizens accused of terrorism. Although most people conceded that this practice was permissible under the Constitution, many in the media and in Congress were highly critical of Bush's plan. Some complained that although Bush might technically have the power in his role as commander-in-chief, he should be more specific regarding the circumstances under which tribunals would be used and the procedures they would follow. Others worried that using military commissions to try accused terrorists sent the wrong message to the world: that America was abandoning its historic commitment to the ideal of due process. These questions continued when captured Taliban and al Qaeda personnel were brought to the American naval base at Guantanamo Bay, Cuba, for detainment in 2002.

The War in Iraq

At President George W. Bush's urging, Congress in October 2002 authorized military action against Iraq. President Bush praised the resolution, declaring that "America speaks with one voice" on Iraq. But Americans were far from united on this issue. Invoking painful memories of the Vietnam War, Senator Robert Byrd (D-West Virginia) asserted, "This is the Tonkin Gulf resolution all over again. Let us stop, look and listen. Let us not give this president or any president unchecked power. Remember the Constitution."[15] President Bush sought to link the invasion of Iraq to the war on terrorism by stressing the need to secure Saddam Hussein's supposed weapons of mass destruction (WMDs), lest they fall into the hands of terrorists. The fact that no stockpiles of chemical or biological weapons were found in Iraq after American troops captured the country took a tremendous toll on President Bush's credibility. Had those weapons been found in Iraq, the president's decision to go to war would have been largely vindicated, and he might well have been politically unassailable. The failure to find WMDs made the president extremely vulnerable, and Democrats would seek to exploit that vulnerability during the 2004 campaign.

The unrelenting media coverage of the war, most of which brought bad news, placed President Bush on the defensive. Of course, despite bad news from Iraq, President Bush was able to secure reelection. Within days after the election, American forces launched an offensive in Fallujah, a city controlled by insurgents opposed to American occupation and the interim Iraqi government supported by the United States. Although the offensive was successful in meeting its specific objectives, it by no means brought an end to the insurgency. An Associated Press poll taken after the election showed that achieving stability in Iraq was the voters' top priority.[16] Clearly, this would be President Bush's most daunting challenge as his second term began. In its post-election issue, *Time* magazine stated the case bluntly: "The bloody mess in Iraq remains George W. Bush's No. 1 responsibility and the one most likely to define his presidential legacy."[17]

13-3i Domestic Powers during Wartime

Just as serious as the constitutional question over who has the power to *make* war is the question of the extent of presidential power within our borders *during* wartime. Do the president's **inherent power** and duty to protect national security override constitutional limitations and the rights of citizens? The Supreme Court's answer to the question has been mixed.

The "Relocation" of Japanese Americans during World War II

Early in World War II, President Franklin D. Roosevelt issued orders authorizing the establishment of zones from which persons the military considered to be security risks could be expelled or excluded. Congressional legislation supported Roosevelt's orders by establishing criminal penalties for violators. Under these executive and congressional mandates, General DeWitt, who headed the Western Defense Command, proclaimed a curfew and issued an order excluding all Japanese Americans from a designated West Coast military area. The exclusion order led first to the imprisonment of some one hundred twenty thousand persons in "assembly centers" surrounded by barbed wire. Later, these Japanese Americans were removed to "relocation centers" in rural areas as far inland as Arkansas.

Although these actions were justified at the time on grounds of military necessity, overwhelming evidence indicates that they were in fact based on the view that all Japanese Americans were "subversive" members of an "enemy race." In spite of the blatant racism reflected in these policies, the Supreme Court upheld both the curfew and the exclusion order.[18] A majority of the justices concluded that, under the pressure of war, the government had a compelling interest justifying such extreme measures. It has now been well established that the forced relocation of thousands of Japanese Americans was not justified on grounds of military necessity and was motivated largely by racial hostility. In 1988, Congress belatedly acknowledged the government's responsibility for this gross miscarriage of justice by awarding reparations to survivors of the internment camps.

Peacetime Threats to National Security

During peacetime, presidential responses to perceived domestic threats to the national security are not as likely to win judicial approval. A good example is the Nixon administration's extensive wiretapping and other forms of electronic surveillance directed at American citizens during the late 1960s and early 1970s. The Supreme Court held that these activities, which were conducted without prior judicial approval, offended the Fourth Amendment prohibition against unreasonable searches and seizures.[19] The Court rejected the Nixon administration's argument that inherent executive power permitted the government to take these actions to obtain intelligence regarding foreign agents acting in the domestic sphere. In 1978, Congress buttressed the Court's decision by adopting the Foreign Intelligence Surveillance Act, which requires government agents to obtain a search warrant before subjecting American citizens to electronic surveillance for the purpose of foreign intelligence.

Detention of American Citizens Suspected of Terrorism

Two months after the terrorist attacks of 9/11, President George W. Bush signed an executive order authorizing the creation of military tribunals for the detention, treatment, and trial of certain noncitizens in the war against terrorism. After the invasion of Afghanistan, hundreds of foreign nationals suspected of fighting for al Qaeda were detained at the U.S. naval base at Guantanamo Bay, Cuba. One of these individuals was Yaser Hamdi, a Saudi national who was also an American citizen because he was born in New Orleans. When military officials discovered that he was an American citizen, they moved him to a military prison in the United States. He was not charged with a crime, but held incommunicado as an "enemy combatant." Hamdi sought a writ of habeas corpus in the federal courts, challenging the legality of his detention. The Bush administration argued that the president had authority as commander-in-chief to detain enemy combatants, even American citizens, and that such detentions were not subject to judicial review.

Commenting on the case, former Justice Department official David Rivkin observed that it was "absolutely, clearly, constitutionally permissible, as a matter of international law, for an enemy combatant, lawful or unlawful, detained in the course of open hostilities, to be held on any charges proffered, for the duration of this particular conflict."[20] Taking the opposite view, Georgetown University law professor Mark Tushnet observed, "The difficulty with the administration's position is that, at least as applied to U.S. citizens, it poses a threat to essentially anyone who the administration chooses to call an enemy combatant."[21] In June 2004, the Supreme Court decided the case of *Hamdi v. Rumsfeld*.[22] The Court stopped short of ruling on the constitutional questions pertaining to presidential power, but did say that Hamdi was entitled to a fair and impartial hearing to determine the factual basis of his detention. Subsequently, Mr. Hamdi renounced his American citizenship and was deported to Saudi Arabia. A similar case, *Rumsfeld v. Padilla*, was dismissed on technical grounds.[23] The Supreme Court managed, at least in the near term, to avoid the troubling constitutional questions raised by indefinite military detention of American citizens suspected of terrorism.

13-4 The Structure of the Presidential Office

The responsibilities of the presidency are so vast, and the expectations of the American people so great, that one person cannot possibly exercise the powers of the presidency. Clearly, the president needs help, which he gets from a variety of supporting offices within the executive branch.

Throughout the first 140 years of the Republic, the president had only a small staff. Not until 1857 did Congress even pass a provision allowing the president to hire a full-time clerk. Early presidents relied mostly on their cabinet members and a few close personal advisers to help them form policy. With the emergence of a more active presidency during Franklin Roosevelt's tenure in office, however, greater staff resources were required. Three main sources of staff assistance are now available to presidents:

- The White House staff
- The Executive Office of the President
- The Cabinet

Presidents generally rely most heavily on the members of the White House staff. They are the president's closest advisers. Cabinet members do not have as much daily access to the president, who usually relies less heavily on them than on the White House staff or the Executive Office of the President.

13-4a THE WHITE HOUSE STAFF

The president usually places his closest advisers in positions on the White House staff. In selecting these staffers, the president does not have to worry as much about their public reputation as he does in choosing members of the cabinet. Congress allows the president great latitude in choosing White House staff, but occasionally rejects cabinet nominees. Each president also has the power to organize the White House staff in whatever manner he chooses. Some have preferred tightly organized structures with only a few close advisers at the top, and others have designed open structures allowing much greater access to the president.

The most important position in the White House is the **chief of staff**. The chief of staff is viewed as the president's right-hand man. Usually, the chief of staff controls the president's calendar, limits access to the president, manages the staff, and helps the president in all aspects of domestic and foreign policy. The most important qualification for the position is loyalty to the president. The chief of staff often serves as the bad guy for the president so that the president can maintain a likable reputation. H. R. Haldeman argued that "Every president needs a son of a bitch, and I'm Nixon's. I get what he wants done, and I take the heat instead of him."[24] Because the chief of staff must say no to so many people, he often serves as a lightning rod for the president. Many have eventually fallen from power because of a scandal: Sherman Adams, Eisenhower's chief, left after being accused of taking gifts from a lobbyist; Haldeman was disgraced by Watergate; and John Sununu, George Bush's chief, was forced out after media attention focused on his use of government jets for private purposes. This job is not easy, and few have made it through an entire four-year presidential term.

The White House staff had grown to more than five hundred people by the time George H.W. Bush took office in 1989. The shape of the organization changes with every president, but generally the president has an adviser who coordinates domestic policy, a liaison staff that lobbies Congress for the president, and a press secretary and a communications director who coordinate public relations and press relations. Any services the president needs in performing the many aspects of the job are essentially provided by the White House staff.

13-4b The Executive Office

The Executive Office of the President (EOP) was formed in 1939 with thirty-seven employees. By 1992, it had grown to more than fifteen hundred employees. Most EOP employees work in the Executive Office Building, a structure right next to the White House. The EOP includes several different units; the three most important are the National Security Council (NSC), the Council of Economic Advisers (CEA), and the Office of Management and Budget (OMB). The National Security Council, formed in 1947, assists the president in handling crises in the international arena. The NSC is composed of the president, the vice president, the secretary of defense, and the secretary of state. The staff of the NSC helps the president interpret the massive amount of information on international events that flows into the White House. The NSC staff appraises the quality of the information, filters out the less meaningful and unsubstantiated stories, and packages the information in a way more useful to the president. The NSC works closely with other parts of the bureaucracy, such as the Department of Defense and the CIA.

The Council of Economic Advisers assists the president in evaluating economic trends and formulating economic policy. Composed of three economists appointed by the president, the council prepares an annual President's Economic Report that analyzes economic developments. The council is designed to help the president anticipate potential weaknesses in the economy and devise policy to maintain economic growth.

The Office of Management and Budget, originally called the Bureau of the Budget, was formed in 1921. The OMB prepares the president's budget proposal to Congress, helps push the proposal through Congress, and analyzes the effects of all new programs on the national debt. Because of the central role the budget plays in the legislative agenda, this power alone would make the OMB one of the most influential units within the federal bureaucracy. The OMB, however, has gained over time other responsibilities that have greatly expanded its power. Franklin Roosevelt, after taking the bureau out of the Treasury Department and placing it in the EOP, required that all new agency proposals receive clearance through the OMB before being sent to Congress. This centralized clearance procedure greatly enhanced the bureau's power. Later, President Reagan required that all new agency rules proposed by the bureaucracy must also receive OMB approval before they can take effect. This combination of budget influence, clearance for agency proposals to Congress, and review of agency rule making has made the OMB the single most important tool for presidential control of domestic policy.

ONLINE 13.8: *The Executive Office of the President*
http://www.whitehouse.gov/administration/eop

13-4c The Cabinet

The president's cabinet consists of the heads of the major executive departments. Originally, the cabinet consisted of the attorney general and the secretaries of state, war, and treasury. The cabinet now includes the heads of the fifteen major executive departments in addition to certain other high-level executive officials. At one time, the cabinet members were close advisers to the president, but their role has gradually changed as the bureaucracy has grown, the powers of the president have expanded, and expectations of the president have increased. The bureaucracy is composed of three million civilian employees with a multitude of programs, so the cabinet members do not have the time to assist the president on a day-to-day basis. Furthermore, recent presidents have not always completely trusted their cabinet members, for two reasons.

First, cabinet members are often chosen for public relations reasons. Presidents, particularly Democrats, are concerned about the symbolism of the appointments. Features such as ethnicity, gender, geographic origin, membership in an interest group, ideological orientation, and prominence within the party are all considered by the president in making an appointment. Because of the concern for balancing the cabinet along these lines, a president may have to seek out people he does not know. Because their prominence gives them an independent power base, cabinet members are not usually part of the president's inner circle of advisers.

A second factor reducing the power of cabinet members as presidential advisers is that many recent presidents have not trusted the bureaucracy, and they are suspicious that cabinet members may be "captured" by the interests they represent. Presidents Nixon and Reagan, in particular, believed that much of the bureaucracy had a liberal, pro-government stance that would thwart their conservative policies if given a chance. If a president has a choice between relying on advice from a White House staffer who has been loyal for a number of years or a cabinet secretary who was only recently brought on the team and may be more sympathetic to the interests of the agency she manages, the president is likely to choose the staffer. Cabinet members are especially likely to be excluded from the most important strategic planning when the president is already hostile toward the programs and political aims of their agency or department.

The influence of a cabinet member ultimately depends on the president. In some cases, such as when Robert Kennedy was John F. Kennedy's attorney general, cabinet members can be extremely influential, but often they are not. The bureaucracy retains access to large volumes of information, expertise, experience, and policy ideas, but often presidents do not fully utilize it because of the lack of trust, the rivalry between agencies, and the vast number of points where information can be cut off on the way to the president. On the other hand, control of the bureaucracy is one of the most important, and most difficult, functions of the president.

13-5 The Functioning Presidency

Although the Constitution has granted the president a variety of powers that permit decisive leadership on foreign policy, it is less generous on the domestic front. Presidents are more likely to become bogged down in battles with Congress over domestic policy. This likelihood can be politically dangerous to a president because legislative gridlock may create the appearance that the president is indecisive or incapable of leadership. In turn, this perception may adversely affect his chance of reelection, ability to get legislation passed, and place in history.

If the president wants to have a long-term effect on domestic policy, he must work with Congress to pass legislation, although the Constitution has provided the president with few resources. The Constitution gives the president the veto power and the right to "give to the Congress information of the state of the Union, and recommend to their consideration such measures as he shall judge necessary and expedient." The veto does provide the president with leverage over legislation, but it is a difficult tool for the president to use in all but the most extreme cases. Because the president must veto the entire bill, this tool is not useful for working out differences of opinion on the details of legislation.

Most of the president's influence over lawmaking has evolved over time as presidents have expanded on the duty to report on the "State of the Union." Most presidents in the first century of the Republic did not use the State of the Union speech or their power to recommend legislative measures as a means of creating their own policy agenda. Some presidents actively attempted to control congressional action on legislation, but most did not. Though the increase in presidential influence over Congress evolved over time, the presidency of Franklin D. Roosevelt radically changed the president's role in the policy process. Partly because of his political ideology but largely because of the devastating economic conditions of the Great Depression, Roosevelt came into office with the most active legislative agenda ever proposed by a president. His first hundred days in office were so productive that they have served as a measure for assessing the efforts of all other presidents. The public now expects the president to come into office with a set of policy preferences that he wants to see enacted.

13-5a The President's Legislative Agenda

The president's **legislative agenda** is the primary tool available for securing and extending his power. Passage of the agenda is the key to the president's effort to be reelected to a second term and to secure his place in history. These goals, along with any campaign promises from his first election, are often the primary motivation for what the president places on the agenda and moves to the top of his priority list. For example, President Reagan's top priority in 1981 was enacting tax cuts. Reagan first proposed these cuts during the campaign of 1980, and the administration assumed that they would stimulate economic growth that would aid Reagan's reelection bid in 1984. Of course, the president's political ideology and vision of good policy also shape the nature of his policy proposals. For example, even though President George H.W. Bush claimed that education was high on his agenda in 1989, he was not interested in creating any costly new programs. Current events also influence the agenda. For example, the oil shortages and huge energy price increases of the 1970s forced President Carter to make energy policy a priority.

Beyond formulating an agenda, the president must push Congress to act on his proposals. That is not an easy job because Congress is a complex organization with a heavy workload separate from the president's agenda. Negotiating with Congress over policy has become increasingly difficult as Congress has become more fragmented and decentralized. Furthermore, because of the decline of partisanship, the president cannot even rely on his own party members to fully support all aspects of his agenda. President Clinton certainly experienced this phenomenon repeatedly during his first two years in office. He had a wide-ranging agenda after taking office in 1993. Most observers later questioned his strategy of beginning his term with such controversial issues as gays in the military and national healthcare reform. Both were controversial, and in both cases no obvious consensus was formed in either public opinion or Congress. President George W. Bush, on the other hand, began his term in 2001 with issues around which he could more easily build: an education initiative and a substantial tax cut.

Political Context

Several factors influence the political situation facing the president. First, does the president have an electoral mandate? Second, does the president face a friendly Congress with a majority of his own party members or a hostile Congress with a majority of the opposition party? Third, is the president at the beginning of a term, late in the first term, or in the second term in office?

Candidates have been propelled into the White House by a wide variety of margins. Some presidents, such as Clinton in 1992, are elected with less than 50 percent of the popular vote, whereas others, such as Johnson in 1964 and Reagan in 1984, received approximately 60 percent of the popular vote. A strong showing in both the popular vote and the electoral college is viewed as a **landslide**. A landslide lends tremendous credibility to a president's claim of a mandate. A **mandate** is the idea that the people have spoken in an election and that they support the president so strongly that they want his agenda to pass. Though the concept of a mandate is so vague that almost every president can claim he has one, if most people believe the claim, it can be a powerful tool in Congress. To use a mandate successfully, the president as a candidate must have expressed a clear set of ideas that form an agenda. This step is important because the president must be able to identify what the people were saying they wanted. Obviously, it is a game of perception, but, nevertheless, the more others believe that the president's victory represented people's approval of a particular set of ideas, the more likely the president will be able to translate a mandate into political capital in Congress. This capital is crucial to passage of the president's agenda.

In no case was a lack of a mandate more obvious than in George W. Bush's election in 2000 and his subsequent inauguration in 2001. Not only did Bush lose the popular vote, the newly appointed chair of the Democratic National Committee, Terry McAuliffe, stated his strong belief that Bush had not legitimately won in Florida. However, President Bush, after assuming office, began his administration without any indication that he held office without public support. After President Bush narrowly won reelection in 2004, some of his supporters characterized the outcome as a "mandate," but few neutral observers could agree with that characterization. Today, with the people of the United States so sharply divided ideologically, landslide elections are unlikely. But a mandate requires more than a "squeaker" like the 2004 election.

The Partisanship of Congress

The partisan makeup of Congress dramatically affects the likelihood of the president's legislative success. Presidents are much more successful when their party has a majority in each chamber. From 1955 to 1994, the Democrats controlled the House of Representatives, so no Republican president since Eisenhower has enjoyed an easy ride in the House. The Senate was Democratic every year from 1955 to 1994 with the exception of the six years from 1981 to 1987. This six-year period of Republican control of the Senate was quite beneficial to President Reagan in that it gave him a strong ally in his battles with the Democratic House.

Unlike Reagan, Republicans Nixon, Ford, and George H.W. Bush had to work with hostile Congresses that were not only willing to defeat or ignore the presidential agenda but were also likely to pass their own measures. Ford and Bush both made extensive use of the veto power in staving off Democratic legislation; and Congress overrode many of Ford's vetoes, though only one of Bush's. Until 1968, when Nixon was elected president and the Democrats retained control of Congress, divided-party government in this country was rare. But in twenty of the twenty-four years between 1968 and the inauguration of Democrat Bill Clinton, presidents have had to deal with Congresses in which at least one chamber had a majority of the opposite party. This long period of divided government made presidential leadership of Congress even more difficult. George W. Bush was unquestionably extremely pleased in November 2002 when Republicans regained control of both houses of Congress.

In devising a strategy for getting his agenda passed, a president can divide each chamber of Congress into four partisan groups:

1. Strong party loyalists of the president's party
2. Weak party loyalists
3. Weak opposition-party members
4. Strong opposition-party members

The president can count on strong party loyalists to be supportive in most legislative battles and strong opposition-party members to almost always work against his agenda. The two decisive groups are the moderates in each party. Most of the president's efforts to put together coalitions to pass his agenda focus on the two moderate groups. For example, President Reagan in 1981 faced a Democratic majority in the House, but he was able to put together successful coalitions. He achieved them by keeping his party in line and wooing conservative Democrats, particularly southerners known as the Boll Weevils.

In 1995, President Clinton faced an especially daunting task in dealing with a Congress that had just come under Republican control via the 1994 midterm elections. In the wake of the Republican victory, the magnitude of which no one had expected, Clinton appealed for cooperation and pledged to "govern from the center." However, the Republicans, who were feeling their oats after capturing both houses of Congress for the first time since 1954, were in no mood to compromise. Rather, they looked eagerly to the 1996 presidential election that they hoped would return the White House to Republican control. Of course, that was not the case. By the end of his term, Clinton's relationship with Congress had plummeted, pushed downward by impeachment, vetoes, and battles that either threatened to shut down, or did in fact shut down, the federal government.

George W. Bush's relationship with Congress, although beginning on a high note, showed signs of deterioration during 2002. The Senate, under the leadership of Tom Daschle after the defection of Vermont Senator Jim Jeffords in 2001, turned down some of the president's judicial appointments and delayed consideration of others. Following his reelection victory in 2004 and Daschle's loss in South Dakota, President Bush could look forward to a slightly more Republican Senate under new leadership, but with no assurance of success in overcoming the threat of a filibuster in the Senate for any judges deemed too conservative by the Democratic leadership.

The Importance of Timing

The timing of a new proposal is extremely important for a president. Even a president who enjoys congressional majorities realizes that a mandate does not last for long. A president must "move it or lose it" in trying to use the mandate to push legislation through Congress in the first hundred days, sometimes referred to as the **honeymoon period**. During the early days of the term, the president still enjoys the benefits of the electoral victory. The press treats a new president with a bit more deference, the members of Congress are still somewhat taken by the new person in the White House, and the general mood is one of high expectations of the new administration. Members of the president's party are likely to believe the president has a mandate, and electorally vulnerable members of the opposition party may be more likely to go along with the president. Recently, the honeymoon period has been getting progressively shorter for each new president as the press has become more aggressive, Congress has become more independent, and the public has become more cynical about politics. For example, Dave Barry, a national humor columnist, was already referring to the Clinton presidency as the "failed Clinton administration" even before Clinton had taken office!

Many questioned whether George W. Bush would have much of a honeymoon period following his contentious election in 2000. However, after assuming office, President Bush embarked on what many in the media referred to as a "charm offensive" with congressional Democrats. Bush attended a Democratic caucus and invited many Democrats to the White House. The initiative seemed to disarm many Democrats and set a decidedly more pleasant tone, at least at the beginning of the term.

Because of the honeymoon phenomenon, presidential proposals are much more likely to pass if they are presented in the first year of the president's first term, and the earlier in the year, the better. One study has shown since 1961 that almost three-fourths of all presidential proposals introduced in the first quarter of the first year have been passed, but only one-fourth of the proposals made in the last six months of the first year have been successful.[25] David Stockman, the budget director for President Reagan in 1981, dramatically emphasized this point: "If bold policies are not swiftly, deftly, and courageously implemented in the first six months, Washington will quickly become engulfed in political disorder...a golden opportunity for permanent conservative policy revision and political alignment could be thoroughly dissipated before the Reagan administration is even up to speed."[26]

The first year stands out as the greatest legislative opportunity for a president. The second year is dominated by political maneuvering in Congress by members of each party preparing for the midterm congressional elections. Though the president is not on any of the midterm election ballots, his performance usually affects the congressional elections. The president's party generally loses seats in the midterm elections. The loss of seats can be devastating for the president if he was already working with a bare party majority or creating fragile coalitions between his party and the moderates of the other party. The third year may be difficult if the midterm losses were too large. The fourth year is usually dominated by the presidential election, with primaries and caucuses starting in February. Consequently, passage of major legislation is unlikely.

A second term is likely to be much different from the first term. The president is immediately tagged with the title of **lame duck** because he cannot run for a third term. Furthermore, a second-term president usually does not enjoy the benefits of a mandate or a honeymoon period. Typically, items from the first-term agenda that were not passed are left over for the second term. Neither Congress, the media, nor the public accepts these leftovers as the basis for a mandate. Unless the president has pushed for new legislation in the campaign, major legislative initiatives are unlikely to be undertaken in the second term. By the last couple of years of the second term, the Washington community usually begins to ignore the president and starts focusing its attention on the election of a new president.

13-5b POWER AND PERSUASION

Despite labels such as the leader of the free world and the most powerful man on earth, the president cannot just issue commands and expect action. Richard Neustadt, a prominent political scholar, argues that "presidential power is the power to persuade."[27] The president has to rely on cooperation from a number of individuals in the political system to get anything done. The president relies on a large White House staff to implement his strategies, but they may not respond perfectly to his requests. Though the president is the head of the administration, the bureaucracy is so large, complex, and, in some cases, legally independent that the president cannot expect policy to be implemented as planned without close supervision, occasional negotiation, and lots of persuasion. Congress is even more independent and willing to aggressively counter the president's wishes. It requires even greater powers of persuasion than the rest of the government. President Harry S. Truman expressed the limits on presidential power in describing how Dwight Eisenhower would feel after taking the office after having been a general: "He'll sit here and he'll say, 'Do this! Do that!' And nothing will happen. Poor Ike—it won't be a bit like the Army. He'll find it very frustrating."[28]

The power of persuasion depends on both the rhetorical skills and political savvy of the president. It involves both the public perception of the president and behind-the-scenes action. A popular president is more likely to be persuasive, but he also has to know how to use his skills. Bargaining with other political leaders, knowing when to compromise, building coalitions that are strong enough to survive but not so large that the president wastes resources, and choosing priorities are vital political skills. Considering the complexity of Congress and the independence of its members, the president has difficulty even knowing which leaders need to be targeted for action.

President Lyndon B. Johnson was known as a master of the legislative game. Through his years of experience in the House and Senate, he had developed a keen sense of how to keep friends happy, never burn bridges with foes, and massage the egos of all of them. A president can help persuade members to stay focused on his agenda through a variety of means, and Johnson was a master of these techniques. One way that presidents can maintain good relations with Congress is through the provision of personal amenities, sometimes known as the "Johnson treatment." For example, Johnson was known for keeping track of members' birthdays, anniversaries, and other significant events along with some of their personal preferences. When he needed a key vote or wanted to reward a member for loyalty, he would offer the presidential seats to the opera on the member's anniversary. Sometimes, the president can attract or retain a key vote by simply making a big display of bringing a legislator to the White House for a personal meeting to demonstrate the member's influence and importance. Although these amenities and personal attention often do not change a hostile member's vote, they help the president focus attention on his agenda and keep loyal members in line.

At other times, a president may need to make more serious overtures to a member of Congress. The president may have to trade votes with a member, release funding for a special project in the member's district, or make legislative concessions. This kind of "horse trading" costs the president more in political terms than the personal-amenities approach, but when it is essential to attain the necessary majority, the president must decide whether the cost is worthwhile. Often, the president must decide whether "half a loaf" is better than none. That this type of trading goes on is a clear indication that the president must continuously work to persuade and cannot simply command.

If all else fails, a president may resort to arm-twisting to keep members in his legislative coalition. But presidents have little to use as threats. Members of Congress enjoy independent power bases supported by congressional committees, personal staffs, the incumbency advantage, and campaign fundraising techniques that do not rely on the party. Therefore, a president has difficulty bullying a member of Congress. Some subtle techniques, however, are useful against members of the president's party and electorally vulnerable members of the opposition. The president can apply direct pressure to a party member by using party financial, technical, and media assistance as a carrot to get a key vote. The president can also use indirect pressure on either group of legislators by contacting interest groups and influential constituents and asking them to apply pressure, either financial or otherwise, on a member. If the president is nationally popular or at least performed well in a member's district in the last election, a presidential visit to the district can be used as either a carrot or a stick. For members of the same party, a visit by a popular president may be useful in the next election. For members of the opposite party, a visit by the president in support of a challenger may be quite a credible threat that may give the president leverage in bargaining for a member's vote.

"Going Public"

As Neustadt's argument about persuasion suggests, popular presidents are more likely to be influential. This concern over presidential popularity has resulted in nearly continuous polling of the public's approval of the president's handling of the job. Because of the number of polls and continual attention to polls by the press, public, and Congress, the president is increasingly facing a "perpetual election."[29] This perpetual election has a dramatic effect on the president's influence. Several studies have shown a strong relationship between presidential popularity and presidential success in Congress. Popularity enhances a president's ability to enact his agenda and avoid vetoes.[30]

Because of its importance for legislative success, presidents focus tremendous resources on "going public."[31] Press conferences, nationally televised presidential addresses, personal appearances, sound bites on the national news, and aggressive courting of the press are all part of the president's appeal to the voters to support his policies and place pressure on Congress. Franklin D. Roosevelt was one of the first to make extensive use of national addresses by broadcasting his "fireside chats" on the radio. Television greatly expanded the president's ability to reach the public. Many view President Reagan, a former actor, as the most successful president in exploiting the mass media and the strategy of going public. Dubbed the Great Communicator, he was quite effective in making national appeals to the public and asking voters to pressure their representatives to support his programs. Because of his personal appeal, he was able to maintain high levels of public support throughout most of his two terms despite a severe recession early in his first term, the bombing of the U.S. Marine compound in Lebanon that killed nearly 250 Marines, and the Iran–Contra scandal.

Not surprisingly, presidents are most successful when they are popular. Generally, the pattern has been one of initially high public support during the honeymoon period immediately after the first election followed by a gradual decline in support throughout the term. If a president is reelected, he usually benefits from a brief period of higher support followed by another gradual decline. Of course, this general pattern is greatly affected by events, and the numbers move up and down almost continuously over time. The public expects the government to provide, in general, peace, security, and prosperity in this country. As one study of the presidency argues, "the public punishes the President more than members of Congress if expectations are not met."[32]

One of the worst things that can happen to a president's public approval is an economic downturn.[33]33 Severe recessions have always had a negative effect on public approval. On the other hand, a crisis can have a positive effect on public approval. For example, before the Iraqi invasion of Kuwait in 1990, President George Bush's public approval numbers were slightly less than 60 percent. After the Iraqi army had been thoroughly routed by the allied forces in early 1991, Bush's public approval ratings

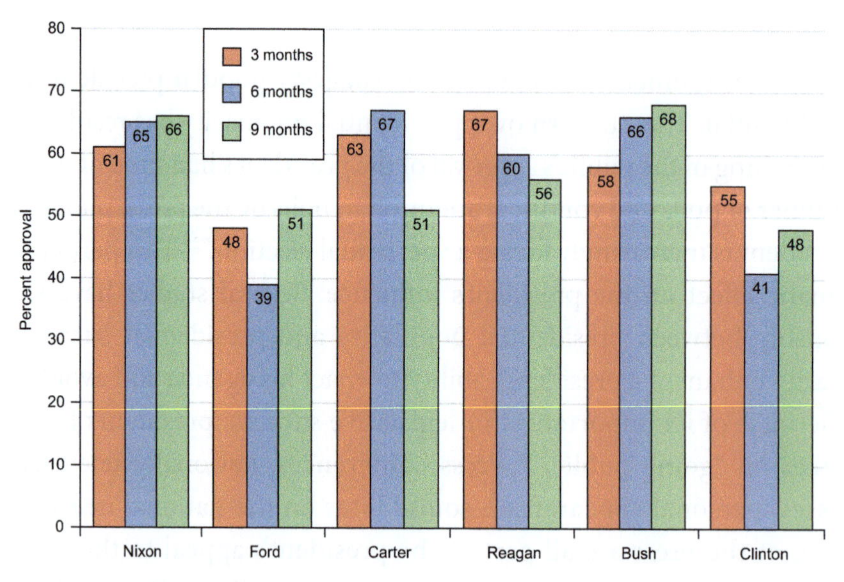

Figure 13-2 *Presidential Approval Ratings after Three Months, Six Months, and Nine Months: Presidents Nixon, Ford, Carter, Reagan, George H.W. Bush, Clinton, and George W. Bush*

Source: **Adapted from surveys by the Gallup Organization.**

skyrocketed to almost 90 percent. However, the deepening recession, the Los Angeles riots, and the lack of any new legislative initiatives combined to cause his approval numbers to drop sharply to less than 40 percent by the time his campaign for reelection began in 1992.[34] Although the public may not always reward the president for what is going well in the country, they are usually quick to punish the president for any problems, especially economic ones. In turn, public approval influences how successful a president will be in achieving legislative success.

Bill Clinton was a master of going public. His ease before the camera and natural style of communication helped bolster his image among voters throughout his presidency despite his having to defend himself against an almost constant stream of criticism regarding a variety of scandals. Even during impeachment, Clinton was able to maintain a high job rating despite quite a low personal approval rating (see Figure 13-2).[35]

13-5c The Budget

Although the president's relationship with Congress has always been difficult, the deficit problems of the 1980s and 1990s exacerbated the tensions between the two branches and the two parties. In the late 1990s and 2000, the tension eased as the deficit was replaced by a surplus for the first time in three decades. Unfortunately, the surplus did not last long—government expenditures increased in response to the terrorist attacks of 9/11, and the economic downturn produced lower-than-expected government revenues.

The budget process is complex and slow; it extends over several different stages involving the president's budget proposal, negotiations over the general shape of the budget, tax considerations, deliberations on appropriations to each different program, the actual expenditure decisions, and oversight of the manner in which the money was used. Furthermore, budget considerations influence every major legislative decision. No new program may be discussed without assessing its effect on the national debt.

Unfortunately, despite the central nature of budget policy in the legislative calendar, the system is not well designed for producing coherent policy. The president has only limited constitutional tools, such as the veto and the right to recommend legislation, to deal with a Congress that divides power between two chambers that are further divided into several committees and subcommittees with power over the budget. The Constitution does not provide for a joint bargaining process among the president, the House, and the Senate. The budget must originate in the House, pass in each chamber in identical form, and be submitted to the president for signing or a veto. The president has a potent weapon in the veto power, but it is a clumsy tool for fighting with Congress over the details of a budget. If Congress passes the president's budget and he does not care for some of the spending decisions, his only choice is to either defeat the entire bill or accept the entire document, including the less-preferred parts.

In 1990, President George H.W. Bush chose to let the government close down for a weekend rather than accept a budget plan that he did not like. National parks closed, government workers were told to stay home from work, and no government checks were mailed out. The president and Congress were both within their constitutional rights in fighting for a desirable budget, but the battle did not look good to the average citizen. The deadlock was to many observers just another symptom of a dysfunctional political system. Both Congress and the president paid a price, in terms of public trust in government, for the provisions of the bill.

President Clinton utilized the budget battle with congressional Republicans to great advantage in 1995 following the Republican victories in 1994. By allowing the Republicans to take the blame for the government shutdown, Clinton was able to skillfully use his communications advantages as president to cast congressional leaders, especially House Speaker Newt Gingrich, as extremists. Many observers attributed Clinton's subsequent election to his ability to recast himself following his battle with Congress.

13-6 Evaluating Presidential Performance

Americans love rankings and ratings. Not surprisingly, scholars like to rate presidents. In 1982, they were polled and their ratings tabulated.[36] The scholars' three favorites were Abraham Lincoln, George Washington, and Franklin D. Roosevelt. Lincoln's greatness was in his leadership and steadfastness through the nation's greatest crisis, the Civil War. Washington's greatness derived from having presided over the creation of a new republic and setting the tone for how the presidency should be conducted. Roosevelt's claim to greatness rests on his decisive leadership through the two greatest challenges this country faced in the twentieth century: the Great Depression and World War II.

According to the survey of scholars, the two worst presidents were Warren G. Harding and Richard Nixon. Harding's main failure was the widespread corruption of his administration—most notably, the infamous Teapot Dome scandal. Nixon, on the other hand, was accused of abusing the power of the presidency. His primary failure was his handling of a very troubling event: the Watergate scandal. Even worse was his cover-up of the whole enterprise. Nevertheless, though little can be offered in defense of Harding, one can find much in Nixon's administration to praise. He negotiated an end to America's involvement in the Vietnam War, made progress in controlling nuclear weapons, and established an important relationship with the People's Republic of China.

When polled in 1991, the American people rated Washington, Lincoln, and Roosevelt among the greatest presidents.[37] But, interestingly, the public gave its highest rating to John F. Kennedy (who did not make the scholars' top ten). To some extent, Kennedy's ongoing popularity is a function of his charisma, his oratorical skill, and the degree to which he inspired America to strive for a "new frontier." Without question, his untimely death at the hands of an assassin has also buttressed his standing in the public mind. One might wonder how Kennedy would be regarded now had he not been assassinated three years after being elected.

Americans tend to think of the great presidents as those who brought an activist approach to the office—what political scientist James David Barber has called the "active-positive" presidency.[38] In Barber's framework, an active-positive president brings a high level of energy and excitement to the office and derives pleasure from being president. He is characterized by a general openness and flexibility and has a warm and engaging personality. Moreover, he has a strong drive to lead and to be judged a success by others. Certainly, John Kennedy exemplified this approach to the office, as did Franklin Roosevelt.

Perhaps a fairer way to evaluate presidents is to determine whether they achieved the goals they set for themselves during their campaigns. Ronald Reagan did not have an activist conception of the presidency. Indeed, he wanted to scale down the activities of the national government. Yet most would agree that, despite certain problems and setbacks, Reagan's presidency was a successful one. Whether Reagan will go down in history as a great president remains to be seen, but strong indications show that history will regard Reagan quite favorably. Certainly, the mass public now renders a favorable judgment of President Reagan.[39] To his many admirers, Reagan was the president who stood up to the Soviet Union and hastened the end of the Cold War.

13-6a Assessing George W. Bush's Presidency

By most standards George W. Bush's first term did not appear to be successful as he approached the election of 2004. His approval rating hovered at or slightly below the 50 percent mark deemed critical for any president seeking reelection. The economic recovery seemed to be stalling out, and the war in Iraq was generating increasingly negative headlines. George W. Bush had assumed office in early 2001 with a full agenda, including reforming Social Security, cutting taxes, and adding a prescription drug component to Medicare. He also brought an expectation that he would unite, rather than divide, the country and reduce partisan fighting. By the end of his first term, he could claim to have worked with the Democrats in Congress to pass the No Child Left Behind legislation, to have developed a prescription drug policy, and to have cut taxes, but not to have managed to close the partisan divide or to have done much with Social Security.

What the president, or anyone else, could not have foreseen, was the terrorist attacks of September 11, 2001. Most observers give President Bush high marks for the way in which he led the country in the aftermath of the attacks. In the understandable wave of concern for national security, Congress approved the USA Patriot Act by an overwhelming margin. By the end of his first term, the Patriot Act and its implementation was a point of strong controversy, with many in and out of government decrying its impact on civil liberties, while others pointed to the lack of a second attack.

Bush won reelection despite a deeply divided public and evaluations of him continued to decline throughout the remainder of his presidency. As the two-front war waged on, public support for the president waned. During his second midterm election, Republicans lost control of both chambers of Congress, turning the last two years of the Bush presidency to mostly adversarial. As is common with lame duck presidents, little significant policy change occurred in the last two years of the Bush presidency, giving way to a sense of needed change among the public.

13-6b Initial Assessments of the Obama Presidency

Assessing an in-office president is difficult. After leaving the office with historically low approval ratings, seven years later President George W. Bush was much more kindly regarded by the public. When a president is still in office, every assessment is tentative because their story is not fully written. Barack Obama entered office on a wave of popularity from an invigorated Democratic base propelled by the campaign slogans of "Hope" and "Change." While a case can be made for Obama having pushed through fairly significant change, the public's embrace of the "hope" element has been fleeting.

The hallmark of Obama's first term was clearly the Affordable Care Act of 2010, commonly called Obamacare. Seventeen years prior, President Clinton made an initial attempt at a national single-payer health care system. Clinton was unsuccessful, and even though the Affordable Care Act did not go nearly as far as the Clinton plan did, President Obama was able to successfully steer the bill through Congress. In doing so he paid dearly, as Republicans took control of the House of Representatives back and made for a contentious second half of his first term. Having secured reelection in 2012, only time will tell if Obama is as successful in his second-term goals as he was in his first.

13-7 Conclusion: Assessing the Presidency as an Institution

American political culture has always been somewhat ambivalent in regard to executive power. The Articles of Confederation did not even provide for a chief executive. The debate among the Framers at the Constitutional Convention made clear that their greatest fear was a tyrant. They carefully devised a method of selecting presidents that was far from the people; the president was to be chosen by a deliberative body picked by state legislatures. On the other hand, the American people have always loved heroes and have looked to heroic individuals to lead the country through times of crisis. The American people have come to expect a great deal from their presidents. Yet presidents, like all other officials in this country, operate with an elaborate set of legal and political constraints.

Not surprisingly, American presidents have trouble maintaining their popularity. The political scientist Paul Light has argued that the job has become a "no-win presidency."[40] The president is limited by the structures originally intended to limit the office. Moreover, he must face the pressure of living up to the expectations to excel in a multiplicity of roles, many of which are in conflict. By most accounts, George Bush (the elder) excelled at the military and diplomatic aspects of his presidency. He was widely perceived as unsuccessful as chief legislator, however, and, in the view of some Republicans, as party leader. Bill Clinton was highly successful as party leader and chief legislator, though his performance in the foreign policy realm was less stellar. At the beginning of his second term as president, George W. Bush appeared to be most successful as crisis manager, chief diplomat, and commander-in-chief, which few would have expected before his becoming president. Here, as in many areas of political life, unforeseen events dictate unexpected roles and responses.

QUESTIONS FOR THOUGHT AND DISCUSSION

1. Is the American presidency too powerful, or is it not powerful enough?
2. Is it better for the country if the same party controls the presidency and Congress?
3. Should the president be given the power to veto specific lines in an appropriations bill?
4. Was President Bush (the elder) constitutionally required to obtain consent from Congress before initiating Operation Desert Storm in 1991?
5. Who was the greatest president since World War II? What makes a great president?
6. Did Congress have good grounds for impeaching President Bill Clinton in 1998? Did the Senate make the correct decision in acquitting him?
7. Should the Constitution be amended to require Senate approval of presidential pardons?
8. How will the Clinton presidency be regarded by historians fifty years from now?
9. How does the administration of George W. Bush differ from that of Bill Clinton?
10. How do the leadership styles of George W. Bush and Bill Clinton compare and contrast?

ENDNOTES

1 *Youngstown Sheet and Tube Co. v. Sawyer*, 343 U.S. 579 (1952).

2 *United States v. Nixon*, 418 U.S. 683 (1974).

3 *New York Times v. United States*, 403 U.S. 713 (1971).

4 *Clinton v. City of New York*, 524 U.S. 417 (1998).

5 Quoted in Sean Higgins, "President Revives Idea for a Line-Item Veto to Help Curb Spending," **Investor's Business Daily**, November 22, 2004.

6 Ibid.

7 Jeffrey M. Jones, "Bill Clinton's Image Suffers as Americans Criticize Pardon," *Gallup News Service*, February 22, 2001.

8 *United States v. Nixon, 418 U.S. 683 (1974).*

9 See, for example, Aaron Wildavsky, "The Two Presidencies." In *The Presidency*, ed. Aaron Wildavsky (Boston: Little, Brown, 1969), p. 230.

10 *United States v. Curtiss-Wright Export Corp.*, 299 U.S. 304 (1936).

11 As reported by Tom Brokaw on the "NBC Nightly News," December 15, 1993.

12 *Dames and Moore v. Regan*, 453 U.S. 654 (1981).

13 *Massachusetts v. Laird*, 400 U.S. 886 (1970).

14 *Crockett v. Reagan*, 558 F. Supp. 893 (D.C. 1982).

15 CNN.com, "Senate Approves Iraq War Resolution," *CNN*, October 11, 2002, http://archives.cnn.com/2002/ALLPOLITICS/10/11/iraq.us/.

16 Will Lester, "AP Poll: Stable Iraq Tops Voter Priorities," *Associated Press*, November 7, 2004.

17 Johanna McGeary, "The Number One Priority," *Time*, November 15, 2004, p. 66.

18 See *Hirabayashi v. United States*, 320 U.S. 81 (1943); *Korematsu v. United States*, 323 U.S. 214 (1944).

19 *United States v. United States District Court*, 407 U.S. 297 (1972).

20 Quoted in Bill Mears, "Supreme Court Looks at 'Enemy Combatants,'" CNN.com, April 28, 2004.

21 Ibid.

22 *Hamdi v. Rumsfeld*, 124 S.Ct. 2633 (2004).

23 *Rumsfeld v. Padilla*, 124 S.Ct. 2711 (2004).

24 Quoted in Benjamin I. Page and Mark P. Petracca, *The American Presidency* (New York: McGraw-Hill, 1983), p. 169.

25 Paul Light, *The President's Agenda* (Baltimore: Johns Hopkins University Press, 1982), p. 44.

26 Ibid., p. 45.

27 Richard Neustadt, *Presidential Power* (New York: John Wiley & Sons, 1980), p. 10.

28 Ibid., p. 9.

29 See Richard A. Brody and Benjamin I. Page, "The Impact of Events on Presidential Popularity." In *Perspectives on the Presidency*, ed. Aaron Wildavsky (Boston: Little, Brown, 1975).

30 See George C. Edwards III, *Presidential Influence in Congress* (San Francisco: W. H. Freeman, 1980); Douglas Rivers and Nancy Rose, "Passing the President's Program: Public Opinion and Presidential Influence in Congress," *American Journal of Political Science*, vol. 29, 1985, pp. 183–96.

31 See, generally, Samuel Kernell, *Going Public: New Strategies of Presidential Leadership*, 3d ed. (Washington, D.C.: CQ Press, 1997).

32 John R. Bond and Richard Fleisher, *The President in the Legislative Arena* (Chicago: University of Chicago Press, 1990), p. 2.

33 Compare Henry C. Kenski, “The Impact of Economic Conditions on Presidential Popularity,” *Journal of Politics*, vol. 39, 1977, pp. 764–73; Douglas A. Hibbs, “On the Demands for Economic Outcomes: Macroeconomic Performance and Mass Political Support in the United States,” *Journal of Politics*, vol. 34, 1982, pp. 426–62; K. Monroe, “Presidential Popularity: An Almon Distributed Lag Model,” *Political Methodology*, vol. 7, 1981, pp. 43–70.

34 See Kernell, *Going Public*.

35 During the Lewinsky scandal, President Clinton’s approval rating ranged from 73 percent in December 1998 to 53 percent in May 1999. During 1999 and 2000, his approval rating ranged in the high 50s to low 60s. The average approval rating for the entire Clinton presidency was 55 percent. These approval ratings are based on regular surveys conducted by the Gallup Organization and can be accessed at www.gallup.com.

36 Arthur Murphy, “Evaluating the Presidents of the United States,” *Presidential Studies Quarterly*, vol. 14, 1984, pp. 117–26.

37 George H. Gallup, Jr. *The Gallup Poll: Public Opinion 1991* (Wilmington, DE: Scholarly Resources, 1992).

38 James David Barber, *The Presidential Character*, 3d ed. (Englewood Cliffs, NJ: Prentice-Hall, 1985).

39 A survey conducted in early 2001 by the Gallup Organization found that the mass public is now most likely to regard Ronald Reagan as the greatest president ever. See Wendy W. Simmons, “Reagan, Kennedy and Lincoln Receive the Most Votes for Greatest U.S. President,” Gallup News Service, February 19, 2001. As we noted in section 13-6, a 1991 Gallup survey identified John F. Kennedy as the leading choice.

40 Paul Light, *The President’s Agenda*, rev. ed. (Baltimore: Johns Hopkins University Press, 1991), p. 202.

Chapter 14

THE SUPREME COURT AND THE FEDERAL JUDICIARY

OUTLINE

Key Terms 542

Expected Learning Outcomes 542

14-1 The "Least Dangerous Branch" 542

- **14-1a** The Power "To Say What the Law Is" 543
- **14-1b** Rules Governing the Resolution of Legal Disputes 545

14-2 The Federal Court System 548

- **14-2a** The Supreme Court 548
- **14-2b** The United States District Courts 549
- **14-2c** The United States Courts of Appeals 549
- **14-2d** Specialized Federal Tribunals 550
- **14-2e** Appointment of Federal Judges 550
- **14-2f** Impeachment of Federal Judges 553

14-3 The Supreme Court and Public Policy: A Brief History 554

- **14-3a** The Marshall Court 555
- **14-3b** The Civil War Era 555
- **14-3c** The Age of Conservative Activism 556
- **14-3d** The Constitutional Battle over the New Deal 556
- **14-3e** The Warren Court 557
- **14-3f** The Burger Court 558
- **14-3g** The Rehnquist Court 558
- **14-3h** The Roberts Court 559

14-4 Supreme Court Decision Making 560

- **14-4a** The Court's Internal Procedures 560
- **14-4b** Factors That Influence the Court's Decisions 564
- **14-4c** Checks on the Supreme Court 566
- **14-4d** Enforcement of Court Decisions 568

14-5 Conclusion: Assessing the Judicial Branch 569

Questions for Thought and Discussion 571

Endnotes 572

KEY TERMS

advisory opinions
affirm
amicus curiae briefs
blocs
briefs
case or controversy principle
certiorari
civil case
concurring opinion
contempt of court
courts-martial
criminal case
defendant
dissenting opinion
judicial activism
judicial restraint
jurisdiction
majority opinion
opinion
Opinion of the Court
oral argument
plaintiff
political questions, doctrine of
precedent
reversal
rule of four
senatorial courtesy
standing
stare decisis, doctrine of
writs

EXPECTED LEARNING OUTCOMES

After reading this chapter and completing the supplemental online materials, students will:

- Describe the constitutional design of the Supreme Court
- Understand the process by which cases make it to the Supreme Court
- Describe the Supreme Court's decision-making process
- Compare the judiciary branch's powers with those of the other branches of government

14-1 THE "LEAST DANGEROUS BRANCH"

One of the principal deficiencies of the national government under the Articles of Confederation was that no court of law was capable of resolving disputes between states or between citizens of different states. Early in the Constitutional Convention of 1787, the delegates unanimously adopted a resolution calling for the creation of a national judiciary. Yet the Constitution they produced said little about the structure, powers, and functions of the third branch of government. Nevertheless, Alexander Hamilton assured the nation that the judiciary would be the "least dangerous branch" because it would have "no influence over either the sword or the purse; no direction of the strength or of the wealth of a society; and can take no active resolution whatever." In Hamilton's view, the judicial branch "may be truly said to have neither force nor will, but merely judgment."[1]

The "mere judgment" of the federal courts has become a much more important source of government power than Hamilton or the other Framers of the Constitution could have ever envisioned. In the modern era, the "least dangerous branch" has become more or less coequal to Congress and the executive branch. In part, this increased importance has come about because the federal courts have emerged as the referee in the ongoing struggle for power between Congress and the president and between the national government and the states. It is also because great questions of public policy are often framed as legal questions for the courts to decide.

As Alexis de Tocqueville observed in 1835: "Scarcely any political question arises in the United States that is not resolved, sooner or later, into a judicial question."[2] That statement proved unusually prophetic in December 2000, when the Supreme Court decided *Bush v. Gore*, which effectively determined the outcome of the presidential election.[3]

ONLINE 14.1 *Cornell's Supreme Court Audio Archives*
http://www.law.cornell.edu/supct/

14-1a The Power "To Say What the Law Is"

The mainstay of judicial power is the authority to interpret the law. The federal courts interpret the statutes enacted by Congress and the regulations promulgated by federal agencies. On occasion, the courts must also interpret executive orders issued by the president and treaties the United States has made with foreign governments. Quite often, the law that must be interpreted to decide a case is vague, ambiguous, or incomplete, particularly with federal statutes. Congress, or any legislature, has difficulty writing a law that provides clear, precise guidance for the courts in all future situations. Moreover, the politics of the legislative process often results in vague, ambiguous, or even self-contradictory statutes because Congress is seeking to satisfy different constituencies with different views about what the law should contain.

Ultimately, the courts must decide what a particular provision of a statute really means in the context of a given set of facts. In assigning meaning to statutes, the courts rely heavily on **precedent**—a law will be interpreted in the way it has already been interpreted. In the absence of precedent, however, a court must use its own discretion to decide the meaning of an unclear law. In doing so, a court, in a sense, makes law. The more Congress leaves the meaning of a statute open to conflicting interpretations, the greater the likelihood that the federal courts will have to engage in lawmaking. With Congress having to make laws dealing with increasingly complex issues, the meaning of legislation is often decided, not surprisingly, in the courts.

Judicial Review

In addition to their power to interpret statutes, regulations, and so forth, the federal courts possess the power to interpret the U.S. Constitution and to invalidate laws and policies that are found to be contrary to the Constitution. This aspect of judicial power, known as judicial review, is a uniquely American invention. Although English common-law courts exercised the power to make law in some instances, no English court claimed the authority to nullify an act of Parliament. Though judicial review is normally associated with the U.S. Supreme Court, nearly all courts of law in this country also possess this power. In fact, judicial review had already been exercised by a few state courts before the adoption of the U.S. Constitution. The Framers, however, did not resolve the question of whether the newly created federal courts should have this power. Article III is silent on the subject. It remained for the Supreme Court, in a bold stroke of legal and political genius, to assume this power for itself and the rest of the federal courts. That bold stroke occurred in *Marbury v. Madison* (1803),[4] the first great case in American constitutional law. In *Marbury*, the Supreme Court struck down as unconstitutional a provision of the Judiciary Act of 1789.[5] Writing for the Court, Chief Justice John Marshall asserted the primacy of the courts in interpreting the Constitution and statutes, observing, "It is emphatically the province and duty of the judicial department to say what the law is."

In the nearly two centuries since the *Marbury* decision, approximately 170 federal statutes, or provisions thereof, have been declared unconstitutional by the Supreme Court. The Court has also invalidated about twelve hundred state and local laws. More than half these declarations have come since 1960, showing the increased activism of the modern Court. When Congress, a state legislature, or a city council debates pending legislation, it must consider whether the law as written will survive judicial review. Failure to exercise due care in the drafting of legislation increases the probability that it will be challenged in court and ultimately invalidated. Of course, it is not unheard of for legislators to enact a law that they know will be struck down in the courts in order to satisfy a certain constituency. When that happens, the legislature can take credit for passing the measure and blame the courts for striking it down.

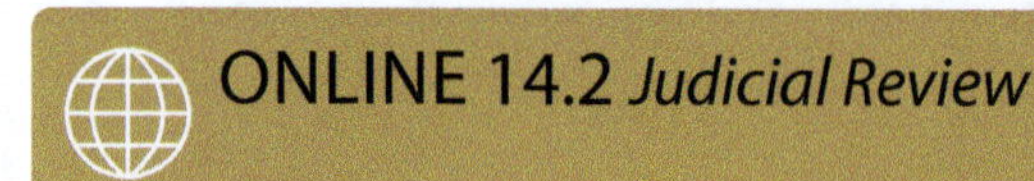

Although the courts sometimes invalidate popular legislation, the American public is generally supportive of judicial review, at least in principle. Yet, from time to time, it is criticized as antidemocratic. Clearly, judicial review is counter-majoritarian, by definition. Whether it is antidemocratic depends on one's definition of *democracy*. If democracy is defined not just in terms of majority rule, but also in terms of individual and minority rights, a case can be made that judicial review is eminently democratic. Some commentators even argue that judicial review is necessary to ensure that the right to vote is not infringed and that channels of political participation remain open to citizens.[6] To the extent that courts use their power to invalidate legislation to maintain the integrity of the democratic process, judicial review is consistent with democracy. On the other hand, when courts employ judicial review merely to impose their own public policy preferences without a sound basis in constitutional interpretation, one can argue that democracy is being usurped.

In making a determination about what the law means and applying it to a concrete situation, a federal court often makes an important public policy decision. Certainly, that was the case in 1973 when the Supreme Court interpreted the right of privacy under the Constitution to be broad enough to allow a woman to choose to terminate an unwanted pregnancy.[7] The Court's landmark decision in *Roe v. Wade* effectively legalized abortion in this country, a major public policy pronouncement. Although *Roe* stands as a legal landmark, the Supreme Court and other federal courts have also made important policy pronouncements in numerous other cases. Thus, public policy making must be regarded as a major function of the federal judiciary.

14-1b Rules Governing the Resolution of Legal Disputes

Few would deny that the courts play an important role in the policy-making process. Yet one must understand that courts make policy in a manner that is unique to the judiciary. Federal judges are not simply legislators in black robes. First, courts are limited to deciding legal disputes and may address only the policy questions that arise in the context of those disputes. A court cannot undertake to make a ruling except in response to a dispute that individuals or groups bring before it. Second, courts observe rules and doctrines that limit the way in which they decide legal disputes. Finally, in certain areas of public policy, such as taxing and spending, foreign affairs, and military policy, the courts have limited, if any, involvement.

Jurisdiction

In law, the **plaintiff** is a party who files a complaint alleging wrongdoing on the part of a **defendant**, who must either admit to the wrong or defend against the accusation. A **civil case** begins when a plaintiff brings a lawsuit, usually seeking monetary damages for an injury that occurred as a result of the defendant's actions. A **criminal case**, on the other hand, begins when the government prosecutes someone for allegedly committing a crime. Of course, not all civil and criminal cases find their way into the federal courts; indeed, the overwhelming majority of cases originate and are finalized in state courts. For a case to be brought

into the federal courts, it must qualify under federal jurisdiction. **Jurisdiction** is, quite simply, the authority of a court of law to hear and decide a case. A court must have jurisdiction, both over the subject matter of a case and the parties to a case, before it may proceed to adjudicate that controversy. The jurisdiction of the federal courts is determined by both the language of Article III of the Constitution and statutes enacted by Congress.

Standing

Ever since the Supreme Court refused to give legal advice to President George Washington, it has been well established that the federal courts do not render **advisory opinions** on hypothetical questions. If the president wishes advice on a legal matter that involves the government, he consults with the attorney general, who heads the Justice Department. If a member of Congress wants a legal opinion on a public matter, she consults with a staff attorney on the relevant congressional committee. The federal courts issue rulings and opinions only as they are necessary to resolve real cases or controversies between adverse parties.

It follows from the **case or controversy principle** that one may not invoke the jurisdiction of a federal court without standing. To have **standing**, a party must have suffered, or be about to suffer, an injury. The injury need not be physical in nature; it may be economic or even aesthetic. For example, a person who has been convicted of a federal crime clearly has standing to challenge the conviction on appeal. The injury the person has sustained is the punishment that follows conviction. In some situations, a person may even have standing to bring a federal lawsuit to prevent the enforcement of a criminal law if being prosecuted under the law would violate his constitutional rights. In this case, the injury would arise from the infringement of constitutional rights. A resident living in a community in which a toxic waste dump will be located would probably have standing to challenge the legality of the dump's intended location. Having standing to sue or to appeal has nothing to do with ultimately winning the case, however. It means only that a suit may be brought.

Political Questions

Even though a litigant may have standing and meets all the other technical requirements, the federal courts may still refuse to consider the merits of the dispute. Under the **doctrine of political questions**, cases may be dismissed if the issues they present are regarded as extremely "political" in nature. Of course, in a broad sense, all the cases that make their way into the federal courts are political in nature. The political questions doctrine really refers to those issues that are likely to draw the courts into a political battle with the executive or legislative branch or are simply more amenable to executive or legislative decision making.

ONLINE 14.3 *The Political Question Doctrine*
http://law2.umkc.edu/faculty/projects/ftrials/conlaw/politicalquestions.html

The doctrine of political questions originated in an 1849 decision in which the Supreme Court refused to take sides in a dispute between two rival governments in Rhode Island—one based on a popular referendum and the other based on an old royal charter. Writing for the Court in that case, Chief Justice Roger B. Taney observed that the argument in the case "turned on political rights and political questions.[8] Not insignificantly, President John Tyler had agreed to send in troops to support the charter government before the case ever went to the Supreme Court.

Perhaps the best-established application of the political questions doctrine is the federal courts' unwillingness to enter the fields of international relations, military affairs, and foreign policy making. This unwillingness was demonstrated in 1970 when the Supreme Court dismissed a suit challenging the constitutionality of the Vietnam War.[9] It was also invoked in 1982 when a federal district judge in Washington, D.C., dismissed a suit brought by members of Congress challenging President Reagan's decision to supply military aid to the government of El Salvador.[10]

In December 2000, some observers thought the Supreme Court would dismiss *Bush v. Gore* on the basis of the political questions doctrine. That expectation proved to be wrong, of course. Although the issues posed in that sensational case were as politically charged as legal issues can be, they were really not the types of issues the modern court has avoided through the political questions doctrine. Since the early 1960s, the Supreme Court has shown a willingness to enter the "political thicket" of campaigns, elections, and voting systems. Most accept the Court's role in policing the democratic process, but certainly many people (especially Democrats) were shocked and dismayed by the Court's closely divided decision in *Bush v. Gore*. Harvard law professor Alan Dershowitz went so far as to accuse the Court of hijacking the election.[11] According to Vincent Bugliosi, "the Court committed the unpardonable sin of being a knowing surrogate for the Republican Party instead of being an impartial arbiter of the law."[12]

The Importance of Precedent

As you have seen, a number of important doctrines limit access to judicial decision making, chief among them standing and political questions. Likewise, a number of important doctrines apply when a federal court has reached "the merits" of a case (the substantive legal question to be resolved) and has to render an interpretation of the law. Most fundamental is the **doctrine of *stare decisis*** ("stand by decided matters"), which refers to the fact that American courts rely heavily on precedent. A long-standing tradition in American courts of law stipulates that they should follow precedent whenever possible, thus maintaining stability and continuity in the law. Justice Louis Brandeis once remarked, "*Stare decisis* is usually the wise policy, because in most matters it is more important that the applicable rule of law be settled than that it be settled right."[13]

Devotion to precedent is considered a hallmark of American law. Obviously, following precedent limits a judge's ability to determine the outcome of a case in the way that she might choose if it were a matter of first impression (a case in which an issue arises for the first time; thus, there is no precedent to follow). Although the doctrine of *stare decisis* applies to constitutional and statutory interpretation, numerous examples exist of the Supreme Court departing from precedent in constitutional matters. Perhaps the most famous **reversal** is *Brown v. Board of Education* (1954), in which the Supreme Court repudiated the "separate but equal" doctrine of *Plessy v. Ferguson* (1896). The separate but equal doctrine had legitimated racial segregation in this country for nearly six decades. Beginning with the *Brown* decision, official segregation was abolished as a denial of the equal protection of the laws required by the Fourteenth Amendment.

14-2 The Federal Court System

Article III of the Constitution provides that "the judicial Power of the United States, shall be vested in one supreme Court, and in such inferior Courts as the Congress may from time to time ordain and establish." Thus, Congress was given the power to create and, to some extent, control the federal court system. When the First Congress convened in early 1789, its first order of business was the creation of a federal judiciary. Not all members of Congress saw the need for lower federal courts, however. Some preferred that state courts, which had existed since the American Revolution, be given the power to decide federal cases. But the advocates of a federal court system prevailed, and the Judiciary Act of 1789 became law. The Judiciary Act laid the foundation for the contemporary federal court system.

ONLINE 14.4 *Organization of the U.S. Court System*

14-2a The Supreme Court

Although Article III provided for the Supreme Court, the Court was not officially established until the adoption of the Judiciary Act. The act provided for a Court composed of a chief justice and five associate justices. The Supreme Court was given the authority to hear certain appeals brought from the lower federal courts and the state courts. The Court was also given the power to issue various kinds of orders, or **writs**, to enforce its decisions. But the Court's powers remained somewhat vague, and its role in the governmental system was unclear. Like many aspects of the new Constitution, the role and powers of the Court had to be worked out in practice.

14-2b The United States District Courts

At the base of the hierarchy created by the Judiciary Act of 1789 were the district courts, which were given limited jurisdiction. The Judiciary Act established thirteen district courts, one for each of the eleven states then in the Union and one each for the parts of Massachusetts and Virginia that were later to become the states of Maine and Kentucky, respectively. Above the district courts were the circuit courts, which were given broader jurisdiction, including the authority to hear suits between citizens of different states. The circuit courts were not staffed by their own judges. Rather, judges of the district courts sat alongside Supreme Court justices, who were required to "ride circuit." Given the difficulty of travel in late-eighteenth-century America, it is not surprising that Supreme Court justices regarded their circuit-riding duties as onerous. Eventually, Congress responded to their complaints, reduced the justices' circuit-riding responsibilities, and staffed the circuits with their own judges. In 1911, the circuit courts were abolished; their responsibilities were transferred to the district courts.

The district courts remain the major trial courts in the federal system. Their principal task is to conduct trials and hearings in civil and criminal cases arising under federal law. Normally, one federal judge presides at such hearings and trials, although federal law permits certain exceptional cases to be decided by panels of three judges. Ninety-four federal judicial districts now exist, with each state allocated at least one. About a third of the states, mainly in the West, have only one district. Most states have two districts. Some—including Tennessee, Florida, Georgia, Illinois, and North Carolina—have three. California, New York, and Texas are the only states with four federal judicial districts. The district courts' caseload has expanded dramatically in recent decades, especially in the filing of civil cases.

14-2c The United States Courts of Appeals

The Judiciary Act of 1789 authorized the party who lost at trial to appeal the ruling to the Supreme Court. As the caseload of the federal courts proliferated, the Supreme Court was unable to handle the number of routine appeals it was receiving. In 1891, Congress created the U.S. courts of appeals to handle routine federal appeals. Not only did this action reduce the caseload of the Supreme Court, but it also allowed the Court to concentrate on the more important cases.

Like the district courts, the U.S. courts of appeals are organized geographically. The nation is divided into twelve circuits, with a number of federal judicial districts comprising each circuit. Each court of appeals hears appeals from the federal districts within its circuit. For example, the U.S. Court of Appeals for the Seventh Circuit, based in Chicago, hears appeals from the district courts located in Illinois, Indiana, and Wisconsin. The Court of Appeals for the District of Columbia Circuit, based in Washington, has the important function of hearing appeals from numerous quasi-judicial bodies in the federal bureaucracy (see Chapter 15, "The Federal Bureaucracy"). A federal circuit court, not to be confused with the D.C. circuit court, hears appeals from certain specialized courts. Appeals in the circuit courts are normally decided by rotating panels of three judges, although under exceptional circumstances these courts decide cases *en banc*, meaning that all judges assigned to the court participate in the decision. On average, twelve judges are assigned to each circuit, although the number varies according to caseload.

14-2d Specialized Federal Tribunals

As federal law has become more complex, Congress has over the years provided for a number of specialized courts. The U.S. Claims Court is responsible for adjudicating civil suits for damages brought against the federal government. The U.S. Court of International Trade adjudicates controversies between the federal government and importers of foreign goods. Finally, the Tax Court performs the important function of interpreting the complex federal tax laws and deciding who prevails in disputes between citizens or corporations and the Internal Revenue Service. Appeals from the Claims Court, the Court of International Trade, and the Tax Court are directed to the Court of Appeals for the Federal Circuit, which represents the thirteenth federal circuit court (again, not to be confused with the D.C. circuit court).

Under the Uniform Code of Military Justice, crimes committed by persons in military service are prosecuted before courts-martial. In 1950, Congress created a civilian court, the U.S. Court of Military Appeals, to review criminal convictions rendered by **courts-martial**. Recently, that court was renamed the Court of Appeals for the Armed Forces. Cases before this tribunal are decided by a panel of five judges.

14-2e Appointment of Federal Judges

All federal judges, including Supreme Court justices, are appointed by the president, with the consent of the Senate, to life terms. The grant of life tenure was intended to make the federal courts independent of partisan forces and public passions so that they could dispense justice impartially according to the law. There is no question that life tenure has the effect of insulating the federal judiciary from political pressures. In the view of many lawyers and litigants who have dealt with the federal courts, life tenure also allows some judges to become haughty, arrogant, and even authoritarian. Yet a strong consensus remains that the Framers' plan for a life-tenured judiciary still makes good sense. In any event, no serious public support exists for changing the system.

Presidential Nomination of Judicial Candidates

The fact that federal judges are life-tenured makes a president's judicial appointments extremely crucial. Yet, given the numbers of federal judges to be appointed in a typical term, presidents have to rely heavily on others to locate nominees. Lower federal court appointments are heavily influenced by patronage, although ideology and, increasingly, race and gender considerations play a role in the selection process. Under the custom known as **senatorial courtesy**, senators from the president's party have traditionally exercised significant influence in the selection of judges for the district courts within their states. Senatorial courtesy has been less important in the nomination of individuals to the courts of appeals and almost irrelevant in the selection of Supreme Court nominees.

Recent presidents have moved away from reliance on home-state senators and increasingly turned to the Justice Department for help in identifying nominees. This change has been coincident with an increased emphasis on the ideology of nominees, as against treating judgeships solely as patronage. Another factor that has lessened the influence of the Senate in the selection process is the concern for increasing the diversity of the federal bench, which, until recently, has been the exclusive preserve of white males. There is reason to believe that allowing senators to pick nominees has helped to maintain the "good old boy network" and undermine efforts to increase the ethnic, racial, and sexual diversity of the judiciary. Although Presidents Carter, George Bush (the elder), and Clinton made clear that they wanted to appoint more women and members of minority groups to the courts, some women's and minority groups have been dissatisfied with the pace of change.[14]

The Senate Confirmation Process

Under the Constitution, the Senate must give its "advice and consent" to presidential nominations to the federal courts. The confirmation process begins in the Senate Judiciary Committee, which conducts a background investigation and then holds a public hearing on the nomination. During the hearing, the nominee appears before the committee to answer questions. Other individuals, often representing interest groups with a perceived stake in the appointment, testify in favor of or in opposition to confirmation. At the conclusion of the hearing, the Judiciary Committee votes on a recommendation to the full Senate. The Senate almost always follows the committee's recommendation.

The Bork Controversy

On July 1, 1987, President Ronald Reagan touched off a national debate by nominating the federal appeals court judge Robert H. Bork to succeed Justice Lewis Powell on the Supreme Court. With Powell's departure, the Supreme Court appeared to be evenly split between liberal and conservative blocs. One vote would be enough, or so it was widely believed, to tip the balance one way or another in any given case. Liberals feared, rightly or wrongly, that Bork, a judicial conservative, would create a conservative majority on the Supreme Court. Unfortunately for President Reagan and his nominee, the Democratic party had regained control of the Senate in the 1986 midterm elections. What transpired was a battle between Senate Democrats and the Reagan administration over the future direction of the Supreme Court.

A long parade of interest groups lined up to testify for and against Bork in the Senate Judiciary Committee. Liberal groups—including feminists, abortion rights activists, environmentalists, civil libertarians, and labor unions—united to wage an extremely effective lobbying and media campaign against Judge Bork. They painted him as a reactionary who, if confirmed, would work to strip Americans of their constitutional rights. Conservative groups, somewhat on the defensive, argued that Bork would help restore the proper balance to government by acting on the premise that in a democracy, legislators—not judges—should make policy. The highlight of the hearings was the testimony of Bork himself, who obliged the committee with detailed discussions of his views on constitutional interpretation. As the hearing continued over twelve days, public opinion began to shift against Bork. The Senate Judiciary Committee narrowly recommended rejection of the nomination, and the full Senate followed suit. The vote on the Senate floor was 58–42, the largest margin by which a Supreme Court nominee has ever been rejected by the Senate.

The Clarence Thomas Ordeal

In one of the most bizarre spectacles ever seen in American politics, President George H.W. Bush's nomination of Judge Clarence Thomas to the Supreme Court in 1991 was nearly derailed by allegations of sexual harassment. Law professor Anita Hill appeared before the Senate Judiciary Committee to testify that Thomas had sexually harassed her when they worked together at the Equal Employment Opportunity Commission in the early 1980s. The nation watched on live television as Hill detailed her charges and Thomas vehemently denied each one. Ultimately, the Judiciary Committee passed the nomination to the Senate without recommendation. The Senate approved Thomas by the vote of 52–48, one of the closest judicial confirmation votes in history.

The Harriet Miers False Start

Presidents always try to appoint nominees to the bench who mirror their own ideology and worldview, but sometimes presidents appoint candidates who are seen as too close to the president. Such was the case with Harriett Miers, President George W. Bush's chief legal counsel, who he initially appointed to replace Sandra Day O'Connor on the bench in 2005. But Miers never served as a judge, and was seen as nothing more than a personal loyalist to Bush with little independent legal philosophy. Even conservative Republicans were off-put by Miers' lack of Supreme Court–relevant experience, and Bush was forced to withdraw her nomination.

Presidential Predictions of Judicial Behavior

Presidents have no way to predict with certainty what their judicial nominees will do after they have been confirmed. Although most judges perform more or less as expected, presidents are not always happy with their judicial appointments. Dwight D. Eisenhower once remarked that his nomination of Earl Warren to become chief justice in 1953 was "the biggest damn fool mistake I ever made." Eisenhower was reacting to the liberalism of the Warren Court as manifested in cases like *Brown v. Board of Education* (1954). As a moderate conservative, Eisenhower found himself at odds with many of the Warren Court's rulings.

14-2f Impeachment of Federal Judges

The only means of removing a federal judge or Supreme Court justice is through the impeachment process provided in the Constitution. First, the House of Representatives must approve one or more articles of impeachment by at least a majority vote. Then, a trial is held in the Senate. To be removed from office, a judge must be convicted by a vote of at least two-thirds of the Senate.

Since 1789, the House of Representatives has initiated impeachment proceedings against fewer than twenty federal judges, and fewer than ten of them have been convicted in the Senate. Only once has a Supreme Court justice been impeached by the House. In 1804, Justice Samuel Chase fell victim to President Jefferson's attempt to control a federal judiciary largely composed of Washington and Adams appointees. Justice Chase had irritated the Jeffersonians by his haughty and arrogant personality and his extreme partisanship. Nevertheless, no evidence existed that he was guilty of any crime. Consequently, Chase narrowly escaped conviction in the Senate.

The Chase affair set an important precedent: a federal judge may not be removed simply for reasons of partisanship, ideology, or personality. Thus, despite strong support in ultraconservative quarters for the impeachment of Chief Justice Earl Warren during the 1960s, there was never any real prospect of Warren's removal. Barring criminal conduct or serious breaches of judicial ethics, federal judges do not have to worry that their decisions might cost them their jobs.

What Americans Think About
The U.S. Supreme Court

Despite some slippage in the 2003–2005 period, the Supreme Court has maintained a fairly high public approval rating throughout the last decade.
"Do you approve or disapprove of the way the Supreme Court is handling its job?"

YEAR	% SAYING "APPROVE"
2003	52%
2005	48%
2006	60%
2007	51%
2008	50%
2009	59%
2010	51%
2011	46%
2012	49%

Source: http://www.gallup.com/poll/4732/supreme-court.aspx

14-3 THE SUPREME COURT AND PUBLIC POLICY: A BRIEF HISTORY

The Supreme Court is now the most visible and prestigious court of law in the United States—indeed, in the entire world. Many of its decisions have an enormous effect on public policy and, ultimately, on the daily lives of Americans. That was not always the case, however. The Court began as a vaguely conceived tribunal, with no cases to decide and no permanent home. Over the years, as the Court's caseload increased, so did its prominence and prestige. Eventually, the Court found a home in the Capitol, although its chambers were less than spectacular. In 1935, the Court moved into its own building, the majestic marble structure across the street from the Capitol. In this "marble temple," the Court hears arguments, holds conferences, and renders decisions on important matters, all the while shielded from the glare of television lights, the stress of press conferences, and the demands of lobbyists.

The first chief justice of the United States was John Jay, a former chief justice of the New York state supreme court and the author of several of *The Federalist Papers*. During Jay's tenure as chief justice, the Court decided few important cases and enjoyed little prestige. The one truly important decision of the Jay Court, *Chisholm v. Georgia* (1793), was overruled by the adoption of the Eleventh Amendment to the

Constitution.[15] Somewhat disgusted, Jay resigned from the Court in 1795. When President John Adams asked Jay to resume his duties as chief justice in 1800, Jay refused, saying that the Court lacked "energy, weight, and dignity."[16]

14-3a The Marshall Court

When John Adams could not get John Jay to resume the chief justiceship, he turned to his secretary of state, John Marshall. Marshall became chief justice in 1801 and held the position until his retirement in 1835. No other individual has had more of an effect on the Supreme Court than Marshall. Under his leadership—indeed, dominance—the Court established its credibility and prestige. Moreover, the Marshall Court set many of the basic precedents of American constitutional law in decisions that still affect the outcome of litigation.

As we noted in section 14-1a, "The Power 'To Say What the Law Is,'" the Supreme Court assumed the power of judicial review in the landmark case of *Marbury v. Madison* in 1803. The *Marbury* decision was the only instance in which the Court under Chief Justice Marshall used its power of judicial review to strike down an act of Congress. The Marshall Court did, however, use its power of judicial review to strike down a number of state laws in some important cases. Perhaps the most important of these was *McCulloch v. Maryland* (1819), in which the Court invalidated an attempt by a state to tax a branch of the Bank of the United States.[17] Nearly as important was *Gibbons v. Ogden* (1824), in which the Court struck down a New York law granting a monopoly to a steamboat company in violation of a federal law granting a license to another company.[18] The decisions in *McCulloch* and *Gibbons* were not only important as assertions of power by the Supreme Court, but were also instrumental in enlarging the powers of Congress vis-à-vis the states. In addition to asserting the power to invalidate state laws, the Marshall Court established its authority to overrule decisions of the highest state appellate courts on questions of federal law, both constitutional and statutory. Thus, under Marshall's leadership, the Supreme Court asserted, expanded, extended, and consolidated its power.

14-3b The Civil War Era

Under John Marshall's successor, Chief Justice Roger B. Taney, the Court damaged its credibility and prestige by an unwise use of judicial review. It occurred in the infamous Dred Scott decision of 1857, the first case since *Marbury v. Madison* in which the Court struck down an act of Congress.[19] In 1820, in an attempt to solve the slavery issue, Congress had adopted the Missouri Compromise, which admitted Missouri to the Union as a *slave state* (one in which slavery would be legal), but prohibited slavery in the western territories north of thirty-six degrees, thirty minutes latitude. In *Dred Scott*, the Supreme Court ruled that the Missouri Compromise arbitrarily deprived slave holders of their property rights and therefore violated the provision of the Fifth Amendment that prohibits government from depriving persons of property without "due process of law." Moreover, the Court held that Congress lacked any power to regulate slavery. This bold exercise of judicial review, well received in the South but roundly condemned in the North, probably hastened the start of the Civil War. In any event, the decision was rendered null and void by the adoption of the Thirteenth and Fourteenth Amendments to the Constitution after the Civil War.

14-3c The Age of Conservative Activism

Judicial review again became a subject of political controversy in the late nineteenth and early twentieth centuries as the Supreme Court exercised its power to limit government activity in the economic realm. During this age of conservative activism (1890–1937), the Court often interpreted the Constitution as prohibiting the governmental regulation of business and other types of progressive reform. For example, in 1895, the Court gutted the Sherman Anti-Trust Act, which Congress had passed in 1890 to curtail industrial monopolies.[20] That same year, the Court struck down a new federal tax on the incomes of the wealthiest Americans, evidently viewing the tax as a manifestation of socialism.[21] The best-known decision of the period is *Lochner v. New York* (1905), in which the Supreme Court struck down a state law regulating working hours in bakeries.[22]

Throughout the early twentieth century, the Supreme Court continued to use its power of judicial review to frustrate state and federal attempts at economic regulation. In 1918, for example, the Court struck down an act of Congress that sought to discourage the industrial exploitation of child labor.[23] In another notable decision in 1923, the Court invoked the "freedom of contract" doctrine it had developed in *Lochner v. New York* and similar cases to invalidate a law authorizing a minimum wage for women and children working in the District of Columbia.[24] This tendency to insulate *laissez-faire* capitalism from government intervention brought the Supreme Court, and its power of judicial review, under an increasing barrage of criticism from populists and progressives.

14-3d The Constitutional Battle over the New Deal

The age of conservative activism entered its final phase in a constitutional showdown between the Supreme Court on one side and Congress and the president on the other. In 1932, in the depths of the Great Depression, Franklin D. Roosevelt was elected president in a landslide over the Republican incumbent, Herbert Hoover. Roosevelt promised the American people a "new deal" from the federal government. A bold departure from the traditional theory of *laissez-faire* capitalism, the New Deal greatly expanded the role of the federal government in the economic life of the nation. Inevitably, the New Deal faced a serious challenge in the Supreme Court, which in the 1930s was still dominated by justices with conservative views on economic matters.

The first New Deal program to be struck down was the National Recovery Administration (NRA). The NRA, the centerpiece of the New Deal, was a powerful government agency with the authority to regulate wages and prices in major industries. In 1935, the Supreme Court held that in passing the act that created the NRA, Congress had gone too far in delegating legislative power to the executive branch.[25] Between 1935 and 1937, the Court declared a host of other New Deal programs unconstitutional.

President Roosevelt responded to the adverse judicial decisions by trying to "pack" the Court with new appointees. Although the infamous Court-packing plan ultimately failed to win approval in Congress, the Supreme Court may have gotten the message. In an abrupt turnabout, the Court approved a key New Deal measure. In 1937, the Court upheld the controversial Wagner Act, which guaranteed industrial workers the right to unionize and bargain collectively with management.[26] The Court's sudden turnabout was the beginning of a constitutional revolution. For decades to come, the Court would no longer interpret the Constitution as a barrier to social and economic legislation. In the late 1930s and 1940s, the Court permitted Congress to enact sweeping legislation affecting labor relations, agricultural production, and social welfare. The Court exercised similar restraint with respect to state laws regulating economic activity.

14-3e THE WARREN COURT

The modern Supreme Court's restraint in the area of economic regulation was counterbalanced by a heightened concern for civil rights and liberties (see Case in Point 14-2). This was especially the case under the leadership of Earl Warren, who served as chief justice from 1953 to 1969. The Warren Court had an enormous effect on civil rights and liberties. Its most notable decision was *Brown v. Board of Education* (1954), in which the Court declared racially segregated public schools unconstitutional.[27] In *Brown* and numerous other decisions, the Warren Court expressed its commitment to ending discrimination against blacks and other minority groups.

The Warren Court used its power of judicial review liberally to expand the rights of not only racial minorities but also persons accused of crimes, members of extremist political groups, and the poor. Moreover, the Court revolutionized American politics by entering the "political thicket" of legislative reapportionment in *Baker v. Carr* (1962) and subsequent cases.[28] In what proved to be the least popular of its many controversial decisions, the Warren Court rendered a series of rulings striking down prayer and Bible-reading exercises in the public schools as a violation of the First Amendment requirement of separation of church and state.[29] Without question, the Warren era represents the most significant period in the Supreme Court's history since the clash over the New Deal in the 1930s. The Warren Court has been praised as heroic and idealistic; it has also been denounced as lawless and accused of "moral imperialism."

ONLINE 14.5 *The Warren Court*
http://www.supremecourthistory.org/history-of-the-court/history-of-the-court-2/the-warren-court-1953-1969/

14-3f THE BURGER COURT

President Nixon's appointment of Chief Justice Warren E. Burger and three associate justices had the effect of tempering the liberal activism of the Warren Court. In numerous cases, the Burger Court limited the decisions of the Warren Court, especially in the criminal justice area. Yet, despite the predictions of some critics, the Burger Court did not stage a counterrevolution in American law. Indeed, it was the Burger Court that handed down the blockbuster decision in *Roe v. Wade* (1973), effectively legalizing abortion throughout the United States. Even Chief Justice Burger, who was clearly much more conservative than his predecessor Earl Warren, concurred in *Roe v. Wade*. Moreover, in a series of decisions beginning with the landmark *Bakke* case of 1978, the Burger Court gave its approval to affirmative action programs to remedy discrimination against minorities. Support for affirmative action is hardly indicative of a reactionary court.

14-3g THE REHNQUIST COURT

In the 1980s, the Supreme Court became increasingly conservative as older members retired and were replaced by justices appointed by Presidents Reagan and George Bush (the elder). In 1986, Associate Justice William Rehnquist was elevated to chief justice when Warren E. Burger retired. The Rehnquist Court has continued the Burger Court's movement to the right, although it has not dismantled most of what was accomplished by the Warren Court in the realm of civil rights and liberties. Indeed, the Court's 5–4 decision in *Texas v. Johnson* (1989), in which the Court struck down a state law making it a crime to burn the American flag, was surprisingly reminiscent of the Warren era.[30] With the retirements of Justices William Brennan and Thurgood Marshall, both of whom were members of the majority in *Texas v. Johnson*, the Rehnquist Court moved further away from the civil liberties commitments of the Warren Court. During the 1990s, the Court's most important effect was in limiting the powers of the national government vis-à-vis the states.[31]

One "Court watcher" has observed that the Rehnquist Court is "the most conservative Supreme Court since before the New Deal."[32] This may well be the case, yet it is a Court that renders liberal decisions with some regularity, due largely to the moderate orientations of Justices Sandra Day O'Connor and Anthony Kennedy. Not only did these justices prevent the Court from overruling *Roe v. Wade*,[33] they provided crucial votes in cases upholding "gay rights,"[34] maintaining a strict separation of church and state,[35] and recognizing the rights of detainees in the war on terrorism.[36] The Rehnquist Court is indeed a conservative Court, but not nearly as conservative as it might be but for President Clinton's two appointments (Ginsburg and Breyer) and the fact that two of three of President Reagan's appointees (O'Connor and Kennedy) turned out to be less conservative than many expected.

14-3h The Roberts Court

Going into the 2004 presidential election, most observers believed that whoever won would likely appoint one or two new members to the Court. For some voters, the future direction of the Court was an important consideration in deciding between candidates Kerry and Bush. Indeed, within days after the 2004 election, the Court announced that Chief Justice Rehnquist was undergoing treatment for thyroid cancer. In the summer of 2005, Justice Sandra Day O'Connor announced her retirement from the Court. Later that summer, Chief Justice Rehnquist passed away. Thus, President George W. Bush was able to appoint two justices to the Court during his second term. John G. Roberts, who President Bush had previously appointed to the D.C. Circuit Court, was appointed chief justice. President Bush chose another federal appeals court judge, Samuel Alito, to fill the vacancy left by Justice O'Connor's retirement. Both Alito and Roberts have proven to be solid conservatives on the Court, but because the justices they replaced were also conservative (less so Justice O'Connor than Chief Justice Rehnquist), their ideological impact on the Court has not been dramatic.

During the spring of 2009, Justice David Souter stepped down, allowing President Obama to make a Supreme Court appointment during his first year in office. Because the Democrats controlled the Senate, President Obama was not constrained to select a candidate who would have strong cross-party appeal. He chose Sonia Sotomayor, also a federal appeals court judge, to fill the vacancy. When she took the oath of office in September 2009, Justice Sotomayor became the first Hispanic and only the third woman to serve on the High Court.

After eight years, it is clear the Roberts Court is a moderately conservative court. At this point it is too early to say whether President Obama will have a major impact on the Court, but with several justices near the end of their careers, he ought to have additional opportunities to appoint new justices. The Roberts Court does not act in a montolithically conservative way, however. 2013 rulings striking down restrictions on same-sex marriage suggest that the Roberts court is slightly less conservative than its predecessor.

14-4 SUPREME COURT DECISION MAKING

The Supreme Court's first session was held in February 1790. It had no cases on the docket and adjourned after ten days. During its first decade (1790–1801), the Court met twice a year for brief terms beginning in February and August. Over the years, the Court's annual sessions have expanded along with its workload and its role in the political and legal system. Since 1917, the Court's annual term has begun on the "first Monday of October." Until 1979, the Court adjourned for the summer, necessitating special sessions to handle urgent cases arising in July, August, or September. Since 1979, however, the Court has stayed in continuous session throughout the year, merely declaring a recess for a summer vacation. Still, the Court observes an annual term beginning on the first Monday of October.

The Constitution permits Congress to decide how many justices will serve on the Court. Initially, Congress set the number at six, but in 1807 the Court was expanded to include seven justices. In 1837, Congress increased the number of justices to nine. During the Civil War, the number of justices was increased to ten. Since 1869, the membership of the Court has remained constant at nine.

14-4a THE COURT'S INTERNAL PROCEDURES

The overwhelming majority of cases the Supreme Court hears come by way of writs of **certiorari** (pronounced "SIR-she-o-rary"), which the Court grants at its discretion. The losing party in a lower court may apply for a writ of certiorari from the Supreme Court as long as the case involves a substantial federal question and the party seeking review has exhausted all other avenues of appeal.

GRANTING CERTIORARI

A grant of certiorari from the Court requires the affirmative vote of at least four justices, the so-called **rule of four**. Getting four justices to agree to review a case is not easy. Each justice is entitled to evaluate a petition for certiorari according to his or her own criteria. However, most justices would seem to follow the criteria enumerated by Justice Sandra Day O'Connor, who has indicated that she considers "the importance of the issue, how likely it is to recur in various courts around the country, and the extent to which other courts considering the issue have reached conflicting holdings on it."[37]

The chances of the Supreme Court granting certiorari in a given case are slim. The odds are somewhat improved if the case originated in a federal court. The chances are even better if the party seeking review is the federal government. Of the more than 7,500 petitions for certiorari coming to it each year, the Court normally grants review in only a couple hundred. In an average term, fewer than one hundred cases are treated as full-opinion decisions. It is difficult to overstate the importance of the fact that the Supreme Court's appellate jurisdiction is almost entirely discretionary.

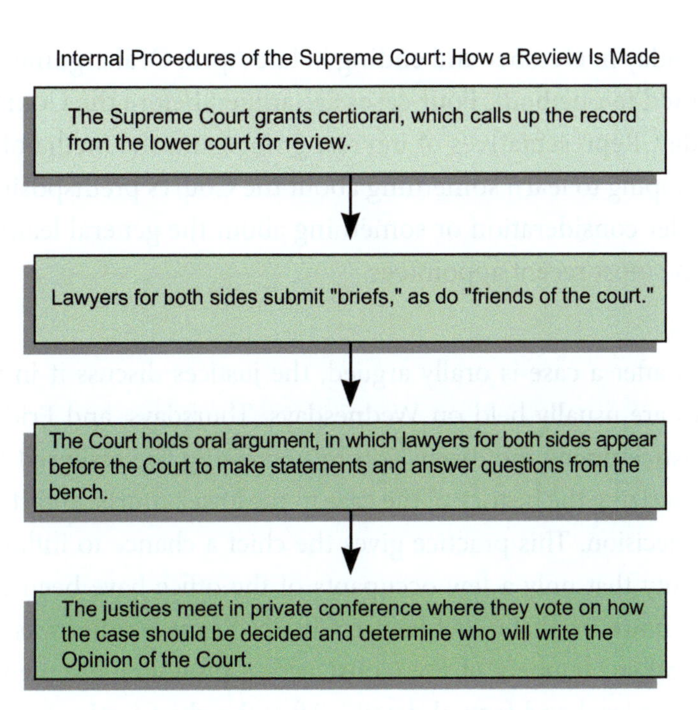

Internal Procedures of the Supreme Court: How a Review Is Made
The Supreme Court grants certiorari, which calls up the record from the lower court for review.
Lawyers for both sides submit "briefs," as do "friends of the court."
The Court holds oral argument, in which lawyers for both sides appear before the Court to make statements and answer questions from the bench.
The justices meet in private conference where they vote on how the case should be decided and determine who will write the Opinion of the Court.

Figure 14-1 *Internal Procedures of the Supreme Court: How a Review Is Made*

Because the continuous stream of certiorari petitions contains a wide range of policy questions, the Court is able to set its own agenda. Agenda setting is, of course, the first phase in any institutional policy-making process. Figure 14-1 summarizes the Court's decision-making process.

Briefs of Counsel

Parties to cases slated for review are required to submit **briefs**, which are written documents containing legal arguments in support of a party's position. By Supreme Court rule, briefs are limited to fifty pages. In addition to the briefs submitted by the direct parties, the Court may permit outside parties to file ***amicus curiae* briefs**. *Amicus* briefs are often filed on behalf of organized groups that have an interest in the outcome of a case. Examples of interest groups that routinely file *amicus* briefs in the Supreme Court are the American Civil Liberties Union (ACLU), the National Association for the Advancement of Colored People (NAACP), the National Rifle Association (NRA), and the American Medical Association (AMA). The federal government often files *amicus* briefs in cases that have national policy significance.

Oral Argument

After the briefs are submitted, the case is scheduled for **oral argument**, a public hearing where lawyers for both sides appear before the Court to make verbal presentations and, more importantly, answer questions from the bench. The oral argument is the only occasion on which lawyers in a case have any direct contact with the justices. Oral arguments are normally held on Mondays, Tuesdays, and Wednesdays beginning on the first Monday in October and ending in late April. Oral argument on a given case is usually limited to one hour. Four cases are argued before the Court on any given oral argument day. Representatives of interest groups and the media often attend the oral argument, hoping to learn something about the Court's predisposition with respect to the case under consideration or something about the general leanings of the justices, especially the most recent appointees.

Conference

Within days after a case is orally argued, the justices discuss it in private conference. Conferences are usually held on Wednesdays, Thursdays, and Fridays. At conference, the chief justice opens the discussion by reviewing the essential facts of the case at hand, summarizing the history of the case in the lower courts, and stating his view about the correct decision. This practice gives the chief a chance to influence his colleagues, an opportunity that only a few occupants of the office have been able to exploit. It is well known, however, that Chief Justice Charles Evans Hughes was on occasion able to overwhelm other members of the Court with a photographic memory that gave him command over legal and factual details. After the chief justice has presented the case, associate justices, speaking in order of seniority, present their views of the case and indicate their votes about the proper judgment. This original vote on the merits is not binding, however, and justices have been known to change their votes before the announcement of the decision. The final vote is not recorded until the decision is formally announced.

The Judgment of the Court

In deciding a case that has been fully argued, the Court has several options. First, the Court may decide that it should not have granted review in the first place, whereupon the case is dismissed. Of course, this situation rarely occurs. Alternatively, the Court may instruct the parties to reargue the case, focusing on somewhat different issues; in this case, the matter is likely to be carried over to the next term and the final decision delayed for at least a year. If the Court decides to render judgment, it either will **affirm** (uphold) or **reverse** (overturn) the decision of the lower court. Alternatively, it may modify the lower court's decision in some respect. Reversal or modification of a lower court decision requires a majority vote; a quorum is six justices. A tie vote (in cases in which one or more justices are unable to participate) always results in the affirmance of the decision under review.

Supreme Court Opinions

After a judgment has been reached, it remains for the decision to be explained and justified in a written **opinion** or opinions. In the early days of the Court, opinions were issued *seriatim*—each justice would produce an opinion reflecting his views of the case. John Marshall, who became chief justice in 1801, instituted the practice of issuing an Opinion of the Court, which reflects the views of at least a majority of the justices. The **Opinion of the Court**, referred to as the **majority opinion** when the Court is not unanimous, has the great advantage of providing a coherent statement of the Court's position to the parties, the lower courts, and the larger legal and political communities. It must be understood, however, that even a unanimous vote in support of a particular judgment does not guarantee that an Opinion of the Court will be issued. Justices can and do differ on the rationales they adopt for voting a particular way. Every justice retains the right to produce an opinion in every case, either for or against the judgment of the Court. A **concurring opinion** is one written in support of the Court's decision; a **dissenting opinion** disagrees with the decision.

Dissenting opinions, although indicative of intellectual conflict on the Court, are important in the development of American law. It is often said that "yesterday's dissent is tomorrow's majority opinion." Although the time lag is much longer than the saying suggests, a number of examples exist of dissents being vindicated by later Court decisions. More frequently, of course, a dissenting vote is merely a defense of a dying position. The modern Supreme Court has seen a dramatic rise in the frequency of dissenting opinions, reflecting both the increased complexity of the law and the demise in consensual norms in the Court itself. The modern Court has become less of a collegial decision-making body and more like "nine separate law firms."

In an effort to obtain a majority opinion, the chief justice, assuming that he is in the majority, either prepares a draft opinion himself or assigns the task to one of his colleagues in the majority. If the chief is in dissent, the responsibility of opinion assignment falls on the senior associate justice in the majority. Sometimes, in a 5–4 decision, a majority opinion may be "rescued" by assigning it to the swing voter, that is, the justice who was most likely to dissent. On the modern Court, the task of writing majority opinions is more or less evenly distributed among the nine justices. However, majority opinions in important decisions are more apt to be authored by the chief justice or a senior member of the Court.

After the opinion has been assigned to one of the justices, work begins on a rough draft. At this stage, the law clerks play an important role by performing legal research and assisting the justice in writing the opinion. When a draft is ready, it is circulated among the justices in the majority for their suggestions and, ultimately, their signatures. A draft opinion that fails to receive the approval of a majority of justices participating in a given decision cannot be characterized as the Opinion of the Court. Accordingly, a draft may be subject to considerable revision before it attains the status of majority opinion.

The Supreme Court announces its major decisions in open court, usually late in the term. A decision is announced by the author of the majority or plurality opinion, who may even read excerpts from that opinion. In important and controversial cases, concurring and dissenting justices also read excerpts from their opinions. When several decisions are to be announced, the justices making the announcements speak in reverse order of their seniority on the Court. After decisions are announced, summaries are released to the media by the Court's public information office. Word of an important Supreme Court decision now often spreads across the nation within minutes of being handed down.

14-4b Factors That Influence the Court's Decisions

Political scientists who have studied Supreme Court decision making have amassed considerable evidence that the Court's decisions are influenced by the ideologies of the justices. This belief is inferred from regularities in the voting behavior of the justices—mainly, the tendency of certain groups of justices to vote as **blocs**. In the late 1980s, for example, the Court was divided into two opposing ideological camps: a liberal bloc composed of Justices Brennan, Marshall, Blackmun, and Stevens; and a conservative bloc composed of Justices Rehnquist, White, O'Connor, Scalia, and Kennedy. In the early 1990s, the Court became increasingly dominated by justices with conservative ideologies. Perhaps the most significant recent ideological shift on the Court occurred when Justices William Brennan and Thurgood Marshall, both staunch liberals, retired in 1990 and 1991, respectively. Their replacements, David Souter and Clarence Thomas, are considerably more conservative. President Clinton's appointment of Justices Ginsburg and Breyer in 1993 and 1994, respectively, moderated the Court's movement to the right. In the 2000s, the court started moving further right, with moderates being replaced by John Roberts and Samuel Alito, but then shifted back to the center with Sonya Sotomayor and Elena Kagan appointed by President Obama.

Although observers tend to characterize Supreme Court decisions and voting patterns in simplistic liberal-conservative terms, judicial "ideology" may well include more than general political attitudes or views on specific issues of public policy (for example, school prayer or abortion). It may also embrace philosophies regarding the proper role of courts in a democratic society. At least for some justices, considerations of **judicial activism** versus **judicial restraint** may weigh as heavily as policy preferences in determining how the vote will be cast in a given case. Justices inclined toward activism are more likely to support the expansion of the Court's jurisdiction and powers and are more likely to embrace innovative constitutional doctrines. Activists are less likely than restraintists to follow precedent or defer to the judgment of elected officials. Judicial activists also are more prone to see cases in terms of their public policy significance rather than as abstract questions of law.

The Political Environment

In addition to the ideologies of the justices, a number of political factors influence Supreme Court decision making (Table 14-1 provides selected characteristics of the justices of the Supreme Court). Although the Supreme Court is ostensibly

TABLE 14-1 Selected Characteristics of the Justices of the Supreme Court

JUSTICE	JOINED COURT	PRIOR POSITION	J.D. DEGREE FROM	POLITICAL PARTY	APPOINTING PRESIDENT
John Paul Stevens	1975	U.S. Court of Appeals	Northwestern	Republican	Ford
Antonin Scalia	1986	U.S. Court of Appeals	Harvard	Republican	Reagan
Anthony M. Kennedy	1987	U.S. Court of Appeals	Harvard	Republican	Reagan
Clarence Thomas	1991	U.S. Court of Appeals	Yale	Republican	Bush (41)
Ruth B. Ginsburg	1993	U.S. Court of Appeals	Columbia	Democrat	Clinton
Stephen G. Breyer	1994	U.S. Court of Appeals	Harvard	Democrat	Clinton
John G. Roberts (CJ)	2005	U.S. Court of Appeals	Harvard	Republican	Bush (43)
Samuel Alito	2005	U.S. Court of Appeals	Yale	Republican	Bush (43)
Sonia Sotomayor	2009	U.S. Court of Appeals	Yale	Democrat	Obama
Elena Kagan	2010	Solicitor General	Harvard	Democrat	Obama

a counter-majoritarian institution, public opinion may occasionally influence the Court. Certainly, ample evidence exists that the actions, or threatened actions, of Congress and the president have an effect on Court decisions. And, in a constitutional system that emphasizes checks and balances, one should not expect that it would be otherwise. The political environment unquestionably imposes constraints on and provides stimuli to, and support for, Supreme Court decision making.

The Internal Politics of the Court

Finally, the Court's decision making is intensely political in the sense that the internal dynamics of the Court are characterized by conflict, bargaining, and compromise—the essence of politics. These activities are difficult to observe because they occur behind the "purple curtain" that separates the Court from its attentive public. Conferences are held in private, votes on certiorari are not routinely made public, and the justices tend to be tight-lipped about what goes on behind the scenes in the "marble temple." Yet from time to time, evidence of the Court's internal politics appears in the form of memoirs, autobiographies, and other writings of the justices and in the occasional interviews the justices and their clerks give to journalists and academicians.

14-4c CHECKS ON THE SUPREME COURT

The concept of checks and balances is one of the fundamental principles of the U.S. Constitution. Each branch of the national government is provided with specific means of limiting the exercise of power by the other branches. For example, the president may veto acts of Congress, which do not become law unless the veto is overridden by a two-thirds vote in both chambers. Although the federal courts, and the Supreme Court in particular, are often characterized as guardians of the Constitution, the judicial branch is by no means immune to the abuse of power. Accordingly, the federal judiciary is subject to checks and balances imposed by Congress and the president. In a constitutional system that seeks to prevent any agency of government from exercising unchecked power, even the Supreme Court is subject to external limitations.

CONSTITUTIONAL AMENDMENT

By far the most effective means of overruling a Supreme Court or any federal court decision is for Congress to use its power of amendment. If Congress disapproves of a particular judicial decision, it may be able to override that decision through a simple statute, but only if the decision was based on statutory interpretation. In *Grove City College v. Bell* (1984), for example, the Court was called on to interpret Title IX of the Education Amendments of 1972, which prohibited sex discrimination by educational institutions receiving federal funds. In *Grove City*, the Court interpreted Title IX narrowly so as to limit a potential plaintiff's ability to sue a college or university for sex discrimination.[38] Congress disapproved of the Court's interpretation of Title IX and effectively nullified the decision by adopting the Civil Rights Restoration Act of 1988 over President Reagan's veto. Because *Grove City College v. Bell* was based on a statute rather than on the Constitution, Congress could overrule the Court by simply amending the statute.

Congress has much more difficulty in overriding a federal court decision based on the U.S. Constitution. Indeed, Congress alone cannot do so. Ever since *Marbury v. Madison*, the U.S. system of government has conceded to the courts the power to authoritatively interpret the nation's charter. A Supreme Court decision interpreting the Constitution is therefore final unless and until one of two events occurs. First, the Court may overrule itself in a later case, which has happened numerous times. Historically, the most notable example was the repudiation of official racial segregation in *Brown v. Board of Education* (1954). The only other way to overturn a constitutional decision of the Supreme Court is through constitutional amendment. This method is not easily done because Article V of the Constitution prescribes a two-thirds majority in both chambers of Congress followed by ratification by three-fourths of the states. Yet four times in our country's history, specific Supreme Court decisions have been overturned in this manner, beginning with a 1793 decision that was reversed by the adoption of the Eleventh Amendment.[39] The infamous *Dred Scott* decision was overturned by the ratification of the Fourteenth Amendment in 1868. The income tax decision of 1895, alluded to in section 14-3c, "The Age of Conservative Activism," was reversed when the Sixteenth Amendment was ratified in 1913.

The most recent instance of a Supreme Court decision being overturned by constitutional amendment took place in 1971. In 1970, Congress enacted a statute lowering the voting age to eighteen in both state and federal elections. The states of Oregon and Texas filed suit under the original jurisdiction of the Supreme Court seeking an injunction preventing the attorney general from enforcing the statute with respect to the states. The Supreme Court ruled that Congress had no power to regulate the voting age in state elections.[40] The Twenty-Sixth Amendment, ratified in 1971, accomplished what Congress was not permitted to do through simple statute.

Over the years, numerous unsuccessful attempts have been made to overrule Supreme Court decisions through constitutional amendments. In 1983, an amendment providing that "the right to an abortion is not secured by this Constitution," obviously aimed at *Roe v. Wade*, failed to pass the Senate by only one vote. In 1971, a proposal designed to overrule the Warren Court's controversial school prayer decisions fell twenty-eight votes short of the necessary two-thirds majority in the House of Representatives. In his 1980 presidential campaign, Ronald Reagan called on Congress to resurrect the School Prayer Amendment, but Congress was unwilling to give the measure serious consideration.

The most recent example of a proposed constitutional amendment aimed at a Supreme Court decision dealt with the emotional public issue of flag burning. As we noted in section 14-3g, "The Rehnquist Court," in 1989, the Court held that burning the American flag as part of a public protest was a form of symbolic speech protected by the First Amendment. Many, including President George Bush (the elder), called on Congress to overrule the Court. Congress considered an amendment that read, "The Congress and the States shall have power to prohibit the physical desecration of the flag of the United States." Votes were taken in both chambers, but neither achieved the necessary two-thirds majority. In the wake of the failed constitutional amendment, Congress adopted a statute making flag desecration a federal offense. As it had done with the Texas law in 1989, the Supreme Court declared the new federal statute unconstitutional.[41]

The Appointment Power

The shared presidential–senatorial power of appointing federal judges is an important means of influencing the judiciary. For example, President Richard Nixon made a significant impact on the Supreme Court and on American constitutional law through his appointment of four justices. During the 1968 presidential campaign, Nixon criticized the Warren Court's liberal decisions, especially in the criminal law area, and promised to appoint "strict constructionists" (widely interpreted to mean "conservatives") to the bench. Nixon's first appointment came in 1969, when Warren E. Burger was selected to succeed Earl Warren as chief justice. In 1970, after the failed nominations of Clement Haynsworth and G. Harold Carswell, Harry Blackmun was appointed to succeed Justice Abe Fortas, who had resigned from the Court in a scandal in 1969. Then, in 1972, Nixon appointed Lewis Powell to fill the vacancy left by Hugo Black's retirement and William Rehnquist to succeed John M. Harlan, who had also retired. The four Nixon appointments had a definite impact on the Supreme Court, although the resulting swing to the right was less dramatic than many observers had predicted.

More recently, Presidents Reagan and George H.W. Bush moved the Court further to the ideological right by their appointments of Justices O'Connor (1981), Scalia (1986), Kennedy (1987), Souter (1990), and Thomas (1991). When Justice Byron White announced his retirement in 1993, President Clinton was given the opportunity to reverse the conservative trend by appointing a more liberal justice to the Court. Clinton chose the federal appeals court judge Ruth Bader Ginsburg to fill the vacancy. Widely seen as a moderate-to-liberal judge, Ginsburg won confirmation easily in the Senate. The year 1994 saw the departure of Justice Harry Blackmun, who had been on the Court since 1970. President Clinton appointed Judge Stephen G. Breyer, of Boston, to fill the vacancy. The appointments of Ginsburg and Breyer prevented the Court from moving further to the right.

Without question, the shared presidential–senatorial power to appoint judges and justices is the most effective means of controlling the federal judiciary. Congress and the president may not be able to achieve immediate results using the appointment power, but they can bring about long-term changes in the Court's direction. The appointment power ensures that the Supreme Court and the other federal courts may not continue to defy a clear national consensus for long.

14-4d Enforcement of Court Decisions

Courts generally have adequate means of enforcing their decisions on the parties directly involved in litigation. Any party who fails to comply with a court order, such as a subpoena or an injunction, may be held in **contempt of court**. The Supreme Court's decisions interpreting the federal Constitution are typically nationwide in scope. For this reason, they automatically elicit the compliance of state and federal judges. Occasionally, one hears of a stubborn federal judge who, for one reason or another, defies a Supreme Court decision, but this phenomenon, although not uncommon in the early days of the Republic, is now an eccentric curiosity.

Courts have greater difficulty enlisting the compliance of the general public, especially when they render unpopular decisions. Despite the Supreme Court's repeated rulings against officially sponsored prayer in the public schools, these activities now continue in some parts of the country. Even after three decades, the Warren Court's school prayer decisions have failed to generate broad public acceptance. Without the assistance of local school officials, the Court can do little to effect compliance with its mandates regarding school prayer unless and until an unhappy parent files a lawsuit.

14-5 Conclusion: Assessing the Judicial Branch

Courts are both legal and political institutions. As legal institutions, they decide cases by following set procedures, applying legal rules, and following legal precedents. As political institutions, they are involved in the authoritative allocation of values, the resolution of conflict, the determination of "who gets what," and the making of public policy. How the courts exercise their political role, however, can be a great source of controversy. In earlier decades, liberals chided the courts for employing judicial review to thwart progressive economic policies. Today, criticism of judicial activism is more likely to come from conservatives who believe that liberals have come to rely on the courts to achieve social policies they could never achieve through legislatures. In both instances the underlying question is: What is the role of a court in a constitutional democracy? The easy answer is that the courts should follow the rule of law and permit the people's elected representatives to legislate as long as legislation does not conflict with constitutional principles. But there is a more difficult question lurking within this easy answer. How should constitutional principles be understood and applied to contemporary issues? On this profound question, liberals and conservatives often disagree. This is why ideology is an important consideration in deciding who should be appointed to the bench and, especially, who should serve on the highest court in the land.

The power and prestige of the Supreme Court—indeed, of the entire federal judiciary—have grown tremendously over the past two centuries. It is no exaggeration to say that the Supreme Court now stands as the most influential tribunal in the world. Nevertheless, the Court works within a constitutional and political system that imposes significant constraints on its power. The Supreme Court can, and often does, speak with finality on important questions of constitutional law and public policy. But it must consider the probable responses of Congress, the president, and, ultimately, the American people. In the long run, the power of the Supreme Court depends on its acceptance within the political culture. Diffuse support for the federal courts is fairly strong, certainly relative to public support for Congress. But this support could be jeopardized by a series of court decisions that run counter to public opinion. Most people are willing to accept court decisions that they do not agree with from time to time, but a continual series of decisions that run counter to the political culture could undermine the legitimacy of the courts as institutions. Of course, the system of checks and balances works to ensure that the federal courts do not stray too far from the ideological mainstream for too long.

American government, especially at the national level, is vastly more powerful and pervasive than the Framers of the Constitution could have imagined. The increased authority of the federal judiciary has kept pace with the growth of governmental activity generally, but it has not placed the Court in a dominant position in the American system of government. Although judges, because they are human beings, are not immune to corruption or the abuse of power, and courts sometimes overstep their traditional bounds, those who worry about the prospect of "government by judiciary" are exaggerating judicial power. Although the federal courts have formidable powers, they cannot raise an army, start a war, create a new government program, or raise anyone's taxes. More than two hundred years after the ratification of the Constitution, Alexander Hamilton's characterization of the federal judiciary as the least dangerous branch of the national government still remains credible.

Questions for Thought and Discussion

1. Is the power of judicial review consistent or inconsistent with the ideals of democracy?

2. Should federal judges have to stand for reelection periodically as most state judges do?

3. How important is it that the federal judiciary mirror the diversity of society?

4. In reviewing presidential nominees to the Supreme Court, what factors should the Senate consider? Is the ideology of the nominee a legitimate consideration?

5. Is it possible for federal judges to determine the intentions of the Framers of the Constitution? How is this done? In interpreting the Constitution, should judges be limited by the intentions of the Framers?

6. Was the Supreme Court justified in intervening in the disputed 2000 presidential election in Florida? Do you agree or disagree with the Court's decision in *Bush v. Gore*?

ENDNOTES

1 Alexander Hamilton, *The Federalist*, No. 78.

2 Alexis de Tocqueville, *Democracy in America*, ed. Phillips Bradley (New York: Knopf, 1944), vol. 1, p. 280.

3 *Bush v. Gore*, 531 U.S. 98 (2000).

4 *Marbury v. Madison*, 5 U.S. 137 (1803).

5 An excellent account of the political context surrounding *Marbury v. Madison* can be found in Jean Edward Smith, *John Marshall: Definer of a Nation* (New York: Henry Holt Co., 1996), Chapter 13.

6 See, for example, John Hart Ely, *Democracy and Distrust: A Theory of Judicial Review* (Cambridge, MA: Harvard University Press, 1980).

7 *Roe v. Wade*, 410 U.S. 113 (1973).

8 *Luther v. Borden*, 48 U.S. 1 (1849).

9 *Massachusetts v. Laird*, 400 U.S. 886 (1970).

10 *Crockett v. Reagan*, 558 F. Supp. 893 (D.C.D.C. 1982).

11 See Alan M. Dershowitz, *Supreme Injustice: How the High Court Hijacked Election 2000* (New York: Oxford University Press, 2001).

12 Vincent Bugliosi, "None Dare Call It Treason," *The Nation*, January 18, 2001.

13 *Burnet v. Coronado Oil and Gas Co.*, 285 U.S. 393 (1932), dissenting opinion.

14 For example, the George H.W. Bush administration (1989–1992) appointed 182 federal judges. Nearly 19 percent of those appointees were women, and 5.5 percent were African Americans.

15 *Chisholm v. Georgia*, 2 U.S. 419 (1793).

16 Quoted in Sandra F. VanBurkleo, "John Jay." In *The Oxford Companion to the Supreme Court of the United States*, ed. Kermit L. Hall (New York: Oxford University Press, 1992), p. 447.

17 *McCulloch v. Maryland*, 17 U.S. 316 (1819).

18 *Gibbons v. Ogden*, 22 U.S. 1 (1824).

19 *Scott v. Sandford*, 60 U.S. 393 (1857).

20 *United States v. E. C. Knight Co.*, 156 U.S. 1 (1895).

21 *Pollock v. Farmer's Loan and Trust Co.*, 158 U.S. 601 (1895).

22 *Lochner v. New York*, 198 U.S. 45 (1905).

23 *Hammer v. Dagenhart*, 247 U.S. 251 (1918).

24 *Adkins v. Children's Hospital*, 261 U.S. 525 (1923).

25 *A. L. A. Schechter Poultry Corp. v. United States*, 295 U.S. 495 (1935).

26 *National Labor Relations Board v. Jones and Laughlin Steel Corp.*, 301 U.S. 1 (1937).

27 *Brown v. Board of Education*, 347 U.S. 483 (1954).

28 *Baker v. Carr*, 369 U.S. 186 (1962).

29 See, for example, *Abington School District v. Schempp*, 374 U.S. 203 (1963).

30 *Texas v. Johnson*, 491 U.S. 397 (1989).

31 See, for example, *United States v. Lopez*, 514 U.S. 549 (1995); *Printz v. United States*, 521 U.S. 898 (1997).

32 Herman Schwartz, "Introduction." In *The Rehnquist Court: Judicial Activism on the Right*, ed. Herman Schwartz (New York: Hill and Wang, 2002), p. 13.

33 See *Planned Parenthood v. Casey*, 505 U.S. 833 (1992).

34 *Romer v. Evans*, 517 U.S. 620 (1996); *Lawrence v. Texas*, 539 U.S. 558 (2003).

35 See, for example, *Santa Fe Independent School District v. Doe*, 530 U.S. 290 (2000).

36 *Rasul v. Bush*, 124 S Ct 2686 (2004).

37 Sandra Day O'Connor, *The Majesty of the Law: Reflections of a Supreme Court Justice* (New York: Random House, 2003), p. 5.

38 *Grove City College v. Bell*, 465 U.S. 555 (1984).

39 *Chisholm v. Georgia*, 2 U.S. 419 (1793).

40 *Oregon v. Mitchell*, 400 U.S. 112 (1970).

41 *United States v. Eichman*, 496 U.S. 310 (1990).

Chapter 15

THE FEDERAL BUREAUCRACY

OUTLINE

Key Terms 576

Expected Learning Outcomes 576

15-1 Bureaucracy and the Growth of Government 576
- **15-1a** What Is Bureaucracy? 579
- **15-1b** Bureaucracy in American Political Thought 580
- **15-1c** The Conservative Aversion to Bureaucracy 580
- **15-1d** Bureaucracy in American Political Culture 581

15-2 The Origin and Development of the Federal Bureaucracy 583
- **15-2a** Expansion of the Cabinet 582
- **15-2b** Emergence of the Regulatory State 583
- **15-2c** Emergence of the Welfare State 585
- **15-2d** Growth of Government during the 1970s 586
- **15-2e** The Reagan Revolution 587
- **15-2f** Reinventing Government? Bureaucracy in the Clinton Years 588
- **15-2g** George W. Bush, the Federal Bureaucracy, and the War on Terrorism 589
- **15-2h** Barack Obama as "Bureaucrat in Chief" 590

15-3 The Structure of the Federal Bureaucracy 591
- **15-3a** The Cabinet-Level Departments 591
- **15-3b** The Independent Agencies 593

15-4 Functions of the Bureaucracy 593
- **15-4a** Rule Making 594
- **15-4b** Adjudication of Disputes 596

15-5 Staffing the Bureaucracy 597
- **15-5a** The Civil Service 597

15-6 Presidential Control of the Bureaucracy 598
- **15-6a** Presidential Appointment and Removal Powers 599

15-7 Congressional Control of the Bureaucracy 603
- **15-7a** Legislative Tools 603
- **15-7b** Legislative Oversight 604

15-8 Legal Constraints on the Bureaucracy 604
- **15-8a** Public Access to Agency Information 605

15-9 Do Bureaucracies Respond to the Public Interest? 606
15-9a Iron Triangles and Issue Networks 606
15-10 Conclusion: Assessing the Bureaucracy 607
Questions for Thought and Discussion 609
Endnotes 610

KEY TERMS

agency point of view
bureaucracy
career civil servants
enabling legislation
independent agencies
legislative veto
meritocracy
modern administrative state
political appointees
sunshine laws
whistle blowers

EXPECTED LEARNING OUTCOMES

After reading this chapter and completing the supplemental online materials, students will:

- Understand the role of bureaucracy in American government
- Compare theories of bureaucratic behavior
- Analyze the effects of bureaucratic behavior on public policy

15-1 BUREAUCRACY AND THE GROWTH OF GOVERNMENT

When the first Congress convened in 1789, the United States consisted of thirteen states stretching along the Atlantic coast. The economy was primarily agricultural, and most of the nation's four million people lived in rural areas. The pace of life was slow. Little was expected from the national government. Consequently, government was small and seldom touched people's lives directly. In 1792, the federal government had approximately eight hundred employees. The total expenditures of the new national government until that time were around $4 million, and the national debt left over from the Revolutionary War stood at just over $77 million. Thus, during the early days of the Republic, the national government essentially followed the dictum often attributed to Thomas Jefferson: "That government is best which governs least."[1]

As the nineteenth century began, the federal government concerned itself mostly with the regulation of foreign trade, internal improvements such as canals and "post roads," and the protection of national security. Such functions as social welfare and education were left to the state and local governments, which, in turn, tended to leave matters of social welfare and education to neighborhoods, churches, and families. Perhaps most fundamentally, the dominant political culture regarded individuals as responsible for their own problems in addition to their own good fortunes. When Alexis de Tocqueville visited America in the 1830s, he was surprised to find so little in the way of government agencies. Tocqueville concluded that in America, "society governs itself for itself."[2]

Of course, things are quite different now. The United States stretches across the continent and beyond into the islands of the Pacific. The nation's population exceeds three hundred million. The United States is the only nation in the world that is now both a military and an industrial superpower. The American people now live in gigantic metropolitan areas—restless hubs of transportation, communications, and business. The pace of life has become extremely quick. Although Americans enjoy a standard of living undreamed of by the Founders, we also experience collective problems that did not greatly trouble the eighteenth century: environmental degradation, crime, racial conflict, and social disorganization, to name just a few. Most Americans now look to government, especially to Washington, D.C., to address these problems. Consequently, the annual federal budget is more than $2.9 trillion and the national debt exceeded $10 trillion for the first time in 2009.[3] The number of federal employees is nearly three million, not counting the armed forces (see Figure 15-1). Perhaps as many as ten million other individuals make their living indirectly from the national government, as consultants or contractors.

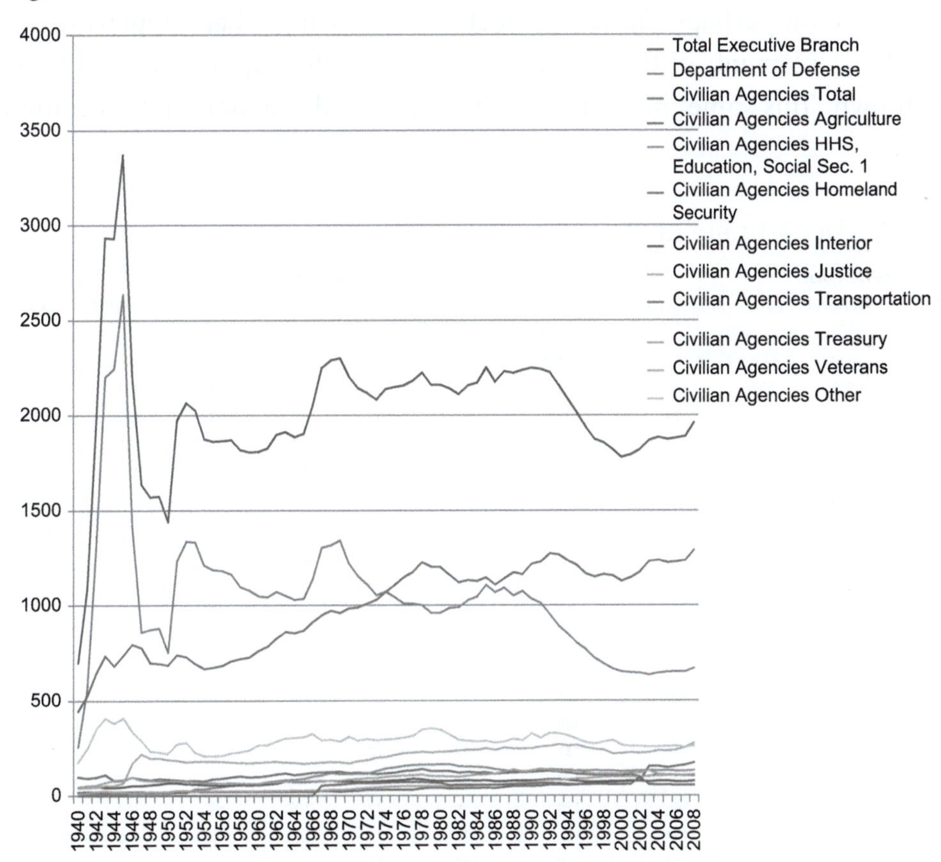

Figure 15-1 *Growth in Federal Civilian Employment by Decade, 1940–2011*
http://www.opm.gov/feddata/HistoricalTables/ExecutiveBranchSince1940.asp

The roughly 2.8 million civilian employees of the federal government staff an enormous bureaucracy encompassing fifteen major government departments and some fifty independent regulatory commissions, executive agencies, and government corporations. In the past four decades, more than two hundred fifty new agencies or bureaus have been added to the federal bureaucracy. Although some consolidation has taken place, few agencies have been eliminated. In all, the national government now has more than two thousand identifiable units. All these bureaucratic entities exist to meet some demand that the American people, or particular interests within society, have made on the national government. (Table 15-1 shows a sampling of federal agencies.)

The extensive bureaucratization of American government has led some commentators to refer to contemporary government as the administrative state.[4] More than simply a collection of offices, the **modern administrative state** consists of "vast, interconnecting webs of complicated administrative systems, regulatory procedures and nameless bureaucrats."[5] Given what government is now expected to do, from agricultural inspection to space exploration, bureaucracy is both necessary and inevitable. Indeed, one can argue that the "administrative state is very much a central factor, perhaps *the* central factor, influencing what happens in contemporary life."[6] Elements of this administrative state often appear to take on a world of their own. This sometimes leads to a very public discussion of its accountability.

TABLE 15.1 U.S. Department of Labor Headquarters

FISCAL YEAR	TOTAL EXECUTIVE BRANCH	DEPARTMENT OF DEFENSE	CIVILIAN AGENCIES									
			TOTAL	AGRICULTURE	HHS, EDUCATION, SOCIAL SEC. 1	HOMELAND SECURITY	INTERIOR	JUSTICE	TRANSPOR-TATION	TREASURY	VETERANS	OTHER
1992	2,225	952	1,274	128	136	56	85	82	64	133	260	329
1993	2,157	891	1,266	124	135	56	85	82	63	127	268	326
1994	2,085	850	1,235	120	133	55	81	83	59	128	262	315
1995	2,012	802	1,210	113	132	56	76	87	58	128	264	297
1996	1,934	768	1,166	110	130	62	71	88	58	118	251	279
1997	1,872	723	1,149	107	131	64	71	93	59	112	243	270
1998	1,856	693	1,163	106	130	68	72	95	59	112	240	281
1999	1,820	666	1,155	105	130	69	73	97	58	113	219	290
2000	1,778	651	1,127	104	126	70	74	98	58	113	220	265
2001	1,792	647	1,145	109	129	73	76	99	59	117	226	258
2002	1,818	645	1,173	98	130	76	77	96	96	118	223	258
2003	1,867	636	1,231	100	131	153	72	102	58	132	226	257
2004	1,882	644	1,238	111	130	153	77	104	57	111	236	257
2005	1,872	649	1,224	108	131	147	76	105	56	108	235	258
2006	1,880	653	1,227	105	129	154	72	107	54	107	239	260
2007	1,888	651	1,237	103	129	159	72	107	54	104	254	254
2008	1,960	670	1,289	104	132	172	76	109	55	106	274	261
2009	2,094	737	1,357	104	139	180	75	113	57	109	297	283
2010	2,133	773	1,360	107	144	183	70	118	58	110	305	265
2011	2,146	774	1,372	104	143	194	77	117	58	108	314	257

Source: http://www.opm.gov/feddata/HistoricalTables/ExecutiveBranchSince1940.asp

When President George W. Bush appointed Congressman Porter Goss (R-Florida) to head the Central Intelligence Agency (CIA) in the fall of 2004, the consensus among most observers was that he was put in place with a clear mandate to provide accountability to what had been perceived as an agency that was out of control.

15-1a What Is Bureaucracy?

A bureau is a government agency or office. Although the term **bureaucracy** literally means "government by agency," the term is commonly employed to describe the collection of agencies a government creates to impose regulations, implement policies, and administer programs. *The American Heritage Dictionary* defines bureaucracy as "administration of a government chiefly through bureaus staffed with nonelective officials." Bureaucracy is a universal phenomenon among advanced societies with well-established governments. German sociologist Max Weber argued that bureaucracy exists in the modern world because it is the most rational way of organizing efforts to achieve collective goals. Whether or not Weber was right, bureaucracy is an inextricable component of modern government.

In the United States, bureaucracy is found at every level of government: local, state, and national. And bureaucracy may be found in all three branches of government: executive, legislative, and judicial. To simplify matters somewhat, this chapter focuses on the collection of agencies that constitute the executive bureaucracy of the national government in addition to the numerous agencies officially classified as independent—that is, not formally part of any of the three branches of government. Indeed, many observers think of the entire executive bureaucracy as a virtual fourth branch of American national government.[7] Constitutionally speaking, this characterization may be incorrect. But considering the difficulties that both the president and Congress can have in controlling agency action, the characterization makes sense.

The federal bureaucracy may seem remote, impersonal, and impenetrable. It is, after all, a large group of American citizens doing a wide variety of jobs for the federal government, from a ranger riding on horseback through a national park to a clerk entering data at a computer terminal inside a massive government building in Washington. The people who operate the federal bureaucracy can be placed in two categories. **Political appointees**, who hold the highest executive positions, come and go with changing presidential administrations. **Career civil servants**—who occupy the middle management, professional, technical, and clerical positions—obtain their jobs on the basis of merit and are protected from being fired for political reasons.

15-1b Bureaucracy in American Political Thought

Whereas the classical liberals of the Enlightenment called for minimal government as a means of promoting individual freedom, liberal theorists of the late-nineteenth and early twentieth centuries sought to justify a broader role for government. Social theorists, such as John Dewey, advocated an expanded governmental role in part to realize the ideal of equality in an economy in which gross disparities exist between rich and poor. For modern liberal economists, like John Maynard Keynes, a greater degree of government intervention is necessary to avoid the wild swings between periods of dramatic growth and periods of recession, or even depression. According to the Keynesian perspective—dominant during the New Deal era—the very survival of capitalism depends on successful government management of the economy. In the decades following the New Deal, the American intellectual community, as exemplified in the work of the economist John Kenneth Galbraith, embraced the concept of proactive government—that is, government committed to progress through regulation, the redistribution of wealth, and planning. In the 1960s, President Lyndon Johnson's Great Society program was based squarely on the assumptions of modern liberalism.

15-1c The Conservative Aversion to Bureaucracy

Conservatives are highly critical of the mammoth bureaucracy that has developed in Washington to implement the policies and programs of modern liberalism. Conservatives view bureaucracy as unnecessary meddling in people's lives, especially in their economic activities. The modern conservative criticism of bureaucracy stems from a pervasive distrust of government and a deep-seated skepticism about what government can do to promote justice, welfare, and progress. Indeed, one fundamental point of division between liberals and conservatives now is their differing view of the role and capabilities of government.

Former President Ronald Reagan was, without question, the most conservative president the United States had seen in decades. Throughout his career in government, which began as the governor of California in the 1960s, Reagan remained sharply critical of big government, "liberal" programs, and the bureaucracy created to implement them. In his 1981 inaugural address, Reagan famously observed, "Government is not the solution to our problem; government is the problem." As president, Reagan sought to scale down the national government and return decision making to the state and local levels. During his first term, he attempted to have Congress abolish the newly created Department of Education, which he saw as both unnecessary bureaucracy and a federal encroachment on a traditionally local function. In failing to abolish the department, Reagan learned what political scientists have long known: *After bureaucracy is created, it is virtually impossible to do away with it!* As one well-known student of public administration has put it, "Government activities tend to go on indefinitely."[8]

As a practical matter, the influence of pluralist politics (the interplay of organized interests) has been even more important in creating and maintaining bureaucracy. You only have to consider the success of numerous interest groups in shaping, perpetuating, and often enlarging government programs created (at least in theory) to advance the public interest. Students of American politics have long recognized that government regulators are apt to be more influenced by the interests of those they regulate than by abstract notions of responsible government.

ONLINE 15.1 *Milton Freidman on Bureaucracy*
http://www.youtube.com/watch?v=8tJHjghAHJg

15-1d Bureaucracy in American Political Culture

Although Americans over the past decades have come to look to Washington to solve their social and economic problems, bureaucracy remains a dirty word in American political culture. To say that an organization is bureaucratic, or to call someone a bureaucrat, is obviously not a compliment. Although most people recognize the necessity of bureaucracy, Americans are deeply critical and suspicious of it. In common parlance, bureaucracy is synonymous with delay and waste, with red tape[9] and the runaround. The business community (particularly small business) tends to be especially vocal in complaining about government regulations and record-keeping requirements. "Anyone who has ever attempted to operate a small business in this country is well aware of the difficulties (not to mention costs) associated with compliance with myriad laws and regulations."[10]

Suffice it to say that American political culture, which has long valued localism and the popular control of government, is not hospitable to bureaucracy. Yet the basic reason that bureaucracy exists is to achieve goals that the people, through their elected representatives, have set for government in the modern age. The American people may dislike bureaucracy, but most of them understand that, given what they expect from government, bureaucracy is inevitable. Yet most also believe, rightly or wrongly, that the federal bureaucracy is beset by "waste, fraud, and abuse." Unfortunately, waste, fraud, and abuse, when they do exist in government agencies, are difficult to detect and eliminate. And, of course, efforts to cut wasteful spending are always subject to being politicized, especially when the agency being targeted is engaged in the delivery of needed social services. As one commentator observed in 2003, "Whenever you talk about [cutting] mandatory spending, it's spun by the groups who oppose true accountability that we are trying to take away entitlements for those who are needy."[11]

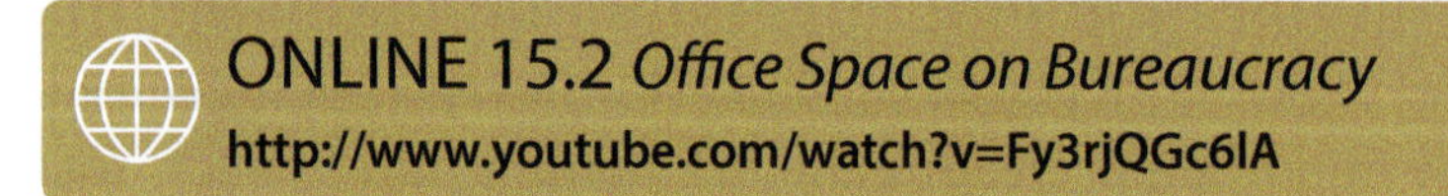

ONLINE 15.2 Office Space on Bureaucracy
http://www.youtube.com/watch?v=Fy3rjQGc6lA

15-2 The Origin and Development of the Federal Bureaucracy

The Constitution says nothing about the president's cabinet, let alone a mammoth federal bureaucracy. Article II, Section 2 merely allows the president, with the advice and consent of the Senate, to appoint "public ministers" and all other "officers of the United States whose appointments are not herein otherwise provided for, and which shall be established by law." In Article I, Section 6, the Constitution does mention "the Treasury," which became one of the three executive departments established by Congress in 1789. In addition to the treasury, President George Washington's administration consisted of two small departments—the Department of State and the Department of War (now the Department of Defense)—and the office of attorney general. Thomas Jefferson, the first secretary of state, had only nine people working for him at the State Department. The Department of War had fewer than eighty civilian employees. Alexander Hamilton, the first secretary of the treasury, had a somewhat larger staff. In all, the first Washington administration employed about eight hundred people.

15-2a Expansion of the Cabinet

Throughout most of the nineteenth century, the idea of limited government prevailed. The national government remained relatively small and did not involve itself much in the lives of the American people. The existing executive departments (state, war, treasury, and attorney general, which became the Justice Department in 1870) performed only the essential functions of government. Social welfare and economic regulation were not considered legitimate concerns of the national government. The three new departments that were added to the national government during the nineteenth century—the post office and the departments of the interior and agriculture—did not represent a significant change in public expectations of the national government.

The Post Office

In 1790, Congress created the post office and placed it under the jurisdiction of the Treasury Department. Much of the growth of the federal bureaucracy during the early nineteenth century is attributable to the expansion of the post office, which grew as the nation expanded westward. The post office became so large and so important that in 1829 Congress removed it from the treasury and made it a separate department. The postmaster general was made a member of the cabinet. In 1970, the Post Office Department was converted into the U.S. Postal Service, an independent agency governed by an eleven-member board, and the postmaster general was removed from the cabinet.

The Department of the Interior

In 1849, President James K. Polk signed a bill creating the new Department of the Interior to take charge of the millions of acres of land being acquired by the federal government in the West. Moreover, the Interior Department, through its Bureau of Indian Affairs, was to handle relations with the Native Americans who lived on much of this land. The Interior Department was also given the responsibility of conducting the decennial census mandated by the Constitution, a function originally performed by the Treasury Department.[12] In 1916, the National Park Service was set up within the Department of the Interior to administer the growing number of national parks and monuments. The park service now operates more than three hundred national parks, monuments, historic sites, battlefields, cemeteries, parkways, and recreational areas, encompassing nearly eighty million acres of public land.

The Department of Agriculture

The Department of Agriculture was established in 1862 to promote food production on the nation's farms. President Abraham Lincoln and Congress created the new department to ensure that the Union Army would have a steady food supply during its war with the Confederacy. Originally, the department assisted farmers through research, planning, and various service programs. It now assists consumers by inspecting and grading meat products. The department also administers the food stamp program, a major welfare program for the poor. The U.S. Forest Service, a bureau within the Department of Agriculture, manages federally owned forest lands, many of which are leased to private companies for logging.

15-2b Emergence of the Regulatory State

Before the twentieth century, the federal bureaucracy was concerned primarily with the essential functions of government and secondarily with providing services to citizens. In the late nineteenth century, America experienced a period of rapid industrialization. Factories and mills sprang up everywhere, mines were dug to extract coal and iron, and railroads were built to carry goods and people westward. At the same time, waves of immigrants looking for better lives were streaming in from Europe. Many immigrants took jobs in mines, mills, or factories or worked on the railroads. Wages were low, and working conditions were often miserable. Children worked side by side with their parents. Those who subscribed to the principle of *laissez-faire* argued that government should not intervene on behalf of workers or consumers. Unrestricted capitalism would, over the long run, produce the greatest good for the greatest number of people. On the other side of the issue were reformers backed by throngs of workers, many of whom were beginning to exercise their right to vote. Pressure was growing for the national government to become actively involved in the regulation of the economy.

The Interstate Commerce Commission

In 1887, Congress created the Interstate Commerce Commission (ICC), the first independent regulatory commission of the national government. The ICC was independent in the sense that commissioners held their positions for fixed terms rather than simply served at the pleasure of the president. The ICC was created, largely at the behest of the nation's farmers, to control price fixing and other unfair practices by the railroads. Over time, the ICC's jurisdiction was expanded to include the trucking industry, bus lines, and even oil and gas pipelines. The ICC controlled rates and enforced antidiscrimination laws in these industries. When these industries were deregulated in the 1980s, there was no longer any need for the commission. The ICC was finally abolished in 1995.

The Department of Labor

Concerns over the plight of the nation's workers led to the creation of the Department of Labor in 1913. The department's mission is to administer programs and enforce laws that improve working conditions and advance employment opportunities. Now, the Department of Labor, through the Bureau of Labor Statistics, compiles important data on the American economy, including the consumer price index and the unemployment rate. The Occupational Safety and Health Administration (OSHA), an agency within the Department of Labor, was established in 1970 to develop and enforce regulations for the safety and health of workers in major industries. Congress has given OSHA the power to make rules that are "reasonably necessary or appropriate to provide safe and healthful employment and places of employment." One of OSHA's principal concerns now is the exposure of workers to hazardous chemicals. OSHA routinely inspects workplaces and issues citations to companies that fail to comply with its regulations. Labor unions and environmentalists strongly support OSHA in these activities, although business interests often resent OSHA's "meddling."

The Federal Trade Commission

In 1914, Congress established the Federal Trade Commission (FTC) as an independent agency, like the ICC. The FTC's creation was supported not only by consumers but also by small businesses threatened by unfair competition from large-scale monopolies. The

FTC was charged with maintaining free and fair competition, specifically by enforcing antitrust laws and preventing deceptive advertising. A major concern of the FTC is now the labeling and packaging of products. The FTC is empowered to investigate claims of unfair practices. It may issue cease-and-desist orders if it finds these types of claims to be valid. It may even file suit in federal court against companies deemed to be acting unlawfully.

ONLINE 15.3 *One State Elected Official's Response to the Federal Regulatory State*
http://www.youtube.com/watch?v=GvOO8HDp_Tk

15-2c Emergence of the Welfare State

No single event in American history had more of an impact on the growth of the federal bureaucracy than did the election of Franklin D. Roosevelt to the presidency in 1932. Roosevelt won the election by promising the American people a "new deal" to cope with the massive poverty and unemployment brought on by the Great Depression. Under the New Deal, Roosevelt and the Democratic Congress established public works programs, such as the Civilian Conservation Corps and the Works Progress Administration, in addition to a variety of regulatory programs affecting agriculture, banking, and heavy industry. All these programs required new bureaucracies, and the size of the federal government grew dramatically as a consequence. The Supreme Court declared unconstitutional several of the laws that established these regulatory programs.[13] The result was a showdown between the president and the Court, which Roosevelt finally won when the Court, perhaps fearing retaliation by Congress and the president, abruptly changed direction in what has been referred to as the "constitutional revolution of 1937." Roosevelt's four-term presidency, which lasted from 1933 until his death in 1945, firmly established the legitimacy of the modern regulatory state.

Although the Constitution authorized Congress to spend money to promote the general welfare, the federal government had traditionally left social welfare problems to the state and local governments. But the Great Depression of the 1930s overwhelmed the ability of state and local governments to provide relief and created widespread demands for the national government to get involved. These demands led to the passage of the Social Security Act of 1935, the federal government's first major foray into the realm of promoting social welfare. The Social Security Act established retirement insurance for older Americans, provided unemployment compensation for laid-off workers, and provided federal supplements to state and local welfare programs. The enactment of the Social Security Act signaled the emergence of another facet of modern government: the welfare state.

The Great Society

In 1965, President Lyndon B. Johnson, a lifelong Democrat and admirer of Roosevelt, launched a broad range of initiatives to achieve what he called the Great Society. Unlike the New Deal, which was conceived during a time of national crisis, the Great Society program was introduced during a period of economic vitality. The president's theme was that America could afford to do a better job of taking care of its people. Johnson, who had been elected in a landslide over the conservative Republican Barry Goldwater, felt that he had a mandate from the American people to enact this program, and Congress evidently agreed. In short order, Johnson proposed and Congress adopted the Medicare program, which provides health insurance for Americans over sixty-five, and Medicaid, which provides health care for the poor. At Johnson's request, Congress greatly increased funding for Aid to Families with Dependent Children (AFDC), which had been established by the Social Security Act in 1935 as a means of helping children whose fathers were deceased. From 1965 to 1969, the federal government doubled the money it spent on AFDC, and the number of AFDC recipients increased by almost 60 percent.

The administration of Social Security, Medicare, Medicaid, and AFDC required a large-scale bureaucracy. Before 1979, these programs were administered by the Department of Health, Education and Welfare, which had been established during the Eisenhower administration. The national government's social welfare programs are now run by the Department of Health and Human Services, which in monetary terms is the largest of the executive departments.

In addition to expanding social welfare programs, Johnson's Great Society program also called for an increased federal role in a number of other areas traditionally relegated to state and local governments: education, transportation, and housing. The Department of Health, Education and Welfare assumed the responsibility of administering the greatly increased federal grants to local schools, but new bureaucracies were created to handle the increased federal role in housing and transportation. In 1965, Congress established the Department of Housing and Urban Development (HUD) to administer programs that provide federal aid for housing and community development. Acting under the mantle of "cooperative federalism," HUD subsidized state and federal low-income housing projects. The Department of Transportation (DOT) was created in 1967 to coordinate policies and administer the transportation programs of the national government, especially urban mass-transit systems.

15-2d Growth of Government during the 1970s

Under President Richard M. Nixon (1969–1974), the Social Security program was expanded, wage and price controls were instituted in an attempt to control inflation, and a number of new regulatory programs were initiated, most significantly in the areas of environmental protection, occupational safety and health, and consumer product safety. Indeed, the period of the early 1970s has been called the Golden Age of Regulation, as new federal agencies generated volumes of new regulations to protect workers, consumers, and endangered species.

By far the most significant bureaucratic development of the Nixon years was the creation of the Environmental Protection Agency (EPA) in 1971. With its broad responsibilities for environmental protection, the EPA quickly became a focal point for political controversy, as environmentalists, business interests, and state and local officials sought to advance or protect their interests. From the outset, critics in business and industry charged that the EPA was imposing unreasonable policies that would threaten the economic health of the nation. On the other hand, environmentalists have often accused the EPA of dragging its feet in the face of political resistance to environmental progress.

In response to the energy crisis of the 1970s, President Carter persuaded Congress in 1977 to enact legislation creating the Department of Energy. The department brought together various federal programs and offices, including the nuclear weapons program previously housed in the Department of Defense. By assuming cabinet-level status, the new agency dramatized the importance of the energy issue at a time when future energy supplies were in doubt. The most significant bureaucratic development of the Carter years was the creation of the Department of Education in 1979. The new department was essentially carved out of the existing Department of Health, Education and Welfare, which was renamed Health and Human Services. The creation of the Department of Education highlighted the increasing federal role in public education, an area that, before the 1960s, had been the nearly exclusive preserve of state and local governments.

15-2e The Reagan Revolution

The election of Ronald Reagan to the presidency in 1980 was a watershed event in American political history. Reagan rode a wave of discontent in American society. To a great extent, the public was frustrated with the performance of the economy, which, shocked by spikes in oil prices, had experienced high levels of inflation combined with recession. Reagan also exploited a degree of popular dissatisfaction with the federal government. Reagan's strongest support came from the business community, which demanded relief from government regulation it regarded as excessive and oppressive. The Reagan administration came to Washington with a clear agenda of reducing the size and scope of the federal government, at least in domestic affairs. The administration sought to curtail regulatory activity and even deregulate industries altogether. It sought to reduce the size of federal welfare programs. President Reagan went so far as to call for the abolition of the recently created departments of education and energy. In his 1981 inaugural address, Reagan observed, "Government is not the solution to our problem; government is the problem."

Under President Reagan (1981–1989), the budgets of social services and regulatory agencies were reduced, but not without tremendous political resistance. The number of new regulations being issued by the federal bureaucracy declined, and entire industries were deregulated. But Reagan's proposals to eliminate the Department of Education and the Department of Energy never gained real traction. As we noted in section 15-1c, "The Conservative Aversion to Bureaucracy," once created, bureaucracy is extremely difficult to dislodge. Moreover, during the Reagan years, the defense budget was increased dramatically, and with it, the number of civilians working for the Pentagon. Despite President Reagan's commitment to downsizing the federal government, federal civilian employment continued to rise during the 1980s, albeit at a slower rate. Federal spending, mainly in the area of defense, rose dramatically and helped to create the massive budget deficits that became the defining political issue of the 1980s.

15-2f Reinventing Government? Bureaucracy in the Clinton Years

A staple of presidential campaigns is that candidates promise to go after the wasteful, inefficient, or corrupt bureaucracy. Many presidents have tried to reform the bureaucracy, most with limited success. Shortly after taking office in January 1993, President Bill Clinton appointed Vice President Al Gore to head a task force named the National Performance Review. Operating under the banner of "reinventing government," Gore and his staff spent six months scouring the federal bureaucracy for waste, inefficiency, and needless or silly regulations. In reporting his findings to the press, Gore displayed a souvenir of his inquiry. Referred to officially as an "ash receiver, tobacco, desk type," Gore's memento was nothing more than a glass ashtray, the kind found in offices and restaurants everywhere. Along with the ash receiver, Gore produced ten pages of federal regulations detailing the procedures government agencies must go through to procure the item. The regulations also contained an interesting requirement for testing the ashtray. First, the ashtray is placed on a maple plank exactly 44.5 millimeters thick. It is then struck with a hammer and steel punch, the point of which is ground to a specified angle. The ashtray must break into no more than thirty-five glass shards, each of which must be at least 6.4 millimeters on any three of its adjacent sides.[14] The National Performance Review generated considerable publicity for the Clinton administration.

During the 2000 presidential campaign, Al Gore made numerous references to the success of the government in reducing federal government employees. Some critics maintained that many of the numbers Gore used as indicators of government reduction in fact reflected cutbacks in the military and its civilian support staff. Moreover, the number of private contractors doing business with the government increased significantly as government functions were increasingly "outsourced." Needless to say, government was hardly reinvented during the Clinton–Gore administration. It would be a rare thing indeed for a president to be able to effect such radical change.

15-2g GEORGE W. BUSH, THE FEDERAL BUREAUCRACY, AND THE WAR ON TERRORISM

As a Republican, President George W. Bush came to Washington with considerable skepticism of the federal bureaucracy. Yet, as is often the case with presidents, uncontrollable events would have a powerful effect on the president's relationship with the bureaucracy. After the terrorist attacks of September 11, 2001, President Bush found himself leading the federal government's efforts to improve domestic security. In this capacity, President Bush interacted with government agencies at all levels. At first Bush seemed to be profoundly impressed by the government's response to the new crisis. He praised the actions of government agencies and supported their requests for additional resources. Bush even used his constitutional and statutory powers to create a new federal office, the Office of Homeland Security, based in the Executive Office of the President, to coordinate federal, state, and local efforts to make the country safe from terrorism.

By the summer of 2002, it had become apparent that there were serious problems with the federal government's homeland security operations. They included serious deficiencies in the Immigration and Naturalization Service, inadequacies in the Customs Service, and an overall lack of coordination among federal law enforcement and intelligence agencies. Many members of Congress called for an overhaul of the national homeland security apparatus. President Bush eventually came to support this idea and the result was the Homeland Security Act of 2002, creating a new cabinet-level department: the Department of Homeland Security. After signing the bill into law in late November 2002, Bush nominated Tom Ridge, who had been serving as director of the temporary Office of Homeland Security, to head the new department.

The creation of the new department represented the largest reorganization of the executive branch in the past five decades. It merged more than twenty existing federal agencies, including the Secret Service, the Coast Guard, the Customs Service, and the Immigration and Naturalization Service, into a new department with more than one hundred seventy-five thousand employees. While the creation of the new department signaled the high priority now assigned to homeland security, the construction of the new department would not be easy. It required the merger of agencies with different computer systems, different operational styles, different leadership structures, and different agency cultures. President Bush called the creation of the new department an "immense task" that would "take time and focus and steady resolve." Senate Republican leader Trent Lott (R-Mississippi) called it a "monstrous undertaking."

In the spring of 2002, the Federal Bureau of Investigation (FBI) came under increasing scrutiny following the revelation that people in senior positions in the agency did not follow through on field agents' concerns about suspected terrorist activities before 9/11. Testifying before the Senate Intelligence Committee in May 2002, FBI Director Robert Mueller admitted that the FBI could have done a better job in piecing together information from the field. Much of the discussion of the FBI's performance and its perceived weaknesses centered on the nature of its bureaucracy. Many expressed the opinion that those promoted to leadership positions were overly interested in "playing it safe" to advance their careers while the best agents remained in the field without promotion to positions of greater authority. The FBI experience pointed to a perennial bureaucratic pathology: the organization loses sight of its mission as people in the organization work to maintain their own status and power within. In response to mounting criticism of the FBI, Director Mueller and Attorney General John Ashcroft (Mueller's boss) announced sweeping structural and procedural changes in the agency. What they hoped for as well, but what is always more difficult to achieve, was *cultural change* within the FBI.

15-2h Barack Obama as "Bureaucrat in Chief"

Much like Bill Clinton before him, Barack Obama came in with an agenda to reform the federal bureaucracy. President Obama believed that lack of regulations, especially oversight of the mortgage and finance industries, led to the conditions that spawned the "Great Recession" of 2008. President Obama came into office promising to rein in the banks, lenders, and underwriters with significantly increased oversight and regulation from the federal government. Conservatives railed against his actions, claiming that regulation had increased so drastically that small businesses could not keep up with them all. Mitt Romney made that point very sharply on the campaign trail in 2012, saying that federal regulation had quadrupled in the Obama term. However, regulations did not increase significantly over the term of his predecessor, George W. Bush.[15] Obama's main thrust has been using the bureaucracy as an outreach and campaign tool. For example, the president has established an online petition site, where any proposal can be submitted and the White House will respond to any petition that receives a threshold number of endorsements.

ONLINE 15.4 *The White House Petition Site*
https://petitions.whitehouse.gov/

15-3 The Structure of the Federal Bureaucracy

The federal bureaucracy now encompasses fifteen major executive departments and a host of **independent agencies**. Each of these departments or agencies is responsible for administering programs, collecting information, or making and enforcing regulations within a specific area of public policy. Unfortunately for the student of American politics, the dividing lines of responsibility and authority in the federal bureaucracy are not always clear. Often, agency responsibilities overlap so that several agencies within the bureaucracy are working on the same issue or problem. For example, more than a hundred different agencies or bureaus of the national government have some responsibility for education policy. Usually, federal agencies cooperate in making policy or running programs, but not always! Just as well-known rivalries exist among the military services, rivalries exist within the federal bureaucracy. Sometimes, these rivalries even occur between bureaus located within the same department.

The fragmented responsibility, interagency rivalries, and, above all, generally unwieldy character of the massive bureaucracy have led presidents to try to reorganize the executive branch. These efforts have been, at best, only moderately successful. Perhaps the most ambitious plan was launched by President Nixon, who wanted to combine all the more than fifty independent agencies into four new executive departments. Nixon was interested in not only simplifying the bureaucratic structure but also achieving more presidential control over the independent agencies. Unfortunately for Nixon, too many powerful, entrenched interests supported the status quo, and the plan never got off the ground.

15-3a The Cabinet-Level Departments

The executive branch is organized into fifteen major departments, each of which is headed by a secretary who is a member of the president's cabinet (see Table 15-2). Although secretaries are primarily accountable to the president, who appoints and may fire them without notice, they are also somewhat accountable to Congress, which appropriates the funding for their departments. Offices within these major departments are called bureaus, or agencies. In some departments, the bureaus and agencies are closely controlled by the appointed officials at the top of the hierarchy. In others, the political appointees at the top find it quite difficult to control the activities

TABLE 15-2 The Fifteen Cabinet-Level Departments

DEPARTMENT	NUMBER OF CIVILIAN EMPLOYEES, 1990 (IN THOUSANDS)	NUMBER OF CIVILIAN EMPLOYEES, 2012 (IN THOUSANDS)	DIFFERENCE, 1990–2012
Agriculture	123	99	–24
Commerce	70	44	–26
Defense	1,034	730	–304
Education	5	4	–1
Energy	18	15	–3
Health and Human Services	124	74	–50
Homeland Security	0	191	191
Housing and Urban Development	14	9	–5
Interior	78	77	–1
Justice	84	117	33
Labor	18	18	0
State	26	41	15
Transportation	67	57	–10
Treasury	159	112	–47
Veterans Affairs	248	323	75
Totals	2,068	1,687	–381

Sources: http://www.opm.gov/policy-data-oversight/data-analysis-documentation/federal-employment-reports/employment-trends-data/2012/september/table-2/. Adapted from U.S. Department of the Census, Statistical Abstract of the United States.

that go on "under" them. The appointed leaders often find that the careerists in their departments have adopted an agency point of view rather than the administration's agenda.[16]

The **agency point of view** stresses protection of the agency's budget, powers, staff, and routines, often at the expense of what elected officials may want. Agencies become quite protective of their "turf" and set in their ways. Presidents and their cabinets come and go, but career bureaucrats seem to stay on forever! The longevity of careerists within a particular bureau or agency is one reason that agencies develop their own, distinctive culture. For example, one study has shown that more than 80 percent of the career civil servants at the highest ranks have risen through the same agency.[17] It is no wonder that they believe in the goals of the agency and the societal need for its programs. In fairness, one must recognize that not everyone working in an agency subscribes to the agency point of view. Many agency managers truly believe that they are working for the public good.[18]

15-3b The Independent Agencies

Congress created the first independent agency in 1887 when it established the Interstate Commerce Commission. Since then, more than sixty other independent agencies have been established. These agencies can be divided into three rough categories: regulatory commissions, government corporations, and administrative agencies (see Table 15-3). The categories are rough because all the independent agencies engage in administration and many of them have some degree of regulatory authority. These agencies are independent in two senses. First, because they are located outside the fifteen major executive departments, they are not under the authority of a member of the cabinet. Second, the heads of these agencies, usually multimember boards or commissions, are appointed by the president for set terms of office. In most cases, they cannot be fired until their terms have expired.[19] This arrangement was intentional—the idea was to give the agencies a degree of freedom from presidential pressure. Much to the chagrin of presidents, this arrangement promotes the development of an agency point of view.

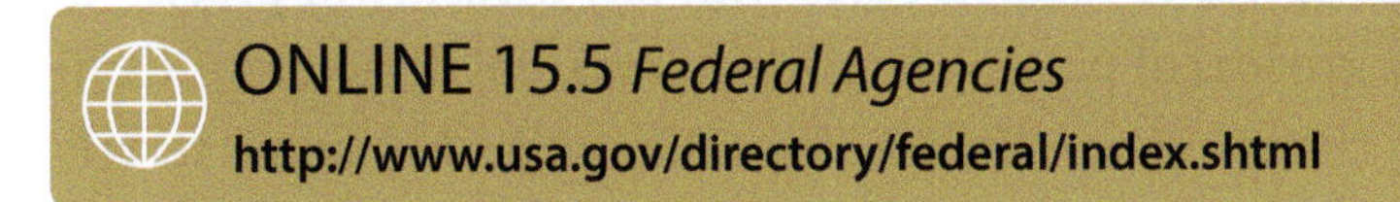

ONLINE 15.5 *Federal Agencies*
http://www.usa.gov/directory/federal/index.shtml

The independent agencies slide in and out of public view. The Federal Communications Commission (FCC), charged with regulating the airwaves, became the subject of controversy in 2004 when it became much more aggressive in policing radio and television programming. After Janet Jackson's infamous "wardrobe malfunction" during the 2004 Super Bowl halftime show, the FCC imposed record-level fines on CBS and its affiliates. FCC Chairman Michael Powell defended the FCC's action, saying, "As countless families gathered around the television to watch one of our nation's most celebrated events, they were rudely greeted with a halftime show stunt more fitting of a burlesque show."[20] When radio personality Howard Stern, the subject of numerous fines for violating the FCC's decency rule, finally abandoned the public airwaves for satellite radio in 2004, he was unmerciful in his criticism of the agency and its chair, Michael Powell. Speaking to thousands of cheering supporters in late 2004, Stern screamed, "Down with the FCC! They have ruined commercial broadcasting."[21]

15-4 Functions of the Bureaucracy

The functions of the bureaucracy can be divided into three broad categories: administration of programs, rule making, and adjudication of disputes. Every agency is involved to some degree in administration—at the least, it has to run itself. Many agencies have been given responsibility for managing government programs designed to meet some social or economic need: for example, agricultural subsidies, veterans' hospitals, school lunch programs, space exploration, delivery of mail, and construction of highways, among others. Some agencies are designed to manage and supervise aspects of the entire federal bureaucracy. For example, the General Services Administration manages and supplies government buildings, the General Accounting Office keeps tabs on agency budgets, and the Office of Personnel Management supervises the hiring of federal employees.

15-4a Rule Making

The broad role now played by the national government makes Congress' job in passing needed legislation much more difficult. The sheer magnitude of problems demanding congressional attention and the practical difficulties of drafting sound regulations now limit Congress' ability to legislate comprehensively, much less effectively. Indeed, this complexity and impracticability, coupled with the pluralistic politics of the legislative process, make it difficult for Congress to fashion rules with any measure of precision. At the same time, the tortuous process of passing legislation makes it difficult for Congress to respond promptly to changing conditions. Thus, Congress has come to rely more and more on "experts" for the development, and the implementation, of regulations. These experts are found in a host of government departments, commissions, agencies, boards, and bureaus that comprise the modern administrative state.

Delegation of Legislative Power

Through a series of broad delegations of its legislative power, Congress has transferred to the federal bureaucracy much of the responsibility for making and enforcing the rules and regulations deemed necessary for a technological society (see Table 15-3). Frequently, the **enabling legislation** creating these agencies provides little more than vague generalities to guide agency rule making. These delegations of power may be desirable or even inevitable, but they do raise serious philosophical and constitutional questions. Most fundamental is the question of representative government. No one votes for the bureaucrats at OSHA who make regulations that affect millions of American workers and businesses.

The Americans with Disabilities Act (ADA) of 1990 provides a recent example of legislative delegation. The ADA, which built on the existing body of federal civil rights law, mandates the elimination of discrimination against individuals with disabilities. A number of federal agencies, including the Department of Justice, the Department of Transportation, the Equal Employment Opportunity Commission (EEOC), and the Federal Communications Commission (FCC), are given extensive regulatory and enforcement powers under the act. One of the many regulations that have been

TABLE 15-3 The Major Federal Regulatory Agencies

AGENCY	YEAR CREATED	FUNCTIONS
Food and Drug Administration (FDA)	1907	Regulates the safety of food, drugs, and cosmetics
Federal Reserve Board (The Fed)	1913	Controls money supply; attempts to stabilize the economy; sets bank reserve requirements
Federal Trade Commission (FTC)	1914	Attempts to prevent false and misleading advertising; monitors business practices affecting fair competition
Federal Deposit Insurance Corporation (FDIC)	1933	Insures deposits in participating banks
Federal Communications Commission (FCC)	1934	Regulates interstate telephone service, cellular phones, broadcasting, and cable television
Securities and Exchange Commission (SEC)	1934	Regulates securities markets, such as the stock market
Federal Power Commission, renamed the Federal Energy Regulatory Commission (FERC) in 1977	1935	Regulates natural gas and oil pipelines and natural gas prices and issues hydroelectric dam licenses
Atomic Energy Commission, changed to Nuclear Regulatory Commission (NRC) in 1975	1947	Licenses and regulates nuclear power plants
Federal Aviation Administration (FAA)	1958	Regulates airline safety
Occupational Safety and Health Administration (OSHA)	1971	Protects workers' safety and health in the workplace
Consumer Product Safety Commission	1972	Regulates the safety of consumer products; recalls unsafe products from the market
Environmental Protection Agency (EPA)	1972	Regulates air, water, and noise pollution

Note: The first federal regulatory commission, the Interstate Commerce Commission, was abolished in 1995. Its functions were transferred to other agencies.

adopted in support of the statute is a final rule prohibiting discrimination on the basis of disability in the provision of state and local government services, which was published in the *Federal Register* by the Justice Department. Twenty-nine pages of the *Federal Register* of July 26, 1991 are devoted to this one rule. Various agencies' regulations implementing the ADA fill hundreds of pages of the *Federal Register*.

Article I of the Constitution vests "all legislative power" in Congress. When Congress delegates legislative power to the executive branch, it can be viewed as violating the implicit separation of powers. In 1935, the Supreme Court struck down an act of Congress on the grounds that it delegated too much legislative power to the bureaucracy without adequate policy guidance.[22] Since then, the Court has not invalidated any federal laws on this basis. In effect, the courts have given Congress *carte blanche* to delegate policy-making authority to the bureaucracy.

Normally, the federal courts permit agencies to interpret their statutory authorities broadly. For example, the Supreme Court has held that the Internal Revenue Service is empowered to revoke the tax-exempt status of private schools that practice racial discrimination, even though the text of Section 501(c)(3) of the Internal Revenue Code suggests otherwise.[23] However, in 2000, the Supreme Court dealt a major blow to the Clinton administration when it held that the Food and Drug Administration did not have the authority to regulate tobacco products. The Court ruled that the FDA has misinterpreted the power granted by Congress under the Food, Drug and Cosmetics Act.[24]

Procedures for Adoption of Rules

Although Congress has delegated broad rule-making authority to the bureaucracy, it has also stipulated the procedures that must be followed in making rules and applying them to concrete cases. These procedures are spelled out in the Administrative Procedures Act (APA), first enacted in 1946 and later amended. The APA requires that the time, place, and procedures for agency rule making be published in the *Federal Register* and that interested parties be afforded the opportunity to submit written arguments to the agency before a proposed rule is finally adopted. Once adopted by the agency, the final rule must be published in the *Federal Register*. In most cases, agencies are required by law to conduct formal public hearings before adopting rules, and they must give the public an opportunity to comment on the proposed rules. Of course, even when a hearing is held, the interests that are adversely affected by a new rule often claim that the agency's rule-making procedures were inadequate.

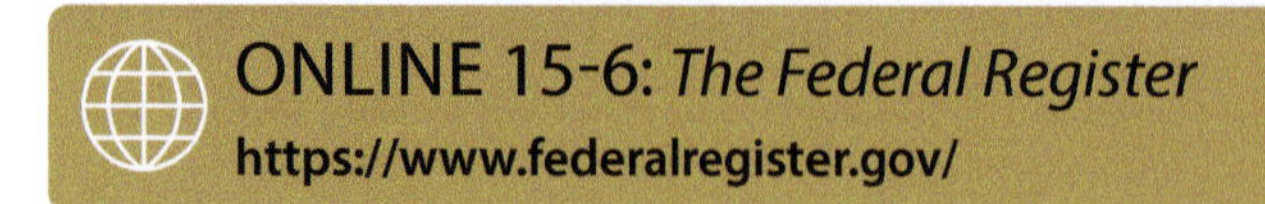

ONLINE 15-6: *The Federal Register*
https://www.federalregister.gov/

15-4b Adjudication of Disputes

Controversies often arise as agencies attempt to apply their rules to affected parties. Before an agency enforces a decision that adversely affects a person, group, or company, it must follow a process provided for in the Administrative Procedures Act. In these instances, agencies take on a judicial, or "quasijudicial," character. Indeed, some agencies employ administrative law judges (ALJs) to decide disputes. Although less elaborate than a civil or criminal trial, a hearing conducted by an ALJ is a formal legal proceeding with its own rules and procedures. Agencies and affected parties are usually represented by counsel, testimony and other evidence are presented, and the losing party has the right to appeal the ALJ's decision to the federal courts. The agencies do not always win these disputes. Although the ALJs are technically the employees of the agency for which they work, they are required by law to act as independent arbiters. Indeed, the law provides that no punitive action may be taken against ALJs for making decisions that run counter to their agencies.

15-5 Staffing the Bureaucracy

In *The Federalist* No. 86, Alexander Hamilton observed, "The true test of a good government is its aptitude and tendency to produce a good administration." Be that as it may, in the early days of the Republic, federal employees were chosen largely on the basis of political patronage. This practice of hiring the political supporters and cronies of the president came to be known as the spoils system, from the adage "to the victor belongs the spoils." Though practiced in greater or lesser degree by all the early presidents, the spoils system was elevated to an art form by President Andrew Jackson. Jackson defended the system as necessary to the implementation of presidential will. In his view, federal officials should be loyal supporters of the president and must remain totally dependent on the president to keep their jobs if the president is to be assured that his policies will be carried out.

By the 1880s, criticism of the spoils system was reaching a crescendo. Reformers argued that the system fostered incompetence and inefficiency. They believed that being a good federal official required much more than being a friend of the president—it required ability, dedication, and special training. Reformers were calling for the creation of a **meritocracy**, a system in which officials are recruited, selected, and retained on the basis of demonstrable merit.

15-5a The Civil Service

The assassination of President James A. Garfield by a frustrated federal job seeker in 1881 spurred Congress to enact civil service reform. The Pendleton Act of 1883 forbade the firing of a federal employee for failing to contribute to a political campaign (a common practice at that time). Moreover, the act created a bipartisan Civil Service Commission to oversee a new federal meritocracy. As a result, approximately 15 percent of federal offices were to be staffed on the basis of competitive examinations, commonly referred to as the civil service exam. After the passage of the legislation, presidents routinely used expansions of the civil service system to protect their political appointees. After a worker was included under civil service, both the person and the job remained in the system. This practice led to a slow increase in the number of workers in the civil service system. Thus, by 1952, after further expansion by the Truman administration, the merit system covered more than 90 percent of all federal jobs.

As a result of reports in 1949 and 1955 by the Hoover Commission, the federal civil service was streamlined, and the operations of numerous agencies were consolidated under the General Services Administration. In an effort to further separate the civil service from partisan politics, Congress enacted the Hatch Act in 1940, which prohibited federal civil service employees from actively participating in or even contributing money to political campaigns. The Hatch Act was criticized by many as an infringement on the First Amendment rights of federal employees. Nevertheless, the act was upheld by the federal courts against constitutional challenges based on the First Amendment.[25] In 1993, Congress amended the Hatch Act to allow for greater political activity by federal employees. Republicans were critical of this change because most federal employees have traditionally supported the Democrats. Allowing greater political participation by federal employees helps the Democratic party, although the effect is probably not that great.

The Civil Service Reform Act of 1978

As the federal bureaucracy grew in size, complexity, and authority, presidential appointees charged with running the major departments found themselves relying more and more on senior civil service personnel. Because almost all these people had come up through the ranks within that department, they tended to have an agency point of view that often differed from the president's political agenda. Presidents of both parties became concerned that they might be losing control of the bureaucracy. These concerns led to the enactment of the Civil Service Reform Act of 1978. The act created the Senior Executive Service, an echelon of approximately eight thousand top managers who can be hired, fired, and transferred more easily than civil service personnel. The idea was to place top department and bureau managers more directly under the control of the president's appointees. Decades later, it does not appear as though the 1978 law has had much effect on the federal bureaucracy. Few members of the Senior Executive Service are fired or transferred. Cabinet members still complain about departments adopting an "agency point of view" rather than the president's.

15-6 Presidential Control of the Bureaucracy

Most recent presidents have entered office with strong suspicions about the bureaucracy. At a minimum, the bureaucracy is a large, unwieldy organization that must be pushed, pulled, pleaded with, threatened, and persuaded into enacting the goals of the president. Moreover, conservative presidents see a bureaucracy full of workers dedicated to the social welfare system and the power of government regulation. Because all recent conservative presidents have campaigned against the perceived excesses of the social welfare system and the prevalence of regulation, their hostility toward much of the bureaucracy is easy to understand. On the other hand, liberals distrust the close relationship between interest groups and government agencies. Liberals also fear that the rigidity of the organization and job safety of the individuals will create obstacles to any new ideas or policy changes. At the same time, all presidents realize that they must rely on the bureaucracy to carry out their wishes and that they depend on the bureaucracy for information. Given the bureaucracy's control over information, technical expertise, close relations with members of Congress, ties with interest groups, and long-term security, presidents may feel that this reliance on the bureaucracy makes them vulnerable.

Presidents have developed three main strategies for dealing with the bureaucracy. First, a president can appoint high-level bureaucrats who are in agreement with him on issues related to the agency's functions. Second, the president can establish a counterbureaucracy within the White House composed of close advisers who will watch over the shoulders of the bureaucrats. Third, the president can depend on policy organizations within the White House to develop new policy. Each of these three methods has its advantages and shortcomings.[26]

15-6a Presidential Appointment and Removal Powers

The powers of removal and nomination are the best tool a president has for asserting control over a stubborn bureaucracy. Presidents control appointments to only 1 percent of all bureaucratic jobs, but the jobs in question are leadership positions at the top of the federal bureaucracy. When a president enters office, it is now assumed that the political appointees of the former president who hold most of the top positions will resign so that the new president, even if he is of the same party, can leave his own imprint on the bureaucracy. Presidents have always insisted on broad power to remove officials in their administrations. With respect to the top-level officials in the major executive departments, the president unquestionably has unbridled removal powers. These officials—secretaries, assistant secretaries, and undersecretaries—are widely understood to be political appointees who serve at the president's pleasure.

In an attempt to force the bureaucracy to adopt its political agenda, the Reagan White House exercised tight control over the process of top-level executive appointments. The Reagan people scrutinized all candidates for high-level administrative posts to ensure that they shared President Reagan's conservative views about the role of the federal government. In some cases, Reagan appointed persons whom he knew were opposed to the programs they would be charged with administering. For example, Anne Burford Gorsuch, who opposed the enforcement of many antipollution regulations, was appointed as director of the Environmental Protection Agency. Rather than confront Congress to try to change the legislation, Reagan sought to avoid controversy by appointing someone who would make the laws less effective by not enforcing them. In contrast, the Clinton White House was less concerned about ideology and more concerned about diversity in making its bureaucratic nominations. Of course, the Clinton administration was much more liberal than its Republican predecessors, but it was also more diverse in terms of race and gender. This increased diversity reflected Clinton's campaign promise to make his administration "look like America."

Although cabinet and subcabinet officials are subject to immediate presidential firing, civil service employees can be fired only for cause, and displeasing the president is not necessarily cause for dismissal. Of course, presidents are seldom aware of the activities of civil service personnel because they occupy the middle and lower rungs of the administrative hierarchy.

Removal of Officials in the Independent Agencies

The independent agencies and commissions pose a more difficult question of presidential removal authority, one that the courts have struggled with over the years. For example, in 1935, the Supreme Court considered whether President Franklin D. Roosevelt could fire a member of the Federal Trade Commission (FTC) solely on policy grounds.[27] In 1931, President Herbert Hoover reappointed William Humphrey to serve on the FTC. According to an act of Congress, Humphrey's seven-year term was subject to presidential curtailment only for malfeasance, inefficiency, or neglect of duty. When Roosevelt took office, he fired Humphrey, believing that the goals of his administration would be better served by people of his own choosing. Although Humphrey died shortly after his removal, the executor of his estate brought suit to recover wages lost between the time of removal and the time of his death. In deciding the case, the Supreme Court held that executive officials performing strictly executive functions could be removed at will by the president. In the case of regulatory commissions, like the FTC, however, Congress had created a quasi-legislative body designed to perform tasks independently of executive control. Thus, the Court said that Congress could regulate the removal of these officials.

In 1958, the Supreme Court expanded on this holding, saying that the unique nature of independent agencies requires that removal must be for cause, whether or not Congress has so stipulated.[28] The latter case involved a member of the War Claims Commission who had been appointed by President Harry S. Truman and who was removed for partisan reasons by President Dwight D. Eisenhower. In disallowing Eisenhower's actions, the Court stated that "it must be inferred that Congress did not want to have hang over the Commission the Damocles' sword of removal by the President for no other reason than that he preferred to have on the Commission men of his own choosing." Thus, the legality of presidential removal of an official in the executive branch depends on the nature of the duties performed by the official in question. Officials performing purely executive functions may be removed by the president at will; those performing quasi-legislative or quasi-judicial functions can be removed only for cause.

Establishing a Counterbureaucracy in the White House

Some presidents have not seen appointment and removal as a strong enough strategy in dealing with the bureaucracy. Mostly, they are concerned that even when an appointee takes office as a loyal supporter of the president's position, over time the appointee will begin to take on an agency point of view. This socialization into the culture of the agency or bureau has several facets. The high-ranking civil servants still provide most of the information and policy alternatives to the appointees. Furthermore, the appointees must work within the bureaucracy on an everyday basis, and they may begin to be more worried about their own turf than the president's agenda, particularly in the area of budget battles. The appointees also work within a small community of persons with an interest in that area: interest groups, members of Congress, policy experts, and other bureaucrats.

To help ensure responsiveness from career civil servants, President Richard Nixon employed a "counterbureaucracy strategy." Because he distrusted the bureaucracy, Nixon established groups within the White House to keep watch on the different bureaus and agencies. The advantage of this system was that Nixon knew that he could trust his counterbureaucracy. These people worked in the White House and thus were not as influenced by the bureaucratic culture. Ironically, this strategy proved ineffective. Even though the top-level agency personnel were Nixon appointees, they were treated as outsiders by the counterbureaucracy in the White House. Clashes cropped up between the two groups, and they had difficulty cooperating to formulate policy or communicate information. As one scholar explained, "the experience of the Nixon years clearly demonstrates that these two approaches (appointment strategy and counterbureaucracy) do not go together. A strong White House staff interested in managing the executive branch is likely to weaken the role of the cabinet officer and vice versa."[29]

White House Policy Organizations

President Nixon also used another strategy to influence the bureaucracy. Rather than rely only on his counterbureaucracy, he appointed a new Office of Telecommunications Policy (OTP) that was responsible for promoting his views in the fast-growing and important area of telecommunications technology. Although the Federal Communications Commission (FCC) existed to handle these types of policies, the OTP served as an "action-forcing mechanism" to shake things up in the policy area.[30] The advantage of this strategy was that Nixon had a like-minded individual running the OTP. Because the FCC is relatively independent from the president, this strategy allowed Nixon greater influence in the area than he would have had otherwise. The disadvantage was that policy development became confused, bogged down in turf wars, and incoherent. Neither group wanted to share information with the other. This strategy is not likely to be effective over the long term. Ultimately, a new president can easily eliminate any temporary White House office, whereas a more permanent, bureaucratic agency would enjoy congressional protection.

Other Presidential Tools for Controlling the Bureaucracy

The president also has a variety of other tools, both formal and informal, that assist him in controlling the bureaucracy. The president's most powerful formal tool is the budget. Because of the budget deficits rampant in the 1980s and 1990s, the budget process has become a dominant force in the policy process. Presidents have increasingly relied on the Office of Management and Budget (OMB) to formulate budget policy. Though Congress may or may not accept the president's budget plan, any bureau or agency wants to avoid budget cuts proposed by the OMB. This threat alone may be enough to convince a stubborn bureau to abide by the president's policy wishes. In addition, any new legislative proposals an agency wants must be cleared by the OMB prior to proposal to Congress. Moreover, since the Reagan administration, the OMB has been used to review the budgetary effect of proposed agency rules. Although the primary justification of OMB review is cost control, this review allows the president, in effect, to veto agency rules or programs he opposes.

Another formal power is the executive order. Though not as forceful as legislation or as permanent, executive orders can require certain changes in the way the bureaucracy implements various policies. President Truman, for example, brought about desegregation of the military by executive order. More recently, President Clinton issued an executive order liberalizing the military's policy restricting service by gay men and lesbians. Clinton's order came only after extensive negotiation with key members of Congress—in particular, Senator Sam Nunn (D-Georgia), who was chairman of the Senate Armed Services Committee. These negotiations resulted in an agreement to adopt a "don't ask, don't tell" policy through executive order. Of course, had it been so inclined, Congress could have passed a bill stating a different policy.

The president has numerous informal means of influence. A president can influence a bureau's legislative proposals by using his prestige to publicly support the agency's request. A president can lend even greater support to an agency's proposal by pushing for it in a State of the Union address to Congress or other public speeches. A popular president may also use personal visits to reward a bureaucracy for its efforts. The chief executive can also use his "bully pulpit" to attack the bureaucracy. This threat alone may sway some bureaucrats to adopt the president's positions.

15-7 CONGRESSIONAL CONTROL OF THE BUREAUCRACY

Although Congress has found it necessary or expedient to delegate much of its legislative authority to the executive branch, it has attempted to maintain control over executive decisions arising out of the exercise of delegated authority. Keep in mind that executive agencies in many cases do not just promulgate but also implement and enforce regulations, the traditional concept of separation of powers notwithstanding. Thus, Congress has attempted, through a variety of mechanisms, to retain control over agency discretion. These mechanisms can be divided into two general categories: formal actions employing the legislative powers of Congress and oversight of the bureaucracy.

15-7a LEGISLATIVE TOOLS

Congress has numerous legislative tools to use in controlling the bureaucracy. Legislation is a cumbersome method because of the difficulty of forming coalitions and the time required to pass a bill, but it is a powerful method. Congress may pass new legislation or attach amendments to other legislation changing certain policies. It may also use its power over the purse to threaten an agency with loss of funding if it does not cooperate. Of course, if Congress is extremely dissatisfied with the performance of a particular agency, it may rewrite the statute that created the agency in the first place. By amending the appropriate statute (or statutes), Congress may enlarge or contract the agency's jurisdiction in addition to the nature and scope of its rule-making authority. Congress could even shift the responsibility for policy from a difficult agency to another, more cooperative one.

The Senate can also influence the bureaucracy through its approval of the president's bureaucratic nominations. Though most nominees are approved by the Senate, the hearings that are held can be used to grill a nominee extensively about a particular policy, organizational structure, or management method. Sometimes, these hearings are concerned more with the battle between the president and Congress than with the qualifications of the nominee, but they also send a message to the bureaucracy about congressional preferences.

One of the more interesting, and certainly the most controversial, of the mechanisms by which Congress has sought to control the bureaucracy is the legislative veto. In existence since the early 1930s, the **legislative veto** is a device whereby Congress, one chamber of Congress, or even one congressional committee can veto agency decisions that are based on delegated authority. A legislative veto provision is written into the original act delegating legislative power to an executive agency. The provision requires that before an agency rule can take effect, it must be approved by Congress. Some provisions require Congress to vote on the measure before it takes effect, but others simply state that the rule will not take effect until Congress has had ninety days in which to consider and possibly reject the regulation. Because legislative vetoes do not always involve bicameral passage and presentment to the president, however, the Supreme Court has said that they are unconstitutional unless they pass both chambers of Congress and are signed by the president.[31] Nevertheless, many legislative veto provisions remain on the books, although no court will enforce them.

15-7b Legislative Oversight

Because the bureaucracy is so large and has so many different programs, Congress has had to develop an institutional process, known as *oversight*, to keep track of the bureaucracy and the implementation of policy. Congress divides the task among the different standing committees according to issue area. For example, the Armed Services Committee performs oversight on the Department of Defense. Oversight involves hearings in which bureaucrats have to defend their actions publicly; investigations by the General Accounting Office and the Congressional Budget Office; annual reports from the bureaucracy to Congress; informal meetings; and responses to demands from the media, constituents, or interest groups. Congress may be concerned about whether policy implementation was consistent with congressional wishes, how the bureaucracy handles individual cases, whether the policy works, how well the bureaucracy serves its customers, or whether money is being wasted.

The more active oversight process has been likened to a police patrol. Under a police patrol system, legislators actively search for problems in the bureaucracy by routinely conducting investigations. In general, most observers do not believe that members of Congress engage in a great deal of police patrol oversight. A less active style in which members of Congress wait for others—such as interest groups, constituents, or the media—to alert them to problems with the bureaucracy has been compared to a fire alarm system. The fire alarm system requires much less work on the part of members, and they can look like heroes when they step in to fix the problem.[32] Congress routinely engages in more fire alarm oversight than police patrol. Some observers argue that the problem with this system is that through constant vigilance, police patrols may prevent some problems within the bureaucracy, but with fire alarm oversight, a problem must become serious enough to cause someone to pull an alarm before Congress gets involved.

15-8 Legal Constraints on the Bureaucracy

Like Congress, the federal courts play an important role in supervising the federal bureaucracy. A fundamental question arising in many cases is whether an agency has acted beyond the scope of its jurisdiction as defined by Congress. In addition to the substantive issues of agency jurisdiction and rule-making authority, administrative actions may raise significant procedural questions. Agency decisions must follow procedural guidelines, so as to prevent arbitrary and capricious action and to safeguard the rights of parties.

Federal agency procedures are generally based on statutory requirements—most notably, the Administrative Procedures Act (APA) of 1946. In addition to the requirements of the APA, the federal courts have applied the Due Process Clause of the Fifth Amendment when statutory procedures have been deemed inadequate to ensure fairness or to protect the rights of individuals. When a federal court reviews an agency decision, it generally attempts to dispose of the case on statutory grounds; for example, by interpreting the APA rather than reach the constitutional due process issue.

15-8a Public Access to Agency Information

Government agencies maintain tremendous stockpiles of information. In a society in which information is power, citizens often want to gain access to these types of data. Although the courts have never held this type of access to be a matter of constitutional right, Congress has created a statutory right of public access under the Freedom of Information Act of 1966 and a right of individual access under the Privacy Act of 1974. Although these acts create exemptions for certain types of secret information, such as sensitive national security material, they nevertheless represent a significant attempt to open up the process of modern governance to the ordinary citizen.

Government in the Sunshine

Much of what bureaucracies do occurs behind the scenes, away from the hot lights of television or the probing questions of interest group spokespersons. In an effort to open the bureaucracy to public scrutiny, Congress passed the Open Meeting Law in 1976. The law requires all meetings and hearings conducted by the bureaucracy to be open to the public, except where matters of diplomacy, national security, military affairs, or trade secrets are being discussed. Moreover, meetings must be announced in advance. The Open Meeting Law parallels the **sunshine laws** that have been adopted by most states. The effort to open up the bureaucracy and "let the sun shine in" is generally applauded by citizens and scholars alike.

Whistle Blowing

One of the most important constraints on bureaucracy is the ability of people within an agency to "blow the whistle" when the agency is acting improperly. Waste, fraud, and mismanagement that cost taxpayers money are the most common problems revealed by **whistle blowers**. Sometimes, the issue goes beyond economics, however, as in the case of workers at nuclear power plants reporting their safety concerns. Of course, whistle blowers run the risk of being punished, formally and informally, by their superiors and colleagues. They can be fired, stripped of their responsibilities, or even deprived of their security clearances. Most difficult perhaps for whistle blowers is being shunned by their coworkers. A 1988 survey found that two-thirds of government workers expressed concern that they would suffer reprisals if they "blew the whistle."[33]

Perhaps the most famous whistle blower in American politics was A. Ernest Fitzgerald, a Pentagon financial analyst who was fired after he told Congress about the extreme cost overruns on the C-5A transport plane being built by Lockheed. Fitzgerald spent a decade in court and incurred more than a million dollars in legal fees before he was able to win back his civil service job. Fitzgerald's case helped place the issue of whistle blowing on the congressional agenda. Recognizing the need to protect whistle blowers, in 1988 Congress passed the Whistleblower Protection Act. President Reagan vetoed this legislation, but his successor, George Bush, signed the bill into law in 1989. The law provides for awards of as much as $250,000 to individuals who blow the whistle on cost overruns by government contractors. The law encourages whistle blowers to come forward by providing financial incentives and legal protection.

15-9 Do Bureaucracies Respond to the Public Interest?

Because the American democracy relies on the bureaucracy to implement the decisions of its elected officials, one major concern with bureaucracy is whether it responds to the public interest. Two of the major theories of the way bureaucracies interact with other political actors in the policy process suggest that a small group of individuals dominates the process at the expense of broader political control by the president and all members of Congress.

15-9a Iron Triangles and Issue Networks

Iron triangles are small policy systems composed of the members of Congress on a particular subcommittee or committee with jurisdiction over an issue, leaders of the interest groups affected by the policy, and the agency responsible for implementing the program. The agency stays in the system because the legislators control the bureaucracy's budget, can stifle unfavorable legislation, and protect the agency from extensive oversight. Because members of Congress choose which committees they prefer and stay on the same committee for years, the system can be maintained over time. Presidents or other outside actors may influence the policy for short periods when the issue is controversial and in the public eye, but the iron triangle can outlast most intrusions and control the administration of the program during normal times.

Somewhat similar to iron triangles but including more people and somewhat less reviled are issue networks, which are composed of a small group of political actors involved in a particular policy area.[34] They include bureaucratic leaders, congressional staff members, interest groups, the media, academics, and researchers in the Washington think tanks who regularly interact on a given issue. Issue networks are not as exclusive as iron triangles, but they do dominate the policy process. A different network exists for each different policy area. In general, expertise and information tend to be the keys to influence within a policy network. Individuals move between the different jobs within the issue network, so the network develops its own language and political culture. Access to others within the network and to key decision makers is crucial to influence, but some individuals may be influential regardless of their official position. In general, power is fragmented, and the bureaucracy may fill the void by trying to develop coalitions of support for certain policies. Most observers would view the issue network as more inclusive than an iron triangle. Furthermore, it may be more likely to serve the public interest than an iron triangle.

15-10 Conclusion: Assessing the Bureaucracy

It is fair to say that the United States has a mammoth bureaucracy that exercises formidable powers. It is not accurate to characterize the bureaucracy as all-powerful or out of control, as some of the more extreme critics of the administrative state are prone to do. To be sure, the federal bureaucracy is large, powerful, and unwieldy, but like all institutions of American government, it is subject to a system of checks and balances. These checks and balances are not spelled out in the Constitution, for the Framers did not anticipate the emergence of a large-scale bureaucracy. Rather, they are a natural outgrowth of the constitutional and statutory powers of Congress, the president, and the courts.

No one is particularly happy with the federal bureaucracy now. Liberals often see the bureaucracy as the protector of corporate interests. Conservatives tend to view the bureaucracy as "big government" meddling where it does not belong. Presidents are often frustrated that the executive branch seems to have a mind of its own. Members of Congress are sometimes disappointed in the way in which legislation is (or is not) implemented. The average person, irrespective of ideology, is likely to believe that the bureaucracy is wasteful, inefficient, and too powerful. This view of the bureaucracy is firmly established in the political culture. Even our popular culture is filled with negative portrayals of bureaucrats and bureaucracies.

Some expert commentators have also been very critical of the federal bureaucracy, although their critiques seldom resemble popular perspectives on the subject.

Many have called for dramatic reorganizations of the executive branch with an emphasis on "flattening the pyramid"—reducing the layers of hierarchy.[35] But many political scientists have defended the federal bureaucracy, charging that popular perceptions of inefficiency and incompetence are based more on myth than reality.[36]

From time to time, government leaders attempt to reform the bureaucracy, as in the case of the National Performance Review under the Clinton administration. These attempts at reform seldom accomplish all that they set out to do. Despite occasional reform efforts, the public continues to perceive the bureaucracy as the epitome of waste, fraud, and abuse. What citizens should keep in mind in evaluating their bureaucracy is what our society would look like without the rules, programs, and services the bureaucracy represents. To the person struggling to maintain a small business, the prospect of less government regulation and red tape could be appealing. But to an industrial worker risking injury on the job, the prospect of curtailing OSHA plant inspections might be more than a little worrisome. Much of what the bureaucracy does has come in response to public demands for the government to address some serious problem. Most of these problems do not go away, but instead require continuing attention. As the aftermath of September 11 demonstrates, particularly in reference to the FBI and the CIA, the nature of bureaucracy itself has become a problem, with its inevitable internal politics and interagency jealousies. This problem often cries out for attention from the public and its elected officials.

Questions for Thought and Discussion

1. Why do Americans generally dislike bureaucracy?

2. Is it possible to imagine a democracy in a mass society without bureaucracy?

3. Can the federal bureaucracy be made more efficient? More accountable? More representative of the American people? To what extent are these goals consistent with one another?

4. Why has Congress found it necessary or desirable to delegate so much regulatory authority to the federal bureaucracy?

5. Do the federal courts do an effective job of ensuring that the bureaucracy respects individual rights and liberties?

Endnotes

1 Although it does not appear in his writings, the following quotation has been attributed to Thomas Jefferson: "That government is best which governs the least, because its people discipline themselves." Later, in his essay *Civil Disobedience* (1846), Henry David Thoreau wrote, "I heartily accept the motto—'That government is best which governs least'; and I should like to see it acted up to more rapidly and systematically."

2 Alexis de Tocqueville, *Democracy in America* (New York: Vintage Books, 1945), vol. 1, p. 59.

3 Office of Management and Budget, online at www.whitehouse.gov/omb.

4 See, for example, Gary Lawson, "The Rise and Rise of the Administrative State," *Harvard Law Review*, vol. 107, 1994, p. 1231.

5 Richard J. Stillman, *Creating the American State: The Moral Reformers and the Modern Administrative World They Made* (Tuscaloosa, AL: University of Alabama Press, 1998), p. 3.

6 Ibid.

7 See, for example, Kenneth J. Meier, *Politics and the Bureaucracy: Policymaking in the Fourth Branch of Government*, 4th ed. (Fort Worth, TX: Harcourt College Publishers, 2000).

8 Herbert Kaufman, *Are Government Organizations Immortal?* (Washington, D.C.: Brookings Institution, 1976), p. 76.

9 The term *red tape* derives from the strips of red tape once used by the British government to bind bundles of official papers. The term now connotes needlessly complicated and time-consuming bureaucratic rules and procedures.

10 John M. Scheb and John M. Scheb, II, *Law and the Administrative Process* (Belmont, CA: Thomson/Wadsworth, 2005), p. 11.

11 Susan Mosychuk of Citizens Against Government Waste, quoted in Christine Hall, "House GOP Targets Waste, Fraud in Government Programs," *CNS News*, May 21, 2003, http://www.cnsnews.com.

12 Today, the census is conducted by the Bureau of the Census, an agency within the Department of Commerce.

13 See, for example, *Schechter Poultry Corp. v. United States*, 295 U.S. 495 (1935); *United States v. Butler*, 297 U.S. 1 (1936); *Carter v. Carter Coal Co.*, 298 U.S. 238 (1936).

14 See Joe Klein, "The Vice-President's Ashtray," *Newsweek*, August 16, 1993, p. 27.

15 J. B. Wogan, "Romney Says Federal Regulations Quadrupled under Obama," Politifact.com, http://www.politifact.com/truth-o-meter/statements/2012/oct/18/mitt-romney/federal-regulations-quadrupled-under-obama/

16 William A. Niskanen, Jr., *Bureaucracy and Representation* (Chicago: Aldine-Atherton, 1971), p. 38.

17 Hugh Heclo, *A Government of Strangers* (Washington, D.C.: Brookings Institution, 1974), pp. 117–18.

18 Barry Z. Posner, and Warren H. Schmidt, "An Updated Look at the Values and Expectations of Federal Government Executives," *Public Administration Review*, vol. 54, January/February 1994, pp. 20–24.

19 *Wiener v. United States*, 357 U.S. 349 (1958).

20 "CBS Stations Fined $550,000 for 'Wardrobe Malfunction,'" Associated Press, September 22, 2004.

21 Verena Dobnik, "Stern Blasts FCC at Satellite Promotion," Associated Press, November 18, 2004.

22 *Schechter Poultry Corp. v. United States*, 295 U.S. 495 (1935).

23 See *Bob Jones University v. United States*, 461 U.S. 574 (1983).

24 *FDA v. Brown and Williamson Corp.*, 529 U.S. 120 (2000).

25 See, for example, *United States v. Harris*, 216 F.2d 690 (5th Cir. 1954).

26 Francis E. Rourke, "The Presidency and the Bureaucracy: Strategic Alternatives." In *The Presidency and the Political System*, ed. Michael Nelson (Washington, D.C.: CQ Press, 1984).

27 *Humphrey's Executor v. United States*, 295 U.S. 602 (1935).

28 *Wiener v. United States*, 357 U.S. 349 (1958).

29 Richard P. Nathan, *The Administrative Presidency* (New York: John Wiley & Sons, 1983).

30 Francis E. Rourke, "The Presidency and the Bureaucracy: Strategic Alternatives," p. 354.

31 *Immigration and Naturalization Service v. Chadha*, 462 U.S. 919 (1986).

32 Mathew McCubbins and Thomas Schwartz, "Congressional Oversight Overlooked: Police Patrols Versus Fire Alarm," *American Journal of Political Science*, vol. 28, 1984, pp. 165–79.

33 Survey reported in Bob Cohn, "New Help for Whistle Blowers," *Newsweek*, June 27, 1988, p. 43.

34 See Hugh Heclo, "Issue Networks and the Executive Establishment." In *The New American Political System*, ed. Anthony King (Washington, D.C.: American Enterprise Institute, 1978).

35 See, for example, Paul C. Light, *Thickening Government: Federal Hierarchy and the Diffusion of Accountability* (Washington, D.C.: Brookings Institution Press, 1995).

36 See, for example, Kenneth J. Meier, *Politics and The Bureaucracy: Policymaking in the Fourth Branch of Government*, 4th ed.; Charles Goodsell, *The Case for Bureaucracy: A Public Administration Polemic*, 4th ed. (Washington, D.C.: CQ Press, 2003).

THE CONSTITUTION OF THE UNITED STATES

We the People of the United States, in Order to form a more perfect Union, establish Justice, insure domestic Tranquility, provide for the common defence, promote the general Welfare, and secure the Blessings of Liberty to ourselves and our Posterity, do ordain and establish this Constitution for the United States of America

ARTICLE. I.

SECTION. 1

All legislative Powers herein granted shall be vested in a Congress of the United States, which shall consist of a Senate and House of Representatives.

SECTION. 2

The House of Representatives shall be composed of Members chosen every second Year by the People of the several States, and the Electors in each State shall have the Qualifications requisite for Electors of the most numerous Branch of the State Legislature.

No Person shall be a Representative who shall not have attained to the Age of twenty five Years, and been seven Years a Citizen of the United States, and who shall not, when elected, be an Inhabitant of that State in which he shall be chosen.

[Representatives and direct Taxes shall be apportioned among the several States which may be included within this Union, according to their respective Numbers, which shall be determined by adding to the whole Number of free Persons, including those bound to Service for a Term of Years, and excluding Indians not taxed, three fifths of all other Persons.]* The actual Enumeration shall be made within three Years after the first Meeting of the Congress of the United States, and within every subsequent Term of ten Years, in such Manner as they shall by Law direct. The Number of Representatives shall not exceed one for every thirty Thousand, but each State shall have at Least one Representative; and until such enumeration shall be made, the State of New Hampshire shall be entitled to chuse three, Massachusetts eight, Rhode-Island and Providence Plantations one, Connecticut five, New-York six, New Jersey four,

Pennsylvania eight, Delaware one, Maryland six, Virginia ten, North Carolina five, South Carolina five, and Georgia three.

When vacancies happen in the Representation from any State, the Executive Authority thereof shall issue Writs of Election to fill such Vacancies.

The House of Representatives shall chuse their Speaker and other Officers; and shall have the sole Power of Impeachment.

Section. 3

The Senate of the United States shall be composed of two Senators from each State, [chosen by the Legislature thereof,]* for six Years; and each Senator shall have one Vote.

Immediately after they shall be assembled in Consequence of the first Election, they shall be divided as equally as may be into three Classes. The Seats of the Senators of the first Class shall be vacated at the Expiration of the second Year, of the second Class at the Expiration of the fourth Year, and of the third Class at the Expiration of the sixth Year, so that one third may be chosen every second Year; [and if Vacancies happen by Resignation, or otherwise, during the Recess of the Legislature of any State, the Executive thereof may make temporary Appointments until the next Meeting of the Legislature, which shall then fill such Vacancies.]*

No Person shall be a Senator who shall not have attained to the Age of thirty Years, and been nine Years a Citizen of the United States, and who shall not, when elected, be an Inhabitant of that State for which he shall be chosen

The Vice President of the United States shall be President of the Senate, but shall have no Vote, unless they be equally divided.

The Senate shall chuse their other Officers, and also a President pro tempore, in the Absence of the Vice President, or when he shall exercise the Office of President of the United States

The Senate shall have the sole Power to try all Impeachments. When sitting for that Purpose, they shall be on Oath or Affirmation. When the President of the United States is tried, the Chief Justice shall preside: And no Person shall be convicted without the Concurrence of two thirds of the Members present.

Judgment in Cases of Impeachment shall not extend further than to removal from Office, and disqualification to hold and enjoy any Office of honor, Trust or Profit under the United States: but the Party convicted shall nevertheless be liable and subject to Indictment, Trial, Judgment and Punishment, according to Law.

Section. 4

The Times, Places and Manner of holding Elections for Senators and Representatives, shall be prescribed in each State by the Legislature thereof; but the Congress may at any time by Law make or alter such Regulations, except as to the Places of chusing Senators.

The Congress shall assemble at least once in every Year, and such Meeting shall be [on the first Monday in December,]* unless they shall by Law appoint a different Day.

Section. 5

Each House shall be the Judge of the Elections, Returns and Qualifications of its own Members, and a Majority of each shall constitute a Quorum to do Business; but a smaller Number may adjourn from day to day, and may be authorized to compel the Attendance of absent Members, in such Manner, and under such Penalties as each House may provide.

Each House may determine the Rules of its Proceedings, punish its Members for disorderly Behaviour, and, with the Concurrence of two thirds, expel a Member.

Each House shall keep a Journal of its Proceedings, and from time to time publish the same, excepting such Parts as may in their Judgment require Secrecy; and the Yeas and Nays of the Members of either House on any question shall, at the Desire of one fifth of those Present, be entered on the Journal.

Neither House, during the Session of Congress, shall, without the Consent of the other, adjourn for more than three days, nor to any other Place than that in which the two Houses shall be sitting.

Section. 6

The Senators and Representatives shall receive a Compensation for their Services, to be ascertained by Law, and paid out of the Treasury of the United States. They shall in all Cases, except Treason, Felony and Breach of the Peace, be privileged from Arrest during their Attendance at the Session of their respective Houses, and in going to and returning from the same; and for any Speech or Debate in either House, they shall not be questioned in any other Place.

No Senator or Representative shall, during the Time for which he was elected, be appointed to any civil Office under the Authority of the United States, which shall have been created, or the Emoluments whereof shall have been encreased during such time; and no Person holding any Office under the United States, shall be a Member of either House during his Continuance in Office.

Section. 7

All Bills for raising Revenue shall originate in the House of Representatives; but the Senate may propose or concur with Amendments as on other Bills

Every Bill which shall have passed the House of Representatives and the Senate, shall, before it become a Law, be presented to the President of the United States; If he approve he shall sign it, but if not he shall return it, with his Objections to that House in which it shall have originated, who shall enter the Objections at large on their Journal, and proceed to reconsider it. If after such Reconsideration two thirds of that House shall agree to pass the Bill, it shall be sent, together with the Objections, to the other House, by which it shall likewise be reconsidered, and if approved by two thirds of that House, it shall become a Law. But in all such Cases the Votes of both Houses shall be determined by Yeas and Nays, and the Names of the Persons voting for and against the Bill shall be entered on the Journal of each House respectively, If any Bill shall not be returned by the President within ten Days (Sundays excepted) after it shall have been presented to him, the Same shall be a Law, in like Manner as if he had signed it, unless the Congress by their Adjournament prevent its Return, in which Case it shall not be a Law

Every Order, Resolution, or Vote to which the Concurrence of the Senate and House of Representatives may be necessary (except on a question of Adjournment) shall be presented to the President of the United States; and before the Same shall take Effect, shall be approved by him, or being disapproved by him, shall be repassed by two thirds of the Senate and House of Representatives, according to the Rules and Limitations prescribed in the Case of a Bill.

Section. 8

The Congress shall have Power To lay and collect Taxes, Duties, Imposts and Excises, to pay the Debts and provide for the common Defence and general Welfare of the United States; but all Duties, Imposts and Excises shall be uniform throughout the United States;

To borrow Money on the credit of the United States;

To regulate Commerce with foreign Nations, and among the several States, and with the Indian Tribes;

To establish an uniform Rule of Naturalization, and uniform Laws on the subject of Bankruptcies throughout the United States;

To coin Money, regulate the Value thereof, and of foreign Coin, and fix the Standard of Weights and Measures;

To provide for the Punishment of counterfeiting the Securities and current Coin of the United States;

To establish Post Offices and post Roads;

To promote the Progress of Science and useful Arts, by securing for limited Times to Authors and Inventors the exclusive Right to their respective Writings and Discoveries;

To constitute Tribunals inferior to the supreme Court;

To define and punish Piracies and Felonies committed on the high Seas, and Offenses against the Law of Nations;

To declare War, grant Letters of Marque and Reprisal, and make Rules concerning Captures on Land and Water;

To raise and support Armies, but no Appropriation of Money to that Use shall be for a longer Term than two Years;

To provide and maintain a Navy;

To make Rules for the Government and Regulation of the land and naval Forces;

To provide for calling forth the Militia to execute the Laws of the Union, suppress Insurrections and repel Invasions;

To provide for organizing, arming, and disciplining, the Militia, and for governing such Part of them as may be employed in the Service of the United States, reserving to the States respectively, the Appointment of the Officers, and the Authority of training the Militia according to the discipline prescribed by Congress;

To exercise exclusive Legislation in all Cases whatsoever, over such District (not exceeding ten Miles square) as may, by Cession of particular States, and the Acceptance of Congress, become the Seat of the Government of the United States, and to exercise like Authority over all Places purchased by the Consent of the Legislature of the State in which the Same shall be, for the Erection of Forts, Magazines, Arsenals, dock-Yards and other needful Buildings;

-And

To make all Laws which shall be necessary and proper for carrying into Execution the foregoing Powers, and all other Powers vested by this Constitution in the Government of the United States, or in any Department or Officer thereof.

Section. 9

The Migration or Importation of such Persons as any of the States now existing shall think proper to admit, shall not be prohibited by the Congress prior to the Year one thousand eight hundred and eight, but a Tax or duty may be imposed on such Importation, not exceeding ten dollars for each Person

The Privilege of the Writ of Habeas Corpus shall not be suspended, unless when in Cases of Rebellion or Invasion the public Safety may require it.

No Bill of Attainder or ex post facto Law shall be passed.

[No Capitation, or other direct, Tax shall be laid, unless in Proportion to the Census or Enumeration herein before directed to be taken.]*

No Tax or Duty shall be laid on Articles exported from any State

No Preference shall be given by any Regulation of Commerce or Revenue to the Ports of one State over those of another: nor shall Vessels bound to, or from, one State, be obliged to enter, clear, or pay Duties in another.

No Money shall be drawn from the Treasury, but in Consequence of Appropriations made by Law; and a regular Statement and Account of the Receipts and Expenditures of all public Money shall be published from time to time.

No Title of Nobility shall be granted by the United States: And no Person holding any Office of Profit or Trust under them, shall, without the Consent of the Congress, accept of any present, Emolument, Office, or Title, of any kind whatever, from any King, Prince, or foreign State.

SECTION. 10

No State shall enter into any Treaty, Alliance, or Confederation; grant Letters of Marque and Reprisal; coin Money; emit Bills of Credit; make any Thing but gold and silver Coin a Tender in Payment of Debts; pass any Bill of Attainder, ex post facto Law, or Law impairing the Obligation of Contracts, or grant any Title of Nobility.

No State shall, without the Consent of the Congress, lay any Imposts or Duties on Imports or Exports, except what may be absolutely necessary for executing it's inspection Laws: and the net Produce of all Duties and Imposts, laid by any State on Imports or Exports, shall be for the Use of the Treasury of the United States; and all such Laws shall be subject to the Revision and Controul of the Congress.

No State shall, without the Consent of Congress, lay any Duty of Tonnage, keep Troops, or Ships of War in time of Peace, enter into any Agreement or Compact with another State, or with a foreign Power, or engage in War, unless actually invaded, or in such imminent Danger as will not admit of delay.

ARTICLE. II.

SECTION. 1

The executive Power shall be vested in a President of the United States of America. He shall hold his Office during the Term of four Years, and, together with the Vice President, chosen for the same Term, be elected, as follows:

Each State shall appoint, in such Manner as the Legislature thereof may direct, a Number of Electors, equal to the whole Number of Senators and Representatives to which the State may be entitled in the Congress: but no Senator or Representative, or Person holding an Office of Trust or Profit under the United States, shall be appointed an Elector.

[The Electors shall meet in their respective States, and vote by Ballot for two Persons, of whom one at least shall not be an Inhabitant of the same State with themselves. And they shall make a List of all the Persons voted for, and of the Number of Votes for each; which List they shall sign and certify, and transmit sealed to the Seat of the Government of the United States, directed to the President of the Senate. The President of the Senate shall, in the Presence of the Senate and House of Representatives, open all the Certificates, and the Votes shall then be counted. The Person having the greatest Number of Votes shall be the President, if such Number be a Majority of the whole Number of Electors appointed; and if there be more than one who have such Majority, and have an equal Number of Votes, then the House of Representatives shall immediately chuse by Ballot one of them for President; and if no Person have a Majority, then from the five highest on the List the said House shall in like Manner chuse the President.

But in chusing the President, the Votes shall be taken by States, the Representation from each State having one Vote; A quorum for this Purpose shall consist of a Member or Members from two thirds of the States, and a Majority of all the States shall be necessary to a Choice. In every Case, after the Choice of the President, the Person having the greatest Number of Votes of the Electors shall be the Vice President. But if there should remain two or more who have equal Votes, the Senate shall chuse from them by Ballot the Vice President.]*

The Congress may determine the Time of chusing the Electors, and the Day on which they shall give their Votes; which Day shall be the same throughout the United States.

No Person except a natural born Citizen, or a Citizen of the United States, at the time of the Adoption of this Constitution, shall be eligible to the Office of President; neither shall any person be eligible to that Office who shall not have attained to the Age of thirty five Years, and been fourteen Years a Resident within the United States

In Case of the Removal of the President from Office, or of his Death, Resignation, or Inability to discharge the Powers and Duties of the said Office, the Same shall devolve on the Vice President, and the Congress may by Law provide for the Case of Removal, Death, Resignation or Inability, both of the President and Vice President, declaring what Officer shall then act as President, and such Officer shall act accordingly, until the Disability be removed, or a President shall be elected.]*

The President shall, at stated Times, receive for his Services, a Compensation, which shall neither be increased nor diminished during the Period for which he shall have been elected, and he shall not receive within that Period any other Emolument from the United States, or any of them.

Before he enter on the Execution of his Office, he shall take the following Oath or Affirmation:"I do solemnly swear (or affirm) that I will faithfully execute the Office of President of the United States, and will to the best of my Ability, preserve, protect and defend the Constitution of the United States."

SECTION. 2

The President shall be Commander in Chief of the Army and Navy of the United States, and of the Militia of the several States, when called into the actual Service of the United States; he may require the Opinion, in writing, of the principal Officer in each of the executive Departments, upon any Subject relating to the Duties of their respective Offices, and he shall have Power to grant Reprieves and Pardons for Offenses against the United States, except in Cases of Impeachment.

He shall have Power, by and with the Advice and Consent of the Senate, to make Treaties, provided two thirds of the Senators present concur; and he shall nominate, and by and with the Advice and Consent of the Senate, shall appoint Ambassadors, other public Ministers and Consuls, Judges of the supreme Court, and all other Officers of the United States, whose Appointments are not herein otherwise provided for, and which shall be established by Law: but the Congress may by Law vest the Appointment of such inferior Officers, as they think proper, in the President alone, in the Courts of Law, or in the Heads of Departments.

The President shall have Power to fill up all Vacancies that may happen during the Recess of the Senate, by granting Commissions which shall expire at the End of their next Session

SECTION. 3

He shall from time to time give to the Congress Information of the State of the Union, and recommend to their Consideration such Measures as he shall judge necessary and expedient; he may, on extraordinary Occasions, convene both Houses, or either of them, and in Case of Disagreement between them, with Respect to the Time of Adjournment, he may adjourn them to such Time as he shall think proper; he shall receive Ambassadors and other public Ministers; he shall take Care that the Laws be faithfully executed, and shall Commission all the Officers of the United States

SECTION. 4

The President, Vice President and all civil Officers of the United States, shall be removed from Office on Impeachment for, and Conviction of, Treason, Bribery, or other high Crimes and Misdemeanors.

ARTICLE. III.

SECTION. 1

The judicial Power of the United States, shall be vested in one supreme Court, and in such inferior Courts as the Congress may from time to time ordain and establish. The Judges, both of the supreme and inferior Courts, shall hold their Offices during good Behaviour, and shall at stated Times, receive for their Services, a Compensation, which shall not be diminished during their Continuance in Office.

SECTION. 2

The judicial Power shall extend to all Cases, in Law and Equity, arising under this Constitution, the Laws of the United States, and Treaties made, or which shall be made, under their Authority; to all Cases affecting Ambassadors, other public Ministers and Consuls; to all Cases of admiralty and maritime Jurisdiction; to Controversies to which the United States shall be a Party; to Controversies between two or more States; - [between a State and Citizens of another State;-]* between Citizens of different States, - between Citizens of the same State claiming Lands under Grants of different States, [and between a State, or the Citizens thereof;- and foreign States, Citizens or Subjects.]*

In all Cases affecting Ambassadors, other public Ministers and Consuls, and those in which a State shall be Party, the supreme Court shall have original Jurisdiction. In all the other Cases before mentioned, the supreme Court shall have appellate Jurisdiction, both as to Law and Fact, with such Exceptions, and under such Regulations as the Congress shall make.

The Trial of all Crimes, except in Cases of Impeachment; shall be by Jury; and such Trial shall be held in the State where the said Crimes shall have been committed; but when not committed within any State, the Trial shall be at such Place or Places as the Congress may by Law have directed.

SECTION. 3

Treason against the United States, shall consist only in levying War against them, or in adhering to their Enemies, giving them Aid and Comfort. No Person shall be convicted of Treason unless on the Testimony of two Witnesses to the same overt Act, or on Confession in open Court.

The Congress shall have Power to declare the Punishment of Treason, but no Attainder of Treason shall work Corruption of Blood, or Forfeiture except during the Life of the Person attainted

ARTICLE. IV.

SECTION. 1

Full Faith and Credit shall be given in each State to the public Acts, Records, and judicial Proceedings of every other State. And the Congress may by general Laws prescribe the Manner in which such Acts, Records and Proceedings shall be proved, and the Effect thereof.

SECTION. 2

The Citizens of each State shall be entitled to all Privileges and Immunities of Citizens in the several States

A Person charged in any State with Treason, Felony, or other Crime, who shall flee from Justice, and be found in another State, shall on Demand of the executive Authority of the State from which he fled, be delivered up, to be removed to the State having Jurisdiction of the Crime.

No Person held to Service or Labour in one State, under the Laws thereof, escaping into another, shall, in Consequence of any Law or Regulation therein, be discharged from such Service or Labour, but shall be delivered up on Claim of the Party to whom such Service or Labour may be due.]*

Section. 3

New States may be admitted by the Congress into this Union; but no new State shall be formed or erected within the Jurisdiction of any other State; nor any State be formed by the Junction of two or more States, or Parts of States, without the Consent of the Legislatures of the States concerned as well as of the Congress.

The Congress shall have Power to dispose of and make all needful Rules and Regulations respecting the Territory or other Property belonging to the United States; and nothing in this Constitution shall be so construed as to Prejudice any Claims of the United States, or of any particular State.

Section. 4

The United States shall guarantee to every State in this Union a Republican Form of Government, and shall protect each of them against Invasion; and on Application of the Legislature, or of the Executive (when the Legislature cannot be convened) against domestic Violence.

Article. V.

The Congress, whenever two thirds of both Houses shall deem it necessary, shall propose Amendments to this Constitution, or, on the Application of the Legislatures of two thirds of the several States, shall call a Convention for proposing Amendments, which in either Case, shall be valid to all Intents and Purposes, as Part of this Constitution, when ratified by the Legislatures of three-fourths of the several States, or by Conventions in three fourths thereof, as the one or the other Mode of Ratification may be proposed by the Congress; Provided that no Amendment which may be made prior to the Year One thousand eight hundred and eight shall in any Manner affect the first and fourth Clauses in the Ninth Section of the first Article; and that no State, without its Consent, shall be deprived of its equal Suffrage in the Senate

Article. VI.

All Debts contracted and Engagements entered into, before the Adoption of this Constitution, shall be as valid against the United States under this Constitution, as under the Confederation

This Constitution, and the Laws of the United States which shall be made in Pursuance thereof; and all Treaties made, or which shall be made, under the Authority of the United States, shall be the supreme Law of the Land; and the Judges in every State shall be bound thereby, any Thing in the Constitution or Laws of any State to the Contrary notwithstanding.

The Senators and Representatives before mentioned, and the Members of the several State Legislatures, and all executive and judicial Officers, both of the United States and of the several States, shall be bound by Oath or Affirmation, to support this Constitution; but no religious Test shall ever be required as a Qualification to any Office or public Trust under the United States

ARTICLE. VII.

The Ratification of the Conventions of nine States, shall be sufficient for the Establishment of this Constitution between the States so ratifying the Same.

Done in Convention by the Unanimous Consent of the States present the Seventeenth Day of September in the Year of our Lord one thousand seven hundred and Eighty seven and of the Independence of the United States of America the Twelfth In Witness whereof We have hereunto subscribed our Names,

Go. Washington--Presidt: and deputy from Virginia

NEW HAMPSHIRE

John Langdon Nicholas Gilman

MASSACHUSETTS

Nathaniel Gorham Rufus King

CONNECTICUT

Wm. Saml. Johnson Roger Sherman

NEW YORK

Alexander Hamilton

NEW JERSEY

Wil: Livingston David Brearley Wm. Paterson Jona: Dayton

PENNSYLVANIA

B Franklin Thomas Mifflin Robt Morris Geo. Clymer Thos. FitzSimons Jared Ingersoll James Wilson Gouv Morris

DELAWARE

Geo: Read Gunning Bedford jun John Dickinson Richard Bassett Jaco: Broom

MARYLAND

James McHenry
Dan of St. Thos. Jenifer Danl Carroll

VIRGINIA

John Blair- James Madison Jr.

North Carolina

Wm. Blount
Richd. Dobbs Spaight Hu Williamson

South Carolina

J. Rutledge
Charles Cotesworth Pinckney Charles Pinckney
Pierce Butler

Georgia

William Few Abr Baldwin

Attest William Jackson Secretary

In Convention Monday September 17th, 1787. Present

The States of New Hampshire, Massachusetts, Connecticut, Mr. Hamilton from New York, New Jersey, Pennsylvania, Delaware, Maryland, Virginia, North Carolina, South Carolina and Georgia.

Resolved,

That the preceeding Constitution be laid before the United States in Congress assembled, and that it is the Opinion of this Convention, that it should afterwards be submitted to a Convention of Delegates, chosen in each State by the People thereof, under the Recommendation of its Legislature, for their Assent and Ratification; and that each Convention assenting to, and ratifying the Same, should give Notice thereof to the United States in Congress assembled. Resolved, That it is the Opinion of this Convention, that as soon as the Conventions of nine States shall have ratified this Constitution, the United States in Congress assembled should fix a Day on which Electors should be appointed by the States which shall have ratified the same, and a Day on which the Electors should assemble to vote for the President, and the Time and Place for commencing Proceedings under this Constitution

That after such Publication the Electors should be appointed, and the Senators and Representatives elected: That the Electors should meet on the Day fixed for the Election of the President, and should transmit their Votes certified, signed, sealed and directed, as the Constitution requires, to the Secretary of the United States in Congress assembled, that the Senators and Representatives should convene at the Time and Place assigned; that the Senators should appoint a President of the Senate, for the sole Purpose of receiving, opening and counting the Votes for President; and, that after he shall be chosen, the Congress, together with the President, should, without Delay, proceed to execute this Constitution

By the unanimous Order of the Convention
Go. Washington-Presidt:
W. JACKSON Secretary.

* Language in brackets has been changed by amendment.

1. The Amendments to the Constitution of the United States as
   Ratified by the States
   Preamble to the Bill of Rights
   Congress of the United States
   begun and held at the City of New-York, on Wednesday the fourth of March,

THE Conventions of a number of the States, having at the time of their adopting the Constitution, expressed a desire, in order to prevent misconstruction or abuse of its powers, that further declaratory and restrictive clauses should be added: And as extending the ground of public confidence in the Government, will best ensure the beneficent ends of its institution

RESOLVED by the Senate and House of Representatives of the United States of America, in Congress assembled, two thirds of both Houses concurring, that the following Articles be proposed to the Legislatures of the several States, as amendments to the Constitution of the United States, all, or any of which Articles, when ratified by three fourths of the said Legislatures, to be valid to all intents and purposes, as part of the said Constitution; viz.

ARTICLES in addition to, and Amendment of the Constitution of the United States of America, proposed by Congress, and ratified by the Legislatures of the several States, pursuant to the fifth Article of the original Constitution.

(*Note*: The first 10 amendments to the Constitution were ratified December 15, 1791, and form what is known as the "Bill of Rights.")

Amendment I.

Congress shall make no law respecting an establishment of religion, or prohibiting the free exercise thereof; or abridging the freedom of speech, or of the press, or the right of the people peaceably to assemble, and to petition the Government for a redress of grievances.

Amendment II.

A well regulated Militia, being necessary to the security of a free State, the right of the people to keep and bear Arms, shall not be infringed.

Amendment III.

No Soldier shall, in time of peace be quartered in any house, without the consent of the Owner, nor in time of war, but in a manner to be prescribed by law.

Amendment IV.

The right of the people to be secure in their persons, houses, papers, and effects, against unreasonable searches and seizures, shall not be violated, and no Warrants shall issue, but upon probable cause, supported by Oath or affirmation, and particularly describing the place to be searched, and the persons or things to be seized.

Amendment V.

No person shall be held to answer for a capital, or otherwise infamous crime, unless on a presentment or indictment of a Grand Jury, except in cases arising in the land or naval forces, or in the Militia, when in actual service in time of War or public danger; nor shall any person be subject for the same offence to be twice put in jeopardy of life or limb; nor shall be compelled in any criminal case to be a witness against himself, nor be deprived of life, liberty, or property, without due process of law; nor shall private property be taken for public use, without just compensation.

Amendment VI.

In all criminal prosecutions, the accused shall enjoy the right to a speedy and public trial, by an impartial jury of the State and district wherein the crime shall have been committed, which district shall have been previously ascertained by law, and to be informed of the nature and cause of the accusation; to be confronted with the witnesses against him; to have compulsory process for obtaining witnesses in his favor, and to have the Assistance of Counsel for his defence.

Amendment VII.

In suits at common law, where the value in controversy shall exceed twenty dollars, the right of trial by jury shall be preserved, and no fact tried by a jury shall be otherwise re-examined in any Court of the United States, than according to the rules of the common law.

Amendment VIII.

Excessive bail shall not be required, nor excessive fines imposed, nor cruel and unusual punishments inflicted.

Amendment IX.

The enumeration in the Constitution, of certain rights, shall not be construed to deny or disparage others retained by the people.

Amendment X.

The powers not delegated to the United States by the Constitution, nor prohibited by it to the States, are reserved to the States respectively, or to the people.

AMENDMENTS 11-27

Amendment XI.

Passed by Congress March 4, 1794. Ratified February 7, 1795.

(*Note:* A portion of Article III, Section 2 of the Constitution was modified by the 11th Amendment.)

The Judicial power of the United States shall not be construed to extend to any suit in law or equity, commenced or prosecuted against one of the United States by Citizens of another State, or by Citizens or Subjects of any Foreign State.

Amendment XII.

Passed by Congress December 9, 1803. Ratified June 15, 1804.

(*Note:* A portion of Article II, Section 1 of the Constitution was changed by the 12th Amendment.)

The Electors shall meet in their respective states, and vote by ballot for President and Vice-President, one of whom, at least, shall not be an inhabitant of the same state with themselves; they shall name in their ballots the person voted for as President, and in distinct ballots the person voted for as Vice-President, and they shall make distinct lists of all persons voted for as President, and of all persons voted for as Vice-President, and of the number of votes for each, which lists they shall sign and certify, and transmit sealed to the seat of the government of the United States, directed to the President of the Senate;-the President of the Senate shall, in the presence of the Senate and House of Representatives, open all the certificates and the votes shall then be counted;-The person having the greatest number of votes for President, shall be the President, if such number be a majority of the whole number of Electors appointed; and if no person have such majority, then from the persons having the highest numbers not exceeding three on the list of those voted for as President, the House of Representatives shall choose immediately, by ballot, the President. But in choosing the President, the votes shall be taken by states, the representation from each state having one vote; a quorum for this purpose shall consist of a member or members from two-thirds of the states, and a majority of all the states shall be necessary to a choice. [And if the House of Representatives shall not choose a President whenever the right of choice shall devolve upon them, before the fourth day of March next following, then the Vice-President shall act as President, as in case of the death or other constitutional disability of the President.-]* The person having the greatest number of votes as Vice-President, shall be the Vice-President, if such number be a majority of the whole number of Electors appointed, and if no person have a majority, then from the two highest numbers on the list, the Senate shall choose the Vice-President; a quorum for the purpose shall consist of two-thirds of the whole number of Senators, and a majority of the whole number shall be necessary to a choice. But no person constitutionally ineligible to the office of President shall be eligible to that of Vice-President of the United States.

*Superseded by Section 3 of the 20th Amendment.

Amendment XIII.

Passed by Congress January 31, 1865. Ratified December 6, 1865.

(*Note*: A portion of Article IV, Section 2 of the Constitution was changed by the 13th Amendment.)

Section 1

Neither slavery nor involuntary servitude, except as a punishment for crime whereof the party shall have been duly convicted, shall exist within the United States, or any place subject to their jurisdiction.

Section 2

Congress shall have power to enforce this article by appropriate legislation.

Amendment XIV.

Passed by Congress June 13, 1866. Ratified July 9, 1868.

(*Note*: Article I, Section 2 of the Constitution was modified by Section 2 of the 14th Amendment.)

Section 1

All persons born or naturalized in the United States and subject to the jurisdiction thereof, are citizens of the United States and of the State wherein they reside. No State shall make or enforce any law which shall abridge the privileges or immunities of citizens of the United States; nor shall any State deprive any person of life, liberty, or property, without due process of law; nor deny to any person within its jurisdiction the equal protection of the laws.

Section 2

Representatives shall be apportioned among the several States according to their respective numbers, counting the whole number of persons in each State, excluding Indians not taxed. But when the right to vote at any election for the choice of electors for President and Vice President of the United States, Representatives in Congress, the Executive and Judicial officers of a State, or the members of the Legislature thereof, is denied to any of the male inhabit ants of such State, [being twenty-one years of age,]* and citizens of the United States, or in any way abridged, except for participation in rebellion, or other crime, the basis of representation therein shall be reduced in the proportion which the number of such male citizens shall bear to the whole number of male citizens twenty-one years of age in such State.

Section 3

No person shall be a Senator or Representative in Congress, or elector of President and Vice President, or hold any office, civil or military, under the United States, or under any State, who, having previously taken an oath, as a member of Congress, or as an officer of the United States, or as a member of any State legislature, or as an executive or judicial officer of any State, to support the Constitution of the United States, shall have engaged in insurrection or rebellion against the same, or given aid or comfort to the enemies thereof. But Congress may by a vote of two-thirds of each House, remove such disability.

Section 4

The validity of the public debt of the United States, authorized by law, including debts incurred for payment of pensions and bounties for services in suppressing insurrection or rebellion, shall not be questioned. But neither the United States nor any State shall assume or pay any debt or obligation incurred in aid of insurrection or rebellion against the United States, or any claim for the loss or emancipation of any slave; but all such debts, obligations and claims shall be held illegal and void.

Section 5

The Congress shall have the power to enforce, by appropriate legislation, the provisions of this article.

*Changed by Section 1 of the 26th Amendment.

Amendment XV.

Passed by Congress February 26, 1869. Ratified February 3, 1870.

Section 1

The right of citizens of the United States to vote shall not be denied or abridged by the United States or by any State on account of race, color, or previous condition of servitude.

Section 2

The Congress shall have the power to enforce this article by appropriate legislation.

Amendment XVI.

Passed by Congress July 2, 1909. Ratified February 3, 1913.

(*Note*: Article I, Section 9 of the Constitution was modified by the 16th Amendment.)

The Congress shall have power to lay and collect taxes on incomes, from whatever source derived, without apportionment among the several States, and without regard to any census or enumeration.

Amendment XVII.

Passed by Congress May 13, 1912. Ratified April 8, 1913.

(*Note*: Article I, Section 3 of the Constitution was modified by the 17th Amendment.)

The Senate of the United States shall be composed of two Senators from each State, elected by the people thereof, for six years; and each Senator shall have one vote. The electors in each State shall have the qualifications requisite for electors of the most numerous branch of the State legislatures.

When vacancies happen in the representation of any State in the Senate, the executive authority of such State shall issue writs of election to fill such vacancies: Provided, That the legislature of any State may empower the executive thereof to make temporary appointments until the people fill the vacancies by election as the legislature may direct. This amendment shall not be so construed as to affect the election or term of any Senator chosen before it becomes valid as part of the Constitution.

Amendment XVIII.

Passed by Congress December 18, 1917. Ratified January 16, 1919. Repealed by the 21 Amendment, December 5, 1933.

Section 1

After one year from the ratification of this article the manufacture, sale, or transportation of intoxicating liquors within, the importation thereof into, or the exportation thereof from the United States and all territory subject to the jurisdiction thereof for beverage purposes is hereby prohibited.

Section 2

The Congress and the several States shall have concurrent power to enforce this article by appropriate legislation.

Section 3

This article shall be inoperative unless it shall have been ratified as an amendment to the Constitution by the legislatures of the several States, as provided in the Constitution, within seven years from the date of the submission hereof to the States by the Congress.

Amendment XIX.

Passed by Congress June 4, 1919. Ratified August 18, 1920.

The right of citizens of the United States to vote shall not be denied or abridged by the United States or by any State on account of sex.

Congress shall have power to enforce this article by appropriate legislation.

Amendment XX.

Passed by Congress March 2, 1932. Ratified January 23, 1933.

(*Note*: Article I, Section 4 of the Constitution was modified by Section 2 of this Amendment. In addition, a portion of the 12th Amendment was superseded by Section 3.)

Section 1

The terms of the President and the Vice President shall end at noon on the 20th day of January, and the terms of Senators and Representatives at noon on the 3d day of January, of the years in which such terms would have ended if this article had not been ratified; and the terms of their successors shall then begin.

Section 2

The Congress shall assemble at least once in every year, and such meeting shall begin at noon on the 3d day of January, unless they shall by law appoint a different day.

Section 3

If, at the time fixed for the beginning of the term of the President, the President elect shall have died, the Vice President elect shall become President. If a President shall not have been chosen before the time fixed for the beginning of his term, or if the President elect shall have failed to qualify, then the Vice President elect shall act as President until a President shall have qualified; and the Congress may by law provide for the case wherein neither a President elect nor a Vice President shall have qualified, declaring who shall then act as President, or the manner in which one who is to act shall be selected, and such person shall act accordingly until a President or Vice President shall have qualified.

Section 4

The Congress may by law provide for the case of the death of any of the persons from whom the House of Representatives may choose a President whenever the right of choice shall have devolved upon them, and for the case of the death of any of the persons from whom the Senate may choose a Vice President whenever the right of choice shall have devolved upon them.

Section 5

Sections 1 and 2 shall take effect on the 15th day of October following the ratification of this article.

Section 6

This article shall be inoperative unless it shall have been ratified as an amendment to the Constitution by the legislatures of three-fourths of the several States within seven years from the date of its submission.

Amendment XXI.

Passed by Congress February 20, 1933. Ratified December 5, 933.

Section 1

The eighteenth article of amendment to the Constitution of the United States is hereby repealed.

Section 2

The transportation or importation into any State, Territory, or possession of the United States for delivery or use therein of intoxicating liquors, in violation of the laws thereof, is hereby prohibited.

Section 3

This article shall be inoperative unless it shall have been ratified as an amendment to the Constitution by conventions in the several States, as provided in the Constitution, within seven years from the date of the submission hereof to the States by the Congress.

Amendment XXII.

Passed by Congress March 21, 1947. Ratified February 27, 951.

Section 1

No person shall be elected to the office of the President more than twice, and no person who has held the office of President, or acted as President, for more than two years of a term to which some other person was elected President shall be elected to the office of President more than once. But this Article shall not apply to any person holding the office of President when this Article was proposed by Congress, and shall not prevent any person who may be holding the office of President, or acting as President, during the term within which this Article becomes operative from holding the office of President or acting as President during the remainder of such term.

Section 2

This article shall be inoperative unless it shall have been ratified as an amendment to the Constitution by the legislatures of three-fourths of the several States within seven years from the date of its submission to the States by the Congress.

Amendment XXIII.

Passed by Congress June 16, 1960. Ratified March 29, 1961.

Section 1

The District constituting the seat of Government of the United States shall appoint in such manner as Congress may direct:

A number of electors of President and Vice President equal to the whole number of Senators and Representatives in Congress to which the District would be entitled if it were a State, but in no event more than the least populous State; they shall be in addition to those appointed by the States, but they shall be considered, for the purposes of the election of President and Vice President, to be electors appointed by a State; and they shall meet in the District and perform such duties as provided by the twelfth article of amendment.

Section 2

The Congress shall have power to enforce this article by appropriate legislation.

Amendment XXIV.

Passed by Congress August 27, 1962. Ratified January 23, 1964.

Section 1

The right of citizens of the United States to vote in any primary or other election for President or Vice President, for electors for President or Vice President, or for Senator or Representative in Congress, shall not be denied or abridged by the United States or any State by reason of failure to pay poll tax or other tax.

Section 2

The Congress shall have power to enforce this article by appropriate legislation.

Amendment XXV.

Passed by Congress July 6, 1965. Ratified February 10, 1967. (*Note*: Article II, Section 1 of the Constitution was modified by the 25th Amendment.)

Section 1

In case of the removal of the President from office or of his death or resignation, the Vice President shall become President.

Section 2

Whenever there is a vacancy in the office of the Vice President, the President shall nominate a Vice President who shall take office upon confirmation by a majority vote of both Houses of Congress.

Section 3

Whenever the President transmits to the President pro tempore of the Senate and the Speaker of the House of Representatives his written declaration that he is unable to discharge the powers and duties of his office, and until he transmits to them a written declaration to the contrary, such powers and duties shall be discharged by the Vice President as Acting President.

Section 4

Whenever the Vice President and a majority of either the principal officers of the executive departments or of such other body as Congress may by law provide, transmit to the President pro tempore of the Senate and the Speaker of the House of Representatives their written declaration that the President is unable to discharge the powers and duties of his office, the Vice President shall immediately assume the powers and duties of the office as Acting President.

Thereafter, when the President transmits to the President pro tempore of the Senate and the Speaker of the House of Representatives his written declaration that no inability exists, he shall resume the powers and duties of his office unless the Vice President and a majority of either the principal officers of the executive department or of such other body as Congress may by law provide, transmit within four days to the President pro tempore of the Senate and the Speaker of the House of Representatives their written declaration that the President is unable to discharge the powers and duties of his office. Thereupon Congress shall decide the issue, assembling within forty-eight hours for that purpose if not in session. If the Congress, within twenty-one days after receipt of the latter written declaration, or, if Congress is not in session, within twenty-one days after Congress is required to assemble, determines by two-thirds vote of both Houses that the President is unable to discharge the powers and duties of his office, the Vice President shall continue to discharge the same as Acting President; otherwise, the President shall resume the powers and duties of his office.

Amendment XXVI.

Passed by Congress March 23, 1971. Ratified July 1, 1971.

(*Note*: Amendment 14, Section 2 of the Constitution was modified by Section 1 of the 26th Amendment.)

Section 1

The right of citizens of the United States, who are eighteen years of age or older, to vote shall not be denied or abridged by the United States or by any State on account of age.

Section 2

The Congress shall have power to enforce this article by appropriate legislation.

Amendment XXVII.

Originally proposed Sept. 25, 1789. Ratified May 7, 1992.

No law, varying the compensation for the services of the Senators and Representatives, shall take effect, until an election of representatives shall have intervened.

Index

A

AARP. *See* American Association of Retired Persons
ABA. *See* American Bar Association
Abolitionism, 293
ACORN. *See* Association of Community Organizations for Reform Now
Active and attentive class, 278
"Active-positive" presidency, 534
Actual malice, 128
ADA. *See* Americans for Democratic Action; Americans With Disabilities Act
Adams, John, 44, 62, 458, 555
Administrative law judges (ALJs), 596
Administrative Procedures Act (APA) of 1946, 605
Advice and consent, 55
Advisory opinions, 546
AFDC. *See* Aid to Families with Dependent Children
Affirm, 562
Affirmative action
  Bakke case, 168
  on behalf of women, 180–181
  judicial decisions, 169
  presidential politics, 169–170
  public attitudes toward, 170
Affordable Care Act, 351, 536
Afghanistan and war on terrorism, 517, 520
AFL. *See* American Federation of Labor
African American president, 490
African American representatives, 463–464
AFSCME. *See* American Federation of State, County, and Municipal Employees
Age Discrimination in Employment Act, 183
Agencies providing assistance to Congress, 475–476
Agency point of view, 592
Agenda, issue on, 229–230
Age, socioeconomic factors, 258–259
Agnew, Spiro T., 222
Agrarian populism, 293–294
Agriculture Committee, 355, 473
Agriculture Department, 437
Aid to Families with Dependent Children (AFDC), 102, 586
Alienation, opinion dysfunction, 261
ALJs. *See* Administrative law judges
Al Qaeda, 520
AMA. *See* American Medical Association
American appetite for socialism, 379
American Association of Retired Persons (AARP), 434
American auto industry, 413
American Bankers Association, 412
American Bar Association (ABA), 404, 412, 414
American cities, murder rate in, 27
American colonies establishment, 40–41
American Constitutional Democracy
  American colonies, establishment, 40–41
  American government, principles, 52
  American Revolution, 42–45
  battle over ratification, 58–60
  Constitutional amendments. *See* Constitutional amendments
  Constitutional convention. *See* Constitutional convention
  Constitution and American Political Culture, 38–40
  Disunited States of America, 45–48
  Framers' Constitution, 55–57
American democracy
  equality and. *See* Equality, and American democracy
  interest groups and, 406–407
  mass media in
    economic decline and media, 214
    ownership and control, 211–212
    political culture, 210–211
American electoral system, 170, 311
American experience, reflection of, 11–13
American federal system, 76, 79–80, 103–107, 313
American Federation of Labor (AFL), 294, 415, 417
American Federation of State, County, and Municipal Employees (AFSCME), 416
American flag, 122, 123
American frontier, individualism of, 22
American government
  growth of, 492
  personification of, 490–494
American Heritage Dictionary, 579
American Independence, 44–45
American Medical Association (AMA), 355, 412, 414, 421
American national character, 23
American national government, 374
American Nations (Woodard), 23
American party system, 373, 374, 399
  development of, 366–367
  early republic, parties in, 367–368
  great realignment of 1932, 371–373
  Populist Revolt, 370–371
  slavery and party realignment, 369–370
American political consensus, 23–28
American political culture, 38–40, 163–164, 581–582
  contours of, 21–22
  democracy. *See* Democracy
  equality in, 26
  evolution, 31
  ideology, 31–33
  institutions and, 28–31
  regional variations in, 22–23
American political system, 365
  media, 231–232
American Revolution, 17
  causes, 42–43
  and Civil War, 255
  contrasting political cultures, 43–44
  independence, 44–45

Americans for Democratic Action (ADA), 420–421, 433
American society, 154
  interest groups and, 406
Americans with Disabilities Act (ADA), 185, 594
American Voter, The, 340
American way of life, 23
Amicus briefs, 435
Amicus curiae briefs, 561
Amnesties, 509
Anarchy, 15
Ancient Greece, culture of, 14
Anderson, John, 375
Anecdotal evidence, 236
Annapolis convention, 47
Anti-Federalists, 58–59, 367
Antiglobalism movement, 302
Anti-Masonic party, 388
Anti-Riot Act of 1968, 288
Anti-Romanism, 24
Anti-Semitism, 24
Antiterrorism and Effective Death Penalty Act, 117
Anti-Vietnam War movement, 296
Antiwar movement, 296–297
Aquino, Corazon, 289
Arab Spring of 2011, 9
Aristocracy, 13
Aristotle, 275
Articles of Confederation, 45–48, 50, 52, 53, 58, 79–81, 495, 536
Aspin, Les, 481
Associational freedom, gay rights *vs.*, 188–189
Association of Community Organizations for Reform Now (ACORN), 404
Association of Trial Lawyers of America, 414
Athenian government, 14
Atlantic seaboard, 44
At-large voting, 172
Atlas Shrugged (Rand), 21
Attitudes, political, 245
Australian ballot, 386
Authoritarianism, 20
Authoritarian regime, 13
Authority, culture and, 11–13
Automobile industry, 413–414
  regulation of, 416
Autonomy, American political consensus, 25–26

B

Baker v. Carr (1962), 70, 557
Balanced response sets, 267
Bandwagon effect, 60
Bank of United States, 84
Barber, James David, 534
Battle over ratification, 58
  federalists *vs.* anti-federalists, 58–59
  ratifying conventions, 59–60
BCRA. *See* Bipartisan Campaign Reform Act
Behavior, voting. *See* Voting, behavior
Beliefs, 244–245
Bellah, Robert, 29
Bell, John, 335
Bernstein, Carl, 229
Bicameral Congress, 54
Bicameral legislatures, 41
Bifurcated trial, 138
"Big Data" election, 326
Bill of attainder, 57, 117
Bill of Rights, 39, 61, 62, 67, 81, 91–92
Bills
  dislodging from committees, 479
  getting to floor, 478–479
  referral, 478
bin Laden, Osama, 20, 517
Bipartisan Campaign Reform Act (BCRA), 329, 484
Birmingham jail, 291
Birthers, 315
Black Codes, 87, 88
Blackhawk Down, 230
Black Panther party, 296
Black-white relations, 151
Block grants, 96
Blocs, 564
Bloggers, 207
Boll Weevils, 527
Bork, Robert H., 510, 552
Boston Tea Party, 43, 290
Bowling Alone (Putnam), 30
Boycott, 289, 295
Boy Scouts' policy, 130
Brady, Jim, 134
Brandeis, Louis, 548
Branzburg v. Hayes, 217
Breaux, John, 470
Breckenridge, John, 335
Brennan, William, 408, 218, 564
Breyer, Stephen G., 568
Briefs of counsel, 561
British parliamentary system, 374
British political parties, 373
British thermal unit (BTU) energy tax, 381
Broadcast media, special case of, 217–220
Broward County, 347
Brownback, Sam, 13
Brown decision, 160–161
Browne, Harry, 377
Brown, Jerry, 316
Brown, John, 293
Brown v. Board of Education (1954), 88, 89, 160, 295, 435, 548, 557, 566
Bryan, William Jennings, 293, 370
BTU energy tax. *See* British thermal unit energy tax
Buchanan, Pat, 300
Buckley v. Valeo, 425
Budget, 532–533
Budget and Impoundment Control Act (1974), 476
Budgetary process, 454
Bugliosi, Vincent, 547
Bull Moose party, 324, 375
Bundling, 317
Bureaucracy. *See* Federal bureaucracy
Bureau of the Budget, 522
Burger Court, 558
Burger, Warren E., 558, 568
Burr, Aaron, 62
Bush, George H. W., 102, 231, 486, 491, 536, 552, 568
  budget, 533
  chief diplomat and foreign policy maker, 493–494
  chief executive role, 492
  chief legislator, 494
  going public, 531–532
  honeymoon period, 527–528
  legislative agenda, 525
  line-item veto, 505, 506
  mandate, 526
  9/11 attack, 517, 520
  Persian Gulf war, 516
  presidential performance evaluation, 535
  presidential war powers, 514
  veto legislation, 503
  war in Iraq, 518
  White House staff, 521
Bush, George W., 20, 101, 285, 415, 226, 553, 559
  administration's approach, 251, 411–412
  bureaucracy, 589
  campaign in Florida, 344
  defend sanctity of marriage, 190

elections, 333, 348–349
exchange of power, 470
media, 212
NAFTA, 417
presidential election, 214
presidential politics, 169
role in election 2000, 300
same-sex marriage, 190
Sixty Minutes news program, 204
supporting for stem cell research, 301
Bush v. Gore, 543, 547
Business interests, 411–412
Business organizations, 412–413
Busing, 167–168
Butterworth, Bob, 344
Byrd, James Jr., 101

C

Cabinet, 523–524
Cabinet, expansion of
agriculture department, 583
fifteen cabinet-level departments, 591–592
interior department, 583
post office, 582–583
Cable News Network (CNN), 205
Cable TV, 205
Calendars, 479–480
Calvinist Protestantism, 40
Campaign
congressional campaigns. *See* Congressional campaigns
electoral environment, 323–324
expectations game, 318
Perennial campaign, 358
raising money for, 316–317, 353
spin control, 318
staff, 317–318
2004, 348–349
Campaign finance laws, 398
Campaign finance reform, 398–399, 484
Candidate-centered campaigns, 398
Candidates
image, 341–342
2008 election, 349–350
2012 election, 351
Cannon, Joe, 460
Capitalism, democracy and, 18–20
Capitalist economy, 18–19
socialist economies *vs.*, 19
Card check legislation, 418
Career civil servants, 579
Carter, Jimmy, 96, 320, 373, 509, 513
amnesty, 509
chief executive role, 492
foreign affairs, 512
prospective and retrospective issue voting, 340
veto legislation, 503
Carter, Stephen, 24
Case/controversy principle, 546
Casework, 450
Categorical grant, 96
Catholic Church, 420
Caucuses, 368
advantages and disadvantages of primaries *vs.*, 390
Caucus system, 389
CBO. *See* Congressional Budget Office
CDA. *See* Communications Decency Act
CEA. *See* Council of Economic Advisers
Central government, unitary system, 80
Central Intelligence Agency (CIA), 511, 579
Centrists, 246
Certiorari, grant of, 560–561
Chain ownership, 211
Chamber of Commerce, 412–413
Charismatic leader, 292
Charles A. Beard, 48–49
Chase, Samuel, 457, 553
Checkbook, controlling government's, 453–456
Checks and balances, 53
system of, 56, 456–457
Cheney, Dick, 190, 411, 464, 470, 492, 502
Chief diplomat, 493–494
Chief executive, 491–492
checking, 456
removal of, 498–500
Chief foreign policy maker, 493–494
Chief legislator, 494
Chief of staff, 521
Chisholm v. Georgia, 554
Christian Coalition, 420
Christian Right, 300–301
Chrysler, 417
CIA. *See* Central Intelligence Agency
CIO. *See* Congress of Industrial Organizations
Circuit courts, 549, 550
Citizen, 15
Citizen journalism, 209
Citizenship, Athenian government and, 14
Citizen's ideology, 340
Civic engagement, 29
Civil case, 545
Civil disobedience, 290–292
Civilian Conservation Corps, 585
Civil liberties, 90–92, 153, 243
and individual freedom, 113
association, freedom of, 129–130
Bill of rights, nationalization, 118–120
crimes, rights of persons accused, 134–138
democratic society, 112–115
First Amendment freedoms, 121–130
freedom of religion, 130–133
original constitution, 116–118
private property, protection of, 121
right of privacy, 138–143
right to keep and bear arms, 133–134
substantive and procedural rights, 115
Civil rights, 113, 151
discrimination
age, 183
against persons with disabilities, 184–185
against poor, 183–184
federalism, 87–89
gay rights, controversy over, 185–191
ideology, 248
national consensus development on, 89
for racial and ethnic groups
Asian Americans, 175–176
Hispanics, 173–174
Native Americans, 174–175
Civil Rights Act
of 1866, 87
of 1875, 154–155
of 1964, 89, 164–166, 170, 295, 432, 451
Civil rights groups, 420
Civil Rights Legislation, 166
Civil rights movement, 5, 161, 295–296, 372
American political culture and, 163–164
role of Martin Luther King, Jr., 162–163

Civil Rights Restoration Act of 1988, 566
Civil Service Reform Act of 1978, 598
Civil War, 154, 324, 387, 555–556
amendments, 62–63, 154
battle between two ideas of federalism, 85
civil rights measures after, 154–155
founding to, 83–86
veto, 503
Clark, Ed, 377
Clay, Henry, 368, 459
Clean-air legislation, 422
Clean Water act, 98
Clear and present danger doctrine, 125
Clear Channel Communications, 219
Clinton, Bill, 267, 285, 300, 376, 380, 381, 226, 230, 456, 500, 536, 588
budget, 476, 533
chief legislator, 494
Congress partisanship, 526–527
crisis manager, 492–493
going public, 532
health insurance and medical cost reduction plan, 415
impeachment, 498–500
and interest groups, 413
job performance ratings, 314–315
labor movement and, 294–295
leadership, 466–467
pardons, 508
scandals, 206
support of NAFTA, 417, 418
survival and eventual triumph in 1992, 315
treaties, 513
veto legislation, 503, 505
Clinton, Hillary Rodham, 349, 415, 416, 462, 499
Clinton v. Jones, 499
Closed primary, 390
CNN. *See* Cable News Network
Coalition, 365
Coattails, 357
Coercive Acts, 43
Coercive federalism, 96–97
Cognitive dissonance, 256
Colonial assemblies, 43
Commander-in-chief, 55, 493
Commerce Clause, 452
Commercial television, 227
Committee action, 478
Committee of the Whole, 480
Committees of Congress
dislodging bills from, 479
and leadership staff, 475
types of, 471–473
Common Cause, 429
Common law, 41
Common Sense (pamphlet), 44
Communications Decency Act (CDA), 127, 220
Communitarians, 29
Compassionate conservatism, 395
Compulsory self-incrimination, 136
Concurring opinion, 563
Condit, Gary, 482
Confederations, 79, 80
Conference, 562
Conference committee, 472–473
Confidential sources, 216–217
Congress, 46, 56, 446
agencies providing assistance to, 475–476
assessing, 486
campaign finance reform, 484
committees, 471–473
controlling government's "checkbook," 453–456
covering, 225–226
foreign policy structures, 511
functions of, 448
institutional development of, 457–462
institution under scrutiny, 481–485
limiting number of terms, 485
maintaining system of checks and balances, 456–457
making laws, 452–453, 476–481
members of, 462–464
organization of. *See* Organization of Congress
partisanship, legislative agenda, 526–527
reforms of, 461, 483–485
representation, 53–54
representing constituents, 449–452
staff, 473–475
and two-party system, 448
veto legislation, 502–505
Congressional Budget and Impoundment Control Act of 1974, 507
Congressional Budget Office (CBO), 98, 454, 476
Congressional campaigns, 352
financing, 353
money, sources of, 354
PACs and, 354–356
Congressional caucus, 368
Congressional elections
earthquakes of 2006 and 2010, 358
national events and, 356–357
scandals, 357
Congressional hearings, 226
Congressional Quarterly Weekly Report, 431
Congressional Research Service (CRS), 476
Congressional *vs.* parliamentary system, 447–448
Congress of Industrial Organizations (CIO), 415, 417
Conservative activism, 556
The Conservative Aversion to Bureaucracy, 588
Conservatives, 32, 33, 247, 250
Constant campaign, 483
Constitution, 66–67, 78, 94, 366
Article III of, 548
Article V of, 566
elitist elements, 57
indirect elections in, 38–40
interest groups and, 407–408
Necessary and Proper Clause in Article I, 82
New Jersey, 92
political culture, 38–40
public opinion and, 240–241
ratification, 58
Constitutional amendments, 60–61
checks on Supreme Court, 566–567
Civil War amendments, 62–63
conferring power on Congress, 453
democratization. *See* Democratization
guaranteeing ERA for women, 178
judicial interpretation, constitutional changes, 64–67
others, 63–64
Tenth and Eleventh Amendments, 62
Twelfth Amendment, 62
Constitutional Convention, 85, 153, 536
conflict and compromise in Philadelphia, 53–54
consensus on basic principles, 50–53
federalism, 52
separation of powers, 53
delegates. *See* Delegates
of 1787, 448, 495, 496, 542

signing Constitution, 54
slavery, 54
Constitutional democracy, 18
Constitutional powers of Congress, 452–453
Constitutional protection of Internet, 220
Constitutional rights, 153
Constitutional theory of presidential power, 501
Consultants, 317
Consumer Product Safety Commission, 595
Contemporary federalism, 99–104
Contemporary mainstream press, 203
Contemporary party system, 373–379
Contemporary political culture, parties and, 399
Contemporary public opinion, 242
Contempt of court, 568
Continental Congress, 44, 45
Controversial program, 96
Convention, 322–323
Cooperative federalism, 99, 100
Corporations PACs, 426, 430
Corporation-without-stock PACs, 426
Council of Economic Advisers (CEA), 522
Council of revision, 496
Counting, 345–347
Coup d'état, 14
Court-packing plan, 67
Courts
checking, 457
circuit, 549, 550
contempt of, 568
federal *vs.* states, 92
internal politics of, 565
internal procedures, 560–564
judgment of, 562
media and, 226–228
role in constitutional democracy, 569
Court's decisions, 457
enforcement of, 568–569
factors influencing, 564–565
Courts-martial, 550
Courts of appeals, United States, 549–550
Coverage of elections, campaigns, and candidates, 228–229
Cox, Archibald, 510
Cracking, 172
Crimes
and criminal justice, 248–249
rights of persons accused of
cruel and unusual punishments, 137–138
Fifth Amendment, protections of, 136
Sixth Amendment rights, 136–137
technology and Fourth Amendment, 135–136
Criminal case, 545
Criminal justice, crime and, 248–249
Crisis manager, 492–493
CRS. *See* Congressional Research Service
Cruel and unusual punishments, 137
Cultural conservative, 33
Cultural war, 249
Culture
and authority, 11–13
changes, 5
German, 11
political. *See* Political culture
Cutback, 97

D

Dade County, 347
Dahl, Robert, 275
Daley, Richard, 391
Damon, Matt, 12
Daschle, Tom, 470
Davis, Gray, 482
Davis, Jefferson, 463
DEA. *See* Drug Enforcement Administration
Dealignment, 397
Dean, Howard, 317
Debates, President, 332–333
Debs, Eugene V., 294
Decentralized power in Congress, 460–462
Decision-making process, 232
Declaration of Independence, 45, 50, 79
Defendant, 545
Defense of Marriage Act (DOMA), 190
Defining events, 258
Degree of racial integration, 167
De jure segregation, 166
Delegates
English constitutional tradition, 49
motives of, 48–49
philosophical influences on, 49
political considerations, 50
Delegate style of representation, 451
Deliberation, 449
Dellinger, David, 296
Demagogue, 240
Democracy, 13–14, 40, 151, 544
and capitalism, 18–20
and human rights, 18
intellectual foundations of modern, 14–16
mass participation in, 274–275
political culture and, 20
regimes, 16–18
role of parties in, 364–366
Democratic-controlled Congress, 231
Democratic institutions, 274
failure of, 158
individualism and support for, 23
Democratic Leadership Council, 393–394
Democratic National Committee, 396–397, 226
Democratic National Convention of 1968, 391
Democratic nomination process (1992), 316, 321
Democratic party, 365, 368–371, 381, 382, 387, 394
in Congress, 381
NEA role in, 415
and organized labor, 417
organized labor and, 416
Democratic plank, 397
Democratic Republican candidates, 367
Democratic Republican party, 369
Democratic society
individual rights
accused, rights of, 115
evolving social contract, 114
natural law, 114
natural rights, 114
substantive and procedural rights, 115
public opinion in, 240
Democratization, 67
eliminating economic restrictions, 69–70
enfranchising African Americans, 68
liberty and equality, constitutional protection, 67
reapportionment, 70
Senate, election of, 68
voting age, 69
women's suffrage, 68–69
Demonstrations, 287
Department of Health, Education and Welfare, 586
Department of Homeland Security (DHS), 78

Department of Housing and Urban development (HUD), 586
Department of Transportation (DOT), 586
Dershowitz, Alan, 547
Descriptive representation, 449
Desegregation, Supreme Court's, 89
Devolution, 99, 103
DHS. *See* Department of Homeland Security
Dictatorship, 13–14
Dimpled chads, 345
Direct democracy, 51
Direct mail, 316, 429, 430
Direct primary, 389
Disaster response, federal–state cooperation, 102–103
Discrimination, 151
basis of sexual orientation, 150
civil rights
age, 183
against persons with disabilities, 184–185
against poor, 183–184
faces of, 152–153
gender. *See* Gender discrimination
private, 152–153
public, 154
racial, 170–173
sex, 177
Discriminatory legislation on racial differences, 177
Dislodging bills from committees, 479
Disputes, adjudication of, 596–597
Dissenting opinion, 563
Distributive articles, 55
District courts, United States, 549
Disunited States of America, 45–48
Divided-party government, 71, 380, 502
Dixiecrats, 372
Doctrine of implied powers, 84
Doctrine of nullification, 86
Doctrine of political questions, 546
Doctrine of secession, 86
Doctrine of *stare decisis*, 547, 548
Dole, Bob, 469
DOMA. *See* Defense of Marriage Act
Donaldson, Sam, 223
DOT. *See* Department of Transportation
Double-barreled question, 267
Double jeopardy, 136
Douglas, Stephen, 335
Draft opinion, 563
Dred Scott case, 153–154
Drudge Report, 499
Drug Enforcement Administration (DEA), 100
Dual federalism, 99
Due Process Clause of Fourteenth Amendment, 91
Due process of law, 63, 556
Dukakis, Michael, 340
Duncan, John, 251
Duval County, 345
Dye, Thomas, 254

E

Earmarks, 455
Earthquakes of 2006 and 2010, 358
Economic conservative, 33
Economic interest groups, 410–411, 429
business interests, 411–412
business organizations, 412–413
organized labor, 415–418
professional associations, 414–415
trade associations, 413–414
Economic liberty, 26
Economic regulation, conflict in federalism, 93
Edelman, Marian Wright, 423
Educational institutions, sex discrimination by, 179–180
Educational system, 409–410
Education Amendments of 1972, Title IX of, 566
Education, federal–state cooperation, 101–102
Education for All Handicapped Children Act of 1975, 184
EEOC. *See* Equal Employment Opportunity Commission
Efficacy, opinion dysfunction, lack of, 261–262
Eighteenth Amendment, 64
Eisenhower, Dwight D., 529, 553
Elazar, Daniel, 22–23
Election campaign, general, 323
electoral environment, 323–324
finance reform of 2002, 329
financing, 326–328
national media campaign, 330–332
presidential debates, 332–333
role of issues, 332
Section 535, 329–330
state-by-state strategies, 325–326
SuperPAC, 330
Elections
congressional elections. *See* Congressional elections
general. *See* General election
importance of, 310–312
influencing, 424–428
presidential campaigns and, 313
presidential debates, 332–333
primary election, 312, 313
realigning, 371
referenda, 313
2000, 469–470
2008, 349–350
2004, 348–349
2012, 350–351
types of, 312–313
Electoral college, 57
Electoral college vote, 334–337
Electoral discrimination, institutionalized, 171–172
Electoral disfranchisement, 157–158
Electoral environment, campaign, 323–324
Electoral federalism, 89–90
Electronic media, 128–129, 200, 209
bloggers, 207
cable and satellite TV, 205
Internet, 206–207
talk radio, 203–204
television broadcast networks, 204
twenty-four-hour television news networks, 205–206
Electronic voting, 481
Eleventh Amendments, 62, 566
Elite-pluralist model, 269
Elites, 13, 14
Emergency Powers Act of 1977, 513
Emerging Republican majority, 372
Employment discrimination, 165
Enabling legislation, 594
End of Liberalis, The (Lowi), 409
Energy tax, 413
English Bill of Rights, 49
Enron Corporation, 411
Enumerated powers, 82
Article I, Section 10, 85
of Congress, 452–453
Environmental group, 433
Environmental movement, 420
Environmental protection, 100
Environmental Protection Agency (EPA), 100, 507, 587, 595
Environment, preserving, 409
EOP. *See* Executive Office of the President

EPA. *See* Environmental Protection Agency
Equal Employment Opportunity Commission (EEOC), 181, 552, 594
Equality, 18
and American democracy
faces of discrimination, 152–153
founding of the republic, 151–152
in American political culture, 26
individualism and, 242–244
Equality of opportunity, 152
Equality of result, 183
Equal Pay Act of 1963, 177
Equal Protection Clause, 87
Equal protection of laws, 63, 153
Equal Rights Amendment (ERA), 60, 178, 297
Era of Good Feelings, 368
Ethnic groups
Asian Americans, 175–176
Hispanics, 173–174
Native Americans, 174–175
European politics on American thinking and values, 151–152
Europe governments, 40
Evidence, anecdotal, 236
Exchange of power (2006), 470
Exclusionary rule, 135
Executive agreements, 513–514
Executive branch of government, 491
Executive Calendar, 479
Executive Office Building, 522
Executive Office of the President (EOP), 522
Executive privilege, 509
Exit poll, 236, 266
Expectations game, campaign, 318
Ex post facto law, 57
Expressive conduct, 122
Expressive individualism, 22

F

FAA. *See* Federal Aviation Administration
Facebook, 207–209
"Failed Clinton administration," 528
Fair Deal, 372
Fair Housing Act of 1968, 451
Fairness Commission, 393
Fairness doctrine, 218
Falwell, Jerry, 300
Family and Medical Leave Act, 297, 418
Family, political socialization, 253–254
FCC. *See* Federal Communications Commission
FDA. *See* Food and Drug Administration
FDIC. *See* Federal Deposit Insurance Corporation
Federal Aviation Administration (FAA), 595
Federal bureaucracy
American political culture, 581–582
American political thought, 580
congressional control of, 603–604
conservative aversion, 580–581
definition, 579
functions of, 593–597
government, growth of, 576–579
iron triangles and issue networks, 606–607
legal constraints, 604–606
origin and development of, 582–590
presidential control of. *See* Presidential control bureaucracy
staff, 597–598
structure of, 591–593
Federal Bureau of Investigation (FBI), 590
Federal civil rights laws, violation of, 182
Federal Communications Commission (FCC), 128, 217–220, 595, 601
Federal courts, 89–91, 98, 544, 548–554
courts of appeals, 549–550
covering, 227
district courts, 549
federal judges, 550–554
mere judgment, 542
specialized federal tribunals, 550
vs. state courts, 92, 101
Supreme Court, 548–549
Federal Deposit Insurance Corporation (FDIC), 595
Federal Education Act of 1972, 177
Federal Election Campaign Act (FECA), 354, 375, 424
Federal Election Commission (FEC), 425
dividing PAC, 426
Federal Emergency Management Agency (FEMA), 78, 103
Federal Energy Regulatory Commission (FERC), 595
Federal funds, denial of, 166
Federal government, 76, 83–85, 97, 386
New Deal programs, 94, 102
states, cities, and, 94–99
Federalism, 52, 76–81, 95–96
civil rights, 87–89
coercive and regulatory, 96–97
conflict in, 93
cooperative, 99, 100
development of, 83–86
to devolution, 97–99
disadvantages of, 106
dual, 99
electoral, 89–90
fiscal, 103–104
marble cake, 99
in modern era, 86–99
nation-centered, 86
and political culture, 106–107
rights of accused, 92
state-centered, 86
Federalism in Constitution, 81–83, 91
federal relationship, 82
supremacy of federal law, 82–83
Federalist candidates, 367
Federalist No. 12, The (Madison), 406–407
Federalist Papers, 59, 240–241
Federalist program, 367
Federalists, 58–59
Federal judges
appointment of, 550–552
impeachment of, 553–554
Federal judiciary, 226
Federal law, 93
supremacy of, 82–83
Federal party system, 384
Federal political campaigns, cost of, 355
Federal Register, 431
Federal regulation of economy, 93
Federal relationship, 82
evolution, 94–99
Federal-state cooperation, 99–103
disaster response and relief, 102–103
education, 101–102
environmental protection, 100
law enforcement, 100–101
welfare, 102
Federal system, 79, 81
advantages of, 104–105
Federal tax code, 329
Federal theory, 103

Federal Trade Commission (FTC), 584–585, 595
Federal tribunals, 550
FEMA. *See* Federal Emergency Management Agency
Female representation in Congress, 462–463
FERC. *See* Federal Energy Regulatory Commission
Fifteenth Amendment, 68
Fifth Amendment, 556
 Just Compensation Clause, 91
Fighting words, 125
Finance reform of 2002, campaign, 329
Financing congressional campaigns, 353–356
"Fireside chats," 531
First Amendment, 91, 407–408, 567
 free exercise of religion, 24
 rights, 330
First Amendment freedoms
 assembly, freedom of, 129
 censorship, free, 124–125
 dangerous ideas, 125
 defamation, 127–128
 electronic media, 128–129
 fighting words, 125–126
 obscenity and pornography, 126–127
 profanity, 126
 protected expression, scope of, 122–124
First Bank of United States, 83
First Continental Congress, 43
First responders, 77
Fiscal federalism, 103–104
Florida county, 348
Florida law, 348
Florida's post-election contest, 344–345
Florida Supreme Court, 227
Food and Drug Administration (FDA), 595
Ford, Gerald, 508
Foreign affairs, specifics of, 512–514
Foreign Intelligence Surveillance Act, 519
Foreign policy
 and military issues, 247–248
 power to make, 510–512
Forrest McDonald, 48–49, 58
Fourteenth Amendment, 63, 68, 87–92, 154, 548, 567
 Due Process Clause, 91
 Equal Protection Clause, 170
 importance of, 87–88
 Section 1 of, 91
 Section 5 of, 87
Fourth Amendment, 519
Fragmentation of power in Congress, 460–462
Framers' Constitution, 79–81, 452
 checks and balances, system of, 56
 individual rights, 57
 new government, institutions of, 55–56
 restrictions on states, 56–57
 undemocratic document, 57
Franken, Al, 471
Franking privilege, 482–483
Fraser, Donald, 392
Freedom, 18
 autonomy and privacy, 25–26
 commitment to individual, 23–24
 faith and, 24–25
Freedom of association, 129–130
Freedom of expression, 121
Freedom of Information Act of 1966, 605
Freedom of press
 broadcast and online media, 217–220
 confidential sources, 216–217
 constitutional protection of Internet, 220
 libel suits, 216
 prohibition against prior restraint, 215
 right to know, 216
Freedom of religion
 church and state, separation of, 130–131
 free exercise of, 132–133
 government, and ideology, 131–132
Free enterprise system, support for, 26
Free Exercise Clause, 132
Free, fair, and open elections, 16
Free riders, 422
 problem, 422–423, 429
Free speech, violation of, 220
Free trade, 411
Frémont, John C., 370
French and Indian War. *See* Seven Years War
French Revolution, 16, 151–152
 Rousseau and, 16
French society, 151–152
Frontloading, 321–322, 394
FTC. *See* Federal Trade Commission
Full Faith and Credit Clause of U.S. Constitution, 190
Fund for a Conservative Majority, 421
Fundraising, 429–430
Furman v. Georgia, 137

G

Gallup, George, 265
Gallup poll, 508
Gandhi, Mohandas, 291
GAO. *See* General Accounting Office
Garraty, John, 49
Garrison, William Lloyd, 369
GATT. *See* General Agreement on Tariffs and Trade
Gay and lesbian Americans, 151
Gay couples
 health benefits for, 31
 rights, 25
Gay marriage, 189–191
 state-imposed bans on, 191
Gay men in Military service, 186–187
Gay rights, 188
 vs. associational freedom, 188–189
Gay rights movement, 297–299
Gazette of the United States, 201
Gender discrimination
 sex discrimination by educational institutions, 179–180
 sexual harassment, 181–182
 women, 178–181
Gender gap, 259
Gender, socioeconomic factors, 259
General Accounting Office (GAO), 476
General Agreement on Tariffs and Trade (GATT), 513
General election, 312
 campaign. *See* Election campaign, general
General Motors, 411, 417
General revenue sharing, 96
General strike, 289
Georgia law, 138
Gephardt, Dick, 482
German culture, 11
Gerrymandering, 173
Gettysburg Address, 279
Gibbons v. Ogden, 84, 85, 411, 555
Gingrich, Newt, 466, 533
 rise and fall of, 467–469
Ginsburg, Ruth Bader, 568
Giuliani, Rudy, 77
Glorious Revolution of 1688, 15, 43
"Going public," 531–532

Golden Age of Regulation, 587
Goldwater, Barry, 382
Gompers, Samuel, 294
Gore, Al, 169, 236–240, 266, 313, 314, 415
elections, 2000, 333
Florida's post-election contest, 344–345
Government
"checkbook," controlling, 453–456
defining, 6–7
democratic form of, 20
purpose of, 7–8
relationship between press and, 221
role in economy, 247
Governmental institutions, 28
Grandfather clause, 157
Grand jury, 136
Grants-in-aid, 95–97
Grassroots lobbying, 431–432
Grassroots party politics, 372
Gray v. Sanders (1963), 279
Great Depression, 258, 371
Great Society, 586
Green party, 375, 377
Greenpeace, 420, 433, 434
Grenada invasion, 216
Gridlock, 409, 502
Grodzins, Morton, 99
Grove City College v. Bell, 566
Gulf of Tonkin Resolution of 1964, 515
Gun control, 134
Gun-Free Schools Act of 1990, 452–453
Gunn, David, 301

H

Habeas corpus, 57
state criminal cases, 117
World War II, 116
Habits of the Heart (Bellah), 29
Haldeman, H. R., 521
Hamdi v. Rumsfeld, 520
Hamilton, Alexander, 54–56, 62, 81, 83, 368, 495, 500–501, 542
Harassment, sexual, 181–182
Harding, Warren G., 534
Hardwick, Michael, 140
Harkin, Tom, 319
Harlan, John M., 568
Harrison, Benjamin, 336
Harrison, William Henry, 497
Hashtag, 210
Hastert, Dennis, 469
Hatch Act, 598
Hate crime, 101
Hayden, Tom, 296
Head of state, president role, 491
Health insurance, 415
Helms, Jesse, 437
Henry, Patrick, 57, 59
Hill, Anita, 552
Hill, Capitol, 483
Hinckley, John, 134
History of U.S. Decision-Making Process on Vietnam Policy, 124
Hitler, Adolf, 14
Hobbes, Thomas, 15, 51, 290
Homeland Security Act of 2002, 589
Homosexual conduct, American political consensus, 25
Homosexuality, 191
Honeymoon period, 527–528
Honeymoon phase, 222
Hoover, Herbert, 371
House Agriculture Committee, 478
House committees, 472–473, 478
House floor
getting bill to, 478–479
procedure, 480–481
House Judiciary Committee, 225
House leadership of Congress, 466–467
House of Representatives, 446, 448, 468, 553, 567
Housing Act of 1949, 95
Housing and Community Development Act of 1974, 96
HUD. *See* Department of Housing and urban development
Hughes, Charles Evans, 215, 562
Human Rights Campaign, 434
Human rights, democracy and, 18
Humphrey, Hubert H., 391
Hurricane Andrew, 102, 492
Hurricane Katrina, 103
Hussein, Saddam, 14, 20, 492, 518
Hyde Amendment, 184
Hyperlocal sites, 212
Hyperpluralism, 409

I

IBM, 411
ICC. *See* Interstate Commerce Commission
Ideological groups, 420–421
Ideological self-identification, issue positions by, 252
Ideology, 31–33, 246–251
civil rights, 248
crime and criminal justice, 248–249
foreign policy and military issues, 247–248
Liberal-Conservative continuum, 246–247
and public policy, 249–251
self-identification, 252
traditional values and institutions, 249
Illegal immigration, issue of, 229–230
Immediacy of information, 209–210
Imminent lawless action, 125
Impeachment, 456, 498
Implied powers, 453
doctrine of, 84
and national supremacy, 83–85
Impoundment, 506–507
Incumbency advantage, 352, 482–483
Independent agencies, 591, 593
Independent voters, 390
rise of, 382–384
Indictment, 136
Individual freedom, commitment to, 23–24
Individualism, 21–22
and equality, 242–244
Individualistic political culture, 22
Individual opinions, 244–263
attitudes and opinions, 245–246
dysfunction, 261–263
ideology. *See* Ideology
political socialization. *See* Political socialization
socioeconomic factors. *See* Socioeconomic factors
values and beliefs, 244–245
Individual participation, levels of, 275–279
Industrial Revolution, 26
Inferior citizenship status of women, 176
Influencing elections, 424–428
Information society, 209
Inherent power, 518–519
Injunction, 215
Inside Politics program, 205
Institutional development of Congress, 457–458
decentralization and fragmentation, 460–462
evolving, 459
strong committee system, 459–460

Institutionalized electoral discrimination, 171–172
Institutions
and American political culture, 28–31
under scrutiny, 481–485
advantages of incumbency, 482–483
constant campaign, 483
proposals for reform, 483–485
traditional values and, 249
"Intellectual" wing of Democratic party, 372
Interest, 404
Interest aggregation, 365
Interest articulation, 365
Interest-group liberalism, 409
Interest groups, 404–405
and American democracy, 406–407
and American society, 406
building coalitions, 434
campaigns and elections influence, 424–428
and constitution, 407–408
fundraising, 428–430
grassroots lobbying, 431–432
hyperpluralism, 409
litigation, 434–435
lobbying, 430–431
pluralism, 408
and political culture, 438–439
and political parties, 405–406
public interest, 409–410
public opinion influence, 432–433
reason for joining, 421–423
role of, 423–435
subgovernments, 436–438
targeting political opposition, 433–434
in United States, 410–421
Intermediary institutions, 28
Internal Security Act of 1940, 130
International relations, "sole organ" in, 511
Internet, 206–207
constitutional protection of, 220
Interstate Commerce Act, 93
Interstate Commerce Commission (ICC), 93, 584
Intolerable Acts, 43
Intolerance, opinion dysfunction, 262–263
Iowa caucus, 319
Iran-Contra Scandal, 512
Iraq
invasion of, 251
under Saddam Hussein, 14
war in, 380, 518
Iron triangles, 435–438
Islam and terrorism, 20
Issue networks, 438
Issues
2008 election, 350
2012 election, 350
voting, 340

J

Jackson, Andrew, 76, 368, 369
Jacksonian Democrats, 369
Jackson, Janet, 219
Jackson, Jesse, 393
Japanese Americans relocation during World War II, 519
Jaworski, Leon, 510
Jay, John, 554
Jefferson, Thomas, 45, 48, 62, 83–84, 130, 291, 311, 367, 453, 458
committees in Congress, 471
executive privilege, 509
impoundment, 506
Jeffords, James, 469–470
Jeffords, Jim, 527
Jews, proportions of, 24
Jim Crow laws, 87–88, 156–157
Johnson, Andrew, 456
impeachment, 498
veto legislation, 503
Johnson, Lyndon B., 67, 96, 102, 295, 391, 529–530
"Johnson treatment," 530
Joint committees, 473
Jones, Paula Corbin, 499
Journalistic professionalism, 212
Judeo-Christian moral tradition, 185
Judicial activism, 564, 569
Judicial behavior, presidential predictions of, 553
Judicial branch, assessing, 569–570
Judicial candidates, presidential nomination of, 551
Judicial decisions, 457
Judicial federalism, 92, 184
Judicial interpretation, constitutional changes, 64–67
Judicial restraint, 564
Judicial review, 543–545
Judiciary Act of 1789, 544, 548, 549
Jurisdiction, 545–546
Just Compensation Clause, Fifth Amendment, 91

K

Kaplan, Robert, 276
Kelo, Susette, 121
Kennedy, Anthony, 559
Kennedy, Edward M., 433–434, 470
Kennedy, John F., 164, 204
cabinet, 523
foreign affairs, 512
presidential performance evaluation, 534
treaties, 513
Kennedy-Nixon debate, 232
Kennedy, Paul, 42
Kennedy, Robert, 391
Kerry, John, 281, 301, 321, 341, 214
King, Martin Luther, Jr., 162–163, 289, 295, 391
and civil disobedience, 291–292
social movement and, 292
Kobach, Kris, 284
Kyllo v. United States, 136

L

Labor
headquarters, 578
organized, 415–418
PACs, 426, 430
Labor movement, 294–295
LaFollette, Robert, 376
Laissez-faire, 26, 32
approach, 93
capitalism, 66–67
economic policy, 294
Lambda Legal Defense and Education Fund, 185
Lame duck, 529
Landslide, 470–471, 525
Law clerks, 563
Law enforcement, 100–101
Lawrence v. Texas, 189
Laws making in Congress, 452–453, 476–478
bill referral, 478
committee action, 478
getting bill to floor, 478–479
Lazio, Rick, 462
Leadership of Congress, 464–471
committee and staff, 475

Leaks, 224–225
"Least dangerous branch," 542–548
Lee, Richard Henry, 45
Legal Defense and Education Fund, 434
Legal disputes, resolution of, 545–546
Legal institutions, court, 569
Legally mandated school segregation, 159–160
Legal reform, 414
Legislation, 413
Legislative agenda, 524–525
  Congress partisanship, 526–527
  political context, 525–526
  timing, 527–529
Legislative veto, 603
Legislature, 41
Legitimacy, 7
Lesbians
  health benefits for, 31
  in military service, 186–187
  rights, 25
Lesbians, gays, bisexuals, and transsexuals (LGBT), 151
Levees, 77
Leviathan (Hobbes), 15, 51
Lewinsky, Monica, 267, 499
Lewinsky scandal, 223
LGBT. *See* Lesbians, gays, bisexuals, and transsexuals
Libel suits, 216
Liberal 527, 329
Liberal-conservative continuum, 246–247
Liberals, 32, 33, 247
  organization, 406
  perspective, 250
Liberator, 369
Libertarian party, 377–378
Libertarians, 32
Liberty, 23
  economic, 26
Library of Congress, 476
Light, Paul, 536
Limited government, 15
Lincoln, Abraham, 13, 86, 255, 303, 456, 514
  Emancipation Proclamation, 63
  presidential performance evaluation, 533–534
Line-item veto, 505–506
Linkage institution, 364
Lipset, Seymour Martin, 254, 286
Literacy test, 157
Literary Digest, 264
Litigation, interest groups, 434–435
Live-in partners, health benefits for, 31
Lobbying, 430–431
  grassroots, 431–432
  hiring, 411
Lochner v. New York, 66, 556
Locke, John, 15, 17, 45, 49, 291
Logic of Collective Action, The (Olson), 422
Lott, Trent, 469, 470
Loyal opposition, 380
Lugar, Richard, 511

M

Madison, James, 48, 50, 53, 61, 367, 406–407, 458, 500–501
Magna Carta, 49
Majority/individual problem, 18
Majority leader, 467, 469
Majority/minority problem, 18, 151
Majority opinion, 562–563
Majority party, 365
Majority rule, 18
Majority whip, 467, 469
Malapportionment, 70
Malcolm X, 278–279
Mandate, 525–526
Marble cake federalism, 99
Marbury v. Madison, 64, 544, 555, 566
Marches, 287
Marcos, Ferdinand, 289, 511
Marital status, socioeconomic factors, 259
Markup session, 478
Marshall Court, 555
Marshall, John, 84–85, 544, 555
Marshall, Margaret H., 189
Marshall, Thurgood, 564
Mason, George, 81
Massachusetts, Shays' Rebellion in, 47–48
Massachusetts Supreme Court, 299
Masses, 13
Mass media, 200, 232
  in American democracy
    economic decline and media, 214
    ownership and control, 211–212
    political culture, 210–211
  development of
    electronic media, 203–207
    news media, 207–208
    print media, 201–203
    ubiquitous media, 208–210
  and making of public policy, 229–231
  press, freedom of. *See* Freedom of press
  prevalence of, 384
Mass participation in democracy, 274–275
Mass protests, 287
Matrix, The, 27
Mayflower Compact, 41, 49
Mcauliff, Terry, 385
McCain, John, 319, 321, 327, 455
  campaign finance reform, 484
McCarthy, Eugene, 391
McCulloch v. Maryland, 65, 84, 85, 555
McGovern–Fraser Commission, 392
McGovern, George, 276, 392
McKinley, William, 293, 370
McLuhan, Marshall, 209
Media
  in American Political System, 231–232
  campaign, 332
  and courts, 226–228
  in United States, 31
Media junkie, 208–209
Medical cost reduction plan, 415
Medicare, 414
Members of Congress, 462–464
Meritocracy, 597
Microsoft, 428
Midterm election, 352
Miers, Harriett, 457, 552–553
Milbrath, Lester, 275, 277
Military issues, foreign policy and, 247–248
Military service
  gay men and lesbians in, 186–187
  women in, 178–179
Miller test, 126
Minority leadership, 467, 469
Minority party, 365
Minority representation in Congress, 463–464
Miranda v. Arizona, 136
Missouri Compromise of 1820, 85
Model Cities, 96
Moderates, 32, 246
Modern administrative state, 578
Modern pluralist theory, 287
Mondale, Walter, 417
Money, sources of, 354
Montgomery bus boycott, 295
Moralistic political culture, 22
Morison, Samuel Eliot, 41

Motor Voter Act, 285–286
MoveOn.org, 317, 329, 406, 424
MoveOn Political Action Committee, 424
Mr. Smith Goes to Washington, 11, 12
Mubarak, Hosni, 9
Multiculturalism, 30
Multiparty system, 373
Multiple referral system, 461
Murder rate in American cities, 27
Murphy Brown television series, 211
Muslim Brotherhood, 10
MySpace, 207

N

NAACP. *See* National Association for the Advancement of Colored People
Nader, Ralph, 313, 375, 377, 423
NAFTA. *See* North American Free Trade Agreement
National Abortion Rights Action League, 419
National Association for the Advancement of Colored People (NAACP), 160, 420
National Association of Manufacturers, 412, 413–414, 429
National Association of Realtors, 421, 427
National Beer Wholesalers Association, 412
National Committee for an Effective Congress, 420–421
National Committee to Preserve Social Security, 434
National community, 386
National Conservative Political Action Committee, 421
National conventions, 388, 391, 395, 396
National Democratic party, 372
National Education Association (NEA)
  role in Democratic party politics, 415
National Environmental Performance Partnership System (NEPPS), 100
National events and congressional elections, 356–357
National Labor Relations Act, 67
National legislature, 446–448
"National" mechanism, 81
National media campaign, 330–332
National Minimum Drinking Age Law of 1984, 97
National Office of Drug Policy, 100
National Organization for Marriage website, 434
National Park Service, 583
National party, 397
  chair, 385
  structure of, 384–388
National party conventions
  delegates, 395–396
  functions of, 396–397
  history of, 388–389
  party reform, 391–394
  primaries, rise of, 389–390
National political conversation, 232
National Public Radio, 218
National Realtors Association, 412
National Recovery Administration (NRA), 557
National Rifle Association (NRA), 134, 425, 427, 428, 430
National Right to Life group, 419
National Security Council (NSC), 522
National security, peacetime threats to, 519
National Wildlife Federation, 420, 422
Nation-centered federalism, 86
Natural law, 15, 114
Natural rights, 15
NEA. *See* National Education Association
Nebraska law, 140
Necessary and Proper Clause, 55
  Article I, 82, 84
NEPPS. *See* National Environmental Performance Partnership System
Neustadt, Richard, 529
New Amsterdam, 23
New Christian Right (NCR), 300
New Deal, 66–67, 294
  agenda, 371
  coalition, 416
New Deal program, 94, 95, 102
  constitutional battle over, 556–557
New Hampshire primary, 320
New Jersey Constitution, 92
New Jersey Plan, 54
News media, 207–208
Newspapers, 201–202
Newsweek, 430
New York Herald, 201
New York Journal, 202
New York Times, The, 202, 211, 212, 215
9/11 attack, 517, 520
9/11 Commission, 226
Nineteenth Amendment, 68–69
Nixon administration, 96
Nixon campaign of 1968, 330–331
Nixon–Kennedy presidential election, 280
Nixon, Richard M., 288, 567, 568
  cabinet, 523
  handling of budget, 476
  impeachment, 498
  impoundment, 506
  against "liberal media," 212
  pardons, 508
  presidential performance evaluation, 534
  prior restraint on press, 215
  Supreme Court, 502
  treaties, 513
  Watergate controversy, 509–510
Nixon White House, 224
No Child Left Behind Act of 2001, 102, 535
Nomination process, 312–314
  building momentum, 319–320
  campaign staff, 317–318
  culmination of, 322–323
  frontloading, 321–322
  getting started, 314–316
  polls, use of, 318–319
  raising money for campaingn, 316–317
  reforms in, 394
  Super Tuesday, 321
Nonconnected PACs, 426, 427
Noneconomic groups, 410
  ideological groups, 420–421
  public interest groups, 421
  single-issue groups, 419–420
Nonmanagement workers, 416
Nonresponse bias, 264
Nonviolent resistance, 295–296
Nonvoting
  evaluating, 286
  explanations for, 285
North American Free Trade Agreement (NAFTA), 294, 381, 417–418, 494, 513
NRA. *See* National Recovery Administration
NRC. *See* Nuclear Regulatory Commission
NSC. *See* National Security Council
Nuclear Regulatory Commission (NRC), 595
Nullification, doctrine of, 86

O

Obama, Barack, 5, 327, 404, 418, 490
  African American representation, 463
  antiwar movement and, 297
  bureaucrat, 590
  chief legislator, 494
  economic crisis, 326
  elections, 151
  electoral vote, 310
  Obamacare referendum of 2010, 471
  presidential performance evaluation, 535–536
  reelection campaign, 213
Obamacare, 536
  referendum of 2010, 471
Obscenity, 126–127
Occupational Safety and Health Administration (OSHA), 584, 595
Occupy Wall Street, 379
O'Connor, Sandra Day, 553, 559, 560
Office of Economic Opportunity (OEO), 506–507
Office of Management and Budget (OMB), 476, 522, 602
Office of Telecommunications Policy (OTP), 601
Oliver, Andrew, 42
Olson, Mancur, 422
Omar, Mullah, 517
OMB. *See* Office of Management and Budget
Ombudsman, 450
One-dimensional liberal-conservative scale, 246
One person, one vote, 70
Online media, special case of, 217–220
Online world and politics, 12
Open primary, 390
Operation Desert Shield, 231
Operation Rescue, 301
Ophthalmologists, 414
Opinions, 245–246, 562
  advisory, 546
  concurring, 563
  of Court, 562, 563
  dysfunction, 261–263
    alienation, 261
    intolerance, 262–263
    lack of efficacy, 261–262
  of individuals. *See* Individual opinions
  measurement, 263–268
  public. *See* Public opinion
Oral argument, 561–562
Organization of Congress, leadership, 464–471
Organized labor, 415–418
Original constitution
  attainder and *ex post facto laws*, bills of, 117–118
  Habeas Corpus, 116–117
OSHA. *See* Occupational Safety and Health Administration
OTP. *See* Office of Telecommunications Policy
Oversight, 456

P

PAC. *See* Political action committees
Packing, 172
Pack journalism, 223
PACs. *See* Political action committees
Panama Canal treaty, 513
Pardons, 500, 508–509
Parenti, Michael, 213
Parks, Rosa, 295
Parliamentary system, congressional *vs.*, 447–448
Participatory democracy, 16
Particularism, 454–456
Parties
  and contemporary political culture, 399
  decline and revitalization of, 397–399
  and governing process, 380–384
Partisan realignment, 365
Partisanship, 253
Partisan strength in states, differences in, 387–388
Party caucus, 466
Party identification, 251
  trends in, 382
  voting behavior, 337–338
Party image, 341
Party in Congress, 381
Party in electorate, 381–384
Party in government, 380–381
Party leader, president role, 494
Party machines, 385–386
Party out of power, 369
Party platform, 397
Party realignment, slavery and, 369–370
Party reform, 391–394
Patient Protection and Affordable Care Act of 2010, 471
Patriot Act, 116, 535
Patronage, 389
Patterson, Thomas, 286
Paula Jones case, 499
Paul, Rand, 210
Paywall, 212
Peaceful character of movement, 295
Peace mission, 511
Peacetime threats to national security, 519
Peer groups, 256
Pentagon Papers Case of 1971, 215, 502
People for the Ethical Treatment of Animals, 420
Perennial campaign, 358
Perks, 483–484
Perot, H. Ross, 279, 281, 300, 376, 418
Perpetual election, 531
Perry, Rick, 351
Persian Gulf War, 516
Personal Responsibility and Work Opportunity Reconciliation Act, 102
Personal staff members, 474–475
Persuasion, power and, 529–532
Photo opportunity, 342
Plaintiff, 545
Pledge of allegiance, 25
Plessy decision, 162
Plessy v. Ferguson, 156, 157, 160, 548
Pluralism, 408, 409
Pocket veto, 503
Police power, 66, 82
Policy deliberation, 449
Policy initiators, 269
Policy laboratories, 104
Policy makers, communicating public opinion to, 269–270
Policy-making process, 99, 408, 545
Policy process, models of public opinion, 269
Policy representation, competing models of, 451–452
Political action committees (PACs), 316, 328, 421, 424–428, 468
  and congressional campaigns, 354–356
  contributors, 427
  growth of, 425
  increase in, 428
Political activists, 277
Political alienation, 261
Political apathy, 276
Political appointees, 579
Political culture
  Constitution and American, 38–40
  contrasting, 43–44

Political culture (*Continued*)
and democracy, 20
importance of, 8–13
interest groups and, 438–439
participation and, 302–303
public opinion and, 242
and societal culture, 10–11
YouTube and, 12
Political efficacy, 254
opinion dysfunction, lack of, 261–262
Political entrepreneurs, 423
Political equality, women's struggle for, 177
Political institutions, 569
Politically selective consumption of media, 214
Political participation, 274–275
continuum of, 276
culture and, 302–303
extraordinary forms of, 287–292
levels of, 275–279
restrictions on females, 462
social movements and, 292–302
through voting, 279–286
Political parties, interest groups and, 405–406
Political process, decision in participation, 278–279
Political questions, doctrine of, 546, 547
Political resources, 278
Political socialization, 29, 251–252
family, 253–254
peer groups, 256
school, 254–256
Political values, 244
Politics, 4–6
and American future, 33
Polk, James K., 514
Pollsters, 235
Polls, use of, 318–319
Poll tax, 69
Popular culture, 11–13
Population, 263–264
Populist Revolt, 370–371
Populists, 32, 416
Pork barrel, 454–456
Pornography, 24
Pornography online, 127
Post Office Department, 583
Potential presidencies, 495
Powell, Colin, 78
Power and persuasion, 529–532
Power elite, 408
Power sharing arrangement, 469–470
Precedent, 543
importance of, 547–548
Pregnant chads, 345
Presidency, 524
aspects of, 510–511
budget, 532–533
chief executive removal, 498–500
creation of, 495–496
as institution, 536
legislative agenda, 524–529
power and persuasion, 529–532
presidential terms, 496–497
Presidential candidate, nomination of, 389
Presidential control bureaucracy
counterbureaucracy strategy, 601
independent agencies, 600–601
OMB, 602
presidential appointment and removal powers, 599–600
White House policy organizations, 601–602
Presidential debates, 332–333
Presidential election campaign, 484
Presidential election of 2000, 342–344
contest period, 347–348
counting, 345–347
Florida's post-election contest, 344–345
U.S. Supreme Court, 348
Presidential news agencies, 222
Presidential office, structure of, 520–521
cabinet, 523–524
EOP, 522
White House staff, 521–522
Presidential performance evaluation, 533–536
Presidential power, scope and limits of
appointment and removal, 507–508
Congress, 502–507
domestic powers, wartime, 518–520
executive privilege, 509–510
foreign policy, 510–512
pardons, 508–509
specifics of foreign affairs, 512–514
theories of, 500–502
war powers, 514–518
Presidential primaries, 389
Presidential succession and disability, 497
Presidential vetoes, 503–505
Presidential war powers, 514
Afghanistan and war on terrorism, 517
Iraq, war, 518
Persian Gulf war (1991), 516
Vietnam war, 515
War Powers Resolution, 515–516
President, roles of, 491–494
Press
conference, 223
freedom of. *See* Freedom of press
vs. government, 221
Press coverage of government
Congress, 225–226
coverage of president, 221–225
media and courts, 226–228
Press secretary, 222
Primaries, 389–390
Primary election, 312, 313
Priming, 268
Print in decline, 212
Print media, 200
contemporary mainstream press, 203
newspapers, 201–202
tabloids, 202–203
yellow journalism, 202
Prior restraint, prohibition against, 215
Privacy Act of 1974, 605
Privacy, right of, 25–26
Private discrimination, 152–153
Private enterprise, 18
Private property, 18
Probable cause, 135
Profanity, 126
Professional associations, 414–415, 426
Programming, content of, 218–220
Progressive, liberals, 33
Progressive movement, 386
Progressive party, 375–376
Prohibition, 64
against prior restraint, 215
Pro-life movement, 301–302
Propaganda, 240
Proportional representation, 173
Prospective voting, 340
Protective tariffs, 46
Protestant churches, 420
Protestant Reformation, 40
Proto-party, 379
Public benefits, 8
Public Broadcasting System (PBS), 218
Public cynicism, 229
Public defender, 137
Public discrimination, 154
Public education, role of, 415
Public interest, 29, 409–410
Public interest group, 421

Public ministers, 582
Public opinion, 235–240
contemporary, 242
in democratic society, 240
dimensions of, 270
influence, interest groups, 432–433
measurement, 263–268
models of, 269
to policy makers, communicating, 269–270
and political culture, 242–244
and public policy, 268–270
and U.S Constitution, 240–241
Public policy
ideology and, 249–251
making of, 229–231
public opinion and, 268–270
Supreme Court and, 554–559
Public relations campaign, 432–433
Public schools, unequal funding of, 183–184
Public television, editorializing by, 218
Pundits, 236
Puritans' ship, 41
Putnam, Robert, 30

Q

Question writing, 266–268
Quorum, 480

R

Race
relations, 151
socioeconomic factors, 259
issue positions by, 260
Race-conscious remedies, 167
Racial discrimination in voting rights, 170–173
Racial equality, 153–154
civil rights, 154–155
measures enacted after civil war, 154–155
for other racial and ethnic groups, 173–176
Civil Rights Act of 1964, 164–166
civil rights movement, 162–164
decline of "separate but equal," 159–161
dismantling segregation, 166–170
racial discrimination in voting rights, 170–173
second-class citizenship, 155–158
Racial groups
Asian Americans, 175–176
Hispanics, 173–174
Native Americans, 174–175
Racial integration, degree of, 167
Racial profiling, 192
Radio stations, editorializing by, 218
Radio talk shows, 270
Rainbow Coalition, 420
Raising money for campaign, 316–317
Rand, Ayn, 21
Random-digit dialing, 265
Random sample, 265
Ratifying conventions, 59–60
Reagan, Ronald, 64, 97, 98, 417, 467, 486, 552, 567, 568, 587
cabinet, 523
chief executive role, 492
international relations, 511
Iran–Contra scandal, 512
line-item veto, 505
media, 212
OMB, 522
presidential performance evaluation, 534
presidential terms, 496–497
revolution, 586–588
victory in 1980, 338
War Powers Resolution, 515–516
Realigning election, 371
Realtor's PAC, 428
Reapportionment, 70
Reasonable time, place, and manner regulations, 129
Reckless disregard of truth, 216
Referenda, elections, 313
Reform party, 376–377
Regionalism, 23
Regional variations in American political culture, 22–23
Region, socioeconomic factors, 257–258
Registration
changes in, 281
reasons for failing to, 284–285
"Regulation of interstate commerce," 165, 411
Regulatory federalism, 96–97
Regulatory state, 26
FTC, 584–585
ICC, 584
labor department, 584
Rehabilitation Act of 1973, 184
Rehnquist Court, 558–559, 567
Rehnquist, William, 457, 558
Reinventing government, 588
Reliability, 267
Religion
conflict over, 24
free exercise of, 24
socioeconomic factors, 257
Religious groups, 420
Renner, Jeremy, 12
Reno, Janet, 499
Reno v. American Civil Liberties Union (1997), 220
Representation function, 449
policy, 451–452
service, 450–451
symbolic, 450
Representative democracy, 18
Representative government, 50
Representative institutions, 16
Republic, 51
Republican House leadership, 329
Republican National Committee, 396
Republican National Convention, 395
Republican party, 324, 366, 370, 371, 373
Republican plank, 397
Republican reforms, 394
Rescue America, 301
Retrospective voting, 340
Revenue Act of 1971, 375
Reversal, 548
of lower court decision, 562
Revolution, 14, 46
American, 17
Articles of Confederation, 80
French, 16
sexual, 10
Revolutionary War, 44
Reynolds v. Sims, 70, 279
Rhode Island legislature, 48
Richardson, Elliot, 510
Rich, Denise, 508
Rich, Marc, 508
Rider, 477
Right of privacy, 25–26, 138
and gay rights, 140–142
reproductive freedom, 139–140
right to die, 142–143
Rights of accused, 92
Right to keep and bear arms, 133
Right-to-work laws, 416
Riots, 287–288
Rivkin, David, 520
Roberts Court, 559
Roberts, John G., 559
Robertson, Pat, 300
Roche, John P., 50
Rodney King verdict, 175
Roeder, Scott, 302

Roe, Jane, 139
Roe v. Wade, 545, 558, 559, 567
Roll Call newsletter, 431
Roman Catholic, proportions of, 24
Romer v. Evans, 187
Romney, Mitt, 349
Roosevel, Teddy, 324
Roosevelt, Franklin D., 64, 66, 67, 94, 294, 331, 371, 416, 456, 496, 556, 557, 585
  foreign affairs, 512
  going public, 531
  presidential performance evaluation, 533–534
  role in policy process, 524
  veto legislation, 503
  World War II, "relocation centers," 519
Roosevelt, Theodore, 376, 501
Roper, Elmo, 265
Rousseau, Jean-Jacques, 16
Ruckelshaus, William, 510
Rugged individualism, 21–22
Rule making
  adoption, procedures, 596
  legislative power, delegation of, 594–596
Rule of four, 560
Rule of law, 26–28
Rules Committee, 478–479
Rumsfeld v. Padilla, 520

S

Sabato, Larry, 229
Safe seat, 460
SALT I treaty, 513
Same-sex marriage, 151, 190
Sample, 264
Sampling
  frame, 265
  plan, 265
  scientific measurement, 265–266
Satellite TV, 205
"Saturday night massacre," 510
Saturday Press, 215
Scabs, 294
Scalia, Antonin, 189
Scandals, 357
Schattschneider, E. E., 364
Schlafly, Phyllis, 297
Schlesinge, Arthur M., 31
School political socialization, 254–256
School segregation, 165–16
Scientific measurement
  interpretation, problems in, 267–268
  question writing, 266–268
  sampling, 265–266
Scott, Dred, 68, 85, 555, 566
Scott v. Sandford, 68
Search warrant, 135, 136
SEC. *See* Securities and Exchange Commission
Secession, doctrine of, 86
Second Bank of United States, 84
Second-class citizenship
  civil rights cases of 1883, 155–156
  electoral disfranchisement, 157–158
  failure of democratic institutions, 158
  Jim Crow laws, 156–157
  lack of protest against, 158–159
Second Continental Congress, 44
Secret ballot, 386
Securities and Exchange Commission (SEC), 595
Seed money, 316
Segregation, dismantling, 166–168
SEIU. *See* Service Employees International Union
Select committees, 473
Selective benefits, 422
Selective incentives, 422–423
Selective incorporation, 119
Senate, 82, 446, 551
  committees, 472–473, 478–479
  confirmation process, 551
  leadership in, 469
Senate Judiciary Committee, 181, 551, 552
Senatorial courtesy, 551
Seniority, 460
Sensational federal trial, 227
Sensationalism, 202
Separate but equal, 157
  Brown decision, 160
  legally mandated school segregation, 159–160
  state challenges to implementation of Brown, 160–161
Separation of powers, principle of, 456
September 11, 2001, terrorist attack, 8, 20
Sequential referral system, 461
Service Employees International Union (SEIU), 416
Service representation, 450–451
Seventeenth Amendment, 68, 449
Seven Years War, 42
Sex and race, issue positions by, 260
Sex discrimination, 177
  by educational institutions, 179–180
Sexual harassment, 181–182
Sexual orientation, 185
Sexual revolution, 10
Sharpton, Al, 320
Shaw v. Reno, 90
Shays' Rebellion, 47–48
Sherman Anti-Trust Act, 556
Sherman, Roger, 54
Shield laws, 216–217
Sierra Club, 420, 422
Single executive, 496
Single-issue groups, 419–420
Single-issue politics, 399
Single-member districts, 448
Sixteenth Amendment, 63
Slander, defined, 127
Slavery
  issues, 293
  and party realignment, 369–370
Smith Act, 130
Social capital, 30
Social class, socioeconomic factors, 256–257
Social contract, 15
Social desirability bias, 268
Social equality, 243
Socialism, 19, 243
  American appetite for, 379
Socialist *vs.* capitalist economy, 19
Socialist Workers parties, 379
Socialization, political. *See* Political socialization
Social media, 208
  and political culture, 13
Social movements, 292–302
Social Security, 405
Social Security Act of 1935, 585
Social welfare, 102
Societal culture, political and, 10–11
Societal institutions, 28, 29–31
Socioeconomic factors, 256–260
  age, 258–259
  gender, 259
  marital status, 259
  race, 259
  region, 257–258
  religion, 257
  social class, 256–257
Sodomy law, 298
Soft money, 398
Soldier of Fortune, 430

SOPA/PIPA. *See* Stop Online Piracy and Protect Intellectual Property Acts
Sound bite, 331
Southern colonies, 41
Sovereign immunity, 62
Sovereignty, 15, 80
Special committees, 473
Spectator activities, 276–277
Spin control, campaign, 318
Spoils system, 368
Staff in Congress, 473–475
Stalin, Joseph, 14
Stamp Act, 42
Stamp Act Congress, 42–43
Standing, 546, 547
Standing committees of Congress, 471–472
Stare decisis, doctrine of, 547, 548
Starr, Ken, 499–500
State action, 91–92
State-by-state campaign strategies, 325–326
State-centered federalism, 86
State convention, 389
State courts, 84, 88, 91
  federal courts *vs.,* 92, 101
State criminal courts, 226
State legislatures, 414
State of nature, 15
State party committee, 327
State party systems, 385–388
States' rights, 62
Steel industry, 413
Stern, Howard, 219
Stewardship theory of presidential power, 501
Stockman, David, 528
Stone, Harlan Fiske, 93
Stop Online Piracy and Protect Intellectual Property Acts (SOPA/PIPA), 220
Straw poll, 263
Strikes, 288–289, 294
Strong committee system, 459–460
Subcommittee Bill of Rights, 461
Subcommittees, 473, 478
Subgovernments, 436
  iron triangles, 436–438
  issue networks, 438
Subpoena, 137
Suffragists, 177
Sunshine laws, 605
Superdelegates, democratic conventions, 349–350
Superdelegate system, 392–393
SuperPAC, 330
Super Tuesday, 321, 393–394
Supremacy Clause, 65, 82, 84
Supremacy of federal law, 82–83
Supreme Court
  appointment power, 567–568
  Article III, 548
  Bill of Rights, 120
  Brown v. Board of Education, 88, 89
  Bush v. Gore, 543
  characteristics of justices, 565
  checks on, 566–568
  child pornography laws, 127
  constitutional amendment, 566–567
  covering, 227–228
  decision making, 560–569
  decisions, 457
  ex post facto, 118
  federal court system, 548–549
  and federal regulation of economy, 93
  fighting words, 125
  Florida Supreme Court, 347–348
  Gibbons v. Ogden, 84, 85
  Hardwick case, 141
  internal politics of, 565
  internal procedures, 560–564
  McCulloch v. Maryland, 84, 85
  Miller test, 126
  opinions, 562–564
  and presidential power, 502
  and public policy, 554–559
  Roe v. Wade, 139
  Texas v. White, 86
  U.S. Supreme Court, 348
Swift Boat Veterans for Truth, 404, 406
Symbolic representation, 450
Symbolic speech, 122
Systematic sample, 266

T

Tabloids, 202–203
Taliban, 8–9
  religion and government fusion, 9
Talk radio, 203–204
Tammany Hall Democratic machine, 386
Taney, Roger B., 547, 555
Tariff, 411
Tax Court, 550
Taxed Enough Already (TEA), 379
Taxes, 413
Tea Act, 43
Teamsters, 416, 426
Tea Party, 379
Tea Party movement, 471
Teixeira, Ruy, 281
Television broadcast networks, 204
Television news networks, 205–206
Television shows, 270
Temporary Assistance for Needy Families (TANF), 102
Tenth Amendment, 62, 81, 82, 93
Term Limits v. Thornton, 485
Terrorism, 589–590
  Afghanistan and war on, 517
  American citizens detention, 520
  Islam and, 20
Terrorist attack, September 11, 2001, 8, 20
Terry, Randall, 301
Texas law, 139
Texas v. Johnson, 558
Texas v. White, 86
Theory, iron triangle, 436
Third parties, 375–376, 378, 379
Third-party candidate, 372
Thomas, Clarence, 485, 552
Thoreau, Henry David, 290
Tiananmen Square, 20
Tiller, George, 301–302
Timing, legislative agenda, 527–529
Tobacco farmers case, subsidies for, 437–438
Tocqueville, Alexis de, 40, 242, 406, 543
Tort, 216
Tracking polls, 318
Trade associations, 413–414, 426
Traditional democratic theory, 269, 287
Traditionalistic political culture, 22–23
Traditional values and institutions, 249
Train, Russell, 507
Transitional government, 44
Treaties, 513
Trial balloons, 224–225
Tripp, Linda, 499
Truman, Harry S., 372, 493, 529
  foreign affairs, 512
Trustee style of representation, 451
Turnout, voting, 280–283
Tushnet, Mark, 520
TV talk shows, 213
TV violence, 219
Twelfth Amendment, 62, 334–335
Twenty-Fifth Amendment, 497
Twenty-Second Amendment, 64
  term limits on Congress, 485
Twenty-Sixth Amendment, 61, 69
Twitter, 210
  and political culture, 12
Two-party system, 367, 374–375, 399
  Congress and, 448

2008 election, 349–350
2008 Landslide, 470–471
2004 campaign, 348–349
2012 election, 351
Two Treatises of Government (Locke), 15, 45, 49
Tyler, John, 497, 547
Tyranny of majority, 56, 241

U

UAW. *See* United Auto Workers
Ubiquitous media, 208–210
UMRA. *See* Unfunded Mandates Reform Act
Unanimous consent agreements, 479
Unfunded mandates, 98–99
Unfunded Mandates Reform Act (UMRA), 98
Unicameral legislature, 46
Union density, 417
Unitary system, 52, 79, 80, 374
United Auto Workers (UAW), 416–417, 433
United States
    courts of appeals, 549–550
    district courts, 549
    economic framework for, 374
    federalism. *See* Federalism
    media in, 31
    terrorists attacks in September 2001, 77, 105
United States v. Curtiss-Wright Export Corporation (1936), 511, 512
Universal suffrage, 17
Unscientific polling, dangers of, 264
USA Today, 202
U.S. Claims Court, 550
U.S. Constitution, 82, 83, 92
U.S. Senate, 68
U.S. Supreme Court, 348
    gay rights movement and, 298

V

Validity, 267
Values, 244
Van Buren, Martin, 369, 388
Vermont Supreme Court, 189
Veto, 41
Vetoes, presidential, 503–505
Vetting, 224
Victory of nation-centered federalism, 86
Vietnam War, 296, 215, 509, 515
Violence
    problem of, 26–28
    TV, 219
Virginia Plan, 53–54
Virtual child pornography, 127
VNS. *See* Voter News Service
Volstead Act, 64
Vote dilution, 171
Voter News Service (VNS), 266, 343
Voter registration, 283
Voting, 275
    behavior
        candidate image, 341–342
        decision, model of, 342, 343
        ideology, 340
        issues, 338–340
        party identification, 337–338
    decision, model of, 342, 343
    individual decision to, 284
    political participation through, 279
    reforming system, 285–286
    rights, 165, 170–173
    turnout, 280–283
Voting-age population (VAP), 280, 281
Voting Rights Act, 170–171, 280, 284, 295, 432, 451, 463
    changes in, 172–173
    of 1965, 68, 89–90

W

Wagner Act, 557
Wag the Dog, 12
Walker, Scott, 295
Wallace, George C., 372, 376
Wall of separation, 130
Wall Street Journal, The, 202
War chest of funds, 385
War Hawk faction, 459
War on drugs, 100
War on terrorism, 230
War Powers Resolution, 515–516
Warren Court, 557–558, 567, 568
Warren, Earl, 279–280, 407, 553, 557
Washington, George, 255, 367, 496, 546
    executive privilege, 509
    presidential performance evaluation, 533–534
Washington Post, 202, 203, 215
Watergate scandal, 357, 398, 221
    controversy, 509–510
    hearings of 1974, 226
Water Pollution Control Act of 1972, 507
Ways and Means Committee, 460
Weapons of mass destruction (WMDs), 518
Web 2.0., 208
Welfare state, 26, 585–586
West, Darrell, 229
West Win, The, 11
Whig party, 369
Whistleblower Protection Act, 606
Whistle blowers, 605
White House policy organizations, 601–602
White House press corps, 222–223
White House staff, 521–522
White primary, 158, 390
Wikileaks, 124
Winner-take-all electoral system, 374
WMDs. *See* Weapons of mass destruction
Women
    gender discrimination
        affirmative action on behalf of, 180–181
        in military service, 178–179
        struggle for political equality, 177–178
    in workforce, 180
    rights of, 25
Women's movement, 297
Woodard, Colin, 23
Woodward, Bob, 203
Workforce, women in, 180
World Trade Center, 209, 517
World Trade Organization, 302
World War II
    Japanese Americans "relocation centers," 519
Wright, Jim, 511
Writs, 548, 560

Y

Yellow journalism, 202
YouTube and political culture, 12

Z

Zeigler, Harmon, 254